THE COMPLETE POETICAL WORKS OF
JAMES WHITCOMB RILEY

THE
COMPLETE POETICAL WORKS
OF
JAMES
WHITCOMB
RILEY

INDIANA UNIVERSITY PRESS
Bloomington & Indianapolis

This book is a publication of

Indiana University Press
601 North Morton Street
Bloomington, Indiana 47404-3797 USA

http://iupress.indiana.edu

Telephone orders 800-842-6796
Fax orders 812-855-7931
Orders by e-mail iuporder@indiana.edu

The paper used in this publication meets the minimum requirements
of American National Standard for Information Sciences—Permanence
of Paper for Printed Library Materials, ANSI Z39.48-1984.

∞TM

Manufactured in the United States of America

Library of Congress Cataloging-in-Publication Data

Riley, James Whitcomb, 1849–1916.
   (Poems)
   The complete poetical works of James Whitcomb Riley.
     p.   cm.
   Includes index.
   ISBN 0-253-34989-3 (cloth).—ISBN 0-253-20777-0 (paper)
   I. Title.
   PS2700   1993
   811'.4—dc20   92-28235

ISBN-13 978-0-253-20777-7 (paper)

   8   9   10   11   14   13   12

CONTENTS

CONTENTS

viii CONTENTS

CONTENTS

CONTENTS

CONTENTS

CONTENTS

CONTENTS

CONTENTS

CONTENTS

CONTENTS

CONTENTS

CONTENTS

CONTENTS

CONTENTS

THE COMPLETE POETICAL WORKS OF
JAMES WHITCOMB RILEY

The
Complete Poetical Works

OF JAMES WHITCOMB RILEY

I

A BACKWARD LOOK

AS I sat smoking, alone, yesterday,
    And lazily leaning back in my
        chair,
Enjoying myself in a general way—
Allowing my thoughts a holiday
From weariness, toil and care,—
My fancies—doubtless, for ventilation—
Left ajar the gates of my mind,—
And Memory, seeing the situation,
    Slipped out in the street of "Auld
        Lang Syne."—

Wandering ever with tireless feet
    Through scenes of silence, and jubilee
Of long-hushed voices; and faces sweet
Were thronging the shadowy side of
        the street
    As far as the eye could see;
Dreaming again, in anticipation,
    The same old dreams of our boy-
        hood's days
That never come true, from the vague
        sensation
    Of walking asleep in the world's
        strange ways.

Away to the house where I was born!
    And there was the selfsame clock
        that ticked

From the close of dusk to the burst of
        morn,
When life-warm hands plucked the
        golden corn
    And helped when the apples were
        picked.
And the "chany dog" on the mantel-
        shelf,
    With the gilded collar and yellow
        eyes,
Looked just as at first, when I hugged
        myself
    Sound asleep with the dear surprise.

And down to the swing in the locust-
        tree,
    Where the grass was worn from the
        trampled ground,
And where "Eck" Skinner, "Old" Carr,
        and three
Or four such other boys used to be
    "Doin' sky-scrapers," or "whirlin'
        round":
And again Bob climbed for the blue-
        bird's nest,
    And again "had shows" in the
        buggy-shed
Of Guymon's barn, where still, un-
        guessed,

The old ghosts romp through the
  best days dead!

And again I gazed from the old school-
  room
With a wistful look, of a long June
  day,
When on my cheek was the hectic
  bloom
Caught of Mischief, as I presume—
He had such a "partial" way,
It seemed, toward me.—And again I
  thought
Of a probable likelihood to be
Kept in after school—for a girl was
  caught
Catching a note from me.

And down through the woods to the
  swimming-hole—
Where the big, white, hollow old
  sycamore grows,—
And we never cared when the water
  was cold,
And always "ducked" the boy that told
On the fellow that tied the clothes.—
When life went so like a dreamy
  rhyme,
That it seems to me now that then
The world was having a jollier time
Than it ever will have again.

2

PHILIPER FLASH

YOUNG Philiper Flash was a prom-
  ising lad,
His intentions were good—but oh, how
  sad
For a person to think
How the veriest pink

And bloom of perfection may turn out
  bad.
Old Flash himself was a moral man,
And prided himself on a moral plan,
Of a maxim as old
As the calf of gold,
Of making that boy do what he was
  told.

And such a good mother had Philiper
  Flash;
Her voice was as soft as the creamy
  plash
Of the milky wave
With its musical lave
That gushed through the holes of her
  patent churn-dash;—
And the excellent woman loved Phil-
  iper so,
She could cry sometimes when he
  stumped his toe,—
And she stroked his hair
With such motherly care
When the dear little angel learned to
  swear.

Old Flash himself would sometimes
  say
That his wife had "such a ridiculous
  way,—
She'd humor that child
Till he'd soon be sp'iled,
And then there'd be the devil to pay!"
And the excellent wife, with a mar-
  tyr's look,
Would tell old Flash himself "he took
No notice at all
Of the bright-eyed doll
Unless when he spanked him for get-
  ting a fall!"

Young Philiper Flash, as time passed
  by,

Grew into "a boy with a roguish eye":
    He could smoke a cigar,
    And seemed by far
The most promising youth.—"He's
    powerful sly,"
Old Flash himself once told a friend,
"Every copper he gets he's sure to
    spend—
And," said he, "don't you know
    If he keeps on so
What a crop of wild oats the boy will
    grow!"

But his dear good mother knew Phil-
    iper's ways
So—well, she managed the money to
    raise;
    And old Flash himself
    Was "laid on the shelf,"
(In the manner of speaking we have
    nowadays).
For "gracious knows, her darling child,
If he went without money he'd soon
    grow wild."
    So Philiper Flash
    With a regular dash
"Swung on to the reins," and went
    "slingin' the cash."

As old Flash himself in his office one
    day,
Was shaving notes in a barberous way,
    At the hour of four
    Death entered the door
And shaved the note on his life, they
    say.
And he had for his grave a magnificent
    tomb,
Though the venturous finger that
    pointed "Gone Home,"
    Looked white and cold
    From being so bold,
As it feared that a popular lie was
    told.

Young Philiper Flash was a man of
    style
When he first began unpacking the
    pile
    Of the dollars and dimes
    Whose jingling chimes
Had clinked to the tune of his father's
    smile;
And he strewed his wealth with such
    lavish hand,
His rakish ways were the talk of the
    land,
    And gossipers wise
    Sat winking their eyes
(A certain foreboding of fresh sur-
    prise).

A "fast young man" was Philiper
    Flash
And wore "loud clothes" and a weak
    mustache,
    And "done the Park,"
    For an "afternoon lark,"
With a very fast horse of "remarkable
    dash."
And Philiper handled a billiard-cue
About as well as the best he knew,
    And used to say
    "He could make it pay
By playing two or three games a day."

And Philiper Flash was his mother's
    joy,
He seemed to her the magic alloy
    That made her glad,
    When her heart was sad,
With the thought that "she lived for
    her darling boy."
His dear good mother wasn't aware
How her darling boy relished a
    "tare."—
    She said "one night
    He gave her a fright
By coming home late and *acting* tight."

Young Philiper Flash, on a winterish
  day,
Was published a bankrupt, so they
  say—
And as far as I know
I suppose it was so,
For matters went on in a singular
  way;
His excellent mother, I think I was
  told,
Died from exposure and want and
  cold;
And Philiper Flash,
With a horrible slash,
Whacked his jugular open and went
  to smash.

3

THE SAME OLD STORY

THE same old story told again—
    The maiden droops her head,
The ripening glow of her crimson
  cheek
  Is answering in her stead.
The pleading tone of a trembling voice
  Is telling her the way
He loved her when his heart was young
  In Youth's sunshiny day:
The trembling tongue, the longing
  tone,
  Imploringly ask why
They can not be as happy now
  As in the days gone by.
And two more hearts, tumultuous
  With overflowing joy,
Are dancing to the music
  Which that dear, provoking boy
Is twanging on his bowstring,
  As, fluttering his wings,

He sends his love-charged arrows
  While merrily he sings:
"Ho! ho! my dainty maiden,
  It surely can not be
You are thinking you are master
  Of your heart, when it is me."
And another gleaming arrow
  Does the little god's behest,
And the dainty little maiden
  Falls upon her lover's breast.
"The same old story told again,"
  And listened o'er and o'er,
Will still be new, and pleasing, too,
  Till "Time shall be no more."

4

TO A BOY WHISTLING

THE smiling face of a happy boy
    With its enchanted key
  Is now unlocking in memory
My store of heartiest joy.

And my lost life again to-day,
  In pleasant colors all aglow,
  From rainbow tints, to pure white
    snow,
Is a panorama sliding away.

The whistled air of a simple tune
  Eddies and whirls my thoughts
    around,
  As fairy balloons of thistle-down
Sail through the air of June.

O happy boy with untaught grace!
  What is there in the world to give
  That can buy one hour of the life
    you live
Or the trivial cause of your smiling
    face!

5
AN OLD FRIEND

HEY, Old Midsummer! are you
here again,
With all your harvest-store of olden
joys,—
Vast overhanging meadow-lands of
rain,
And drowsy dawns, and noons when
golden grain
Nods in the sun, and lazy truant
boys
Drift ever listlessly adown the day,
Too full of joy to rest, and dreams to
play.

The same old Summer, with the same
old smile
Beaming upon us in the same old
way
We knew in childhood! Though a
weary while

Since that far time, yet memories recon-
cile
The heart with odorous breaths of
clover hay;
And again I hear the doves, and the
sun streams through
The old barn door just as it used to do.

And so it seems like welcoming a
friend—
An old, *old* friend, upon his coming
home
From some far country—coming home
to spend
Long, loitering days with me: And I
extend
My hand in rapturous glee:—And
so you've come!—
Ho, I'm so glad! Come in and take
a chair:
Well, this is just like *old* times, I de-
clare!

6

WHAT SMITH KNEW ABOUT FARMING

THERE wasn't two purtier farms in the state
Than the couple of which I'm about to relate;—
Jinin' each other—belongin' to Brown,
And jest at the edge of a flourishin' town.
Brown was a man, as I understand,
That allus had handled a good 'eal o' land,
And was sharp as a tack in drivin' a trade—
For that's the way most of his money was made.
And all the grounds and the orchards about
His two pet farms was all tricked out
With poppies and posies
And sweet-smellin' rosies;
And hundreds o' kinds
Of all sorts o' vines,
To tickle the most horticultural minds;

And little dwarf trees not as thick as your wrist
With ripe apples on 'em as big as your fist:
And peaches—Siberian crabs and pears,
And quinces—Well! *any* fruit *any* tree bears;
And the purtiest stream—jest a-swimmin' with fish
And—*jest a'most everything heart could wish!*
The purtiest orch'rds—I wish you could see
How purty they was, fer I know it 'ud be
A regular treat!—but I'll go ahead with
My story! A man by the name o' Smith—
(A bad name to rhyme,
But I reckon that I'm
Not goin' back on a Smith! nary time!)
'At hadn't a soul of kin nor kith,
And more money than he knowed what to do with,—
So he comes a-ridin' along one day,
And *he* says to Brown, in his offhand way—
Who was trainin' some newfangled vines round a bay-
Winder—"Howdy-do—look-a-here—say:
What'll you take fer this property here?—
I'm talkin' o' leavin' the city this year,
And I want to be
Where the air is free,
And I'll *buy* this place, if it ain't too dear!"—
Well—they grumbled and jawed aroun'—
"I don't like to part with the place," says Brown;
"Well," says Smith, a-jerkin' his head,
"That house yonder—bricks painted red—
Jest like this'n—a *purtier view*—
Who is it owns *it?*" "That's mine too,"
Says Brown, as he winked at a hole in his shoe,
"But I'll tell you right here jest what I *kin* do:—
If you'll pay the figgers I'll sell *it* to you."
Smith went over and looked at the place—
Badgered with Brown, and argied the case—
Thought that Brown's figgers was rather too tall,
But, findin' that Brown wasn't goin' to fall,
In final agreed,
So they drawed up the deed
Fer the farm and the fixtures—the live stock an' all.
And so Smith moved from the city as soon
As he possibly could—But "the man in the moon"
Knowed more'n Smith o' farmin' pursuits,

And jest to convince you, and have no disputes,
How little he knowed,
I'll tell you his "mode,"
As he called it, o' raisin' "the best that growed,"
In the way o' potatoes—
Cucumbers—tomatoes,
And squashes as lengthy as young alligators.
'Twas allus a curious thing to me
How big a fool a feller kin be
When he gits on a farm after leavin' a town!—
Expectin' to raise himself up to renown,
And reap fer himself agricultural fame,
By growin' of squashes—*without any shame*—
As useless and long as a technical name.
To make the soil pure,
And certainly sure,
He plastered the ground with patent manure.
He had cultivators, and double-hoss plows,
And patent machines fer milkin' his cows;
And patent hay-forks—patent measures and weights,
And new patent back-action hinges fer gates,
And barn locks and latches, and such little dribs,
And patents to keep the rats out o' the cribs—
Reapers and mowers,
And patent grain sowers;
And drillers
And tillers
And cucumber hillers,
And horries;—and had patent rollers and scrapers,
And took about ten agricultural papers.
So you can imagine how matters turned out:
But *Brown* didn't have not a shadder o' doubt
That Smith didn't know what he was about
When he said that "the *old* way to farm was played out."
But Smith worked ahead,
And when any one said
That the *old* way o' workin' was better instead
O' his "modern idees," he allus turned red,
And wanted to know
What made people so
Infernally anxious to hear theirselves crow?
And guessed that he'd manage to hoe his own row.
Brown he come onc't and leant over the fence,

And told Smith that he couldn't see any sense
In goin' to such a tremendous expense
Fer the sake o' such no-account experiments:—
"That'll never make corn!
As shore's you're born
It'll come out the leetlest end of the horn!"
Says Brown, as he pulled off a big roastin'-ear
From a stalk of his own
That had tribble outgrown
Smith's poor yaller shoots, and says he, "Looky here!
This corn was raised in the old-fashioned way,
And I rather imagine that *this* corn'll pay
Expenses fer *raisin'* it!—What do you say?"
Brown got him then to look over his crop.—
His luck that season had been tip-top!
And you may surmise
Smith opened his eyes
And let out a look o' the wildest surprise
When Brown showed him punkins as big as the lies
He was stuffin' him with—about offers he's had
Fer his farm: "I don't want to sell very bad,"
He says, but says he,
"Mr. Smith, you kin see
Fer yourself how matters is standin' with me,
I understand farmin' and I'd better stay,
You know, on my farm;—I'm a-makin' it pay—
I oughtn't to grumble!—I reckon I'll clear
Away over four thousand dollars this year."
And that was the reason, he made it appear,
Why he didn't care about sellin' his farm,
And hinted at his havin' done himself harm
In sellin' the other, and wanted to know
If Smith wouldn't sell back ag'in to him.—So
Smith took the bait, and says he, "Mr. Brown,
I wouldn't *sell* out but we might swap aroun'—
How'll you trade your place fer mine?"
(Purty sharp way o' comin' the shine
Over Smith! Wasn't it?) Well, sir, this Brown
Played out his hand and brought Smithy down—
Traded with him an', workin' it cute,
Raked in two thousand dollars to boot
As slick as a whistle, an' that wasn't all,—
He managed to trade back ag'in the next fall,—

And the next—and the next—as long as Smith stayed
He reaped with his harvests an annual trade.—
Why, I reckon that Brown must 'a' easily made—
On an *average*—nearly two thousand a year—
Together he made over seven thousand—clear.—
Till Mr. Smith found he was losin' his health
In as big a proportion, almost, as his wealth;
So at last he concluded to move back to town,
And sold back his farm to this same Mr. Brown
At very low figgers, by gittin' it down.
Further'n this I have nothin' to say
Than merely advisin' the Smiths fer to stay
In their grocery stores in flourishin' towns
And leave agriculture alone—and the Browns.

7

A POET'S WOOING

I woo'd a woman once,
But she was sharper than an eastern
wind.
—TENNYSON.

"WHAT may I do to make you
glad,
To make you glad and free,
Till your light smiles glance
And your bright eyes dance
Like sunbeams on the sea?
Read some rhyme that is blithe
and gay
Of a bright May morn and a
marriage day?"
And she sighed in a listless way she
had,—
"Do not read—it will make me sad!"

"What shall I do to make you glad—
To make you glad and gay,
Till your eyes gleam bright
As the stars at night
When as light as the light of day?—

Sing some song as I twang the
strings
Of my sweet guitar through its
wanderings?"
And she sighed in the weary way she
had,—
"Do not sing—it will make me sad!"

"What can I do to make you glad—
As glad as glad can be,
Till your clear eyes seem
Like the rays that gleam
And glint through a dew-decked
tree?—
Will it please you, dear, that I
now begin
A grand old air on my violin?"
And she spoke again in the follow-
ing way,—
"Yes, oh yes, it would please me,
sir;
I would be so glad you'd play
Some grand old march—in char-
acter,—
And then as you march away
I will no longer thus be sad,
But oh, so glad—so glad—so glad!"

8

MAN'S DEVOTION

A LOVER said, "O Maiden, love
    me well,
For I must go away:
And should *another* ever come to tell
Of love—What *will* you say?"

And she let fall a royal robe of hair
    That folded on his arm
And made a golden pillow for her
    there;
    Her face—as bright a charm

As ever setting held in kingly crown—
    Made answer with a look,
And reading it, the lover bended down,
    And, trusting, "kissed the book."

He took a fond farewell and went
    away.
    And slow the time went by—
So weary—dreary was it, day by day
    To love, and wait, and sigh.

She kissed his pictured face sometimes,
    and said:
"O Lips, so cold and dumb,
I would that you would tell me, if not
    dead,
    Why, why do you not come?"

The picture, smiling, stared her in the
    face
    Unmoved—e'en with the touch
Of tear-drops—*hers*—bejeweling the
    case—
    'Twas plain—she loved him much.

And, thus she grew to think of him as
    gay

And joyous all the while,
And *she* was sorrowing—"Ah, wella-
    day!"
But pictures *always* smile!

And years—dull years—in dull monot-
    ony
    As ever went and came,
Still weaving changes on unceasingly,
    And changing, changed her name.

Was she untrue?—She oftentimes was
    glad
    And happy as a wife;
But *one* remembrance oftentimes made
    sad
    Her matrimonial life.—

Though its few years were hardly
    noted, when
    Again her path was strown
With thorns—the roses swept away
    again,
    And she again alone!

And then—alas! ah *then!*—her lover
    came:
"I come to claim you now—
My Darling, for I know *you* are the
    same,
    And I have kept *my* vow

Through these long, long, long years,
    and now no more
    Shall we asundered be!"
She staggered back and, sinking to the
    floor,
    Cried in her agony:

"I have been false!" she moaned, "*I* am
    not true—
    I am not worthy now,
Nor ever can I be a wife to *you*—
    For I have broke my vow!"

And as she kneeled there, sobbing at
  his feet,
He calmly spoke—no sign
Betrayed his inward agony—"I count
  you meet
To be a wife of mine!"

And raised her up forgiven, though
  untrue;
As fond he gazed on her,
She sighed,—"*So happy!*" And she
  never knew
He was a *widower.*

9

A BALLAD

WITH A SERIOUS CONCLUSION

CROWD about me, little children—
    Come and cluster 'round my knee
While I tell a little story
That happened once with me.

My father he had gone away
  A-sailing on the foam,
Leaving me—the merest infant—
And my mother dear at home;

For my father was a sailor,
  And he sailed the ocean o'er
For full five years ere yet again
He reached his native shore.

And I had grown up rugged
  And healthy day by day,
Though I was but a puny babe
When father went away.

Poor mother she would kiss me
And look at me and sigh

So strangely, oft I wondered
And would ask the reason why.

And she would answer sadly,
  Between her sobs and tears,—
"You look so like your father,
  Far away so many years!"

And then she would caress me
  And brush my hair away,
And tell me not to question,
But to run about my play.

Thus I went playing thoughtfully—
  For that my mother said,—
"You look so like your father!"
Kept ringing in my head.

So, ranging once the golden sands
  That looked out on the sea,
I called aloud, "My father dear,
  Come back to ma and me!"

Then I saw a glancing shadow
  On the sand, and heard the shriek
Of a sea-gull flying seaward,
  And I heard a gruff voice speak:—

"Ay, ay, my little shipmate,
  I thought I heard you hail;
Were you trumpeting that sea-gull,
  Or do you see a sail?"

And as rough and gruff a sailor
  As ever sailed the sea
Was standing near grotesquely
  And leering dreadfully.

I replied, though I was frightened,
  "It was my father dear
I was calling for across the sea—
  I think he didn't hear."

And then the sailor leered again
  In such a frightful way,
And made so many faces
  I was little loath to stay:

But he started fiercely toward me—
  Then made a sudden halt
And roared, *"I* think he heard you!"
  And turned a somersault.

Then a wild fear overcame me,
  And I flew off like the wind,
Shrieking *"Mother!"*—and the sailor
  Just a little way behind!

And then my mother heard me,
  And I saw her shade her eyes,
Looking toward me from the doorway,
  Transfixed with pale surprise

For a moment—then her features
  Glowed with all their wonted charms
As the sailor overtook me,
  And I fainted in her arms.

When I awoke to reason
  I shuddered with affright
Till I felt my mother's presence
  With a thrill of wild delight—

Till, amid a shower of kisses
  Falling glad as summer rain,
A muffled thunder rumbled,—
  "Is he coming 'round again?"

Then I shrieked and clung unto her,
  While her features flushed and
     burned
As she told me it was father
  From a foreign land returned.

   .   .   .   .   .   .

I said—when I was calm again,
  And thoughtfully once more
Had dwelt upon my mother's words
  Of just the day before,—

"I *don't* look like my father,
  As you told me yesterday—
I know I don't—or father
  Would have run the other way."

10

THE OLD TIMES WERE THE
BEST

FRIENDS, my heart is half aweary
  Of its happiness to-night:
Though your songs are gay and cheery,
  And your spirits feather-light,
There's a ghostly music haunting
  Still the heart of every guest
And a voiceless chorus chanting
  That the Old Times were the best.

CHORUS

All about is bright and pleasant
  With the sound of song and jest,
Yet a feeling's ever present
  That the Old Times were the best.

11

A SUMMER AFTERNOON

A LANGUID atmosphere, a lazy
  breeze,
With labored respiration, moves the
  wheat
From distant reaches, till the golden
  seas
  Break in crisp whispers at my feet.

My book, neglected of an idle mind,
  Hides for a moment from the eyes
    of men;
Or, lightly opened by a critic wind,
  Affrightedly reviews itself again.

Off through the haze that dances in the
    shine
  The warm sun showers in the open
    glade,
The forest lies, a silhouette design
  Dimmed through and through with
    shade.

A dreamy day; and tranquilly I lie
  At anchor from all storms of mental
    strain;
With absent vision, gazing at the sky,
  "Like one that hears it rain."

The Katydid, so boisterous last night,
  Clinging, inverted, in uneasy poise,
Beneath a wheat-blade, has forgotten
    quite
  If "Katy *did* or *didn't*" make a noise.

The twitter, sometimes, of a wayward
    bird
  That checks the song abruptly at the
    sound,
And mildly, chiding echoes that have
    stirred,
  Sink into silence, all the more pro-
    found.

And drowsily I hear the plaintive
    strain
  Of some poor dove . . . Why, I can
    scarcely keep
My heavy eyelids—there it is again—
  "Coo-coo!"—I mustn't—"Coo-coo!"
    fall asleep!

12

AT LAST

A DARK, tempestuous night; the
    stars shut in
  With shrouds of fog; an inky, jet-
    black blot
The firmament; and where the moon
    has been
  An hour agone seems like the dark-
    est spot.
The weird wind—furious at its demon
    game—
Rattles one's fancy like a window-
    frame.

A care-worn face peers out into the
    dark,
  And childish faces—frightened at the
    gloom—
Grow awed and vacant as they turn to
    mark
  The father's as he passes through the
    room:
The gate latch clatters, and wee baby
    Bess
Whispers, "The doctor's tummin' now,
    I dess!"

The father turns; a sharp, swift flash
    of pain
  Flits o'er his face: "Amanda, child!
    I said
A moment since—I see I must *again*—
  Go take your little sisters off to bed!
There, Effie, Rose, and *Clara mustn't
    cry!*"
"I tan't he'p it—I'm fyaid 'at mama'll
    die!"

What are his feelings, when this man
    alone

Sits in the silence, glaring in the grate
That sobs and sighs on in an undertone
As stoical—immovable as Fate,
While muffled voices from the sick one's room
Come in like heralds of a dreaded doom?

The door-latch jingles: in the doorway stands
The doctor, while the draft puffs in a breath—
The dead coals leap to life, and clap their hands,
The flames flash up. A face as pale as death

Turns slowly—teeth tight clenched, and with a look
The doctor, through his specs, reads like a book.

"Come, brace up, Major!"—"Let me know the worst!"
"W'y you're the biggest fool I ever saw—
Here, Major—take a little brandy first—
There! She's a *boy*—I mean *he* is—hurrah!"
"Wake up the other girls—and shout for joy—
Eureka is his name—I've found A BOY!"

13

FARMER WHIPPLE—BACHELOR

IT'S a mystery to see me—a man o' fifty-four,
   Who's lived a cross old bachelor fer thirty year' and more—
A-lookin' glad and smilin'! And they's none o' you can say
That you can guess the reason why I feel so good to-day!

I must tell you all about it! But I'll have to deviate
A little in beginnin', so's to set the matter straight
As to how it comes to happen that I never took a wife—
Kindo' "crawfish" from the Present to the Springtime of my life!

I was brought up in the country: Of a family of five—
Three brothers and a sister—I'm the only one alive,—
Fer they all died little babies; and 'twas one o' Mother's ways,
You know, to want a daughter; so she took a girl to raise.

The sweetest little thing she was, with rosy cheeks, and fat—
We was little chunks o' shavers then about as high as that!
But someway we sort o' *suited*-like! and Mother she'd declare
She never laid her eyes on a more lovin' pair

Than *we* was! So we growed up side by side fer thirteen year',
And every hour of it she growed to me more dear!—
W'y, even Father's dyin', as he did, I do believe
Warn't more affectin' to me than it was to see her grieve!

I was then a lad o' twenty; and I felt a flash o' pride
In thinkin' all depended on *me* now to pervide
Fer mother and fer Mary; and I went about the place
With sleeves rolled up—and workin', with a mighty smilin' face.—

Fer *somepin' else* was workin'! but not a word I said
Of a certain sort o' notion that was runnin' through my head,—
"Some day I'd maybe marry, and a *brother's* love was one
Thing—a *lover's* was another!" was the way the notion run!

I remember onc't in harvest, when the "cradle-in' " was done,
(When the harvest of my summers mounted up to twenty-one),
I was ridin' home with Mary at the closin' o' the day—
A-chawin' straws and thinkin', in a lover's lazy way!

And Mary's cheeks was burnin' like the sunset down the lane:
I noticed she was thinkin', too, and ast her to explain.
Well—when she turned and *kissed* me, *with her arms around me—law!*
I'd a bigger load o' Heaven than I had a load o' straw!

I don't p'tend to learnin', but I'll tell you what's a fac',
They's a mighty truthful sayin' somers in a' almanac—
Er *somers*—'bout "puore happiness"—perhaps some folks'll laugh
At the idy—"only lastin' jest two seconds and a half."—

But it's jest as true as preachin'!—fer that was a *sister's* kiss,
And a sister's lovin' confidence a-tellin' to me this:—
"*She* was happy, *bein' promised to the son o' Farmer Brown.*"—
And my feelin's struck a pardnership with sunset and went down!

I don't know *how* I acted, and I don't know *what* I said,—
Fer my heart seemed jest a-turnin' to an ice-cold lump o' lead;
And the hosses kind o' glimmered before me in the road,
And the lines fell from my fingers—And that was all I knowed—

Fer—well, I don't know *how* long—They's a dim rememberence
Of a sound o' snortin' horses, and a stake-and-ridered fence
A-whizzin' past, and wheat-sheaves a-dancin' in the air,
And Mary screamin' "Murder!" and a-runnin' up to where

I was layin' by the roadside, and the wagon upside down
A-leanin' on the gate-post, with the wheels a-whirlin' roun'!
And I tried to raise and meet her, but I couldn't, with a vague
Sort o' notion comin' to me that I had a broken leg.

Well, the women nussed me through it; but many a time I'd sigh
As I'd keep a-gittin' better instid o' goin' to die,
And wonder what was left *me* worth livin' fer below,
When the girl I loved was married to another, don't you know!

And my thoughts was as rebellious as the folks was good and kind
When Brown and Mary married—Railly must 'a' been my *mind*
Was kind o' out o' kilter!—fer I hated Brown, you see,
Worse'n *pizen*—and the feller whittled crutches out fer *me*—

And done a thousand little ac's o' kindness and respec'—
And me a-wishin' all the time that I could break his neck!
My relief was like a mourner's when the funeral is done
When they moved to Illinois in the Fall o' Forty-one.

Then I went to work in airnest—I had nothin' much in view
But to drownd out rickollections—and it kep' me busy, too!
But I slowly thrived and prospered, tel Mother used to say
She expected yit to see me a wealthy man some day.

Then I'd think how little *money* was, compared to happiness—
And who'd be left to use it when I died I couldn't guess!
But I've still kep' speculatin' and a-gainin' year by year,
Tel I'm payin' half the taxes in the county, mighty near!

Well!—A year ago er better, a letter comes to hand
Astin' how I'd like to dicker fer some Illinois land—
"The feller that had owned it," it went ahead to state,
"Had jest deceased, insolvent, leavin' chance to speculate,"—

And then it closed by sayin' that I'd "better come and see."—
I'd never been West, anyhow—a'most too wild fer *me*,
I'd allus had a notion; but a lawyer here in town
Said I'd find myself mistakend when I come to look around.

So I bids good-by to Mother, and I jumps aboard the train,
A-thinkin' what I'd bring her when I come back home again—
And ef she'd had an idy what the present was to be,
I think it's more'n likely she'd 'a' went along with me!

Cars is awful tejus ridin', fer all they go so fast!
But finally they called out my stoppin'-place at last:
And that night, at the tavern, I dreamp' I was a train
O' cars, and *skeered* at somepin', runnin' down a country lane!

Well, in the morning airly—after huntin' up the man—
The lawyer who was wantin' to swap the piece o' land—
We started fer the country; and I ast the history
Of the farm—its former owner—and so forth, etcetery!

And—well—it was inter*est*in'—I su'prised him, I suppose,
By the loud and frequent manner in which I blowed my nose!—
But his su'prise was greater, and it made him wonder more,
When I kissed and hugged the widder when she met us at the door!—

It was Mary: . . . They's a feelin' a-hidin' down in here—
Of course I can't explain it, ner ever make it clear.—
It was with us in that meetin', I don't want you to fergit!
And it makes me kind o' nervous when I think about it yit!

I *bought* that farm, and *deeded* it, afore I left the town,
With "title clear to mansions in the skies," to Mary Brown!
And fu'thermore, I took her and the *childern*—fer you see,
They'd never seed their Grandma—and I fetched 'em home with me.

So *now* you've got an idy why a man o' fifty-four,
Who's lived a cross old bachelor for thirty year' and more
Is a-lookin' glad and smilin'!—And I've jest come into town
To git a pair o' license fer to *marry* Mary Brown.

14

MY JOLLY FRIEND'S SECRET

AH, friend of mine, how goes it
  Since you've taken you a mate?—
Your smile, though, plainly shows it
  Is a very happy state!
Dan Cupid's necromancy!
  You must sit you down and dine,
And lubricate your fancy
  With a glass or two of wine.

And as you have "deserted,"
  As my other chums have done,
While I laugh alone diverted,
  As you drop off one by one—
And I've remained unwedded,
  Till—you see—look here—that I'm,
In a manner, "snatched bald-headed"
  By the sportive hand of Time!

I'm an "old 'un!" yes, but wrinkles
  Are not so plenty, quite,
As to cover up the twinkles
  Of the *boy*—ain't I right?

Yet, there are ghosts of kisses
Under this mustache of mine
My mem'ry only misses
When I drown 'em out with wine.

From acknowledgment so ample,
You would hardly take me for
What I am—a perfect sample
Of a "jolly bachelor";
Not a bachelor has being
When he laughs at married life
But his heart and soul's agreeing
That he ought to have a wife!

Ah, ha! old chum, this claret,
Like Fatima, holds the key
Of the old Blue-Beardish garret
Of my hidden mystery!
Did you say you'd like to listen?
Ah, my boy! the *"Sad No More!"*
And the tear-drops that will glisten—
Turn the catch upon the door,

And sit you down beside me,
And put yourself at ease—
I'll trouble you to slide me
That wine decanter, please;
The path is kind o' mazy
Where my fancies have to go,
And my heart gets sort o' lazy
On the journey—don't you know?

Let me see—when I was twenty—
It's a lordly age, my boy,
When a fellow's money's plenty,
And the leisure to enjoy—
And a girl—with hair as golden
As—*that;* and lips—well—quite
As red as *this* I'm holdin'
Between you and the light.

And eyes and a complexion—
Ah, heavens!—le'-me-see—

Well,—just in this connection,—
Did you lock that door for me?
Did I start in recitation
My past life to recall?
Well, *that's* an indication
I am purty tight—that's all!

15

THE SPEEDING OF THE KING'S
SPITE

A KING—estranged from his loving
    Queen
By a foolish royal whim—
Tired and sick of the dull routine
Of matters surrounding him—
Issued a mandate in this wise:—
*"The dower of my daughter's hand
I will give to him who holds this prize,
The strangest thing in the land."*

But the King, sad sooth! in this grim
    decree
Had a motive low and mean;—
'Twas a royal piece of chicanery
To harry and spite the Queen;
For King though he was, and beyond
    compare,
He had ruled all things save one—
Then blamed the Queen that his only
    heir
Was a daughter—not a son.

The girl had grown, in the mother's
    care,
Like a bud in the shine and shower
That drinks of the wine of the balmy
    air
Till it blooms into matchless flower;
Her waist was the rose's stem that bore
The flower—and the flower's per-
    fume—

That ripens on till it bulges o'er
With its wealth of bud and bloom.

And she had a lover—lowly sprung,—
But a purer, nobler heart
Never spake in a courtlier tongue
Or wooed with a dearer art:
And the fair pair paled at the King's
decree;
But the smiling Fates contrived
To have them wed, in a secrecy
That the Queen *herself* connived—

While the grim King's heralds scoured
the land
And the countries roundabout,
Shouting aloud, at the King's com-
mand,
A challenge to knave or lout,
Prince or peasant,—"The mighty King
Would have ye understand
That he who shows him the strangest
thing
Shall have his daughter's hand!"

And thousands flocked to the royal
throne,
Bringing a thousand things
Strange and curious;—One, a bone—
The hinge of a fairy's wings;
And one, the glass of a mermaid queen,
Gemmed with a diamond dew,
Where, down in its reflex, dimly seen,
Her face smiled out at you.

One brought a cluster of some strange
date,
With a subtle and searching tang
That seemed, as you tasted, to pene-
trate
The heart like a serpent's fang;
And back you fell for a spell entranced,
As cold as a corpse of stone,

And heard your brains, as they laughed
and danced
And talked in an undertone.

One brought a bird that could whistle
a tune
So piercingly pure and sweet,
That tears would fall from the eyes of
the moon
In dewdrops at its feet,
And the winds would sigh at the sweet
refrain,
Till they swooned in an ecstasy,
To waken again in a hurricane
Of riot and jubilee.

One brought a lute that was wrought
of a shell
Luminous as the shine
Of a new-born star in a dewy dell,—
And its strings were strands of wine
That sprayed at the Fancy's touch and
fused,
As your listening spirit leant
Drunken through with the airs that
oozed
From the o'ersweet instrument.

One brought a tablet of ivory
Whereon no thing was writ,—
But, at night—and the dazzled eyes
would see
Flickering lines o'er it,—
And each, as you read from the magic
tome,
Lightened and died in flame,
And the memory held but a golden
poem
Too beautiful to name.

Till it seemed all marvels that ever
were known
Or dreamed of under the sun

Were brought and displayed at the
    royal throne,
And put by, one by one;—
Till a graybeard monster came to the
    King—
Haggard and wrinkled and old—
And spread to his gaze this wondrous
    thing,—
A gossamer veil of gold.—

Strangely   marvelous — mocking   the
    gaze
Like a tangle of bright sunshine,
Dipping a million glittering rays
In a baptism divine:
And a maiden, sheened in this gauze
    attire—
Sifting a glance of her eye—
Dazzled men's souls with a fierce de-
    sire
To kiss and caress her and—die.

And the grim King swore by his royal
    beard
That the veil had won the prize,
While the gray old monster blinked
    and leered
With his lashless, red-rimmed eyes,
As the fainting form of the princess
    fell,
And the mother's heart went wild,
Throbbing and swelling a muffled knell
For the dead hopes of her child.

But her clouded face with a faint
    smile shone,
As suddenly, through the throng,
Pushing his way to the royal throne,
A fair youth strode along,
While a strange smile hovered about
    his eyes,
As he said to the grim old King:—
"The veil of gold must lose the prize;
For *I* have a stranger thing."

He bent and whispered a sentence
    brief;
But the monarch shook his head,
With a look expressive of unbelief—
"It can't be so," he said;
"Or give me proof; and I, the King,
    Give you my daughter's hand,—
For certes THAT *is* a stranger thing—
    The strangest thing in the land!"

Then the fair youth, turning, caught
    the Queen
In a rapturous caress,
While his lithe form towered in lordly
    mien,
As he said in a brief address:—
"My fair bride's mother is this; and, lo,
    As you stare in your royal awe,
By this pure kiss do I proudly show
    A love for a mother-in-law!"

Then a thaw set in the old King's
    mood,
And a sweet Spring freshet came
Into his eyes, and his heart renewed
    Its love for the favored dame:
But often he has been heard to declare
    That "he never could clearly see
How, in the deuce, such a strange
    affair
Could have ended so happily!"

16

JOB WORK

"WRITE me a rhyme of the pres-
        ent time"
And the poet took his pen
And wrote such lines as the miser
    minds
Hide in the hearts of men.

He grew enthused, as the poets used
When their fingers kissed the strings
Of some sweet lyre, and caught the fire
True inspiration brings,

And sang the song of a nation's
          wrong—
Of the patriot's galling chain,
And the glad release that the angel,
          Peace,
Has given him again.

He sang the lay of religion's sway,
Where a hundred creeds clasp hands
And shout in glee such a symphony
That the whole world understands.

He struck the key of monopoly,
And sang of her swift decay,
And traveled the track of the railway
          back
With a blithesome roundelay—

Of the tranquil bliss of a true love
          kiss;
And painted the picture, too,
Of the wedded life, and the patient
          wife,
And the husband fond and true;

And sang the joy that a noble boy
Brings to a father's soul,
Who lets the wine as a mocker shine
Stagnated in the bowl.

And he stabbed his pen in the ink
          again,
And wrote, with a writhing frown,
"This is the end." "And now, my
          friend,
You may print it—upside down!"

17

PRIVATE THEATRICALS

A QUITE convincing axiom
    Is, "Life is like a play";
For, turning back its pages some
    Few dog-eared years away,
        I find where I
        Committed my
Love-tale—with brackets where to sigh.

I feel an idle interest
    To read again the page;
I enter, as a lover dressed,
    At twenty years of age,
        And play the part
        With throbbing heart,
And all an actor's glowing art.

And she who plays my Lady-love
    Excels!—Her loving glance
Has power her audience to move—
    I am her audience.—
        Her acting tact,
        To tell the fact,
"Brings down the house" in every act.

And often we defy the curse
    Of storms and thunder-showers,
To meet together and rehearse
    This little play of ours—
        I think, when she
        "Makes love" to me,
She kisses very naturally!

.   .   .   .   .   .

Yes; it's convincing—rather—
    That "Life is like a play":
I am playing "Heavy Father"
    In a "Screaming Farce" to-day,
        That so "brings down
        The house," I frown,
And fain would "ring the curtain
          down."

18

PLAIN SERMONS

I SAW a man—and envied him be-
side—
Because of this world's goods he had
great store;
But even as I envied him, he died,
And left me envious of him no more.

I saw another man—and envied still—
Because he was content with frugal
lot;
But as I envied him, the rich man's
will
Bequeathed him all, and envy I for-
got.

Yet still another man I saw, and he
I envied for a calm and tranquil
mind
That nothing fretted in the least de-
gree—
Until, alas! I found that he was
blind.

What vanity is envy! for I find
I have been rich in dross of thought,
and poor
In that I was a fool, and lastly blind—
For never having seen myself before!

19

"TRADIN' JOE"

I'M one o' these cur'ous kind o' chaps
You think you know when you
don't, perhaps!
I hain't no fool—ner I don't p'tend
To be so smart I could rickommend

Myself fer a *congerssman*, my friend!—
But I'm kind o' betwixt-and-between,
you know,—
One o' these fellers 'at folks call "slow."
And I'll say jest here I'm kind o'
queer
Regardin' things 'at I *see* and *hear*,—
Fer I'm *thick* o' hearin' *sometimes,* and
It's hard to git me to understand;
But other times it hain't, you bet!
Fer I don't sleep with both eyes shet!

I've swapped a power in stock, and so
The neighbors calls me "Tradin' Joe"—
And I'm goin' to tell you 'bout a
trade,—
And one o' the best I ever made:

Folks has gone so fur's to say
'At I'm well fixed, in a *worldly* way,
And *bein'* so, and a *widower,*
It's not su'prisin', as you'll infer,
I'm purty handy among the sect—
Widders especially, rickollect!
And I won't deny that along o' late
I've hankered a heap fer the married
state—
But some way o' 'nother the longer we
wait
The harder it is to discover a mate.

Marshall Thomas,—a friend o' mine,
Doin' some in the tradin' line,
But a'most too *young* to know it all—
On'y at *picnics* er some *ball!*—
Says to me, in a banterin' way,
As we was a-loadin' stock one day,—
"You're a-huntin' a wife, and I want
you to see
My girl's mother, at Kankakee!—
She hain't over forty—good-lookin' and
spry,
And jest the woman to fill your eye!

And I'm a-goin' there Sund'y,—and
now," says he,
"I want to take you along with *me;*
And you marry *her,* and," he says, "by
'shaw!
You'll hev me fer yer son-in-law!"
I studied a while, and says I, "Well, I'll
First have to see ef she suits my style;
And ef she does, you kin bet your life
Your mother-in-law will be my wife!"

Well, Sund'y come; and I fixed up
some—
Putt on a collar—I did, by gum!—
Got down my "plug," and my satin
vest—
(You wouldn't know me to see me
dressed!—
But any one knows ef you got the
clothes
You kin go in the crowd wher' the best
of 'em goes!)
And I greeced my boots, and combed
my hair
Keerfully over the bald place there;
And Marshall Thomas and me that
day
Eat our dinners with Widder Gray
And her girl Han'! * * *

Well, jest a glance
O' the widder's smilin' countenance,
A-cuttin' up chicken and big pot-pies,
Would make a man hungry in Para-
dise!
And passin' p'serves and jelly and cake
'At would make an *angel's* appetite
ache!—
Pourin' out coffee as yaller as gold—
Twic't as much as the cup could hold—
La! it was rich!—And then she'd say,
"Take some o' *this!*" in her coaxin'
way,

Tell ef I'd been a hoss I'd 'a' *foundered,*
shore,
And jest dropped dead on her white-
oak floor!

Well, the way I talked would 'a' done
you good,
Ef you'd 'a' been there to 'a' under-
stood;
Tel I noticed Hanner and Marshall,
they
Was a-noticin' me in a cur'ous way;
So I says to myse'f, says I, "Now, Joe,
The best thing fer you is to jest go
slow!"
And I simmered down, and let them
do
The bulk o' the talkin' the evening
through.

And Marshall was still in a talkative
gait
When he left, that evening—tolable
late.
"How do you like her?" he says to me;
Says I, "She suits, to a 't-y-*Tee'!*"
And then I ast how matters stood
With him in the *opposite* neighber-
hood?
"Bully!" he says; "I ruther guess
I'll finally git her to say the 'yes.'
I named it to her to-night, and she
Kind o' smiled, and said *'she'd see'*—
And that's a purty good sign!" says he:
"Yes," says I, "you're ahead o' *me!*"
And then he laughed, and said, *"Go
in!"*
And patted me on the shoulder ag'in.

Well, ever sense then I've been ridin' a
good
Deal through the Kankakee neighber-
hood;

And I make it convenient sometimes to
stop
And hitch a few minutes, and kind o'
drop
In at the widder's, and talk o' the
crop
And one thing o' 'nother. And week
afore last
The notion struck me, as I drove past,
I'd stop at the place and state my
case—
Might as well do it at first as last!

I felt first-rate; so I hitched at the gate,
And went up to the house; and,
strange to relate,
Marshall Thomas had dropped in,
too.—
"Glad to see you, sir, how do you do?"
He says, says he! Well—it *sounded
queer:*
And when Han' told me to take a
cheer,
Marshall got up and putt out o' the
room—
And motioned his hand fer the *widder*
to come.
I didn't say nothin' fer quite a spell,
But thinks I to myse'f, "There's a dog
in the well!"
And Han' *she* smiled so cur'ous at
me—
Says I, "What's up?" And she says,
says she,
"Marshall's been at me to marry ag'in,
And I told him 'no,' jest as you come
in."
Well, somepin' o' 'nother in that girl's
voice
Says to me, "Joseph, here's your
choice!"
And another minute her guileless breast
Was lovin'ly throbbin' ag'in my vest!—

And then I kissed her, and heerd a
smack
Come like a' echo a-flutterin' back,
And we looked around, and in full
view
Marshall was kissin' the widder, too!
Well, we all of us laughed, in our
glad su'prise,
Tel the tears come *a-streamin'* out of
our eyes!
And when Marsh said " 'Twas the
squarest trade
That ever me and him had made,"
We both shuck hands, 'y jucks! and
swore
We'd stick together ferevermore.
And old Squire Chipman tuck us the
trip:
And Marshall and me's in pardnership!

20

DOT LEEDLE BOY

OT'S a leedle Gristmas story
Dot I told der leedle folks—
Und I vant you stop dot laughin'
Und grackin' funny jokes!—
So help me Peter-Moses!
Ot's no time for monkey-shine,
Ober I vast told you somedings
Of dot leedle boy of mine!

Ot vas von cold Vinter vedder,
Ven der snow vas all about—
Dot you have to chop der hatchet
Eef you got der sauerkraut!
Und der cheekens on der hind leg
Vas standin' in der shine
Der sun shmile out dot morning
On dot leedle boy of mine.

He vas yoost a leedle baby
  Not bigger as a doll
Dot time I got acquaintet—
  Ach! you ought to heard 'im squall!—
I grackys! dot's der moosic
  Ot make me feel so fine
Ven first I vas been marriet—
  Oh, dot leedle boy of mine!

He look yoost like his fader!—
  So, ven der vimmen said,
"Vot a purty leedle baby!"
  Katrina shake der head. . . .
I dink she must 'a' notice
  Dot der baby vas a-gryin',
Und she cover up der blankets
  Of dot leedle boy of mine.

Vel, ven he vas got bigger,
  Dot he grawl und bump his nose,
Und make der table over,
  Und molasses on his glothes—
Dot make 'im all der sveeter,—
  So I say to my Katrine,
"Better you vas quit a-shpankin'
  Dot leedle boy of mine!"

No more he vas older
  As about a dozen months
He speak der English language
  Und der German—bote at vonce!
Und he dringk his glass of lager
  Like a Londsman fon der Rhine—
Und I klingk my glass togeder
  Mit dot leedle boy of mine!

I vish you could 'a' seen id—
  Ven he glimb up on der chair
Und shmash der lookin'-glasses
  Ven he try to comb his hair
Mit a hammer!—Und Katrina
  Say, "Dot's an ugly sign!"

But I laugh und vink my fingers
  At dot leedle boy of mine.

But vonce, dot Vinter morning,
  He shlip out in der snow
Mitout no stockin's on 'im.—
  He say he "vant to go
Und fly some mit der birdies!"
  Und ve give 'im medi-cine
Ven he catch der "parrygoric"—
  Dot leedle boy of mine!

Und so I set und nurse 'im,
  Vile der Gristmas vas come roun',
Und I told 'im 'bout "Kriss Kringle,"
  How he come der chimbly down:
Und I ask 'im eef he love 'im
  Eef he bring 'im someding fine?
"Nicht besser as mein fader,"
  Say dot leedle boy of mine.—

Und he put his arms aroun' me
  Und hug so close und tight,
I hear der gclock a-tickin'
  All der balance of der night! . . .
Someding make me feel so funny
  Ven I say to my Katrine,
"Let us go und fill der stockin's
  Of dot leedle boy of mine."

Vell.—Ve buyed a leedle horses
  Dot you pull 'im mit a shtring,
Und a leedle fancy jay-bird—
  Eef you vant to hear 'im sing
You took 'im by der topknot
  Und yoost blow in behine—
Und dot make much *spectakel*
  For dot leedle boy of mine!

Und gandies, nuts und raizens—
  Und I buy a leedle drum
Dot I vant to hear 'im rattle
  Ven der Gristmas morning come!

Und a leedle shmall tin rooster
　Dot vould crow so loud und fine
Ven he sqveeze 'im in der morning,
　Dot leedle boy of mine!

Und—vile ve vas a-fixin'—
　Dot leedle boy vake out!
I t'ought he been a-dreamin'
　"Kriss Kringle" vas about,—
For he say—*"Dot's him!—I see 'im*
　Mit der shtars dot make der shine!"
Und he yoost keep on a-gryin'—
　Dot leedle boy of mine,—

Und gottin' vorse und vorser—
　Und tumble on der bed!
So—ven der doctor seen id,
　He kindo' shake his head,
Und feel his pulse—und visper,
　"Der boy is a-dyin'."
You dink I could *believe* id?—
　Dot leedle boy of mine?

I told you, friends—dot's someding,
　Der last time dot he speak
Und say, *"Goot-by, Kriss Kringle!"*
　—dot make me feel so veak
I yoost kneel down und drimble,
　Und bur-sed out a-gryin',
"Mein Gott, mein Gott in Himmel!—
　Dot leedle boy of mine!"

　.　　.　　.　　.　　.　　.

Der sun don't shine *dot* Gristmas!
　. . . Eef dot leedle boy vould *liff'd*—
No deefer-in'! for *Heaven* vas
　His leedle Gristmas gift!
Und der *rooster*, und der *gandy*,
　Und me—und my Katrine—
Und der jay-bird—is a-vaiting
　For dot leedle boy of mine.

21

I SMOKE MY PIPE

I CAN'T extend to every friend
　In need a helping hand—
No matter though I wish it so,
　'Tis not as Fortune planned;
But haply may I fancy they
　Are men of different stripe
Than others think who hint and
　wink,—
　And so—I smoke my pipe!

A golden coal to crown the bowl—
　My pipe and I alone,—
I sit and muse with idler views
　Perchance than I should own:—
It might be worse to own the
　purse
Whose glutted bowels gripe
　In little qualms of stinted alms;
And so I smoke my pipe.

And if inclined to moor my mind
　And cast the anchor Hope,
A puff of breath will put to death
　The morbid misanthrope
That lurks inside—as errors hide
　In standing forms of type
To mar at birth some line of worth;
　And so I smoke my pipe.

The subtle stings misfortune flings
　Can give me little pain
When my narcotic spell has wrought
　This quiet in my brain:
When I can waste the past in taste
　So luscious and so ripe
That like an elf I hug myself;
　And so I smoke my pipe.

And wrapped in shrouds of drifting
    clouds
I watch the phantom's flight,
Till alien eyes from Paradise
    Smile on me as I write:
And I forgive the wrongs that live,
    As lightly as I wipe
Away the tear that rises here;
    And so I smoke my pipe.

Here are not pansies and buttercups
    only—
Brambles and briers as keen as a
    knife;
And a Heart, ravenous, trails in the
    wood
For the meal have he must,—Red
    Riding-Hood!

22

RED RIDING-HOOD

SWEET little myth of the nursery
    story—
Earliest love of mine infantile breast,
Be something tangible, bloom in thy
    glory
Into existence, as thou art addressed!
Hasten! appear to me, guileless and
    good—
Thou art so dear to me, Red Riding-
    Hood!

Azure-blue eyes, in a marvel of won-
    der,
    Over the dawn of a blush breaking
        out;
Sensitive nose, with a little smile under
    Trying to hide in a blossoming
        pout—
Couldn't be serious, try as you would,
Little mysterious Red Riding-Hood!

Hah! little girl, it is desolate, lonely,
    Out in this bloomy old forest of
        Life!—

23

IF I KNEW WHAT POETS KNOW

IF I knew what poets know,
    Would I write a rhyme
Of the buds that never blow
    In the summer-time?
Would I sing of golden seeds
Springing up in ironweeds?
And of rain-drops turned to snow,
If I knew what poets know?

Did I know what poets do,
    Would I sing a song
Sadder than the pigeon's coo
    When the days are long?
Where I found a heart in pain,
I would make it glad again;
And the false should be the true,
Did I know what poets do.

If I knew what poets know,
    I would find a theme
Sweeter than the placid flow
    Of the fairest dream:
I would sing of love that lives
On the errors it forgives;
And the world would better grow
If I knew what poets know.

24

AN OLD SWEETHEART OF MINE

AN old sweetheart of mine!—Is this her presence here with me,
Or but a vain creation of a lover's memory?
A fair, illusive vision that would vanish into air
Dared I even touch the silence with the whisper of a prayer?

Nay, let me then believe in all the blended false and true—
The semblance of the *old* love and the substance of the *new,*—`
The *then* of changeless sunny days—the *now* of shower and shine—
But Love forever smiling—as that old sweetheart of mine.

This ever-restful sense of *home,* though shouts ring in the hall.—
The easy chair—the old book-shelves and prints along the wall;
The rare *Habanas* in their box, or gaunt church-warden-stem
That often wags, above the jar, derisively at them.

As one who cons at evening o'er an album, all alone,
And muses on the faces of the friends that he has known,
So I turn the leaves of Fancy, till, in shadowy design,
I find the smiling features of an old sweetheart of mine.

The lamplight seems to glimmer with a flicker of surprise,
As I turn it low—to rest me of the dazzle in my eyes,
And light my pipe in silence, save a sigh that seems to yoke
Its fate with my tobacco and to vanish with the smoke.

'Tis a *fragrant* retrospection,—for the loving thoughts that start
Into being are like perfume from the blossom of the heart;
And to dream the old dreams over is a luxury divine—
When my truant fancies wander with that old sweetheart of mine.

Though I hear beneath my study, like a fluttering of wings,
The voices of my children and the mother as she sings—
I feel no twinge of conscience to deny me any theme
When Care has cast her anchor in the harbor of a dream—

In fact, to speak in earnest, I believe it adds a charm
To spice the good a trifle with a little dust of harm,—
For I find an extra flavor in Memory's mellow wine
That makes me drink the deeper to that old sweetheart of mine.

O Childhood-days enchanted! O the magic of the Spring!—
With all green boughs to blossom white, and all bluebirds to sing!
When all the air, to toss and quaff, made life a jubilee
And changed the children's song and laugh to shrieks of ecstasy.

With eyes half closed in clouds that ooze from lips that taste, as well,
The peppermint and cinnamon, I hear the old School bell,
And from "Recess" romp in again from "Blackman's" broken line,
To smile, behind my "lesson," at that old sweetheart of mine.

A face of lily beauty, with a form of airy grace,
Floats out of my tobacco as the Genii from the vase;
And I thrill beneath the glances of a pair of azure eyes
As glowing as the summer and as tender as the skies.

I can see the pink sunbonnet and the little checkered dress
She wore when first I kissed her and she answered the caress
With the written declaration that, "as surely as the vine
Grew 'round the stump," she loved me—that old sweetheart of mine.

Again I made her presents, in a really helpless way,—
The big "Rhode Island Greening"—I was hungry, too, that day!—
But I follow her from Spelling, with her hand behind her—so—
And I slip the apple in it—and the Teacher doesn't know!

I give my *treasures* to her—all,—my pencil—blue-and-red;—
And, if little girls played marbles, *mine* should all be *hers,* instead!
But *she* gave me her *photograph,* and printed "Ever Thine"
Across the back—in blue-and-red—that old sweetheart of mine!

And again I feel the pressure of her slender little hand,
As we used to talk together of the future we had planned,—
When I should be a poet, and with nothing else to do
But write the tender verses that she set the music to . . .

When we should live together in a cozy little cot
Hid in a nest of roses, with a fairy garden-spot,
Where the vines were ever fruited, and the weather ever fine,
And the birds were ever singing for that old sweetheart of mine.

When I should be her lover forever and a day,
And she my faithful sweetheart till the golden hair was gray;
And we should be so happy that when either's lips were dumb
They would not smile in Heaven till the other's kiss had come.

But, ah! my dream is broken by a step upon the stair,
And the door is softly opened, and—my wife is standing there:
Yet with eagerness and rapture all my visions I resign,—
To greet the *living* presence of that old sweetheart of mine.

25

SQUIRE HAWKINS'S STORY

I HAIN'T no hand at tellin' tales,
    Er spinnin' yarns, as the sailors say;
Someway o' 'nother, language fails
To slide fer me in the oily way
That *lawyers* has; and I wisht it would,
Fer I've got somepin' that I call good;
But bein' only a country squire,
I've learned to listen and admire,
Ruther preferrin' to be addressed
Than talk myse'f—but I'll do my best:—

Old Jeff Thompson—well, I'll say,
Was the clos'test man I ever saw!—
Rich as cream, but the porest pay,
And the meanest man to work fer—
    La!
I've knowed that man to work one "hand"—
Fer little er nothin', you understand—
From four o'clock in the morning light
Tel eight and nine o'clock at night,
And then find fault with his appetite!
He'd drive all over the neighborhood
To miss the place where a toll-gate stood,
And slip in town, by some old road
That no two men in the county knowed,
With a jag o' wood, and a sack o' wheat,
That wouldn't burn and you couldn't eat!

And the trades he'd make, 'll I jest declare,
Was enough to make a preacher swear!
And then he'd hitch, and hang about
Tel the lights in the toll-gate was blowed out,
And then the turnpike he'd turn in
And sneak his way back home ag'in!

Some folks hint, and I make no doubt,
That that's what wore his old wife out—
Toilin' away from day to day
And year to year, through heat and cold,
Uncomplainin'—the same old way
The martyrs died in the days of old;
And a-clingin', too, as the martyrs done,
To one fixed faith, and her *only* one,—
Little Patience, the sweetest child
That ever wept unrickonciled,
Er felt the pain and the ache and sting
That only a mother's death can bring.

Patience Thompson!—I think that name
Must 'a' come from a power above,
Fer it seemed to fit her jest the same
As a *gaiter* would, er a fine kid glove!
And to see that girl, with all the care
Of the household on her—I de-clare
It was *oudacious,* the work she'd do,
And the thousand plans that she'd putt through;
And sing like a medder-lark all day long,
And drowned her cares in the joys o' song;

And *laugh* sometimes tel the farmer's
    "hand,"
Away fur off in the fields, would stand
A-listenin', with the plow half drawn,
Tel the coaxin' echoes called him on;
And the furries seemed, in his dreamy
    eyes,
Like foot-paths a-leadin' to Paradise,
As off through the hazy atmosphere
The call fer dinner reached his ear.

Now *love's* as cunnin' a little thing
As a hummin'-bird upon the wing,
And as liable to poke his nose
Jest where folks would least suppose,—
And more'n likely build his nest
Right in the heart you'd leave un-
    guessed,
And live and thrive at your expense—
At least, that's *my* experience.
And old Jeff Thompson often thought,
In his se'fish way, that the quiet John
Was a stiddy chap, as a farm-hand
    ought
To always be,—fer the airliest dawn
Found John busy—and *"easy,"* too,
Whenever his *wages* would fall due!—
To sum him up with a final touch,
He *eat* so little and *worked* so much,
That old Jeff laughed to hisse'f and
    said,
"He makes *me* money and airns his
    bread!"

But John, fer all of his quietude,
Would sometimes drap a word er so
That none but *Patience* understood,
And none but her was *meant* to
    know!—
Maybe at meal-times John would say,
As the sugar-bowl come down his way,
"Thanky, no; *my* coffee's sweet
Enough fer *me!"* with sich conceit,
She'd know at once, without no doubt,

He meant because *she* poured it out;
And smile and blush, and all sich stuff,
And ast ef it was *"strong* enough?"
And git the answer, neat and trim,
"It *couldn't* be too 'strong' fer *him!"*

And so things went fer 'bout a year,
Tel John, at last, found pluck to go
And pour his tale in the old man's
    ear—
And ef it had been *hot lead,* I know
It couldn't 'a' raised a louder fuss,
Ner 'a' riled the old man's temper wuss!
He jest *lit* in, and cussed and swore,
And lunged and rared, and ripped and
    tore,
And told John jest to leave his door,
And not to darken it no more!
But Patience cried, with eyes all wet,
"Remember, John, and don't ferget,
Whatever comes, I love you yet!"
But the old man thought, in his se'fish
    way,
"I'll see her married rich some day;
And *that,"* thinks he, "is money fer
    me—
And my will's *law,* as it ought to be!"

So when, in the course of a month er so,
A *widower,* with a farm er two,
Comes to Jeff's, w'y, the folks, you
    know,
Had to *talk*—as the folks'll do:
It was the talk of the neighberhood—
Patience and *John,* and *their* affairs;—
And this old chap with a few gray hairs
Had "cut John out," it was understood.
And some folks reckoned "Patience,
    too,
Knowed what *she* was a-goin' to do—
It was *like* her—la! indeed!—
All *she* loved was *dollars* and *cents*—
Like old *Jeff*—and they saw no need
Fer *John* to pine at *her* negligence!"

But others said, in a *kinder* way,
They missed the songs she used to
    sing—
They missed the smiles that used to
    play
Over her face, and the laughin' ring
Of her glad voice—that *every*thing
Of her *old* se'f seemed dead and gone,
And this was the ghost that they gazed
    on!

Tel finally it was noised about
There was a *weddin'* soon to be
Down at Jeff's; and the "cat was out"
Shore enough!—'Ll the *Jee-mum-nee!*
It *riled* me when John told me so,—
Fer *I was* a *friend o' John's,* you know;
And his trimblin' voice jest broke in
    two—
As a feller's voice'll sometimes do.—
And I says, says I, "Ef I know my biz—
And I think I know what *jestice* is,—
I've read *some* law—and I'd advise
A man like you to wipe his eyes
And square his jaws and start *ag'in,*
Fer jestice is a-goin' to win!"
And it wasn't long tel his eyes had
    cleared
As blue as the skies, and the *sun* ap-
    peared
In the shape of a good old-fashioned
    smile
That I hadn't seen fer a long, long
    while.

So we talked on fer a' hour er more,
And sunned ourselves in the open
    door,—
Tel a hoss-and-buggy down the road
Come a-drivin' up, that I guess John
    knowed,—
Fer he winked and says, "I'll dessap-
    pear—

They'd smell a mice ef they saw *me*
    here!"
And he thumbed his nose at the old
    gray mare,
And hid hisse'f in the house some-
    where.

Well.—The rig drove up: and I raised
    my head
As old Jeff hollered to me and said
That "him and his old friend there had
    come
To see ef the squire was at home."
. . . I told 'em "I was; and I *aimed* to be
At every chance of a weddin'-fee!"
And then I laughed—and they laughed,
    too,—
Fer that was the object they had in
    view.
"Would I be on hands at eight that
    night?"
They ast; and 's-I, "You're mighty
    right,
I'll be on hand!" And then I *bu'st*
Out a-laughin' my very wu'st,—
And so did they, as they wheeled away
And drove to'rds town in a cloud o'
    dust.
Then I shet the door, and me and John
Laughed and *laughed,* and jest *laughed*
    on,
Tel Mother drapped her specs, and *by*
Jeewhillikers! I thought she'd *die!—*
And she couldn't 'a' told, I'll bet my
    hat,
What on earth she was laughin' at!

But all o' the fun o' the tale hain't
    done!—
Fer a drizzlin' rain had jest begun,
And a-havin' 'bout four mile' to ride,
I jest concluded I'd better light
Out fer Jeff's and save my hide,—

Fer *it was a-goin' to storm, that night!*
So we went down to the barn, and John
Saddled my beast, and I got on;
And he told me somepin' to not ferget,
And when I left, he was *laughin'* yet.

And, 'proachin' on to my journey's end,
The great big draps o' the rain come
 down,
And the thunder growled in a way to
 lend
An awful look to the lowerin 'frown
The dull sky wore; and the lightnin'
 glanced
Tel my old mare jest *more'n* pranced,
And tossed her head, and bugged her
 eyes
To about four times their natchurl size,
As the big black lips of the clouds 'ud
 drap
Out some oath of a thunderclap,
And threaten on in an undertone
That chilled a feller clean to the bone!

But I struck shelter soon enough
To save myse'f. And the house was
 jammed
With the women-folks, and the wed-
 din'-stuff: —
A great, long table, fairly *crammed*
With big pound-cakes—and chops and
 steaks—
And roasts and stews—and stumick-
 aches
Of every fashion, form, and size,
From twisters up to punkin-pies!
And candies, oranges, and figs,
And reezins,—all the "whilligigs"
And "jim-cracks" that the law allows
On sich occasions!—Bobs and bows
Of gigglin' girls, with corkscrew curls,
And fancy ribbons, reds and blues,
And "beau-ketchers" and "curliques"
To beat the world! And seven o'clock

Brought old Jeff;—and brought—*the*
 groom,—
With a sideboard-collar on, and stock
That choked him so, he hadn't room
To *swaller* in, er even sneeze,
Er clear his th'oat with any ease
Er comfort—and a good square cough
Would saw his Adam's apple off!

But as fer *Patience—My!* Oomh-
 oomh!—
I never saw her look so sweet!—
Her face was cream and roses, too;
And then them eyes o' heavenly blue
Jest made an angel all complete!
And when she split 'em up in smiles
And splintered 'em around the room,
And danced acrost and met the groom,
And *laughed out loud*—It kind o' spiles
My language when I come to that—
Fer, as she laid away his hat,
Thinks I, *"The papers hid inside*
Of that said hat must make a bride
A happy one fer all her life,
Er else a wrecked and wretched wife!"
And, someway, then, I thought of
 John,—
Then looked towards *Patience.* . . .
 She was *gone!*—
The door stood open, and the rain
Was dashin' in; and sharp and plain
Above the storm we heerd a cry—
A ringin', laughin', loud "Good-by!"
That died away, as fleet and fast
A hoss's hoofs went splashin' past!
And that was all. 'Twas done that
 quick! . . .
You've heerd o' fellers "lookin' sick"?
I wisht you'd seen *the groom* jest then—
I wisht you'd seen them two old men,
With starin' eyes that fairly *glared*
At one another, and the scared
And empty faces of the crowd,—

I wisht you could 'a' been allowed
To jest look on and see it all,—
And heerd the girls and women bawl
And wring their hands; and heerd old
    Jeff
A-cussin' as he swung hisse'f
Upon his hoss, who champed his bit
As though old Nick had holt of it:
And cheek by jowl the two old wrecks
Rode off as though they'd break their
    necks.

And as we all stood starin' out
Into the night, I felt the brush
Of some one's hand, and turned about,
And heerd a voice that whispered,
    "Hush!—
They're waitin' in the kitchen, and
You're wanted. Don't you understand?"
Well, ef my memory serves me now,
I think I winked.—Well, anyhow,
I left the crowd a-gawkin' there,
And jest slipped off around to where
The back door opened, and went in,
And turned and shet the door ag'in,
And maybe locked it—couldn't swear,—
A woman's arms around me makes
Me liable to make mistakes.—
I read a marriage license nex',
But as I didn't have my specs
I jest inferred it was all right,
And tied the knot so mortal-tight
That Patience and my old friend John
Was safe enough from that time on!

Well, now, I might go on and tell
How all the joke at last leaked out,
And how the youngsters raised the yell
And rode the happy groom about
Upon their shoulders; how the bride
Was kissed a hunderd times beside
The one I give her,—tel she cried
And laughed untel she like to died!
I might go on and tell you all

About the supper—and the ball.—
You'd ought to see me twist my heel
Through jest one old Furginny reel
Afore you die! er tromp the strings
Of some old fiddle tel she sings
Some old cowtillion, don't you know,
That putts the devil in yer toe!

We kep' the dancin' up tel four
O'clock, I reckon—maybe more.—
We hardly heerd the thunders roar,
Er thought about the storm that
    blowed—
And them two fellers on the road!
Tel all at onc't we heerd the door
Bu'st open, and a voice that swore,—
And old Jeff Thompson tuck the floor.
He shuck hisse'f and looked around
Like some old dog about half-
    drowned—
His hat, I reckon, weighed ten pound
To say the least, and I'll say, shore,
His overcoat weighed fifty more—
The wettest man you ever saw,
To have so dry a son-in-law!

He sized it all; and Patience laid
Her hand in John's, and looked afraid,
And waited. And a stiller set
O' folks, I know, you never met
In any court room, where with dread
They wait to hear a verdick read.

The old man turned his eyes on me:
"And have you married 'em?" says he.
I nodded "Yes." "Well, that'll do,"
He says, "and now we're th'ough with
    you,—
You jest clear out, and I decide
And promise to be satisfied!"
He hadn't nothin' more to say.
I saw, of course, how matters lay,
And left. But as I rode away
I heerd the roosters crow fer day.

26

A COUNTRY PATHWAY

I COME upon it suddenly, alone—
    A little pathway winding in the
        weeds
That fringe the roadside; and with
        dreams my own,
    I wander as it leads.

Full wistfully along the slender way,
    Through summer tan of freckled
        shade and shine,
I take the path that leads me as it
        may—
    Its every choice is mine.

A chipmunk, or a sudden-whirring
        quail,
    Is startled by my step as on I fare—
A garter-snake across the dusty trail
    Glances and—is not there.

Above the arching jimson-weeds flare
        twos
    And twos of sallow-yellow butter-
        flies,
Like blooms of lorn primroses blowing
        loose
    When autumn winds arise.

The trail dips—dwindles—broadens
        then, and lifts
    Itself astride a cross-road dubiously,
And, from the fennel marge beyond it,
        drifts
    Still onward, beckoning me.

And though it needs must lure me mile
        on mile
    Out of the public highway, still I go,

My thoughts, far in advance in Indian
        file,
    Allure me even so.

Why, I am as a long-lost boy that went
    At dusk to bring the cattle to the
        bars,
And was not found again, though
        Heaven lent
    His mother all the stars

With which to seek him through that
        awful night
    O years of nights as vain!—Stars
        never rise
But well might miss their glitter in the
        light
    Of tears in mother-eyes!

So—on, with quickened breaths, I fol-
        low still—
    My avant-courier must be obeyed!
Thus am I led, and thus the path, at
        will,
    Invites me to invade

A meadow's precincts, where my dar-
        ing guide
    Clambers the steps of an old-fash-
        ioned stile,
And stumbles down again, the other
        side,
    To gambol there a while.

In pranks of hide-and-seek, as on ahead
    I see it running, while the clover-
        stalks
Shake rosy fists at me, as though they
        said—
    "You dog our country walks

"And mutilate us with your walking-
        stick!—
    We will not suffer tamely what you
        do,

And warn you at your peril,—for we'll
    sick
Our bumblebees on you!"

But I smile back, in airy noncha-
    lance,—
  The more determined on my way-
    ward quest,
As some bright memory a moment
    dawns
  A morning in my breast—

Sending a thrill that hurries me along
  In faulty similes of childish skips,
Enthused with lithe contortions of a
    song
  Performing on my lips.

In wild meanderings o'er pasture
    wealth—
  Erratic wanderings through dead'-
    ning lands,
Where sly old brambles, plucking me
    by stealth,
  Put berries in my hands:

Or the path climbs a boulder—wades
    a slough—
  Or, rollicking through buttercups
    and flags,
Goes gaily dancing o'er a deep bayou
  On old tree-trunks and snags:

Or, at the creek, leads o'er a limpid
    pool
  Upon a bridge the stream itself has
    made,
With some Spring-freshet for the
    mighty tool
  That its foundation laid.

I pause a moment here to bend and
    muse,

With dreamy eyes, on my reflection,
    where
A boat-backed bug drifts on a helpless
    cruise,
  Or wildly oars the air,

As, dimly seen, the pirate of the
    brook—
  The pike, whose jaunty hulk de-
    notes his speed—
Swings pivoting about, with wary look
  Of low and cunning greed.

Till, filled with other thought, I turn
    again
  To where the pathway enters in a
    realm
Of lordly woodland, under sovereign
    reign
  Of towering oak and elm.

A puritanic quiet here reviles
  The almost whispered warble from
    the hedge,
And takes a locust's rasping voice and
    files
  The silence to an edge.

In such a solitude my somber way
  Strays like a misanthrope within a
    gloom
Of his own shadows—till the perfect
    day
  Bursts into sudden bloom,

And crowns a long, declining stretch
    of space,
  Where King Corn's armies lie with
    flags unfurled,
And where the valley's dint in Nature's
    face
  Dimples a smiling world.

And lo! through mists that may not
    be dispelled,
I see an old farm homestead, as in
    dreams,
Where, like a gem in costly setting
    held,
The old log cabin gleams.

. . .   .

O darling Pathway! lead me bravely on
    Adown your valley-way, and run be-
    fore
Among the roses crowding up the lawn
    And thronging at the door,—

And carry up the echo there that shall
    Arouse the drowsy dog, that he may
    bay
The household out to greet the prod-
    igal
That wanders home to-day.

27

THE OLD GUITAR

NEGLECTED now is the old guitar
    And moldering into decay;
Fretted with many a rift and scar
    That the dull dust hides away,
While the spider spins a silver star
    In its silent lips to-day.

The keys hold only nerveless strings—
    The sinews of brave old airs
Are pulseless now; and the scarf that
    clings
So closely here declares
A sad regret in its ravelings
    And the faded hue it wears.

But the old guitar, with a lenient grace,
    Has cherished a smile for me;
And its features hint of a fairer face
    That comes with a memory
Of a flower-and-perfume-haunted place
    And a moonlit balcony.

Music sweeter than words confess,
    Or the minstrel's powers invent,
Thrilled here once at the light caress
    Of the fairy hands that lent
This excuse for the kiss I press
    On the dear old instrument.

The rose of pearl with the jeweled
    stem
Still blooms; and the tiny sets
In the circle all are here; the gem
    In the keys, and the silver frets;
But the dainty fingers that danced o'er
    them—
Alas for the heart's regrets!—

Alas for the loosened strings to-day,
    And the wounds of rift and scar
On a worn old heart, with its rounde-
    lay
Enthralled with a stronger bar
That Fate weaves on, through a dull
    decay
Like that of the old guitar!

28

"FRIDAY AFTERNOON"

TO WILLIAM MORRIS PIERSON

[1868-1870]

OF the wealth of facts and fancies
    That our memories may recall,
The old school-day romances
    Are the dearest, after all!—

When some sweet thought revises
  The half-forgotten tune
That opened "Exercises"
  On "Friday Afternoon."

We seem to hear the clicking
  Of the pencil and the pen,
And the solemn, ceaseless ticking
  Of the timepiece ticking then;
And we note the watchful master,
  As he waves the warning rod,
With our own heart beating faster
  Than the boy's who threw the wad.

Some little hand uplifted,
  And the creaking of a shoe:—
A problem left unsifted
  For the teacher's hand to do:
The murmured hum of learning—
  And the flutter of a book;
The smell of something burning,
  And the school's inquiring look.

The bashful boy in blushes;
  And the girl, with glancing eyes,
Who hides her smiles, and hushes
  The laugh about to rise,—
Then, with a quick invention,
  Assumes a serious face,
To meet the words, "Attention!
  Every scholar in his place!"

The opening song, page 20.—
  Ah! dear old "Golden Wreath,"
You willed your sweets in plenty;
  And some who look beneath
The leaves of Time will linger,
  And loving tears will start,
As Fancy trails her finger
  O'er the index of the heart.

"Good News from Home"—We hear it
  Welling tremulous, yet clear

And holy as the spirit
  Of the song we used to hear—
"Good news for me"—(A throbbing
  And an aching melody)—
"Has come across the"—(sobbing,
  Yea, and salty) "dark blue sea!"

Or the pæan "Scotland's burning!"
  With its mighty surge and swell
Of chorus, still returning
  To its universal yell—
Till we're almost glad to drop to
  Something sad and full of pain—
And "Skip verse three," and stop, too,
  Ere our hearts are broke again.

Then "the big girls' " compositions,
  With their doubt, and hope, and
    glow
Of heart and face,—conditions
  Of "the big boys"—even so,—
When themes of "Spring," and "Sum-
    mer"
And of "Fall," and "Winter-time"
Droop our heads and hold us dumber
  Than the sleigh-bell's fancied chime.

Elocutionary science—
  (Still in changeless infancy!)—
With its "Cataline's Defiance,"
  And "The Banner of the Free":
Or, lured from Grandma's attic,
  A ramshackle "rocker" there,
Adds a skreek of the dramatic
  To the poet's "Old Arm-Chair."

Or the "Speech of Logan" shifts us
  From the pathos, to the fire;
And Tell (with Gessler) lifts us
  Many noble notches higher.—
Till a youngster, far from sunny,
  With sad eyes of watery blue,
Winds up with something "funny,"
  Like "Cock-a-doodle-do!"

Then a dialogue—selected
  For its realistic worth:—
The Cruel Boy detected
  With a turtle turned to earth
Back downward; and, in pleading,
  The Good Boy—strangely gay
At such a sad proceeding—
  Says, "Turn him over, pray!"

So the exercises taper
  Through gradations of delight
To the reading of "The Paper,"
  Which is entertaining—quite!
For it goes ahead and mentions
  "If a certain Mr. O.
Has serious intentions
  That he ought to tell her so."

It also "Asks permission
  To intimate to 'John'
The dubious condition
  Of the ground he's standing on";
And, dropping the suggestion
  To "mind what he's about,"
It stuns him with the question:
  "Does his mother know he's out?"

And among the contributions
  To this "Academic Press"
Are "Versified Effusions"
  By—"Our lady editress"—
Which fact is proudly stated
  By the *Chief* of the concern,—
"Though the verse communicated
  Bears the pen-name 'Fanny Fern.'"

.   .   .   .

When all has been recited,
  And the teacher's bell is heard,
And visitors, invited,
  Have dropped a kindly word,
A hush of holy feeling

Falls down upon us there,
  As though the day were kneeling,
With the twilight for the prayer.

.   .   .   .

Midst the wealth of facts and fancies
  That our memories may recall,
Thus the old school-day romances
  Are the dearest, after all!—
When some sweet thought revises
  The half-forgotten tune
That opened "Exercises,"
  On "Friday Afternoon."

29

"JOHNSON'S BOY"

THE world is turned ag'in' me,
  And people says, "They guess
That nothin' else is in me
  But pure maliciousness!"
I git the blame for doin'
  What other chaps destroy,
And I'm a-goin' to ruin
  Because I'm "Johnson's boy."

That ain't my *name*—I'd ruther
  They'd call me *Ike* or *Pat*—
But they've forgot the other—
  And so have *I*, for that!
I reckon it's as handy,
  When Nibsy breaks his toy,
Or some one steals his candy,
  To say 'twas *"Johnson's boy!"*

You can't git any water
  At the pump, and find the spout
So durn chuck-full o' mortar
  That you have to bore it out;

You tackle any scholar
   In Wisdom's wise employ,
And I'll bet you half a dollar
   He'll say it's "Johnson's boy!"

Folks don't know how I suffer
   In my uncomplainin' way—
They think I'm gittin' tougher
   And tougher every day.
Last Sunday night, when Flinder
   Was a-shoutin' out for joy,
And some one shook the winder,
   He prayed for "Johnson's boy."

I'm tired of bein' follered
   By farmers every day,
And then o' bein' collared
   For coaxin' hounds away;
Hounds always plays me double—
   It's a trick they all enjoy—
To git me into trouble,
   Because I'm "Johnson's boy."

But if I git to Heaven,
   I hope the Lord'll see
Some boy has been perfect,
   And lay it on to me;
I'll swell the song sonorous,
   And clap my wings for joy,
And sail off on the chorus—
   "Hurrah, for 'Johnson's boy!'"

30

HER BEAUTIFUL HANDS

O YOUR hands—they are strangely
      fair!
Fair—for the jewels that sparkle
   there,—
Fair—for the witchery of the spell
That ivory keys alone can tell;

But when their delicate touches rest
Here in my own do I love them best,
As I clasp with eager, acquisitive spans
My glorious treasure of beautiful hands!

Marvelous — wonderful — beautiful
   hands!
They can coax roses to bloom in the
   strands
Of your brown tresses; and ribbons
   will twine,
Under mysterious touches of thine,
Into such knots as entangle the soul
And fetter the heart under such a con-
   trol
As only the strength of my love under-
   stands—
My passionate love for your beautiful
   hands.

As I remember the first fair touch
Of those beautiful hands that I love so
   much,
I seem to thrill as I then was thrilled,
Kissing the glove that I found un-
   filled—
When I met your gaze, and the queenly
   bow,
As you said to me, laughingly, "Keep
   it now!" . . .
And dazed and alone in a dream I
   stand,
Kissing this ghost of your beautiful
   hand.

When first I loved, in the long ago,
And held your hand as I told you so—
Pressed and caressed it and gave it a
   kiss
And said "I could die for a hand like
   this!"
Little I dreamed love's fullness yet
Had to ripen when eyes were wet

And prayers were vain in their wild
demands
For one warm touch of your beautiful
hands.

. . . .

Beautiful Hands!—O Beautiful Hands!
Could you reach out of the alien lands
Where you are lingering, and give me,
to-night,
Only a touch—were it ever so light—
My heart were soothed, and my weary
brain
Would lull itself into rest again;
For there is no solace the world com-
mands
Like the caress of your beautiful hands.

31

NATURAL PERVERSITIES

I AM not prone to moralize
In scientific doubt
On certain facts that Nature tries
To puzzle us about,—
For I am no philosopher
Of wise elucidation,
But speak of things as they occur,
From simple observation.

I notice *little* things—to wit:—
I never missed a train
Because I didn't *run* for it;
I never knew it rain
That my umbrella wasn't lent,—
Or, when in my possession,
The sun but wore, to all intent,
A jocular expression.

I never knew a creditor
To dun me for a debt

But I was "cramped" or "bu'sted"; o'
I never knew one yet,
When I had plenty in my purse,
To make the least invasion,—
As I, accordingly perverse,
Have courted no occasion.

Nor do I claim to comprehend
What Nature has in view
In giving us the very friend
To trust we oughtn't to.—
But so it is: The trusty gun
Disastrously exploded
Is always sure to be the one
We didn't think was loaded.

Our moaning is another's mirth,—
And what is worse by half,
We say the funniest thing on earth
And never raise a laugh:
'Mid friends that love us over well,
And sparkling jests and liquor,
Our hearts somehow are liable
To melt in tears the quicker.

We reach the wrong when most we
seek
The right; in like effect,
We stay the strong and not the weak—
Do most when we neglect.—
Neglected genius—truth be said—
As wild and quick as tinder,
The more you seek to help ahead
The more you seem to hinder.

I've known the least the greatest, too—
And, on the selfsame plan,
The biggest fool I ever knew
Was quite a little man:
We find we ought, and then we
won't—'
We prove a thing, then doubt it,—
Know *everything* but when we don't
Know *anything* about it.

32

THE SILENT VICTORS

May 30, 1878

*Dying for victory, cheer on cheer
Thundered on his eager ear.*
                    —Charles L. Holstein.

I

DEEP, tender, firm and true, the
      Nation's heart
Throbs for her gallant heroes passed
      away,
Who in grim Battle's drama played
      their part,
And slumber here to-day.—

Warm hearts that beat their lives out
      at the shrine
Of Freedom, while our country held
      its breath
As brave battalions wheeled themselves
      in line
And marched upon their death:

When Freedom's Flag, its natal wounds
      scarce healed,
      Was torn from peaceful winds and
      flung again
To shudder in the storm of battle-
      field—
      The elements of men,—

When every star that glittered was a
      mark
      For Treason's ball, and every rip-
      pling bar
Of red and white was sullied with the
      dark
      And purple stain of war:

When angry guns, like famished beasts
      of prey,
Were howling o'er their gory feast
      of lives,
And sending dismal echoes far away
To mothers, maids, and wives:—

The mother, kneeling in the empty
      night,
With pleading hands uplifted for the
      son
Who, even as she prayed, had fought
      the fight—
The victory had won:

The wife, with trembling hand that
      wrote to say
The babe was waiting for the sire's
      caress—
The letter meeting that upon the
      way,—
The babe was fatherless:

The maiden, with her lips, in fancy,
      pressed
Against the brow once dewy with
      her breath,
Now lying numb, unknown, and un-
      caressed
Save by the dews of death.

II

What meed of tribute can the poet pay
The Soldier, but to trail the ivy-vine
Of idle rhyme above his grave to-day
In epitaph design?—

Or wreathe with laurel-words the icy
      brows
That ache no longer with a dream
      of fame,

But, pillowed lowly in the narrow
  house,
  Renowned beyond the name.

The dewy tear-drops of the night may
  fall,
  And tender morning with her shin-
    ing hand
May brush them from the grasses
    green and tall
  That undulate the land.—

Yet song of Peace nor din of toil and
    thrift,
  Nor chanted honors, with the flowers
    we heap,
Can yield us hope the Hero's head to
    lift
  Out of its dreamless sleep:

The dear old Flag, whose faintest flut-
    ter flies
  A stirring echo through each patriot
    breast,
Can never coax to life the folded eyes
  That saw its wrongs redressed—

That watched it waver when the fight
    was hot,
  And blazed with newer courage to
    its aid,
Regardless of the shower of shell and
    shot
  Through which the charge was
    made;—

And when, at last, they saw it plume
    its wings,
  Like some proud bird in stormy ele-
    ment,
And soar untrammeled on its wander-
    ings,
  They closed in death, content.

III

O Mother, you who miss the smiling
    face
  Of that dear boy who vanished from
    your sight,
And left you weeping o'er the vacant
    place
  He used to fill at night,—

Who left you dazed, bewildered, on a
    day
  That echoed wild huzzas, and roar
    of guns
That drowned the farewell words you
    tried to say
  To incoherent ones;—

Be glad and proud you had the life to
    give—
  Be comforted through all the years
    to come,—
Your country has a longer life to live,
  Your son a better home.

O Widow, weeping o'er the orphaned
    child,
  Who only lifts his questioning eyes
    to send
A keener pang to grief unreconciled,—
  Teach him to comprehend

He had a father brave enough to stand
  Before the fire of Treason's blazing
    gun,
That, dying, he might will the rich old
    land
  Of Freedom to his son.

And, Maiden, living on through lonely
    years
  In fealty to love's enduring ties,—

With strong faith gleaming through
　　the tender tears
That gather in your eyes,

Look up! and own, in gratefulness of
　　prayer,
　　Submission to the will of Heaven's
　　High Host:—
I see your Angel-soldier pacing there,
　　Expectant at his post.—

I see the rank and file of armies vast,
　　That muster under one supreme con-
　　trol;
I hear the trumpet sound the signal-
　　blast—
　　The calling of the roll—

The grand divisions falling into line
　　And forming, under voice of One
　　alone
Who gives command, and joins with
　　tongue divine
　　The hymn that shakes the Throne.

IV

And thus, in tribute to the forms that
　　rest
　　In their last, camping-ground, we
　　strew the bloom
And fragrance of the flowers they
　　loved the best,
　　In silence o'er the tomb.

With reverent hands we twine the
　　Hero's wreath
　　And clasp it tenderly on stake or
　　stone
That stands the sentinel for each be-
　　neath
　　Whose glory is our own.

While in the violet that greets the sun,
　　We see the azure eye of some lost
　　boy;
And in the rose the ruddy cheek of one
　　We kissed in childish joy,—

Recalling, haply, when he marched
　　away,
　　He laughed his loudest though his
　　eyes were wet.—
The kiss he gave his mother's brow
　　that day
　　Is there and burning yet:

And through the storm of grief around
　　her tossed,
　　One ray of saddest comfort she may
　　see,—
Four hundred thousand sons like hers
　　were lost
　　To weeping Liberty.

.　　.　　.　　.　　.　　.　　.

But draw aside the drapery of gloom,
　　And let the sunshine chase the clouds
　　away
And gild with brighter glory every
　　tomb
　　We decorate to-day:

And in the holy silence reigning round,
　　While prayers of perfume bless the
　　atmosphere,
Where loyal souls of love and faith are
　　found,
　　Thank God that Peace is here!

And let each angry impulse that may
　　start,
　　Be smothered out of every loyal
　　breast;
And, rocked within the cradle of the
　　heart,
　　Let every sorrow rest.

33

SCRAPS

THERE'S a habit I have nurtured,
    From the sentimental time
When my life was like a story,
    And my heart a happy rhyme,—
Of clipping from the paper,
    Or magazine, perhaps,
The idle songs of dreamers,
    Which I treasure as my scraps.

They hide among my letters,
    And they find a cozy nest
In the bosom of my wrapper,
    And the pockets of my vest;
They clamber in my fingers
    Till my dreams of wealth relapse
In fairer dreams than Fortune's
    Though I find them only scraps.

Sometimes I find, in tatters
    Like a beggar, form as fair
As ever gave to Heaven
    The treasure of a prayer;
And words all dim and faded,
    And obliterate in part,
Grow into fadeless meanings
    That are printed on the heart.

Sometimes a childish jingle
    Flings an echo, sweet and clear,
And thrills me as I listen
    To the laughs I used to hear;
And I catch the gleam of faces,
    And the glimmer of glad eyes
That peep at me expectant
    O'er the walls of Paradise.

O syllables of measure!
    Though you wheel yourselves in line,
And await the further order
    Of this eager voice of mine;

You are powerless to follow
    O'er the field my fancy maps,
So I lead you back to silence
    Feeling you are only scraps.

34

AUGUST

A DAY of torpor in the sullen heat
    Of Summer's passion: In the slug-
        gish stream
The panting cattle lave their lazy feet,
    With drowsy eyes, and dream.

Long since the winds have died, and
        in the sky
    There lives no cloud to hint of Na-
        ture's grief;
The sun glares ever like an evil eye,
    And withers flower and leaf.

Upon the gleaming harvest-field remote
    The thresher lies deserted, like some
        old
Dismantled galleon that hangs afloat
    Upon a sea of gold.

The yearning cry of some bewildered
        bird
    Above an empty nest, and truant
        boys
Along the river's shady margin heard—
    A harmony of noise—

A melody of wrangling voices blent
    With liquid laughter, and with rip-
        pling calls
Of piping lips and thrilling echoes sent
    To mimic waterfalls.

And through the hazy veil the at-
        mosphere
    Has draped about the gleaming face
        of Day,

The sifted glances of the sun appear
In splinterings of spray.

The dusty highway, like a cloud of
    dawn,
    Trails o'er the hillside, and the
        passer-by,
A tired ghost in misty shroud, toils on
His journey to the sky.

And down across the valley's drooping
    sweep
    Withdrawn to farthest limit of the
        glade,
The forest stands in silence, drinking
    deep
    Its purple wine of shade.

The gossamer floats up on phantom
    wing;
    The sailor-vision voyages the skies
And carries into chaos everything
    That freights the weary eyes:

Till, throbbing on and on, the pulse of
    heat
    Increases — reaches — passes fever's
        height,
And Day slinks into slumber, cool and
    sweet,
    Within the arms of Night.

35

DEAD IN SIGHT OF FAME

Died—*Early morning of September
5, 1876, and in the gleaming dawn of
"name and fame," Hamilton J. Dunbar.*

DEAD! Dead! Dead!
    We thought him ours alone;
And were so proud to see him tread

The rounds of fame, and lift his head
    Where sunlight ever shone;
But now our aching eyes are dim,
And look through tears in vain for him.

Name! Name! Name!
    It was his diadem;
Nor ever tarnish-taint of shame
Could dim its luster—like a flame
    Reflected in a gem,
He wears it blazing on his brow
Within the courts of Heaven now.

Tears! Tears! Tears!
    Like dews upon the leaf
That bursts at last—from out the years
The blossom of a trust appears
    That blooms above the grief;
And mother, brother, wife and child
Will see it and be reconciled.

36

IN THE DARK

O IN the depths of midnight
    What fancies haunt the brain!
When even the sigh of the sleeper
    Sounds like a sob of pain.

A sense of awe and of wonder
    I may never well define,—
For the thoughts that come in the
        shadows
    Never come in the shine.

The old clock down in the parlor
    Like a sleepless mourner grieves,
And the seconds drip in the silence
    As the rain drips from the eaves.

And I think of the hands that signal
The hours there in the gloom,
And wonder what angel watchers
Wait in the darkened room.

And I think of the smiling faces
That used to watch and wait,
Till the click of the clock was an-
swered
By the click of the opening gate.—

They are not there now in the eve-
ning—
Morning or noon—not there;
Yet I know that they keep their vigil,
And wait for me Somewhere.

37

THE IRON HORSE

NO song is mine of Arab steed—
My courser is of nobler blood,
And cleaner limb and fleeter speed,
And greater strength and hardihood
Than ever cantered wild and free
Across the plains of Araby.

Go search the level desert land
From Sana on to Samarcand—
Wherever Persian prince has been,
Or Dervish, Sheik, or Bedouin,
And I defy you there to point
Me out a steed the half so fine—
From tip of ear to pastern-joint
As this old iron horse of mine.

You do not know what beauty is—
You do not know what gentleness
His answer is to my caress!—

Why, look upon this gait of his,—
A touch upon his iron rein—
He moves with such a stately grace
The sunlight on his burnished mane
Is barely shaken in its place;
And at a touch he changes pace,
And, gliding backward, stops again.

And talk of mettle—Ah! my friend,
Such passion smolders in his breast
That when awakened it will send
A thrill of rapture wilder than
E'er palpitated heart of man
When flaming at its mightiest.
And there's a fierceness in his ire—
A maddened majesty that leaps
Along his veins in blood of fire,
Until the path his vision sweeps
Spins out behind him like a thread
Unraveled from the reel of time,
As, wheeling on his course sublime,
The earth revolves beneath his tread.

Then stretch away, my gallant steed!
Thy mission is a noble one:
Thou bear'st the father to the son,
And sweet relief to bitter need;
Thou bear'st the stranger to his friends;
Thou bear'st the pilgrim to the
shrine,
And back again the prayer he sends
That God will prosper me and
mine,—
The star that on thy forehead gleams
Has blossomed in our brightest dreams.

Then speed thee on thy glorious race!
The mother waits thy ringing pace;
The father leans an anxious ear
The thunder of thy hooves to hear;
The lover listens, far away,
To catch thy keen exultant neigh;

And, where thy breathings roll and rise,
The husband strains his eager eyes,
And laugh of wife and baby-glee
Ring out to greet and welcome thee.
Then stretch away! and when at last
    The master's hand shall gently check
Thy mighty speed, and hold thee fast,
    The world will pat thee on the neck.

38

DEAD LEAVES

DAWN

AS though a gipsy maiden with dim
    look,
    Sat crooning by the roadside of the
        year,
    So, Autumn, in thy strangeness, thou
        art here
To read dark fortunes for us from the
    book.
Of fate; thou flingest in the crinkled
    brook
    The trembling maple's gold, and
        frosty-clear
    Thy mocking laughter thrills the at-
        mosphere,
And drifting on its current calls the
    rook
To other lands. As one who wades,
    alone,
    Deep in the dusk, and hears the
        minor talk
Of distant melody, and finds the tone,
    In some weird way compelling him
        to stalk
The paths of childhood over,—so I
    moan,
    And like a troubled sleeper, groping,
        walk.

DUSK

THE frightened herds of clouds
    across the sky
    Trample the sunshine down, and
        chase the day
    Into the dusky forest-lands of gray
And somber twilight. Far, and faint,
    and high
The wild goose trails his harrow, with
    a cry
    Sad as the wail of some poor cast-
        away
Who sees a vessel drifting far astray
Of his last hope, and lays him down to
    die.
The children, riotous from school,
    grow bold
    And quarrel with the wind, whose
        angry gust
Plucks off the summer hat, and flaps
    the fold
    Of many a crimson cloak, and twirls
        the dust
In spiral shapes grotesque, and dims
    the gold
    Of gleaming tresses with the blur of
        rust.

NIGHT

FUNEREAL Darkness, drear and
    desolate,
    Muffles the world. The moaning of
        the wind
    Is piteous with sobs of saddest kind;
And laughter is a phantom at the gate
Of memory. The long-neglected grate
    Within sprouts into flame and lights
        the mind
    With hopes and wishes long ago re-
        fined

To ashes,—long departed friends await
  Our words of welcome: and our lips
    are dumb
And powerless to greet the ones that
    press
  Old kisses there. The baby beats its
    drum,
And fancy marches to the dear caress
  Of mother-arms, and all the gleeful
    hum
Of home intrudes upon our loneliness.

39

OVER THE EYES OF GLADNESS

The voice of One hath spoken,
  And the bended reed is bruised—
The golden bowl is broken,
  And the silver cord is loosed.

OVER the eyes of gladness
  The lids of sorrow fall,
And the light of mirth is darkened
  Under the funeral pall.

The hearts that throbbed with rapture
  In dreams of the future years,
Are wakened from their slumbers,
  And their visions drowned in tears.

.   .   .   .

Two buds on the bough in the morn-
    ing—
  Twin buds in the smiling sun,
But the frost of death has fallen
  And blighted the bloom of one.

One leaf of life still folded
  Has fallen from the stem,
Leaving the symbol teaching
  There still are two of them,—

For though—through Time's grada-
    tions,
  The *living* bud may burst,—
The *withered* one is gathered,
  And blooms in Heaven first.

40

ONLY A DREAM

ONLY a dream!
      Her head is bent
Over the keys of the instrument,
While her trembling fingers go astray
In the foolish tune she tries to play.
He smiles in his heart, though his deep,
    sad eyes
Never change to a glad surprise
As he finds the answer he seeks con-
    fessed
In glowing features, and heaving breast.

Only a dream!
      Though the *fête* is grand,
And a hundred hearts at her command,
She takes no part, for her soul is sick
Of the Coquette's art and the Serpent's
    trick,—
She someway feels she would like to
    fling
Her sins away as a robe, and spring
Up like a lily pure and white,
And bloom alone for *him* to-night.

Only a dream
      That the fancy weaves.
The lids unfold like the rose's leaves,
And the upraised eyes are moist and
    mild
As the prayerful eyes of a drowsy child.
Does she remember the spell they once

Wrought in the past a few short
    months?
Haply not—yet her lover's eyes
Never change to the glad surprise.

Only a dream!
        He winds her form
Close in the coil of his curving arm,
And whirls her away in a gust of sound
As wild and sweet as the poets found
In the paradise where the silken tent
Of the Persian blooms in the Orient,—
While ever the chords of the music
    seem
Whispering sadly,—"Only a dream!"

41

OUR LITTLE GIRL

HER heart knew naught of sorrow,
    Nor the vaguest taint of sin—
'Twas an ever-blooming blossom
    Of the purity within:
And her hands knew only touches
    Of the mother's gentle care,
And the kisses and caresses
    Through the interludes of prayer.

Her baby-feet had journeyed
    Such a little distance here,
They could have found no briers
    In the path to interfere;
The little cross she carried
    Could not weary her, we know,
For it lay as lightly on her
    As a shadow on the snow.

And yet the way before us—
    O how empty now and drear!—
How ev'n the dews of roses
    Seem as dripping tears for her!

And the song-birds all seem crying,
    As the winds cry and the rain,
All sobbingly,—"We want—we want
    Our little girl again!"

42

THE FUNNY LITTLE FELLOW

'TWAS a Funny Little Fellow
    Of the very purest type,
For he had a heart as mellow
    As an apple over ripe;
And the brightest little twinkle
    When a funny thing occurred,
And the lightest little tinkle
    Of a laugh you ever heard!

His smile was like the glitter
    Of the sun in tropic lands,
And his talk a sweeter twitter
    Than the swallow understands;
Hear him sing—and tell a story—
    Snap a joke—ignite a pun,—
'Twas a capture—rapture—glory,
    An explosion—all in one!

Though he hadn't any money—
    That condiment which tends
To make a fellow "honey"
    For the palate of his friends;—
Sweet simples he compounded—
    Sovereign antidotes for sin
Or taint,—a faith unbounded
    That his friends were genuine.

He wasn't honored, maybe—
    For his songs of praise were slim,—
Yet I never knew a baby
    That wouldn't crow for him;

I never knew a mother
But urged a kindly claim
Upon him as a brother,
At the mention of his name.

The sick have ceased their sighing,
And have even found the grace
Of a smile when they were dying
As they looked upon his face;
And I've seen his eyes of laughter
Melt in tears that only ran
As though, swift-dancing after,
Came the Funny Little Man.

He laughed away the sorrow
And he laughed away the gloom
We are all so prone to borrow
From the darkness of the tomb;
And he laughed across the ocean
Of a happy life, and passed,
With a laugh of glad emotion,
Into Paradise at last.

And I think the Angels knew him,
And had gathered to await
His coming, and run to him
Through the widely opened Gate,
With their faces gleaming sunny
For his laughter-loving sake,
And thinking, "What a funny
Little Angel he will make!"

43

SONG OF THE NEW YEAR

I HEARD the bells at midnight
Ring in the dawning year;
And above the clanging chorus
Of the song, I seemed to hear
A choir of mystic voices
Flinging echoes, ringing clear,

From a band of angels winging
Through the haunted atmosphere:
"Ring out the shame and sorrow,
And the misery and sin,
That the dawning of the morrow
May in peace be ushered in."

And I thought of all the trials
The departed years had cost,
And the blooming hopes and pleasures
That are withered now and lost;
And with joy I drank the music
Stealing o'er the feeling there
As the spirit song came pealing
On the silence everywhere:
"Ring out the shame and sorrow,
And the misery and sin,
That the dawning of the morrow
May in peace be ushered in."

And I listened as a lover
To an utterance that flows
In syllables like dewdrops
From the red lips of a rose,
Till the anthem, fainter growing,
Climbing higher, chiming on
Up the rounds of happy rhyming,
Slowly vanished in the dawn:
"Ring out the shame and sorrow,
And the misery and sin,
That the dawning of the morrow
May in peace be ushered in."

Then I raised my eyes to Heaven,
And with trembling lips I pled
For a blessing for the living
And a pardon for the dead;
And like a ghost of music
Slowly whispered—lowly sung—
Came the echo pure and holy
In the happy angel tongue:
"Ring out the shame and sorrow.
And the misery and sin,

And the dawn of every morrow
  Will in peace be ushered in."

44

A LETTER TO A FRIEND

THE past is like a story
  I have listened to in dreams
That vanished in the glory
  Of the Morning's early gleams;
And—at my shadow glancing—
  I feel a loss of strength,
As the Day of Life advancing
  Leaves it shorn of half its length.

But it's all in vain to worry
  At the rapid race of Time—
And he flies in such a flurry
  When I trip him with a rhyme,
I'll bother him no longer
  Than to thank you for the thought
That "my fame is growing stronger
  As you really think it ought."

And though I fall below it,
  I might know as much of mirth
To live and die a poet
  Of unacknowledged worth;
For Fame is but a vagrant—
  Though a loyal one and brave,
And his laurels ne'er so fragrant
  As when scattered o'er the grave.

45

LINES FOR AN ALBUM

I WOULD not trace the hackneyed
    phrase
Of shallow words and empty praise,
And prate of "peace" till one might
    think
My foolish pen was drunk with ink.

Nor will I here the wish express
Of "lasting love and happiness,"
And "cloudless skies"—for after all
"Into each life some rain must fall."
—No. Keep the empty page below,
In my remembrance, white as snow—
Nor sigh to know the secret prayer
My spirit hand has written there.

46

TO ANNIE

WHEN the lids of dusk are falling
    O'er the dreamy eyes of day,
And the whippoorwills are calling,
  And the lesson laid away,—
May Mem'ry soft and tender
  As the prelude of the night,
Bend over you and render
  As tranquil a delight.

47

FAME

I

ONCE, in a dream, I saw a man
    With haggard face and tangled
      hair,
And eyes that nursed as wild a care
  As gaunt Starvation ever can;
And in his hand he held a wand
  Whose magic touch gave life and
      thought
Unto a form his fancy wrought
And robed with coloring so grand,
  It seemed the reflex of some child
  Of Heaven, fair and undefiled—
  A face of purity and love—
  To woo him into worlds above:

And as I gazed with dazzled eyes,
A gleaming smile lit up his lips
As his bright soul from its eclipse
Went flashing into Paradise.
Then tardy Fame came through the
    door
And found a picture—nothing more.

II

And once I saw a man, alone,
    In abject poverty, with hand
Uplifted o'er a block of stone
That took a shape at his command
And smiled upon him, fair and good—
A perfect work of womanhood,
Save that the eyes might never weep,
Nor weary hands be crossed in sleep,
Nor hair that fell from crown to wrist,
Be brushed away, caressed and kissed.
And as in awe I gazed on her,
    I saw the sculptor's chisel fall—
    I saw him sink, without a moan,
    Sink lifeless at the feet of stone,
And lie there like a worshiper.
    Fame crossed the threshold of the
        hall,
    And found a statue—that was all.

III

And once I saw a man who drew
    A gloom about him like a cloak,
And wandered aimlessly. The few
    Who spoke of him at all but spoke
Disparagingly of a mind
The Fates had faultily designed:
Too indolent for modern times—
    Too fanciful, and full of whims—
For, talking to himself in rhymes,
    And scrawling never-heard-of hymns,

The idle life to which he clung
Was worthless as the songs he sung!
I saw him, in my vision, filled
    With rapture o'er a spray of bloom
    The wind threw in his lonely room;
And of the sweet perfume it spilled
He drank to drunkenness, and flung
His long hair back, and laughed and
    sung
And clapped his hands as children do
At fairy tales they listen to,
While from his flying quill there
    dripped
Such music on his manuscript
That he who listens to the words
May close his eyes and dream the birds
Are twittering on every hand
A language he can understand.
He journeyed on through life, un-
    known,
Without one friend to call his own;
He tired. No kindly hand to press
The cooling touch of tenderness
Upon his burning brow, nor lift
To his parched lips God's freest gift—
No sympathetic sob or sigh
Of trembling lips—no sorrowing eye
Looked out through tears to see him
    die.
And Fame her greenest laurels brought
To crown a head that heeded not.

And this is Fame! A thing, indeed,
That only comes when least the need:
The wisest minds of every age
The book of life from page to page
Have searched in vain; each lesson
    conned
Will promise it the page beyond—
Until the last, when dusk of night
Falls over it, and reason's light
Is smothered by that unknown friend
Who signs his *nom de plume*, The End.

48

AN EMPTY NEST

I FIND an old deserted nest,
　Half-hidden in the underbrush:
A withered leaf, in phantom jest,
　Has nestled in it like a thrush
With weary, palpitating breast.

I muse as one in sad surprise
　Who seeks his childhood's home
　　once more,
And finds it in a strange disguise
　Of vacant rooms and naked floor,
With sudden tear-drops in his eyes.

An empty nest! It used to bear
　A happy burden, when the breeze
Of summer rocked it, and a pair
　Of merry tattlers told the trees
What treasures they had hidden there.

But Fancy, flitting through the gleams
　Of youth's sunshiny atmosphere,
Has fallen in the past, and seems,
　Like this poor leaflet nestled here,—
A phantom guest of empty dreams.

49

MY FATHER'S HALLS

MY father's halls, so rich and rare,
　Are desolate and bleak and
　　bare;
My father's heart and halls are one,
Since I, their life and light, am gone.

O, valiant knight, with hand of steel
And heart of gold, hear my appeal:
Release me from the spoiler's charms,
And bear me to my father's arms.

50

THE HARP OF THE MINSTREL

THE harp of the minstrel has never
　a tone
As sad as the song in his bosom to-
　night,
For the magical touch of his fingers
　alone
　Can not waken the echoes that
　　breathe it aright;
But oh! as the smile of the moon may
　impart
A sorrow to one in an alien clime,
Let the light of the melody fall on the
　heart,
　And cadence his grief into musical
　　rhyme.

The faces have faded, the eyes have
　grown dim
　That once were his passionate love
　　and his pride;
And alas! all the smiles that once blos-
　somed for him
　Have fallen away as the flowers have
　　died.
The hands that entwined him the
　laureate's wreath
　And crowned him with fame in the
　　long, long ago,
Like the laurels are withered and
　folded beneath
　The grass and the stubble—the frost
　　and the snow.

Then sigh, if thou wilt, as the whis-
　pering strings
　Strive ever in vain for the utterance
　　clear,
And think of the sorrowful spirit that
　sings,

And jewel the song with the gem
   of a tear.
For the harp of the minstrel has never
   a tone
As sad as the song in his bosom to-
   night,
And the magical touch of his fingers
   alone
Can not waken the echoes that
   breathe it aright.

51

HONEY DRIPPING FROM THE COMB

HOW slight a thing may set one's
   fancy drifting
Upon the dead sea of the Past!—A
   view—
Sometimes an odor—or a rooster lifting
   A far-off *"Ooh! ooh-ooh!"*

And suddenly we find ourselves astray
   In some wood's-pasture of the Long
   Ago—
Or idly dream again upon a day
   Of rest we used to know.

I bit an apple but a moment since—
   A wilted apple that the worm had
   spurned,—
Yet hidden in the taste were happy
   hints
   Of good old days returned.—

And so my heart, like some enraptured
   lute,
   Tinkles a tune so tender and com-
   plete,
God's blessing must be resting on the
   fruit—
   So bitter, yet so sweet!

52

JOHN WALSH

A STRANGE life—strangely passed!
   We may not read the soul
When God has folded up the scroll
   In death at last.
We may not—dare not say of one
Whose task of life as well was done
As he could do it,—"This is lost,
And prayers may never pay the cost."

Who listens to the song
   That sings within the breast,
   Should ever hear the good expressed
     Above the wrong.
And he who leans an eager ear
To catch the discord, he will hear
The echoes of his own weak heart
Beat out the most discordant part.

Whose tender heart could build
   Affection's bower above
   A heart where baby nests of love
     Were ever filled,—
With upward growth may reach and
   twine
About the children, grown divine,
That once were his a time so brief
His very joy was more than grief.

O Sorrow—"Peace, be still!"
   God reads the riddle right;
   And we who grope in constant night
     But serve His will;
And when sometime the doubt is gone,
And darkness blossoms into dawn,—
"God keeps the good," we then will
   say:
" 'Tis but the dross He throws away."

53

ORLIE WILDE

A GODDESS, with a siren's grace,—
A sun-haired girl on a craggy
place
Above a bay where fish-boats lay
Drifting about like birds of prey.

Wrought   was   she   of   a   painter's
dream,—
Wise only as are artists wise,
My artist-friend, Rolf Herschkelhiem,
With deep sad eyes of oversize,
And face of melancholy guise.

I pressed him that he tell to me
This masterpiece's history.
He turned—*re*turned—and thus be-
guiled
Me with the tale of Orlie Wilde:—

"We artists live ideally:
We breed our firmest facts of air;
We make our own reality—
We dream a thing and it is so.
The fairest scenes we ever see
Are mirages of memory;
The sweetest thoughts we ever know
We plagiarize from Long Ago:
And as the girl on canvas there
Is marvelously rare and fair,
'Tis only inasmuch as she
Is dumb and may not speak to me!"
He tapped me with his mahlstick—then
The picture,—and went on again:

"Orlie Wilde, the fisher's child—
I see her yet, as fair and mild
As ever nursling summer day
Dreamed on the bosom of the bay:

For I was twenty then, and went
Alone and long-haired—all content
With promises of sounding name
And fantasies of future fame,
And thoughts that now my mind dis-
cards
As editor a fledgling bard's.

"At evening once I chanced to go,
With pencil and portfolio,
Adown the street of silver sand
That winds beneath this craggy land,
To make a sketch of some old scurf
Of driftage, nosing through the surf
A splintered mast, with knarl and
strand
Of rigging-rope and tattered threads
Of flag and streamer and of sail
That fluttered idly in the gale
Or whipped themselves to sadder
shreds.
The while I wrought, half listlessly,
On my dismantled subject, came
A sea-bird, settling on the same
With plaintive moan, as though that he
Had lost his mate upon the sea;
And—with my melancholy trend—
It brought dim dreams half under-
stood—
It wrought upon my morbid mood,—
I thought of my own voyagings
That had no end—that have no end.—
And, like the sea-bird, I made moan
That I was loveless and alone.
And when at last with weary wings
It went upon its wanderings,
With upturned face I watched its
flight
Until this picture met my sight:
A goddess, with a siren's grace,—
A sun-haired girl on a craggy place
Above a bay where fish-boats lay
Drifting about like birds of prey.

"In airy poise she, gazing, stood
A matchless form of womanhood,
That brought a thought that if for me
Such eyes had sought across the sea,
I could have swum the widest tide
That ever mariner defied,
And, at the shore, could on have gone
To that high crag she stood upon,
To there entreat and say, 'My Sweet,
Behold thy servant at thy feet.'
And to my soul I said: 'Above,
There stands the idol of thy love!'

"In this rapt, awed, ecstatic state
I gazed—till lo! I was aware
A fisherman had joined her there—
A weary man, with halting gait,
Who toiled beneath a basket's weight:
Her father, as I guessed, for she
Had run to meet him gleefully
And ta'en his burden to herself,
That perched upon her shoulder's shelf
So lightly that she, tripping, neared
A jutting crag and disappeared;
But she left the echo of a song
That thrills me yet, and will as long
As I have being! . . .

            . . . "Evenings came
And went,—but each the same—the
    same:
She watched above, and even so
I stood there watching from below;
Till, grown so bold at last, I sung,—
(What matter now the theme there-
    of!)—
It brought an answer from her
    tongue—
Faint as the murmur of a dove,
Yet all the more the song of love. . . .

"I turned and looked upon the bay,
With palm to forehead—eyes a-blur

In the sea's smile—meant but for
    her!—
I saw the fish-boats far away
In misty distance, lightly drawn
In chalk-dots on the horizon—
Looked back at her, long, wistfully,—
And, pushing off an empty skiff,
I beckoned her to quit the cliff
And yield me her rare company
Upon a little pleasure-cruise.—
She stood, as loathful to refuse,
To muse for full a moment's time,—
Then answered back in pantomime
'She feared some danger from the sea
Were she discovered thus with me.'
I motioned then to ask her if
I might not join her on the cliff;
And back again, with graceful wave
Of lifted arm, she answer gave
'She feared some danger from the sea.'

"Impatient, piqued, impetuous, I
Sprang in the boat, and flung 'Good-by'
From pouted mouth with angry hand,
And madly pulled away from land
With lusty stroke, despite that she
Held out her hands entreatingly;
And when far out, with covert eye
I shoreward glanced, I saw her fly
In reckless haste adown the crag,
Her hair a-flutter like a flag
Of gold that danced across the strand
In little mists of silver sand.
All curious I, pausing, tried
To fancy what it all implied,—
When suddenly I found my feet
Were wet; and, underneath the seat
On which I sat, I heard the sound
Of gurgling waters, and I found
The boat aleak alarmingly. . . .
I turned and looked upon the sea,
Whose every wave seemed mocking
    me;

I saw the fishers' sails once more—
In dimmer distance than before;
I saw the sea-bird wheeling by,
With foolish wish that *I* could fly:
I thought of firm earth, home and
    friends—
I thought of everything that tends
To drive a man to frenzy and
To wholly lose his own command;
I thought of all my waywardness—
Thought of a mother's deep distress;
Of youthful follies yet unpurged—
Sins, as the seas, about me surged—
Thought of the printer's ready pen
To-morrow drowning me again;—
A million things without a name—
I thought of everything but—Fame. . . .

"A memory yet is in my mind,
So keenly clear and sharp-defined,
I picture every phase and line
Of life and death, and neither mine,—
While some fair seraph, golden-haired,
Bends over me,—with white arms
    bared,
That strongly plait themselves about
My drowning weight and lift me out—
With joy too great for words to state
Or tongue to dare articulate!

"And this seraphic ocean-child
And heroine was Orlie Wilde:
And thus it was I came to hear
Her voice's music in my ear—
Ay, thus it was Fate paved the way
That I walk desolate to-day!" . . .

The artist paused and bowed his face
Within his palms a little space,
While reverently on his form
I bent my gaze and marked a storm
That shook his frame as wrathfully
As some typhoon of agony,

And fraught with sobs—the more pro-
    found
For that peculiar laughing sound
We hear when strong men weep. . . .
    I leant
With warmest sympathy—I bent
To stroke with soothing hand his brow,
He murmuring—" 'Tis over now!—
And shall I tie the silken thread
Of my frail romance?" "Yes," I said.—
He faintly smiled; and then, with brow
In kneading palm, as one in dread—
His tasseled cap pushed from his
    head;—
" 'Her voice's music,' I repeat,"
He said,—" 'twas sweet—O passing
    sweet!—
Though she herself, in uttering
Its melody, proved not the thing
Of loveliness my dreams made meet
For me—there, yearning, at her feet—
Prone at her feet—a worshiper,—
For lo! she spake a tongue," moaned
he,
"Unknown to me;—unknown to me
As mine to her—as mine to her."

54

THAT OTHER MAUD MULLER

MAUD MULLER worked at mak-
    ing hay,
And cleared her forty cents a day.

Her clothes were coarse, but her health
    was fine,
And so she worked in the sweet sun-
shine

Singing as glad as a bird in May
"Barbara Allen" the livelong day.

She often glanced at the far-off town,
And wondered if eggs were up or
down.

And the sweet song died of a strange
disease,
Leaving a phantom taste of cheese,

And an appetite and a nameless ache
For soda-water and ginger cake.

The Judge rode slowly into view—
Stopped his horse in the shade and
threw

His fine-cut out, while the blushing
Maud
Marveled much at the kind he
"chawed."

"He was dry as a fish," he said with a
wink,
"And kind o' thought that a good
square drink

Would brace him up." So the cup was
filled
With the crystal wine that old spring
spilled;

And she gave it him with a sun-
browned hand.
"Thanks," said the Judge in accents
bland;

"A thousand thanks! for a sweeter
draught,
From a fairer hand"—but there he
laughed.

And the sweet girl stood in the sun
that day,
And raked the Judge instead of the
hay.

55

A MAN OF MANY PARTS

IT was a man of many parts,
    Who in his coffer mind
Had stored the Classics and the Arts
    And Sciences combined;
The purest gems of poesy
    Came flashing from his pen—
The wholesome truths of History
    He gave his fellow men.

He knew the stars from "Dog" to
        Mars;
    And he could tell you, too,
Their distances—as though the cars
    Had often checked him through—
And time 'twould take to reach the sun,
    Or by the "Milky Way,"
Drop in upon the moon, or run
    The homeward trip, or stay.

With Logic at his fingers' ends,
    Theology in mind,
He often entertained his friends
    Until they died resigned;
And with inquiring mind intent
    Upon Alchemic arts
A dynamite experiment—

.   .   .   .

A man of many parts!

56

THE FROG

WHO am I but the Frog—the
        Frog!
My realm is the dark bayou,
And my throne is the muddy and moss-
        grown log
    That the poison-vine clings to—

And the blacksnakes slide in the slimy
        tide
    Where the ghost of the moon looks
        blue.

What am I but a King—a King!—
    For the royal robes I wear—
A scepter, too, and a signet-ring,
    As vassals and serfs declare:
And a voice, god wot, that is equaled
        not
    In the wide world anywhere!

I can talk to the Night—the Night!—
    Under her big black wing
She tells me the tale of the world out-
        right,
    And the secret of everything;
For she knows you all, from the time
        you crawl
    To the doom that death will bring.

The Storm swoops down, and he blows
        —and blows,—
    While I drum on his swollen cheek,
And croak in his angered eye that
        glows
    With the lurid lightning's streak;
While the rushes drown in the watery
        frown
    That his bursting passions leak.

And I can see through the sky—the
        sky—
    As clear as a piece of glass;
And I can tell you the how and why
    Of the things that come to pass—
And whether the dead are there in-
        stead,
    Or under the graveyard grass.

To your Sovereign lord all hail—all
        hail!—

To your Prince on his throne so
        grim!
Let the moon swing low, and the high
        stars trail
    Their heads in the dust to him;
And the wide world sing: Long live
        the King,
    And grace to his royal whim!

57

DEAD SELVES

HOW many of my selves are dead?
    The ghosts of many haunt me:
        Lo,
The baby in the tiny bed
With rockers on, is blanketed
    And sleeping in the long ago;
And so I ask, with shaking head,
How many of my selves are dead?

A little face with drowsy eyes
    And lisping lips comes mistily
From out the faded past, and tries
The prayers a mother breathed with
        sighs
    Of anxious care in teaching me;
But face and form and prayers have
        fled—
How many of my selves are dead?

The little naked feet that slipped
    In truant paths, and led the way
Through dead'ning pasture-lands, and
        tripped
O'er tangled poison-vines, and dipped
    In streams forbidden—where are
        they?
In vain I listen for their tread—
How many of my selves are dead?

The awkward boy the teacher caught
    Inditing letters filled with love,
Who was compelled, for all he fought,
To read aloud each tender thought
    Of "Sugar Lump" and "Turtle
        Dove."
I wonder where he hides his head—
How many of my selves are dead?

The earnest features of a youth
    With manly fringe on lip and chin,
With eager tongue to tell the truth,
To offer love and life, forsooth,
    So brave was he to woo and win;
A prouder man was never wed—
How many of my selves are dead?

The great, strong hands so all-inclined
    To welcome toil, or smooth the care
From mother-brows, or quick to find
A leisure-scrap of any kind,
    To toss the baby in the air,
Or clap at babbling things it said—
How many of my selves are dead?

The pact of brawn and scheming
        brain—
    Conspiring in the plots of wealth,
Still delving, till the lengthened chain,
Unwindlassed in the mines of gain,
    Recoils with dregs of ruined health
And pain and poverty instead—
How many of my selves are dead?

The faltering step, the faded hair—
    Head, heart and soul, all echoing
With maundering fancies that declare
That life and love were never there,
    Nor ever joy in anything,
Nor wounded heart that ever bled—
How many of my selves are dead?

So many of my selves are dead,
    That, bending here above the brink
Of my last grave, with dizzy head,
I find my spirit comforted
    For all the idle things I think:
It can but be a peaceful bed,
Since all my other selves are dead.

58

A DREAM OF LONG AGO

LYING listless in the mosses
    Underneath a tree that tosses
Flakes of sunshine, and embosses
    Its green shadow with the snow—
Drowsy-eyed, I sink in slumber
Born of fancies without number—
Tangled fancies that encumber
    Me with dreams of long ago.

Ripples of the river singing;
And the water-lilies swinging
Bells of Parian, and ringing
    Peals of perfume faint and fine,
While old forms and fairy faces
Leap from out their hiding-places
In the past, with glad embraces
    Fraught with kisses sweet as wine.

Willows dip their slender fingers
O'er the little fisher's stringers,
While he baits his hook and lingers
    Till the shadows gather dim;
And afar off comes a calling
Like the sounds of water falling,
With the lazy echoes drawling
    Messages of haste to him.

Little naked feet that tinkle
Through the stubble-fields, and twinkle

Down the winding road, and sprinkle
  Little mists of dusty rain,
While in pasture-lands the cattle
Cease their grazing with a rattle
Of the bells whose clappers tattle
  To their masters down the lane.

Trees that hold their tempting treas-
    ures
O'er the orchard's hedge embrasures,
Furnish their forbidden pleasures
  As in Eden lands of old;
And the coming of the master
Indicates a like disaster
To the frightened heart that faster
  Beats pulsations manifold.

Puckered lips whose pipings tingle
In staccato notes that mingle
Musically with the jingle-
  Haunted winds that lightly fan
Mellow twilights, crimson-tinted
By the sun, and picture-printed
Like a book that sweetly hinted
  Of the Nights Arabian.

Porticoes with columns plaited
And entwined with vines and freighted
With a bloom all radiated
  With the light of moon and star;
Where some tender voice is winging
In sad flights of song, and singing
To the dancing fingers flinging
  Dripping from the sweet guitar.

Would my dreams were never taken
From me: that with faith unshaken
I might sleep and never waken
  On a weary world of woe!
Links of love would never sever
As I dreamed them, never, never!
I would glide along forever
  Through the dreams of long ago.

59

CRAQUEODOOM

THE Crankadox leaned o'er the edge
    of the moon
And wistfully gazed on the sea
Where the Gryxabodill madly whistled
    a tune
  To the air of "Ti-fol-de-ding-dee."
The quavering shriek of the Fly-up-the-
    creek
  Was fitfully wafted afar
To the Queen of the Wunks as she
    powdered her cheek
  With the pulverized rays of a star.

The Gool closed his ear on the voice
    of the Grig,
  And his heart it grew heavy as lead
As he marked the Baldekin adjusting
    his wing
  On the opposite side of his head,
And the air it grew chill as the Gryxa-
    bodill
  Raised his dank, dripping fins to the
    skies,
And plead with the Plunk for the use
    of her bill
  To pick the tears out of his eyes.

The ghost of the Zhack flitted by in a
    trance,
  And the Squidjum hid under a tub
As he heard the loud hooves of the
    Hooken advance
  With a rub-a-dub—dub-a-dub—dub!
And the Crankadox cried, as he lay
    down and died,
  "My fate there is none to bewail,"
While the Queen of the Wunks drifted
    over the tide
  With a long piece of crape to her
    tail.

60

JUNE

O QUEENLY month of indolent
    repose!
I drink thy breath in sips of rare per-
    fume,
As in thy downy lap of clover-bloom
I nestle like a drowsy child and doze
The lazy hours away. The zephyr
    throws
The shifting shuttle of the Summer's
    loom
And weaves a damask-work of gleam
    and gloom
Before thy listless feet. The lily blows
A bugle-call of fragrance o'er the glade;
    And, wheeling into ranks, with
        plume and spear,
Thy harvest-armies gather on parade;
    While, faint and far away, yet pure
        and clear,
A voice calls out of alien lands of
    shade:—
    All hail the Peerless Goddess of the
        Year!

61

WASH LOWRY'S REMINISCENCE

A ND you're the poet of this con-
    cern?
I've seed your name in print
A dozen times, but I'll be dern
I'd 'a' never 'a' took the hint
O' the size you are—fer I'd pictured
    you
A kind of a tallish man—
Dark-complected and sallor too,
    And on the consumpted plan.

'Stid o' that you're little and small,
    With a milk-and-water face—
'Thout no snap in your eyes at all,
    Er nothin' to suit the case!
Kind o' look like a—I don't know—
    One o' these fair-ground chaps
That runs a thingamajig to blow,
    Er a candy-stand perhaps.

'Ll I've allus thought that poetry
    Was a sort of a—some disease—
Fer I knowed a poet once, and he
    Was techy and hard to please,
And moody-like, and kind o' sad
    And didn't seem to mix
With other folks—like his health was
    bad,
    Er his liver out o' fix.

Used to teach fer a livelihood—
    There's folks in Pipe Crick yit
Remembers him—and he was good
    At cipherin' I'll admit—
And posted up in G'ography
    But when it comes to tact,
And gittin' along with the school, you
    see,
    He fizzled, and that's a fact!

Boarded with us fer fourteen months
    And in all that time I'll say
We never catched him a-sleepin' once
    Er idle a single day.
But shucks! It made him worse and
    worse
    A-writin' rhymes and stuff,
And the school committee used to furse
    'At the school warn't good enough.

He warn't as strict as he ought to been,
    And never was known to whip,
Or even to keep a scholard in
    At work at his penmanship;

'Stid o' that he'd learn 'em notes,
  And have 'em every day,
Spilin' hymns and a-splittin' th'oats
  With his "Do-sol-fa-me-ra!"

Tel finally it was jest agreed
  We'd have to let him go,
And we all felt bad—we did indeed,
  When we come to tell him so;
Fer I remember, he turned so white,
  And smiled so sad, somehow,
I someway felt it wasn't right,
  And I'm shore it wasn't now!

He hadn't no complaints at all—
  He bid the school adieu,
And all o' the scholards great and
    small
  Was mighty sorry too!
And when he closed that afternoon
  They sung some lines that he
Had writ a purpose, to some old tune
  That suited the case, you see.

And then he lingered and delayed
  And wouldn't go away—
And shet himself in his room and
    stayed
  A-writin' from day to day;
And kep' a-gittin' stranger still,
  And thinner all the time,
You know, as any feller will
  On nothin' else but rhyme.

He didn't seem adzactly right,
  Er like he was crossed in love,
He'd work away night after night,
  And walk the floor above;
We'd hear him read and talk, and sing
  So lonesome-like and low,
My woman's cried like ever'thing—
  'Way in the night, you know.

And when at last he tuck to bed
  He'd have his ink and pen;
"So's he could coat the muse" he said,
  "He'd die contented then";
And jest before he past away
  He read with dyin' gaze
The epitaph that stands to-day
  To show you where he lays.

And ever sence then I've allus thought
  That poetry's some disease,
And them like you that's got it ought
  To watch their q's and p's;
And leave the sweets of rhyme, to sup
  On the wholesome draughts of toil,
And git your health recruited up
  By plowin' in rougher soil.

62

THE ANCIENT PRINTERMAN

"O PRINTERMAN of sallow face,
    And look of absent guile,
Is it the 'copy' on your 'case'
    That causes you to smile?
Or is it some old treasure scrap
    You cull from Memory's file?

"I fain would guess its mystery—
    For often I can trace
A fellow dreamer's history
    Whene'er it haunts the face;
Your fancy's running riot
    In a retrospective race!

"Ah, Printerman, you're straying
    Afar from 'stick' and type—
Your heart has 'gone a-maying,'
    And you taste old kisses, ripe
Again on lips that pucker
    At your old asthmatic pipe!

"You are dreaming of old pleasures
  That have faded from your view;
And the music-burdened measures
  Of the laughs you listen to
Are now but angel-echoes—
  O, have I spoken true?"

The ancient Printer hinted
  With a motion full of grace
To where the words were printed
  On a card above his "case,"—
"I am deaf and dumb!" I left him
  With a smile upon his face.

63

PRIOR TO MISS BELLE'S APPEARANCE

WHAT makes you come *here* fer,
      Mister,
  So much to *our* house?—*Say?*
Come to see our big sister!—
An' Charley he says 'at you kissed her
  An' he ketched you, th'uther day!—
Didn' you, Charley?—But we p'omised
      Belle
An' crossed our heart to never to tell—
'Cause *she* gived us some o' them-er
Chawk'lut-drops 'at you bringed to her!

Charley he's my little b'uther—
  An' we has a-mostest fun,
Don't we, Charley?—Our Muther,
Whenever we whips one anuther,
  Tries to whip *us*—an' we *run*—
Don't we, Charley?—An' nen, bime-by,
Nen she gives us cake—an' pie—
Don't she, Charley?—when we come
      in
An' p'omise never to do it ag'in!

He's named Charley.—I'm *Willie*—
  An' I'm got the purtiest name!
But Uncle Bob *he* calls me "Billy"—
  Don't he, Charley?—'N' our filly
We named "Billy," the same
Ist like me! An' our Ma said
'At "Bob puts foolishnuss into our
      head!"—
Didn' she, Charley?—An' *she* don't
      know
Much about *boys!*—'Cause Bob said so!

Baby's a funniest feller!
  Nain't no hair on his head—
Is they, Charley?—It's meller
Wite up there! An' ef Belle er
  Us ask wuz *we* that way, Ma said,—
"Yes; an' yer *Pa's* head wuz soft as
      that,
An' it's that way yet!"—An' Pa grabs
      his hat
An' says, "Yes, children, she's right
      about Pa—
'Cause that's the reason he married yer
      Ma!"

An' our Ma says 'at "Belle couldn'
  Ketch nothin' at all but ist *'bows'!'*—
An' *Pa* says 'at "you're soft as pud-
      dun!"—
An' *Uncle Bob* says "you're a good-
      un—
  'Cause he can tell by yer nose!"—
Didn' he, Charley?—An' when Belle'll
      play
In the poller on th' pianer, some day,
Bob makes up funny songs about you,
Till she gits mad—like he wants her
      to!

Our sister *Fanny* she's *'leven*
  Years old! 'At's mucher 'an *I*—
Ain't it, Charley? . . . I'm seven!—

But our sister Fanny's in *Heaven!*
  Nere's where you go ef you die!—
Don't you, Charley?—Nen you has
    wings—
Ist like Fanny!—an' *purtiest things!*—
Don't you, Charley?—An' nen you can
    fly—
Ist fly—an' *ever*'thing! . . . Wisht *I'd*
    die!

64

WHEN MOTHER COMBED MY HAIR

WHEN Memory, with gentle
      hand,
Has led me to that foreign land
Of childhood days, I long to be
Again the boy on bended knee,
With head a-bow, and drowsy smile
Hid in a mother's lap the while,
With tender touch and kindly care,
She bends above and combs my hair.

Ere threats of Time, or ghosts of cares
Had paled it to the hue it wears,
Its tangled threads of amber light
Fell o'er a forehead, fair and white,
That only knew the light caress
Of loving hands, or sudden press
Of kisses that were sifted there
The times when mother combed my
    hair.

But its last gleams of gold have slipped
Away; and Sorrow's manuscript
Is fashioned of the snowy brow—
So lined and underscored now
That you, to see it, scarce would guess
It e'er had felt the fond caress

Of loving lips, or known the care
Of those dear hands that combed my
    hair.

.   .   .   .

I am so tired! Let me be
A moment at my mother's knee;
One moment—that I may forget
The trials waiting for me yet:
One moment free from every pain—
O! Mother! Comb my hair again!
And I will, oh, so humbly bow,
For I've a wife that combs it now.

65

A WRANGDILLION

DEXERY-TETHERY! down in the
      dike,
  Under the ooze and the slime,
Nestles the wraith of a reticent Gryke,
  Blubbering bubbles of rhyme:
Though the reeds touch him and tickle
      his teeth—
  Though the Graigroll and the Cheest
Pluck at the leaves of his laureate-
      wreath,
  Nothing affects him the least.

He sinks to the dregs in the dead o' the
      night,
  And he shuffles the shadows about
As he gathers the stars in a nest of de-
      light
  And sets there and hatches them out:
The Zhederrill peers from his watery
      mine
  In scorn with the Will-o'-the-wisp,
As he twinkles his eyes in a whisper of
      shine
  That ends in a luminous lisp.

The Morning is born like a baby of
   gold,
And it lies in a spasm of pink,
And rallies the Cheest for the horrible
   cold
He has dragged to the willowy brink,

The Gryke blots his tears with a scrap
   of his grief,
And growls at the wary Graigroll
As he twunkers a tune on a Tiljicum
   leaf
And hums like a telegraph pole.

66

GEORGE MULLEN'S CONFESSION

FOR the sake of guilty conscience, and the heart that ticks the time
   Of the clockworks of my nature, I desire to say that I'm
A weak and sinful creature, as regards my daily walk
The last five years and better. It ain't worth while to talk—

I've been too mean to tell it! I've been so hard, you see,
And full of pride, and—onry—now there's the word for me—
Just onry—and to show you, I'll give my history
With vital points in question, and I think you'll all agree.

I was always stiff and stubborn since I could recollect,
And had an awful temper, and never would reflect;
And always into trouble—I remember once at school
The teacher tried to flog me, and I reversed that rule.

O I was bad I tell you! And it's a funny move
That a fellow wild as I was could ever fall in love;
And it's a funny notion that an animal like me,
Under a girl's weak fingers was as tame as tame could be!

But it's so, and sets me thinking of the easy way she had
Of cooling down my temper—though I'd be fighting mad.
"My Lion Queen" I called her—when a spell of mine occurred
She'd come in a den of feelings and quell them with a word.

I'll tell you how she loved me—and what her people thought:
When I asked to marry Annie they said "they reckoned not—
That I cut too many didoes and monkey-shines to suit
Their idea of a son-in-law, and I could go, to boot!"

I tell you that thing riled me! Why, I felt my face turn white,
And my teeth shut like a steel trap, and the fingers of my right
Hand pained me with their pressure—all the rest's a mystery
Till I heard my Annie saying—"I'm going, too, you see."

We were coming through the gateway, and she wavered for a spell
When she heard her mother crying and her raving father yell
That she wa'n't no child of his'n—like an actor in a play
We saw at Independence, coming through the other day.

Well! that's the way we started. And for days and weeks and months
And even years we journeyed on, regretting never once
Of starting out together upon the path of life—
A kind o' sort o' husband, but a mighty loving wife,—

And the cutest little baby—little Grace—I see her now
A-standin' on the pig-pen as her mother milked the cow—
And I can hear her shouting—as I stood unloading straw,—
"I'm ain't as big as papa, but I'm biggerest'n ma."

Now folks that never married don't seem to understand
That a little baby's language is the sweetest ever planned—
Why, I tell you it's pure music, and I'll just go on to say
That I sometimes have a notion that the angels talk that way!

There's a chapter in this story I'd be happy to destroy;
I could burn it up before you with a mighty sight of joy;
But I'll go ahead and give it—not in detail, no, my friend,
For it takes five years of reading before you find the end.

My Annie's folks relented—at least, in some degree;
They sent one time for Annie, but they didn't send for me.
The old man wrote the message with a heart as hot and dry
As a furnace—"Annie Mullen, come and see your mother die."

I saw the slur intended—why I fancied I could see
The old man shoot the insult like a poison dart at me;
And in that heat of passion I swore an inward oath
That if Annie pleased her father she could never please us both.

I watched her—dark and sullen—as she hurried on her shawl;
I watched her—calm and cruel, though I saw her tear-drops fall;
I watched her—cold and heartless, though I heard her moaning, call
For mercy from high Heaven—and I smiled throughout it all.

Why even when she kissed me, and her tears were on my brow,
As she murmured, "George, forgive me—I must go to mother now!"
Such hate there was within me that I answered not at all,
But calm, and cold and cruel, I smiled throughout it all.

But a shadow in the doorway caught my eye, and then the face
Full of innocence and sunshine of little baby Grace.
And I snatched her up and kissed her, and I softened through and through
For a minute when she told me "I must kiss her muvver too."

I remember, at the starting, how I tried to freeze again
As I watched them slowly driving down the little crooked lane—
When Annie shouted something that ended in a cry,
And how I tried to whistle and it fizzled in a sigh.

I remember running after, with a glimmer in my sight—
Pretending I'd discovered that the traces wasn't right;
And the last that I remember, as they disappeared from view,
Was little Grace a-calling, "I see papa! Howdy-do!"

And left alone to ponder, I again took up my hate
For the old man who would chuckle that I was desolate;
And I mouthed my wrongs in mutters till my pride called up the pain
His last insult had given me—until I smiled again

Till the wild beast in my nature was raging in the den—
With no one now to quell it, and I wrote a letter then
Full of hissing things, and heated with so hot a heat of hate
That my pen flashed out black lightning at a most terrific rate.

I wrote that "she had wronged me when she went away from me—
Though to see her dying mother 'twas her father's victory,
And a woman that could waver when her husband's pride was rent
Was no longer worthy of it." And I shut the house and went.

To tell of my long exile would be of little good—
Though I couldn't half-way tell it, and I wouldn't if I could!
I could tell of California—of a wild and vicious life;
Of trackless plains, and mountains, and the Indian's scalping-knife.

I could tell of gloomy forests howling wild with threats of death;
I could tell of fiery deserts that have scorched me with their breath;
I could tell of wretched outcasts by the hundreds, great and small,
And could claim the nasty honor of the greatest of them all.

I could tell of toil and hardship; and of sickness and disease,
And hollow-eyed starvation, but I tell you, friend, that these
Are trifles in comparison with what a fellow feels
With that bloodhound, Remorsefulness, forever at his heels.

I remember—worn and weary of the long, long years of care,
When the frost of time was making early harvest of my hair—
I remember, wrecked and hopeless of a rest beneath the sky,
My resolve to quit the country, and to seek the East, and die.

I remember my long journey, like a dull, oppressive dream,
Across the empty prairies till I caught the distant gleam
Of a city in the beauty of its broad and shining stream
On whose bosom, flocked together, float the mighty swans of steam.

I remember drifting with them till I found myself again
In the rush and roar and rattle of the engine and the train;
And when from my surroundings something spoke of child and wife,
It seemed the train was rumbling through a tunnel in my life.

Then I remember something—like a sudden burst of light—
That don't exactly tell it, but I couldn't tell it right—
A something clinging to me with its arms around my ncek—
A little girl, for instance—or an angel, I expect—

For she kissed me, cried and called me "her dear papa," and I felt
My heart was pure virgin gold, and just about to melt—
And so it did—it melted in a mist of gleaming rain
When she took my hand and whispered, "My mama's on the train."

There's some things I can dwell on, and get off pretty well,
But the balance of this story I know I couldn't tell;
So I ain't going to try it, for to tell the reason why—
I'm so chicken-hearted lately I'd be certain 'most to cry.

67

"TIRED OUT"

"TIRED out!" Yet face and brow
  Do not look aweary now,
And the eyelids lie like two
Pure, white rose-leaves washed with dew.

Was her life so hard a task?—
Strange that we forget to ask
What the lips now dumb for aye
Could have told us yesterday!

"Tired out!" A faded scrawl
Pinned upon the ragged shawl—
Nothing else to leave a clue

Even of a friend or two,
Who might come to fold the hands,
Or smooth back the dripping strands
Of her tresses, or to wet
Them anew with fond regret.

"Tired out!" We can but guess
Of her little happiness—
Long ago, in some fair land,
When a lover held her hand
In the dream that frees us all,
Soon or later, from its thrall—
Be it either false or true,
We, at last, must tire, too.

68

HARLIE

FOLD the little waxen hands
Lightly. Let your warmest tears
Speak regrets, but never fears,—
Heaven understands!
Let the sad heart, o'er the tomb,
Lift again and burst in bloom
Fragrant with a prayer as sweet
As the lily at your feet.

Bend and kiss the folded eyes—
They are only feigning sleep
While their truant glances peep
Into Paradise.
See, the face, though cold and white,
Holds a hint of some delight
E'en with Death, whose finger-tips
Rest upon the frozen lips.

When, within the years to come,
Vanished echoes live once more—
Pattering footsteps on the floor,
And the sounds of home,—

Let your arms in fancy fold
Little Harlie as of old—
As of old and as he waits
At the City's golden gates.

69

SAY SOMETHING TO ME

SAY something to me! I've waited
so long—
Waited and wondered in vain;
Only a sentence would fall like a song
Over this listening pain,—
Over a silence that glowers and
frowns,—
Even my pencil to-night
Slips in the dews of my sorrow and
wounds
Each tender word that I write.

Say something to me—if only to tell
Me you remember the past;
Let the sweet words, like the notes of
a bell,
Ring out my vigil at last.
O it were better, far better than this
Doubt and distrust in the breast,—
For in the wine of a fanciful kiss
I could taste Heaven, and—rest.

Say something to me! I kneel and I
plead,
In my wild need, for a word;
If my poor heart from this silence were
freed,
I could soar up like a bird
In the glad morning, and twitter and
sing,
Carol and warble and cry
Blithe as the lark as he cruises awing
Over the deeps of the sky.

70
LEONAINIE

LEONAINIE—Angels named her;
    And they took the light
Of the laughing stars and framed her
    In a smile of white;
        And they made her hair of gloomy
        Midnight, and her eyes of bloomy
        Moonshine, and they brought her
            to me
    In the solemn night.—

In a solemn night of summer,
    When my heart of gloom
Blossomed up to greet the comer
    Like a rose in bloom;
        All forebodings that distressed me
        I forgot as Joy caressed me—
        (*Lying* Joy! that caught and
            pressed me
    In the arms of doom!)

Only spake the little lisper
    In the Angel-tongue;
Yet I, listening, heard her whisper,—
    "Songs are only sung
        Here below that they may grieve
            you—
        Tales but told you to deceive
            you,—
        So must Leonainie leave you
    While her love is young."

Then God smiled and it was morning.
    Matchless and supreme
Heaven's glory seemed adorning
    Earth with its esteem:
        Every heart but mine seemed
            gifted
        With the voice of prayer, and
            lifted
        Where my Leonainie drifted
    From me like a dream.

71
A TEST OF LOVE

"Now who shall say he loves me not."

HE wooed her first in an atmosphere
    Of tender and low-breathed sighs;
But the pang of her laugh went cutting
    clear
    To the soul of the enterprise;
"You beg so pert for the kiss you seek
    It reminds me, John," she said,
"Of a poodle pet that jumps to 'speak'
    For a crumb or a crust of bread."

And flashing up, with the blush that
    flushed
His face like a tableau-light,
Came a bitter threat that his white lips
    hushed
    To a chill, hoarse-voiced "Good
    night!"
And again her laugh, like a knell that
    tolled,
    And a wide-eyed mock surprise,—
"Why, John," she said, "you have
    taken cold
    In the chill air of your sighs!"

And then he turned, and with teeth
    tight-clenched,
    He told her he hated her,—
That his love for her from his heart he
    wrenched
    Like a corpse from a sepulcher.
And then she called him "a ghoul all
    red
    With the quintessence of crimes"—
"But I know you love me now," she
    said,
    And kissed him a hundred times.

72

FATHER WILLIAM

A NEW VERSION BY LEE O. HARRIS AND
JAMES WHITCOMB RILEY

"YOU are old, Father William, and
though one would think
All the veins in your body were dry,
Yet the end of your nose is red as a
pink;
I beg your indulgence, but why?"

"You see," Father William replied, "in
my youth—
'Tis a thing I must ever regret—
It worried me so to keep up with the
truth
That my nose has a flush on it yet."

"You are old," said the youth, "and I
grieve to detect
A feverish gleam in your eye;
Yet I'm willing to give you full time to
reflect.
Now, pray, can you answer me
why?"

"Alas," said the sage, "I was tempted to
choose
Me a wife in my earlier years,
And the grief, when I think that she
didn't refuse,
Has reddened my eyelids with tears."

"You are old, Father William," the
young man said,
"And you never touch wine, you de-
clare,
Yet you sleep with your feet at the
head of the bed;
Now answer me that if you dare."

"In my youth," said the sage, "I was
told it was true,
That the world turned around in the
night;
I cherished the lesson, my boy, and I
knew
That at morning my feet would be
right."

"You are old," said the youth, "and it
grieved me to note,
As you recently fell through the
door,
That 'full as a goose' had been chalked
on your coat;
Now answer me that I implore."

"My boy," said the sage, "I have an-
swered you fair,
While you stuck to the point in dis-
pute,
But this is a personal matter, and there
Is my answer—the toe of my boot."

73

WHAT THE WIND SAID

I MUSE to-day, in a listless way,
   In the gleam of a summer land;
I close my eyes as a lover may
   At the touch of his sweetheart's hand,
And I hear these things in the whisper-
      ings
   Of the zephyrs round me fanned:—

I am the Wind, and I rule mankind,
   And I hold a sovereign reign
Over the lands, as God designed,
   And the waters they contain:
Lo! the bound of the wide world round
   Falleth in my domain!

I was born on a stormy morn
In a kingdom walled with snow,
Whose crystal cities laugh to scorn
The proudest the world can show;
And the daylight's glare is frozen there
In the breath of the blasts that blow.

Life to me was a jubilee
From the first of my youthful days:
Clinking my icy toys with glee—
Playing my childish plays;
Filling my hands with the silver sands
To scatter a thousand ways:

Chasing the flakes that the Polar shakes
From his shaggy coat of white,
Or hunting the trace of the track he
makes
And sweeping it from sight,
As he turned to glare from the slippery
stair
Of the iceberg's farthest height.

Till I grew so strong that I strayed ere
long
From my home of ice and chill;
With an eager heart and a merry song
I traveled the snows until
I heard the thaws in the ice-crag's jaws
Crunched with a hungry will;

And the angry crash of the waves that
dash
Themselves on the jaggèd shore
Where the splintered masts of the ice-
wrecks flash,
And the frightened breakers roar
In wild unrest on the ocean's breast
For a thousand leagues or more.

And the grand old sea invited me
With a million beckoning hands,
And I spread my wings for a flight as
free

As ever a sailor plans
When his thoughts are wild and his
heart beguiled
With the dreams of foreign lands.

I passed a ship on its homeward trip,
With a weary and toil-worn crew;
And I kissed their flag with a welcome
lip,
And so glad a gale I blew
That the sailors quaffed their grog and
laughed
At the work I made them do.

I drifted by where sea-groves lie
Like brides in the fond caress
Of the warm sunshine and the tender
sky—
Where the ocean, passionless
And tranquil, lies like a child whose
eyes
Are blurred with drowsiness.

I drank the air and the perfume there,
And bathed in a fountain's spray;
And I smoothed the wings and the
plumage rare
Of a bird for his roundelay,
And fluttered a rag from a signal-crag
For a wretched castaway.

With a sea-gull resting on my breast,
I launched on a madder flight:
And I lashed the waves to a wild un-
rest,
And howled with a fierce delight
Till the daylight slept; and I wailed
and wept
Like a fretful babe all night.

For I heard the boom of a gun strike
doom;
And the gleam of a blood-red star

Glared at me through the mirk and
  gloom
From the lighthouse tower afar;
And I held my breath at the shriek of
  death
That came from the harbor bar.

For I am the Wind, and I rule man-
  kind,
And I hold a sovereign reign
Over the lands, as God designed,
And the waters they contain:
Lo! the bound of the wide world round
  Falleth in my domain!

I journeyed on, when the night was
  gone,
  O'er a coast of oak and pine;
And I followed a path that a stream
  had drawn
Through a land of vale and vine,
And here and there was a village fair
In a nest of shade and shine.

I passed o'er lakes where the sunshine
  shakes
  And shivers his golden lance
On the glittering shield of the wave
  that breaks
  Where the fish-boats dip and dance,
And the trader sails where the mist un-
  veils
The glory of old romance.

I joyed to stand where the jeweled
  hand
Of the maiden-morning lies
On the tawny brow of the mountain-
  land.
  Where the eagle shrieks and cries,
And holds his throne to himself alone
From the light of human eyes.

Adown deep glades where the forest
  shades
  Are dim as the dusk of day—
Where only the foot of the wild beast
  wades,
  Or the Indian dares to stray,
As the blacksnakes glide through the
  reeds and hide
In the swamp-depths grim and gray.

And I turned and fled from the place
  of dread
  To the far-off haunts of men.
"In the city's heart is rest," I said,—
  But I found it not, and when
I saw but care and vice reign there
I was filled with wrath again:

And I blew a spark in the midnight
  dark
Till it flashed to an angry flame
And scarred the sky with a lurid mark
  As red as the blush of shame:
And a hint of hell was the dying yell
That up from the ruins came.

The bells went wild, and the black
  smoke piled
  Its pillars against the night,
Till I gathered them, like flocks de-
  filed,
  And scattered them left and right,
While the holocaust's red tresses tossed
As a maddened Fury's might.

"Ye overthrown!" did I jeer and
  groan—
  "Ho! who is your master?—say!—
Ye shapes that writhe in the slag and
  moan
  Your slow-charred souls away—
Ye worse than worst of things ac-
  curst—
Ye dead leaves of a day!"

I am the Wind, and I rule mankind,
And I hold a sovereign reign
Over the lands, as God designed,
And the waters they contain:
Lo! the bound of the wide world round
Falleth in my domain!

. . . .

I wake, as one from a dream half done,
And gaze with a dazzled eye
On an autumn leaf like a scrap of sun
That the wind goes whirling by,
While afar I hear, with a chill of fear,
The winter storm-king sigh.

74

MORTON

THE warm pulse of the nation has
grown chill;
The muffled heart of Freedom, like
a knell,
Throbs solemnly for one whose earthly
will
Wrought every mission well.

Whose glowing reason towered above
the sea
Of dark disaster like a beacon light,
And led the Ship of State, unscathed
and free,
Out of the gulfs of night.

When Treason, rabid-mouthed, and
fanged with steel,
Lay growling o'er the bones of fallen
braves,
And when beneath the tyrant's iron
heel
Were ground the hearts of slaves,

And War, with all his train of horrors,
leapt
Across the fortress-walls of Liberty
With havoc e'en the marble goddess
wept
With tears of blood to see.

Throughout it all his brave and kingly
mind
Kept loyal vigil o'er the patriot's
vow,
And yet the flag he lifted to the wind
Is drooping o'er him now.

And Peace—all pallid from the battle-
field
When first again it hovered o'er the
land
And found his voice above it like a
shield,
Had nestled in his hand.

. . . .

O throne of State and gilded Senate
halls—
Though thousands throng your aisles
and galleries—
How empty are ye! and what silence
falls
On your hilarities!

And yet, though great the loss to us
appears,
The consolation sweetens all our
pain—
Though hushed the voice, through all
the coming years
Its echoes will remain.

75

AN AUTUMNAL
EXTRAVAGANZA

WITH a sweeter voice than birds
    Dare to twitter in their sleep,
Pipe for me a tune of words,
    Till my dancing fancies leap
Into freedom vaster far
Than the realms of Reason are!
Sing for me with wilder fire
    Than the lover ever sung,
From the time he twanged the lyre
    When the world was baby-young.

O my maiden Autumn, you—
You have filled me through and
        through
With a passion so intense,
All of earthly eloquence
    Fails, and falls, and swoons away
In your presence. Like as one
Who essays to look the sun
    Fairly in the face, I say,
Though my eyes you dazzle blind
Greater dazzled is my mind.
So, my Autumn, let me kneel
    At your feet and worship you!
Be my sweetheart; let me feel
    Your caress; and tell me too
Why your smiles bewilder me—
Glancing into laughter, then
Trancing into calm again,
Till your meaning drowning lies
In the dim depths of your eyes.
Let me see the things you see
Down the depths of mystery!
Blow aside the hazy veil
    From the daylight of your face
With the fragrance-ladened gale
    Of your spicy breath and chase
Every dimple to its place.

Lift your gipsy finger-tips
To the roses of your lips,
And fling down to me a bud—
    But an unblown kiss—but one—
It shall blossom in my blood,
    Even after life is done—
When I dare to touch the brow
Your rare hair is veiling now—
When the rich, red-golden strands
Of the treasure in my hands
Shall be all of worldly worth
Heaven lifted from the earth,
Like a banner to have set
On its highest minaret.

76

THE ROSE

IT tossed its head at the wooing
    breeze;
    And the sun, like a bashful swain,
Beamed on it through the waving trees
    With a passion all in vain,—
For my rose laughed in a crimson glee,
And hid in the leaves in wait for me.

The honey-bee came there to sing
    His love through the languid hours,
And vaunt of his hives, as a proud old
        king
    Might boast of his palace-towers:
But my rose bowed in a mockery,
And hid in the leaves in wait for me.

The humming-bird, like a courtier gay,
    Dipped down with a dalliant song,
And twanged his wings through the
        roundelay
    Of love the whole day long:

Yet my rose turned from his min-
    strelsy
And hid in the leaves in wait for me.

The firefly came in the twilight dim
    My red, red rose to woo—
Till quenched was the flame of love
    in him,
    And the light of his lantern too,
As my rose wept with dewdrops three
And hid in the leaves in wait for me.

And I said: I will cull my own sweet
    rose—
    Some day I will claim as mine
The priceless worth of the flower that
    knows
    No change, but a bloom divine—
The bloom of a fadeless constancy
That hides in the leaves in wait for
    me!

But time passed by in a strange dis-
    guise,
    And I marked it not, but lay
In a lazy dream, with drowsy eyes,
    Till the summer slipped away,
And a chill wind sang in a minor key:
"Where is the rose that waits for
    thee?"

·   ·   ·   ·   ·   ·   ·

I dream to-day, o'er a purple stain
    Of bloom on a withered stalk,
Pelted down by the autumn rain
    In the dust of the garden-walk,
That an Angel-rose in the world to be
Will hide in the leaves in wait for me.

77

THE MERMAN

I

WHO would be
    A merman gay,
    Singing alone,
    Sitting alone,
With a mermaid's knee,
    For instance—hey—
    For a throne?

II

I would be a merman gay;
    I would sit and sing the whole day
        long;
I would fill my lungs with the strong-
        est brine,
    And squirt it up in a spray of song,
And soak my head in my liquid voice;
    I'd curl my tail in curves divine,
And let each curve in a kink rejoice.
    I'd tackle the mermaids under the
        sea,
And yank 'em around till they yanked
        me,
        Sportively, sportively;
And then we would wiggle away,
        away,
To the pea-green groves on the coast
        of day,
    Chasing each other sportively.

III

There would be neither moon nor star;
But the waves would twang like a wet
        guitar—
Low thunder and thrum in the dark-
        ness grum—
    Neither moon nor star;

We would shriek aloud in the dismal
    dales—
Shriek at each other and squawk and
    squeal,
"All night!" rakishly, rakishly;
They would pelt me with oysters and
    wiggletails,
Laughing and clapping their hands at
    me,
"All night!" prankishly, prank-
    ishly;
But I would toss them back in mine,
Lobsters and turtles of quaint design;
Then leaping out in an abrupt way,
I'd snatch them bald in my devilish
    glee,
And skip away when they snatched at
    me,
    Fiendishly, fiendishly.
O, what a jolly life I'd lead,
Ah, what a "bang-up" life indeed!
Soft are the mermaids under the sea—
We would live merrily, merrily.

78

THE RAINY MORNING

THE dawn of the day was dreary,
    And the lowering clouds o'erhead
Wept in a silent sorrow
    Where the sweet sunshine lay dead;
And a wind came out of the eastward
    Like an endless sigh of pain,
And the leaves fell down in the path-
    way
And writhed in the falling rain.

I had tried in a brave endeavor
    To chord my harp with the sun,

But the strings would slacken ever,
    And the task was a weary one:
And so, like a child impatient
    And sick of a discontent,
I bowed in a shower of tear-drops
    And mourned with the instrument.

And lo! as I bowed, the splendor
    Of the sun bent over me,
With a touch as warm and tender
    As a father's hand might be:
And, even as I felt its presence,
    My clouded soul grew bright,
And the tears, like the rain of morning,
    Melted in mists of light.

79

WE ARE NOT ALWAYS GLAD
WHEN WE SMILE

WE are not always glad when we
    smile:
Though we wear a fair face and are .
    gay,
    And the world we deceive
    May not ever believe
We could laugh in a happier way.—
Yet, down in the deeps of the soul,
    Ofttimes, with our faces aglow,
    There's an ache and a moan
    That we know of alone,
And as only the hopeless may know.

We are not always glad when we
    smile,—
    For the heart, in a tempest of pain,
    May live in the guise
    Of a smile in the eyes
As a rainbow may live in the rain;

And the stormiest night of our woe
  May hang out a radiant star
  Whose light in the sky
  Of despair is a lie
As black as the thunder-clouds are.

We are not always glad when we
    smile!—
  But the conscience is quick to record,
  All the sorrow and sin
  We are hiding within
Is plain in the sight of the Lord:
And ever, O ever, till pride
And evasion shall cease to defile
  The sacred recess
  Of the soul, we confess
We are not always glad when we
    smile.

80

A SUMMER SUNRISE

AFTER LEE O. HARRIS

THE master-hand whose pencils
    trace
This wondrous landscape of the
    morn,
Is but the sun, whose glowing face.
Reflects the rapture and the grace
  Of inspiration Heaven-born.

And yet with vision-dazzled eyes,
  I see the lotus-lands of old,
Where odorous breezes fall and rise,
And mountains, peering in the skies,
  Stand ankle-deep in lakes of gold.

And, spangled with the shine and
    shade,
  I see the rivers raveled out
In strands of silver, slowly fade
In threads of light along the glade
  Where truant roses hide and pout.

The tamarind on gleaming sands
  Droops drowsily beneath the heat;
And bowed as though aweary, stands
The stately palm, with lazy hands
  That fold their shadows round his
    feet.

And mistily, as through a veil,
  I catch the glances of a sea
Of sapphire, dimpled with a gale
Toward Colch's blowing, where the
    sail
  Of Jason's Argo beckons me.

And gazing on and farther yet,
  I see the isles enchanted, bright
With fretted spire and parapet,
And gilded mosque and minaret,
  That glitter in the crimson light.

But as I gaze, the city's walls
  Are keenly smitten with a gleam
Of pallid splendor, that appalls
The fancy as the ruin falls
  In ashen embers of a dream.

Yet over all the waking earth
  The tears of night are brushed away,
And eyes are lit with love and mirth,
And benisons of richest worth
  Go up to bless the new-born day.

81

DAS KRIST KINDEL

I HAD fed the fire and stirred it, till the sparkles in delight
  Snapped their saucy little fingers at the chill December night;
And in dressing-gown and slippers, I had tilted back "my throne"—
The old split-bottomed rocker—and was musing all alone.

I could hear the hungry Winter prowling round the outer door,
And the tread of muffled footsteps on the white piazza floor;
But the sounds came to me only as the murmur of a stream
That mingled with the current of a lazy-flowing dream.

Like a fragrant incense rising, curled the smoke of my cigar,
With the lamplight gleaming through it like a mist-enfolded star;—
And as I gazed, the vapor like a curtain rolled away,
With a sound of bells that tinkled, and the clatter of a sleigh.

And in a vision, painted like a picture in the air,
I saw the elfish figure of a man with frosty hair—
A quaint old man that chuckled with a laugh as he appeared,
And with ruddy cheeks like embers in the ashes of his beard.

He poised himself grotesquely, in an attitude of mirth,
On a damask-covered hassock that was sitting on the hearth;
And at a magic signal of his stubby little thumb,
I saw the fireplace changing to a bright proscenium.

And looking there, I marveled as I saw a mimic stage
Alive with little actors of a very tender age;
And some so very tiny that they tottered as they walked,
And lisped and purled and gurgled like the brooklets, when they talked.

And their faces were like lilies, and their eyes like purest dew,
And their tresses like the shadows that the shine is woven through;
And they each had little burdens, and a little tale to tell
Of fairy lore, and giants, and delights delectable.

And they mixed and intermingled, weaving melody with joy,
Till the magic circle clustered round a blooming baby-boy;
And they threw aside their treasures in an ecstasy of glee,
And bent, with dazzled faces and with parted lips, to see.

'Twas a wondrous little fellow, with a dainty double-chin,
And chubby cheeks, and dimples for the smiles to blossom in;
And he looked as ripe and rosy, on his bed of straw and reeds,
As a mellow little pippin that had tumbled in the weeds.

And I saw the happy mother, and a group surrounding her
That knelt with costly presents of frankincense and myrrh;
And I thrilled with awe and wonder, as a murmur on the air
Came drifting o'er the hearing in a melody of prayer:—

By the splendor in the heavens, and the hush upon the sea,
And the majesty of silence reigning over Galilee,—
We feel Thy kingly presence, and we humbly bow the knee
And lift our hearts and voices in gratefulness to Thee.

Thy messenger has spoken, and our doubts have fled and gone
As the dark and spectral shadows of the night before the dawn;
And, in the kindly shelter of the light around us drawn,
We would nestle down forever in the breast we lean upon.

You have given us a shepherd—You have given us a guide,
And the light of Heaven grew dimmer when You sent him from Your side,—
But he comes to lead Thy children where the gates will open wide
To welcome his returning when his works are glorified.

By the splendor in the heavens, and the hush upon the sea,
And the majesty of silence reigning over Galilee,—
We feel Thy kingly presence, and we humbly bow the knee
And lift our hearts and voices in gratefulness to Thee.

Then the vision, slowly failing, with the words of the refrain,
Fell swooning in the moonlight through the frosty window-pane;
And I heard the clock proclaiming, like an eager sentinel
Who brings the world good tidings,—"It is Christmas—all is well!"

82

AN OLD YEAR'S ADDRESS

"I HAVE twankled the strings of the
   twinkering rain;
I have burnished the meteor's mail;

I have bridled the wind
When he whinnied and whined
With a bunch of stars tied to his tail;
But my sky-rocket hopes, hanging over
   the past,
Must fuzzle and fazzle and fizzle at
   last!"

I had waded far out in a drizzling
    dream,
And my fancies had spattered my
    eyes
    With a vision of dread,
    With a number ten head,
    And a form of diminutive size—
That wavered and wagged in a singu-
    lar way
As he wound himself up and pro-
    ceeded to say,—

"I have trimmed all my corns with the
    blade of the moon;
I have picked every tooth with a star:
    And I thrill to recall
    That I went through it all
Like a tune through a tickled guitar.
I have ripped up the rainbow and rav-
    eled the ends
When the sun and myself were par-
    ticular friends."

And pausing again, and producing a
    sponge
And wiping the tears from his eyes,
    He sank in a chair
    With a technical air
That he struggled in vain to dis-
    guise,—
For a sigh that he breathed, as I over
    him leant,
Was haunted and hot with a pepper-
    mint scent.

"Alas!" he continued in quavering
    tones
As a pang rippled over his face,
    "The life was too fast
    For the pleasure to last
In my very unfortunate case;
And I'm going"—he said as he turned
    to adjust

A fuse in his bosom,—"I'm going to—
    BUST!"

I shrieked and awoke with the sullen
    che-boom
    Of a five-pounder filling my ears;
    And a roseate bloom
    Of a light in the room
I saw through the mist of my tears,—
But my guest of the night never saw
    the display,
He had fuzzled and fazzled and fizzled
    away!

83

A NEW YEAR'S PLAINT

In words like weeds, I'll wrap me o'er,
Like coarsest clothes against the cold;
But that large grief which these en-
    fold
Is given in outline and no more.
    —TENNYSON.

THE bells that lift their yawning
    throats
    And lolling tongues with wrangling
    cries
Flung up in harsh, discordant notes,
    As though in anger, at the skies,—
Are filled with echoings replete,
    With purest tinkles of delight—
So I would have a something sweet
    Ring in the song I sing to-night.

As when a blotch of ugly guise
    On some poor artist's naked floor
Becomes a picture in his eyes,
    And he forgets that he is poor,—
So I look out upon the night,
    That ushers in the dawning year,

And in a vacant blur of light
I see these fantasies appear.

I see a home whose windows gleam
Like facets of a mighty gem
That some poor king's distorted dream
Has fastened in his diadem.
And I behold a throng that reels
In revelry of dance and mirth,
With hearts of love beneath their heels,
And in their bosoms hearts of earth.

O Luxury, as false and grand
As in the mystic tales of old,
When genii answered man's command,
And built of nothing halls of gold!
O Banquet, bright with pallid jets,
And tropic blooms, and vases caught
In palms of naked statuettes,
Ye can not color as ye ought!

For, crouching in the storm without,
I see the figure of a child,
In little ragged roundabout,
Who stares with eyes that never
smiled—
And he, in fancy can but taste
The dainties of the kingly fare,
And pick the crumbs that go to waste
Where none have learned to kneel in
prayer.

Go, Pride, and throw your goblet
down—
The "merry greeting" best appears
On loving lips that never drown
Its worth but in the wine of tears;
Go, close your coffers like your hearts,
And shut your hearts against the
poor,
Go, strut through all your pretty parts
But take the "Welcome" from your
door.

LUTHER BENSON

POOR victim of that vulture curse
That hovers o'er the universe,
With ready talons quick to strike
In every human heart alike,
And cruel beak to stab and tear
In virtue's vitals everywhere,—
You need no sympathy of mine
To aid you, for a strength divine
Encircles you, and lifts you clear
Above this earthly atmosphere.

And yet I can but call you poor,
As, looking through the open door
Of your sad life, I only see
A broad landscape of misery,
And catch through mists of pitying
tears
The ruins of your younger years,
I see a father's shielding arm
Thrown round you in a wild alarm—
Struck down, and powerless to free
Or aid you in your agony.

I see a happy home grow dark
And desolate—the latest spark
Of hope is passing in eclipse—
The prayer upon a mother's lips
Has fallen with her latest breath
In ashes on the lips of death—
I see a penitent who reels,
And writhes, and clasps his hands, and
kneels,
And moans for mercy for the sake
Of that fond heart he dared to break.

And lo! as when in Galilee
A voice above the troubled sea

Commanded "Peace; be still!" the flood
That rolled in tempest-waves of blood
Within you, fell in calm so sweet
It ripples round the Saviour's feet;
And all your noble nature thrilled
With brightest hope and faith, and
    filled
Your thirsty soul with joy and peace
And praise to Him who gave release.

Because I saw her, in a sleep
As dark and desolate and deep
And fleeting as the taunting night
That flings a vision of delight
To some lorn martyr as he lies
In slumber ere the day he dies—
Because she vanished like a gleam
Of glory, do I call her "Dream."

85

"DREAM"

BECAUSE her eyes were far too
    deep
And holy for a laugh to leap
Across the brink where sorrow tried
To drown within the amber tide;
Because the looks, whose ripples kissed
The trembling lids through tender mist,
Were dazzled with a radiant gleam—
Because of this I called her "Dream."

Because the roses growing wild
About her features when she smiled
Were ever dewed with tears that fell
With tenderness ineffable;
Because her lips might spill a kiss
That, dripping in a world like this,
Would tincture death's myrrh-bitter
    stream
To sweetness—so I called her "Dream."

Because I could not understand
The magic touches of a hand
That seemed, beneath her strange con-
    trol,
To smooth the plumage of the soul
And calm it, till, with folded wings,
It half forgot its flutterings,
And, nestled in her palm, did seem
To trill a song that called her "Dream."

86

WHEN EVENING SHADOWS
FALL

WHEN evening shadows fall,
    She hangs her cares away
Like empty garments on the wall
    That hides her from the day;
And while old memories throng,
    And vanished voices call,
She lifts her grateful heart in song
    When evening shadows fall.

Her weary hands forget
    The burdens of the day.
The weight of sorrow and regret
    In music rolls away;
And from the day's dull tomb,
    That holds her in its thrall,
Her soul springs up in lily bloom
    When evening shadows fall.

O weary heart and hand,
    Go bravely to the strife—
No victory is half so grand
    As that which conquers life!
One day shall yet be thine—
    The day that waits for all
Whose prayerful eyes are things divine
    When evening shadows fall.

87

YLLADMAR

HER hair was, oh, so dense a blur
    Of darkness, midnight envied
        her;
And stars grew dimmer in the skies
To see the glory of her eyes;
And all the summer rain of light
That showered from the moon at night
Fell o'er her features as the gloom
Of twilight o'er a lily-bloom.

The crimson fruitage of her lips
Was ripe and lush with sweeter wine
Than burgundy or muscadine
Or vintage that the burgher sips
In some old garden on the Rhine:
And I to taste of it could well
Believe my heart a crucible
Of molten love—and I could feel
The drunken soul within me reel
And rock and stagger till it fell.

And do you wonder that I bowed
Before her splendor as a cloud
Of storm the golden-sandaled sun
Had set his conquering foot upon?
And did she will it, I could lie
In writhing rapture down and die
A death so full of precious pain
I'd waken up to die again.

88

A FANTASY

A FANTASY that came to me
    As wild and wantonly designed
As ever any dream might be
    Unraveled from a madman's mind,—

A tangle-work of tissue, wrought
By cunning of the spider-brain,
And woven, in an hour of pain,
To trap the giddy flies of thought.

I stood beneath a summer moon
    All swollen to uncanny girth,
And hanging, like the sun at noon,
    Above the center of the earth;
But with a sad and sallow light,
    As it had sickened of the night
And fallen in a pallid swoon.
Around me I could hear the rush
    Of sullen wings, and feel the whir
Of unseen wings apast me brush
    Like phantoms round a sepulcher;
And, like a carpeting of plush,
    A lawn unrolled beneath my feet,
    Bespangled o'er with flowers as sweet
To look upon as those that nod
Within the garden-fields of God,
But odorless as those that blow
In ashes in the shades below.

And on my hearing fell a storm
    Of gusty music, sadder yet
    Than every whimper of regret
That sobbing utterance could form,
    And patched with scraps of sound
        that seemed
    Torn out of tunes that demons
        dreamed,
    And pitched to such a piercing key,
    It stabbed the ear with agony;
    And when at last it lulled and died,
    I stood aghast and terrified.
I shuddered and I shut my eyes,
    And still could see, and feel aware
    Some mystic presence waited there;
And staring, with a dazed surprise,
    I saw a creature so divine
    That never subtle thought of mine
May reproduce to inner sight
So fair a vision of delight.

A syllable of dew that drips
From out a lily's laughing lips
Could not be sweeter than the word
I listened to, yet never heard.—
For, oh, the woman hiding there
Within the shadows of her hair,
Spake to me in an undertone
So delicate, my soul alone
But understood it as a moan
Of some weak melody of wind
A heavenward breeze had left behind.

A tracery of trees, grotesque
    Against the sky, behind her seen,
Like shapeless shapes of arabesque
    Wrought in an Oriental screen;
And tall, austere and statuesque
    She loomed before it—e'en as though
    The spirit-hand of Angelo
    Had chiseled her to life complete,
    With chips of moonshine round her
        feet.
And I grew jealous of the dusk,
    To see it softly touch her face,
    As lover-like, with fond embrace,
It folded round her like a husk:
But when the glitter of her hand,
    Like wasted glory, beckoned me,
    My eyes grew blurred and dull and
        dim—
    My vision failed—I could not see—
I could not stir—I could but stand,
    Till, quivering in every limb,
    I flung me prone, as though to swim
The tide of grass whose waves of
        green
    Went rolling ocean-wide between
My helpless shipwrecked heart and
        her
    Who claimed me for a worshiper.

And writhing thus in my despair,
    I heard a weird, unearthly sound,

That seemed to lift me from the
        ground
And hold me floating in the air.
I looked, and lo! I saw her bow
    Above a harp within her hands;
A crown of blossoms bound her brow,
    And on her harp were twisted
        strands
Of silken starlight, rippling o'er
With music never heard before
By mortal ears; and, at the strain,
I felt my Spirit snap its chain
And break away,—and I could see
It as it turned and fled from me
To greet its mistress, where she smiled
To see the phantom dancing wild
And wizard-like before the spell
Her mystic fingers knew so well.

89

A DREAM

I DREAMED I was a spider;
    A big, fat, hungry spider;
A lusty, rusty spider
    With a dozen palsied limbs;
With a dozen limbs that dangled
Where three wretched flies were tan-
        gled
And their buzzing wings were strangled
    In the middle of their hymns.

And I mocked them like a demon—
A demoniacal demon
Who delights to be a demon
    For the sake of sin alone;
And with fondly false embraces
Did I weave my mystic laces
Round their horror-stricken faces
    Till I muffled every groan.

And I smiled to see them weeping,
For to see an insect weeping,
Sadly, sorrowfully weeping,
    Fattens every spider's mirth;
And to note a fly's heart quaking,
And with anguish ever aching
Till you see it slowly breaking
    Is the sweetest thing on earth.

I experienced a pleasure,
Such a highly-flavored pleasure,
Such intoxicating pleasure,
    That I drank of it like wine;
And my mortal soul engages
That no spider on the pages
Of the history of ages
    Felt a rapture more divine.

I careened around and capered—
Madly, mystically capered—
For three days and nights I capered
    Round my web in wild delight;
Till with fierce ambition burning,
And an inward thirst and yearning
I hastened my returning
    With a fiendish appetite.

And I found my victims dying,
"Ha," they whispered, "we are dying!"
Faintly whispered, "we are dying,
    And our earthly course is run."
And the scene was so impressing
That I breathed a special blessing,
As I killed them with caressing
    And devoured them one by one.

90
DREAMER, SAY

DREAMER, say, will you dream for
    me
A wild sweet dream of a foreign
    land,

Whose border sips of a foaming sea
    With lips of coral and silver sand;
Where warm winds loll on the shady
    deeps,
Or lave themselves in the tearful mist
The great wild wave of the breaker
    weeps
    O'er crags of opal and amethyst?

Dreamer, say, will you dream a dream
    Of tropic shades in the lands of shine,
Where the lily leans o'er an amber
    stream
    That flows like a rill of wasted
    wine,—
Where the palm-trees, lifting their
    shields of green,
    Parry the shafts of the Indian sun
Whose splintering vengeance falls be-
    tween
    The reeds below where the waters
    run?

Dreamer, say, will you dream of love
    That lives in a land of sweet per-
    fume,
Where the stars drip down from the
    skies above
    In molten spatters of bud and
    bloom?
Where never the weary eyes are wet,
    And never a sob in the balmy air,
And only the laugh of the paroquet
    Breaks the sleep of the silence
    there?

91
BRYANT

THE harp has fallen from the mas-
    ter's hand;
Mute is the music, voiceless are the
    strings,

Save such faint discord as the wild
    wind flings
In sad Æolian murmurs through the
    land.
The tide of melody, whose billows
    grand
    Flowed o'er the world in clearest
      utterings,
    Now, in receding current, sobs and
      sings
That song we never wholly under-
    stand.
* * O, eyes where glorious prophecies
    belong,
    And gracious reverence to humbly
      bow,
And kingly spirit, proud, and pure,
    and strong;
    O, pallid minstrel with the laureled
      brow,
And lips so long attuned to sacred
    song,
    How sweet must be the Heavenly
      anthem now!

92

BABYHOOD

HEIGH-HO! Babyhood! Tell me
    where you linger!
    Let's toddle home again, for we have
      gone astray;
Take this eager hand of mine and lead
    me by the finger
    Back to the lotus-lands of the far-
    away!

Turn back the leaves of life.—Don't
    read the story.—
    Let's find the pictures, and fancy all
    the rest;

We can fill the written pages with a
    brighter glory
Than old Time, the story-teller, at
    his very best.

Turn to the brook where the honey-
    suckle tipping
    O'er its vase of perfume spills it on
    the breeze,
And the bee and humming-bird in ec-
    stasy are sipping
    From the fairy flagons of the bloom-
    ing locust-trees.

Turn to the lane where we used to
    "teeter-totter,"
    Printing little foot-palms in the mel-
    low mold—
Laughing at the lazy cattle wading in
    the water
    Where the ripples dimple round the
    buttercups of gold;

Where the dusky turtle lies basking
    on the gravel
    Of the sunny sand-bar in the middle
    tide,
And the ghostly dragon-fly pauses in
    his travel
    To rest like a blossom where the
    water-lily died.

Heigh-ho! Babyhood! Tell me where
    you linger!
    Let's toddle home again, for we have
    gone astray;
Take this eager hand of mine and lead
    me by the finger
    Back to the lotus-lands of the far-
    away!

93

LIBERTY

NEW CASTLE, JULY 4, 1878

I

FOR a hundred years the pulse of
    time
Has throbbed for Liberty;
For a hundred years the grand old
    clime
Columbia has been free;
    For a hundred years our country's
        love,
    The Stars and Stripes, has waved
        above.

Away far out on the gulf of years—
Misty and faint and white
Through the fogs of wrong—a sail ap-
    pears,
    And the Mayflower heaves in sight,
    And drifts again, with its little
        flock
    Of a hundred souls, on Plymouth
        Rock.

Do you see them there—as long, long
    since—
Through the lens of History;
Do you see them there as their chief-
    tain prints
    In the snow his bended knee,
    And lifts his voice through the
        wintry blast
    In thanks for a peaceful home at
        last?

Though the skies are dark and the
    coast is bleak,
And the storm is wild and fierce,
Its frozen flake on the upturned cheek
Of the Pilgrim melts in tears,

And the dawn that springs from
    the darkness there
Is the morning light of an an-
    swered prayer.
The morning light of the day of Peace
That gladdens the aching eyes,
And gives to the soul that sweet re-
    lease
That the present verifies,—
    Nor a snow so deep, nor a wind
        so chill
    To quench the flame of a free-
        man's will!

II

Days of toil when the bleeding hand
    Of the pioneer grew numb,
When the untilled tracts of the barren
    land
    Where the weary ones had come
    Could offer nought from a fruit-
        ful soil
    To stay the strength of the
        stranger's toil.

Days of pain, when the heart beat low,
    And the empty hours went by
Pitiless, with the wail of woe
    And the moan of Hunger's cry—
    When the trembling hands up-
        raised in prayer
    Had only the strength to hold them
        there.

Days when the voice of hope had fled—
Days when the eyes grown weak
Were folded to, and the tears they shed
Were frost on a frozen cheek—
    When the story bent down from
        the skies and gave
    A shroud of snow for the Pilgrim's
        grave.

Days at last when the smiling sun
Glanced down from a summer sky,
And a music rang where the rivers
    run,
And the waves went laughing by;
    And the rose peeped over the
        mossy bank
    While the wild deer stood in the
        stream and drank.

And the birds sang out so loud and
        good,
    In a symphony so clear
And pure and sweet that the woodman
        stood
    With his ax upraised to hear,
    And to shape the words of the
        tongue unknown
    Into a language all his own:—

1

Sing! every bird, to-day!
    Sing for the sky so clear,
    And the gracious breath of the at-
        mosphere
Shall waft our cares away.
Sing! sing! for the sunshine free;
Sing through the land from sea to sea;
Lift each voice in the highest key
    And sing for Liberty!

2

Sing for the arms that fling
    Their fetters in the dust
    And lift their hands in higher trust
Unto the one Great King;
Sing for the patriot heart and hand;
Sing for the country they have planned;
Sing that the world may understand
    This is Freedom's land!

3

Sing in the tones of prayer,
    Sing till the soaring soul
    Shall float above the world's control
In Freedom everywhere!
Sing for the good that is to be,
Sing for the eyes that are to see
The land where man at last is free,
    O sing for Liberty!

III

A holy quiet reigned, save where the
        hand
Of labor sent a murmur through the
        land,
And happy voices in a harmony
Taught every lisping breeze a melody.
A nest of cabins, where the smoke up-
        curled
A breathing incense to the other world.
A land of languor from the sun of
        noon,
That fainted slowly to the pallid moon,
Till stars, thick-scattered in the garden-
        land
Of Heaven by the great Jehovah's hand,
Had blossomed into light to look upon
The dusky warrior with his arrow
        drawn,
As skulking from the covert of the
        night
With serpent cunning and a fiend's de-
        light,
With murderous spirit, and a yell of
        hate
The voice of Hell might tremble to
        translate:
When the fond mother's tender lullaby
Went quavering in shrieks all suddenly,
And baby-lips were dabbled with the
        stain
Of crimson at the bosom of the slain,

And peaceful homes and fortunes
    ruined—lost
In smoldering embers of the holocaust.
Yet on and on, through years of gloom
    and strife,
Our country struggled into stronger
    life;
Till colonies, like footprints in the sand,
Marked Freedom's pathway winding
    through the land—
And not the footprints to be swept
    away
Before the storm we hatched in Boston
    Bay,—
But footprints where the path of war
    begun
That led to Bunker Hill and Lexing-
    ton,—
For he who "dared to lead where others
    dared
To follow" found the promise there de-
    clared
Of Liberty, in blood of Freedom's host
Baptized to Father, Son, and Holy
    Ghost!

Oh, there were times when every pa-
    triot breast
Was riotous with sentiments expressed
In tones that swelled in volume till the
    sound
Of lusty war itself was well-nigh
    drowned.
Oh, those were times when happy eyes
    with tears
Brimmed o'er as all the misty doubts
    and fears
Were washed away, and Hope with
    gracious mien,
Reigned from her throne again a sov-
    ereign queen.
Until at last, upon a day like this

When flowers were blushing at the
    summer's kiss,
And when the sky was cloudless as the
    face
Of some sweet infant in its angel
    grace,—
There came a sound of music, thrown
    afloat
Upon the balmy air—a clanging note
Reiterated from the brazen throat
Of Independence Bell: A sound so
    sweet,
The clamoring throngs of people in the
    streets
Were stilled as at the solemn voice of
    prayer,
And heads were bowed, and lips were
    moving there
That made no sound—until the spell
    had passed,
And then, as when all sudden comes
    the blast
Of some tornado, came the cheer on
    cheer
Of every eager voice, while far and
    near
The echoing bells upon the atmosphere
Set glorious rumors floating, till the ear
Of every listening patriot tingled clear,
And thrilled with joy and jubilee to
    hear.

I

Stir all your echoes up,
    O Independence Bell,
And pour from your inverted cup
    The song we love so well.

Lift high your happy voice,
    And swing your iron tongue
Till syllables of praise rejoice
    That never yet were sung.

Ring in the gleaming dawn
Of Freedom—Toll the knell
Of Tyranny, and then ring on,
O Independence Bell.—

Ring on, and drown the moan
Above the patriot slain,
Till sorrow's voice shall catch the tone
And join the glad refrain.

Ring out the wounds of wrong
And rankle in the breast;
Your music like a slumber-song
Will lull revenge to rest.

Ring out from Occident
To Orient, and peal
From continent to continent
The mighty joy you feel.

Ring! Independence Bell!
Ring on till worlds to be
Shall listen to the tale you tell
Of love and Liberty!

IV

O Liberty—the dearest word
A bleeding country ever heard,—
We lay our hopes upon thy shrine
And offer up our lives for thine.
You gave us many happy years
Of peace and plenty ere the tears
A mourning country wept were dried
Above the graves of those who died
Upon thy threshold. And again
When newer wars were bred, and men
Went marching in the cannon's breath
And died for thee and loved the death,
While, high above them, gleaming
  bright,
The dear old flag remained in sight,
And lighted up their dying eyes

With smiles that brightened paradise.
O Liberty, it is thy power
To gladden us in every hour
Of gloom, and lead us by thy hand
As little children through a land
Of bud and blossom; while the days
Are filled with sunshine, and thy praise
Is warbled in the roundelays
Of joyous birds, and in the song
Of waters, murmuring along
The paths of peace, whose flowery
  fringe
Has roses finding deeper tinge
Of crimson, looking on themselves
Reflected—leaning from the shelves
Of cliff and crag and mossy mound
Of emerald splendor shadow-
  drowned.—
We hail thy presence, as you come
With bugle blast and rolling drum,
And booming guns and shouts of gle
Commingled in a symphony
That thrills the worlds that throng t
  see
The glory of thy pageantry.
And with thy praise, we breathe a
  prayer
That God who leaves you in our care
May favor us from this day on
With thy dear presence—till the dawn
Of Heaven, breaking on thy face,
Lights up thy first abiding place.

94

TOM VAN ARDEN

TOM VAN ARDEN, my old friend,
  Our warm fellowship is one
Far too old to comprehend
  Where its bond was first begun:
Mirage-like before my gaze

Gleams a land of other days,
Where two truant boys, astray,
Dream their lazy lives away.

There's a vision, in the guise
Of Midsummer, where the Past
Like a weary beggar lies
In the shadow Time has cast;
And as blends the bloom of trees
With the drowsy hum of bees,
Fragrant thoughts and murmurs
blend,
Tom Van Arden, my old friend.

Tom Van Arden, my old friend,
All the pleasures we have known
Thrill me now as I extend
This old hand and grasp your own—
Feeling, in the rude caress,
All affection's tenderness;
Feeling, though the touch be
rough,
Our old souls are soft enough.

So we'll make a mellow hour:
Fill your pipe, and taste the wine—
Warp your face, if it be sour,
I can spare a smile from mine;
If it sharpen up your wit,
Let me feel the edge of it—
I have eager ears to lend,
Tom Van Arden, my old friend.

Tom Van Arden, my old friend,
Are we "lucky dogs," indeed?
Are we all that we pretend
In the jolly life we lead?—
Bachelors, we must confess,
Boast of "single blessedness"
To the world, but not alone—
Man's best sorrow is his own!

And the saddest truth is this,—
Life to us has never proved
What we tasted in the kiss

Of the women we have loved:
Vainly we congratulate
Our escape from such a fate
As their lying lips could send,
Tom Van Arden, my old friend!

Tom Van Arden, my old friend,
Hearts, like fruit upon the stem,
Ripen sweetest, I contend,
As the frost falls over them:
Your regard for me to-day
Makes November taste of May,
And through every vein of rhyme
Pours the blood of summer-time.

When our souls are cramped with
youth
Happiness seems far away
In the future, while, in truth,
We look back on it to-day
Through our tears, nor dare to
boast,—
"Better to have loved and lost!"
Broken hearts are hard to mend,
Tom Van Arden, my old friend.

Tom Van Arden, my old friend,
I grow prosy, and you tire;
Fill the glasses while I bend
To prod up the failing fire. . . .
You are restless:—I presume
There's a dampness in the room.—
Much of warmth our nature begs,
With rheumatics in our legs! . . .

Humph! the legs we used to fling
Limber-jointed in the dance,
When we heard the fiddle ring
Up the curtain of Romance,
And in crowded public halls
Played with hearts like jugglers'
balls.
Feats of mountebanks, depend!—
Tom Van Arden, my old friend.

Tom Van Arden, my old friend,
Pardon, then, this theme of mine:
While the firelight leaps to lend
   Higher color to the wine,—
I propose a health to those
Who have *homes,* and home's re-
      pose,
Wife- and child-love without end!
. . . Tom Van Arden, my old
   friend.

95

T. C. PHILIPS

O NOBLE heart, and brave impet-
   uous hand!
So all engrossed in work of public
   weal

Thou couldst not pause thy own dis-
   tress to feel
While maladies of Wrong oppressed
   the land.
The hopes that marshaled at thy pen's
   command
   To cheer the Right, had not the
      power to heal
The ever-aching wounds thou didst
   conceal
Beneath a front so stoically bland
That no one guessed thy inward agony,—
   Until the Master, leaning from His
      throne,
   Heard some soul wailing in an un-
      dertone,
And bending lower down, discovered
      thee,
   And clasped thy weary hand within
      His own
And lifted thee to rest eternally.

96

A DREAM UNFINISHED

O NLY a dream unfinished; only a form at rest
   With weary hands clasped lightly over a peaceful breast.

And the lonesome light of summer through the open doorway falls,
But it wakes no laugh in the parlor—no voice in the vacant halls.

It throws no spell of music over the slumbrous air;
It meets no step on the carpet—no form in the easy chair.

It finds no queenly presence blessing the solitude
With the gracious benediction of royal womanhood.

It finds no willowy figure tilting the cage that swings
With the little pale canary that forgets the song he sings.

No face at the open window to welcome the fragrant breeze;
No touch at the old piano to waken the sleeping keys.

The idle book lies open, and the folded leaf is pressed
Over the half-told story while death relates the rest.

Only a dream unfinished; only a form at rest,
With weary hands clasped lightly over a peaceful breast.

The light steals into the corner where the darkest shadows are,
And sweeps with its golden fingers the strings of the mute guitar.

And over the drooping mosses it clambers the rustic stand,
And over the ivy's tresses it trails a trembling hand.

But it brings no smile from the darkness—it calls no face from the gloom—
No song flows out of the silence that aches in the empty room.

And we look in vain for the dawning in the depths of our despair,
Where the weary voice goes wailing through the empty aisles of prayer.

And the hands reach out through the darkness for the touches we have known
When the icy palms lay warmly in the pressure of our own:

When the folded eyes were gleaming with a glory God designed
To light a way to Heaven by the smiles they left behind.

Only a dream unfinished; only a form at rest
With weary hands clasped lightly over a peaceful breast.

97

A CHILD'S HOME—LONG AGO

READ AT AN OLD SETTLERS' MEETING AT
OAKLAND, INDIANA, AUGUST 3, 1878.

THE terse old maxim of the poet's
pen,
"What constitutes a state? High-
minded men,"
Holds such a wealth of truth, when
one reflects,
It seems more like a sermon than a text.
Yet looking dimly backward o'er the
years
Where first the face of progress,
through our tears,
Smiles on us, where within the forest
gloom
The bud of Indiana bursts in bloom;
We can but see, from Lake of Michi-
gan,
To where Ohio rolls, the work of
man—
From where our eastern boundary-line
is pressed,
To where the Wabash revels on the
west;
A broad expanse of fair and fertile
land,

Like some rich landscape, from a master's hand,
That in its rustic frame, we well might call
The fairest picture on Columbia's wall—
A picture now—a masterpiece divine,
That, ere the artist's hand in its design
Had traced this loveliness, was but a blot
Of ugly pigment on a barren spot—
A blur of color on a hueless ground
Where scarce a hint of beauty could be found.
But patiently the hand of labor wrought,
And from each touch new inspiration caught;
Toiled on through disadvantages untold,
And at each onward step found firmer hold,
And obstacles that threatened long delay
He climbed above and went upon his way,
Until at last, exulting, he could see
The sweet reward of patient industry;
And beauties he had hardly dared to dream,
In hill and vale, and cliff and winding stream,
Spread out before his vision, till the soul
Within him seemed to leap beyond control,
And hover over lands the genii made
Of sifted sunshine and of dew-washed shade.

And who, indeed, that loves his native state,
Has not a heart to throb and palpitate
With ecstasy, as o'er her wintry past,
He sees the sun of summer dawn at last,
And catches, through the misty shower of light,
Dim glimpses of the orchards' bloom of white,
And fields beyond where, waving empty sleeves,
The "scarecrow" beckons to the feathered thieves
That perch, and perk their nimble heads away,
And flit away with harsh, discordant cry,
Or shading with his hand, his dazzled eyes,
Looks out across the deadened paradise,
Where wild flowers blossom, and the ivy clings,
And from the ruined oak the grapevine swings,
While high above upon the leafless tree
The red-head drummer beats his reveille,
And, like an army thronging at the sound,
The soldier corn-stalks on their battle ground
March on to harvest victories, and flaunt
Their banners o'er the battlements of want!

And musing thus to-day, the pioneer
Whose brawny arm has grubbed a pathway here,
Stands, haply; with his vision backward turned
To where the log-heap of the past was burned,

And sees again, as in some shadowy
    dream,
The wild deer bending o'er the hidden
    stream,
Or sniffing, with his antlers lifted high,
The gawky crane, as he comes trailing
    by,
And drops in shallow tides below to
    wade
On tilting legs through dusky depths
    of shade,
While just across the glossy otter slips
Like some wet shadow 'neath the rip-
    ple's lips
As, drifting from the thicket-hid bayou,
The wild duck paddles past his ren-
    dezvous,
And overhead the beech and sycamore,
That lean their giant forms from either
    shore,
Clasps hands and bow their heads, as
    though to bless
In whispered prayer the sleeping wil-
    derness.
A scene of such magnificent expanse
Of nameless grandeur that the utter-
    ance
Of even feathered orators is faint.
For here the dove's most melancholy
    plaint
Invokes no echo, and the killdeer's call
Swoons in the murmur of the water-
    fall
That, faint and far away and unde-
    fined,
Falls like a ghost f sound upon the
    mind.
The voice of natι 's very self drops
    low,
As though she whispered of the long
    ago,
When down the wandering stream the
    rude canoe

Of some lone trapper glided into view,
And loitered down the watery path
    that led
Through forest depths that only knew
    the tread
Of savage beasts; and wild barbarians
That skulked about with blood upon
    their hands
And murder in their hearts. The light
    of day
Might barely pierce the gloominess that
    lay
Like some dark pall across the water's
    face,
And folded all the land in its embrace;
The panther's whimper, and the bear's
    low growl—
The snake's sharp rattle, and the wolf's
    wild howl;
The owl's grim chuckle, as it rose and
    fell
In alternation with the Indian's yell,
Made fitting prelude for the gory plays
That were enacted in the early days.

But fancy, soaring o'er the storm of
    grief
Like that lone bird that brought the
    olive leaf,
Brings only peace—an amulet whose
    spell
Works stranger marvels than the
    tongue can tell—
For o'er the vision, like a mirage, falls
The old log cabin with its dingy walls,
And crippled chimney with its crutch-
    like prop
Beneath a sagging shoulder at the top:
The coonskin battened fast on either
    side—
The wisps of leaf-tobacco—"cut-and-
    dried";

The yellow strands of quartered apples, hung
In rich festoons that tangle in among
The morning-glory vines that clamber o'er
The little clapboard roof above the door:
The old well-sweep that drops a courtesy
To every thirsting soul so graciously,
The stranger, as he drains the dripping gourd,
Intuitively murmurs, "Thank the Lord!"
Again through mists of memory arise
The simple scenes of home before the eyes:—
The happy mother, humming, with her wheel,
The dear old melodies that used to steal
So drowsily upon the summer air,
The house-dog hid his bone, forgot his care,
And nestled at her feet, to dream, perchance,
Some cooling dream of winter-time romance:
The square of sunshine through the open door
That notched its edge across the puncheon floor,
And made a golden coverlet whereon
The god of slumber had a picture drawn
Of Babyhood, in all the loveliness
Of dimpled cheek and limb and linsey dress:
The bough-filled fireplace, and the mantel wide,
Its fire-scorched ankles stretched on either side,

Where, perched upon its shoulders 'neath the joist,
The old clock hiccoughed, harsh and husky-voiced,
And snarled the premonition, dire and dread,
When it should hammer Time upon the head:
Tomatoes, red and yellow, in a row,
Preserved not then for diet, but for show,—
Like rare and precious jewels in the rough
Whose worth was not appraised at half enough:
The jars of jelly, with their dusty tops;
The bunch of pennyroyal; the cordial drops;
The flask of camphor, and the vial of squills,
The box of buttons, garden-seeds, and pills;
And, ending all the mantel's bric-à-brac,
The old, time-honored "Family Almanack."
And Memory, with a mother's touch of love,
Climbs with us to the dusky loft above,
Where drowsily we trail our fingers in
The mealy treasures of the harvest bin;
And, feeling with our hands the open track,
We pat the bag of barley on the back;
And, groping onward through the mellow gloom,
We catch the hidden apple's faint perfume,
And, mingling with it, fragrant hints of pear
And musky melon ripening somewhere.
Again we stretch our limbs upon the bed

Where first our simple childish prayers
were said;
And while, without, the gallant cricket
trills
A challenge to the solemn whippoor-
wills,
And, filing on the chorus with his glee,
The katydid whets all the harmony
To feather-edge of incoherent song,
We drop asleep, and peacefully along
The current of our dreams we glide
away
To the dim harbor of another day,
Where brown toil waits for us, and
where labor stands
To welcome us with rough and horny
hands.

And who will mock the rude, unpol-
ished ways
That swayed us in the good old-fash-
ioned days
When labor wore the badge of man-
hood, set
Upon his tawny brow in pearls of
sweat?
Who dares to-day to turn a scornful eye
On labor in his swarthy majesty?
Or wreathe about his lips the sneer
of pride
Where brawny toil stands towering at
his side?
By industry alone we gauge the worth
Of all the richer nations of the earth;
And side by side with honesty and toil
Prosperity walks round the furrowed
soil
That belts the world, and o'er the ocean
ledge
Tilts up the horn of plenty on its edge.
'Tis not the subject fawning to the
king,
'Tis not the citizen, low cowering

Before the throne of state.—'Twas
God's intent
Each man should be a king—a presi-
dent;
And while through human veins the
blood of pride
Shall ebb and flow in Labor's rolling
tide,
The brow of toil shall wear the diadem,
And justice gleaming there, the central
gem,
Shall radiate the time when we shall
see
Each man rewarded as his works shall
be.
Thank God for this bright promise!
Lift the voice
Till all the waiting multitudes rejoice;
Reach out across the sea and clap your
hands
Till voices waken out of foreign lands
To join the song, while listening
Heaven waits
To roll an answering anthem through
the gates.

98

WHEN I DO MOCK

WHEN I do mock the blackness
of the night
With my despair—outweep the very
dews
And wash my wan cheeks stark of all
delight,
Denying every counsel of dear use
In mine embittered state; with infinite
Perversity, mine eyes drink in no
sight
Of pleasance that nor moon nor stars
refuse

In silver largess and gold twinklings
    bright;—
I question me what mannered brain is
    mine
That it doth trick me of the very
    food
It panteth for—the very meat and wine
That yet should plump my starvèd
    soul with good
And comfortable plethora of ease,
That I might drowse away such rhymes
    as these.

99

THE HIGHEST GOOD

TO attain the highest good
    Of true man and womanhood,
Simply do your honest best—
God with joy will do the rest.

100

EZRA HOUSE

[*These lines was writ, in ruther high
sperits, jest at the close of what's called
the Anti Bellum Days, and more to
be a-foolin' than anything else,—though
they is more er less facts in it. But
some of the boys, at the time we was
all a-singin' it, fer Ezry's benefit, to the
old tune of "The Oak and the Ash and
the Bonny Willer Tree," got it struck
off in the weekly, without leave er li-
sence of mine; and so sence they's allus
some of 'em left to rigg me about it
yit, I might as well claim the thing
right here and now, so here goes. I give
it jest as it appeard, fixed up and gram-* matisized *consider'ble, as the editer
told me he took the liburty of doin',
in that sturling old home paper* THE
ADVANCE—*as sound a paper yit to-day
and as stanch and abul as you'll find in
a hunderd.*]

COME listen, good people, while a
    story I do tell,
Of the sad fate of one which I knew so
    passing well;
He enlisted at McCordsville, to battle
    in the South,
And protect his country's union; his
    name was Ezra House.

He was a young school-teacher, and ed-
    ucated high
In regards to Ray's arithmetic, and also
    Algebra:
He give good satisfaction, but at his
    country's call
He dropped his position, his Algebra
    and all.

"It's oh, I'm going to leave you, kind
    scholars," he said—
For he wrote a composition the last
    day and read;
And it brought many tears in the eyes
    of the school,
To say nothing of his sweetheart he
    was going to leave so soon.

"I have many recollections to take
    with me away,
Of the merry transpirations in the
    schoolroom so gay;
And of all that's past and gone I will
    never regret
I went to serve my country at the first
    of the outset!"

He was a good penman, and the lines
that he wrote
On that sad occasion was too fine for
me to quote,—
For I was there and heard it, and I
ever will recall
It brought the happy tears to the eyes
of us all.

And when he left, his sweetheart she
fainted away,
And said she could never forget the
sad day
When her lover so noble, and galliant
and gay,
Said "Fare you well, my true love!"
and went marching away.

But he hadn't been gone for more than
two months,
When the sad news come—"he was in
a skirmish once,
And a cruel Rebel ball had wounded
him full sore
In the region of the chin, through the
canteen he wore."

But his health recruited up, and his
wounds they got well,
But whilst he was in battle at Bull Run
or Malvern Hill,
The news come again, so sorrowful to
hear—
"A sliver from a bombshell cut off his
right ear."

But he stuck to the boys, and it's often
he would write,
That "he wasn't afraid for his country
to fight."
But oh, had he returned on a furlough,
I believe
He would not, to-day, have such cause
to grieve.

For in another battle—the name I never
heard—
He was guarding the wagons when an
accident occurred,—
A comrade who was under the influ-
ence of drink,
Shot him with a musket through the
right cheek, I think.

But his dear life was spared; but it
hadn't been for long,
Till a cruel Rebel colonel come riding
along,
And struck him with his sword, as
many do suppose,
For his cap-rim was cut off, and also
his nose.

But Providence, who watches o'er the
noble and the brave,
Snatched him once more from the
jaws of the grave;
And just a little while before the close
of the war,
He sent his picture home to his girl
away so far.

And she fell into decline, and she wrote
in reply,
"She had seen his face again and was
ready to die";
And she wanted him to promise, when
she was in her tomb,
He would only visit that by the light
of the moon.

But he never returned at the close of
the war,
And the boys that got back said he
hadn't the heart;
But he got a position in a powder-mill,
and said
He hoped to meet the doom that his
country denied.

101

THE VISION OF RABBI BEN ISAAC

FOR three score years my wandering
feet have strayed
Along a path wherein no footprint
lay
Of Him, who of the cross a guide-
board made
To point me out the way.

With open eyes I dreamed that I was
dead—
Dead to all outward semblance,
though I lay
With some old scrap of reason in my
head
That would not fade away.

And peering up in wonderment I saw
My floating spirit plume its wings
elate,
Yet gazing upward with a look of awe,
It seemed to hesitate.

"Go on!" I called to it. "Leap into
space,
And sweep a way to glory with thy
wings!"
"Alas!" it answered back, with troubled
face,
"They are such trembling things!"

And hovering above me, spread them
wide,
And all their glossy plumage o'er
my eyes
Shook out in downy splendor, crimson-
dyed
With hues of Paradise.

"Nay, glorious things are they," I cried
amazed,
And veiled my vision from their daz-
zling light—
"So, get thee gone—their maker must
be praised"—
And upward through the night

It lifted like a meteor, and sailed
Across the gulf of darkness like a
flame,
While down the smoldering wake be-
hind it trailed
The ashes of my name.

It called to me—not larger than a flake
Of starlight did it glimmer through
the gloom—
"Pray for me," fell the voice, "for
Jesus' sake!
I see the heavens bloom."

And loathful to myself I whispered
then,
As wholly from my gaze the glim-
mer went—
"O Lord, through Christ, receive my
soul, Amen."
And like an instrument

Of music in some heavenly tumult
tipped,
Outpouring the elixir of its voice,
Down-showering upon my senses
dripped
The utterance, "Rejoice!

"God listens, for the angels at the door
Are swarming out and in and out
again,
And o'er and round about me ever-
more
They sing 'Good will to men!'"

Then suddenly the voice in quaverings
  Fell wailingly—"Alas! for I alone
Of all the glorious throng have tar-
    nished wings
  That Heaven will not own.

"The angel Truth has pityingly said
  That every plume impure Christ
    will condemn,
And that the stain self-righteousness is
    red
  As blood on all of them."

Then to my soul I cried aloud: "Re-
    turn
  That I may bow my head in holier
    prayer,
And all the recompense of good I earn
  Shall blossom everywhere."

"Not so." It answered, as in some sur-
    prise—
  "The angel Faith has whispered
    'Look above,'
And shading with her wings my daz-
    zled eyes,
  Points out the angel Love,

"Who, weeping, bends above me, and
    her tears
  Baptize me, and her sister Mercy
    trips
Along the golden clouds, and Christ
    appears
  With sorrow on His lips"—

Then silence, and as one who vainly
    wars
  With inner strife: "Come back to
    me!" I cried,
And pealing down a pathway of the
    stars
  A ringing voice replied—

"Now is thy soul's probation so com-
    plete
  It may but answer thee with one
    farewell";
And, filtered through the gloom, lo! at
    my feet
  A snow-white feather fell.

102

DAN PAINE

O LD friend of mine, whose chiming
      name
  Has been the burthen of a rhyme
Within my heart since first I came
  To know thee in thy mellow prime:
    With warm emotions in my breast
    That can but coldly be expressed,
    And hopes and wishes wild and
      vain,
    I reach my hand to thee, Dan
      Paine.

In fancy, as I sit alone
  In gloomy fellowship with care,
I hear again thy cheery tone,
  And wheel for thee an easy chair;
    And from my hand the pencil
      falls—
    My book upon the carpet sprawls,
    As eager soul and heart and brain
    Leap up to welcome thee, Dan
      Paine.

A something gentle in thy mien,
  A something tender in thy voice,
Has made my trouble so serene,
  I can but weep, from very choice.
    And even then my tears, I guess,
    Hold more of sweet than bitterness,

And more of gleaming shine than
rain,
Because of thy bright smile, Dan
Paine.

The wrinkles that the years have spun
And tangled round thy tawny face,
Are kinked with laughter, every one,
And fashioned in a mirthful grace.
And though the twinkle of thine
eyes
Is keen as frost when Summer
dies,
It can not long as frost remain
While thy warm soul shines out,
Dan Paine.

And so I drain a health to thee:—
May merry Joy and jolly Mirth
Like children clamber on thy knee,
And ride thee round the happy earth!
And when, at last, the hand of
Fate
Shall lift the latch of Canaan's
gate,
And usher me in thy domain,
Smile on me just as now, Dan
Paine.

103

OLD HEC'S IDOLATRY

HEIGH-O! our jolly tilts at New
World song!—
What was the poem indeed! and where
the bard—
"Stabbing his ink-pot ever, not his
heart,"
As Hector phrased it contumeliously,
Mouthing and munching, at the or-
chard-stile,

A water-cored rambo whose spirted
juice
Glanced, sprayed and flecked the sun-
light as he mouth'd
And muncht, and muncht and
mouth'd. All loved the man!
"Our Hector" as his *Alma Mater* oozed
It into utterance—"Old Hec" said we
Who knew him, hide-and-tallow, hoof-
and-horn!
So he: "O ay! my soul! our New World
song—
The tweedle-deedles of our modern
school—
A school of minnows,—not one gamy
bass—
To hook the angler, not the angler
him.
Here! all ye little fishes: tweedle-dee!
Soh! one—along the vasty stream of
time—
Glints to the surface with a gasp,—
and, lo,
A bubble! and he thinks, 'My eye!—
see there,
Ye little fishes,—there's a song I've
sung!'
Another gapes: another bubble; then
He thinks: 'Well, is it not a wondrous
art
To breathe a great immortal poem like
that!'
And then another—and another still—
And yet another,—till from brim to
brim
The tide is postuled over with a pest
Of bubbles—bursting bubbles! Ay! O
ay!"
So, bluff old Hec. And we, who knew
his mood
Had ramped its worst—unless we
roused it yet
To ire's horiffickest insanity

By some inane, unguarded reference
To "verse beragged in Hoosier dia-
    lect"—
(A strangely unforgotten coinage of
Old Hec's, long years agone)—we, so,
    forbore
A word, each glimpsing each, as down
    we sank,
Couched limply in the orchard's sel-
    vage, where—
The rambo finished and the soggy core
Zippt at a sapphire wasp with waist
    more slim
Than any slender lady's, of old wars,
Pent fasting for long sennights in tall
    towers
That overtop the undercringing seas—
With one accordant voice, the while he
    creased
His scroll of manuscript, we said, "Go
    on."
Then Hector thus:

AN IDYL OF THE KING

Erewhile, as Autumn, to King Ar-
    thur's court
Came Raelus, clamoring: "Lo, has our
    house
Been sacked and pillaged by a lawless
    band
Of robber knaves, led on by Alstanés,
The Night-Flower named, because of
    her fair face,
All like a lily gleaming in the dusk
Of her dark hair—and like a lily
    brimmed
With dewy eyes that drip their limpid
    smiles
Like poison out, for by them has been
    wro't
My elder brother's doom, as much I
    fear.

While three days gone was holden har-
    vest-feast
At Lynion Castle—clinging like a gull
High up the gray cliffs of Caerleon—
Came, leaf-like lifted from the plain
    below
As by a twisted wind, a rustling pack
Of bandit pillagers, with Alstanés
Bright-fluttering like a red leaf in the
    front.
And ere we were aware of fell intent—
Not knowing whether it was friend or
    foe—
We found us in their toils, and all the
    house
In place of guests held only prisoners—
Save that the host, my brother, wro't
    upon
By the strange beauty of the robber
    queen,
Was left unfettered, but by silken
    threads
Of fine-spun flatteries and wanton
    smiles
Of the enchantress, till her villain
    thieves
Had rifled as they willed and signal
    given
To get to horse again. And so they
    went—
Their leader flinging backward, as she
    rode,
A kiss to my mad brother—mad since
    then,—
For from that sorry hour he but talked
Of Alstanés, and her rare beauty, and
Her purity—ay, even that he said
Was star-white, and should light his
    life with love
Or leave him groping blindly in its
    quest
Thro' all eternity. So, sighing, he
Went wandering about till set of sun,

Then got to horse, and bade us all
  farewell;
And with his glamoured eyes bent
  trancedly
Upon the tumbled sands that marked
  the way
The robber-woman went, he turned
  and chased
His long black shadow o'er the edge of
  night."

—So Raelus, all seemingly befret
With such concern as nipped his utter-
  ance
In scraps of speech: at which Sir
  Lancelot,
Lifting a slow smile to the King, and
  then
Turning his cool eye on the youth—
  "And you
Would track this siren-robber to her
  hold
And rout her rascal followers, and free
Your brother from the meshes of this
  queen
Of hearts—for there you doubtless
  think him?" "Ay!"
Foamed Raelus, cheek flushed and eye
  aflame,—
"So even have I tracked, and found
  them, too,
And know their burrow, shrouded in
  a copse,
Where, faring in my brother's quest, I
  heard
The nicker of his horse, and followed
  on,
And found him tethered in a thicket
  wild,
As tangled in its tress of leaf and limb
As is a madman's hair; and down the
  path
That parted it and ran across a knoll

And dipped again, all suddenly I came
Upon a cave, wide-yawning 'neath a
  beard
Of tangled moss and vine, whence is-
  suing
I heard, blown o'er my senses faint and
  clear
As whiffs of summer wind, my
  brother's voice
Lilting a love-song, with the burden
  tricked
With dainty warblings of·a woman's
  tongue:
And even as I listening bent, I heard
Such peals of wanton merriment as
  made
My own heart flutter as a bird that
  beats
For freedom at the bars that prison it.
So turned I then and fled as one who
  flies
To save himself alone—forgetful all
Of that my dearer self—my brother.—
  O!"—
Breaking as sharply as the icy blade
That loosens from the eave to slice the
  air
And splinter into scales of flying frost—
"Thy help! Thy help! A dozen goodly
  knights—
Ay, even that, if so it be their hearts
Are hungry as my own to right the
  wrong!"

So Raelus. And Arthur graciously
Gave ear to him, and, patient, heard
  him thro',
And pitied him, and granted all he
  asked;
Then took his hand and held it, say-
  ing, "Strong
And ever stronger may its grasp be
  knit

About the sword that flashes in the
cause
Of good."
     Thus Raelus, on the mor-
row's front,
Trapped like a knight and shining
like a star,
Pranced from the archway of the court,
and led
His glittering lances down the gleam-
ing road
That river-like ran winding till it
slipped
Out of the palace view and spilled their
shields
Like twinkling bubbles o'er the moun-
tain brim.

Then happed it that as Raelus rode,
his tongue
Kept even pace and cantered ever on
Right merrily. His brother, as he said,
Had such an idle soul within his
breast—
Such shallowness of fancy for his heart
To drift about in—that he well be-
lieved
Its anchor would lay hold on any smile
The lees of womanhood might offer
him.
As for himself, he loved his brother
well,
Yet had far liefer see him stark and
white
In marble death than that his veins
should burn
With such vitality as spent its flame
So garishly it knew no steady blaze,
But ever wavered round as veered the
wind
Of his conceit; for he had made his
boast—

Tho' to his own shame did he speak
of it—
That with a wink he could buy every
smile
That virtue owned. So tattled Raelus
Till, heated with his theme, he lifted
voice
And sang the song, "The Light of
Woman's Eyes!"

"O bright is gleaming morn on moun-
tain height;
And bright the moon, slipt from its
sheath of night,—
   But brighter is the light of woman's
   eyes.

"And bright the dewdrop, trembling
on the lip
Of some red rose, or lily petal-tip,
   Or lash of pink,—but brighter
   woman's eyes.

"Bright is the firefly's ever-drifting
spark
That throbs its pulse of light out in the
dark;
   And bright the stars,—but brighter
   woman's eyes."

"Bright morn or even; bright or moon
or star,
And all the many twinkling lights that
are,—
   O brighter than ye all are woman's
   eyes."

So Raelus sang.—And they who rode
with him
Bewildered were, and even as he sang
Went straggling, twos and threes, and
fell behind

To whisper wonderingly, "Is he a
fool?"
And "Does he waver in his mind?"
and "Does
The newness of adventure dazzle
him?"
So spake they each to each, till far be-
yond,
With but one loathful knight in com-
pany,
They saw him quit the beaten track,
and turn
Into the grassy margin of a wood.
And loitering, they fell in mocking jest
Of their strange leader! "See! why,
see!" said one,—
"He needs no help to fight his hornets'
nest,
But one brave knight to squire him!"
—pointing on
To where fared on the two and disap-
peared.
"O ay!" said one, "belike he is some
old
War-battered knight of long-forgotten
age,
That, bursting from his chrysalis, the
grave,
Comes back to show us tricks we never
dreamed!"
"Or haply," said another, with a
laugh,—
"He rides ahead to tell them that he
comes
And shrive them ere his courage catches
up."
And merry made they all, and each in
turn
Filliped a witty pellet at his head:
Until, at last, their shadows shrunk
away
And shortened 'neath them and the
hour was noon,

They flung them from their horses
listlessly
Within the grassy margin of the wood
Where had passed Raelus an hour
agone:
And, hungered, spied a rustic; and they
sent
To have them such refreshment as
might be
Found at the nearest farm,—where, as
it chanced,
Was had most wholesome meat, and
milk, and bread;
And honey, too, celled in its fretted
vase
Of gummy gold and dripping nectar-
sweet
As dreamed-of kisses from the lips of
love;
Wine, too, was broughten, rosy as the
dawn
That ushers in the morning of the
heart;
And tawny, mellow pear, whose golden
ore
Fell molten on the tongue and oozed
away
In creamy and delicious nothingness;
And netted melon, musky as the breath
Of breezes blown from out the Orient;
And purple clusterings of plum and
grape,
Blurred with a dust dissolving at the
touch
Like flakes the fairies had snowed over
them.
And as the idlers basked, with toast
and song
And graceful dalliance and wanton jest,
A sound of trampling hooves and jing-
ling reins
Brake sudden, stilled them; and from
out a dim

Path leading from the bosky wood there
        came
A troop of mounted damsels, nigh a
        score,
Led by a queenly girl, in crimson clad,
With lissome figure lithe and willowy,
And face as fair and sweet and pure
        withal
As might a maiden lily-blossom be
Ere it has learned the sin of perfect
        bloom:
Her hair, blown backward like a silken
        scarf
And fondled by the sun, was glossier
And bluer black than any raven's wing.
"And O!" she laughed, not knowing
        she was heard
By any but her fellows: "Men are
        fools!"
Then drawing rein, and wheeling sud-
        denly,
Her charger mincing backward,—"Rae-
        lus—
My Raelus is greater than ye all,
Since he is such a fool that he forgets
He is a man, and lets his tongue of
        love
Run babbling like a silly child's; and,
        pah!
I puff him to the winds like thistle-
        down!"
And, wheeling as she spake, found star-
        ing up,
Wide-eyed and wondering, a group of
        knights,
Half lifted, as their elbows propped
        their heads,
Half lying; and one, smirker than the
        rest,
Stood bowing very low, with upturned
        eyes
Lit with a twinkling smile: "Fair lady
        —and

Most gracious gentlewomen"—seeing
        that
The others drew them back as tho'
        abashed
And veiled their faces with all mod-
        esty,
Tho' she, their leader, showed not any
        qualm,—
"Since all unwittingly we overheard
Your latest speech, and since we know
        at last
'All men are fools,' right glad indeed
        am I
That such a nest of us remains for you
To vanquish with those eyes." Then,
        serious,
That she nor smiled nor winced, nor
        anything—
"Your pardon will be to me as a
        shower
Of gracious rain unto a panting
        drouth."
So bowed in humblest reverence; at
        which
The damsel, turning to her followers,
Laughed musically,—"See! he proves
        my words!"
Whereat the others joined with inward
        glee
Her pealing mirth; and in the merri-
        ment
The knights chimed, too, and he, the
        vanquished one,
Till all the wood rang as at hunting-
        tide
When bugle-rumors float about the air
And echoes leap and revel in delight.
Then spake the vanquished knight,
        with mental eye
Sweeping the vantage-ground that
        chance had gained,—
"Your further pardon, lady: Since the
        name

Of Raelus fell from those lips of thine,
We fain would know of him. He led
    us here,
And as he went the way wherefrom
    your path
Emerges, haply you may tell us where
He may be found?"
              "What! Raelus?" she cried,—
"He comes with you?—The brave Sir
    Raelus?—
That mighty champion?—that gallant
    knight?—
That peerless wonder of all nobleness?
Then proud am I to greet ye, knowing
    that;
And, certes, had I known of it ere now,
Then had I proffered you more cour-
    tesy
And told you, ere the asking, that he
    bides
The coming of his friends a league
    from this,
Hard by a reedy mere, where in high
    tune
We left him singing, nigh an hour
    agone."
Then, as she lightly wheeled her horse
    about
And signal gave to her companions
To follow, gaily cried: "Tell Raelus
His cousin sends to him her sad fare-
    wells
And fond regrets, and kisses many
    as
His valorous deeds are numbered in
    her heart."
And with "Fair morrow to ye, gentle
    knights!"
Her steed's hooves struck the highway
    at a bound;
And dimly thro' the dust they saw her
    lead
Her fluttering cavalcade as recklessly

As might a queen of Araby, fleet-
    horsed,
Skim o'er the level sands of Syria.
So vanished. And the knights with
    one accord
Put foot in stirrup, and, with puzzled
    minds
And many-channeled marvelings, filed
    in
The woody path, and fared them on
    and on
Thro' denser glooms, and ways more
    intricate;
Till, mystified at last and wholly lost,
They made full halt, and would have
    turned them back
But that a sudden voice brake on their
    ears
All piteous and wailing, as distressed:
And, following these cries, they sharply
    came
Upon an open road that circled round
A reedy flat and sodden tract of sedge,
Moated with stagnant water, crusted
    thick
With slimy moss, wherein were wrig-
    gling things
Entangled, and blind bubbles bulging
    up
And bursting where from middle way
    upshot
A tree-trunk, with its knarled and
    warty hands
As tho' upheld to clutch at sliding
    snakes
Or nip the wet wings of the dragon-
    fly.
Here gazing, lo! they saw their com-
    rade, he
That had gone on with Raelus; and he
Was tugging to fling back into its place
A heavy log that once had spanned the
    pool

And made a footway to the sedgy flat
Whence came the bitter wailing cries
   they heard.
Then hastened they to join him in his
   task;
But, panting, as they asked of Raelus,
All winded with his work, yet jollier
Than meadow-lark at morn, he sent
   his voice
In such a twittering of merriment,
The wail of sorrow died and laughter
   strewed
Its grave with melody.
                   "O Raelus!
Rare Raelus!" he cried and clapped his
   hands,
And even in the weeds that edged the
   pool
Fell wrestling with his mirth.—"Why,
   Raelus,"
He said, when he at last could speak
   again,
"Drew magnet-like—you know that
   talk of his,—
And so, adhesive, did I cling and cling
Until I found us in your far advance,
And, hidden in the wood, I stayed to
   say
'Twas better we should bide your com-
   ing. 'No.'
Then on again; and still a second
   time—
'Shall we not bide their coming?' 'No!'
   he said;
And on again, until the third; and
   'No—
We'll push a little further.' As we did;
And, sudden, came upon an open
   glade—
There to the northward,—by a thicket
   bound:
Then he dismounted, giving me his
   rein,

And, charging me to keep myself con-
   cealed,
And if he were not back a certain time
To ride for you and search where he
   had gone,
He crossed the opening and passed
   from sight
Within the thicket. I was curious:
And so, dismounting, tethered our two
   steeds
And followed him; and, creeping wa-
   rily,
Came on him where—unseen of him—
   I saw
Him pause before the cave himself de-
   scribed
Before us yesternoon. And here he
   put
His fingers to his lips and gave a call
Bird-like and quavering: at which a
   face,
As radiant as summer sun at morn,
Parted the viny curtains of the cave;
And then, a moment later, came in
   view
A woman even fairer than my sight
Might understand. 'What! dare you
   come again?'
As, lifting up her eyes all flashingly,
She scorched him with a look of hate.
   —'Begone!
Or have you—traitor, villain, knave,
   and cur,—
Bro't minions of the law to carry out
The vengeance of your whimpering
   jealousy?'
Then Raelus, all cowering before
Her queenly anger, faltered: 'Hear me
   yet;
I do not threaten. But your love—
   your love!—
O give me that. I know you pure as
   dew:

Your love! Your love!—The smile that
    has gone out
And left my soul a midnight of de-
    spair!—
Your love or life! For I have èven
    now
Your stronghold girt about with cer-
    tain doom
If you but waver in your choice.—Your
    love!'
At which, as quick as tho't, leapt on
    him there
A strong man from the covert of the
    gloom;
And others, like to him, from here and
    there
Came skurrying. I, turning, would
    have fled,
But found myself as suddenly beset
And tied and tumbled there with Rae-
    lus.
And him they haltered by his squirm-
    ing heels
Until he did confess such villainy
As made me wonder if his wits were
    sound—
Confessed himself a renegade—a thief—
Ay, even one of them, save that he
    knew
Not that nice honor even thieves may
    claim
Among themselves.—And so ran on
    thro' such
A catalogue of littlenesses, I
For deafest shame had even stopped
    my ears
But that my wrists were lockt. And
    when he came
To his confession of his lie at court,
By which was gained our knightly
    sympathy
And valiant service on this fools' cru-
    sade,

I seemed to feel the redness of my
    blush
Soak thro' my very soul. There I brake
    in:
'Fair lady and most gallant,—to my
    shame
Do I admit we have been duped by
    such
An ingrate as this bundled lump of
    flesh
That I am helpless to rise up and
    spurn:
Unbind me, and I promise such
    amends
As knightly hands may deign to wreak
    upon
A thing so vile as he.' Then, laughing,
    she:
'First tell me, by your honor, where
    await
Your knightly brothers and my en-
    emies.'
To which I answered, truthfully, I
    knew
Not where you lingered, but not close
    at hand
I was assured. Then all abrupt, she
    turned:
'Get every one within! We ride at
    once!'
And scarce a dozen minutes ere they
    came
Outpouring from the cave in such a
    guise
As made me smile from very wonder-
    ment.—
From head to heel in woman's dress
    they came,
Clad richly, too, and trapped and
    tricked withal
As maidenly, but in the face and
    hand,
As ever damsels flock at holiday.

Then were their chargers bro't, ca-
parisoned
In keeping; and they mounted, lifting
us,
Still bounden, with much jest and
mockery
Of soft caress and wanton blandish-
ments,
As tho' they were of sex their dress de-
clared.
And so they carried us until they came
Upon the road there as it nicks the
copse;
And so drew rein, dismounted, leaving
some
To guard their horses; hurried us across
This footway to the middle of the flat.
Here Raelus was bounden to a tree,
Stript to the waist; my fetters cut, and
then
A long, keen switch put in my hand,
and 'Strike!
Strike as all duty bids you!' said the
queen.
And so I did, with right good will at
first;
Till, softened as I heard the wretch's
prayers
Of anguish, I at last withheld my
hand.
'What! tiring?' chirpt the queen: 'Give
me the stick!'
And swish, and swish, and mercy how
it rained!
Then all the others, forming circlewise,
Danced round and round the howling
wretch, and jeered
And japed at him, and mocked and
scoffed at him,
And spat upon him. And I turned
away
And hid my face; then raised it plead-
ingly:

Nor would they listen my appeal for
him;
But left him so, and thonged and took
me back
Across the mere, and drew the bridge,
that none
Might go to him, and carried me with
them
Far on their way, and freed me once
again;
And back I turned, tho' loath, to suc-
cor him."
And even as he ceased they heard the
wail
Break out anew, and crossed without a
word,
And Raelus they found, and without
word
They loosed him. And he brake away
and ran
As runs a lie the truth is hard upon.

Thus did it fare with Raelus. And they
Who knew of it said naught at court
of it,
Nor from that day spake ever of him
once,
Nor heard of him again, nor cared to
hear.

104

A MOTHER-SONG

MOTHER, O mother! forever I cry
for you,
  Sing the old song I may never for-
get;
Even in slumber I murmur and sigh
for you.—
  Mother, O mother,
     Sing low, "Little brother,
Sleep, for thy mother bends over thee
yet!"

Mother, O mother! the years are so
    lonely,
Filled but with weariness, doubt and
    regret!
Can't you come back to me—for to-
    night only,
    Mother, my mother,
      And sing, "Little brother,
Sleep, for thy mother bends over thee
    yet!"

Mother, O mother! of old I had never
    One wish denied me, nor trouble to
    fret;
Now—must I cry out all vainly for-
    ever,—
    Mother, sweet mother,
      O sing, "Little brother,
Sleep, for thy mother bends over thee
    yet!"

Mother, O mother! must longing and
    sorrow
    Leave me in darkness, with eyes ever
    wet,
And never the hope of a meeting to-
    morrow?
    Answer me, mother,
      And sing, "Little brother,
Sleep, for thy mother bends over thee
    yet!"

105

THE LOST PATH

ALONE they walked—their fingers
    knit together,
    And swaying listlessly as might a
    swing
Wherein Dan Cupid dangled in the
    weather
    Of some sun-flooded afternoon of
    Spring.

Within the clover-fields the tickled
    cricket
Laughed lightly as they loitered
    down the lane,
And from the covert of the hazel-
    thicket
The squirrel peeped and laughed at
    them again.

The bumblebee that tipped the lily-
    vases
Along the roadside in the shadows
    dim,
Went following the blossoms of their
    faces
As though their sweets must needs
    be shared with him.

Between the pasture bars the wonder-
    ing cattle
Stared wistfully, and from their mel-
    low bells
Shook out a welcoming whose dreamy
    rattle
Fell swooningly away in faint fare-
    wells.

And though at last the gloom of night
    fell o'er them,
And folded all the landscape from
    their eyes,
They only knew the dusky path before
    them
Was leading safely on to Paradise.

106

MY BRIDE THAT IS TO BE

O SOUL of mine, look out and see
    My bride, my bride that is to
    be!—
Reach out with mad, impatient
    hands,

And draw aside futurity
As one might draw a veil aside—
  And so unveil her where she stands
Madonna-like and glorified—
  The queen of undiscovered lands
Of love, to where she beckons me—
My bride, my bride that is to be.

The shadow of a willow-tree
  That wavers on a garden-wall
  In summer-time may never fall
In attitude as gracefully
As my fair bride that is to be;—
  Nor ever Autumn's leaves of brown
As lightly flutter to the lawn
As fall her fairy-feet upon
  The path of love she loiters down.—
O'er drops of dew she walks, and
      yet
Not one may stain her sandal wet—
Ay, she might *dance* upon the way
Nor crush a single drop to spray,
So airy-like she seems to me,—
My bride, my bride that is to be.

I know not if her eyes are light
As summer skies or dark as night,—
I only know that they are dim
  With mystery: In vain I peer
  To make their hidden meaning
      clear,
  While o'er their surface, like a
      tear
That ripples to the silken brim,
A look of longing seems to swim
  All worn and weary-like to me;
And then, as suddenly, my sight
Is blinded with a smile so bright,
  Through folded lids I still may
      see
My bride, my bride that is to be.

Her face is like a night of June
Upon whose brow the crescent-moon
Hangs pendent in a diadem
Of stars, with envy lighting them.—
  And, like a wild cascade, her hair
Floods neck and shoulder, arm and
      wrist,
Till only through a gleaming mist
  I seem to see a Siren there,
With lips of love and melody
  And open arms and heaving breast
  Wherein I fling myself to rest,
The while my heart cries hopelessly
For my fair bride that is to be.

      .   .   .   .·

Nay, foolish heart and blinded eyes!
My bride hath need of no disguise.—
  But, rather, let her come to me
In such a form as bent above
  My pillow when, in infancy,
I knew not anything but love.—
O let her come from out the lands
  Of Womanhood—not fairy isles,—
And let her come with Woman's
      hands
  And Woman's eyes of tears and
      smiles,—
With Woman's hopefulness and grace
Of patience lighting up her face:
And let her diadem be wrought
Of kindly deed and prayerful thought,
That ever over all distress
May beam the light of cheerfulness.—
And let her feet be brave to fare
The labyrinths of doubt and care,
That, following, my own may find
The path to Heaven God designed.—
O let her come like this to me—
My bride—my bride that is to be.

107

LULLABY

THE maple strews the embers of its
    leaves
O'er the laggard swallows nestled
    'neath the eaves;
And the moody cricket falters in his
    cry—Baby-bye!—
And the lid of night is falling o'er the
    sky—Baby-bye!—
    The lid of night is falling o'er the
    sky!

The rose is lying pallid, and the cup
Of the frosted calla-lily folded up;
And the breezes through the garden
    sob and sigh—Baby-bye!—
O'er the sleeping blooms of Summer
    where they lie—Baby-bye!—
    O'er the sleeping blooms of summer
    where they lie!

Yet, Baby—O my Baby, for your sake
This heart of mine is ever wide awake,
And my love may never droop a
    drowsy eye—Baby-bye!—
Till your own are wet above me when
    I die—Baby-bye!—
    Till your own are wet above me
    when I die.

108

THE ROMAUNT OF KING
MORDAMEER

HO! did ye hear of Mordameer,
    The King of Slumberland!
A lotus-crown upon his brow—
    A poppy in his hand,

And all the elves that people dreams
To bow at his command.

His throne is wrought of blackest night,
    Enriched with rare designs
Wherein the blazing comet runs
    And writhes and wreathes and twines
About a crescent angel-face
    That ever smiling shines.

The dais is of woven rays
    Of starlight fringed with shade,
And jeweled o'er with gems of dew,
    And dyed and interlaid
With every gleaming tint and hue
    Of which the flowers are made.

And when the day has died away
    In darkness o'er the land,
The King bends down his dusky face
    And takes the sleeper's hand,
And lightly o'er his folded eyes
    He waves his magic wand.

And lo! within his princely home,
    Upon his downy bed,
With soft and silken coverlets
    And curtains round him spread,
The rich man rolls in troubled sleep,
    And moans in restless dread:

His eyes are closed, yet Mordameer
    May see their stony stare
As plainly fixed in agony
    As though the orbs were bare
And glaring at the wizard throng
    That fills the empty air:—

A thousand shapes, with phantom
    japes,
Dance o'er the sleeper's sight,—
With fingers bony-like and lean,
    And faces pinched and white,

And withered cheeks, and sunken eyes
  With ever-ravening sight.

And such the dreams that Mordameer
  Brings to the child of Pride,—
The worn and wasted forms that he
  Hath stinted and denied—
Of those who filled his coffers up
  And empty-handed died.

And then again he waves his wand:
  And from his lair of straw
The felon, with his fettered limbs,
  Starts up with fear and awe,
And stares with starting eyes upon
  A vision of the law:

A grim procession passes by,
  The while he glares in fear—
With faces, from a wanton's smile
  Down to a demon's leer,—
The woman marching at the front,
  The hangman at the rear.

All ways are clear to Mordameer:
  The ocean knows his tread;
His feet are free on land or sea:—
  Above the sailor's head
He hangs a dream of home, and bends
  Above his cottage-bed:

And, nestled in the mother's arms,
  A child, surpassing fair,
In slumber lies, its tiny hands
  Entangled in her hair,
And round its face a smile that moves
  Its lips as though in prayer.

And lo! the good king feasts its eyes
  With fruits from foreign shores,
And pink-lipped shells that ever mock
  The ocean as it roars;
And in the mother's arms he folds
  The form that she adores.

Through all the hovels of the poor
  He steals with noiseless tread,
And presses kisses o'er and o'er
  Where sorrow's tears are shed,
Till old caresses live once more
  That are forever dead.

Above the soldier in his tent
  Are glorious battles fought;
And o'er the prince's velvet couch,
  And o'er the peasant's cot,
And o'er the pallet of disease
  His wondrous spells are wrought.

He bends him o'er the artist's cot,
  And fills his dazzled mind
With airy forms that float about
  Like clouds in summer wind,
O'er landscapes that the angels wrought
  And God Himself designed.

And drifting through the poet's dreams
  The seraph trails her wings,
And fills the chancels of his soul
  With heavenly whisperings,
Till, swooning with delight, he hears
  The song he never sings.

He walks the wide world's every way,
  This monarch grand and grim;
All paths that reach the human heart,
  However faint and dim,
He journeys, for the darkest night
  Is light as day to him.

And thus the lordly Mordameer
  Rules o'er his mystic realm,
With gems from out the star's red core
  To light his diadem,
And kings and emperors to kneel
  And kiss his garment's hem.

For once, upon a night of dreams,
  Adown the aisles of space

I strayed so far that I forgot
Mine own abiding-place,
And wandered into Slumberland,
And met him face to face.

109

DEARTH

I HOLD your trembling hand to-
night—and yet
I may not know what wealth of bliss
is mine,
My heart is such a curious design
Of trust and jealousy! Your eyes are
wet—
So must I think they jewel some re-
gret,—
And lo, the loving arms that round
me twine
Cling only as the tendrils of a vine
Whose fruit has long been gathered: I
forget,
While crimson clusters of your kisses
press
Their wine out on my lips, my
royal fare
Of rapture, since blind fancy needs
must guess
They once poured out their sweet-
ness otherwhere,
With fuller flavoring of happiness
Than e'en your broken sobs may
now declare.

110

THE SONG I NEVER SING

AS when in dreams we sometimes
hear
A melody so faint and fine
And musically sweet and clear,

It flavors all the atmosphere
With harmony divine,—
So, often in my waking dreams,
I hear a melody that seems
Like fairy voices whispering
To me the song I never sing.

Sometimes when brooding o'er the
years
My lavish youth has thrown away—
When all the glowing past appears
But as a mirage that my tears
Have crumbled to decay,—
I thrill to find the ache and pain
Of my remorse is stilled again,
As, forward bent and listening,
I hear the song I never sing.

A murmuring of rhythmic words,
Adrift on tunes whose currents flow
Melodious with the trill of birds,
And far-off lowing of the herds
In lands of long ago;
And every sound the truant loves
Comes to me like the coo of doves
When first in blooming fields of
Spring
I heard the song I never sing.

The echoes of old voices, wound
In limpid streams of laughter where
The river Time runs bubble-crowned,
And giddy eddies ripple round
The lilies growing there;
Where roses, bending o'er the
brink,
Drain their own kisses as they
drink,
And ivies climb and twine and
cling
About the song I never sing.

An ocean-surge of sound that falls
As though a tide of heavenly art

Had tempested the gleaming halls
And crested o'er the golden walls
  In showers on my heart. . . .
    Thus—thus, with open arms and
      eyes
    Uplifted toward the alien skies,
    Forgetting every earthly thing,
    I hear the song I never sing.

O nameless lay, sing clear and strong,
  Pour down thy melody divine
Till purifying floods of song
Have washed away the stains of wrong
    That dim this soul of mine!
    O woo me near and nearer thee,
    Till my glad lips may catch the
      key,
    And, with a voice unwavering,
    Join in the song I never sing.

III

UNSPOKEN

O   HE can hold her hand, and full
     and fair
  Look in her face and fling her smile
    for smile,
  And loosen from his lips such words
    the while
As make him wonder how his tongue
    may dare
Such dalliance. And when in wordless
    prayer
  His heart lies gasping, he can recon-
    cile
  His talk to that glib, recitative style
The silly gossip chatters everywhere.
But O, one utterance—one stormy word
  Is fastened down in silence pitiless;
No struggling murmur of it ever
    heard—

No echo welling out of his distress
To plead aloud its mission long de-
    ferred,
And leap up fountain-like in thank-
    fulness.

Yet he is bold enough in dreams—last
    night
He held her in his arms, and in the
    strands
Of her down-streaming hair he
    bathed his hands,
And fretted it in golden foam, as
    bright
And billowy it floated o'er his sight.
  Her breath was like a breeze of
    fairy-lands
  That reels above a bed of bloom and
    fans
Its fragrant life away in sheer delight.
So even did he whisper through the
    sighs
  That quavered as his spirit stayed to
    drain
The mad intoxication of her eyes;
  Then felt a pang of pleasure keen
    as pain—
A barb of ecstasy, shot arrow-wise,
  In such a kiss as cleft his heart in
    twain.

But waking, when the morning of her
    face
  Shines full upon him, voiceless has
    he grown,
  Save that inanimately mirthful tone
That ripples ever on its foolish race
And finds nor rest nor joyance in the
    chase.
    And so it is a never-ending moan
    Wails on unheard, unheeded and un-
      known
But by the echoes of its hiding-place.

What poverty like this?—to laugh, and
    sing,
And babble like a brook in summer-
    time;
To circle o'er the world on airy wing,

Or clamber into Heaven on rounds
    of rhyme,
When in the soul, forever lingering,
There lives a love unspeakably sub-
    lime.

112

THANKSGIVING DAY AT HUNCHLEY'S

IF you never heard of Hunchley, I would say in his behalf,
    He's as jovial a bachelor as ever raised a laugh,
And as fond of boon companions, yet withal as tried and true
A gentleman of honor as the writer ever knew.

And if he has a weakness, as a weakness it depends
On a certain strength of kindness he bestows upon his friends;
Being simple, undesigning, and of courteous address,
All hearts are open to him and his friends are numberless.

And this is how it happened some discrepancies befell
At the late Thanksgiving dinner which began at his hotel,
Where, it seems, the guests invited were selected more to be
In keeping with his bounty than the laws of harmony.

For there among the number were two rivals of the press,
Who had paragraphed each other with prolonged maliciousness,
And in their respective columns had a thousand times declared
That the other fellow "daresn't," when the other fellow dared.

And cheek by jowl together were two members of the bar,
Politically, legally, and socially at war,
Who denounced each other daily, and in every local phrase
That could make the matter binding all the balance of their days.

Of the medical fraternity ("fraternity" is good)
There were four or five disciples of the healing brotherhood—
Botanic and eclectic, and some others that persist
In orthographic wranglings, such as "homeopathist";

And an ordinary actor, and an actor of renown,
Whose cue, it seemed, for smiling was the other actor's frown;

And the most loquacious author my remembrance can recall,
And a little bench-leg poet that couldn't talk at all.

In fact the guests assembled, as they gathered round the feast
Wore expressions such as savored not of thankfulness the least,
And to a close observer were suggestive of the dread
And shadowy disaster that was hanging overhead.

Now the simple Mr. Hunchley had invited, with the rest,
A melancholy pastor, and, in honor of the guest
And the notable occasion, he desired a special "grace,"
Which the thankful pastor offered with a very thankless face.

And at this unhappy juncture came a journalistic pun,
Which the rival designated as a most atrocious one,
At which the grim projector, with a covert look of hate,
Shook a little dust of "fine-cut" in the other fellow's plate.

And the viands circulated, with a sudden gust of wit
From a lawyer—instituted for the other's benefit,—
Then the victim spun a story with exasperating mirth
That reflected his opponent as of small judicial worth.

Then a medical discussion on the stomach swelled the gale
And the literary appetite began to droop and fail;
While a sportive reminiscence from the absented-minded host
Blanched the features of the pastor to the pallor of a ghost.

And a deep sonorous murmur slowly grew, and grew, and grew
Till the similes that suited it were singularly few,—
For even now at leisure, and with nothing else to do,
A task of lesser promise I can say I never knew.

I have heard the tread of armies as they marched upon the foe,
And, among the Alps, have listened to the avalanche of snow;
I have leaned upon Niagara, and heard the wailing tide
Where it leaps its awful chasm in unending suicide:

I have heard the trampling footsteps of the roaring hurricane
As he lashed his tail of lightning, and tossed his shaggy mane;
I have heard the cannonading of the devastating storm,
And the falling politician howling loudly for reform:

But no mystic voice of terror ever bred of Nature's law
Could awake the sense of wonder and dismay, and doubt and awe
That thrilled my inmost being as the conversation swelled
To a mad, chaotic focus in which everybody yelled.

There's a vision in my fancy, misty-like and undefined,
Of an actor with his collar loose and sticking up behind,
And another (though I hesitate to chronicle the fact)
Writhing underneath the table in a wild contortion act.

There's a shadowy remembrance of a group of three or four
Who were seemingly dissecting another on the floor;
And the form of Mr. Hunchley dancing round a couple more,
And a phantom with a chicken-leg a-breaking for the door.

And here my memory wavers—I recall the heated breath
Of the gentleman who held me with the very grip of death,
And as my reeling pencil scrawls the scene of my release
I'm as full of glad thanksgiving as my soul is full of peace.

But this is how it happened these discrepancies befell
At the late Thanksgiving dinner Hunchley gave at his hotel,
Where, it seems, the guests invited were selected more to be
In keeping with his bounty than the laws of harmony.

113

APART

I

THEY stood on either side the gate—
  Though fastened with the hands
    of fate
A touch might lift the latch's weight.

The moonlight, with a faded grace,
Fell o'er the whiteness of her face
Like some soiled veil of bridal lace.

The fan she held went fluttering
About her mouth on restless wing
As though it were a wounded thing.

And in her breast an ache of dread
Held back the word she would have
  said,
And sent a weary sigh instead.

II

He waited, with his eager eyes
Half muffled in a weak disguise
Of carelessness and cold surprise.

Within his breast he heard the moan:
"How desolate and all alone,
And pitiless my heart has grown!"

And yet a nameless ache of dread
Held back the word he would have said,
And sent a weary sigh instead.

The long, black shadows of the trees
Whose branches wavered in the breeze,
Fell o'er them like their destinies.

They parted. Yet the wild wind saith
That two fair ghosts with failing breath
Walk hand in hand the path of death.

114

TOIL

HE had toiled away for a weary
    while,
Through day's dull glare and night's
    deep gloom;
And many a long and lonesome mile
He had paced in the round of his dis-
    mal room;
He had fared on hunger—had drunk
    of pain
As the drouthy earth might drink of
    rain;
And the brow he leaned in his trem-
    bling palm
Throbbed with a misery so intense
That never again did it seem that calm
Might come to him with the gracious
    balm
Of old-time languor and indolence.
And he said, "I will leave the tale half
    told,
And leave the song for the winds to
    sing;
And the pen—that pitiless blade of
    gold
That stabs my heart like a dagger-
    sting—
I will drive to the hilt through the ink-
    stand's top
And spill its blood to the last black
    drop!"

Then he masked his voice with a laugh,
    and went
Out in the world with a lawless grace—
With a brazen lie in his eyes and face
Told in a smile of glad content:
He roved the round of pleasures
    through,
And tasted each as it pleased him to;
He joined old songs, and the clink and
    din
Of the revelers at the banquet hall;
And he tripped his feet where the vio-
    lin
Spun its waltz for the carnival;
He looked, bedazed, on the luring wile
And the siren-light of a woman's smile,
And peered in her eyes as a diver might
Peer in the sea ere he leaps outright,—
Caught his breath, with a glance above,
And dropped full-length in the depths
    of love.

.   .   .   .

'Tis well if ever the false lights die
On the alien coasts where our wreck'd
    hopes lie!
'Tis well to feel, through the blinding
    rain,
Our outflung hands touch earth again!
So the castaway came, safe from doom,
Back at last to his lonely room,
Filled with its treasure of work to do
And radiant with the light and bloom
Of the summer sun and his glad soul,
    too!
And sweet as ever the song of birds,
Over his work he sang these words:—
"O friends are good, with their princely
    ways,
And royal hearts they are goodly
    things;
And fellowship, in the long dark days

When the drear soul cowers with
    drooping wings,
Is a thing to yearn for.—*Mirth* is
    good,—
For a ringing laugh is a rhythmic cry
Blown like a hail from the Angelhood
To the barque of the lone soul drifting
    by.—
Goodly, too, is a mute caress
Of woman's hands and their tender-
    ness—
The warm breath wet with the dews of
    love—
The vine-like arms, and the fruit there-
    of—
The touch that thrills, and the kiss that
    melts,—
But Toil is sweeter than all things else."

115

HIS ROOM

I'M home again, my dear old Room,
    I'm home again, and happy, too,
As, peering through the brightening
    gloom,
    I find myself alone with you:
        Though brief my stay, nor far
            away,
        I missed you—missed you night
            and day—
        As wildly yearned for you as
            now.—
        Old Room, how are you, anyhow?

My easy chair, with open arms,
    Awaits me just within the door;
The littered carpet's woven charms
    Have never seemed so bright be-
        fore,—
        The old rosettes and mignonettes
        And ivy-leaves and violets,

Look up as pure and fresh of hue
    As though baptized in morning-
        dew.

Old Room, to me your homely walls
    Fold round me like the arms of love,
And over all my being falls
    A blessing pure as from above—
        Even as a nestling child caressed
        And lulled upon a loving breast,
        With folded eyes, too glad to weep
        And yet too sad for dreams or
            sleep.

You've been so kind to me, old Room—
    So patient in your tender care,
My drooping heart in fullest bloom
    Has blossomed for you unaware;
        And who but you had cared to
            woo
        A heart so dark, and heavy too,
        As in the past you lifted mine
        From out the shadow to the
            shine?

For I was but a wayward boy
    When first you gladly welcomed me
And taught me work was truer joy
    Than rioting incessantly:
        And thus the din that stormed
            within
        The old guitar and violin
        Has fallen in a fainter tone
        And sweeter, for your sake alone.

Though in my absence I have stood
    In festal halls a favored guest,
I missed, in this old quietude,
    My worthy work and worthy rest—
        By *this* I know that long ago
        You loved me first, and told me so
        In art's mute eloquence of speech
        The voice of praise may never
            reach.

For lips and eyes in truth's disguise
  Confuse the faces of my friends,
Till old affection's fondest ties
  I find unraveling at the ends;
    But, as I turn to you, and learn
    To meet my griefs with less con-
        cern,
    Your love seems all I have to keep
    Me smiling lest I needs must weep.

Yet I am happy, and would fain
  Forget the world and all its woes;
So set me to my tasks again,
  Old Room, and lull me to repose:
    And as we glide adown the tide
    Of dreams, forever side by side,
    I'll hold your hands as lovers do
    Their sweethearts' and talk love to
        you.

116

TO LEONAINIE

In memory of Leonainie, infant daugh-
ter of W. B. and Lotta Titus, these
lines are tenderly inscribed.

"LEONAINIE!" angels missed her—
    Baby angels—they
Who behind the stars had kissed her
    E'er she came away;
And their little, wandering faces
Drooped o'er Heaven's hiding-places
Whiter than the lily-vases
    On the Sabbath day.

"Leonainie!" crying, crying,
    Crying through the night,
Till her lisping lips replying,
    Laughing with delight,
Drew us nearer yet, and nearer

That we might the better hear her
Baby-words, and love her dearer
    Hearing not aright.

Only spake the little lisper
    In the Angel-tongue,
Fainter than a fairy-whisper
    Murmured in among
Dewy blossoms covered over
With the fragrant tufts of clover,
Where the minstrel honey-rover
    Twanged his wings and sung.

"Leonainie!"—And the glimmer
    Of her starry eyes
Faded, and the world grew dimmer
    E'en as Paradise
Blossomed with a glory brighter
Than the waning stars, and whiter
Than the dying moon, and lighter
    Than the morning skies.

117

THE SHOWER

THE landscape, like the awed face
    of a child
Grew curiously blurred; a hush of
        death
Fell on the fields, and in the darkened
        wild
    The zephyr held its breath.

No wavering glamour-work of light
        and shade
    Dappled the shivering surface of the
        brook;
The frightened ripples in their ambus-
        cade
    Of willows trilled and shook.

The sullen day grew darker, and anon
  Dim flashes of pent anger lit the
    sky;
With rumbling wheels of wrath came
    rolling on
  The storm's artillery.

The cloud above put on its blackest
    frown,
  And then, as with a vengeful cry of
    pain,
The lightning snatched it, ripped and
    flung it down
  In raveled shreds of rain:

While I, transfigured by some won-
    drous art,
  Bowed with the thirsty lilies to the
    sod,
My empty soul brimmed over, and my
    heart
  Drenched with the love of God.

118

YE SCHOLAR

HO! ho! Ye Scholar recketh not
    how lean
  His lank frame waxeth in ye hectic
    gloom
That smeareth o'er ye dim walls of
    his room
  His wavering shadow! Shut is he, I
    ween,
Like as a withered nosegay, in between
  Ye musty, mildewed leaves of some
    volume
  Of ancient lore ye moth and he con-
    sume
In jointure. Yet a something in his
    mien

Forbids all mockery, though quaint
    is he,
And eke fantastical in form and face
  As that Old Knight ye Tale of Chiv-
    alry
Made mad immortally, yet spared ye
    grace
Of some rare virtue which we sigh
    to see,
  And pour our laughter out most ten-
    derly.

119

DEATH IS DEAD

AND did you know our old friend
    Death is dead?
  Ah me! he died last night; my ghost
    was there,
  And all his phantom-friends from
    everywhere
Were sorrowfully grouped about his
    bed.
"I die; God help the living now!" he
    said
  With such a ghastly pathos, I de-
    clare
  The tears oozed from the blind eyes
    of the air
And spattered on his face in gouts of
    red.
And then he smiled—the dear old bony
    smile
  That glittered on us in that crazy
    whim
When first our daring feet leapt the
    defile
Of life and ran so eagerly to him:
And so he smiled upon us, even while
  The kind old sockets grew forever
    dim.

120

TOM JOHNSON'S QUIT

A PASSEL o' the boys last night—
       An' me amongst 'em—kind o'
          got
To talkin' Temper'nce left an' right,
   An' workin' up "blue-ribbon," *hot;*
An' while we was a-countin' jes'
   How many hed gone into hit
An' signed the pledge, some feller
      says,—
   "Tom Johnson's quit!"

We laughed, of course—'cause Tom,
      you know,
   Has spiled more whisky, boy an' man,
And seed more trouble, high an' low,
   Than any chap but Tom could stand:
And so, says I, *"He's* too nigh dead
   Fer Temper'nce to benefit!"
The feller sighed ag'in, and said—
   "Tom Johnson's quit!"

We all *liked* Tom, an' that was why
   We sort o' simmered down ag'in,
And ast the feller ser'ously
   Ef he wa'n't tryin' to draw us in:
He shuck his head—tuck off his hat—
   Helt up his hand an' opened hit,
An' says, says he, "I'll *swear* to that—
   Tom Johnson's quit!"

Well, we was stumpt, an' tickled, too,—
   Because we knowed ef Tom *hed*
      signed
There wa'n't no man 'at wore the
      "blue"
   'At was more honester inclined:
An' then and there we kind o' riz,—
   The hull dern gang of us 'at bit—
An' th'owed our hats and let 'er
      whiz,—
      "Tom Johnson's quit!"

I've heerd 'em holler when the balls
   Was buzzin' 'round us wus'n bees,
An' when the ole flag on the walls
   Was flappin' o'er the enemy's,
I've heerd a-many a wild "hooray"
   'At made my heart git up an' git—
But Lord!—to hear 'em shout that
      way!—
   "Tom Johnson's quit!"

But when we saw the chap 'at fetched
   The news wa'n't jinin' in the cheer,
But stood there solemn-like, an' reched
   An' kind o' wiped away a tear,
We someway sort o' stilled ag'in,
   And listened—I kin hear him yit,
His voice a-wobblin' with his chin,—
   "Tom Johnson's quit!"

"I hain't a-givin' you no game—
   I wisht I was! . . . An hour ago,
This operator—what's his name—
   The one 'at works at night, you
      know?—
Went out to flag that Ten Express,
   And sees a man in front of hit
Th'ow up his hands an' stagger—yes,—
   "Tom Johnson's quit!"

121

THE LITTLE DEAD MAN

YET NOT SO DEAD AS ANOTHER

I

IT was a little dead man,
   At peace with all the earth;
Yet I never saw a dead man
   So seeming near to mirth.

His hands were meekly hidden,
   At his very last request—

The right in his hip pocket,
And the other in his vest.

His collar was thrown open,
And he wore his easy clothes—
Had his ordinary boots on,
With rosin on the toes.

II

And so the little dead man
Lay coffined for the tomb.
The hearse was at the doorway—
The mourners in the room—

When suddenly a stranger,
Who had called the day before
With a book beneath his elbow,
Entered softly at the door,

And stood before the mourners
In his bold and brazen might,
A note-book in the left hand
And a pencil in the right.

And he turned him to the mourners
With a business air, and said:
"I must really beg your pardon,
But the gentleman that's dead

"Was kind enough to tell me,
If I'd call around to-day
He'd be prepared to listen
To all I had to say.

"And in view of that engagement,
I would gently intimate
(As it may pitch the funeral
Some dozen hours late,)

"That you have my indulgence,"
And with eyelids downward thrown,

They left the little dead man
And the agent all alone.

As only stars may lighten
Up the grandeur of the plains,
And the mountains where the mid-
night
In her mystic beauty reigns,

So the stars must shed their glory
O'er imagination's vales,
And illuminate the story
Where the poet's pencil fails.

.   .   .   .

But there was a little dead man—
Ah! so very dead indeed,
They fastened down his coffin lid
With most judicious speed.

And they whose latest office
Was to shroud his form from sight,
Saw a note-book in the left hand,
And a pencil in the right.

122

OLD-FASHIONED ROSES

THEY ain't no style about 'em,
    And they're sort o' pale and
        faded
Yit the doorway here, without 'em,
    Would be lonesomer, and shaded
        With a good 'eal blacker shadder
            Than the morning-glories makes,
        And the sunshine would look
            sadder
            Fer their good old-fashion' sakes.

I like 'em 'cause they kind o'
    Sort o' *make* a feller like 'em!

And I tell you, when I find a
  Bunch out whur the sun kin strike
     'em,
    It allus sets me thinkin'
    O' the ones 'at used to grow
And peek in through the chinkin'
  O' the cabin, don't you know!

And then I think o' mother,
  And how she ust to love 'em—
When they wuzn't any other,
  'Less she found 'em up above 'em!
    And her eyes, afore she shut 'em,
      Whispered with a smile and said
    We must pick a bunch and putt
      'em
    In her hand when she wuz dead.

But, as I wuz a-sayin',
  They ain't no style about 'em
Very gaudy er displayin',
  But I wouldn't be without 'em,—
    'Cause I'm happier in these posies,
      And hollyhawks and sich,
    Than the hummin'-bird 'at noses
    In the roses of the rich.

123

THE EMPTY SONG

"WHAT have we but an empty
     song?"
  Said the minstrel, as he bent
To stay the fingers that trailed along
  The strings of her instrument.

"The clasp of your hand is warm in
    mine,
  And your breath on my brow is
    wet—

I have drunk of your lips as men drink
    wine,
  But my heart is thirsty yet."

The starlight shivered a little space,
  And the sigh of the wind uprose
And blew a cloud o'er the moon's wan
    face,
  And swooned back in repose.

   .   .   .   .

The years ooze on in a stagnant flood:
  One drifts as the winds allow;
And one writes rhymes with his heart's
    own blood,
  But his soul is thirsty now.

124

A ROSE IN OCTOBER ·

AN IMITATION OF MAGAZINE POETRY

I

I STRAYED, all alone, where the
    Autumn
Had swept, in her petulant wrath:
All the flowers, that had bloomed in the
    garden,
  She had gathered, and flung in her
    path.
And I saw the dead face of the lily,
  Struck down, by the rain and the
    sleet,
And the pink, with her lashes yet
    weeping,
  Drooped low in the dust, at my feet.

II

The leaves on the branches still swing-
    ing,
  Were blanched with the crimson of
    death;

And the vines that still clung to the
  trellis,
Were palsied, and shook at a breath.
And I sighed: "So hath fate, like the
  Autumn,
Swept over my path, till I see,
As I walk through life's desolate gar-
  den
Not a rose is left blooming for me!"

III

"Heigho!" said a voice of low laugh-
  ter—
"How blind are you poets!"   And
  there,
At the gate, just in front of me, lean-
  ing,
Stood Rosalind May, I declare!
I stammered, confused, for the mo-
  ment;
But was blest for the rest of my life,
For my Rose of October there prom-
  ised
She'd bloom for me aye, as—my
  wife.

125

ROMANCIN'

I' B'EN a-kindo' *"musin',"* as the feller
    says, and I'm
About o' the conclusion that they hain't
  no better time,
When you come to cipher on it, than
  the times we ust to know
When we swore our first *"dog-gone-it"*
  sorto' solum-like and low!

You git my idy, do you?—*Little* tads,
  you understand—

Jest a-wishin' thue and thue you that
  you on'y wuz a *man.—*
Yit here I am, this minit, even sixty, to
  a day,
And fergittin' all that's in it, wishin'
  jest the other way!

I hain't no hand to lectur' on the times,
  er *dim*onstrate
Whare the trouble is, er hector and
  domineer with Fate,—
But when I git so flurried, and so pes-
  tered-like and blue,
And so rail owdacious worried, let me
  tell you what I do!—

I jest gee-haw the hosses, and onhook
  the swingle-tree,
Whare the hazel-bushes tosses down
  theyr shadders over me;
And I draw my plug o' navy, and I
  climb the fence, and set
Jest a-thinkin' here, i gravy! tel my
  eyes is wringin'-wet!

Tho' I still kin see the trouble o' the
  presunt, I kin see—
Kindo' like my sight wuz double—all
  the things that *ust* to be;
And the flutter o' the robin and the
  teeter o' the wren
Sets   the   willer-branches   bobbin'
  "howdy-do" thum *Now* to *Then!*

The deadnin' and the thicket's jest
  a-bilin' full of June,
Thum the rattle o' the cricket, to the
  yallar-hammer's tune;
And the catbird in the bottom, and the
  sapsuck on the snag,
Seems ef they can't—od-rot 'em!—jest
  do nothin' else but brag!

They's music in the twitter of the blue-
  bird and the jay,
And that sassy little critter jest a-*peckin'*
  all the day;
They's music in the "flicker," and they's
  music in the thrush,
And they's music in the snicker o' the
  chipmunk in the brush!

They's music *all around* me!—And I
  go back, in a dream
Sweeter yit than ever found me fast
  asleep,—and in the stream
That ust to split the medder whare
  the dandylions growed,
I stand knee-deep, and redder than the
  sunset down the road.

Then's when I' b'en a-fishin'!—And
  they's other fellers, too,
With theyr hick'ry-poles a-swishin' out
  behind 'em; and a few
Little "shiners" on our stringers, with
  theyr tails tiptoein' bloom,
As we dance 'em in our fingers all the
  happy jurney home.

I kin see us, true to Natur', thum the
  time we started out,
With a biscuit and a 'tater in our little
  "round-about"!—
I kin see our lines a-tanglin', and our
  elbows in a jam,
And our naked legs a-danglin' thum
  the apern o' the dam.

I kin see the honeysuckle climbin' up
  around the mill,
And kin hear the worter chuckle, and
  the wheel a-growlin' still;
And thum the bank below it I kin
  steal the old canoe,
And jest git in and row it like the
  miller ust to do.

W'y, I git my fancy focused on the
  past so mortul plane
I kin even smell the locus'-blossoms
  bloomin' in the lane;
And I hear the cow-bells clinkin'
  sweeter tunes 'n "Monkey-musk"
Fer the lightnin'-bugs a-blinkin' and
  a-dancin' in the dusk.

And when I've kep' on "musin'," as
  the feller says, tel I'm
Firm-fixed in the conclusion that they
  hain't no better time,
When you come to cipher on it, than
  the *old* times,—I de-clare
I kin wake and say "dog-gone-it!" jest
  as soft as any prayer!

126

THE LITTLE OLD POEM THAT NOBODY READS

THE little old poem that nobody
    reads
  Blooms in a crowded space,
Like a ground-vine blossom, so low
    in the weeds
  That nobody sees its face—
    Unless, perchance, the reader's eye
    Stares through a yawn, and hur-
      ries by,
      For no one wants, or loves, or
        heeds
      The little old poem that nobody
        reads.

The little old poem that nobody reads
  Was written—where?—and when?
Maybe a hand of goodly deeds
  Thrilled as it held the pen:

Maybe the fountain whence it came
Was a heart brimmed o'er with tears of shame,
And maybe its creed is the worst of creeds—
The little old poem that nobody reads.

But, little old poem that nobody reads,
Holding you here above
The wound of a heart that warmly bleeds
For all that knows not love,
I well believe if the old World knew
As dear a friend as I find in you,
That friend would tell it that all it needs
Is the little old poem that nobody reads.

127

A SLEEPING BEAUTY

I

AN alien wind that blew and blew
Over the fields where the ripe grain grew,

Sending ripples of shine and shade
That crept and crouched at her feet and played.

The sea-like summer washed the moss
Till the sun-drenched lilies hung like floss,

Draping the throne of green and gold
That lulled her there like a queen of old.

II

Was it the hum of a bumblebee,
Or the long-hushed bugle eerily

Winding a call to the daring Prince
Lost in the wood long ages since?—

A dim old wood, with a palace rare
Hidden away in its depths somewhere!

Was it the Princess, tranced in sleep,
Awaiting her lover's touch to leap

Into the arms that bent above?
To thaw his heart with the breath of love—

And cloy his lips, through her waking tears,
With the dead-ripe kiss of a hundred years!

III

An alien wind that blew and blew.—
I had blurred my eyes as the artists do,

Coaxing life to a half-sketched face,
Or dreaming bloom for a grassy place.

The bee droned on in an undertone;
And a shadow-bird trailed all alone

Across the wheat, while a liquid cry
Dripped from above, as it went by.

What to her was the far-off whir
Of the quail's quick wing or the chipmunk's chirr?—

What to her was the shade that slid
Over the hill where the reapers hid?—

Or what the hunter, with one foot
  raised,
As he turned to go—yet, pausing,
  gazed?

128

LEEDLE DUTCH BABY

LEEDLE Dutch baby haff come ter
  town!
Jabber und jump till der day gone
  down—
Jabber und sphlutter und sphlit hees
  jaws—
Vot a Dutch baby dees Londsmon vas!
I dink dose mout' vas leedle too vide
Ober he laugh fon dot also-side!
Haff got blenty off deemple und
  vrown?—
Hey! leedle Dutchman come ter town!

Leedle Dutch baby, I dink me proud
Ober your fader can schquall dot loud
Ven he vas leedle Dutch baby like you
Und yoost don't gare, like he alvays
  do!—
Guess ven dey vean him on beer, you
  bet
Dot's der because dot he aind veaned
  yet!—
Vot you said off he dringk you
  down?—
Hey! leedle Dutchman come ter town!

Leedle Dutch baby, yoost schquall
  avay—
Schquall fon preakfast till gisterday!
Better you all time gry und shout
Dan shmile me vonce fon der coffin
  out!
Vot I gare off you keek my nose

Downside-up mit your heels und toes—
Downside, oder der oopside-down?—
Hey! leedle Dutchman come ter town!

129

LINES

ON HEARING A COW BAWL IN A DEEP FIT
  OF DEJECTION ON THE EVENING OF
  JULY 3, A. D. 1879

PORTENTOUS sound! mysteriously
  vast
And awful in the grandeur of refrain
That lifts the listener's hair as it swells
  past,
  And pours in turbid currents down
  the lane.

The small boy at the wood-pile, in a
  dream
  Slow trails the meat-rind o'er the list-
  less saw;
The chickens roosting o'er him on the
  beam
  Uplift their drowsy heads with coo-
  tered awe.

The "gung-oigh!" of the pump is
  strangely stilled:
  The smoke-house door bangs once
  emphatic'ly,
Then bangs no more, but leaves the
  silence filled
  With one lorn plaint's despotic min-
  strelsy.

Yet I would join thy sorrowing madri-
  gal,
  Most melancholy cow, and sing of
  thee

Full-hearted through my tears, for,
    after all,
'Tis very kine in you to sing for me.

130

FRIEND OF A WAYWARD HOUR

FRIEND of a wayward hour, you
    came
Like some good ghost, and went the
    same;
And I within the haunted place
Sit smiling on your vanished face,
    And talking with—your name.

But thrice the pressure of your hand—
First hail—congratulations—and
Your last "God bless you!" as the train
That brought you snatched you back
    again
    Into the unknown land.

"God bless me?" Why, your very
    prayer
Was answered ere you asked it there,
I know—for when you came to lend
Me your kind hand, and call me friend,
    God blessed me unaware.

131

LINES

ON RECEIVING A PRESENT FROM AN
UNKNOWN FRIEND

THOU little naked statuette,
    With fairy head a-tip,
And eyelids ever downward let,

And silence on thy lip,
    Thou comest from a friend un-
        known,
    Nor wilt confess,
    E'en in mute syllables of stone,
    That friend's address.

And so, still pools of gratitude
    I pour out at thy feet;
And could it mirror back thy nude
    Perfection half as sweet
        As rests within this heart of
            mine.
    That friend unknown,
    Why, smiles would light that face
        of thine
        And warm the stone.

132

PAN

THIS Pan is but an idle god, I guess,
    Since all the fair midsummer of
        my dreams
He loiters listlessly by woody
    streams,
Soaking the lush glooms up with lazi-
    ness;
Or drowsing while the maiden-winds
    caress
        Him prankishly, and powder him
            with gleams
        Of sifted sunshine. And he ever
            seems
Drugged with a joy unutterable—un-
    less
    His low pipes whistle hints of it far
        out
Across the ripples to the dragon-fly
    That, like a wind-born blossom
        blown about,

Drops quiveringly down, as though to
　　die—
Then lifts and wavers on, as if in
　　doubt
Whether to fan his wings or fly
　　without.

133

WHEN OUR BABY DIED

WHEN our baby died—
　　My Ma she ist cried an' cried!
Yes 'n' my Pa *he* cried, too—
An' *I* cried—An' me an' you.—
An' I 'tended like my doll
She cried too—An' ever'—all—
O ist *ever'body* cried
　　When our baby died!

When our baby died—
Nen I got to took a ride!
An' we all ist rode an' rode
Clean to Heav'n where baby goed—
Mighty nigh!—An' nen Ma she
Cried ag'in—an' Pa—an' me.—
All but ist the *Angels* cried
　　When our baby died!

134

A FULL HARVEST

SEEMS like a feller'd ort'o jes' to-day
　　Git down and roll and waller,
　　　don't you know,
　In that-air stubble, and flop up and
　　　crow,
Seein' sich crops! I'll undertake to
　　say
There're no wheat's ever turned out
　　thataway

Afore this season!—Folks is keer-
　　less, though,
And too fergitful—'caze we'd ort'o
　　show
More thankfulness!—Jes' looky hyon-
　　der, hey?—
And watch that little reaper wadin'
　　thue
That last old yaller hunk o' harvest-
　　ground—
Jes natchur'ly a-slicin' it in two
Like honeycomb, and gaumin' it
　　around
The field—like it had nothin' else to
　　do
On'y jes' waste it all on me and you!

135

MY BACHELOR CHUM

A CORPULENT man is my bache-
　　lor chum,
　With a neck apoplectic and thick—
An abdomen on him as big as a
　　drum,
And a fist big enough for the stick;
With a walk that for grace is clear out
　　of the case,
And a wobble uncertain—as though
His little bow-legs had forgotten the
　　pace
That in youth used to favor him so.

He is forty, at least; and the top of his
　　head
Is a bald and a glittering thing;
And his nose and his two chubby
　　cheeks are as red
As three rival roses in spring:
His mouth is a grin with the corners
　　tucked in,

And his laugh is so breezy and bright
That it ripples his features and dimples his chin
With a billowy look of delight.

He is fond of declaring he "don't care a straw"—
That "the ills of a bachelor's life
Are blisses, compared with a mother-in-law,
And a boarding-school miss for a wife!"
So he smokes and he drinks, and he jokes and he winks,
And he dines and he wines, all alone,
With a thumb ever ready to snap as he thinks
Of the comforts he never has known.

But up in his den—(Ah, my bachelor chum!)—
I have sat with him there in the gloom,
When the laugh of his lips died away to become
But a phantom of mirth in the room.
And to look on him there you would love him, for all
His ridiculous ways, and be dumb
As the little girl-face that smiles down from the wall
On the tears of my bachelor chum.

136

TOMMY SMITH

DIMPLE - CHEEKED and rosy-lipped,
With his cap-rim backward tipped,
Still in fancy I can see

Little Tommy smile on me—
Little Tommy Smith.

Little unsung Tommy Smith—
Scarce a name to rhyme it with;
Yet most tenderly to me
Something sings unceasingly—
Little Tommy Smith.

On the verge of some far land
Still forever does he stand,
With his cap-rim rakishly
Tilted; so he smiles on me—
Little Tommy Smith.

Elder-blooms contrast the grace
Of the rover's radiant face—
Whistling back, in mimicry,
"Old—Bob—White!" all liquidly—
Little Tommy Smith.

O my jaunty statuette
Of first love, I see you yet,
Though you smile so mistily,
It is but through tears I see,
Little Tommy Smith.

But, with crown tipped back behind,
And the glad hand of the wind
Smoothing back your hair, I see
Heaven's best angel smile on me,—
Little Tommy Smith.

137

THE LAUGHTER OF THE RAIN

The rain sounds like a laugh to me—
A low laugh poured out limpidly.

MY very soul smiles as I listen to
The low, mysterious laughter of the rain,
Poured musically over heart and brain

Till sodden care, soaked with it through
  and through,
Sinks; and, with wings wet with it as
  with dew,
  My spirit flutters up, with every
    stain
  Rinsed from its plumage, and as
    white again
As when the old laugh of the rain was
  new.
  Then laugh on, happy Rain! laugh
    louder yet!—
Laugh out in torrent-bursts of watery
  mirth;
  Unlock thy lips of purple cloud, and
    let
Thy liquid merriment baptize the earth,
  And wash the sad face of the world,
    and set
  The universe to music dripping-
    wet!

138

ETERNITY

O WHAT a weary while it is to
    stand,
  Telling the countless ages o'er and
    o'er,
  Till all the finger-tips held out be-
    fore
Our dazzled eyes by heaven's starry
  hand
Drop one by one, yet at some dread
  command
  Are held again, and counted ever-
    more!
  How feverish the music seems to
    pour
Along the throbbing veins of anthems
  grand!

And how the cherubim sing on and
  on—
The seraphim and angels—still in
  white—
  Still harping—still enraptured—far
    withdrawn
In hovering armies tranced in endless
  flight!
  . . . God's mercy! is there never
    dusk or dawn,
  Or any crumb of gloom to feed upon?

139

LAST WORDS

HE left me for a foreign land:
    I could not even free
One little tear to gem the hand
  That God had given me;
For "I will follow soon, my dear,"
  I laughed with girlish air,—
"The sun that cheers our pathway here
  Shall beam upon us there!"

And so we parted. . . . Listen, God!—
  I may not even free
One little tear to dew the sod
  Where, sleeping peacefully,
He waits in foreign lands—my dear!
  But prophecy and prayer,—
"The sun that cheers our pathway here
  Shall beam upon us—*there!*"

140

AT BAY

DESPERATE, at last I stand
    Ready, Fate, with open hand
To grasp yours, or to strike
Blow for blow—just as you like.

You have dogged me day by day—
Chased me when a child at play:
Even from the mother-nest
Pushed me when I needed rest.

You have crouched along my track
Like a hound, and hurled me back,
While your dog's-tongue lapped the
    blood
Of my murdered babyhood.

Pitilessly, year by year,
From the farthest past to here,
You have fallen like a blight
On each blossom of delight.

You have risen up between
Me and every hope serene
That has promised rest at last
From the trials of the past.

You have shut the light of day
From my present—stolen away
All my faith in better things
Than sheer desperation brings.

But as now I come to know
That I may no farther go,
I have turned—not to resist,
But to greet you hand or fist.

141

A WORN-OUT PENCIL

WELLADAY!
    Here I lay
You at rest—all worn away,
    O my pencil, to the tip
    Of our old companionship!

Memory
Sighs to see
What you are, and used to be,

Looking backward to the time
When you wrote your earliest
    rhyme!—

When I sat
Filing at
Your first point, and dreaming that
    Your initial song should be
    Worthy of posterity.

With regret
I forget
If the song be living yet,
    Yet remember, vaguely now,
    It was honest, anyhow.

You have brought
Me a thought—
Truer yet was never taught,—
    That the silent song is best,
    And the unsung worthiest.

So if I,
When I die,
May as uncomplainingly
    Drop aside as now you do,
    Write of me, as I of you:—

Here lies one
Who begun
Life a-singing, heard of none;
    And he died, satisfied,
    With his dead songs by his side.

142

GOD BLESS US EVERY ONE

"GOD bless us every one!" prayed
    Tiny Tim
Crippled, and dwarfed of body, yet
    so tall
Of soul, we tiptoe earth to look on him,
    High towering over all.

He loved the loveless world, nor
        dreamed indeed
That it, at best, could give to him,
        the while,
But pitying glances, when his only
        need
    Was but a cheery smile.

And thus he prayed, "God bless us
        every one!"—
Enfolding all the creeds within the
        span
Of his child-heart; and so, despising
        none,
    Was nearer saint than man.

I like to fancy God, in Paradise,
    Lifting a finger o'er the rhythmic
        swing
Of chiming harp and song, with eager
        eyes
    Turned earthward, listening—

The Anthem stilled—the Angels lean-
        ing there
    Above the golden walls—the morn-
        ing sun
Of Christmas bursting flower-like with
        the prayer,
    "God bless us every one!"

Tel I jest clum down in a craw-
        fish-hole,
    Weary at hart, and sick at soul!

"Dozed away fer an hour,
    And I tackled the thing ag'in:
        And I sung, and sung,
        Tel I knowed my lung
    Was jest about give in;
        And then, thinks I, ef hit don't
            rain now,
    They's nothin' in singin', anyhow!

"Onc't in a while some farmer
    Would come a-drivin' past;
        And he'd hear my cry,
        And stop and sigh—
    Tel I jest laid back, at last,
        And I hollered rain tel I thought
            my th'oat
    Would bust wide open at ever'
            note!

"But I fetched her!—O I fetched her!—
    'Cause a little while ago,
        As I kindo' set,
        With one eye shet,
    And a-singin' soft and low,
        A voice drapped down on my
            fevered brain,
    A-sayin',—'Ef you'll jest hush I'll
        rain!' "

143

THE TREE-TOAD

" 'SCUR'OUS-LIKE," said the tree-
        toad,
    "I've twittered fer rain all day;
        And I got up soon,
        And hollered tel noon—
    But the sun, hit blazed away,

144

LAUGHING SONG

SING us something full of laughter;
    Tune your harp, and twang the
        strings
Till your glad voice, chirping after,
    Mates the song the robin sings:

Loose your lips and let them flutter
　　Like the wings of wanton birds,—
Though they naught but laughter
　　utter,
　　Laugh, and we'll not miss the
　　words.

Sing in ringing tones that mingle
　　In a melody that flings
Joyous echoes in a jingle
　　Sweeter than the minstrel sings:
Sing of Winter, Spring or Summer,
　　Clang of war, or low of herds;
Trill of cricket, roll of drummer—
　　Laugh, and we'll not miss the
　　words.

Like the lisping laughter glancing
　　From the meadow brooks and
　　springs,
Or the river's ripples dancing
　　To the tune the current sings—
Sing of Now, and the Hereafter;
　　Let your glad song, like the birds',
Overflow with limpid laughter—
　　Laugh, and we'll not miss the
　　words.

145

THE WITCH OF ERKMURDEN

I

WHO cantereth forth in the night
　　　so late—
　　So late in the night, and so nigh the
　　dawn?
'Tis The Witch of Erkmurden who
　　leapeth the gate
Of the old churchyard where the three
　　Sprites wait
　　Till the whir of her broom is gone.

And who peereth down from the bel-
　　fry tall,
　　With the ghost-white face and the
　　ghastly stare,
With lean hands clinched in the
　　grated wall
Where the red vine rasps and the
　　rank leaves fall,
　　And the clock-stroke drowns his
　　prayer?

II

The wee babe wails, and the storm
　　grows loud,
　　Nor deeper the dark of the night
　　may be,
For the lightning's claw, with a great
　　wet cloud,
Hath wiped the moon and the wild-
　　eyed crowd
　　Of the stars out wrathfully.

Knuckled and kinked as the hunch-
　　back shade
　　Of a thorn-tree bendeth the bedlam
　　old
Over the couch where the mother-
　　maid,
With her prayerful eyes, and the babe
　　are laid,
　　Waiting the doom untold.

"Mother, O Mother, I only crave
　　Mercy for him and the babe—not
　　me!"
"Hush! for it maketh my brain to rave
Of my two white shrouds, and my
　　one wide grave,
　　And a mound for my children
　　three."

"Mother, O Mother, I only pray
　　Pity for him who is son to thee

And more than my brother.—" "Wilt
  hush, I say!
Though I meet thee not at the Judg-
  ment Day,
  I will bury my children three!"

"Then hark! O Mother, I hear his
  cry—
  Hear his curse from the church-
  tower now,—
'Ride thou witch till thy hate shall
  die,
Yet hell as Heaven eternally
  Be sealed to such as thou!' "

An infant's wail—then a laugh, god
  wot,
  That strangled the echoes of deep-
  est hell;
And a thousand shuttles of lightning
  shot,
And the moon bulged out like a great
  red blot,
  And a shower of blood-stars fell.

III

There is one wide grave scooped un-
  der the eaves—
  Under the eaves as they weep and
  weep;
And, veiled by the mist that the dead
  storm weaves,
The hag bends low, and the earth
  receives
  Mother and child asleep.

There's the print of the hand at either
  throat,
  And the frothy ooze at the lips of
  each,
But both smile up where the new
  stars float,

And the moon sails out like a silver
  boat
  Unloosed from a stormy beach.

IV

Bright was the morn when the sexton
  gray
  Twirled the rope of the old church-
  bell,—
But it answered not, and he tugged
  away—
And lo, at his feet a dead man lay—
  Dropped down with a single knell.

And the scared wight found, in the
  lean hand gripped,
  A scrip which read: "O the grave
  is wide,
But it empty waits, for the low eaves
  dripped
Their prayerful tears, and the three
  Sprites slipped
  Away with my babe and bride."

146

THE BALLAD OF SMILES
AND TEARS

BY LEE O. HARRIS AND
JAMES WHITCOMB RILEY

I

WHEN the gleeful Spring on
  dancing feet
Pranks the sward of the forest
  aisles,
And the bluebird pipes from his old
  retreat,
  O then may the glad face bloom
  with smiles:

But whenever the wind of winter
piles
The drifting snow on the frozen
meres,
And the feet are worn with the
weary miles,
Then hearts that are heavy may
melt in tears.

II

When the soul is brimmed with a joy
too sweet
To waste like that of a laughing
child's,
When the lips of love for the first
time meet,
O then may the glad face bloom
with smiles;
But whenever the kiss of love de-
files,
And friendship wanes with the
waning years,
When faith has perished, and hope
beguiles,
Then hearts that are heavy may
melt in tears.

III

When the brow is crowned and the
song complete,
And the minstrel's guerdon recon-
ciles
The victor-soul to the heart's defeat,
O then may the glad face bloom
with smiles:
But whenever the world in scorn
compiles
Its ready pages of scoffs and jeers,
And the brain is weary of envy's
wiles,
Then hearts that are heavy may
melt in tears.

L'ENVOY

When the eyelids droop like a drowsy
child's,
O then may the glad face bloom with
smiles:
But whenever the waking is fraught
with fears,
Then hearts that are heavy may melt
in tears.

147

THIS MAN JONES

THIS man Jones was what you'd
call
A feller 'at had no sand at all;
Kind o' consumpted, and undersize,
And sallor-complected, with big sad
eyes
And a kind-of-a-sort-of-a hang-dog
style,
And a sneakin' sort-of-a half-way
smile
'At kind o' give him away to us
As a preacher, maybe, er somepin'
wuss.

Didn't take with the gang—well, no—
But still we managed to use him,
though,—
Coddin' the gilly along the rout',
And drivin' the stakes 'at he pulled
out—
Fer I was one of the bosses then,
And of course stood in with the can-
vasmen;
And the way we put up jobs, you
know,
On this man Jones jes' beat the show!

Ust to rattle him scandalous,
And keep the feller a-dodgin' us,

And a-shyin' round half skeered to
    death,
And afeerd to whimper above his
    breath;
Give him a cussin', and then a kick,
And then a kind-of-a backhand lick—
Jes' fer the fun of seein' him climb
Around with a head on most the time.

But what was the curioust thing to
    me,
Was along o' the party—let me see,—
Who was our "Lion Queen" last
    year?—
Mamzelle Zanty, or De La Pierre?—
Well, no matter—a stunnin' mash,
With a red-ripe lip, and a long eye-
    lash,
And a figger sich as the angels owns—
And one too many fer this man Jones.

He'd allus wake in the afternoon,
As the band waltzed in on the lion-
    tune,
And there, from the time 'at she'd
    go in
Till she'd back out of the cage ag'in,
He'd stand, shaky and limber-kneed—
'Specially when she come to "feed
The beasts raw meat with her naked
    hand"—
And all that business, you understand.

And it *was* resky in that den—
Fer I think she juggled three cubs
    then,
And a big "green" lion 'at used to
    smash
Collar-bones fer old Frank Nash;
And I reckon now she hain't fergot
The afternoon old "Nero" sot
His paws on *her!*—but as fer me,
It's a sort-of-a mixed-up mystery:—

Kind o' remember an awful roar,
And see her back fer the bolted door—
See the cage rock—heerd her call
"God have mercy!" and that was all—
Fer they ain't no livin' man can tell
What it's like when a thousand yell
In female tones, and a thousand more
Howl in bass till their throats is sore!

But the keeper said 'at dragged her
    out,
They heerd some feller laugh and
    shout—
"Save her! Quick! I've got the cuss!"
And yit she waked and smiled on *us!*
And we daren't flinch, fer the doctor
    said,
Seein' as this man Jones was dead,
Better to jes' not let her know
Nothin' o' that fer a week or so.

148

WAIT

WE know, O faltering heart,
    Thy need is great:
But weary is the way that leads to
    art,
And all who journey there must bear
    their part—
Must bear their part, and—wait.

The way is wild and steep,
    And desolate:
No flowers blossom there, nor lilies
    peep
Above the walls to warn you, as you
    weep,
With one white whisper—"Wait."

You will find thorns, alas!
    And keen as fate:

And, reaching from rank fens of
    withered grass,
Briers will clutch your feet, nor let
    you pass—
And you must wait—must wait.

And though with failing sight
    You see the gate
Of Promise locked and barred, with
    swarthy Night
Guarding the golden keys of morning-
    light,—
Press bravely on—and wait.

The blurred leaves of life and love
That our wet eyes bend above,
Lisp nor laughter on the lips:
Two white rose-leaves now eclipse
Such of glances as the chance
Dimple dances in advance.
Darling! Darling! tell us why
You do neither laugh nor cry;
Even though you moaned in pain,
We could be so glad again!
What unchanging smile is this
That we shudder so to kiss?
    Hearts are leaning low to glean
    All your meaning, Lelloine.

149

LELLOINE

I

TINY queen,
    Lelloine!
Little eyes laugh out between
    Dimpled fingers that were busy
But a weary moment since
    Mischief-making—for she is a
Match for Puck, the fairy prince!
She must ever be advancing
Some new prank; and laughing, danc-
    ing,
    Disappearing at the door,
Like a sunbeam leaving shaded
    All that was so bright before—
Like a sunbeam leaving faded
    Flowers on the floor.
O, you joking, dear provoking,
    Little laughing Lelloine!

II

Calm, serene,
Lelloine!
Lying lily-like between

150

A DREAM OF AUTUMN

MELLOW hazes, lowly trailing
    Over wood and meadow, veil-
        ing
Somber skies, with wild fowl sailing
    Sailor-like to foreign lands;
And the north wind overleaping
Summer's brink, and flood-like sweep-
    ing
Wrecks of roses where the weeping-
    Willows wring their helpless hands.

Flared, like Titan torches flinging
Flakes of flame and embers, spring-
    ing
From the vale, the trees stand swing-
    ing
    In the moaning atmosphere;
While in dead'ning lands the lowing
Of the cattle, sadder growing,
Fills the sense to overflowing
    With the sorrow of the year.

Sorrowfully, yet the sweeter
Sings the brook in rippled meter
Under boughs that lithely teeter
    Lorn birds, answering from the
        shores
Through the viny, shady-shiny
Interspaces, shot with tiny
Flying motes that fleck the winy
    Wave-engraven sycamores.

Fields of ragged stubble, wrangled
With rank weeds, and shocks of
        tangled
Corn, with crests like rent plumes
        dangled
    Over Harvest's battle-plain;
And the sudden whir and whistle
Of the quail that, like a missile,
Whizzes over thorn and thistle,
    And, a missile, drops again.

Muffled voices, hid in thickets
Where the redbird stops to stick its
Ruddy beak betwixt the pickets
    Of the truant's rustic trap;
And the sound of laughter ringing
Where, within the wild vine swing-
        ing,
Climb Bacchante's schoolmates, fling-
        ing
    Purple clusters in her lap.

Rich as wine, the sunset flashes
Round the tilted world, and dashes
Up the sloping West, and splashes
    Red foam over sky and sea—
Till my dream of Autumn, paling
In the splendor all-prevailing,
Like a sallow leaf goes sailing
    Down the silence solemnly.

151

SINCE MY MOTHER DIED

SINCE my mother died, the tone
    Of my voice has fainter grown,
And my words, so strangely few,
Are as strange to me as you.
Something like a lens is drawn
Over all I look upon,
And the world is O so wide,
    Since my mother died.

Since my mother died, my face
Knows not any resting-place,
Save in visions, lightly pressed
In its old accustomed rest
On her shoulder. But I wake
With a never-ending ache
In my heart, and naught beside, .
    Since my mother died.

Since my mother died, the years
Have been dropping like my tears,
Till the bloom is washed away
From my cheeks, and slow decay
Seams the corners of my eyes,
Where my childish laughter lies
Drowned in tears that never dried
    Since my mother died.

Since my mother died, my feet
Falter in the crowded street,
With bewildered steps that seem
Tangled in some grassy dream,
And, in busy haunts of men,
Slowly down the past again
Do I wander weary-eyed,
    Since my mother died.

Since my mother died, O friends!
No one leads me now, or lends
Me a kindly word, or touch

Of the hands I need so much;
No one counsels me, or cares
For my trials, doubts, despairs,
And the world is O so wide,
    Since my mother died.

152

BELLS JANGLED

I LIE low-coiled in a nest of dreams;
    The lamp gleams dim i' the
        odorous gloom,
And the stars at the casement leak
    long gleams
    Of misty light through the haunted
        room
Where I lie low-coiled in dreams.

The night winds ooze o'er my dusk-
    drowned face
    In a dewy flood that ebbs and
        flows,
Washing a surf of dim white lace
    Under my throat and the dark red
        rose
In the shade of my dusk-drowned
    face.

There's a silken strand of some strange
    sound
    Slipping out of a skein of song:
Eerily as a call unwound
    From a fairy bugle, it slides along
In a silken strand of sound.

There's the tinkling drip of a faint
    guitar;
    There's a gurgling flute, and a blar-
        ing horn
Blowing bubbles of tune afar

O'er the misty heights of the hills of
    morn,
To the drip of a faint guitar.

And I dream that I neither sleep nor
    wake—
    Careless am I if I wake or sleep,
For my soul floats out on the waves
    that break
    In crests of song on the shoreless
        deep
Where I neither sleep nor wake.

153

DUSK SONG—THE BEETLE

THE shrilling locust slowly sheathes
    His dagger-voice, and creeps
        away
Beneath the brooding leaves where
    breathes
    The zephyr of the dying day:
One naked star has waded through
    The purple shallows of the night,
And faltering as falls the dew
    It drips its misty light.

O'er garden blooms,
    On tides of musk,
The beetle booms adown the glooms
And bumps along the dusk.

The katydid is rasping at
    The silence from the tangled broom:
On drunken wings the flitting bat
    Goes staggering athwart the gloom;
The toadstool bulges through the
    weeds,
    And lavishly to left and right
The fireflies, like golden seeds,
    Are sown about the night.

O'er slumbrous blooms,
  On floods of musk,
The beetle booms adown the glooms
  Aud bumps along the dusk.

The primrose flares its baby-hands
  Wide open, as the empty moon,
Slow lifted from the underlands,
  Drifts up the azure-arched lagoon;
The shadows on the garden walk
  Are frayed with rifts of silver light;
And, trickling down the poppy-stalk,
  The dewdrop streaks the night.

O'er folded blooms,
  On swirls of musk,
The beetle booms adown the glooms
  And bumps along the dusk.

154

SLEEP

THOU drowsy god, whose blurred
  eyes, half awink,
  Muse on me,—drifting out upon thy
    dreams,
  I lave my soul as in enchanted
    streams
Where reveling satyrs pipe along the
    brink,
And, tipsy with the melody they
    drink,
  Uplift their dangling hooves and
    down the beams
  Of sunshine dance like motes. Thy
    languor seems
An ocean-depth of love wherein I
    sink
  Like some fond Argonaut, right
    willingly,—
Because of wooing eyes upturned to
    mine,

And siren-arms that coil their sor-
    cery
About my neck, with kisses so divine,
  The heavens reel above me, and the
    sea
Swallows and licks its wet lips over
    me.

155

MARTHY ELLEN

THEY'S nothin' in the name to
  strike
A feller more'n common like!
'Taint liable to git no praise
Ner nothin' like it nowadays;
An' yit that name o' her'n is jest
As purty as the purtiest—
And more'n that, I'm here to say
I'll live a-thinkin' thataway
  And die fer Marthy Ellen!

It may be I was prejudust
In favor of it from the fust—
'Cause I kin ricollect jest how
We met, and hear her mother now
A-callin' of her down the road—
And, aggervatin' little toad!—
I see her now, jest sort o' half-
Way disapp'inted, turn and laugh
  And mock her—"Marthy Ellen!"

Our people never had no fuss,
And yit they never tuck to us;
We neighbered back and foreds some;
Until they see she liked to come
To our house—and me and her
Was jest together ever'whur
And all the time—and when they'd see
That I liked her and she liked me,
  They'd holler "Marthy Ellen!"

When we growed up, and they shet
    down
On me and her a-runnin' roun'
Together, and her father said
He'd never leave her nary red,
So he'p him, ef she married me,
And so on—and her mother she
Jest agged the gyrl, and said she
    'lowed
She'd ruther see her in her shroud,
    I *writ* to Marthy Ellen—

That is, I kind o' tuck my pen
In hand, and stated whur and when
The undersigned would be that night,
With two good hosses, saddled right
Fer lively travelin', in case
Her folks 'ud like to jine the race.
She sent the same note back, and
    writ
"The rose is red!" right under it—
"Your'n allus, Marthy Ellen."

That's all, I reckon—Nothin' more
To tell but what you've heerd afore—
The same old story, sweeter though
Fer all the trouble, don't you know.
Old-fashioned name! and yit it's jest
As purty as the purtiest;
And more'n that, I'm here to say
I'll live a-thinkin' thataway,
    And die fer Marthy Ellen!

156

THE LITTLE TOWN O' TAILHOLT

YOU kin boast about yer cities, and
    their stiddy growth and size,
And brag about yer County-seats, and
    business enterprise,

And railroads, and factories, and all
    sich foolery—
But the little Town o' Tailholt is big
    enough fer me!

You kin harp about yer churches, with
    their steeples in the clouds,
And gas about yer graded streets, and
    blow about yer crowds;
You kin talk about yer "*theaters*," and
    all you've got to see—
But the little Town o' Tailholt is *show*
    enough fer me!

They hain't no *style* in our town—hit's
    little-like and small—
They hain't no "*churches*," nuther,—
    jes' the meetin'-house is all;
They's no sidewalks, to speak of—but
    the highway's allus free,
And the little Town o' Tailholt is
    wide enough fer me!

Some finds it discommodin'-like, I'm
    willing to admit
To hev but one post-office, and a
    womern keepin' hit,
And the drug-store, and shoe-shop, and
    grocery, all three—
But the little Town o' Tailholt is
    handy 'nough fer me!

You kin smile and turn yer nose up,
    and joke and hev yer fun,
And laugh and holler "Tail-holts is
    better holts'n none!"
Ef the city suits you better, w'y, hit's
    where you'd ort'o be—
But the little Town o' Tailholt's good
    enough fer me!

157

WHERE SHALL WE LAND?

Where shall we land you, sweet?
                        —SWINBURNE.

ALL listlessly we float
        Out seaward in the boat
That beareth Love.
Our sails of purest snow
Bend to the blue below
And to the blue above.
        Where shall we land?

We drift upon a tide
Shoreless on every side,
        Save where the eye
Of Fancy sweeps far lands
Shelved slopingly with sands
        Of gold and porphyry.
                Where shall we land?

The fairy isles we see,
Loom up so mistily—
        So vaguely fair,
We do not care to break
Fresh bubbles in our wake
        To bend our course for there.
                Where shall we land?

The warm winds of the deep
Have lulled our sails to sleep,
        And so we glide
Careless of wave or wind,
Or change of any kind,
        Or turn of any tide.
                Where shall we land?

We droop our dreamy eyes
Where our reflection lies
        Steeped in the sea,
And, in an endless fit

Of languor, smile on it
        And its sweet mimicry.
                Where shall we land?

"Where shall we land?" God's grace!
I know not any place
        So fair as this—
Swung here between the blue
Of sea and sky, with you
        To ask me, with a kiss,
                "Where shall we land?"

158

HOPE

HOPE, bending o'er me one time,
        snowed the flakes
    Of her white touches on my folded
        sight,
And whispered, half rebukingly,
        "What makes
    My little girl so sorrowful to-night?"

O scarce did I unclasp my lids, or
        lift
    Their tear-glued fringes, as with
        blind embrace
I caught within my arms the mother-
        gift,
    And with wild kisses dappled all
        her face.

That was a baby dream of long
        ago:
    My fate is fanged with frost, and
        tongued with flame:
My woman-soul, chased naked through
        the snow,
    Stumbles and staggers on without
        an aim.

And yet, here in my agony, sometimes
A faint voice reaches down from
   some far height,
And whispers through a glamouring
   of rhymes,—
"What makes my little girl so sad
   to-night?"

159

THE LITTLE TINY KICKSHAW

—And any little tiny kickshaw.
                              –SHAKESPEARE.

O THE little tiny kickshaw that
   Mither sent tae me,
'Tis sweeter than the sugar-plum that
   reepens on the tree,
Wi' denty flavorin's o' spice an' musky
   rosemarie,
The little tiny kickshaw that Mither
   sent tae me.

'Tis luscious wi' the stalen tang o'
   fruits frae ower the sea,
An' e'en its fragrance gars me laugh
   wi' langin' lip an' ee,
Till a' its frazen scheen o' white maun
   melten hinnie be—
Sae weel I luve the kickshaw that
   Mither sent tae me.

O I luve the tiny kickshaw, an' I
   smack my lips wi' glee,
Aye mickle do I luve the taste o' sic a
   luxourie,
But maist I luve the luvein han'ş that
   could the giftie gie
O' the little tiny kickshaw that Mither
   sent tae me.

160

DEATH

LO, I am dying! And to feel the
   King
Of Terrors fasten on me, steeps all
   sense
Of life, and love, and loss, and every-
   thing,
In such deep calms of restful indo-
   lence,
His keenest fangs of pain are sweet to
   me
As fusèd kisses of mad lovers' lips
When, flung shut-eyed in spasmed
   ecstasy,
They feel the world spin past them in
   eclipse,
And so thank God with ever-tighten-
   ing lids!
But what I see, the soul of me forbids
All utterance of; and what I hear and
   feel,
The rattle in my throat could ill re-
   veal
Though it were music to your ears as
   to
Mine own.—Press closer—closer—I
   have grown
So great, your puny arms about me
   thrown
Seem powerless to hold me here with
   you;—
I slip away—I waver—and—I fall—
Christ! What a plunge! Where am I
   dropping? All
My breath bursts into dust—I can not
   cry—
I whirl—I reel and veer up overhead,
And drop flat-faced against—against—
   the sky—
Soh, bless me! I am dead!

161

TO THE WINE-GOD MERLUS

A Toast of Jucklet's

HO! ho! thou jolly god, with kinkèd
lips
And laughter-streaming eyes, thou
liftest up
The heart of me like any wassail-cup,
And from its teeming brim, in foam-
ing drips,
Thou blowest all my cares. I cry to
thee,
Between the sips:—Drink long and
lustily;
Drink thou my ripest joys, my richest
mirth,
My maddest staves of wanton min-
strelsy;
Drink every song I've tinkered here
on earth
With any patch of music; drink! and
be
Thou drainer of my soul, and to the
lees
Drink all my lover-thrills and ecstasies;
And with a final gulp—ho! ho!—drink
me,
And roll me o'er thy tongue eternally.

162

THE GINOINE AR-TICKLE

TALKIN' o' poetry,—There're few
men yit
'At's got the stuff b'iled down so's
it'll pour
Out sorgum-like, and keeps a year and
more
Jes' sweeter ever' time you tackle it!

Why, all the jinglin' truck 'at hes been
writ
Fer twenty year and better is so pore
You cain't find no sap in it any
more
'N you'd find juice in puff-balls!—
And I'd Quit!
What people wants is facts, I apper-
hend;
And naked Natur is the thing to
give
Your writin' bottom, eh? And I con-
tend
'At honest work is allus bound to
live.
Now them's my views; 'cause you kin
recommend
Sich poetry as that from end to end.

163

A BRIDE

"OI AM weary!" she sighed, as
her billowy
Hair she unloosed in a torrent of
gold
That rippled and fell o'er a figure as
willowy,
Graceful and fair as a goddess of
old:
Over her jewels she flung herself
drearily,
Crumpled the laces that snowed on
her breast,
Crushed with her fingers the lily that
wearily
Clung in her hair like a dove in its
nest.
—And naught but her shadowy
form in the mirror
To kneel in dumb agony down
and weep near her!

"Weary?"—of what? Could we
fathom the mystery?—
Lift up the lashes weighed down by
her tears
And wash with their dews one white
face from her history,
Set like a gem in the red rust of
years?
Nothing will rest her—unless he who
died of her
Strayed from his grave, and, in place
of the groom,
Tipping her face, kneeling there by the
side of her,
Drained the old kiss to the dregs of
his doom.
—And naught but that shadowy
form in the mirror
To kneel in dumb agony down
and weep near her!

Whistle us something old and gray—
Some toothless tune of the bygone
years—
Some bald old song that limps to-day
With a walking-stick this vale of
tears.
Whistle a stave of the good old
days,
E'er the fur stood up in a thou-
sand ways
On the listener's pelt as he ripped
and tore,
And diddle - dee - blank - blanked
Pinafore.

CHORUS

Whistle us something old, you know!
Pucker your lips with the old-time
twist,
And whistle the jigs of the long ago,
Or the old hornpipes that you used
to whist.

164

STANZAS FOR A NEW SONG

WHISTLE us something old, you
know!
Pucker your lips with the old-time
twist,
And whistle the jigs of the long
ago,
Or the old hornpipes that you used
to whist.
Some old, old tune that we oft
averred
Was a little the oldest thing we'd
heard
Since "the bob-tailed nag" was a
frisky colt,
In the babbling days of old "Ben
Bolt."

165

LINES TO AN ONSETTLED
YOUNG MAN

"O, WHAT is Life at last," says
you,
"'At woman-folks and man-folks too,
Cain't oncomplainin', worry through?

"An' what is Love, 'at no one yit
'At's monkeyed with it kin forgit,
Er gits fat on remember'n hit?

"An' what is Death?"—W'y, looky
hyur—
Ef Life an' Love don't suit you, sir,
Hit's jes' the thing yer lookin' fer!

166

PLANTATION HYMN

HEAR dat rum'lin' in de sky!
  Hol' fas', brudders, till you git
    dah!
O, dat's de good Lord walkin' by,
  Hol' fas', brudders, till you git dah!

CHORUS

Mahster! Jesus!
You done come down to please us,
And dahs de good Lord sees us,
  As he goes walkin' by!

See dat lightnin' lick his tongue?
  Hol' fas', brudders, till you git dah!
'Spec he taste de song 'ut de angels
    sung—
  Hol' fas', brudders, till you git dah!

De big black clouds is bust in two,
  Hol' fas', brudders, till you git dah!
And dahs de 'postles peekin' frue,
  Hol' fas', brudders, till you git dah!

Know dem angels ev'ry one,
  Hol' fas', brudders, till you git dah!
Kase dey's got wings and we'se got
    none,
  Hol' fas', brudders, till you git dah!

CHORUS

Mahster! Jesus!
You done come down to please us,
And dahs de good Lord sees us,
  As he goes walkin' by!

167

LAWYER AND CHILD

HOW large was Alexander, father,
  That parties designate
The historic gentleman as rather
  Inordinately great?

Why, son, to speak with conscientious
  Regard for history,
Waiving all claims, of course, to
    heights pretentious,—
  About the size of me.

168

THE LOST KISS

I PUT by the half-written poem,
  While the pen, idly trailed in my
    hand,
Writes on,—"Had I words to complete
    it,
  Who'd read it, or who'd under-
    stand?"
But the little bare feet on the stairway,
  And the faint, smothered laugh in
    the hall,
And the eery-low lisp on the silence,
  Cry up to me over it all.

So I gather it up—where was broken
  The tear-faded thread of my theme,
Telling how, as one night I sat writ-
    ing,
  A fairy broke in on my dream,
A little inquisitive fairy—
  My own little girl, with the gold
Of the sun in her hair, and the dewy
  Blue eyes of the fairies of old.

'Twas the dear little girl that I
    scolded—
"For was it a moment like this,"
I said, "when she knew I was busy,
    To come romping in for a kiss?—
Come rowdying up from her mother,
    And clamoring there at my knee
For 'One 'ittle kiss for my dolly,
    And one 'ittle uzzer for me!' "

God, pity the heart that repelled her,
    And the cold hand that turned her
        away,
And take, from the lips that denied
    her,
    This answerless prayer of to-day!
Take, Lord, from my mem'ry forever
    That pitiful sob of despair,
And the patter and trip of the little
    bare feet,
    And the one piercing cry on the
        stair!

I put by the half-written poem,
    While the pen, idly trailed in my
        hand,
Writes on,—"Had I words to complete
    it,
    Who'd read it, or who'd under-
        stand?"
But the little bare feet on the stairway,
    And the faint, smothered laugh in
        the hall,
And the eery-low lisp on the silence,
    Cry up to me over it all.

169

MICHAEL FLYNN AND THE
BABY

LUK at 'ere, ould baby,—who
    Shak's the fist av 'im at you?
Who's the spalpeen wid the stim

Av his poipe a pokin' 'im?
Who's the divil grinnin' 'ere
In the eyes av yez, me dear?
Arrah! darlint, spake and soy
Don't yez know yer feyther—boy?

Wheer's the gab yer mither had
Whin she blarneyed yer ould dad
Wid her tricks and 'ily words
Loike the liltin' av the birds?
Wheer's the tongue av Michael Flynn,
And the capers av the chin
He's a-waggin' at yez?—Hoy?
Don't yez know yer feyther—boy?

Arrah! baby, wid the eyes
Av the saints in Paradise,
And Saint Patrick's own bald pate,
Is it yer too howly swate
To be changin' words because
It's the hod, and not the cross,
Ornamints me showlder?—soy?
Don't yez know yer feyther—boy?

170

ON A SPLENDUD MATCH

[*On the night of the marraige of the
foregoin' couple, which shall be
nameless here, these lines was ca'mly
dashed off in the albun of the happy
bride whilse the shivver-ree was goin'
on outside the residence.*]

HE was warned aginst the
    womern—
She was warned aginst the *man.*—
And ef *that* won't make a weddin',
    W'y, they's nothin' else that can!

171

THE SINGER

WHILE with Ambition's hectic flame
He wastes the midnight oil,
And dreams, high-throned on heights of fame,
To rest him from his toil,—

Death's Angel, like a vast eclipse,
Above him spreads her wings,
And fans the embers of his lips
To ashes as he sings.

172

GUINEVERE

WHAT is it I am waiting for?
My footfall in the corridor
Jars upward through the night, and swings
The brazen silence till it rings
Like any bell. My weak knees faint
Before the sad face of my saint,
And, 'twixt my lifted eyes and tears,
Dim lists of mounted cavaliers
Swim past. . . . A nodding plume that dips
To brush the dead prayers from my lips
Like dust—. God's mercy! rid my sight
Of Launcelot, or blind me quite!
I know what duty is! Ah, Christ!
The memory of our latest tryst
Is fanged within my very soul! . . .
I swear to you, in all control
I held myself! . . . 'Twas love, I wis,
That sprang upon that kiss of his,
And drank and drained it to the lees
Of three God-shaken destinies.
'Twas love, I tell you, wild, insane,
Stark mad and babbling, wanton, vain—
But tell me, Where is Arthur?—or,
What is it I am waiting for?

173

THE WEREWIFE

SHE came to me in a dazzling guise
Of gleaming tresses and glimmering eyes,
With long, limp lashes that drooped and made
For their baleful glances bowers of shade;
And a face so white—so white and sleek
That the roses blooming in either cheek
Flamed and burned with a crimson glow
Redder than ruddiest roses blow—
Redder than blood of the roses know
That Autumn spills in the drifted snow.
And what could my fluttering, moth-winged soul
Do but hover in her control?—
With its little, bewildered bead-eyes fixed
Where the gold and the white and the crimson mixed?
And when the tune of her low laugh went
Up from that ivory instrument
That you would have called her throat,
I swear

The notes built nests in her gilded
hair,
And nestled and whistled and twit-
tered there,
And wooed me and won me to my
despair.
And thus it was that she lured me on,
Till the latest gasp of my love was
gone,
And my soul lay dead, with a loath-
ing face
Turned in vain from her dread em-
brace,—
For even its poor dead eyes could see
Her sharp teeth sheathed in the flesh
of me,
And her dripping lips, as she turned
to shake
The red froth off that her greed did
make,
As my heart gripped hold of a death-
less ache,
And the kiss of her stung like the
fang of a snake.

174

THE BAN

I

STRANGE dreams of what I used
to be,
And what I dreamed I *would* be,
swim
Before my vision, faint and dim
As misty distances we see
In pictured scenes of fairy lands;
And ever on, with empty hands,
And eyes that ever lie to me,
And smiles that no one understands,
I grope adown my destiny.

II

Some say I waver as I walk
Along the crowded thoroughfares;
And some leer in my eyes, and talk
Of dulness, while I see in theirs—
Like fishes' eyes, alive or dead—
But surfaces of vacancy—
Blank disks that never seem to see,
But glint and glow and glare instead.

III

The ragged shawl I wear is wet
With driving, dripping rains, and yet
It seems a royal raiment, where,
Through twisted torrents of my hair,
I see rare gems that gleam and shine
Like jewels in a stream of wine;
The gaping shoes that clothe my feet
Are golden sandals, and the shrine
Where courtiers grovel and repeat
Vain prayers, and where, in joy there-
at,
A fair Prince doffs his plumèd hat,
And kneels, and names me all things
sweet.

IV

Sometimes the sun shines, and the lull
Of winter noon is like a tune
The stars might twinkle to the moon
If night were white and beautiful—
For when the clangor of the town
And strife of traffic softens down,
The wakeful hunger that I nurse,
In listening, forgets to curse,
Until—ah, joy! with drooping head
I drowse, and dream that I am dead
And buried safe beyond their eyes
Who either pity or despise.

175

AN IDIOT

I'M on'y thist a' idiot—
  That's what folks calls a feller what
Ain't got no mind
Of any kind,
Ner don't know nothin' he's forgot.—
  I'm one o' *them*—But I know why
  The bees buzz *this* way when they
    fly,—
  'Cause honey it gits on their
    wings.
  Ain't thumbs and fingers funny
    things?

What's money? Hooh! it's thist a
    hole
Punched in a round thing 'at won't
    roll
  'Cause they's a string
  Poked through the thing
And fastened round your neck—that's
    all!
  Ef I could git my money off,
  I'd buy whole lots o' whoopin'-
    cough
  And give it to the boy next door
  Who died 'cause he ain't got no
    more.

What is it when you die? *I* know,—
You can't wake up ag'in, ner go
  To sleep no more—
  Ner kick, ner snore,
Ner lay and look and watch it snow;
  And when folks slaps and pinches
    you—
  You don't keer nothin' *what* they
    do.
  No honey on the *angels'* wings!
  Ain't thumbs and fingers funny
    things?

176

AN ORDER FOR A SONG

MAKE me a song of all good
  things,
And fill it full of murmurings,
Of merry voices, such as we
Remember in our infancy;
But make it tender, for the sake
Of hearts that brood and tears that
    break,
And tune it with the harmony,
  The sighs of sorrow make.

Make me a song of summer-time,
And pour such music down the rhyme
As ripples over gleaming sands
And grassy brinks of meadow-lands;
But make it very sweet and low,
For need of them that sorrow so,
Because they reap with empty hands
  The dreams of long ago.

Make me a song of such a tone,
That when we croon it all alone,
The tears of longing as they drip,
Will break in laughter on the lip;
And make it, oh, so pure and clear
And jubilant that every ear   ,
Shall drink its rapture sip by sip,
  And Heaven lean to hear.

177

THE CONQUEROR

HE hears the whir of the battle-
  drum,
  And the shrill-voiced fife, and the
    bugle-call,

With a thirsty spirit that drinks it all
As men might drink the wine
    poured from
Old wicker flagons raimented
With the rust and dust of ages dead.

He plunges into the crimson sea
Of carnage, and with a dauntless
    pride,
He swims, with his good star, side by
    side,
To the blood-sprayed heights of Vic-
    tory,
Where never his glory waxes dim,
Though a woman's weak hand con-
    quers him.

And high and alone—as the sculptor
    makes
Him set in stone that the world may
    see—
He sits there, crowned eternally,
And sheltered under a flag that
    shakes
Her silken stripes and her silver stars
Into a tangle of endless wars.

Of woman's hair, nor grip with
    jealousy
To find her face turned elsewhere
    smilingly.

With slumbrous lids, and mouth in
    mute repose,
And lips that yearn no more for any
    kiss—
Though it might drip, as from the red-
    lipped rose
The dewdrop drips, 'twere not so
    sweet as this
Unutterable density of rest
That reigns in every vein of brain
    and breast!

And thus—soaked with still laughter
    through and through—
I lie here dreaming of the forms
    that pass
Above my grave, to drop, with tears,
    a few
White flowers that but curdle the
    green grass;—
And if they read such sermons,
    they could see
How I do pity them that pity me.

178

AFTER DEATH

A FANCY

AH! this delights me more than
    words could tell,—
To just lie stark and still, with
    folded hands
That tremble not at greeting or fare-
    well,
Nor fumble foolishly in loosened
    strands

179

THE MAD LOVER

MY eyes are feverish and dull;
    I'm tired, and my throat hurts
    so!
And life has grown so pitiful—
    So very pitiful, I know
Not any hope of rest or peace,
    But just to live on, ache by ache,
Feeling my heart click on, nor cease,
    Nor ever wholly break.

You smiled so sweetly, Miriam Wayne,
  I could not help but love your smile,
And fair as sunshine after rain
  It glimmered on me all the while;
Why, it did soak as summer light
  Through all my life, until, indeed,
I ripened as an apple might
  From golden rind to seed.

Fate never wrought so pitiless
  An evil, as when first your eyes
Poured back in mine the tenderness
  That made the world a Paradise—
For Miriam, remembering
  The warm white hands that lay in
      mine
Like wisps of sunshine vanishing—
  Your kisses, spilled like wine

Down over forehead, face and lips,
  Till I lay drunken with delight
From crown of soul to finger-tips—
  . . . Shriek, Memory, in mad
      affright!—
Howl at the moon like any hound!
  Yelp "love" and "liar" every breath,
And "Heaven is lost and hell is
      found!"
  So moan yourself to death!

180

TO ROBERT BURNS

SWEET Singer that I loe the maist
      O' ony, sin' wi' eager haste
I smacket bairn-lips ower the taste
      O' hinnied sang,
I hail thee, though a blessed ghaist
      In Heaven lang!

For, weel I ken, nae cantie phrase,
Nor courtly airs, nor lairdly ways,

Could gar me freer blame, or praise,
      Or proffer hand,
Where "Rantin' Robbie" and his lays
      Thegither stand.

And sae these hamely lines I send,
Wi' jinglin' words at ilka end,
In echo o' the sangs that wend
      Frae thee to me
Like simmer-brooks, wi' mony a bend
      O' wimplin' glee.

In fancy, as, wi' dewy een,
I part the clouds aboon the scene
Where thou wast born, and peer
      atween,
      I see nae spot
In a' the Hielands half sae green
      And unforgot!

I see nae storied castle-hall,
Wi' banners flauntin' ower the wall
And serf and page in ready call,
      Sae grand to me
As ane puir cotter's hut, wi' all
      Its poverty.

There where the simple daisy grew
Sae bonnie sweet, and modest, too,
Thy liltin' filled its wee head fu'
      O' sic a grace,
It aye is weepin' tears o' dew
      Wi' droopit face.

Frae where the heather bluebells fling
Their sangs o' fragrance to the Spring,
To where the lavrock soars to sing,
      Still lives thy strain,
For a' the birds are twittering
      Sangs like thine ain.

And aye, by light o' sun or moon,
By banks o' Ayr, or Bonnie Doon,

The waters lilt nae tender tune
  But sweeter seems
Because they poured their limpid rune
  Through a' thy dreams.

Wi' brimmin' lip, and laughin' ee,
Thou shookest even Grief wi' glee,
Yet had nae niggart sympathy
  Where Sorrow bowed,
But gavest a' thy tears as free
  As a' thy gowd.

And sae it is we loe thy name
To see bleeze up wi' sic a flame,
That a' pretentious stars o' fame
  Maun blink asklent,
To see how simple worth may shame
  Their brightest glent.

181

HER VALENTINE

SOMEBODY'S sent a funny little
  valentine to me.
It's a bunch of baby-roses in a vase of
  filigree,
And hovering above them—just as
  cute as he can be—
Is a fairy cupid tangled in a scarf of
  poetry.

And the prankish little fellow looks so
  knowing in his glee,
With his golden bow and arrow, aim-
  ing most unerringly
At a pair of hearts so labeled that I
  may read and see
That one is meant for "One Who
  Loves," and one is meant for me.

But I know the lad who sent it! It's
  as plain as A-B-C!—

For the roses they are *blushing,* and the
  vase stands *awkwardly,*
And the little god above it—though as
  cute as he can be—
Can not breathe the lightest whisper
  of his burning love for me.

182

SONGS TUNELESS

I

HE kisses me! Ah, now, at last,
  He says good night as it should
    be,
His great warm eyes bent yearn-
    ingly
Above my face—his arms locked fast
About me, and mine own eyes dim
With happy tears for love of him.

He kisses me! Last night, beneath
  A swarm of stars, he said I stood
  His one fair form of womanhood,
And springing, shut me in the sheath
  Of a caress that almost hid
  Me from the good his kisses did.

He kisses me! He kisses me!
  This is the sweetest song I know,
  And so I sing it very low
And faint, and O so tenderly
  That, though you listen, none but
    he
  May hear it as he kisses me.

II

"How can I make you love me
    more?"—
  A thousand times she asks me this,
  Her lips uplifted with the kiss

That I have tasted o'er and o'er,
Till now I drain it with no sense
Other than utter indolence.

"How can I make you love me
    more?"—
A thousand times her questioning
    face
Has nestled in its resting-place
Unanswered, till, though I adore
This thing of being loved, I doubt
Not I could get along without.

"How can she make me love her
    more?"—
Ah! little woman, if, indeed,
I might be frank as is the need
Of frankness, I would fall before
Her very feet, and there confess
My love were more if hers were less.

III

Since I am old I have no care
To babble silly tales of when
I loved, and lied, as other men
Have done, who boasted here and
    there,
They would have died for the fair
    thing
They after murdered, marrying.

Since I am old I reason thus—
No thing survives, of all the past,
But just regret enough to last
Us till the clods have smothered us;—
Then, with our dead loves, side by
    side,
We may, perhaps, be satisfied.

Since I am old, and strive to blow
Alive the embers of my youth
And early loves, I find, in sooth,

An old man's heart may burn so low,
'Tis better just to calmly sit
And rake the ashes over it.

183

SISTER JONES'S CONFESSION

I THOUGHT the deacon liked me,
    yit
I warn't adzackly shore of it—
Fer, mind ye, time and time ag'in,
When jiners 'ud be comin' in,
I'd seed him shakin' hands as free
With all the sistern as with me!
But jurin' last Revival, where
He called on *me* to lead in prayer
An' kneeled there with me, side by
    side,
A-whisper'n' "he felt sanctified .
Jes' tetchin' of my gyarment's hem,"—
That settled things as fur as them-
Thare *other* wimmin was concerned!—
And—well!—I know I must 'a' turned
A dozen colors!—*Flurried?—la!—*
No mortal sinner never saw
A gladder widder than the one
A-kneelin' there and wonderun'
Who'd pray!—So glad, upon my word,
I railly couldn't thank the Lord!

184

THE DEAD JOKE AND THE
FUNNY MAN

LONG years ago, a funny man,
    Flushed with a strange delight,
Sat down and wrote a funny thing
    All in the solemn night;
And as he wrote he clapped his hands
    And laughed with all his might

For it was such a funny thing,
O such a very funny thing,
This wonderfully funny thing,
He
    Laughed
      Outright.

And so it was this funny man
Printed this funny thing—
Forgot it, too, nor ever thought
   It worth remembering,
Till but a day or two ago.
   (Ah! what may changes bring!)
      He found this selfsame funny
         thing
      In an exchange—"O funny thing!"
      He cried, "You dear old funny
         thing!"
And
    Sobbed
      Outright.

185

SLEEP

ORPHANED, I cry to thee:
   Sweet Sleep! O kneel and be
A mother unto me!
  Calm thou my childish fears;
Fold—fold mine eyelids to, all tenderly,
  And dry my tears.

Come, Sleep, all drowsy-eyed
And faint with languor, slide
Thy dim face down beside
  Mine own, and let me rest
And nestle in thy heart, and there
    abide,
  A favored guest.

Good night to every care,
And shadow of despair!

Good night to all things where
  Within is no delight!—
Sleep opens her dark arms, and,
  swooning there,
  I sob: Good night—good night!

186

ONE ANGEL

"A HOMELY little woman with big
  hands":
'Twas thus she named herself, and
  shook her head
All solemnly, the day that we were
  wed,
While I   well, I laughed lightly as I
  said,—
"No prince am I astray from fairy
  lands,
O, 'homely little woman with big
  hands'!"

"My homely little woman with big
  hands"
I called her ever after,—first, intent
On irony and admonition blent;
Then out of—since she smiled—pure
  merriment;
And lastly, from sheer lack of repri-
  mands.
Brave, homely little woman with big
  hands!

My homely little woman with big
  hands,
Somehow, grew almost beautiful to
  me
As time went by.   Her features I
  could see
Grow ever fairer; and so tenderly

The strong hands clung, their touches
    were commands,
Dear homely little woman with big
    hands!

.   .   .   .

A homely little woman, with big hands
    Folded all patiently across her
        breast—
    The plain face fair and beautiful in
        rest—
    But O, the lips that answer not
        when pressed!
"Make me," I cry to God, who under-
        stands,
"A homely little angel with big
        hands!"

187

LAUGHTER

WITHIN the coziest corner of my
    dreams
    He sits, high-throned above all gods
        that be
    Portrayed in marble-cold mythology,
Since from his joyous eyes a twinkle
    gleams
So warm with life and light it ever
    seems
    Spraying in mists of sunshine over
        me,
    And mingled with such rippling ec-
        stasy
As overleaps his lips in laughing
    streams.
    Ho! look on him, and say if he be
        old

Or youthful! Hand in hand with gray
    old Time
    He toddled when an infant; and, be-
        hold!—
He hath not aged, but to the lusty
    prime
    Of babyhood—his brow a trifle
        bold—
    His hair a raveled nimbus of gray
    gold.

188

AN INVOCATION

SWEET Sleep, with mellow palms
    trailed listlessly
    Above mine eyelids, folding out the
        light
    Of coming day, and shutting in the
        night
That gave but now such wondrous
    dreams to me—
Bide with me yet with thy dear sor-
    cery,
    Until once more I grow forgetful
        quite
    Of all the cares that blur my waking
        sight
With dim, regretful tears! I beg of
    thee
To lift again thy wand with magic
    filled,
    And filter through my faith the
        words: Behold,
Aladdin, as thou badest me, I build
    A new dream o'er the ruins of the
        old—
Thine all eternal palace, silver-silled,
    And walled with harps, and roofed
        with crowns of gold!

189
FROM BELOW

IN the dim summer night they were
   leaning alone
From the balcony over the walk;
He, careless enough, one had guessed
   by the tone
Of his voice and his murmurous talk;
And she—well, her laugh flowed as
   sweet to the breeze
As the voice of the faint violin
That ran, with a ripple of ivory keys,
Through the opera warbled within.

.   .   .   .

In the odorous locust-boughs trailed
   o'er the eaves,
The nightingale paused in his tune,
And the mute katydid hid away in the
   leaves
That were turned from the smile of
   the moon:
And the man sat alone, with his fin-
   gers clenched tight
O'er a heart that had failed in its
   beat,
While the passers-by saw but a spatter
   of light
Where he dropped his cigar in the
   street.

190
GLAMOUR

WAS it in the misty twilight, or
   the midnight or the morning,
Or was it in the glare of noon, or
   dazzle of the day,
That, half asleep and half awake, and
   without word or warning,

My fancy, slowly slipping earthly an-
   chor, sailed away?

O leave me and my lazy dream a little
   while together,
Blending each within the other as
   we waken in the dawn,
With languid lids anointed by the
   balmy summer weather
As it wells above the casement that
   our vision swoons upon!

Linger with me yet a little, O my lazy
   dream! nor leave me;
Though we hear the swallows twit-
   ter, it is only in their sleep:
And I want you just to cling to me
   and love me and deceive me
A little ere the morning when I
   waken but to weep.

Ah! dream of mine, I see you growing
   clearer yet and clearer;
Your fairy face comes back again
   from out the misty past,
And your smile shines on before you
   till, approaching ever nearer, ·
It gilds your grave into a glorious
   trysting-place at last.

And you lean there—waiting for me—
   here's the dainty rose-leaf letter
That you sent me, saying, "Meet me
   here, and share my deep delight,
For my love by this long silence is so
   truer, purer, better,
That you will taste of Heaven when
   you touch my lips to-night."

Was it in the misty twilight, or the
   midnight, or the morning,
Or was it in the glare of noon, or
   dazzle of the day,

That, half asleep and half awake, and
    without word or warning,
My fancy, slowly slipping earthly
    anchor, sailed away?

191

SILENCE

THOUSANDS and thousands of
    hushed years ago,
Out on the edge of Chaos, all alone
I stood on peaks of vapor, high up-
    thrown
Above a sea that knew nor ebb nor
    flow,
Nor any motion won of winds that
    blow,
Nor any sound of watery wail or
    moan,
Nor lisp of wave, nor wandering
    undertone
Of any tide lost in the night below.
So still it was, I mind me, as I laid
    My thirsty ear against mine own
    faint sigh
To drink of that, I sipped it, half
    afraid
'Twas but the ghost of a dead voice
    spilled by
The one starved star that tottered
    through the shade
And came tiptoeing toward me down
    the sky.

192

PUCK

O IT was Puck! I saw him yester-
    night
Swung up betwixt a phlox-top and
    the rim

Of a low crescent moon that cradled
    him,
Whirring his rakish wings with all his
    might,
And pursing his wee mouth, that
    dimpled white
And red, as though some dagger
    keen and slim
Had stung him there, while ever
    faint and dim
His eery warblings piped his high de-
    light:
Till I, grown jubilant, shrill answer
    made,
At which all suddenly he dropped
    from view;
And peering after, 'neath the ever-
    glade,
What was it, do you think, I saw
    him do?
I saw him peeling dewdrops with a
    blade
Of starshine sharpened on his bat-
    wing shoe.

193

A MORTUL PRAYER

OH! Thou that veileth from all eyes
    The glory of Thy face,
And setteth throned behind the skies
    In Thy abiding-place:
Though I but dimly reco'nize
    Thy purposes of grace;
And though with weak and waver-
    ing
    Deserts, and vex'd with fears,
I lift the hands I can not wring
    All dry of sorrow's tears,
Make puore my prayers that daily wing
    Theyr way unto Thy ears!

Oh! with the hand that tames the flood
  And smooths the storm to rest,
Make ba'mmy dews of all the blood
  That stormeth in my brest,
And so refresh my hart to bud
  And bloom the loveliest.
Lull all the clammer of my soul
  To silunce; bring release
Unto the brane still in controle
  Of doubts; bid sin to cease,
And let the waves of pashun roll
  And kiss the shores of peace.

Make me to love my feller man—
  Yea, though his bitterness
Doth bite as only adders can—
  Let *me* the fault confess,
And go to him and clasp his hand
  And love him none the less.
So keep me, Lord, ferever free
  From vane concete er whim;
And he whose pius eyes can see
  My faults, however dim,—
Oh! let him pray the least fer me,
  And me the most fer him.

194

A ROUGH SKETCH

I CAUGHT, for a second, across the
      crowd—
Just for a second, and barely that—
A face, pox-pitted and evil-browed,
  Hid in the shade of a slouch-rim'd
      hat—
    With small gray eyes, of a look as
        keen
    As the long, sharp nose that grew
        between.

And I said: 'Tis a sketch of Nature's
      own,
  Drawn i' the dark o' the moon, I
      swear,
On a tatter of Fate that the winds have
      blown
  Hither and thither and everywhere—
    With its keen little sinister eyes of
        gray,
    And nose like the beak of a bird
        of prey!

195

GRANDFATHER SQUEERS

"MY grandfather Squeers," said
      The Raggedy Man,
As he solemnly lighted his pipe and
      began—

"The most indestructible man, for his
      years,
And the grandest on earth, was my
    grandfather Squeers!

"He said, when he rounded his three-
      score-and-ten,
'I've the hang of it now and can do it
    again!'

"He had frozen his heels so repeatedly,
      he
Could tell by them just what the
    weather would be;

"And would laugh and declare, 'while
    the Almanac would
Most falsely prognosticate, *he* never
    could!'

"Such a hale constitution had grand-
father Squeers
That, though he'd used *'navy'* for sixty-
odd years,

"He still chewed a dime's worth six
days of the week,
While the seventh he passed with a
chew in each cheek.

"Then my grandfather Squeers had a
singular knack
Of sitting around on the small of his
back.

"With his legs like a letter Y stretched
o'er the grate
Wherein 'twas his custom to ex-pec-tor-
ate.

"He was fond of tobacco in *manifold*
ways,
And would sit on the door-step, of
sunshiny days,

"And smoke leaf-tobacco he'd raised
strictly for
The pipe he'd used all through the
Mexican War."

And The Raggedy Man said, refilling
the bowl
Of his *own* pipe and leisurely picking
a coal

From the stove with his finger and
thumb, "You can see
What a tee-nacious habit he's fastened
on me!

"And my grandfather Squeers took a
special delight
In pruning his corns every Saturday
night

"With a horn-handled razor, whose
edge he excused
By saying 'twas one that his grand-
father used;

"And, though deeply etched in the
haft of the same
Was the ever-euphonious Wostenholm's
name,

" 'Twas my grandfather's custom to
boast of the blade
As 'a Seth Thomas razor—the best ever
made!'

"No Old Settlers' Meeting, or Pioneers'
Fair,
Was complete without grandfather
Squeers in the chair,

"To lead off the program by telling
folks how
'He used to shoot deer where the
Court-house stands now'—

"How 'he felt, of a truth, to live over
the past,
When the country was wild and un-
broken and vast,

" 'That the little log cabin was just
plenty fine
For himself, his companion, and fam-
bly of nine!—

" 'When they didn't have even a pump,
or a tin,
But drunk surface-water, year out and
year in,

" 'From the old-fashioned gourd that
was sweeter, by odds,
Than the goblets of gold at the lips of
the gods!' "

Then The Raggedy Man paused to
    plaintively say
It was clockin' along to'rds the close
    of the day—

And he'd *ought* to get back to his
    work on the lawn,—
Then dreamily blubbered his pipe and
    went on:

"His teeth were imperfect—my grand-
    father owned
That he couldn't eat oysters unless
    they were 'boned';

"And his eyes were so weak, and so
    feeble of sight,
He couldn't sleep with them unless,
    every night,

"He put on his spectacles—all he pos-
    sessed,—
Three pairs—with his goggles on top
    of the rest.

"And my grandfather always, retiring
    at night,
Blew down the lamp-chimney to put
    out the light;

"Then he'd curl up on edge like a
    shaving, in bed,
And puff and smoke pipes in his sleep,
    it is said:

"And would snore oftentimes, as the
    legends relate,
Till his folks were wrought up to a
    terrible state,—

"Then he'd snort, and rear up, and
    roll over; and there
In the subsequent hush they could hear
    him chew air.

"And so glaringly bald was the top of
    his head
That many's the time he has musingly
    said,

"As his eyes journeyed o'er its reflex in
    the glass,—-
'I must set out a few signs of *Keep Off
    the Grass!'*

"So remarkably deaf was my grand-
    father Squeers
That he had to wear lightning-rods
    over his ears

"To even hear thunder—and often-
    times then
He was forced to request it to thunder
    again."

196

MY LADDIE WI' THE BASHFU' GRACE

MY laddie wi' the bashfu' grace,
    That darena spak the tender loe
That glints o'er a' thy bonny face
    Like winter sunset on the snow,—
Gin ye wad only tak my hand,
    And ask, wi' pressure fond and
        true,
My heart—my heart wad understand,
    And gie its loe to you.

But sin' ye winna spak me free,
    Or darena tak the langin' tip
O' ain puir finger,—come to me
    In mirk o' nicht and touch my lip—
Then a' the glowin' universe
    Will bloom wi' stars, and flow'rs,
        and a',
And God's ain sel' abide wi' us,
    Nor ever gang awa'.

197

A TRESS OF HAIR

THIS tress of hair my sweetheart
        sent to me,
And so I bent above it tenderly
    And kissed the dainty bow
That bound the wisp of sunshine,
        thrilled forsooth,
Because her lips had nestled there—in
        truth,
    She told me so.

And I remember, reading that, the
        flush
That fevered all my face, and the
        heart's hush
    And hurry in my ears;
And how the letter trembled and grew
        blurred
Until my eyes could read no other
        word—
    For happy tears.

This tress of hair! Why, I did hug and
        hold
It here against my heart, and call it
        gold
    With Heaven's own luster lit;
And I did stroke and smooth its gleam-
        ing strands,
And pet and fondle it with foolish
        hands,
    And talk to it!

And now I pray God's blessing may
        alight
Upon the orange flowers she wears to-
        night.
    Her features—keep them fair,
Dear Lord, but let her lips not quite
        forget

The love they kindled once is gilding
        yet
This tress of hair.

198

THE PASSING OF A HEART

O TOUCH me with your hands—
        For pity's sake!
My brow throbs ever on with such an
        ache
As only your cool touch may take
        away;
And so, I pray
    You, touch me with your
        hands!

Touch—touch me with your hands.—
        Smooth back the hair
You once caressed, and kissed, and
        called so fair
That I did dream its gold would wear
        alway,
And lo, to-day—
    O touch me with your hands!

Just touch me with your hands,
        And let them press
My weary eyelids with the old caress,
Aud lull me till I sleep. Then go
        your way,
That Death may say:
    He touched her with his
        hands.

199

AN OLD-TIMER

HERE where the wayward stream
        Is restful as a dream,
    And where the banks o'erlook

A pool from out whose deeps
My pleased face upward peeps,
    I cast my hook.

Silence and sunshine blent!—
A Sabbath-like content
    Of wood and wave;—a free-
Hand landscape grandly wrought
Of Summer's brightest thought
    And mastery.—

For here form, light and shade,
And color—all are laid
    With skill so rarely fine,
The eye may even see
The ripple tremblingly
    Lip at the line.

I mark the dragon-fly
Flit waveringly by
    In ever-veering flight,
Till, in a hush profound,
I see him eddy round
    The "cork," and—'light!

Ho! with the boy's faith then
Brimming my heart again,
    And knowing, soon or late,
The "nibble" yet shall roll
Its thrills along the pole,
    I—breathless—wait.

200

ERE I WENT MAD

ERE I went mad—
    O you may never guess what
        dreams I had!
Such hosts of happy things did come
    to me.
One time, it seemed, I knelt at some
    one's knee,

My wee lips threaded with a strand of
    prayer,
With kinks of kisses in it here and
    there
To stay and tangle it the while I knit
A mother's long-forgotten name in it.
Be sure, I dreamed it all, but I was
    glad
—Ere I went mad!

Ere I went mad,
I dreamed there came to me a fair-
    faced lad,
Who led me by the wrist where blos-
    soms grew
In grassy lands, and where the skies
    were blue
As his own eyes. And he did lisp and
    sing,
And weave me wreaths where I sat
    marveling
What little prince it was that crowned
    me queen
And caught my face so cunningly be-
    tween
His dimple-dinted hands, and kept me
    glad
—Ere I went mad!

Ere I went mad,
Not even winter weather made me sad.
I dreamed, indeed, the skies were ne'er
    so dull
That *his* smile might not make them
    beautiful.
And now, it seemed, he had grown O
    so fair
And straight and strong that, when he
    smoothed my hair,
I felt as any lily with drooped head
That leans, in fields of grain unhar-
    vested,

By some lithe stalk of barley—pure
and glad
—Ere I went mad!

Ere I went mad,
The last of all the happy dreams I had
Was of a peerless king—a conqueror—
Who crowned me with a kiss, and
throned me for
One hour! Ah, God of Mercy! what
a dream
To tincture life with! Yet I made no
scream
As I awakened—with these eyes you
see,
That may not smile till love comes
back to me,
And lulls me back to those old dreams
I had
—Ere I went mad!

Through the coils like the blood in the
veins of a man:
And from dark silken billows that
girdled her free,
Her shoulder welled up like the moon
from the sea.

Oh, her beauty was such, as I knelt,
with the tips
Of the fingers uplifted she snatched
from my lips,
And saw the white flood of her wrath
as it dashed
O'er the features, that one moment
later had flashed
From my vision forever, I raised not
a knee
Till I had thanked God for so rescu-
ing me.

201

OH, HER BEAUTY

OH, her beauty was such that it
dazzled my eyes
Like a dreamer's, who, gazing in day-
dying skies,
Sees the snow of the clouds and the
gold of the sun
And the blue of the heavens all
blended in one
Indescribable luster of glorious light,
Swooning into the moon of a mid-
summer night.

Oh, her beauty was such that I
fancied her hair
Was a cloud of the tempest, tied up
with a glare
Of pale purple lightning, that darted
and ran

202

THE SUMMER-TIME

O THE Summer-time to-day
Makes my words
Jes' flip up and fly away
Like the birds!
—'Tain't no use to try to sing,
With yer language on the
wing,
Jes' too glad fer anything
But to stray
Where it may
Thue the sunny summer weather of
the day!

Lordy! what a Summer-time
Fer to sing!
But my words flops out o' rhyme,
And they wing
Furder yit beyent the view

Than the swallers ever flew,
Er a mortal wanted to—
'Less his eye
Struck the sky
Ez he kind o' sort o' thought he'd like
to fly!

Ef I *could* sing—sweet and low—
And my tongue
Could *twitter,* don't you know,—
Ez I sung
Of the Summer-time, 'y Jings!
All the words and birds and
things
That kin warble, and hes
wings,
Would jes' swear
And declare
That they never heerd sich singin'
anywhere!

203

SONG OF PARTING

SAY farewell, and let me go:
Shatter every vow!
All the future can bestow
Will be welcome now!
And if this fair hand I touch
I have worshiped overmuch,
It was my mistake—and so,
Say farewell, and let me go.

Say farewell, and let me go:
Murmur no regret,
Stay your tear-drops ere they flow—
Do not waste them yet!
They might pour as pours the
rain,
And not wash away the pain:—

I have tried them and I know.—
Say farewell, and let me go.

Say farewell, and let me go:
Think me not untrue—
True as truth is, even so
I am true to you!
If the ghost of love may stay
Where my fond heart dies to-day,
I am with you alway—so,
Say farewell, and let me go.

204

THE WANDERING JEW

THE stars are failing, and the sky
Is like a field of faded flowers
The winds on weary wings go by;
The moon hides, and the tempest
lowers;
And still through every clime
and age
I wander on a pilgrimage
That all men know an idle
quest,
For that the goal I seek is—
REST!

I hear the voice of summer streams,
And, following, I find the brink
Of cooling springs, with childish
dreams
Returning as I bend to drink—
But suddenly, with startled
eyes,
My face looks on its grim dis-
guise
Of long gray beard; and so, dis-
tressed,
I hasten on, nor taste of rest.

I come upon a merry group
Of children in the dusky wood,
Who answer back the owlet's whoop,
That laughs as it had understood;
    And I would pause a little
        space,
    But that each happy blossom-
        face
    Is like to one *His* hands have
        blessed
    Who sent me forth in search of
        rest.

Sometimes I fain would stay my feet
In shady lanes, where huddled kine
Couch in the grasses cool and sweet,
    And lift their patient eyes to mine;
    But I, for thoughts that ever
        then
    Go back to Bethlehem again,
    Must needs fare on my weary
        quest,
    And weep for very need of rest.

Is there no end? I plead in vain:
Lost worlds nor living answer me.
Since Pontius Pilate's awful reign
    Have I not passed eternity?
    Have I not drunk the fetid
        breath
    Of every fevered phase of death,
    And come unscathed through
        every pest
    And scourge and plague that
        promised rest?

Have I not seen the stars go out
    That shed their light o'er Galilee,
And mighty kingdoms tossed about
    And crumbled clod-like in the sea?
    Dead ashes of dead ages blow
    And cover me like drifting
        snow,

And time laughs on as 'twere a
    jest
That I have any need of rest.

205

THE USED-TO-BE

BEYOND the purple, hazy trees
    Of summer's utmost boundaries;
Beyond the sands—beyond the seas—
Beyond the range of eyes like these,
    And only in the reach of the
    Enraptured gaze of Memory,
    There lies a land, long lost to me,—
    The land of Used-to-be!

A land enchanted—such as swung
In golden seas when sirens clung
Along their dripping brinks, and sung
To Jason in that mystic tongue
    That dazed men with its melody—
    O such a land, with such a sea
    Kissing its shores eternally,
    Is the fair Used-to-be.

A land where music ever girds
The air with belts of singing-birds,
And sows all sounds with such sweet
    words,
That even in the low of herds
    A meaning lives so sweet to me,
    Lost laughter ripples limpidly
    From lips brimmed over with the
        glee
    Of rare old Used-to-be.

Lost laughter, and the whistled tunes
Of boyhood's mouth of crescent runes,
That rounded, through long after-
    noons,
To serenading plenilunes—

When starlight fell so mistily
That, peering up from bended knee,
I dreamed 'twas bridal drapery
Snowed over Used-to-be.

O land of love and dreamy thoughts,
And shining fields, and shady spots
Of coolest, greenest grassy plots,
Embossed with wild forget-me-nots!—
And all ye blooms that longingly
Lift your fair faces up to me
Out of the past, I kiss in ye
The lips of Used-to-be.

206

AT UTTER LOAF

I

AN afternoon as ripe with heat
As might the golden pippin be
With mellowness if at my feet
It dropped now from the apple-tree
My hammock swings in lazily.

II

The boughs about me spread a shade
That shields me from the sun, but
weaves
With breezy shuttles through the
leaves
Blue rifts of skies, to gleam and fade
Upon the eyes that only see
Just of themselves, all drowsily.

III

Above me drifts the fallen skein
Of some tired spider, looped and
blown,

As fragile as a strand of rain,
Across the air, and upward thrown
By breaths of hay-fields newly
mown—
So glimmering it is and fine,
I doubt these drowsy eyes of mine.

IV

Far-off and faint as voices pent
In mines, and heard from under-
ground,
Come murmurs as of discontent,
And clamorings of sullen sound
The city sends me, as, I guess,
To vex me, though they do but bless
Me in my drowsy fastnesses.

V

I have no care. I only know
My hammock hides and holds me
here
In lands of shade a prisoner:
While lazily the breezes blow
Light leaves of sunshine over me,
And back and forth and to and fro
I swing, enwrapped in some hushed
glee,
Smiling at all things drowsily.

207

MY OLD FRIEND

YOU'VE a manner all so mellow,
My old friend,
That it cheers and warms a fellow,
My old friend,
Just to meet and greet you, and
Feel the pressure of a hand
That one may understand,
My old friend.

Though dimmed in youthful splendor,
    My old friend,
Your smiles are still as tender,
    My old friend,
And your eyes as true a blue
As your childhood ever knew,
And your laugh as merry, too,
    My old friend.

For though your hair is faded,
    My old friend,
And your step a trifle jaded,
    My old friend,
Old Time, with all his lures
In the trophies he secures,
Leaves young that heart of yours,
    My old friend.

And so it is you cheer me,
    My old friend,
For to know you and be near you,
    My old friend,
Makes my hopes of clearer light,
And my faith of surer sight,
And my soul a purer white,
    My old friend.

208

KISSING THE ROD

O HEART of mine, we shouldn't
    Worry so!
What we've missed of calm we couldn't
    Have, you know!
What we've met of stormy pain,
And of sorrow's driving rain,
We can better meet again,
    If it blow!

We have erred in that dark hour
    We have known,

When our tears fell with the shower,
    All alone!—
Were not shine and shower blent
As the gracious Master meant?—
Let us temper our content
    With His own.

For, we know, not every morrow
    Can be sad;
So, forgetting all the sorrow
    We have had,
Let us fold away our fears,
And put by our foolish tears,
And through all the coming years
    Just be glad.

209

THE RIVAL

I SO loved once, when Death came
    by I hid
    Away my face,
And all my sweetheart's tresses she
    undid
    To make my hiding-place.

The dread shade passed me thus un-
    heeding; and
    I turned me then
To calm my love—kiss down her
    shielding hand
    And comfort her again.

And lo! she answered not: And she
    did sit
    All fixedly,
With her fair face and the sweet smile
    of it,
    In love with Death, not me.

210

THE LIGHT OF LOVE

SONG

THE clouds have deepened o'er the
   night
Till, through the dark profound,
The moon is but a stain of light,
   And all the stars are drowned;
And all the stars are drowned, my
      love,
   And all the skies are drear;
But what care we for light above,
   If light of love is here?

The wind is like a wounded thing
   That beats about the gloom
With baffled breast and drooping
      wing,
   And wail of deepest doom;
And wail of deepest doom, my love;
   But what have we to fear
From night, or rain, or winds above,
   With love and laughter here?

211

LET SOMETHING GOOD BE
SAID

WHEN over the fair fame of
   friend or foe
The shadow of disgrace shall fall,
      instead
Of words of blame, or proof of thus
      and so,
   Let something good be said.

Forget not that no fellow-being yet
   May fall so low but love may lift
      his head:

Even the cheek of shame with tears
      is wet,
   If something good be said.

No generous heart may vainly turn
      aside
   In ways of sympathy; no soul so
      dead
But may awaken strong·and glorified,
   If something good be said.

And so I charge ye, by the thorny
      crown,
   And by the cross on which the
      Saviour bled,
And by your own soul's hope of fair
      renown,
   Let something good be said!

212

THE OLD HAND-ORGAN

HARSH-VOICED it was, and shrill
   and high,
   With hesitating stops and stutters,
As though the vagrant melody,
   Playing so long about the gutters,
   Had been infected with some low
   Malignant type of vertigo.

A stark-eyed man that stared the sun
   Square in the face, and without
      winking;
His soldier cap pushed back, and one
   Scarred hand that grasped the
      crank, unshrinking—
   But from the jingling discord
      made
   By shamefaced pennies as he
      played.

213

HOME AT NIGHT

WHEN chirping crickets fainter
cry,
And pale stars blossom in the sky,
And twilight's gloom has dimmed the
bloom
And blurred the butterfly:

When locust-blossoms fleck the walk,
And up the tiger-lily stalk
The glowworm crawls and clings and
falls
And glimmers down the garden-walls:

When buzzing things, with double
wings
Of crisp and raspish flutterings,
Go whizzing by so very nigh
One thinks of fangs and stings:—

O then, within, is stilled the din
Of crib she rocks the baby in,
And heart and gate and latch's weight
Are lifted—and the lips of Kate.

214

A DREAM OF INSPIRATION

TO loll back, in a misty hammock,
swung
From tip to tip of a slim crescent
moon
That gems some royal-purple night
of June—
To dream of songs that never have
been sung
Since the first stars were stilled and
God was young

And Heaven as lonesome as a lone-
some tune:
To lie thus, lost to earth, with lids
aswoon;
By curious, cool winds back and for-
ward flung,
With fluttering hair, blurred eyes,
and utter ease
Adrift like lazy blood through every
vein;
And then,—the pulse of unvoiced
melodies
Timing the raptured sense to some re-
frain
That knows nor words, nor rhymes,
nor euphonies,
Save Fancy's hinted chime of un-
known seas.

215

THE PIPER'S SON

IN olden days there dwelt a piper's
son,
Hight Thomas, who, belike from in-
digence,
Or utter lack of virtuous preference
Of honorable means of thrift, did,
one
Weak hour of temptation—(weaker
none!)—
Put by ye promptings of his better
sense,
And rashly gat him o'er a neighbor's
fence
Wherein ye corner was a paling run
About a goodly pig; and thence he
lured,
All surreptitiously, ye hapless beast,
And had it slaughtered, salted down,
and cured—

Yea, even tricked and garnished for
  ye feast,
Ere yet ye red-eyed Law had him im-
  mured,
And round and soundly justice-of-
  ye-peaced.

216

HIS LAST PICTURE

THE skies have grown troubled and
  dreary;
The clouds gather fold upon fold;
The hand of the painter is weary
And the pencil has dropped from its
  hold:
The easel still leans in the grasses,
  And the palette beside on the lawn,
But the rain o'er the sketch as it passes
  Weeps low—for the artist is gone.

The flowers whose fairy-like features
  Smiled up in his own as he wrought,
And the leaves and the ferns were his
    teachers,
  And the tints of the sun what they
    taught;
The low-swinging vines, and the
    mosses—
  The shadow-filled boughs of the
    trees,
And the blossomy spray as it tosses
  The song of the bird to the breeze.

The silent white laugh of the lily
  He learned; and the smile of the
    rose
Glowed back on his spirit until he
  Had mastered the blush as it glows;
And his pencil has touched and
  caressed them,

And kissed them, through breaths
  of perfume,
To the canvas that yet shall have
  blessed them
With years of unwithering bloom.

Then come!—Leave his palette and
  brushes
And easel there, just as his hand
Has left them, ere through the dark
  hushes
Of death, to the shadowy land,
He wended his way, happy-hearted
  As when, in his youth, his rapt eyes
Swept the pathway of Fame where it
    started,
  To where it wound into the skies.

217

A VARIATION

I AM tired of this!
  Nothing else but loving!
Nothing else but kiss and kiss,
  Coo, and turtle-doving!
    Can't you change the order some?
    Hate me just a little—come!

Lay aside your "dears,"
  "Darlings," "kings," and "princes!"
Call me knave, and dry your tears—
  Nothing in me winces,—
    Call me something low and base—
    Something that will suit the case!

Wish I had your eyes
  And their drooping lashes!
I would dry their teary lies
  Up with lightning-flashes—
    Make your sobbing lips unsheathe
    All the glitter of your teeth!

Can't you lift one word—
  With some pang of laughter—
Louder than the drowsy bird
Crooning 'neath the rafter?
  Just one bitter word, to shriek
  Madly at me as I speak!

How I hate the fair
  Beauty of your forehead!
How I hate your fragrant hair!
How I hate the torrid
  Touches of your splendid lips,
  And the kiss that drips and drips!

Ah, you pale at last!
  And your face is lifted
Like a white sail to the blast,
  And your hands are shifted
  Into fists: and, towering thus,
  You are simply glorious!

Now before me looms
  Something more than human;
Something more than beauty blooms
  In the wrath of Woman—
  Something to bow down before
  Reverently and adore.

218

THERE IS A NEED

THERE is a need for every ache or
    pain
  That falls unto our lot. No heart
    may bleed
That resignation may not heal again
    And teach us—there's a need.

There is a need for every tear that
    drips
  Adown the face of sorrow. None
    may heed,

But weeping washes whiter on the lips
  Our prayers—and there's a
    need.

There is a need for weariness and
    dearth
Of all that brings delight. At top-
    most speed
Of pleasure sobs may break amid our
    mirth
  Unheard—and there's a need.

There is a need for all the growing
    load
Of agony we bear as years succeed;
For lo, the Master's footprints in the
    road
  Before us—There's a need.

219

TO A SKULL

TURN your face this way;
  I'm not weary of it—
Every hour of every day
  More and more I love it—
Grinning in that jolly guise
Of bare bones and empty eyes!

Was this hollow dome,
  Where I tap my finger,
Once the spirit's narrow home—
  Where you loved to linger,
Hiding, as to-day are we,
From the selfsame destiny?

O'er and o'er again
  Have I put the query—
Was existence so in vain
  That you look so cheery?—
Death of such a benefit
That you smile, possessing it?

Did your throbbing brow
  Tire of all the flutter
Of such fancyings as now
  You, at last, may utter
In that grin so grimly bland
Only death can understand?

Has the shallow glee
  Of old dreams of pleasure
Left you ever wholly free
  To float out, at leisure,
O'er the shoreless, trackless trance
Of unsounded circumstance?

Only this I read
  In your changeless features,—
You, at least, have gained a meed
  Held from living creatures:
You have naught to ask.—Beside,
You do grin so satisfied!

220

THE VOICES

DOWN in the night I hear them:
  The Voices—unknown—un-
      guessed,—
That whisper, and lisp, and murmur,
  And will not let me rest.—

Voices that seem to question,
  In unknown words, of me,
Of fabulous ventures, and hopes and
      dreams
  Of this and the World to be.

Voices of mirth and music,
  As in sumptuous homes; and sounds
Of mourning, as of gathering friends
  In country burial-grounds.

Cadence of maiden voices—
  Their lovers' blent with these;
And of little children singing,
  As under orchard trees.

And often, up from the chaos
  Of my deepest dreams, I hear
Sounds of their phantom laughter
  Filling the atmosphere:

They call to me from the darkness;
  They cry to me from the gloom,
Till I start sometimes from my pillow
  And peer through the haunted room;

When the face of the moon at the
      window
  Wears a pallor like my own,
And seems to be listening with me
  To the low, mysterious tone,—

The low, mysterious clamor
  Of voices that seem to be
Striving in vain to whisper
  Of secret things to me;—

Of a something dread to be warned of;
  Of a rapture yet withheld;
Or hints of the marvelous beauty
  Of songs unsyllabled.

But ever and ever the meaning
  Falters and fails and dies,
And only the silence quavers
  With the sorrow of my sighs.

And I answer:—O Voices, ye may not
  Make me to understand
Till my own voice, mingling with you,
  Laughs in the Shadow-land.

221

MY HENRY

H E'S jes' a great, big, awk'ard,
    hulkin'
Feller,—humped, and sort o' sulkin'-
Like, and ruther still-appearin'—
Kind-as-ef he wuzn't keerin'
    Whether school helt out er not—
    That's my Henry, to a dot!

Allus kind o' liked him—whether
Childern, er growed-up together!
Fifteen year' ago and better,
'Fore he ever knowed a letter,
    Run acrosst the little fool
    In my Primer-class at school.

When the Teacher wuzn't lookin',
He'd be th'owin' wads; er crookin'
Pins; er sprinklin' pepper, more'n
Likely, on the stove; er borin'
    Gimlet-holes up thue his desk—
    Nothin' *that* boy wouldn't resk!

But, somehow, as I was goin'
On to say, he seemed so knowin',
Other ways, and cute and cunnin'—
Allus wuz a notion runnin'
    Thue my giddy, fool-head he
    Jes' had be'n cut out fer me!

Don't go much on *prophesyin'*,
But last night whilse I wuz fryin'
Supper, with that man a-pitchin'
Little Marthy round the kitchen,
    Think-says-I, "Them baby's eyes
    Is my Henry's, jes' p'cise!"

222

LOVE'S AS BROAD AS LONG

L OOKY here!—you fellers—you
    Poets I'm a-talkin' to,—
Allus rhymin', right er wrong,
'Bout your "little" love, and "long"—
'Pears to me 'at nary one
Of you fellers gits much fun
Out o' lovin'—tryin' to fit
Out some fool-receet fer it!—
    Love's as broad as long!

Now, I 'low 'at love's a thing
You cain't jes' set down and sing
Out your order fer, and say
You'll hev yourn a certain way;
And how "long" a slice you'll take,
Er how short—'cause love don't make
No distinctions, and you'll find,
When it comes, it's all one kind—
    Jes' as broad as long!

Fust, one of you'll p'tend
"Love's no idle song," and send
Up his voice in jes' the song
He's th'owed up on—"Love me long!"
Now, they hain't no womern needs
No sich talk as that!—er heeds
Sich advice as would infer
You hed any doubts o' her!
    Love's as broad as long.

Ner I don't see any use,
Er occasion, er excuse
Fer some other chap to say,
In his passioneter way,
"Love me madly, as of yore!"—
'Cause I've seed sich love afore,
'At got fellers down, and jes'
Wooled 'em round till they confessed
    Love was broad as long.

No; I'll tell you: You jes' let
Love alone, and you kin bet,
When the time comes, Love'll be
Right on hands as punctchully
As he was the day Eve sot
Waitin', in the gyarden-spot,
Fer ole Adam jes' to go
On ahead and tell her so!
    Love's as broad as long!

223

LOCKERBIE STREET

SUCH a dear little street it is, nestled
    away
From the noise of the city and heat of
    the day,
In cool shady coverts of whispering
    trees,
With their leaves lifted up to shake
    hands with the breeze
Which in all its wide wanderings never
    may meet
With a resting-place fairer than Lock-
    erbie Street!

There is such a relief, from the clangor
    and din
Of the heart of the town, to go loiter-
    ing in
Through the dim, narrow walks, with
    the sheltering shade
Of the trees waving over the long
    promenade,
And littering lightly the ways of our
    feet
With the gold of the sunshine of Lock-
    erbie Street.

And the nights that come down the
    dark pathways of dusk,

With the stars in their tresses, and
    odors of musk
In their moon-woven raiments, be-
    spangled with dews,
And looped up with lilies for lovers to
    use
In the songs that they sing to the
    tinkle and beat
Of their sweet serenadings through
    Lockerbie Street.

O my Lockerbie Street! You are fair
    to be seen—
Be it noon of the day, or the rare and
    serene
Afternoon of the night—you are one to
    my heart,
And I love you above all the phrases of
    art,
For no language could frame and no
    lips could repeat
My rhyme-haunted raptures of Lock-
    erbie Street.

224

THE OLD, OLD WISH

LAST night, in some lost mood of
        meditation,
    The while my dreamy vision ranged
        the far
Unfathomable arches of creation,
    I saw a falling star:

And as my eyes swept round the path
        it embered
    With the swift-dying glory of its
        glow,
With sudden intuition I remembered
    A wish of long ago—

A wish that, were it made—so ran the
　　fancy
Of credulous young lover and of
　　lass—
As fell a star, by some strange necro-
　　mancy,
　　Would surely come to pass.

And, of itself, the wish, reiterated
A thousand times in youth, flashed
　　o'er my brain,
And, like the star, as soon obliterated,
　　Dropped into night again.

For my old heart had wished for the
　　unending
Devotion of a little maid of nine—
And that the girl-heart, with the
　　woman's blending,
　　Might be forever mine.

And so it was, with eyelids raised, and
　　weighty
With ripest clusterings of sorrow's
　　dew,
I cried aloud through Heaven: "O
　　little Katie!
　　When will my wish come
　　true?"

225

A LIFE-LESSON

THERE! little girl; don't cry!
　　They have broken your doll, I
　　know;
　　And your tea-set blue,
　　And your play-house, too,
Are things of the long ago;
　　But childish troubles will soon
　　pass by.—
　　There! little girl; don't cry!

There! little girl; don't cry!
　　They have broken your slate, I
　　know;
　　And the glad, wild ways
　　Of your schoolgirl days
Are things of the long ago;
　　But life and love will soon come
　　by.—
　　There! little girl; don't cry!

There! little girl; don't cry!
　　They have broken your heart, I
　　know;
　　And the rainbow gleams
　　Of your youthful dreams
Are things of the long ago;
　　But Heaven holds all for which
　　you sigh.—
　　There! little girl; don't cry!

226

A WATER-COLOR

LOW hidden in among the forest
　　trees
An artist's tilted easel, ankle-deep
In tousled ferns and mosses, and in
　　these
A fluffy water-spaniel, half asleep
　　Beside a sketch-book and a fallen
　　hat—
　　A little wicker flask tossed into
　　that.

A sense of utter carelessness and grace
Of pure abandon in the slumb'rous
　　scene,—
As if the June, all hoydenish of face,
　　Had romped herself to sleep there on
　　the green,

And brink and sagging bridge and
sliding stream
Were just romantic parcels of her
dream.

227

UNKNOWN FRIENDS

O FRIENDS of mine, whose kindly
words come to me
Voiced only in lost lisps of ink and
pen,
If I had power to tell the good you do
me,
And how the blood you warm goes
laughing through me,
My tongue would babble baby-talk
again.

And I would toddle round the world
to meet you—
Fall at your feet, and clamber to
your knees
And with glad, happy hands would
reach and greet you,
And twine my arms about you, and
entreat you
For leave to weave a thousand
rhymes like these—

A thousand rhymes enwrought of
nought but presses
Of cherry-lip and apple-cheek and
chin,
And pats of honeyed palms, and rare
caresses,
And all the sweets of which as Fancy
guesses
She folds away her wings and
swoons therein.

228

THE SONG OF YESTERDAY

I

BUT yesterday
I looked away
O'er happy lands, where sunshine lay
In golden blots,
Inlaid with spots
Of shade and wild forget-me-nots.

My head was fair
With flaxen hair,
And fragrant breezes, faint and rare,
And, warm with drouth
From out the south,
Blew all my curls across my mouth.

And, cool and sweet,
My naked feet
Found dewy pathways through the
wheat;
And out again
Where, down the lane,
The dust was dimpled with the rain.

II

But yesterday!—
Adream, astray,
From morning's red to evening's gray,
O'er dales and hills
Of daffodils
And lorn sweet-fluting whippoorwills.

I knew nor cares
Nor tears nor prayers—
A mortal god, crowned unawares
With sunset—and
A scepter-wand
Of apple-blossoms in my hand!

The dewy blue
Of twilight grew
To purple, with a star or two
Whose lisping rays
Failed in the blaze
Of sudden fireflies through the haze.

III

But yesterday
I heard the lay
Of summer birds, when I, as they
With breast and wing,
All quivering
With life and love, could only sing.

My head was leant
Where, with it, blent
A maiden's, o'er her instrument;
While all the night,
From vale to height,
Was filled with echoes of delight.

And all our dreams
Were lit with gleams
Of that lost land of reedy streams,
Along whose brim
Forever swim
Pan's lilies, laughing up at him.

IV

But yesterday! . . .
O blooms of May,
And summer roses—where away?
O stars above;
And lips of love,
And all the honeyed sweets thereof!—

O lad and lass,
And orchard pass,
And briered lane, and daisied grass!

O gleam and gloom,
And woodland bloom,
And breezy breaths of all perfume!—

No more for me
Or mine shall be
Thy raptures,—save in memory,—
No more—no more—
Till through the Door
Of Glory gleam the days of yore.

229

AN END

GO away from me—do! I am tired
of you!—
That I loved you last May isn't this
season, too;
And, you know, every spring there's
a new bird to sing
In the nest of the old, and a ghost on
the wing!

Now, don't you assert that I'm simply a
flirt—
And it's babyish for you to say that I
hurt,
And my words are a dart, when they're
only a part
Of your own fickle nature committed
to heart.

It was all a mistake, and I don't want
to make
The silly thing over for your silly
sake—
Though I really once may have been
such a dunce
As to fancy you loved me, some far-
away months.

So, go away—do! I am tired clean
through,
And you can't make me even feel sorry
for you—
For, with us, every spring there's a
new bird to sing
In the nest of the old, and a ghost on
the wing.

230

HER CHOICE

"MY love or hate—choose which
you will,"
He says; and o'er the window-sill
The rose-bush, jostled by the wind,
Rasps at his hands, close-clenched be-
hind,
As she makes answer, smiling clear
As is the day,—"Your hate, my dear!"

An interval of silence—so
Intensely still, the cattle's low
Across the field's remotest rim
Comes like a near moan up to him,
While o'er the open sill once more
The rose-bush rasps him as before.

Then, with an impulse strange and
new
To him, he says: " 'Tis wise of you
To choose thus—for by such a choice
You lose so little, that,"—his voice
Breaks suddenly—the rose-bush stirs—
But ah! his hands are—safe in hers.

231

OUR OWN

THEY walk here with us, hand in
hand;
We gossip, knee by knee;

They tell us all that they have
planned—
Of all their joys to be,—
And, laughing, leave us: And, to-day,
All desolate we cry
Across wide waves of voiceless graves—
Good-by! Good-by! Good-by!

232

THE DRUM

O THE drum!
There is some
Intonation in thy grum
Monotony of utterance that strikes the
spirit dumb,
As we hear
Through the clear
And unclouded atmosphere,
Thy palpitating syllables roll in upon
the ear!

There's a part
Of the art
Of thy music-throbbing heart
That thrills a something in us that
awakens with a start,
And in rhyme
With the chime
And exactitude of time,
Goes marching on to glory to thy mel-
ody sublime.

And the guest
Of the breast
That thy rolling robs of rest
Is a patriotic spirit as a Continental
dressed;
And he looms
From the glooms
Of a century of tombs,
And the blood he spilled at Lexington
in living beauty blooms.

And his eyes
    Wear the guise
        Of a purpose pure and wise,
As the love of them is lifted to a some-
            thing in the skies
That is bright
    Red and white,
        With a blur of starry light,
As it laughs in silken ripples to the
        breezes day and night.

There are deep
    Hushes creep
        O'er the pulses as they leap,
As thy tumult, fainter growing, on the
            silence falls asleep,
While the prayer
    Rising there
        Wills the sea and earth and
            air
As a heritage to Freedom's sons and
        daughters everywhere.

Then, with sound
    As profound
        As the thunderings resound,
Come thy wild reverberations in a throe
            that shakes the ground,
And a cry
    Flung on high,
        Like the flag it flutters by,
Wings rapturously upward till it nes-
        tles in the sky.

O the drum!
    There is some
        Intonation in thy grum
Monotony of utterance that strikes the
            spirit dumb,
As we hear,
    Through the clear
        And unclouded atmosphere,
Thy palpitating syllables roll in upon
        the ear!

233

A CASE IN P'INT

WE don't go much on lawin'
    Here in around the mines?—
Well, now, you're jest hurrahin'
    Like the wind amongst the pines!
Of course we allus aim to
    Give "the prisoner" a chance—
Though sometimes a jury's game to
    Ring a verdict in advonce!

What wuz his name—this feller
    'At stold the Jedge's mare
Last spring?—wuz tryin' to sell her
    Down here at Rip and Tear,
When "Faro Bill" dropped on him,
    And bagged him, sound and good
And biznesslike, dog-gone him,
    As the constable a-could!

Well, anyway, his trial
    Wuz a case in p'int:—He pled
"Not guilty"—a denial
    'At his attorney said
Could be substantiated
    On the grounds, 'at when the mare
Wuz "stold," as claimed and stated,
    The defendant wuzn't square,—

But he'd be'n a testifyin',
    Round the raw edge of a spree
At Stutsman's bar, a-tryin'
    To hold one drink in three,
To "Jim-jams"; and he reckoned
    'At his client's moral tone
Could not be classed as second
    To the Jedge's—er his own.

"That savin'-clause is timely,"
    Says the Jedge, a-turnin' back
To color as sublimely
    As I've seed him turn a jack.—

"But," says he to the defendant,
"Ef you didn't 'steal' the mare
I'll ask ef your attendant
'Pharos William,' didn't swear

"You *wuzn't* 'full' when captured?"
Then, a-drawin' of his gun,
The Jedge went on, enraptured
With the trail 'at he'd begun,—
"I'll tax your re-collection
To enquire ef you know
That hoss left my protection
On'y jes' five hours ago?—

"In consequence, it follers,
No man as drunk as you—
And I'll bet a hundred dollars
To the opposition's two!—
Could sober to the beauty
Of the standerd you present
This writin'—hence my duty
Plainly is—to circumvent—"

And afore the jury knowed it,
Bang! his gun went!—"And I'll
       ask,"
He went on, as he th'owed it
Up to finish out his task,
"Ef it's mortal?"—then, betrayin'
Some emotion, with a bow,
He closed by simply sayin'—
"You can take the witness now!"

234

OLE BULL

DEAD; IN BERGEN, NORWAY;
AUGUST 18, 1880

THE minstrel's mystic wand
    Has fallen from his hand;
Stilled is the tuneful shell;

The airs he used to play
For us but yesterday
Have failed and died away
    In sad farewell.

Forgive—O noble heart,
Whose pure and gracious art
    Enraptured, all these years,
Sang sweet, and sweeter yet
Above all sounds that fret,
And all sobs of regret—
    Forgive our tears!

Forgive us, weeping thus
That thou art gone from us—
    Because thy song divine,
Too, with the master, gone,
Leaves us to listen on
In silence till the dawn
    That now is thine.

235

A WRAITH OF SUMMER-TIME

IN its color, shade and shine,
    'Twas a summer warm as wine,
With an effervescent flavoring of
    flowered bough and vine,
And a fragrance and a taste
Of ripe roses gone to waste,
And a dreamy sense of sun- and moon-
    and starlight interlaced.

'Twas a summer such as broods
O'er enchanted solitudes,
Where the hand of Fancy leads us
    through voluptuary moods,
And with lavish love outpours
All the wealth of out-of-doors,
And woos our feet o'er velvet paths and
    honeysuckle floors.

'Twas a summer-time long dead,—
And its roses, white and red,
And its reeds and water-lilies down
    along the river-bed,—
O they all are ghostly things—
For the ripple never sings,
And the rocking lily never even rustles
    as it rings!

236

JACK THE GIANT-KILLER

Bad Boy's Version

TELL you a story—an' it's a fac':—
    Wunst wuz a little boy, name wuz
        Jack,
An' he had sword an' buckle an' strap
Maked of gold, an' a " 'visibul cap";
An' he killed Gi'nts 'at et whole cows—
Th' horns an' all—an' pigs an' sows!
But Jack, his golding sword wuz, oh!
So awful sharp 'at he could go
An' cut th' ole Gi'nts clean in two
'Fore 'ey knowed what he wuz goin'
    to do!
An' *one* ole Gi'nt, he had four
Heads, an' name wuz "Bumblebore"—
An' he wuz feared o' Jack—'cause he,
Jack, he killed six—five—ten—three,
An' all o' th' uther ole Gi'nts but him:
An' thay wuz a place Jack haf to swim
'Fore he could git t' ole "Bumble-
    bore"—
Nen thay wuz "griffuns" at the door:
But Jack, he thist plunged in an' swum
Clean acrost; an' when he come
To th' uther side, he thist put on
His " 'visibul cap," an' nen, dog-gone!
You couldn't see him at all!—An' so
He slewed the "griffuns"—*boff,* you
    know!

Nen wuz a horn hunged over his head,
High on th' wall, an' words 'at read,—
"Whoever kin this trumput blow
Shall cause the Gi'nt's overth'ow!"
An' Jack, he thist reached up an'
    blowed
The stuffin' out of it! an' th'owed
Th' castul gates wide open, an'
Nen tuk his gold sword in his han',
An' thist marched in t' ole "Bumble-
    bore,"
An', 'fore he knowed, he put 'bout four
Heads on him—an' chopped 'em off,
    too!—
Wisht 'at *I'd* been Jack!—don't you?

237

REQUIESCAT

BE it life, be it death, there is nearing
    the dawn of a glorious day,
When the murmurs of doubt we are
    hearing
    In silence shall dwindle away;
And the hush and content that we
    covet—
    The rest that we need, and the sleep
That abides with the eyelids that love
    it,
    Shall come as we weep.

We shall listen no more to the sobbing
Of sorrowing lips, and the sound
In our pillows at night of the throb-
    bing
Of feverish hearts will have found
The quiet beyond understanding,
    The rush and the moan of the rain,
That shall beat on the shingles, de-
    manding
    Admittance in vain.

The hand on the dial shall number
  The hours unmarked; and the bell
Shall waken us not from the slumber
  That knows neither tolling of knell
Nor the peals of glad melody showered
  Like roses of song o'er the pave
Where the bride and the groom walk
    their flowered
  Green way to the grave.

In that dawn, when it breaks, we shall
    wonder
No more why the heavens send back
To our prayers but the answer of thun-
    der,
  And the lightning-scrawl, writ on the
    black
Of the storm in a language no mortal
  May read till his questioning sight
Shall have pierced through the inner-
    most portal
  Of death to the light.

238

AT SEA

YEA, we go down to sea in ships—
    But Hope remains behind,
And Love, with laughter on his lips,
    And Peace, of passive mind;
While out across the deeps of night,
    With lifted sails of prayer,
We voyage off in quest of light,
    Nor find it anywhere.

O Thou who wroughtest earth and
    sea,
    Yet keepest from our eyes
The shores of an eternity
    In calms of Paradise,

Blow back upon our foolish quest
  With all the driving rain
Of blinding tears and wild unrest,
  And waft us home again!

239

SOMEP'N COMMON-LIKE

SOMEP'N 'at's common-like, and
    good
And plain, and easy understood;
Somep'n 'at folks like me and you
Kin understand, and relish, too,
And find some sermint in 'at hits
The spot, and sticks and benefits.

We don't need nothin' extry fine;
'Cause, take the run o' minds like
    mine,
And we'll go more on good horse-
    sense
Than all your flowery eloquence;
And we'll jedge best of honest acts
By Nature's statement of the facts.

So when you're wantin' to express
Your misery, er happiness,
Er anything 'at's wuth the time
O' telling in plain talk er rhyme—
Jes' sort o' let your subject run
As ef the Lord wuz listenun.

240

BLIND

YOU think it is a sorry thing
    That I am blind. Your pitying
Is welcome to me; yet indeed,
I think I have but little need

Of it. Though you may marvel much
That *we,* who see by sense of touch
And taste and hearing, see things *you*
May never look upon; and true
Is it that even in the scent
Of blossoms *we* find something meant
No eyes have in their faces read,
Or wept to see interpreted.

And you might think it strange if now
I told you you were smiling. How
Do I know that? I hold your hand—
Its language I can understand—
Give both to me, and I will show
You many other things I know.
Listen: We never met before
Till now?—Well, you are something
　　lower
Than five-feet-eight in height; and you
Are slender; and your eyes are blue—
Your mother's eyes—your mother's
　　hair—
Your mother's likeness everywhere
Save in your walk—and that is quite
Your father's; nervous.—Am I right?
I thought so. And you used to sing,
But have neglected everything
Of vocalism—though you may
Still thrum on the guitar, and play
A little on the violin,—
I know that by the callus in
The finger-tips of your left hand—
And, by the by, though nature planned
You as most men, you are, I see,
"*Left*-handed," too,—the mystery
Is clear, though,—your right arm has
　　been
Broken, to "break" the left one in.
And so, you see, though blind of sight,
I still have ways of seeing quite
Too well for you to sympathize
Excessively, with your good eyes.—
Though *once,* perhaps, to be sincere,

Within the whole asylum here,
From cupola to basement hall,
I was the blindest of them all!

Let us move farther down the walk—
The man here waiting hears my talk,
And is disturbed; besides, he may
Not be quite friendly anyway.
In fact—(this will be far enough;
Sit down)—the man just spoken of
Was once a friend of mine. He came
For treatment here from Burlingame—
A rich though brilliant student there,
Who read his eyes out of repair,
And groped his way up here, where
　　we
Became acquainted, and where he
Met one of our girl-teachers, and,
If you'll believe me, asked her hand
In marriage, though the girl was blind
As I am—and the girl *declined.*
Odd, wasn't it? Look, you can see
Him waiting there. Fine, isn't he?
And handsome, eloquently wide
And high of brow, and dignified
With every outward grace, his sight
Restored to him, clear and bright
As day-dawn; waiting, waiting still
For the blind girl that never will
Be wife of his. How do I know?
You will recall a while ago
I told you he and I were friends.
In all that friendship comprehends,
I *was* his friend, I swear! why, now,
Remembering his love, and how
His confidence was all my own,
I hear, in fancy, the low tone
Of his deep voice, so full of pride
And passion, yet so pacified
With his affliction, that it seems
An utterance sent out of dreams
Of saddest melody, withal
So sorrowfully musical

It was, and is, must ever be—
But I'm digressing, pardon me.
I knew not anything of love
In those days, but of that above
All worldly passion,—for my art—
Music,—and that, with all my heart
And soul, blent in a love too great
For words of mine to estimate.
And though among my pupils she
Whose love my friend sought came to
    me,
I only knew her fingers' touch
Because they loitered overmuch
In simple scales, and needs must be
Untangled almost constantly.
But she was bright in other ways,
And quick of thought; with ready plays
Of wit, and with a voice as sweet
To listen to as one might meet
In any oratorio—
And once I gravely told her so,—
And, at my words, her limpid tone
Of laughter faltered to a moan,
And fell from that into a sigh
That quavered all so wearily,
That I, without the tear that crept
Between the keys, had known she
    wept;
And yet the hand I reached for then
She caught away, and laughed again.
And when that evening I strolled
With my old friend, I, smiling, told
Him I believed the girl and he
Were matched and mated perfectly:
He was so noble; she, so fair
Of speech, and womanly of air;
He, strong, ambitious; she, as mild
And artless even as a child;
And with a nature, I was sure,
As worshipful as it was pure
And sweet, and brimmed with tender
    things
Beyond his rarest fancyings.

He stopped me solemnly. He knew,
He said, how good, and just, and true
Was all I said of her; but as
For his own virtues, let them pass,
Since they were nothing to the one
That he had set his heart upon;
For but that morning she had turned
Forever from him. Then I learned
That for a month he had delayed
His going from us, with no aid
Of hope to hold him,—meeting still
Her ever-firm denial, till
Not even in his new-found sight
He found one comfort or delight.
And as his voice broke there, I felt
The brother-heart within me melt
In warm compassion for his own
That throbbed so utterly alone.
And then a sudden fancy hit
Along my brain; and coupling it
With a belief that I, indeed,
Might help my friend in his great need,
I warmly said that I would go
Myself, if he decided so,
And see her for him—that I knew
My pleadings would be listened to
Most seriously, and that she
Should love him, listening to me.
Go; bless me! And that was the last—
The last time his warm hand shut fast
Within my own—so empty since,
That the remembered finger-prints
I've kissed a thousand times, and wet
Them with the tears of all regret!

I know not how to rightly tell
How fared my quest, and what befell
Me, coming in the presence of
That blind girl, and her blinder love.
I know but little else than that
Above the chair in which she sat
I leant—reached for, and found her
    hand,

And held it for a moment, and
Took up the other—held them both—
As might a friend, I will take oath:
Spoke leisurely, as might a man
Praying for no thing other than
He thinks Heaven's justice:—She was
    blind,
I said, and yet a noble mind
Most truly loved her; one whose fond
Clear-sighted vision looked beyond
The bounds of her infirmity,
And saw the woman, perfectly
Modeled, and wrought out pure and
    true
And lovable. She quailed, and drew
Her hands away, but closer still
I caught them. "Rack me as you will!"
She   cried   out   sharply—"Call   me
    'blind'—
Love ever is—I am resigned!
Blind is your friend; as blind as he
Am I—but blindest of the three—
Yea, blind as death—you will not see
My love for you is killing me!"

There is a memory that may
Not ever wholly fade away
From out my heart, so bright and
    fair
The light of it still glimmers there.
Why, it did seem as though my sight
Flamed back upon me, dazzling white
And godlike. Not one other word
Of hers I listened for or heard,
But I *saw* songs sung in her eyes
Till they did swoon up drowning-wise,
As my mad lips did strike her own,
And we flashed one, and one alone!
Ah! was it treachery for me
To kneel there, drinking eagerly
That torrent-flow of words that swept
Out laughingly the tears she wept?—

Sweet words! O sweeter far, maybe,
Than light of day to those that see,—
God knows, who did the rapture send
To me, and hold it from my friend.
And we were married half a year
Ago.—And he is—waiting here,
Heedless of that—or anything,
But just that he is lingering
To say good-by to her, and bow—
As you may see him doing now,—
For there's her footstep in the hall;
God bless her!—help him!—save us
    all!

241

JUST AS OF OLD

JUST as of old! The world rolls on
    and on;
The day dies into night—night into
    dawn—
Dawn into dusk—through centuries
    untold.—
    Just as of old.

Time loiters not. The river ever flows,
Its brink of white with blossoms or
    with snows;
Its tide or warm with spring or winter
    cold:
    Just as of old.

Lo! where is the beginning, where the
    end
Of living, loving, longing? *Listen,*
    friend!—
God answers with a silence of pure
    gold—
    Just as of old.

242

THE PRAYER PERFECT

DEAR Lord! kind Lord!
Gracious Lord! I pray
Thou wilt look on all I love,
Tenderly to-day!
Weed their hearts of weariness;
Scatter every care
Down a wake of angel-wings
Winnowing the air.

Bring unto the sorrowing
All release from pain;
Let the lips of laughter
Overflow again;
And with all the needy
O divide, I pray,
This vast treasure of content
That is mine to-day!

243

MONSIEUR LE SECRETAIRE

[JOHN CLARK RIDPATH]

MON cher Monsieur le Secretaire,
Your song flits with me every-
where;
It lights on Fancy's prow and sings
Me on divinest voyagings:
And when my ruler love would fain
Be laid upon it—high again
It mounts, and hugs itself from me
With rapturous wings—still dwindling-
ly—
On!—on! till but a *ghost* is there
Of song, Monsieur le Secretaire!

244

A PHANTOM

LITTLE baby, you have wandered
far away,
And your fairy face comes back to me
to-day,
But I can not feel the strands
Of your tresses, nor the play
Of the dainty velvet-touches of your
hands.

Little baby, you were mine to hug and
hold;
Now your arms cling not about me as
of old—
O my dream of rest come true,
And my richer wealth than gold,
And the surest hope of Heaven that
I knew!

O for the lisp long silent, and the
tone
Of merriment once mingled with my
own—
For the laughter of your lips,
And the kisses plucked and thrown
In the lavish wastings of your finger-
tips!

Little baby, O as then, come back to
me,
And be again just as you used to
be,
For this phantom of you stands
All too cold and silently,
And will not kiss nor touch me with
its hands.

245

WHAT REDRESS

I PRAY you, do not use this thing
    For vengeance; but if questioning
What wound, when dealt your human-
    kind,
Goes deepest,—surely he will find
Who wrongs *you,* loving *him* no less—
There's nothing hurts like tenderness.

246

A LOST LOVE

'TWAS a summer ago when he left
    me here—
A summer of smiles, with never a tear
Till I said to him, with a sob, my
    dear,—
    Good-by, my lover; good-by!

For I loved him, O as the stars love
    night!
And my cheeks for him flashed red and
    white
When first he called me his Heart's de-
    light,—
    Good-by, my lover; good-by!

The touch of his hand was a thing di-
    vine
As he sat with me in the soft moon-
    shine
And drank of my love as men drink
    wine,—
    Good-by, my lover; good-by!

And never a night as I knelt in prayer,
In thought as white as our own souls
    were,

But in fancy he came and he kissed me
    there,—
    Good-by, my lover; good-by!

But now—ah, *now!* what an empty
    place
My whole heart is!—Of the old em-
    brace
And the kiss I loved there lives no
    trace—
    Good-by, my lover; good-by!

He sailed not over the stormy sea,
And he went not down in the waves—
    not he—
But O, he is lost—for he married me—
    Good-by, my lover; good-by!

247

LET US FORGET

LET us forget. What matters it that
    we
Once reigned o'er happy realms of
    long ago,
And talked of love, and let our voices
    low,
And ruled for some brief sessions roy-
    ally?
What if we sung, or laughed, or wept
    maybe?
It has availed not anything, and so
Let it go by that we may better know
How poor a thing is lost to you and
    me.
But yesterday I kissed your lips, and
    yet
Did thrill you not enough to shake the
    dew
From your drenched lids—and
    missed, with no regret,

Your kiss shot back, with sharp breaths
    failing you:
And so, to-day, while our worn eyes
    are wet
With all this waste of tears, let us
    forget!

248

THE SHOEMAKER

THOU Poet, who, like any lark,
    Dost whet thy beak and trill
From misty morn till murky dark,
    Nor ever pipe thy fill:
Hast thou not, in thy cheery note,
    One poor chirp to confer—
One verseful twitter to devote
    Unto the Shoe-ma-ker?

At early dawn he doth peg in
    His noble work and brave;
And eke from cark and worldly sin
    He seeketh soles to save;
And all day long, with quip and song,
    Thus stitcheth he the way
Our feet may know the right from
    wrong
    Nor ever go astray.

Soak kip in mind the Shoe-ma-ker,
    Nor slight his lasting frame:
Alway he waxeth tenderer
    In warmth of our acclaim;—
Ay, more than any artisan
    We glory in his art
Who ne'er, to help the under man,
    Neglects the upper part.

But toe the mark for him, and heel
    Respond to thee in kine—
Or kid—or calf, shouldst thou reveal
    A taste so superfine:

Thus let him jest—join in his laugh—
    Draw on his stock, and be
A shoer'd there's no rival half-
    Sole liberal as he.

Then, Poet, hail the Shoe-ma-ker
    For all his goodly deeds,—
Yea, bless him free for booting thee—
    The first of all thy needs!
And when at last his eyes grow dim,
    And nerveless drops his clamp,
In golden shoon pray think of him
    Upon his latest tramp.

249

IN THE CORRIDOR

AH! at last alone, love!
    Now the band may play
Till its sweetest tone, love,
    Swoons and dies away!
They who most will miss us
    We're not caring for—
Who of them could kiss us
    In the corridor?

Had we only known, dear,
    Ere this long delay,
Just how all alone, dear,
    We might waltz away,
. Then for hours, like this, love,
    We are longing for,
We'd have still to kiss, love,
    In the corridor!

Nestle in my heart, love;
    Hug and hold me close—
Time will come to part, love,
    Ere a fellow knows;
There! the Strauss is ended—
    Whirl across the floor,
Isn't waltzing splendid
    In the corridor?

250

SUSPENSE

A WOMAN'S figure, on a ground
   of night
Inlaid with sallow stars that dimly
   stare
Down in the lonesome eyes, uplifted
   there
As in vague hope some alien lance of
   light
Might pierce their woe. The tears that
   blind her sight—
The salt and bitter blood of her
   despair—
Her hands toss back through tor-
   rents of her hair
And grip toward God with anguish
   infinite.
And O the carven mouth, with all
   its great
Intensity of longing frozen fast
In such a smile as well may desig-
   nate
The slowly murdered heart, that, to
   the last,
Conceals each newer wound, and
   back at Fate
Throbs Love's eternal lie—"Lo, I
   can wait!"

251

A NONSENSE RHYME

RINGLETY-JING!
   And what will we sing?
Some little crinkety-crankety thing
   That rhymes and chimes,
   And skips, sometimes,
As though wound up with a kink in
   the spring.

Grunkety-krung!
And chunkety-plung!
Sing the song that the bullfrog sung,—
   A song of the soul
   Of a mad tadpole
That met his fate in a leaky bowl:
And it's O for the first false wiggle he
   made
In a sea of pale pink lemonade!
   And it's O for the thirst
   Within him pent,
   And the hopes that burst
   As his reason went—
When his strong arm failed and his
   strength was spent!

   Sing, O sing
Of the things that cling,
And the claws that clutch and the
   fangs that sting—
   Till the tadpole's tongue
   And his tail upflung
Quavered and failed with a song un-
   sung!
   O the dank despair in the
   rank morass,
   Where the crawfish crouch in
   the cringing grass,
   And the long limp rune of the loon
   wails on
   For the mad, sad soul
   Of a bad tadpole
      Forever lost and gone!

   Jinglety-jee!
   And now we'll see
What the last of the lay shall be,
   As the dismal tip of the tune, O
   friends,
   Swoons away and the long tale
   ends.
   And it's O and alack!
   For the tangled legs

And the spangled back
　　Of the green grig's eggs,
And the unstrung strain
　　Of the strange refrain
That the winds wind up like a strand
　　of rain!

And it's O,
　　Also,
For the ears wreathed low,
Like a laurel-wreath on the lifted brow
Of the frog that chants of the why and
　　how,
　　And the wherefore too, and the
　　　thus and so
　　Of the wail he weaves in a woof
　　　of woe!
Twangle, then, with your wrangling
　　strings,
The tinkling links of a thousand
　　things!
And clang the pang of a maddening
　　moan
Till the Echo, hid in a land unknown,
　　Shall leap as he hears, and hoot
　　and hoo
　　　Like the wretched wraith of a
　　　Whoopty-Doo!

252

LOUELLA WAINIE

LOUELLA WAINIE! where are
　　you?
Do you not hear me as I cry?
Dusk is falling; I feel the dew;
　　And the dark will be here by and
　　by:
　　I hear no thing but the owl's hoo-
　　hoo! .
Louella Wainie! where are you?

Hand in hand to the pasture bars
　　We came loitering, Lou and I,
Long ere the fireflies coaxed the stars
　　Out of their hiding-place on high.
　　O how sadly the cattle moo!
Louella Wainie! where are you?

Laughingly we parted here—
　　"I will go this way," said she,
"And you will go that way, my dear"—
　　Kissing her dainty hand at me—
　　And the hazels hid her from my
　　view.
Louella Wainie! where are you?

Is there ever a sadder thing
　　Than to stand on the farther brink
Of twilight, hearing the marsh-frogs
　　sing?
　　Nothing could sadder be, I think!
　　And ah! how the night-fog chills
　　one through.
Louella Wainie! where are you?

Water-lilies and oozy leaves—
　　Lazy bubbles that bulge and stare
Up at the moon through the gloom it
　　weaves
　　Out of the willows waving there!
　　Is it despair I am wading through?
Louella Wainie! where are you?

Louella Wainie, listen to me,
　　Listen, and send me some reply,
For so will I call unceasingly
　　Till death shall answer me by and
　　by—
　　Answer, and help me to find you
　　too!
Louella Wainie! where are you?

253

FOR YOU

FOR you, I could forget the gay
  Delirium of merriment,
And let my laughter die away
In endless silence of content.
  I could forget, for your dear sake,
  The utter emptiness and ache
  Of every loss I ever knew.—
  What could I not forget for you?

I could forget the just deserts
  Of mine own sins, and so erase
The tear that burns, the smile that
    hurts,
  And all that mars and masks my
    face.
    For your fair sake I could for-
      get
    The bonds of life that chafe and
      fret,
    Nor care if death were false or
      true.—
    What could I not forget for you?

What could I not forget? Ah me!
  One thing I know would still abide
Forever in my memory,
    Though all of love were lost be-
      side—
    I yet would feel how first the
      wine
    Of your sweet lips made fools of
      mine
    Until they sung, all drunken
      through—
    "What could I not forget for
      you?"

254

MY FIRST SPECTACLES

AT first I laughed—for it was quite
  An oddity to see
My reflex looking from the glass
Through spectacles at me.

But as I gazed I really found
  They so improved my sight
That many wrinkles in my face
  Were mixed with my delight;

And many streaks of silver, too,
  Were gleaming in my hair,
With quite a hint of baldness that
  I never dreamed was there.

And as I readjusted them
  And winked in slow surprise,
A something like a mist had come
  Between them and my eyes.

And, peering vainly still, the old
  Optician said to me,
The while he took them from my nose
  And wiped them hastily:

"Jes' now, of course, your eyes is apt
  To water some—but where
Is any man's on earth that won't
  The first he has to wear?"

255

THE TEXT

THE text: Love thou thy fellow
  man!
  He may have sinned;—One proof
  indeed,

He is thy fellow, reach thy hand
And help him in his need!

Love thou thy fellow man. He may
Have wronged thee—then, the less
    excuse
Thou hast for wronging him. Obey
What he has dared refuse!

Love thou thy fellow man—for, be
His life a light or heavy load,
No less he needs the love of thee
To help him on his road.

256

AN OUT-WORN SAPPHO

HOW tired I am! I sink down all
    alone
Here by the wayside of the Present.
    Lo,
Even as a child I hide my face and
    moan—
A little girl that may no farther go:
The path above me only seems to
    grow
    More rugged, climbing still, and
        ever briered
With keener thorns of pain than
    these below;
And O the bleeding feet that falter
    so
And are so very tired!

Why, I have journeyed from the far-off
    Lands
Of Babyhood—where baby-lilies
    blew
Their trumpets in mine ears, and filled
    my hands

With treasures of perfume and
    honey-dew,
And where the orchard shadows
    ever drew
Their cool arms round me when
    my cheeks were fired
With too much joy, and lulled mine
    eyelids to,
And only let the starshine trickle
    through
In sprays, when I was tired!

Yet I remember, when the butterfly
    Went flickering about me like a
        flame
That quenched itself in roses suddenly,
    How oft I wished that *I* might blaze
        the same,
And in some rose-wreath nestle with
    my name,
    While all the world looked on it
        and admired.—
Poor moth!—Along my wavering
    flight toward fame
The winds drive backward, and my
    wings are lame
    And broken, bruised and tired!

I hardly know the path from those old
    times;
    I know at first it was a smoother one
Than this that hurries past me now,
    and climbs
So high, its far cliffs even hide the
    sun
And shroud in gloom my journey
    scarce begun.
    I could not do quite all the world
        required—
    I could not do quite all I should
        have done,
And in my eagerness I have outrun
    My strength—and I am tired. . . .

Just tired! But when of old I had the
    stay
Of mother-hands, O very sweet in-
    deed
It was to dream that all the weary way
    I should but follow where I now
        must lead—
For long ago they left me in my
    need,
    And, groping on alone, I tripped
        and mired
Among rank grasses where the ser-
    pents breed
In knotted coils about the feet of
    speed.—
    There first it was I tired.

And yet I staggered on, and bore my
    load
Right gallantly: The sun, in sum-
    mer-time,
In lazy belts came slipping down the
    road
To woo me on, with many a glim-
    mering rhyme
Rained from the golden rim of
    some fair clime,
    That, hovering beyond the clouds,
        inspired
My failing heart with fancies so
    sublime
I half forgot my path of dust and
    grime,
    Though I was growing tired.

And there were many voices cheering
    me:
I listened to sweet praises where the
    wind
Went laughing o'er my shoulders glee-
    fully
And scattering my love-songs far be-
    hind;—

Until, at last, I thought the world
    so kind—
So rich in all my yearning soul
    desired—
So generous—so loyally inclined,
I grew to love and trust it. . . . I
    was blind—
    Yea, blind as I was tired!

And yet one hand held me in crea-
    ture-touch:
And O, how fain it was, how true
    and strong,
How it did hold my heart up like a
    crutch,
Till, in my dreams, I joyed to walk
    along
The toilsome way, contented with
    a song—
    'Twas all of earthly things I had
        acquired,
And 'twas enough, I feigned, or
    right or wrong,
Since, binding me to man—a mortal
    thong—
    It stayed me, growing tired. . . .

Yea, I had e'en resigned me to the strait
Of earthly rulership—had bowed
    my head
Acceptant of the master-mind—the
    great
One lover—lord of all,—the per-
    fected
Kiss-comrade of my soul;—had
    stammering said
    My prayers to him;—all—all that
        he desired
I rendered sacredly as we were
    wed.—
Nay—nay!—'twas but a myth I
    worshipèd.—
    And—God of love!—how tired!

For, O my friends, to lose the latest
grasp—
To feel the last hope slipping from
its hold—
To feel the one fond hand within your
clasp
Fall slack, and loosen with a touch
so cold
Its pressure may not warm you as
of old
Before the light of love had thus
expired—
To know your tears are worthless,
though they rolled
Their torrents out in molten drops
of gold.—
God's pity! I am tired!

And I must rest.—Yet do not say "She
died,"
In speaking of me, sleeping here
alone.
I kiss the grassy grave I sink beside,
And close mine eyes in slumber all
mine own:
Hereafter I shall neither sob nor
moan
Nor murmur one complaint;—all
I desired,
And failed in life to find, will now
be known—
So let me dream. Good night! And
on the stone
Say simply: She was tired.

257

WILLIAM BROWN

"HE bore the name of William
Brown"—
His name, at least, did not go down

With him that day
He went the way
Of certain death where duty lay.

He looked his fate full in the face—
He saw his watery resting-place
Undaunted, and
With firmer hand
Held others' hopes in sure com-
mand.—

The hopes of full three hundred
lives—
Aye, babes unborn, and promised
wives!
"The odds are dread,"
He must have said,
"Here, God, is one poor life in-
stead."

No time for praying overmuch—
No time for tears, or woman's touch
Of tenderness,
Or child's caress—
His last "God bless them!" stopped
at "bless"—

Thus man and engine, nerved with
steel,
Clasped iron hands for woe or weal,
And so went down
Where dark waves drown
All but the name of William Brown.

258

THE NINE LITTLE GOBLINS

THEY all climbed up on a high
board-fence—
Nine little goblins, with green-glass
eyes—
Nine little goblins that had no sense,

And couldn't tell coppers from cold
　　mince pies;
And they all climbed up on the
　　fence, and sat—
And I asked them what they were
　　staring at.

And the first one said, as he scratched
　　his head
With a queer little arm that reached
　　out of his ear
And rasped its claws in his hair so
　　red—
"This is what this little arm is fer!"
　　And he scratched and stared, and
　　　the next one said,
　　"How on earth do *you* scratch
　　　your head?"

And he laughed like the screech of a
　　rusty hinge—
Laughed and laughed till his face
　　grew black;
And when he choked, with a final
　　twinge
Of his stifling laughter, he thumped
　　his back
　　With a fist that grew on the end
　　　of his tail
　　Till the breath came back to his
　　　lips so pale.

And the third little goblin leered
　　round at me—
And there were no lids on his eyes
　　at all,—
And he clucked one eye, and he says,
　　says he,
　　"What is the style of your socks this
　　　fall?"
　　And he clapped his heels—and I
　　　sighed to see
　　That he had hands where his feet
　　　should be.

Then a bald-faced goblin, gray and
　　grim,
Bowed his head, and I saw him slip
His eyebrows off, as I looked at him,
And paste them over his upper lip;
　　And then he moaned in remorse-
　　　ful pain—
　　"Would—Ah, would I'd me brows
　　　again!"

And then the whole of the goblin band
　　Rocked on the fence-top to and fro,
And clung, in a long row, hand in
　　hand,
　　Singing the songs that they used to
　　　know—
　　Singing the songs that their
　　　grandsires sung
　　In the goo-goo days of the goblin-
　　　tongue.

And ever they kept their green-glass
　　eyes
Fixed on me with a stony stare—
Till my own grew glazed with a dread
　　surmise,
　　And my hat whooped up on my
　　　lifted hair,
　　And I felt the heart in my breast
　　　snap to,
　　As you've heard the lid of a snuff-
　　　box do.

And they sang: "You're asleep! There
　　is no board-fence,
And never a goblin with green-glass
　　eyes!—
'Tis only a vision the mind invents
　　After a supper of cold mince pies.—
　　And you're doomed to dream this
　　　way," they said,—
　　"*And you shan't wake up till
　　　you're clean plum dead!*"

259

WHY

WHY are they written—all these
      lovers' rhymes?
I catch faint perfumes of the blos-
      soms white
That maidens drape their tresses
      with at night,
And, through dim smiles of beauty
      and the din
Of the musicians' harp and violin,
I hear, enwound and blended with
      the dance,
The voice whose echo is this utter-
      ance,—
Why are they written—all these lovers'
      rhymes?

Why are they written—all these lovers'
      rhymes?
I see but vacant windows, curtained
      o'er
With webs whose architects forever-
      more
Race up and down their slender
      threads to bind
The buzzing fly's wings whirless,
      and to wind
The living victim in his winding
      sheet.—
I shudder, and with whispering lips
      repeat,
Why are they written—all these lovers'
      rhymes?

Why are they written—all these lovers'
      rhymes?
What will you have for answer?—
      Shall I say
That he who sings the merriest
      roundelay

Hath neither joy nor hope?—and
      he who sings
The lightest, sweetest, tenderest of
      things
But utters moan on moan of keen-
      est pain,
So aches his heart to ask and ask
      in vain,
Why are they written—all these lovers'
      rhymes?

260

THE TOUCH OF LOVING
HANDS

IMITATED

LIGHT falls the rain-drop on the
      fallen leaf,
And light o'er harvest-plain and gar-
      nered sheaf—
   But lightlier falls the touch of lov-
      ing hands.

Light falls the dusk of mild midsum-
      mer night,
And light the first star's faltering lance
      of light
   On glimmering lawns,—but lightlier
      loving hands.

And light the feathery flake of early
      snows,
Or wisp of thistle-down that no wind
      blows,
   And light the dew,—but lightlier
      loving hands.

Light-falling dusk, or dew, or sum-
      mer rain,

Or down of snow or thistle—all are
    vain,—
Far lightlier falls the touch of lov-
    ing hands.

261

THE OLD SCHOOL-CHUM

HE puts the poem by, to say
    His eyes are not themselves to-
day!

A sudden glamour o'er his sight—
A something vague, indefinite—

An oft-recurring blur that blinds
The printed meaning of the lines,

And leaves the mind all dusk and dim
In swimming darkness—strange to
    him!

It is not childishness, I guess,—
Yet something of the tenderness

That used to wet his lashes when
A boy seems troubling him again;—

The old emotion, sweet and wild,
That drove him truant when a child,

That he might hide the tears that fell
Above the lesson—"Little Nell."

And so it is he puts aside
The poem he has vainly tried

To follow; and, as one who sighs
In failure, through a poor disguise

Of smiles, he dries his tears, to say
His eyes are not themselves to-day.

262

A CUP OF TEA

I HAVE sipped, with drooping lashes,
    Dreamy draughts of Verzenay;
I have flourished brandy-smashes
    In the wildest sort of way;
I have joked with "Tom and Jerry"
    Till "wee hours ayont the twal"—
But I've found my tea the very
    Safest tipple of them all!

'Tis a mystical potation
    That exceeds in warmth of glow
And divine exhilaration
    All the drugs of long ago—
All of old magicians' potions—
    Of Medea's philtered spells—
Or of fabled isles and oceans
    Where the Lotos-eater dwells!

Though I've reveled o'er late lunches
    With blasé dramatic stars,
And absorbed their wit and punches
    And the fumes of their cigars—
Drank in the latest story,
    With a cocktail either end,—
I have drained a deeper glory
    In a cup of tea, my friend.

Green, Black, Moyune, Formosa,
    Congou, Amboy, Pingsuey—
No odds the name it knows—ah,
    Fill a cup of it for me!
And, as I clink my china
    Against your goblet's brim,
My tea in steam shall twine a
    Fragrant laurel round its rim.

263

TO THE SERENADER

TINKLE on, O sweet guitar,
 Let the dancing fingers
Loiter where the low notes are
Blended with the singer's:
Let the midnight pour the moon's
 Mellow wine of glory
Down upon him through the tune's
 Old romantic story!

I am listening, my love,
 Through the cautious lattice,
Wondering why the stars above
 All are blinking at us;
Wondering if his eyes from there
 Catch the moonbeam's shimmer
As it lights the robe I wear
 With a ghostly glimmer.

Lilt thy song, and lute away
 In the wildest fashion:—
Pour thy rippling roundelay
 O'er the heights of passion!—·
Flash it down the fretted strings
 Till thy mad lips, missing
All but smothered whisperings,
 Press this rose I'm kissing.

264

WHAT A DEAD MAN SAID

HEAR what a dead man said to me.
 His lips moved not, and the eye-
 lids lay
Shut as the leaves of a white rose may
Ere the wan bud blooms out perfectly;
And the lifeless hands they were stiffly
 crossed

As they always cross them over the
 breast
When the soul goes nude and the
 corpse is dressed;
And over the form, in its long sleep
 lost,
From forehead down to the pointed
 feet
That peaked the foot of the winding-
 sheet,
Pallid patience and perfect rest.—
It was the voice of a dream, may be,
But it seemed that the dead man said
 to me:
"I, indeed, am the man that died
Yesternight—and you weep for this;
But, lo, I am with you, side by side,
As we have walked when the summer
 sun
Made the smiles of our faces one,
And touched our lips with the same
 warm kiss.
Do not doubt that I tell you true—
I am the man you once called friend,
And caught my hand when I came
 to you,
And loosed it only because the end
Of the path I walked of a sudden
 stopped—
And a dead man's hand must needs
 be dropped—
And I—though it's strange to think
 so now—
I have wept, as you weep for me,
And pressed hot palms to my aching
 brow
And moaned through the long night
 ceaselessly.

Yet have I lived to forget my pain,
As you will live to be glad again—
Though never so glad as this hour
 am I,

Tasting a rapture of delight
Vast as the heavens are infinite,
And dear as the hour I came to die.
Living and loving, I dreamed my cup
Brimmed sometimes, and with marvel-
    ings
I have lifted and tipped it up
And drunk to the dregs of all sweet
    things.
Living, 'twas but a *dream* of bliss—
Now I *realize* all it is;
And now my only shadow of grief
Is that I may not give relief
Unto those living and dreaming on,
And woo them graveward, as I have
    gone,
And show death's loveliness,—for they
Shudder and shrink as they walk this
    way,
Never dreaming that all they dread
Is their purest delight when dead."

Thus it was, or it seemed to be,
That the voice of the dead man spoke
    to me.

265

A TEST

'TWAS a test I designed, in a quiet
    conceit
Of myself, and the thoroughly fixed
    and complete
Satisfaction I felt in the utter control
Of the guileless young heart of the
    girl of my soul.

So—we parted. I said it were better
    we should—
That she could forget me—I knew
    that she could;

For I never was worthy so tender a
    heart,
And so for her sake it were better to
    part.

She averted her gaze, and she sighed
    and looked sad
As I held out my hand—for the ring
    that she had—
With the bitterer speech that I hoped
    she might be
Resigned to look up and be happy
    with me.

'Twas a test, as I said—but God pity
    your grief,
At a moment like this when a smile
    of relief
Shall leap to the lips of the woman
    you prize,
And no mist of distress in her glori-
    ous eyes.

266

A SONG FOR CHRISTMAS

CHANT me a rhyme of Christ-
    mas—
Sing me a jovial song,—
And though it is filled with laughter,
Let it be pure and strong.

Let it be clear and ringing,
    And though it mirthful be,
Let a low, sweet voice of pathos
Run through the melody.

Sing of the hearts brimmed over
    With the story of the day—
Of the echo of childish voices
    That will not die away.—

Of the blare of the tasseled bugle,
  And the timeless clatter and beat
Of the drum that throbs to muster
  Squadrons of scampering feet.

But O let your voice fall fainter,
  Till, blent with a minor tone,
You temper your song with the beauty
  Of the pity Christ hath shown:

And sing one verse for the voiceless;
  And yet, ere the song be done,
A verse for the ears that hear not,
  And a verse for the sightless one:

For though it be time for singing
  A merry Christmas glce,
Let a low, sweet voice of pathos
  Run through the melody.

267

SUN AND RAIN

ALL day the sun and rain have been
  as friends,
  Each vying with the other which
    shall be
  Most generous in dowering earth and
    sea
With their glad wealth, till each, as it
  descends,
Is mingled with the other, where it
  blends
  In one warm, glimmering mist that
    falls on me
  As once God's smile fell over Galilee.
The lily-cup, filled with it, droops and
  bends
  Like some white saint beside a sylvan
    shrine

In silent prayer; the roses at my feet,
  Baptized with it as with a crimson
    wine,
Gleam radiant in grasses grown so
  sweet,
  The blossoms lift, with tenderness
    divine,
  Their wet eyes heavenward with
    these of mine.

268

WITH HER FACE

WITH her face between his hands!
  Was it any wonder she
Stood atiptoe tremblingly?
As his lips along the strands
Of her hair went lavishing
Tides of kisses, such as swing
Love's arms to like iron bands.—
With her face between his hands!

And the hands—the hands that pressed
  The glad face—Ah! where are they?
  Folded limp, and laid away
Idly over idle breast?
He whose kisses drenched her hair,
As he caught and held her there,
In Love's alien, lost lands,
With her face between his hands?

Was it long and long ago,
  When her face was not as now,
  Dim with tears? nor wan her brow
As a winter-night of snow?
Nay, anointing still the strands
Of her hair, his kisses flow
Flood-wise, as she dreaming stands,
With her face between his hands.

269

MY NIGHT

HUSH! hush! list, heart of mine,
    and hearken low!
You do not guess how tender is the
    Night,
And in what faintest murmurs of
    delight
Her deep, dim-throated utterances flow
Across the memories of long-ago!
    Hark! do your senses catch the ex-
    quisite
    Staccatos of a bird that dreams he
    sings?
Nay, then, you hear not rightly,—'tis a
    blur
Of misty love-notes, laughs and whis-
    perings
The Night pours o'er the lips that
    fondle her,
    And· that faint breeze, filled with all
    fragrant sighs,—
    That is her breath that quavers lover-
    wise—
O blessed sweetheart, with thy swart,
    sweet kiss,
Baptize me, drown me in black swirls
    of bliss!

270

THE HOUR BEFORE THE DAWN

THE hour before the dawn!
    O ye who grope therein, with
    fear and dread
And agony of soul, be comforted,
Knowing, ere long, the darkness will
    be gone,
    And down its dusky aisles the
    light be shed;

Therefore, in utter trust, fare on—fare
    on,
    This hour before the dawn!

271

THE OLD YEAR AND THE NEW

I

AS one in sorrow looks upon
    The dead face of a loyal friend,
By the dim light of New Year's dawn
I saw the Old Year end.

Upon the pallid features lay
    The dear old smile—so warm and
        bright
Ere thus its cheer had died away
    In ashes of delight.

The hands that I had learned to love
    With strength of passion half divine,
Were folded now, all heedless of
    The emptiness of mine.

The eyes that once had shed their
        bright
    Sweet looks like sunshine, now were
        dull,
And ever lidded from the light
    That made them beautiful.

II

The chimes of bells were in the air,
    And sounds of mirth in hall and
        street,
With pealing laughter everywhere
    And throb of dancing feet:

The mirth and the convivial din
    Of revelers in wanton glee,
With tunes of harp and violin
    In tangled harmony.

But with a sense of nameless dread,
　I turned me, from the merry face
Of this newcomer, to my dead;
　And, kneeling there a space,

I sobbed aloud, all tearfully:—
　By this dear face so fixed and cold,
O Lord, let not this New Year be
　As happy as the old!

272

GOOD-BY, OLD YEAR

GOOD-BY, Old Year!
　　Good-by!
We have been happy—you and I;
　We have been glad in many ways;
And now, that you have come to die,
　Remembering our happy days,
'Tis hard to say, "Good-by—
　Good-by, Old Year!
　　Good-by!"

Good-by, Old Year!
　　Good-by!
We have seen sorrow—you and I—
　Such hopeless sorrow, grief and care,
That now, that you have come to die,
　Remembering our old despair,
'Tis sweet to say, "Good-by—
　Good-by, Old Year!
　　Good-by!"

273

AS CREATED

THERE'S a space for good to bloom
　　in
Every heart of man or woman,—

And however wild or human,
　Or however brimmed with gall,
Never heart may beat without it;
And the darkest heart to doubt it
Has something good about it
　After all.

274

SOMEDAY

SOMEDAY:—So many tearful eyes
　Are watching for thy dawning
　　light;
So many faces toward the skies
　Are weary of the night!

So many failing prayers that reel
　And stagger upward through the
　　storm,
And yearning hands that reach and feel
　No pressure true and warm.

So many hearts whose crimson wine
　Is wasted to a purple stain
And blurred and streaked with drops
　　of brine
　Upon the lips of Pain.

Oh, come to them!—these weary ones!
　Or if thou still must bide a while,
Make stronger yet the hope that runs
　Before thy coming smile:

And haste and find them where they
　　wait—
　Let summer-winds blow down that
　　way,
And all they long for, soon or late,
　Bring round to them, someday.

275

FALSE AND TRUE

ONE said: "Here is my hand to
    lean upon
As long as you may need it." And
    one said:
"Believe me true to you till I am
    dead."
And one, whose dainty way it was to
    fawn
About my face, with mellow fingers
    drawn
Most soothingly o'er brow and droop-
    ing head,
Sighed tremulously: "Till my breath
    is fled
Know I am faithful!" . . . Now, all
    these are gone
And many like to them—and yet I
    make
No bitter moan above their grassy
    graves—
Alas! they are not dead for me to
    take
Such sorry comfort!—but my heart be-
    haves
Most graciously, since one who never
    spake
A vow is true to me for true love's
    sake.

276

A BALLAD FROM APRIL

I AM dazed and bewildered with liv-
    ing
A life but an intricate skein
Of hopes and despairs and thanksgiv-
    ing

Wound up and unraveled again—
Till it seems, whether waking or sleep-
    ing,
I am wondering ever the while
At a something that smiles when I'm
    weeping,
And a something that weeps when
    I smile.

And I walk through the world as one
    dreaming
Who knows not the night from the
    day,
For I look on the stars that are gleam-
    ing,
And lo, they have vanished away:
And I look on the sweet-summer day-
    light,
And e'en as I gaze it is fled,
And, veiled in a cold, misty, gray light,
The winter is there in its stead.

I feel in my palms the warm fingers
Of numberless friends—and I look,
And lo, not a one of them lingers
To give back the pleasure he took;
And I lift my sad eyes to the faces
All tenderly fixed on my own,
But they wither away in grimaces
That scorn me, and leave me alone.

And I turn to the woman that told me
Her love would live on until death—
But her arms they no longer enfold
    me,
Though barely the dew of her breath
Is dry on the forehead so pallid
That droops like the weariest thing
O'er this most inharmonious ballad
That ever a sorrow may sing.

So I'm dazed and bewildered with liv-
    ing
A life but an intricate skein

Of hopes and despairs and thanksgiv-
ing
Wound up and unraveled again—
Till it seems, whether waking or sleep-
ing,
I am wondering ever the while
At a something that smiles when I'm
weeping
And a something that weeps when I
smile.

277

WHEN DE FOLKS IS GONE

WHAT dat scratchin' at de
kitchen do'?
Done heah'n dat foh an hour er mo'!
Tell you, Mr. Niggah, das sho's you'
bo'n,
Hit's mighty lonesome waitin' when de
folks is gone!

Blame my trap! how de wind do blow!
An' dis is das de night foh de witches,
sho'!
Dey's trouble gon' to waste when de
old slut whine,
An' you heah de cat a-spittin' when de
moon don't shine!

Chune my fiddle, an' de bridge go
"bang!"
An' I lef' 'er right back whah she allus
hang,
An' de tribble snap short an' de apern
split
When dey no mortal man wah a-tetch-
in' hit!

Dah! *Now,* what? How de ole j'ice
cracks!

'Spec' dis house, ef hit tell plain fac's,
'Ud talk about de ha'nts wid dey long
tails on
What das'n't on'y come when de folks
is gone!

What I tuk an' done ef a sho'-'nuff
ghos'
Pop right up by de ole bed-pos'?
What dat shinin' fru de front do'
crack? . . .
God bress de Lo'd! hit's de folks got
back!

278

THE TWINS

ONE'S the pictur' of his Pa,
And the *other* of her Ma—
Jes' the bossest pair o' babies 'at a mor-
tal ever saw!
And we love 'em as the bees
Loves the blossoms on the trees,
A-ridin' and a-rompin' in the breeze!

One's got her Mammy's eyes—
Soft and blue as Apurl-skies—
With the same sort of a *smile,* like—
Yes, and mouth about her size,—
Dimples, too, in cheek and chin,
'At my lips jes' *wallers* in,
A-goin' to work, er gittin' home ag'in

And the *other*—Well, they say
That he's got his Daddy's way
O' bein' ruther soberfied, er ruther ex-
try gay,—
That he eether cries his best,

Er he laughs his howlin'est—
Like all he lacked was buttons and a
    vest!

Look at *her!*—and look at *him!*—
Talk about yer "Cheru-*bim!*"
Roll 'em up in dreams together, rosy
    arm and chubby limb!
O we love 'em as the bees
Loves the blossoms on the trees,
A-ridin' and a-rompin' in the breeze!

279

THE ORCHARD LANDS OF LONG AGO

THE orchard lands of Long Ago!
    O drowsy winds, awake, and blow
The snowy blossoms back to me,
And all the buds that used to be!
Blow back along the grassy ways
Of truant feet, and lift the haze
Of happy summer from the trees
That trail their tresses in the seas
Of grain that float and overflow
The orchard lands of Long Ago!

Blow back the melody that slips
In lazy laughter from the lips
That marvel much if any kiss
Is sweeter than the apple's is.
Blow back the twitter of the birds—
The lisp, the titter, and the words
Of merriment that found the shine
Of summer-time a glorious wine
That drenched the leaves that loved it
    so,
In orchard lands of Long Ago!

O memory! alight and sing
Where rosy-bellied pippins cling,

And golden russets glint and gleam,
As, in the old Arabian dream,
The fruits of that enchanted tree
The glad Aladdin robbed for me!
And, drowsy winds, awake and fan
My blood as when it overran
A heart ripe as the apples grow
In orchard lands of Long Ago!

280

BRUDDER SIMS

DAH'S Brudder Sims! Dast slam
    yo' Bible shet
    An' lef' dat man alone—kase he's de
        boss
    Ob all de preachahs ev' I come
        across!
Day's no twis' in dat gospil book, I
    bet,
Ut Brudder Sims cain't splanify, an'
    set
        You' min' at eaze! W'at's Moses an'
            de Laws?
    W'at's fo'ty days an' nights ut Noey
        toss
Aroun' de Dil-ooge?—W'at dem Chil-
    len et
De Lo'd rain down? W'at s'prise
    ole Joney so
In dat whale's inna'ds?—W'at dat lad-
    dah mean
    Ut Jacop see?—an' wha' dat laddah
        go?—
Who clim dat laddah?—Wha' dat lad-
    dah lean?—
    An' wha' dat laddah now? "Dast
        chalk yo' toe
    Wid Faith," sez Brudder Sims, "an'
        den you know!"

281

DEFORMED

CROUCHED at the corner of the
street
She sits all day, with face too white
And hands too wasted to be sweet
In anybody's sight.

Her form is shrunken, and a pair
Of crutches leaning at her side
Are crossed like homely hands in
prayer
At quiet eventide.

Her eyes—two lustrous, weary things—
Have learned a look that ever aches,
Despite the ready jinglings
The passer's penny makes.

And, noting this, I pause and muse
If any precious promise touch
This heart that has so much to lose
If dreaming overmuch—

And, in a vision, mistily
Her future womanhood appears,—
A picture framed with agony
And drenched with ceaseless tears—

Where never lover comes to claim
The hand outheld so yearningly—
The laughing babe that lisps her name
Is but a fantasy!

And, brooding thus, all swift and wild
A daring fancy, strangely sweet,
Comes o'er me, that the crippled child
That crouches at my feet—

Has found her head a resting-place
Upon my shoulder, while my kiss
Across the pallor of her face
Leaves crimson trails of bliss.

282

WHILE THE MUSICIAN PLAYED

O IT was but a dream I had
While the musician played!—
And here the sky, and here the glad
Old ocean kissed the glade;
And here the laughing ripples ran,
And here the roses grew
That threw a kiss to every man
That voyaged with the crew.

Our silken sails in lazy folds
Drooped in the breathless breeze:
As o'er a field of marigolds
Our eyes swam o'er the seas;
While here the eddies lisped and purled
Around the island's rim,
And up from out the underworld
We saw the mermen swim.

And it was dawn and middle-day
And midnight—for the moon
On silver rounds across the bay
Had climbed the skies of June,—
And there the glowing, glorious king
Of day ruled o'er his realm,
With stars of midnight glittering
About his diadem.

The sea-gull reeled on languid wing
In circles round the mast,
We heard the songs the sirens sing
As we went sailing past;
And up and down the golden sands
A thousand fairy throngs
Flung at us from their flashing hands
The echoes of their songs.

O it was but a dream I had
While the musician played!—
For here the sky, and here the glad
Old ocean kissed the glade;

And here the laughing ripples ran,
    And here the roses grew
That threw a kiss to every man
    That voyaged with the crew.

283

FAITH

THE sea was breaking at my feet,
    And looking out across the tide,
Where placid waves and heaven meet,
    I thought me of the Other Side.

For on the beach on which I stood
    Were wastes of sands, and wash, and
        roar,
Low clouds, and gloom, and solitude,
    And wrecks, and ruins—nothing
        more.

"O, tell me if beyond the sea
    A heavenly port there is!" I cried,
And back the echoes laughingly
    "There is! there is!" replied.

284

BE OUR FORTUNES AS THEY MAY

BE our fortunes as they may,
    Touched with loss or sorrow,
Saddest eyes that weep to-day
    May be glad to-morrow.

Yesterday the rain was here,
    And the winds were blowing—
Sky and earth and atmosphere
    Brimmed and overflowing.

But to-day the sun is out,
    And the drear November
We were then so vexed about
    Now we scarce remember.

Yesterday you lost a friend—
    Bless your heart and love it!—
For you scarce could comprehend
    All the aching of it;—

But I sing to you and say:
    Let the lost friend sorrow—
Here's another come to-day,
    Others may to-morrow.

285

A HINT OF SPRING

'TWAS but a hint of Spring—for
        still
The atmosphere was sharp and chill,
Save where the genial sunshine smote
The shoulders of my overcoat,
And o'er the snow beneath my feet
Laid spectral fences down the street.

My *shadow*, even, seemed to be
Elate with some new buoyancy,
And bowed and bobbed in my advance
With trippingest extravagance,
And, when the birds chirpt out some-
        where,
It seemed to wheel with me and stare.

Above I heard a rasping stir—
And on a roof the carpenter
Was perched, and prodding rusty
        leaves
From out the choked and dripping
        eaves—
And some one, hammering about,
Was taking all the windows out.

Old scraps of shingles fell before
The noisy mansion's open door;
And wrangling children raked the yard,
And labored much, and laughed as
      hard,
And fired the burning trash I smelt
And sniffed again—so good I felt!

286

LAST NIGHT—AND THIS

LAST night—how deep the darkness
      was!
And well I knew its depths, because
I waded it from shore to shore,
Thinking to reach the light no more.

She would not even touch my hand.—
The winds rose and the cedars fanned
The moon out, and the stars fled back
In heaven and hid—and all was black!

But ah! To-night a summons came,
Signed with a tear-drop for a name,—
For as I wondering kissed it, lo,
A line beneath it told me so.

And *now*—the moon hangs over me
A disk of dazzling brilliancy,
And every star-tip stabs my sight
With splintered glitterings of light!

287

LITTLE GIRLY-GIRL

LITTLE Girly-Girl, of you
      Still forever I am dreaming.—
Laughing eyes of limpid blue—
      Tresses glimmering and gleaming

Like glad waters running over
Shelving shallows, rimmed with clover,
      Trembling where the eddies whirl,
      Gurgling, "Little Girly-Girl!"

For your name it came to me
      Down the brink of brooks that
         brought it
Out of Paradise—and we—
      Love and I—we, leaning, caught it
From the ripples romping nigh us,
And the bubbles bumping by us
      Over shoals of pebbled pearl,
      Lilting, "Little Girly-Girl!"

That was long and long ago,
      But in memory the tender
Winds of summer weather blow,
      And the roses burst in splendor;
And the meadow's grassy billows
Break in blossoms round the willows
      Where the currents curve and curl,
      Calling, "Little Girly-Girl!"

288

CLOSE THE BOOK

CLOSE the book, and leave the tale
      All unfinished. It is best:
Brighter fancy will not fail
      To relate the rest.

We have read it on and on,
      Till each character, in sooth,
By the master-touches drawn,
      Is a living truth.

Leave it so, and let us sit,
      With the volume laid away—
Cut no other leaf of it,
      But as Fancy may.—

Then the friends that we have met
In its pages will endure,
And the villain, even yet,
May be white and pure.

Close the book, and leave the tale
All unfinished. It is best:
Brighter fancy will not fail
To relate the rest.

289

THE MOTHER SAINTED

FAIR girl, fond wife, and dear
Young mother, sleeping here
So quietly,—
Tell us what dream is thine—
What miracle divine
Is wrought in thee!

Once—was it yesterday,
Or but one hour away?—
The folded hands
Were quick to greet our own—
Now—are they God's alone?
Who understands?

Who, bending low to fold
The fingers as of old
In pressure warm,
But muses,—"Surely she
Will reach one touch to me,
And break the charm!"

And yet she does not stir;—
Such silence lies on her
We hear the drip
Of tear-drops as we press
Our kisses answerless
On brow and lip.

Not e'en the yearning touch
Of lips she loved so much
She made their breath
One with her own, will she
Give answer to and be
Wooed back from death.

And though he kneel and plead
Who was her greatest need,
And on her cheek
Lay the soft baby-face
In its old resting-place,
She will not speak.

So brave she was, and good—
In worth of womanhood
So like the snow—
She, smiling, gave her life
To blend the name of wife
With mother.—So,

God sees in her a worth
Too great for this dull earth,
And, beckoning, stands
At Heaven's open gate
Where all His angels wait
With welcoming hands.

Then, like her, reconciled,
O parent, husband, child,
And mourning friend,—
Smile out as smiles the light
Of day above the night,
And—wait the end.

290

THE LOST THRILL

I GROW so weary, someway, of all
things
That love and loving have vouch-
safed to me,

Since now all dreamed-of sweets of
  ecstasy
Am I possessed of: The caress that
  clings—
The lips that mix with mine with
  murmurings
No language may interpret, and the
  free,
Unfettered brood of kisses, hungrily
Feasting in swarms on honey blos-
  somings
Of passion's fullest flower—For yet I
  miss
The essence that alone makes love
  divine—
The subtle flavoring no tang of this
  Weak wine of melody may here de-
  fine:—
A something found and lost in the
  first kiss
A lover ever poured through lips of
  mine.

291

REACH YOUR HAND TO ME

REACH your hand to me, my
  friend,
  With its heartiest caress—
Sometime there will come an end
  To its present faithfulness—
    Sometime I may ask in vain
    For the touch of it again,
    When between us land or sea
    Holds it ever back from me.

Sometime I may need it so,
  Groping somewhere in the night,
It will seem to me as though
  Just a touch, however light,
    Would make all the darkness day,

And along some sunny way
Lead me through an April-shower
Of my tears to this fair hour.

O the present is too sweet
  To go on forever thus!
Round the corner of the street
  Who can say what waits for us?—
  Meeting—greeting, night and day,
  Faring each the selfsame way—
  Still somewhere the path must
    end—
  Reach your hand to me, my
    friend!

292

WE MUST GET HOME

WE must get home! How could
  we stray like this?—
So far from home, we know not where
  it is,—
Only in some fair, apple-blossomy
  place
Of children's faces—and the mother's
  face—
We dimly dream it, till the vision
  clears
Even in the eyes of fancy, glad with
  tears.

We must get home—for we have
  been away
So long, it seems forever and a day!
And O so very homesick we have
  grown,
The laughter of the world is like a
  moan
In our tired hearing, and its song as
  vain,—
We must get home—we must get
  home again!

We must get home! With heart and
soul we yearn
To find the long-lost pathway, and
return! . . .
The child's shout lifted from the quest-
ing band
Of old folk, faring weary, hand in
hand,
But faces brightening, as if clouds at
last
Were showering sunshine on us as
they passed.

We must get home: It hurts so, stay-
ing here,
Where fond hearts must be wept out
tear by tear,
And where to wear wet lashes means,
at best,
When most our lack, the least our
hope of rest—
When most our need of joy, the more
our pain—
We must get home—we must get
home again!

We must get home—home to the
simple things—
The morning-glories twirling up the
strings
And bugling color, as they blared in
blue-
And-white o'er garden-gates we scam-
pered through;
The long grape-arbor, with its under-
shade
Blue as the green and purple overlaid.

We must get home: All is so quiet
there:
The touch of loving hands on brow
and hair—
Dim rooms, wherein the sunshine is
made mild—

The lost love of the mother and the
child
Restored in restful lullabies of rain,—
We must get home—we must get
home again!

The rows of sweetcorn and the China
beans
Beyond the lettuce-beds where, tower-
ing, leans
The giant sunflower in barbaric pride
Guarding the barn-door and the lane
outside;
The honeysuckles, midst the holly-
hocks,
That clamber almost to the martin-
box.

We must get home, where, as we nod
and drowse,
Time humors us and tiptoes through
the house,
And loves us best when sleeping baby-
wise,
With dreams—not tear-drops—brim-
ming our clenched eyes,—
Pure dreams that know nor taint nor
earthly stain—
We must get home—we must get
home again!

We must get home! There only may
we find
The little playmates that we left be-
hind,—
Some racing down the road; some by
the brook;
Some droning at their desks, with
wistful look
Across the fields and orchards—farther
still
Where laughs and weeps the old wheel
at the mill.

We must get home! The willow-
    whistle's call
Trills crisp and liquid as the water-
    fall—
Mocking the trillers in the cherry-
    trees
And making discord of such rhymes
    as these,
That know nor lilt nor cadence but
    the birds
First warbled—then all poets after-
    wards.

We must get home; and, unremem-
    bering there
All gain of all ambition otherwhere,
Rest—from the feverish victory, and
    the crown
Of conquest whose waste glory weighs
    us down.—
Fame's fairest gifts we toss back with
    disdain—
We must get home—we must get
    home again!

We must get home again—we must
    —we must!—
(Our rainy faces pelted in the dust)
Creep back from the vain quest
    through endless strife
To find not anywhere in all of life
A happier happiness than blest us
    then. . . .
We must get home—we must get
    home again!

293
MABEL

SWEET little face, so full of slum-
        ber now—
    Sweet lips unlifted now with any
        kiss—

Sweet dimpled cheek and chin, and
    snowy brow,—
    What quietude is this?

O speak! Have you forgotten, yester-
    day,
    How gladly you came running to
        the gate
To meet us in the old familiar way,
    So joyous—so elate—

So filled with wildest glee, yet so
    serene
    With innocence of song and childish
        chat,
With all the dear caresses in between—
    Have you forgotten that?

Have you forgotten, knowing gentler
    charms,
    The boisterous love of one you ran
        to greet
When you last met, who caught you in
        his arms
    And kissed you, in the street?

Not very many days have passed since
    then,
    And yet between that kiss and him
        there lies
No pathway of return—unless again,
    In streets of Paradise,

Your eager feet come twinkling down
    the gold
    Of some bright thoroughfare ethereal,
To meet and greet him there just as of
    old.—
    Till then, farewell—farewell.

294
AT DUSK

A SOMETHING quiet and subdued
   In all the faces that we meet;
A sense of rest, a solitude
O'er all the crowded street;
   The very noises seem to be
   Crude utterings of harmony,
   And all we hear, and all we see,
Has in it something sweet.

Thoughts come to us as from a
   dream
Of some long-vanished yesterday;
The voices of the children seem
Like ours, when young as they;
   The hand of Charity extends
   To meet Misfortune's, where it
   blends,
   Veiled by the dusk—and oh, my
   friends,
Would it were dusk alway!

295

ANOTHER RIDE FROM GHENT TO AIX

WE sprang for the side-holts—my gripsack and I—
   It dangled—I dangled—we both dangled by.
"Good speed!" cried mine host, as we landed at last—
"Speed?" chuckled the watch we went lumbering past;
Behind shut the switch, and out through the rear door
I glared while we waited a half hour more.

I had missed the express that went thundering down
Ten minutes before to my next lecture town;
And my only hope left was to catch this "wild freight,"
Which the landlord remarked was "most luckily late—
But the twenty miles distance was easily done,
If they run half as fast as they usually run!"

Not a word to each other—we struck a snail's pace—
Conductor and brakeman ne'er changing a place—
Save at the next watering-tank, where they all
Got out—strolled about—cut their names on the wall,
Or listlessly loitered on down to the pile
Of sawed wood just beyond us, to doze for a while.

'Twas high noon at starting, but while we drew near
"Arcady," I said, "We'll not make it, I fear!
I must strike Aix by eight, and it's three o'clock now;
Let me stoke up that engine, and I'll show you how!"

At which the conductor, with patience sublime,
Smiled up from his novel with, "Plenty of time!"

At "Trask," as we jolted stock-still as a stone,
I heard a cow bawl in a five o'clock tone;
And the steam from the saw-mill looked misty and thin,
And the snarl of the saw had been stifled within:
And a frowzy-haired boy, with a hat full of chips,
Came out and stared up with a smile on his lips.

At "Booneville," I groaned, "Can't I telegraph on?"
No! Why? " 'Cause the telegraph-man had just gone
To visit his folks in Almo"—and one heard
The sharp snap of my teeth through the throat of a word,
That I dragged for a mile and a half up the track,
And strangled it there, and came skulkingly back.

Again we were off. It was twilight, and more,
As we rolled o'er a bridge where beneath us the roar
Of a river came up with so wooing an air
I mechanic'ly strapped myself fast in my chair
As a brakeman slid open the door for more light,
Saying: "Captain, brace up, for your town is in sight!"

"How they'll greet me!"—and all in a moment—"che-wang!"
And the train stopped again, with a bump and a bang.
What was it? "The section-hands, just in advance."
And I spit on my hands, and I rolled up my pants,
And I clumb like an imp that the fiends had let loose
Up out of the depths of that deadly caboose.

I ran the train's length—I lept safe to the ground—
And the legend still lives that for five miles around
They heard my voice hailing the hand-car that yanked
Me aboard at my bidding, and gallantly cranked,
As I groveled and clung, with my eyes in eclipse,
And a rim of red foam round my rapturous lips.

Then I cast loose my ulster—each ear-tab let fall—
Kicked off both my shoes—let go arctics and all—
Stood up with the boys—leaned—patted each head

As it bobbed up and down with the speed that we sped;
Clapped my hands—laughed and sang—any noise, bad or good,
Till at length into Aix we rotated and stood.

And all I remember is friends flocking round
As I unsheathed my head from a hole in the ground;
And no voice but was praising that hand-car divine,
As I rubbed down its spokes with that lecture of mine,
Which (the citizens voted by common consent)
Was no more than its due. 'Twas the lecture they meant.

296

THE RIPEST PEACH

THE ripest peach is highest on the
      tree—
And so her love, beyond the reach of
   me,
Is dearest in my sight. Sweet breezes,
   bow
Her heart down to me where I wor-
   ship now!

She looms aloft where every eye may
   see
The ripest peach is highest on the tree.
Such fruitage as her love I know, alas!
I may not reach here from the orchard
   grass.

I drink the sunshine showered past her
   lips
As roses drain the dewdrop as it drips.
The ripest peach is highest on the tree,
And so mine eyes gaze upward eagerly.

Why—why do I not turn away in
   wrath
And pluck some heart here hanging in
   my path?—

Love's lower boughs bend with them—
      but, ah me!
The ripest peach is highest on the tree!

297

BEDOUIN

O LOVE is like an untamed
      steed!—
So hot of heart and wild of speed,
And with fierce freedom so in love,
The desert is not vast enough,
With all its leagues of glimmering
   sands,
To pasture it! Ah, that my hands
Were more than human in their
   strength,
That my deft lariat at length
Might safely noose this splendid thing
That so defies all conquering!
Ho! but to see it whirl and reel—
The sands spurt forward—and to feel
The quivering tension of the thong
That throned me high, with shriek
   and song!
To grapple tufts of tossing mane—
To spurn it to its feet again,
And then, sans saddle, rein or bit,
To lash the mad life out of it!

298

A DITTY OF NO TONE—

Piped to the Spirit of John Keats

I

WOULD that my lips might pour
      out in thy praise
A fitting melody—an air sublime,—
A song sun-washed and draped in
      dreamy haze—
The floss and velvet of luxurious
      rhyme:
A lay wrought of warm languors, and
      o'er-brimmed
   With balminess, and fragrance of
      wild flowers
   Such as the droning bee ne'er
      wearies of—
Such thoughts as might be hymned
   To thee from this midsummer land
      of ours
      Through shower and sunshine,
      blent for very love.

II

Deep silences in woody aisles where-
      through
   Cool paths go loitering, and where
      the trill
Of best-remembered birds hath some-
      thing new
   In cadence for the hearing—linger-
      ing still
Through all the open day that lies be-
      yond;
   Reaches of pasture-lands, vine-
      wreathen oaks,
      Majestic still in pathos of decay;—
The road—the wayside pond

Wherein the dragon-fly an instant
      soaks
   His filmy wing-tips ere he flits
      away.

III

And I would pluck from out the dank,
      rich mold,
   Thick-shaded from the sun of noon,
      the long
Lithe stalks of barley, topped with
      ruddy gold,
And braid them in the meshes of my
      song;
And with them I would tangle wheat
      and rye,
And wisps of greenest grass the katy-
      did
   E'er crept beneath the blades of,
      sulkily,
As harvest-hands went by;
   And weave of all, as wildest fancy
      bid,
      A crown of mingled song and
      bloom for thee.

299

THE SPHINX

I KNOW all about the Sphinx—
   I know even what she thinks,
Staring with her stony eyes
Up forever at the skies.

For last night I dreamed that she
Told me all the mystery—
Why for æons mute she sat:—
She was just cut out for that!

300

MOTHER GOOSE

DEAR Mother Goose! most moth-
   erly and dear
Of all good mothers who have laps
      wherein
   We children nestle safest from all
      sin,—
I cuddle to thy bosom, with no fear
There to confess that though thy cap
      be queer,
   And thy curls gimlety, and thy
      cheeks thin,
And though the winkered mole upon
      thy chin
Tickles thy very nose-tip,—still to hear
The jolly jingles of mine infancy
Crooned by thee, makes mine eager
      arms, as now,
   To twine about thy neck, full ten-
      derly
Drawing the dear old face down, that
      thy brow
   May dip into my purest kiss, and
      be
Crowned ever with the baby-love of
      me.

301

IN THE HEART OF JUNE

IN the heart of June, love,
   You and I together,
On from dawn till noon, love,
   Laughing with the weather;
Blending both our souls, love,
   In the selfsame tune,
Drinking all life holds, love,
   In the heart of June.

In the heart of June, love,
   With its golden weather,
Underneath the moon, love,
   You and I together.
Ah! how sweet to seem, love,
   Drugged and half aswoon
With this luscious dream, love,
   In the heart of June.

302

MY BOY

YOU smile and you smoke your
   cigar, my boy;
You walk with a languid swing;
You tinkle and tune your guitar, my
      boy,
   And lift up your voice and sing;
The midnight moon is a friend of
      yours,
   And a serenade your joy—
And it's only an age like mine that
      cures
   A trouble like yours, my boy!

303

THE ASSASSIN

FLING him amongst the cobbles of
   the street
   Midmost along a mob's most turbid
      tide;
   Stun him with tumult upon every
      side—
Wrangling of hoarsened voices that re-
      peat
His awful guilt and howl for vengeance
      meet;
   Let white-faced women stare, all
      torrid-eyed,

With hair blown forward, and with
    jaws dropped wide,
And some face like his mother's glim-
    mer sweet
An instant in the hot core of his eyes.
Then snatch him with claw hands,
    and thong his head
That he may look no way but toward
    the skies
That glower lividly and crackle
    red,—
There let some knuckled fist of light-
    ning rise—
Draw backward flickeringly and
    knock him dead.

304

BECAUSE

WHY did we meet long years of
    yore?
And why did we strike hands and
    say:
"We will be friends, and nothing
    more";
Why are we musing thus to-day?
    Because because was just because,
    And no one knew just why it was.

Why did I say good-by to you?
Why did I sail across the main?
Why did I love not heaven's own blue
Until I touched these shores again?
    Because because was just because,
    And you nor I knew why it was.

Why are my arms about you now,
And happy tears upon your cheek?
And why my kisses on your brow?
    Look up in thankfulness and speak!
    Because because was just because,
    And only God knew why it was.

305

PANSIES

PANSIES! Pansies! How I love you,
    pansies!
Jaunty-faced, laughing-lipped and
    dewy-eyed with glee;
Would my song but blossom out in
    little five-leaf stanzas
        As delicate in fancies
        As your beauty is to me!

But my eyes shall smile on you, and
    my hands infold you,
    Pet, caress, and lift you to the lips
        that love you so,
That, shut ever in the years that may
    mildew or mold you,
        My fancy shall behold you
        Fair as in the long ago.

306

BABY'S DYING

BABY'S dying,
    Do not stir—
    Let her spirit lightly float
Through the sighing
    Lips of her—
    Still the murmur in the throat;
Let the moan of grief be curbed—
Baby must not be disturbed!

Baby's dying,
    Do not stir—
    Let her pure life lightly swim
Through the sighing
    Lips of her—
    Out from us and up to HIM—
Let her leave us with that smile—
Kiss and miss her after while.

307

AN EMPTY GLOVE

I

AN empty glove—long withering
in the grasp
Of Time's cold palm. I lift it to
my lips,—
And lo, once more I thrill beneath its
clasp,
In fancy, as with odorous finger-tips
It reaches from the years that used
to be
And proffers back love, life and
all, to me.

II

Ah! beautiful she was beyond belief:
Her face was fair and lustrous as
the moon's;
Her eyes—too large for small delight
or grief,—
The smiles of them were Laughter's
afternoons;
Their tears were April showers,
and their love—
All sweetest speech swoons ere it
speaks thereof.

III

White-fruited cocoa shown against the
shell
Were not so white as was her brow
below
The cloven tresses of the hair that fell
Across her neck and shoulders of
nude snow;
Her cheeks—chaste pallor, with a
crimson stain—
Her mouth was like a red rose
rinsed with rain.

IV

And this was she my fancy held as
good—
As fair and lovable—in every wise
As peerless in pure worth of womanhood
As was her wondrous beauty in
men's eyes.—
Yet, all alone, I kiss this empty
glove—
The poor husk of the hand I loved
—and love.

308

TO THE CRICKET

THE chiming seas may clang; and
Tubal Cain
May clink his tinkling metals as he
may;
Or Pan may sit and pipe his breath
away;
Or Orpheus wake his most entrancing
strain
Till not a note of melody remain!—
But thou, O cricket, with thy rounde-
lay,
Shalt laugh them all to scorn! So
wilt thou, pray
Trill me thy glad song o'er and o'er
again:
I shall not weary; there is purest
worth
In thy sweet prattle, since it sings the
lone
Heart home again. Thy warbling
hath no dearth
Of childish memories—no harsher tone
Than we might listen to in gentlest
mirth,
Thou poor plebeian minstrel of the
hearth.

309

THE OLD-FASHIONED BIBLE

HOW dear to my heart are the
scenes of my childhood
That now but in mem'ry I sadly re-
view;
The old meeting-house at the edge of
the wildwood,
The rail fence and horses all tethered
thereto;
The low, sloping roof, and the bell in
the steeple,
The doves that came fluttering out
overhead
As it solemnly gathered the God-fear-
ing people
To hear the old Bible my grandfather
read.
The old-fashioned Bible—
The dust-covered Bible—
The leathern-bound Bible my grand-
father read.

The blessed old volume! The face bent
above it—
As now I recall it—is gravely severe,
Though the reverent eye that droops
downward to love it
Makes grander the text through the
lens of a tear,
And, as down his features it trickles
and glistens,
The cough of the deacon is still, and
his head
Like a haloèd patriarch's leans as he
listens
To hear the old Bible my grandfather
read.
The old-fashioned Bible—
The dust-covered Bible—
The leathern-bound Bible my grand-
father read.

Ah! who shall look backward with
scorn and derision
And scoff the old book though it
uselessly lies
In the dust of the past, while this
newer revision
Lisps on of a hope and a home in
the skies?
Shall the voice of the Master be stifled
and riven?
Shall we hear but a tithe of the
words He has said,
When so long He has, listening, leaned
out of Heaven
To hear the old Bible my grandfather
read?
The old-fashioned Bible—
The dust-covered Bible—
The leathern-bound Bible my grand-
father read.

310

THE LAND OF USED-TO-BE

AND where's the Land of Used-to-
be, does little baby wonder?
Oh, we will clap a magic saddle over
"Poppie's" knee
And ride away around the world, and
in and out and under
The whole of all the golden sunny
Summer-time and see.

Leisurely and lazy-like we'll jostle on
our journey,
And let the pony bathe his hooves
and cool them in the dew,
As he sidles down the shady way, and
lags along the ferny
And green, grassy edges of the lane
we travel through.

And then we'll canter on to catch the
    bauble of the thistle
As it bumps among the butterflies
    and glimmers down the sun,
To leave us laughing, all content to
    hear the robin whistle
Or guess what Katydid is saying
    little Katy's done.

And pausing here a minute, where we
    hear the squirrel chuckle
As he darts from out the underbrush
    and scampers up the tree,
We will gather buds and locust-blos-
    soms, leaves and honeysuckle,
To wreathe around our foreheads,
    riding into Used-to-be;—

For here's the very rim of it that we
    go swinging over—
Don't you hear the Fairy bugles, and
    the tinkle of the bells,
And see the baby-bumblebees that tum-
    ble in the clover
And dangle from the tilted pinks
    and tipsy pimpernels?

And don't you see the merry faces of
    the daffodillies,
And the jolly Johnny-jump-ups, and
    the buttercups a-glee,
And the low, lolling ripples ring
    around the water-lilies?—
All greeting us with laughter, to the
    Land of Used-to-be!

And here among the blossoms of the
    blooming vines and grasses,
With a haze forever hanging in the
    sky forever blue,
And with a breeze from over seas to
    kiss us as it passes,
We will romp around forever as the
    airy Elfins do!

For all the elves of earth and air are
    swarming here together—
The prankish Puck, King Oberon,
    and Queen Titania too;
And dear old Mother Goose herself, as
    sunny as the weather,
Comes dancing down the dewy
    walks to welcome me and you!

311

JUST TO BE GOOD

JUST to be good—
    This is enough—enough!
O we who find sin's billows wild and
    rough,
Do we not feel how more than any
    gold
Would be the blameless life we led of
    old
While yet our lips knew but a mother's
    kiss!
    Ah! though we miss
    All else but this,
        To be good is enough!

It is enough—
    Enough—just to be good!
To lift our hearts where they are un-
    derstood,
To let the thirst for worldly power and
    place
Go unappeased; to smile back in God's
    face
With the glad lips our mothers used to
    kiss.
    Ah! though we miss
    All else but this,
        To be good is enough!

312

A LOUNGER

HE leaned against a lamp-post, lost
   In some mysterious reverie:
His head was bowed; his arms were
      crossed;
He yawned, and glanced evasively:
Uncrossed his arms, and slowly put
   Them back again, and scratched his
      side—
Shifted his weight from foot to foot,
And gazed out no-ward, idle-eyed.

Grotesque of form and face and dress,
   And picturesque in every way—
A figure that from day to day
Drooped with a limper laziness;
A figure such as artists lean,
   In pictures where distress is seen,
Against low hovels where we guess
No happiness has ever been.

313

MR. WHAT'S-HIS-NAME

THEY called him Mr. What's-his-
      name:
From where he was, or why he came,
Or when, or what he found to do,
Nobody in the city knew.

He lived, it seemed, shut up alone
In a low hovel of his own;
There cooked his meals and made his
      bed,
Careless of all his neighbors said.

His neighbors, too, said many things
Expressive of grave wonderings,
Since none of them had ever been
Within his doors, or peered therein.

In fact, grown watchful, they became
Assured that Mr. What's-his-name
Was up to something wrong—indeed,
Small doubt of it, we all agreed.

At night were heard strange noises
      there,
When honest people everywhere
Had long retired; and his light
Was often seen to burn all night.

He left his house but seldom—then
Would always hurry back again,
As though he feared some stranger's
      knock,
Finding him gone, might burst the
      lock.

Besides, he carried, every day,
At the one hour he went away,
A basket, with the contents hid
Beneath its woven willow lid.

And so we grew to greatly blame
This wary Mr. What's-his-name,
And look on him with such distrust
His actions seemed to sanction just.

But when he died—he died one day—
Dropped in the street while on his way
To that old wretched hut of his—
You'll think it strange—perhaps it is—

But when we lifted him, and past
The threshold of his home at last,
No man of all the crowd but stepped
With   reverence,—ay,   *quailed*   and
      wept!

What was it? Just a shriek of pain
I pray to never hear again—

A withered woman, old and bowed,
That fell and crawled and cried
aloud—

And kissed the dead man's matted
hair—
Lifted his face and kissed him there—
Called to him, as she clutched his hand,
In words no one could understand.

Insane? Yes.—Well, we, searching,
found
An unsigned letter, in a round
Free hand, within the dead man's
breast:
"Look to my mother—*I'm* at rest.

"You'll find my money safely hid
Under the lining of the lid
Of my work-basket. It is hers,
And God will bless her ministers!"

And some day—though he died un-
known—
If through the City by the Throne
I walk, all cleansed of earthly shame,
I'll ask for Mr. What's-his-name.

314

UNCOMFORTED

LELLOINE! Lelloine! Don't you
    hear me calling?
Calling through the night for you,
    and calling through the day;
Calling when the dawn is here, and
    when the dusk is falling—
Calling for my Lelloine the angels
    lured away!

Lelloine! I call and listen, starting
    from my pillow—

In the hush of midnight, Lelloine!
    I cry,
And o'er the rainy window-pane I hear
    the weeping willow
Trail its dripping leaves like baby-
    fingers in reply.

Lelloine, I miss the glimmer of your
    glossy tresses,
I miss the dainty velvet palms that
    nestled in my own;
And all my mother-soul went out in
    answerless caresses,
And a storm of tears and kisses when
    you left me here alone.

I have prayed, O Lelloine, but Heaven
    will not hear me,
I can not gain one sign from Him
    who leads you by the hand;
And O it seems that ne'er again His
    mercy will come near me—
That He will never see my need, nor
    ever understand.

Won't you listen, Lelloine?—just a lit-
    tle leaning
O'er the walls of Paradise—lean and
    hear my prayer,
And interpret death to Him in all its
    awful meaning,
And tell Him you are lonely without
    your mother there.

315

MY WHITE BREAD

DEM good old days done past and
    gone
In old Ca'line wha I wuz bo'n
W'en my old Misst'ess she fust sayd,
    "Yo's a-eatin' yo' white braid!"
Oh, dem's de times uts done gone by

W'en de nights shine cla, an' de coon
        clim' high,
An' I sop my soul in 'possum-pie,
    Das a-eatin' my white braid!

It's dem's de nights ut I cross my legs
An' pat de flo' ez I twis' de pegs
O' de banjo up twil de gals all sayd,
    "Yo's a-eatin' yo' white braid!"
Oh, dem's de times ut I usen fo' to blow
On de long reeds cut in de old by-o,
An' de frogs jine in like dey glad fo'
        to know
    I's a-eatin' my white braid.

An' I shet my eyes fo' to conjuh up
Dem good ole days ut fills my cup
Wid de times ut fust ole Misst'ess
        sayd,
    "Yo's a-eatin' yo' white braid!"
Oh, dem's de dreams ut I fines de best;
An' bald an' gray ez a hornet's nest,
I drap my head on de good Lord's
        breast,
    Says a-eatin' my white braid!

316

HE AND I

JUST drifting on together—
        He and I—
As through the balmy weather
        Of July
    Drift two thistle-tufts embedded
    Each in each—by zephyrs wedded—
    Touring upward, giddy-headed,
        For the sky.

And, veering up and onward,
        Do we seem
Forever drifting dawnward
        In a dream,
Where we meet song-birds that know
        us,
And the winds their kisses blow us,
While the years flow far below us
        Like a stream.

And we are happy—very—
        He and I—
Aye, even glad and merry
        Though on high
    The heavens are sometimes shrouded
    By the midnight storm, and clouded
    Till the pallid moon is crowded
        From the sky.

My spirit ne'er expresses
        Any choice
But to clothe him with caresses
        And rejoice;
    And as he laughs, it is in
    Such a tone the moonbeams glisten
    And the stars come out to listen
        To his voice.

And so, whate'er the weather,
        He and I,—
With our lives linked thus together,
        Float and fly
    As two thistle-tufts embedded
    Each in each—by zephyrs wedded—
    Touring upward, giddy-headed,
        For the sky.

317

FROM A BALLOON

HO! we are loose. Hear how they
        shout,
And how their clamor dwindles out
Beneath us to the merest hum
Of earthly acclamation. Come,

Lean with me here and look below—
Why, bless you, man! don't tremble so!
There is no need of fear up here—
Not higher than the buzzard swings
About upon the atmosphere
With drowsy eyes and open wings!
There, steady, now, and feast your
    eyes;—
See, we are tranced—we do not rise;
It is the earth that sinks from us:
But when I first beheld it thus,
And felt the breezes downward flow,
And heard all noises fail and die,
Until but silence and the sky
Above, around me, and below,—
Why, like you now, I swooned almost,
With mingled awe and fear and glee—
As giddy as an hour-old ghost
That stares into eternity.

318

A TWINTORETTE

HO! my little maiden
    With the glossy tresses,
Come thou and dance with me
    A measure all divine;
Let my breast be laden
    With but thy caresses—
Come thou and glancingly
    Mate thy face with mine.

Thou shalt trill a rondel,
    While my lips are purling
Some dainty twitterings
    Sweeter than the birds';
And, with arms that fondle
    Each as we go twirling,
We will kiss, with twitterings,
    Lisps and loving words.

319

WHAT THEY SAID

WHISPERING to themselves
    apart,
They who knew her said of her,
"Dying of a broken heart—
Death her only comforter—
    For the man she loved is dead—
    She will follow soon!" they said.

Beautiful? Ah! brush the dust
    From Raphael's fairest face,
And restore it, as it must
    First have smiled back from its place
    On his easel as he leant
    Wrapt in awe and wonderment!

Why, to kiss the very hem
    Of the mourning-weeds she wore,
Like the winds that rustled them,
    I had gone the round world o'er;
    And to touch her hand I swear
    All things dareless I would dare!

But unto themselves apart,
    Whispering, they said of her,
"Dying of a broken heart—
Death her only comforter—
    For the man she loved is dead—
    She will follow soon!" they said.

So I mutely turned away,
    Turned with sorrow and despair,
Yearning still from day to day
    For that woman dying there,
    Till at last, by longing led,
    I returned to find her—dead?

"Dead?"—I know that word would tell
    Rhyming there—but in this case
"Wed" rhymes equally as well

In the very selfsame place—
And, in fact, the latter word
Is the one she had preferred.

Yet unto themselves apart,
Whisp'ring they had said of her—
"Dying of a broken heart—
Death her only comforter—
For the man she loved is dead—
"She will follow soon!" they said.

320

AFTER THE FROST

AFTER the frost! O the rose is dead,
And the weeds lie pied in the
garden-bed,
And the peach tree's shade in the wan
sunshine,
Faint as the veins in these hands of
mine,
Streaks the gray of the orchard wall
Where the vine rasps loose, and the last
leaves fall,
And the bare boughs writhe, and the
winds are lost—
After the frost—the frost!

After the frost! O the weary head
And the hands and the heart are
quietèd;
And the lips we loved are locked at
last,
And kiss not back, though the rain
falls fast
And the lashes drip, and the soul
makes moan,
And on through the dead leaves walks
alone
Where the bare boughs writhe and the
winds are lost—
After the frost—the frost!

321

CHARLES H. PHILIPS

OBIT NOVEMBER 5TH, 1881

O FRIEND! There is no way
To bid farewell to thee!
The words that we would say
Above thy grave to-day
Still falter and delay
'And fail us utterly.

When walking with us here,
The hand we loved to press
Was gentle, and sincere
As thy frank eyes were clear
Through every smile and tear
Of pleasure and distress.

In years, young; yet in thought
Mature; thy spirit, free,
And fired with fervor caught
Of thy proud sire, who fought
His way to fame, and taught
Its toilsome way to thee.

So even thou hast gained
The victory God-given—
Yea, as our cheeks are stained
With tears, and our souls pained
And mute, thou hast attained
Thy high reward in Heaven!

322

WHEN IT RAINS

WHEN it rains, and with the rain
Never bird has heart to sing,
And across the window-pane
Is no sunlight glimmering;

When the pitiless refrain
  Brings a tremor to the lips,
Our tears are like the rain
  As it drips, drips, drips—
  Like the sad, unceasing rain as it
    drips.

When the light of heaven's blue
  Is blurred and blotted quite,
And the dreary day to you
  Is but a long twilight;
When it seems that ne'er again
  Shall the sun break its eclipse,
Our tears are like the rain
  As it drips, drips, drips—
  Like the endless, friendless rain as it
    drips.

When it rains! weary heart,
  O be of better cheer!
The leaden clouds will part,
  And the morrow will be clear;
Take up your load again,
  With a prayer upon your lips,
Thanking Heaven for the rain
  As it drips, drips, drips—
  With the golden bow of promise as
    it drips.

323

AN ASSASSIN

CAT LIKE he creeps along where
      ways are dim,
From covert unto covert's secrecy;
His shadow in the moonlight shrinks
      from him
  And crouches warily.

He hugs strange envies to his breast,
      and nurses
Wild hatreds, till the murderous
      hand he grips
Falls, quivering with the tension of the
      curses
He launches from his lips.

Drenched in his victim's blood he
      holds high revel;
He mocks at justice, and in all men's
      eyes
Insults his God—and no one but the
      devil
  Is sorry when he dies.

324

BEST OF ALL

OF all good gifts that the Lord lets
      fall,
Is not silence the best of all?

The deep, sweet hush when the song
      is closed,
And every sound but a voiceless ghost;

And every sigh, as we listening leant,
A breathless quiet of vast content?

The laughs we laughed have a purer
      ring
With but their memory echoing;

And the joys we voiced, and the words
      we said,
Seem so dearer for being dead.

So of all good gifts that the Lord lets
      fall,
Is not silence the best of all?

325

MR. SILBERBERG

AND LITTLE JULIUS

I LIKE me yet dot leedle chile
   Vich climb my lap up in to-day,
Unt took my cheap cigair avay,
Unt laugh unt kiss me, purty-whvile,—
Possescially I like dose mout'
   Vich taste his moder's like—unt
      so,
Eef my cigair it gone glean out
   —Yust let it go!

Vat I caire den for *any*ding?
   Der "HERALDT" schlip out fon my
      handt
Unt all my odvairtizement standt
Mitout new changements boddering;
   I only t'ink—I haf me dis
      One leedle boy to pet unt love
Unt play me vit, unt hug unt kiss—
   Unt dot's enough!

Der plans unt pairposes I vear
   Out in der vorld all fades avay,
Unt vit der beeznis of der day
I got me den no time to spare;
   Der caires of trade vas caires no
      more—
      Dem cash accoundts dey dodge
         me by,
Unt vit my chile I roll der floor,
   Unt laugh unt gry!

Ach! frient! dem childens is der ones
   Dot got some happy times—you
      bet!—
Dot's vy ven I been growed up yet
I visht I schtill been leedle vonce!

Unt ven dot leedle roozter tries
   Dem baby-tricks I used to do,
My mout' it vater, unt my eyes
   Dey vater too!

Unt all der summer-time unt spring
   Of childhoodt it come back to me,
   So dot it vas a dream I see
Ven I yust look at anyding!
   Unt ven dot leedle boy run' by,
      I t'ink "Dot's *me,*" fon hour to
         hour
   Schtill chasing yet dose butterfly
      Fon flower to flower!

Oxpose I vas lots money vairt,
   Vit blenty schtone-front schtore to
      rent,
   Unt mor'gages at twelf-per tcent.,
Unt diamondts in my ruffled shairt,—
   I make a'signment of all dot,
      Unt tairn it over vit a schmile
Aber you please—but, don'd forgot,
   I keep dot chile!

326

THE HEREAFTER

HEREAFTER! O we need not
   waste
   Our smiles or tears, whate'er be-
      fall:
No happiness but holds a taste
   Of something sweeter, after all;—
No depth of agony but feels
   Some fragment of abiding trust,—
Whatever Death unlocks or seals,
   The mute beyond is just.

327

THE LOVING CUP

TRANCED in the glamour of a
    dream
Where banquet-lights and fancies
    gleam,
And ripest wit and wine abound,
And pledges hale go round and
    round,—
Lo, dazzled with enchanted rays—
As in the golden olden days
Sir Galahad—my eyes swim up
To greet your splendor, Loving Cup!

What is the secret of your art,
Linking together hand and heart
Your myriad votaries who do
Themselves most honor honoring you?
What gracious service have you done
To win the name that you have
    won?—
Kissing it back from tuneful lips
That sing your praise between the
    sips!

Your spicy breath, O Loving Cup,
That, like an incense steaming up,
Full-freighted with a fragrance fine
As ever swooned on sense of mine,
Is rare enough.—But then, ah me!
How rarer every memory
That, rising with it, wreathes and
    blends
In forms and faces of my friends!

O Loving Cup! in fancy still,
I clasp their hands, and feel the thrill
Of fellowship that still endures
While lips are theirs and wine is
    yours!
And while my memory journeys down

The years that lead to Boston Town,
Abide where first were rendered up
Our mutual loves, O Loving Cup!

328

EROS

THE storm of love has burst at last
    Full on me: All the world, be-
        fore,
Was like an alien, unknown shore
Along whose verge I laughing
        passed.—
But now—I laugh not any more,—
Bowed with a silence vast in weight
    As that which falls on one who
        stands
For the first time on ocean sands,
Seeing and feeling all the great
    Awe of the waves as they wash the
        lands
And billow and wallow and undulate.

329

THE QUIET LODGER

THE man that rooms next door to
        me:
    Two weeks ago, this very night,
He took possession quietly,
    As any other lodger might—
        But why the room next mine
            should so
        Attract him I was vexed to
            know,—
    Because his quietude, in fine,
    Was far superior to mine.

"Now, I like quiet, truth to tell,
    A tranquil life is sweet to me—
But *this,*" I sneered, "suits me too
        well.—
He shuts his door so noiselessly,
    And glides about so very mute,
    In each mysterious pursuit,
    His silence is oppressive, and
    Too deep for me to understand."

Sometimes, forgetting book or pen,
    I've found my head in breathless
        poise
Lifted, and dropped in shame again,
    Hearing some alien ghost of noise—
    Some   smothered   sound   that
        seemed to be
    A trunk-lid dropped unguardedly,
    Or the crisp writhings of some
        quire
    Of manuscript thrust in the fire.

Then I have climbed, and closed in
        vain
    My transom, opening in the hall;
Or close against the window-pane
    Have pressed my fevered face,—but
        all
    The day or night without held
        not
    A   sight   or   sound   or   counter-
        thought
    To set my mind one instant free
    Of this man's silent mastery.

And often I have paced the floor
    With muttering anger, far at night,
Hearing, and cursing, o'er and o'er,
    The muffled noises, and the light
    And   tireless   movements   of   this
        guest
    Whose silence raged above my
        rest

Hoarser   than   howling   storms   at
        sea—
    The man that rooms next door to
        me.

But twice or thrice, upon the stair,
    I've   seen   his   face—most   strangely
        wan,—
Each time upon me unaware
    He came—smooth'd past me, and
        was gone.—
    So like a whisper he went by,
    I listened after, ear and eye,
    Nor could my chafing fancy tell
    The meaning of one syllable.

Last night I caught him, face to face,—
    He entering his room, and I
Glaring from mine: He paused a space
    And met my scowl all shrinkingly,
    But with full gentleness: The key
    Turned in his door—and I could
        see
    It tremblingly withdrawn and put
    Inside,   and   then—the   door   was
        shut.

Then   silence.   *Silence!*—why,   last
        night
    The silence was tumultuous,
And   thundered   on   till   broad   day-
        light;—
    O never has it stunned me thus!—
    It rolls, and moans, and mumbles
        yet.—
    Ah, God! how loud may silence
        get
    When   man   mocks   at   a   brother
        man
    Who answers but as silence can!

The silence grew, and grew, and grew,
    Till at high noon to-day 'twas heard

Throughout the house; and men
  flocked through
The echoing halls, with faces
  blurred
With pallor, gloom, and fear, and
  awe,
And shuddering at what they
  saw,—
The quiet lodger, as he lay
Stark of the life he cast away.

. . . . . .

So strange to-night—those voices there,
Where all so quiet was before:
They say the face has not a care
Nor sorrow in it any more. . . .
  His latest scrawl:—"Forgive me—
    You
  Who prayed, 'They know not
    what they do!' "
My tears will never let me see
This man that rooms next door to
  me!

330

THE BROOK-SONG

LITTLE brook! Little brook!
    You have such a happy look—
Such a very merry manner, as you
    swerve and curve and
    crook—
  And your ripples, one and
    one,
  Reach each other's hands and
    run
Like laughing little children in the
  sun!

  Little brook, sing to me:
  Sing about a bumblebee
That tumbled from a lily-bell and

  grumbled mumblingly,
  Because he wet the film
  Of his wings, and had to
    swim,
While the water-bugs raced round and
    laughed at him!

  Little brook—sing a song
  Of a leaf that sailed along
Down the golden-braided center of
    your current swift and
    strong,
  And a dragon-fly that lit
  On the tilting rim of it,
And rode away and wasn't scared a
    bit.

  And sing—how oft in glee
  Came a truant boy like me,
Who loved to lean and listen to your
    lilting melody,
  Till the gurgle and refrain
  Of your music in his brain
Wrought a happiness as keen to him
    as pain.

  Little brook—laugh and leap!
  Do not let the dreamer weep:
Sing him all the songs of summer till
    he sink in softest sleep;
  And then sing soft and low
  Through his dreams of long
    ago—
Sing back to him the rest he used to
    know!

331

BIN A-FISHIN'

W'EN de sun's gone down, an' de
    moon is riz,
Bin a-fishin'! Bin a-fishin'!

It's I's aguine 'down wha' the by-o is!
Bin a-fishin' all night long!

CHORUS

Bin a-fishin'! Bin a-fishin'!
Bin a-fishin' clean fum de dusk of
    night
Twel away 'long on in de mornin'
    light.

Bait my hook, un I plunk her down!
Bin a-fishin'! Bin a-fishin'!
Un I lay dat catfish weigh five pound!
Bin a-fishin' all night long!

CHORUS

Folks tells me ut a sucker won't bite,
Bin a-fishin'! Bin a-fishin'!
Yit I lif' out fo' last Chuesday night,
Bin a-fishin' all night long!

CHORUS

Little fish nibble un de big fish come;
Bin a-fishin'! Bin a-fishin'!
"Go way, little fish! I want some!"
Bin a-fishin' all night long!

CHORUS

Sez de bullfrog, "D-runk!" sez de ole
    owl "Whoo!"
Bin a-fishin'! Bin a-fishin'!
'Spec, Mr. Nigger, dey's a-meanin'
    you,
Bin a-fishin' all night long!

CHORUS

332

UNCLE DAN'L IN TOWN OVER
SUNDAY

I CAIN'T git used to city ways—
    Ner never could, I' bet my hat!
Jevver know jes' whur I was raised?—
Raised on a farm! D' ever tell you
    that?
Was undoubtatly, I declare!
And now, on Sunday—fun to spare
Around a farm! Why jes' to set
Up on the top three-cornered rail
Of Pap's old place, nigh La Fayette,
I'd swap my soul off, hide and tail!
You fellers in the city here,
You don't know nothin'!—S'pose to-
    day,
This clatterin' Sunday, you waked up
Without no jinglin'-janglin' bells,
Ner rattlin' of the milkman's cup,
Ner any swarm of screechin' birds
Like these here English swallers—
    S'pose
Ut you could miss all noise like those,
And git shet o' thinkin' of 'em after-
    werds,
And then, in the country, wake and
    hear
Nothin' but silence—wake and see
Nothin' but green woods fur and
    near?—
What sort o' Sunday would that
    be? . . .
Wisht I hed you home with me!
Now think! The laziest of all days—
To git up any time—er sleep—
Er jes' lay round and watch the haze
A-dancin' 'crost the wheat, and keep
My pipe a-goern laisurely,
And puff and whiff as pleases me—
And ef I leave a trail of smoke

Clean through the house, no one to say
"Wah! throw that nasty thing away;
Hev some regyard fer decency!"
To walk round barefoot, if you choose;
Er saw the fiddle—er dig some bait
And go a-fishin'—er pitch hoss shoes
Out in the shade somewhurs, and wait
For dinner-time, with an appetite
Ut folks in town cain't equal quite!
To laze around the barn and poke
Fer hens' nests—er git up a match
Betwixt the boys, and watch 'em
    scratch
And rassle round, and sweat and swear
And quarrel to their hearts' content;
And me a-jes' a-settin' there
A-hatchin' out more devilment!
What sort o' Sunday would that
    be? . . .
Wisht I hed you home with me!

333

EMERSON

CONCORD, APRIL 27, 1882

WHAT shall we say? In quietude,
    Within his home, in dreams
        unguessed,
He lies; the grief a nation would
    Evince must be repressed.

Nor meet is it the loud acclaim
    His countrymen would raise—that
        he
Has left the riches of his fame
    The whole world's legacy.

Then, prayerful, let us pause until
    We find, as grateful spirits can,
The way most worthy to fulfil
    The tribute due the man.

Think what were best in his regard
    Who voyaged life in such a cause:
Our simplest faith were best reward—
    Our silence, best applause.

334

YOUR VIOLIN

YOUR violin! Ah me!
    'Twas fashioned o'er the sea,
In storied Italy—
    What matter where?
It is its voice that sways
And thrills me as it plays
The airs of other days—
    The days that were!

Then let your magic bow
Glide lightly to and fro.—
I close my eyes, and so,
    In vast content,
I kiss my hand to you,
And to the tunes we knew
Of old, as well as to
    Your instrument!

Poured out of some dim dream
Of lulling sounds that seem
Like ripples of a stream
    Twanged lightly by
The slender, tender hands
Of weeping-willow wands
That droop where gleaming sands
    And pebbles lie.

A melody that swoons
In all the truant tunes
Long listless afternoons
    Lure from the breeze,
When woodland boughs are stirred,
And moaning doves are heard,
And laughter afterward
    Beneath the trees.

Through all the chorusing,
I hear on leaves of spring
The drip and pattering
Of April skies,
With echoes faint and sweet
As baby-angel feet
Might wake along a street
Of Paradise.

335

SOLDIERS HERE TO-DAY

I

SOLDIERS and saviors of the homes
   we love;
Heroes and patriots who marched
   away,
And who marched back, and who
   marched on above—
All—all are here to-day!

By the dear cause you fought for—
   you are here;
At summons of bugle, and the drum
Whose palpitating syllables were ne'er
More musical, you come!

Here—by the stars that bloom in fields
   of blue,
And by the bird above with shield-
   ing wings;
And by the flag that floats out over
   you,
   With silken beckonings—

Ay, here beneath its folds are gathered
   all
Who warred unscathed for blessings
   that it gave—

Still blessed its champion, though it
   but fall
A shadow on his grave!

II

We greet you, Victors, as in vast array
You gather from the scenes of strife
   and death—
From spectral fortress-walls where curls
   away
The cannon's latest breath.

We greet you—from the crumbling
   battlements
Where once again the old flag feels
   the breeze
Stroke out its tattered stripes and
   smooth its rents
With rippling ecstasies.

From living tombs where every hope
   seemed lost—
With famine quarantined by bris-
   tling guns—
The prison-pens — the guards — the
   "dead-line" crossed
By—riddled skeletons!

From furrowed plains, sown thick with
   bursting shells—
From mountain gorge, and toppling
   crags o'erhead—
From wards of pestilential hospitals,
   And trenches of the dead.

III

In fancy all are here. The night is
   o'er,
And through dissolving mists the
   morning gleams;
And clustered round their hearths we
   see once more
The heroes of our dreams.

Strong, tawny faces, some, and some
    are fair,
And some are marked with age's
    latest prime,
And, seer-like, browed and aureoled
    with hair
As hoar as winter-time.

The faces of fond lovers, glorified—
    The faces of the husband and the
        wife—
The babe's face nestled at the mother's
        side,
    And smiling back at life;

A bloom of happiness in every cheek—
    A thrill of tingling joy in every
        vein—
In every soul a rapture they will seek
    In Heaven, and find again!

IV

'Tis not a vision only—we who pay
    But the poor tribute of our praises
        here
Are equal sharers in the guerdon they
    Purchased at price so dear.

The angel, Peace, o'er all uplifts her
    hand,
    Waving the olive, and with heavenly
        eyes
Shedding a light of love o'er sea and
    land
    As sunshine from the skies—

Her figure pedestaled on Freedom's
    soil—
    Her sandals kissed with seas of
        golden grain—
Queen of a realm of joy-requited toil
    That glories in her reign.

O blessed land of labor and reward!
    O gracious Ruler, let Thy reign en-
        dure;
In pruning-hook and plough-share beat
        the sword,
    And reap the harvest sure!

336

A WINDY DAY

THE dawn was a dawn of splendor,
        And the blue of the morning
            skies
Was as placid and deep and tender
        As the blue of a baby's eyes;
The sunshine flooded the mountain,
        And flashed over land and sea
Like the spray of a glittering foun-
        tain.—
    But the wind—the wind—Ah me!

Like a weird invisible spirit,
    It swooped in its airy flight;
And the earth, as the stress drew
        near it,
    Quailed as in mute affright;
The grass in the green fields
        quivered—
    The waves of the smitten brook
Chillily shuddered and shivered,
    And the reeds bowed down and
        shook.

Like a sorrowful miserere
    It sobbed, and it blew and blew,
Till the leaves on the trees looked
        weary,
    And my prayers were weary, too;
And then, like the sunshine's glimmer
    That failed in the awful strain,
All the hope of my eyes grew dimmer
    In a spatter of spiteful rain.

337

SHADOW AND SHINE

STORMS of the winter, and deep-
    ening snows,
When will you end? I said,
For the soul within me was numb
    with woes,
And my heart uncomforted.
When will you cease, O dismal days?
When will you set me free?
For the frozen world and its desolate
    ways
Are all unloved of me!

I waited long, but the answer came—
The kiss of the sunshine lay
Warm as a flame on the lips that frame
The song in my heart to-day.
Blossoms of summer-time waved in
    the air,
Glimmers of sun in the sea;
Fair thoughts followed me everywhere,
And the world was dear to me.

338

THE OLD SWIMMIN'-HOLE

OH! the old swimmin'-hole! whare
    the crick so still and deep
Looked like a baby-river that was lay-
    ing half asleep,
And the gurgle of the worter round
    the drift jest below
Sounded like the laugh of something
    we onc't ust to know
Before we could remember anything
    but the eyes
Of the angels lookin' out as we left
    Paradise;

But the merry days of youth is beyond
    our controle,
And it's hard to part ferever with the
    old swimmin'-hole.

Oh! the old swimmin'-hole! In the
    happy days of yore,
When I ust to lean above it on the
    old sickamore,
Oh! it showed me a face in its warm
    sunny tide
That gazed back at me so gay and
    glorified,
It made me love myself, as I leaped to
    caress
My shadder smilin' up at me with sich
    tenderness.
But them days is past and gone, and
    old Time's tuck his toll
From the old man come back to the
    old swimmin'-hole.

Oh! the old swimmin'-hole! In the
    long, lazy days
When the humdrum of school made
    so many run-a-ways,
How plesant was the jurney down the
    old dusty lane,
Whare the tracks of our bare feet was
    all printed so plane
You could tell by the dent of the heel
    . and the sole
They was lots o' fun on hands at the
    old swimmin'-hole.
But the lost joys is past! Let your
    tears in sorrow roll
Like the rain that ust to dapple up the
    old swimmin'-hole.

Thare the bullrushes growed, and the
    cattails so tall,
And the sunshine and shadder fell over
    it all;

And it mottled the worter with amber
and gold
Tel the glad lilies rocked in the ripples
that rolled;
And the snake-feeder's four gauzy
wings fluttered by
Like the ghost of a daisy dropped out
of the sky,
Or a wownded apple-blossom in the
breeze's controle
As it cut acrost some orchurd to'rds the
old swimmin'-hole.

Oh! the old swimmin'-hole! When I
last saw the place,
The scenes was all changed, like the
change in my face;
The bridge of the railroad now crosses
the spot
Whare the old divin'-log lays sunk and
fergot.
And I stray down the banks whare the
trees ust to be—
But never again will theyr shade
shelter me!
And I wish in my sorrow I could strip
to the soul,
And dive off in my grave like the old
swimmin'-hole.

339

THOUGHTS FER THE DIS-
CURAGED FARMER

THE summer winds is sniffin' round
the bloomin' locus' trees;
And the clover in the pastur is a big
day fer the bees,
And they been a-swiggin' honey, above
board and on the sly,
Tel they stutter in theyr buzzin' and
stagger as they fly.

The flicker on the fence-rail 'pears to
jest spit on his wings
And roll up his feathers, by the sassy
way he sings;
And the hoss-fly is a-whettin'-up his
forelegs fer biz,
And the off-mare is a-switchin' all of
her tale they is.

You can hear the blackbirds jawin' as
they foller up the plow—
Oh, theyr bound to git theyr brekfast,
and theyr not a-carin' how;
So they quarrel in the furries, and they
quarrel on the wing—
But theyr peaceabler in pot-pies than
any other thing:
And it's when I git my shotgun
drawed up in stiddy rest,
She's as full of tribbelation as a yeller-
jacket's nest;
And a few shots before dinner, when
the sun's a-shinin' right,
Seems to kindo-sorto' sharpen up a
feller's appetite!

They's been a heap o' rain, but the
sun's out to-day,
And the clouds of the wet spell is all
cleared away,
And the woods is all the greener, and
the grass is greener still;
It may rain again to-morry, but I don't
think it will.
Some says the crops is ruined, and the
corn's drownded out,
And propha-sy the wheat will be a
failure, without doubt;
But the kind Providence that has never
failed us yet,
Will be on hands onc't more at the
'leventh hour, I bet!

Does the medder-lark complane, as he
    swims high and dry
Through the waves of the wind and
    the blue of the sky?
Does the quail set up and whissel in a
    disappinted way,
Er hang his head in silunce, and sor-
    row all the day?
Is the chipmuck's health a-failin'?—
    does he walk, er does he run?
Don't the buzzards ooze around up
    thare jest like they've allus done?
Is they anything the matter with the
    rooster's lungs er voice?
Ort a mortul be complanin' when
    dumb animals rejoice?

Then let us, one and all, be contentud
    with our lot;
The June is here this morning, and
    the sun is shining hot.
Oh! let us fill our harts up with the
    glory of the day,
And banish ev'ry doubt and care and
    sorrow fur away!
Whatever be our station, with Provi-
    dence fer guide,
Sich fine circumstances ort to make us
    satisfied;
Fer the world is full of roses, and the
    roses full of dew,
And the dew is full of heavenly love
    that drips fer me and you.

340

A GOOD-BY

"GOOD-BY, my friend!"
    He takes her hand—
The pressures blend:
    They understand

But vaguely why, with droop-
    ing eye,
Each moans — "Good-by! —
    Good-by!"

"Dear friend, good-by!"
    O she could smile
If she might cry
    A little while!—
She says, "I *ought* to smile—but
    I—
Forgive me — *There!* — Good-
    by!"

" 'Good-by?' Ah, no:
    I hate," says he,
"These 'good-bys' so!"
    "And *I*," says she,
    "Detest them so—why, I should
    die
    Were this a *real* 'good-by'!"

341

A SUMMER'S DAY

THE Summer's put the idy in
    My head that I'm a boy ag'in;
And all around's so bright and gay
I want to put my team away,
And jest git out whare I can lay
And soak my hide full of the day!
But work is work, and must be done—
Yit, as I work, I have my fun,
Jest fancyin' these furries here
Is childhood's paths onc't more so
    dear:—
And so I walk through medder-lands,
    And country lanes, and swampy
    trails
Whare long bullrushes bresh my
    hands;
And, tilted on the ridered rails

Of deadnin' fences, "Old Bob White"
Whissels his name in high delight,
And whirs away. I wunder still,
Whichever way a boy's feet will—
Whare trees has fell, with tangled tops
    Whare dead leaves shakes, I stop fer
        breth,
Heerin' the acorn as it drops—
    H'istin' my chin up still as deth,
And watchin' clos't, with upturned
    eyes,
The tree whare Mr. Squirrel tries
To hide hisse'f above the limb,
But lets his own tale tell on him.
I wunder on in deeper glooms—
    Git hungry, hearin' female cries
From old farmhouses, whare perfumes
    Of harvest dinners seems to rise
And ta'nt a feller, hart and brane,
With memories he can't explane.

I wunder through the underbresh,
    Whare pig-tracks, pintin' to'rds the
        crick,
Is picked and printed in the fresh
    Black bottom-lands, like wimmern
        pick
Theyr pie-crusts with a fork, some
    way,
When bakin' fer camp-meetin' day.

I wunder on and on and on,
Tel my gray hair and beard is gone,
And ev'ry wrinkle on my brow
Is rubbed clean out and shaddered now
With curls as brown and fare and fine
As tenderls of the wild grape-vine
That ust to climb the highest tree
To keep the ripest ones fer me.
I wunder still, and here I am
Wadin' the ford below the dam—
The worter chucklin' round my knee
    At hornet-welt and bramble-scratch,

And me a-slippin' 'crost to see
    Ef Tyner's plums is ripe, and size
The old man's wortermelon-patch,
    With juicy mouth and drouthy
        eyes.
Then, after sich a day of mirth
And happiness as worlds is wurth—
    So tired that Heaven seems nigh
        about,—
The sweetest tiredness on earth
    Is to git home and flatten out—
So tired you can't lay flat enugh,
And sorto' wish that you could spred
Out like molasses on the bed,
And jest drip off the aidges in
The dreams that never comes ag'in.

342

A HYMB OF FAITH

O, THOU that doth all things de-
    vise
And fashon fer the best,
He'p us who sees with mortul eyes
To overlook the rest.

They's times, of course, we grope in
    doubt,
    And in afflictions sore;
So knock the louder, Lord, without,
    And we'll unlock the door.

Make us to feel, when times looks bad
    And tears in pitty melts,
Thou wast the only he'p we had
    When they was nothin' else.

Death comes alike to ev'ry man
    That ever was borned on earth;
Then let us do the best we can
    To live fer all life's wurth.

Ef storms and tempusts dred to see
  Makes black the heavens ore,
They done the same in Galilee
  Two thousand years before.

But after all, the golden sun
  Poured out its floods on them
That watched and waited fer the One
  Then borned in Bethlyham.

Also, the star of holy writ
  Made noonday of the night,
Whilse other stars that looked at it
  Was envious with delight.

The sages then in wurship bowed,
  From ev'ry clime so fare;
O, sinner, think of that glad crowd
  That congergated thare!

They was content to fall in ranks
  With One that knowed the way
From good old Jurden's stormy banks
  Clean up to Jedgmunt Day.

No matter, then, how all is mixed
  In our near-sighted eyes,
All things is fer the best, and fixed
  Out straight in Paradise.

Then take things as God sends 'em
    here,
  And, ef we live er die,
Be more and more contenteder,
  Without a-astin' why.

O, Thou that doth all things devise
  And fashon fer the best,
He'p us who sees with mortul eyes
  To overlook the rest.

343

AT BROAD RIPPLE

AH, luxury! Beyond the heat
    And dust of town, with dan-
      gling feet,
Astride the rock below the dam,
In the cool shadows where the calm
Rests on the stream again, and all
Is silent save the waterfall,—
I bait my hook and cast my line,
And feel the best of life is mine.

No high ambition may I claim—
I angle not for lordly game
Of trout, or bass, or wary bream—
A black perch reaches the extreme
Of my desires; and "goggle-eyes"
Are not a thing that I despise;
A sunfish, or a "chub," or "cat"—
A "silver-side"—yea, even that!

In eloquent tranquillity
The waters lisp and talk to me.
Sometimes, far out, the surface breaks,
As some proud bass an instant shakes
His glittering armor in the sun,
And romping ripples, one by one,
Come dallying across the space
Where undulates my smiling face.

The river's story flowing by,
Forever sweet to ear and eye,
Forever tenderly begun—
Forever new and never done.
Thus lulled and sheltered in a shade
Where never feverish cares invade,
I bait my hook and cast my line,
And feel the best of life is mine.

344

THE COUNTRY EDITOR

A THOUGHTFUL brow and face
    —of sallow hue,
But warm with welcome, as we find
    him there,
Throned in his old misnomered
    "easy chair,"
Scrawling a "leader," or a book-review;
Or staring through the roof for some-
    thing new
With which to lift a wretched rival's
    hair,
Or blow some petty clique in empty
    air
And snap the party-ligaments in two.
A man he is deserving well of
    thee,—
So be compassionate—yea, pay thy
    dues,
Nor pamper him with thy spring-
    poetry,
But haul him wood, or something he
    can use;
And promptly act, nor tarry long
    when he
Gnaweth his pen and glareth
    rabidly.

345

WORTERMELON TIME

OLD wortermelon time is a-comin' round ag'in,
    And they ain't no man a-livin' any tickleder'n me,
Fer the way I hanker after wortermelons is a sin—
    Which is the why and wharefore, as you can plainly see.

Oh! it's in the sandy soil wortermelons does the best,
    And it's thare they'll lay and waller in the sunshine and the dew
Tel they wear all the green streaks clean off of theyr breast;
    And you bet I ain't a-findin' any fault with them; air you?

They ain't no better thing in the vegetable line;
    And they don't need much 'tendin', as ev'ry farmer knows;
And when theyr ripe and ready fer to pluck from the vine,
    I want to say to you theyr the best fruit that grows.

It's some likes the yeller-core, and some likes the red,
    And it's some says "The Little Californy" is the best;
But the sweetest slice of all I ever wedged in my head,
    Is the old "Edingburg Mounting-sprout," of the West.

You don't want no punkins nigh your wortermelon vines—
    'Cause, some-way-another, they'll spile your melons, shore;—

I've seed 'em taste like punkins, from the core to the rines,
    Which may be a fact you have heerd of before.

But your melons that's raised right and 'tended to with care,
    You can walk around amongst 'em with a parent's pride and joy,
And thump 'em on the heads with as fatherly a air
    As ef each one of them was your little girl er boy.

I joy in my hart jest to hear that rippin' sound
    When you split one down the back and jolt the halves in two,
And the friends you love the best is gethered all around—
    And you says unto your sweethart, "Oh, here's the core fer you!"

And I like to slice 'em up in big pieces fer 'em all,
    Espeshally the childern, and watch theyr high delight
As one by one the rines with theyr pink notches falls,
    And they holler fer some more, with unquenched appetite.

Boys takes to it natchurl, and I like to see 'em eat—
    A slice of wortermelon's like a frenchharp in theyr hands,
And when they "saw" it through theyr mouth sich music can't be beat—
    'Cause it's music both the sperit and the stummick understands.

Oh, they's more in wortermelons than the purty-colored meat,
    And the overflowin' sweetness of the worter squshed betwixt
The up'ard and the down'ard motions of a feller's teeth,
    And it's the taste of ripe old age and juicy childhood mixed.

Fer I never taste a melon but my thoughts flies away
    To the summer-time of youth; and again I see the dawn,
And the fadin' afternoon of the long summer day,
    And the dusk and dew a-fallin', and the night a-comin' on.

And thare's the corn around us, and the lispin' leaves and trees,
    And the stars a-peekin' down on us as still as silver mice,
And us boys in the wortermelons on our hands and knees,
    And the new-moon hangin' ore us like a yeller-cored slice.

Oh! it's wortermelon time is a-comin' round ag'in,
    And they ain't no man a-livin' any tickleder'n me,
Fer the way I hanker after wortermelons is a sin—
    Which is the why and wharefore, as you can plainly see.

346

A SONG OF THE CRUISE

O THE sun and the rain, and the
　　rain and the sun!
There'll be sunshine again when the
　　tempest is done;
And the storm will beat back when the
　　shining is past;
But in some happy haven we'll anchor
　　at last.
　　　　Then murmur no more,
　　　　In lull or in roar,
But smile and be brave till the voyage
　　is o'er.

O the rain and the sun, and the sun
　　and the rain!
When the tempest is done, then the
　　sunshine again;
And in rapture we'll ride through the
　　stormiest gales,
For God's hand's on the helm and His
　　breath in the sails.
　　　　Then murmur no more,
　　　　In lull or in roar,
But smile and be brave till the voyage
　　is o'er.

347

MY PHILOSOFY

I AIN'T, ner don't p'tend to be,
　　Much posted on philosofy;
But thare is times, when all alone,
I work out idees of my own.
And of these same thare is a few
I'd like to jest refer to you—
Pervidin' that you don't object
To listen clos't and rickollect.

I allus argy that a m..
Who does about the best he can
Is plenty good enugh to suit
This lower mundane institute—
No matter ef his daily walk
Is subject fer his neghbor's talk,
And critic-minds of ev'ry whim
Jest all git up and go fer him!

I knowed a feller onc't that had
The yeller-janders mighty bad,—
And each and ev'ry friend he'd meet
Would stop and give him some receet
Fer cuorin' of 'em. But he'd say
He kindo' thought they'd go away
Without no medicin', and boast
That he'd git well without one doste.

He kep' a-yellerin' on—and they
Perdictin' that he'd die some day
Before he knowed it! Tuck his bed,
The feller did, and lost his head,
And wundered in his mind a spell—
Then rallied, and, at last, got well,
But ev'ry friend that said he'd die
Went back on him eternally!

It's natchurl enugh, I guess,
When some gits more and some gits
　　less,
Fer them-uns on the slimmest side
To claim it ain't a fare divide;
And I've knowed some to lay and wait,
And git up soon, and set up late,
To ketch some feller they could hate
Fer goin' at a faster gait.

The signs is bad when folks commence
A-findin' fault with Providence,
And balkin' 'cause the earth don't
　　shake
At ev'ry prancin' step they take.
No man is grate tel he can see
How less than little he would be

Ef stripped to self, and stark and bare
He hung his sign out anywhare.

My doctern is to lay aside
Contensions, and be satisfied:
Jest do your best, and praise er blame
That follers that, counts jest the same.
I've allus noticed grate success
Is mixed with troubles, more er less,
And it's the man who does the best
That gits more kicks than all the rest.

348

WHEN AGE COMES ON

WHEN Age comes on!—
  The deepening dusk is where
    the dawn
Once glittered splendid, and the
    dew,
In honey-drips from red rose-lips,
  Was kissed away by me and you.—

And now across the frosty lawn
Black footprints trail, and Age comes
    on—
    And Age comes on!
  And biting wild-winds whistle
    through
Our tattered hopes—and Age comes
    on!

    When Age comes on!—
O tide of raptures, long withdrawn,
  Flow back in summer floods, and
    fling
Here at our feet our childhood sweet,
  And all the songs we used to
    sing! . . .
Old loves, old friends—all dead and
    gone—
Our old faith lost—and Age comes
    on—
    And Age comes on!
  Poor hearts! have we not anything
But longings left when Age comes
    on?

349

THE CIRCUS-DAY PARADE

OH! the Circus-Day Parade! How the bugles played and played!
  And how the glossy horses tossed their flossy manes and neighed,
As the rattle and the rhyme of the tenor-drummer's time
Filled all the hungry hearts of us with melody sublime!

How the grand band-wagon shone with a splendor all its own,
And glittered with a glory that our dreams had never known!
And how the boys behind, high and low of every kind,
Marched in unconscious capture, with a rapture undefined!

How the horsemen, two and two, with their plumes of white and blue
And crimson, gold and purple, nodding by at me and you,
Waved the banners that they bore, as the knights in days of yore,
Till our glad eyes gleamed and glistened like the spangles that they wore!

How the graceless-graceful stride of the elephant was eyed,
And the capers of the little horse that cantered at his side!
How the shambling camels, tame to the plaudits of their fame,
With listless eyes came silent, masticating as they came.

How the cages jolted past, with each wagon battened fast,
And the mystery within it only hinted of at last
From the little grated square in the rear, and nosing there
The snout of some strange animal that sniffed the outer air!

And, last of all, The Clown, making mirth for all the town,
With his lips curved ever upward and his eyebrows ever down,
And his chief attention paid to the little mule that played
A tattoo on the dashboard with his heels, in the Parade.

Oh! the Circus-Day Parade! How the bugles played and played!
And how the glossy horses tossed their flossy manes and neighed,
As the rattle and the rhyme of the tenor-drummer's time
Filled all the hungry hearts of us with melody sublime!

350

WHEN THE FROST IS ON THE PUNKIN

WHEN the frost is on the punkin and the fodder's in the shock,
    And you hear the kyouck and gobble of the struttin' turkey-cock,
And the clackin' of the guineys, and the cluckin' of the hens,
And the rooster's hallylooer as he tiptoes on the fence;
O, it's then's the times a feller is a-feelin' at his best,
With the risin' sun to greet him from a night of peaceful rest,
As he leaves the house, bareheaded, and goes out to feed the stock,
When the frost is on the punkin and the fodder's in the shock.

They's something kindo' harty-like about the atmusfere
When the heat of summer's over and the coolin' fall is here—
Of course we miss the flowers, and the blossums on the trees,
And the mumble of the hummin'-birds and buzzin' of the bees;
But the air's so appetizin'; and the landscape through the haze
Of a crisp and sunny morning of the airly autumn days

Is a pictur' that no painter has the colorin' to mock—
When the frost is on the punkin and the fodder's in the shock.

The husky, rusty russel of the tossels of the corn,
And the raspin' of the tangled leaves, as golden as the morn;
The stubble in the furries—kindo' lonesome-like, but still
A-preachin' sermons to us of the barns they growed to fill;
The strawstack in the medder, and the reaper in the shed;
The hosses in theyr stalls below—the clover overhead!—
O, it sets my hart a-clickin' like the tickin' of a clock,
When the frost is on the punkin and the fodder's in the shock!

Then your apples all is gethered, and the ones a feller keeps
Is poured around the celler-floor in red and yeller heaps;
And your cider-makin' 's over, and your wimmern-folks is through
With their mince and apple-butter, and theyr souse and saussage, too! . . .
I don't know how to tell it—but ef sich a thing could be
As the Angels wantin' boardin', and they'd call around on *me*—
I'd want to 'commodate 'em—all the whole-indurin' flock—
When the frost is on the punkin and the fodder's in the shock!

351

THAT NIGHT

YOU and I, and that night, with its
    perfume and glory!—
The scent of the locusts—the light
    of the moon;
And the violin weaving the waltzers a
    story,
Enmeshing their feet in the weft of
    the tune,
  Till their shadows uncertain
  Reeled round on the curtain,
While under the trellis we drank in
    the June.

Soaked through with the midnight the
    cedars were sleeping,
Their shadowy tresses outlined in
    the bright

Crystal, moon-smitten mists, where the
    fountain's heart, leaping
Forever, forever burst, full with de-
    light;
  And its lisp on my spirit
  Fell faint as that near it
Whose love like a lily bloomed out
    in the night.

O your glove was an odorous sachet of
    blisses!
The breath of your fan was a breeze
    from Cathay!
And the rose at your throat was a nest
    of spilled kisses!—
And the music!—in fancy I hear it
    to-day,
  As I sit here, confessing
  Our secret, and blessing
My rival who found us, and waltzed
    you away.

352

THE BAT

I

THOU dread, uncanny thing,
    With fuzzy breast and leathern
        wing,
In mad, zigzagging flight,
Notching the dusk, and buffeting
The black cheeks of the night,
    With grim delight!

II

What witch's hand unhasps
    Thy keen claw-cornered wings
From under the barn roof, and flings
Thee forth, with chattering gasps,
    To scud the air,
And nip the ladybug, and tear
Her children's hearts out unaware?

III

The glowworm's glimmer, and the
        bright,
Sad pulsings of the firefly's light,
    Are banquet lights to thee.
O less than bird, and worse than
        beast,
Thou Devil's self, or brat, at least,
    Grate not thy teeth at me!

353

ON THE DEATH OF LITTLE
MAHALA ASHCRAFT

"LITTLE Haly! Little Haly!" cheeps
    the robin in the tree;
"Little Haly!" sighs the clover, "Little
    Haly!" moans the bee;

"Little Haly! Little Haly!" calls the
    killdeer at twilight;
And the katydids and crickets hollers
    "Haly!" all the night.

The sunflowers and the hollyhawks
    droops over the garden fence;
The old path down the garden walks
    still holds her footprints' dents;
And the well-sweep's swingin' bucket
    seems to wait fer her to come
And start it on its wortery errant down
    the old beegum.

The beehives all is quiet; and the little
    Jersey steer,
When any one comes nigh it, acts so
    lonesome-like and queer;
And the little Banty chickens kindo'
    cutters faint and low,
Like the hand that now was feedin'
    'em was one they didn't know.

They's sorrow in the waivin' leaves
    of all the apple trees;
And sorrow in the harvest-sheaves, and
    sorrow in the breeze;
And sorrow in the twitter of the swal-
    lers 'round the shed;
And all the song her redbird sings is
    "Little Haly's dead!"

The medder 'pears to miss her, and the
    pathway through the grass,
Whare the dewdrops ust to kiss her
    little bare feet as she passed;
And the old pin in the gate-post seems
    to kindo'-sorto' doubt
That Haly's little sunburnt hands'll
    ever pull it out.

Did her father er her mother ever
    love her more'n me,

Er her sisters er her brother prize her
  love more tendurly?
I question—and what answer?—only
  tears, and tears alone,
And ev'ry neghbor's eyes is full o'
  tear-drops as my own.

"Little Haly! Little Haly!" cheeps the
  robin in the tree;
"Little Haly!" sighs the clover, "Little
  Haly!" moans the bee;
"Little Haly! Little Haly!" calls the
  killdeer at twilight,
And the katydids and crickets hollers
  "Haly!" all the night.

354

THE MULBERRY TREE

O, IT'S many's the scenes which is
  dear to my mind
As I think of my childhood so long
  left behind;
The home of my birth, with its old
  puncheon-floor,
And the bright morning-glorys that
  growed round the door;
The warped clabboard roof whare the
  rain it run off
Into streams of sweet dreams as I laid
  in the loft,
Countin' all of the joys that was dear-
  est to me,
And a-thinkin' the most of the mul-
  berry tree.

And to-day as I dream, with both eyes
  wide-awake,
I can see the old tree, and its limbs as
  they shake,
And the long purple berries that
  rained on the ground

Whare the pastur' was bald whare we
  trommpt it around.
And again, peekin' up through the
  thick leafy shade,
I can see the glad smiles of the friends
  when I strayed
With my little bare feet from my own
  mother's knee
To foller them off to the mulberry tree.

Leanin' up in the forks, I can see the
  old rail,
And the boy climbin' up it, claw,
  tooth, and toenail,
And in fancy can hear, as he spits on
  his hands,
The ring of his laugh and the rip of
  his pants.
But that rail led to glory, as certin and
  shore
As I'll never climb thare by that rout'
  any more—
What was all the green lauruls of
  Fame unto me,
With my brows in the boughs of the
  mulberry tree!

Then it's who can fergit the old mul-
  berry tree
That he knowed in the days when his
  thoughts was as free
As the flutterin' wings of the birds
  that flew out
Of the tall wavin' tops as the boys
  come about?
O, a crowd of my memories, laughin'
  and gay,
Is a-climbin' the fence of that pastur'
  to-day,
And a-pantin' with joy, as us boys ust
  to be,
They go racin' acrost fer the mulberry
  tree.

355

AUGUST

O MELLOW month and merry
    month,
  Let me make love to you,
And follow you around the world
  As knights their ladies do.
I thought your sisters beautiful,
  Both May and April, too,
But April she had rainy eyes,
  And May had eyes of blue.

And June—I liked the singing
  Of her lips—and liked her smile—

But all her songs were promises
  Of something, after while;
And July's face—the lights and shades
  That may not long beguile
With alternations o'er the wheat
  The dreamer at the stile.

But you!—ah, you are tropical,
  Your beauty is so rare;
Your eyes are clearer, deeper eyes
  Than any, anywhere;
Mysterious, imperious,
  Deliriously fair,
O listless Andalusian maid,
  With bangles in your hair!

356

TO MY OLD FRIEND, WILLIAM LEACHMAN

FER forty year and better you have been a friend to me,
    Through days of sore afflictions and dire adversity,
You allus had a kind word of counsul to impart,
Which was like a healin' 'intment to the sorrow of my hart.

When I buried my first womern, William Leachman, it was you
Had the only consolation that I could listen to—
Fer I knowed you had gone through it and had rallied from the blow,
And when you said I'd do the same, I knowed you'd ort to know.

But that time I'll long remember; how I wundered here and thare—
Through the settin'-room and kitchen, and out in the open air—
And the snowflakes whirlin', whirlin', and the fields a frozen glare,
And the neghbors' sleds and wagons congergatin' ev'rywhare.

I turned my eyes to'rds heaven, but the sun was hid away;
I turned my eyes to'rds earth again, but all was cold and gray;
And the clock, like ice a-crackin', clickt the icy hours in two—
And my eyes'd never thawed out ef it hadn't been fer you!

We set thare by the smoke-house—me and you out thare alone—
Me a-thinkin'—you a-talkin' in a soothin' undertone—

You a-talkin'—me a-thinkin' of the summers long ago,
And a-writin' "Marthy—Marthy" with my finger in the snow!

William Leachman, I can see you jest as plane as I could then;
And your hand is on my shoulder, and you rouse me up again;
And I see the tears a-drippin' from your own eyes, as you say:
"Be rickonciled and bear it—we but linger fer a day!"

At the last Old Settlers' Meetin' we went j'intly, you and me—
Your hosses and my wagon, as you wanted it to be;
And sence I can remember, from the time we've neghbored here,
In all sich friendly actions you have double-done your sheer.

It was better than the meetin', too, that nine-mile talk we had
Of the times when we first settled here and travel was so bad;
When we had to go on hoss-back, and sometimes on "Shanks's mare,"
And "blaze" a road fer them behind that had to travel thare.

And now we was a-trottin' 'long a level gravel pike,
In a big two-hoss road-wagon, jest as easy as you like—
Two of us on the front seat, and our wimmern-folks behind,
A-settin' in theyr Winsor-cheers in perfect peace of mind!

And we pinted out old landmarks, nearly faded out of sight:—
Thare they ust to rob the stage-coach; thare Gash Morgan had the fight
With the old stag-deer that pronged him—how he battled fer his life,
And lived to prove the story by the handle of his knife.

Thare the first griss-mill was put up in the Settlement, and we
Had tuck our grindin' to it in the Fall of Forty-three—
When we tuck our rifles with us, techin' elbows all the way,
And a-stickin' right together ev'ry minute, night and day.

Thare ust to stand the tavern that they called the "Travelers' Rest,"
And thare, beyent the covered bridge, "The Counterfitters' Nest"—
Whare they claimed the house was ha'nted—that a man was murdered thare,
And buried underneath the floor, er 'round the place somewhere.

And the old Plank-road they laid along in Fifty-one er two—
You know we talked about the times when the old road was new:
How "Uncle Sam" put down that road and never taxed the State
Was a problum, don't you rickollect, we couldn't *dim*onstrate?

Ways was devius, William Leachman, that me and you has past;
But as I found you true at first, I find you true at last;
And, now the time's a-comin' mighty nigh our jurney's end,
I want to throw wide open all my soul to you, my friend.

With the stren'th of all my bein', and the heat of hart and brane,
And ev'ry livin' drop of blood in artery and vane,
I love you and respect you, and I venerate your name,
Fer the name of William Leachman and True Manhood's jest the same!

357

THE GUIDE

IMITATED

WE rode across the level plain—
  We—my sagacious guide and
    I.—
He knew the earth—the air—the sky;
He knew when it would blow or rain,
And when the weather would be dry:
The bended blades of grass spake out
To him when Redskins were about;
The wagon tracks would tell him too,
The very day that they rolled through:
He knew their burden—whence they
  came—
If any horse along were lame,
And what its owner ought to do;
He knew when it would snow; he
  knew,
By some strange intuition, when
The buffalo would overflow
The prairies like a flood, and then
Recede in their stampede again.
He knew all things—yea, he did know
The brand of liquor in my flask,
And many times did tilt it up,
Nor halt or hesitate one whit,
Nor pause to slip the silver cup
From off its crystal base, nor ask

Why I preferred to drink from it.
And more and more I plied him, and
Did query of him o'er and o'er,
And seek to lure from him the lore
By which the man did understand
These hidden things of sky and land:
And, wrought upon, he sudden drew
His bridle—wheeled, and caught my
  hand—
Pressed it, as one that loved me true,
And bade me listen.
. . . . There be few
Like tales as strange to listen to!
He told me all—How, when a child,
The Indians stole him—there he
  laughed—
"They stole me and I stole their craft!"
Then slowly winked both eyes, and
  smiled,
And went on ramblingly,—"And
  they—
They reared me, and I ran away—
'Twas winter, and the weather wild;
And, caught up in the awful snows
That bury wilderness and plain,
I struggled on until I froze
My feet ere human hands again
Were reached to me in my distress,—
And lo, since then not any rain
May fall upon me anywhere,
Nor any cyclone's cussedness
Slip up behind me unaware,—

Nor any change of cold, or heat,
Or blow, or snow, but I do know
It's coming, days and days before;—
I know it by my frozen feet—
I know it by my itching heels,
And by the agony one feels
Who knows that scratching nevermore
Will bring to him the old and sweet
Relief he knew ere thus endowed
With knowledge that a certain cloud
Will burst with storm on such a day,
And when a snow will fall, and—nay,
I speak not falsely when I say
That by my tingling heels and toes
I measure time, and can disclose
The date of month—the week—and lo,
The very day and minute—yea—
Look at your watch!—An houi ago
And twenty minutes I did say
Unto myself with bitter laugh,
'In less than one hour and a half
Will I be drunken!' Is it so?"

358

SUTTER'S CLAIM

SAY! *you* feller! *You*—
    With that spade and the pick!—
What do you 'pose to do
    On this side o' the crick?
Goin' to tackle this claim?   Well, I
        reckon
You'll let up ag'in, purty quick!

No bluff, understand,—
    But the same has been tried,
And the claim never panned—
    Or the fellers has lied,—
For they tell of a dozen that tried it,
    And quit it most onsatisfied.

The luck's dead ag'in it!—
    The first man I see
That stuck a pick in it
    Proved *that* thing to me,—
For he sort o' took down, and got
        homesick,
And went back whar he'd orto be!

Then others they worked it
    Some—more or less,
But finally shirked it,
    In grades of distress,—
With an eye out—a jaw or skull busted,
    Or some sort o' seriousness.

The *last* one was plucky—
    He wasn't afeerd,
And bragged he was "lucky,"
    And said that "he'd heerd
A heap of bluff-talk," and swore awk-
        ward
He'd work any claim that he keered!

Don't you strike nary lick
    With that pick till I'm through;
This-here feller talked slick
    And as peart-like as you!
And he says: "I'll abide here
    As long as I please!"

But he didn't. . . . He died here—
    And I'm his disease!

359

DOLORES

LITHE-ARMED, and with satin-
    soft shoulders
    As white as the cream-crested wave;
With a gaze dazing every beholder's,
    She holds every gazer a slave:

Her hair, a fair haze, is outfloated
And flared in the air like a flame;
Bare-breasted, bare-browed and bare-
    throated—
Too smooth for the soothliest name.

She wiles you with wine, and wrings
    for you
Ripe juices of citron and grape;
She lifts up her lute and sings for you
Till the soul of you seeks no escape;
And you revel and reel with mad
    laughter,
And fall at her feet, at her beck,
And the scar of her sandal thereafter
You wear like a gyve round your
    neck.

360

MY FIDDLE

MY fiddle?—Well, I kindo' keep
    her handy, don't you know!
Though I ain't so much inclined to
    tromp the strings and switch the
    bow
As I was before the timber of my el-
    bows got so dry,
And my fingers was more limber-like
    and caperish and spry;
        Yit I can plonk and plunk and
            plink,
        And tune her up and play,
        And jest lean back and laugh
            and wink
        At ev'ry rainy day!

My playin' 's only middlin'—tunes I
    picked up when a boy—
The kindo'-sorto' fiddlin' that the folks
    call "cordaroy";

"The Old Fat Gal," and "Rye-straw,"
    and "My Sailyor's on the Sea,"
Is the old cowtillions *I* "saw" when the
    ch'ice is left to me;
        And so I plunk and plonk and
            plink,
        And rosum-up my bow
        And play the tunes that makes
            you think
        The devil's in your toe!

I was allus a-romancin', do-less boy, to
    tell the truth,
A-fiddlin' and a-dancin', and a-wastin'
    of my youth,
And a-actin' and a-cuttin'-up all sorts
    o' silly pranks
That wasn't worth a button of any-
    body's thanks!
        But they tell me, when I used
            to plink
        And plonk and plunk and
            play,
        My music seemed to have the
            kink
        O' drivin' cares away!

That's how this here old fiddle's won
    my hart's indurin' love!
From the strings acrost her middle, to
    the schreechin' keys above—
From her "apern," over "bridge," and
    to the ribbon round her throat,
She's a wooin', cooin' pigeon, singin'
    "Love me" ev'ry note!
        And so I pat her neck, and
            plink
        Her strings with lovin'
            hands,—
        And, list'nin' clos't, I some-
            times think
        She kindo' understands!

361

NORTH AND SOUTH

OF the North I wove a dream,
  All bespangled with the gleam
Of the glancing wings of swallows
Dipping ripples in a stream,
That, like·a tide of wine,
Wound through lands of shade and
  shine
Where purple grapes hung bursting on
  the vine.

And where orchard-boughs were bent
Till their tawny fruitage blent
  With the golden wake that marked
  the
Way the happy reapers went;
Where the dawn died into noon
As the May-mists into June,
And the dusk fell like a sweet face in
  a swoon.

Of the South I dreamed: And there
Came a vision clear and fair
  As the marvelous enchantments
Of the mirage of the air;
And I saw the bayou-trees,
With their lavish draperies,
Hang heavy o'er the moon-washed cy-
  press-knees.

Peering from lush fens of rice,
I beheld the Negro's eyes,
  Lit with that old superstition
Death itself can not disguise;
And I saw the palm-tree nod
Like an Oriental god,
And the cotton froth and bubble from
  the pod.

And I dreamed that North and South,
With a sigh of dew and drouth,
  Blew each unto the other

The salute of lip and mouth;
And I wakened, awed and thrilled—
Every doubting murmur stilled
In the silence of the dream I found ful-
  filled.

362

THE DAYS GONE BY

O THE days gone by! O the days
  gone by!
The apples in the orchard, and the
  pathway through the rye;
The chirrup of the robin, and the
  whistle of the quail
As he piped across the meadows sweet
  as any nightingale;
When the bloom was on the clover,
  and the blue was in the sky,
And my happy heart brimmed over, in
  the days gone by.

In the days gone by, when my naked
  feet were tripped
By the honeysuckle tangles where the
  water-lilies dipped,
And the ripples of the river lipped the
  moss along the brink
Where the placid-eyed and lazy-footed
  cattle came to drink,
And the tilting snipe stood fearless of
  the truant's wayward cry
And the splashing of the swimmer, in
  the days gone by.

O the days gone by! O the days gone
  by!
The music of the laughing lip, the
  luster of the eye;
The childish faith in fairies, and Alad-
  din's magic ring—
The simple, soul-reposing, glad belief
  in every thing,—

When life was like a story holding
　　neither sob nor sigh,
In the golden olden glory of the days
　　gone by.

363

THE CLOVER

SOME sings of the lilly, and daisy,
　　and rose,
And the pansies and pinks that the
　　Summer-time throws
In the green grassy lap of the medder
　　that lays
Blinkin' up at the skyes through the
　　sunshiny days;
But what is the lilly and all of the
　　rest
Of the flowers, to a man with a hart
　　in his brest
That was dipped brimmin' full of the
　　honey and dew
Of the sweet clover-blossoms his baby-
　　hood knew?

I never set eyes on a clover-field now,
Er fool round a stable, er climb in the
　　mow,
But my childhood comes back jest as
　　clear and as plane
As the smell of the clover I'm sniffin'
　　again;
And I wunder away in a barefooted
　　dream,
Whare I tangle my toes in the blos-
　　soms that gleam
With the dew of the dawn of the
　　morning of love
Ere it wept ore the graves that I'm
　　weepin' above.

And so I love clover—it seems like a
　　part
Of the sacerdest sorrows and joys of
　　my hart;
And wharever it blossoms, oh, thare let
　　me bow
And thank the good God as I'm thank-
　　in' Him now;
And I pray to Him still fer the stren'th
　　when I die,
To go out in the clover and tell it
　　good-by,
And lovin'ly nestle my face in its bloom
While my soul slips away on a breth
　　of purfume.

364

GEORGE A. CARR

O PLAYMATE of the far-away
　　And dear delights of Boyhood's
　　　day,
And friend and comrade true and tried
Through length of years of life beside,
I bid you thus a fond farewell
Too deep for words or tears to tell.

But though I lose you, nevermore
To greet you at the open door,
To grasp your hand or see your smile,
I shall be thankful all the while
Because your love and loyalty
Have made a happier world for me.

So rest you, Playmate, in that land
Still hidden from us by His hand,
Where you may know again in truth
All of the glad days of your youth—
As when in days of endless ease
We played beneath the apple trees.

365

THE SOUTH WIND AND THE SUN

O THE South Wind and the Sun!
    How each loved the other one—
Full of fancy—full of folly—
    Full of jollity and fun!
How they romped and ran about,
Like two boys when school is out,
With glowing face, and lisping lip,
Low laugh, and lifted shout!

And the South Wind—he was dressed
    With a ribbon round his breast
That floated, flapped and fluttered
    In a riotous unrest,
And a drapery of mist
From the shoulder and the wrist
Flowing backward with the motion
Of the waving hand he kissed.

And the Sun had on a crown
    Wrought of gilded thistle-down,
And a scarf of velvet vapor,
    And a raveled-rainbow gown;
And his tinsel-tangled hair,
Tossed and lost upon the air,
Was glossier and flossier
    Than any anywhere.

And the South Wind's eyes were two
    Little dancing drops of dew,
As he puffed his cheeks, and pursed
    his lips,
And blew and blew and blew!
And the Sun's—like diamond-stone,
Brighter yet than ever known,
As he knit his brows and held his
    breath,
And shone and shone and shone!

And this pair of merry fays
Wandered through the summer days;
Arm in arm they went together
    Over heights of morning haze—
Over slanting slopes of lawn
Then went on and on and on,
Where the daisies looked like star-
    tracks
Trailing up and down the dawn.

And where'er they found the top
Of a wheat-stalk droop and lop
They chucked it underneath the chin
    And praised the lavish crop.
Till it lifted with the pride
Of the heads it grew beside,
And then the South Wind and the Sun
    Went onward satisfied.

Over meadow-lands they tripped,
Where the dandelions dipped
In crimson foam of clover-bloom,
    And dripped and dripped and
        dripped;
And they clinched the bumble-
        stings,
Gauming honey on their wings,
And bundling them in lily-bells,
    With maudlin murmurings.

And the humming-bird, that hung
    Like a jewel up among
The tilted honeysuckle-horns,
    They mesmerized, and swung
In the palpitating air,
Drowsed with odors strange and
    rare,
And, with whispered laughter, slipped
    away,
And left him hanging there.

And they braided blades of grass
Where the truant had to pass;
And they wriggled through the rushes

And the reeds of the morass,
Where they danced, in rapture sweet,
O'er the leaves that laid a street
Of undulant mosaic for
The touches of their feet.

By the brook with mossy brink
Where the cattle came to drink,
They trilled and piped and whistled
With the thrush and bobolink,
Till the kine, in listless pause,
Switched their tails in mute applause,
With lifted heads, and dreamy eyes,
And bubble-dripping jaws.

And where the melons grew,
Streaked with yellow, green and
  blue,
These jolly sprites went wandering
Through spangled paths of dew;
And the melons, here and there,
They made love to, everywhere,
Turning their pink souls to crimson
With caresses fond and fair.

Over orchard walls they went,
Where the fruited boughs were bent
Till they brushed the sward beneath
  them
Where the shine and shadow blent;
And the great green pear they shook
Till the sallow hue forsook
Its features, and the gleam of gold
Laughed out in every nook.

And they stroked the downy cheek
Of the peach, and smoothed it sleek,
And flushed it into splendor;
And, with many an elfish freak,
Gave the russet's rust a wipe—
Prankt the rambo with a stripe,
And the wine-sap blushed its reddest
As they spanked the pippins ripe.

Through the woven ambuscade
That the twining vines had made,
They found the grapes, in clusters,
Drinking up the shine and shade—
Plumpt, like tiny skins of wine,
With a vintage so divine
That the tongue of fancy tingled
With the tang of muscadine.

And the golden-banded bees,
Droning o'er the flowery leas,
They bridled, reined, and rode away
Across the fragrant breeze,
Till in hollow oak and elm
They had groomed and stabled them
In waxen stalls that oozed with dews
Of rose and lily-stem.

Where the dusty highway leads,
High above the wayside weeds,
They sowed the air with butterflies
Like blooming flower-seeds,
Till the dull grasshopper sprung
Half a man's height up, and hung
Tranced in the heat, with whirring
  wings,
And sung and sung and sung!

And they loitered, hand in hand,
Where the snipe along the sand
Of the river ran to meet them
As the ripple meets the land,
Till the dragon-fly, in light
Gauzy armor, burnished bright,
Came tilting down the waters
In a wild, bewildered flight.

And they heard the killdee's call,
And afar, the waterfall,
But the rustle of a falling leaf
They heard above it all;
And the trailing willow crept
Deeper in the tide that swept

The leafy shallop to the shore,
And wept and wept and wept!

And the fairy vessel veered
From its moorings—tacked and
steered
For the center of the current—
Sailed away and disappeared:
And the burthen that it bore
From the long-enchanted shore—
"Alas! the South Wind and the Sun!"
I murmur evermore.

For the South Wind and the Sun,
Each so loves the other one,
For all his jolly folly
And frivolity and fun,
That our love for them they weigh
As their fickle fancies may,
And when at last we love them most,
They laugh and sail away.

366

WHERE-AWAY

O THE Lands of Where-Away!
Tell us—tell us—where are they?
Through the darkness and the dawn
We have journeyed on and on—
From the cradle to the cross—
From possession unto loss.—
Seeking still, from day to day,
For the Lands of Where-Away.

When our baby-feet were first
Planted where the daisies burst,
And the greenest grasses grew
In the fields we wandered through,—
On, with childish discontent,
Ever on and on we went,
Hoping still to pass, some day,
O'er the verge of Where-Away.

Roses laid their velvet lips
On our own, with fragrant sips;
But their kisses held us not,
All their sweetness we forgot;—
Though the brambles in our track
Plucked at us to hold us back—
"Just ahead," we used to say,
"Lie the Lands of Where-Away."

Children at the pasture-bars,
Through the dusk, like glimmering
stars,
Waved their hands that we should bide
With them over eventide:
Down the dark their voices failed
Falteringly, as they hailed,
And died into yesterday—
Night ahead and—Where-Away?

Twining arms about us thrown—
Warm caresses, all our own,
Can but stay us for a spell—
Love hath little new to tell
To the soul in need supreme,
Aching ever with the dream
Of the endless bliss it may
Find in Lands of Where-Away!

367

THE SMITTEN PURIST

*And the Charming Miss Smith's Effect
Upon Him*

THWEET Poethy! let me *lithp*
forthwith,
That I may thhing of the name of
Smith—
Which name, alath!
In Harmony hath

No adequate rhyme, letht you grant
  me thith,—
That the thimple thibillant thound of
  eth—
(Which to thave my thoul, I can not
  expreth!)
Thuth I may thhingingly,
Wooingly and winningly
Thu—thu—thound in the name of
  Smith.

O give me a name that will rhyme
  with Smith,—
For wild and weird ath the sthrange
  name ith,
  I would sthrangle a sthrain
  And a thad refrain
Faint and sthweet ath a whithpered
  kissth;
I would thhing thome thong for the
  mythtic mitth
Who beareth the thingular name of
  Smith—
  The dathzlingly brilli-ant,
  Rarely rethilliant
Ap—pup—pellation of Smith!

O had I a name that would rhyme with
  Smith—
Thome rhythmical tincture of retho-
  nant blith—
  Thome melody rare
  Ath the cherubth blare
On them little trumpeths they're foolin'
  with—
I would thit me down, and I'd thhing
  like thith
Of the girl of the thingular name of
  Smith—
  The sthrangely curiouth,
  Rich and luxuriouth
Pup—patronymic of Smith!

368

CHRISTINE'S SONG

UP in Tentoleena Land—
    Tentoleena! Tentoleena!
All the Dollies, hand in hand,
    Mina, Nainie, and Serena,
Dance the Fairy fancy dances,
With glad songs and starry glances,
Lisping roundelays; and, after,
Bird-like interludes of laughter
Strewn and scattered o'er the lawn
Their gilt sandals twinkle on
Through light mists of silver sand—
    Up in Tentoleena Land.

Up in Tentoleena Land—
    Tentoleena! Tentoleena!
Blares the eery Elfin band—
    Trumpet, harp and concertina—
Larkspur bugle—honeysuckle
Cornet, with a quickstep chuckle
In its golden throat; and, maybe,
Lilies-of-the-valley they be
Baby-silver-bells that chime
Musically all the time,
Tossed about from hand to hand—
    Up in Tentoleena Land.

Up in Tentoleena Land—
    Tentoleena! Tentoleena!
Dollies dark, and blond and bland—
    Sweet as musk-rose or verbena—
Sweet as moon-blown daffodillies,
Or wave-jostled water-lilies
Yearning to'rd the rose-mouths, ready
Leaning o'er the river's eddy,—
Dance, and glancing fling to you,
Through these lines you listen to,
Kisses blown from lip and hand
    Out of Tentoleena Land!

369

DEAR HANDS

THE touches of her hands are like
    the fall
Of velvet snowflakes; like the touch
    of down
The peach just brushes 'gainst the gar-
    den wall;
The flossy fondlings of the thistle-wisp
    Caught in the crinkle of a leaf of
    brown
The blighting frost hath turned from
    green to crisp.

Soft as the falling of the dusk at
    night,
The touches of her hands, and the de-
    light—
    The touches of her hands!
The touches of her hands are like the
    dew
That falls so softly down no one e'er
    knew
The touch thereof save lovers like to
    one
Astray in lights where ranged Endym-
    ion.

O rarely soft, the touches of her hands,
As drowsy zephyrs in enchanted
    lands;
    Or pulse of dying fay; or fairy
    sighs;
Or—in between the midnight and the
    dawn,
When long unrest and tears and fears
    are gone—
    Sleep, smoothing down the lids of
    weary eyes.

370

WINTER FANCIES

I

WINTER without
    And warmth within;
The winds may shout
    And the storm begin;
The snows may pack
    At the window-pane,
And the skies grow black,
    And the sun remain
Hidden away
    The livelong day—
But here—in here is the warmth of
    May!

II

Swoop your spitefulest
    Up the flue,
    Wild Winds—do!
What in the world do I care for you?
    O delightfulest
    Weather of all,
    Howl and squall,
And shake the trees till the last leaves
    fall!

III

The joy one feels,
    In an easy-chair,
Cocking his heels
    In the dancing air
That wreathes the rim of a roaring
    stove
Whose heat loves better than hearts
    can love,
Will not permit
    The coldest day
    To drive away
The fire in his blood, and the bliss of it!

IV

Then blow, Winds, blow!
　And rave and shriek,
And snarl and snow,
　Till your breath grows weak—
While here in my room
　I'm as snugly shut
As a glad little worm
　In the heart of a nut!

371

"A BRAVE REFRAIN"

WHEN snow is here, and the
　　trees look weird,
And the knuckled twigs are gloved
　with frost;
When the breath congeals in the
　drover's beard,
And the old pathway to the barn is
　lost;
When the rooster's crow is sad to hear,
　And the stamp of the stabled horse
　is vain,
And the tone of the cow-bell grieves
　the ear—
　O then is the time for a brave re-
　frain!

When the gears hang stiff on the har-
　ness-peg,
　And the tallow gleams in frozen
　streaks;
And the old hen stands on a lonesome
　leg,
　And the pump sounds hoarse and
　the handle squeaks;
When the wood-pile lies in a shrouded
　heap,
　And the frost is scratched from the
　window-pane

And anxious eyes from the inside
　peep—
　O then is the time for a brave re-
　frain!

When the ax-helve warms at the chim-
　ney-jamb,
　And hobnailed shoes on the hearth
　below,
And the house-cat curls in a slumber
　calm,
　And the eight-day clock ticks loud
　and slow;
When the harsh broom-handle jabs the
　ceil
　'Neath the kitchen-loft, and the
　drowsy brain
Sniffs the breath of the morning
　meal—
　O then is the time for a brave re-
　frain!

ENVOI

When the skillet seethes, and a blub-
　bering hot
Tilts the lid of the coffee-pot,
And the scent of the buckwheat cake
　grows plain—
　O then is the time for a brave refrain!

372

AS I SIT IN THE SILENCE

MANY pleasures of Youth have
　　been buoyantly sung—
　And, borne on the winds of delight,
　may they beat
With their palpitant wings at the
　hearts of the Young,
　And in bosoms of Age find as warm
　a retreat!—

Yet sweetest of all of the musical
  throng,
Though least of the numbers that
  upward aspire,
Is the one rising now into wavering
  song,
As I sit in the silence and gaze in the
  fire.

'Tis a Winter long dead that be-
  leaguers my door
And muffles his steps in the snows
  of the past:
And I see, in the embers I'm dreaming
  before,
  Lost faces of love as they looked on
  me last:—
The round, laughing eyes of the desk-
  mate of old
  Gleam out for a moment with truant
  desire—
Then fade and are lost in a City of
  Gold,
  As I sit in the silence and gaze in the
  fire.

And then comes the face, peering back
  in my own,
  Of a shy little girl, with her lids
  drooping low,
As she faltering tells, in a far-away
  tone,
  The ghost of a story of long, long
  ago.—
Then her dewy blue eyes they are
  lifted again;
  But I see their glad light slowly fail
  and expire,
As I reach and cry to her in vain, all in
  vain!—
  As I sit in the silence and gaze in the
  fire.

Then the face of a Mother looks back,
  through the mist
  Of the tears that are welling; and,
  lucent with light,
I see the dear smile of the lips I have
  kissed
  As she knelt by my cradle at morn-
  ing and night;
And my arms are outheld, with a
  yearning too wild
  For any but God in His love to in-
  spire,
As she pleads at the foot of His throne
  for her child,—
  As I sit in the silence and gaze in
  the fire.

O pathos of rapture! O glorious pain!
  My heart is a blossom of joy over-
  run
With a shower of tears, as a lily with
  rain
  That weeps in the shadow and
  laughs in the sun.
The blight of the frost may descend on
  the tree,
  And the leaf and the flower may fall
  and expire,
But ever and ever love blossoms for
  me,
  As I sit in the silence and gaze in
  the fire.

373

LONGFELLOW'S LOVE FOR THE CHILDREN

AWAKE, he loved their voices,
    And wove them into his rhyme;
And the music of their laughter
  Was with him all the time.

Though he knew the tongues of na-
 tions,
And their meanings all were dear,
The prattle and lisp of a little child
Was the sweetest for him to hear.

374

A SONG OF LONG AGO

A SONG of Long Ago:
 Sing it lightly—sing it low—
Sing it softly—like the lisping of the
 lips we used to know
When our baby-laughter spilled
From the glad hearts ever filled
With music blithe as robin ever trilled!

Let the fragrant summer breeze,
And the leaves of locust-trees,
And the apple-buds and -blossoms, and
 the wings of honey-bees,
All palpitate with glee,
Till the happy harmony
Brings back each childish joy to you
 and me

Let the eyes of fancy turn
Where the tumbled pippins burn
Like embers in the orchard's lap of
 tangled grass and fern,—
There let the old path wind
In and out, and on behind
The cider-press that chuckles as we
 grind.

Blend in the song the moan
Of the dove that grieves alone,
And the wild whir of the locust, and
 the bumble's drowsy drone;
And the low of cows that call
Through the pasture-bars when all
The landscape fades away at evenfall.

Then, far away and clear,
Through the dusky atmosphere,
Let the wailing of the killdee be the
 only sound we hear:
O sad and sweet and low
As the memory may know
Is the glad-pathetic song of Long Ago!

375

UNLESS

WHO has not *wanted* does not
 guess
What plenty is.—Who has not
 groped
In depths of doubt and hopelessness
Has never truly hoped.—
Unless, sometimes, a shadow falls
 Upon his mirth, and veils his sight,
 And from the darkness drifts the
  light
Of love at intervals.

And that most dear of everything,
 I hold, is love; and who can sit
With lightest heart and laugh and sing,
 Knows not the worth of it.—
Unless, in some strange throng, per-
 chance,
 He feels how thrilling sweet it is,
 One yearning look that answers his—
The troth of glance and glance.

Who knows not pain, knows not, alas!
 What pleasure is.—Who knows not
  of
The bitter cup that will not pass,
 Knows not the taste of love.
O souls that thirst, and hearts that fast,
 And natures faint with famishing,
 God lift and lead and safely bring
You to your own at last!

376

WHEN EARLY MARCH SEEMS MIDDLE MAY

WHEN country roads begin to
    thaw
In mottled spots of damp and dust,
And fences by the margin draw
Along the frosty crust
Their graphic silhouettes, I say,
The Spring is coming round this way.

When morning-time is bright with sun
    And keen with wind, and both con-
        fuse
The dancing, glancing eyes of one
    With tears that ooze and ooze—
And nose-tips weep as well as they,
The Spring is coming round this way.

When suddenly some shadow-bird
    Goes wavering beneath the gaze,
And through the hedge the moan is
        heard
Of kine that fain would graze
In grasses new, I smile and say,
The Spring is coming round this way.

When knotted horse-tails are untied,
    And teamsters whistle here and
        there,
And clumsy mitts are laid aside
    And choppers' hands are bare,
And chips are thick where children
        play,
The Spring is coming round this way.

When through the twigs the farmer
    tramps,
    And troughs are chunked beneath
    the trees,

And fragrant hints of sugar-camps
    Astray in every breeze,—
When early March seems middle May,
The Spring is coming round this way.

When coughs are changed to laughs,
    and when
    Our frowns melt into smiles of glee,
And all our blood thaws out again
    In streams of ecstasy,
And poets wreak their roundelay,
The Spring is coming round this way.

377

THE MUSKINGUM VALLEY

THE Muskingum Valley!—How
    longin' the gaze
A feller throws back on its long sum-
    mer days,
When the smiles of its blossoms and
    my smiles wuz one-
And-the-same, from the rise to the set
    o' the sun:
Wher' the hills sloped as soft as the
    dawn down to noon,
And the river run by like an old fiddle-
    tune,
And the hours glided past as the bub-
    bles 'ud glide,
All so loaferin'-like, 'long the path o'
    the tide.

In the Muskingum Valley—it 'peared
    like the skies
Looked lovin' on me as my own
    mother's eyes,
While the laughin'-sad song of the
    stream seemed to be
Like a lullaby angels was wastin' on
    me—

Tel, swimmin' the air, like the gossa-
mer's thread,
'Twixt the blue underneath and the
blue overhead,
My thoughts went astray in that so-
to-speak realm
Wher' Sleep bared her breast as a
piller fer them.

In the Muskingum Valley, though far,
far a-way,
I know that the winter is bleak there
to-day—
No bloom ner perfume on the brambles
er trees—
Wher' the buds ust to bloom, now the
icicles freeze.—
That the grass is all hid 'long the side
of the road
Wher' the deep snow has drifted and
shifted and blowed—
And I feel in my life the same changes
is there,—
The frost in my heart, and the snow
in my hair.

But, Muskingum Valley! my memory
sees
Not the white on the ground, but the
green in the trees—
Not the froze'-over gorge, but the cur-
rent, as clear
And warm as the drop that has jes'
trickled here;
Not the choked-up ravine, and the
hills topped with snow,
But the grass and the blossoms I
knowed long ago
When my little bare feet wundered
down wher' the stream
In the Muskingum Valley flowed on
like a dream.

378

SERENADE—TO NORA

THE moonlight is failin'—
        The sad stars are palin'—
The black wings av night are a-
        dhroopin' an' trailin';
The wind's miserere
Sounds lonesome an' dreary;
The katydid's dumb an' the nightin-
        gale's weary.

Troth, Nora! I'm wadin'
The grass an' paradin'
The dews at your dure, wid my swate
        serenadin',
Alone and forsaken,
Whilst you're never wakin'
To tell me you're wid me an' I am
        mistaken!

Don't think that my singin'
It's wrong to be flingin'
Forninst av the dreams that the Angels
        are bringin';
For if your pure spirit
Might waken and hear it,
You'd never be draamin' the Saints
        could come near it!

Then lave off your slaapin'—
The pulse av me's laapin'
To have the two eyes av yez down on
        me paapin'.
Och, Nora! It's hopin'
Your windy ye'll open
And light up the night where the
        heart av me's gropin'.

379

THE LITTLE WHITE HEARSE

AS the little white hearse went glim-
mering by—
The man on the coal-cart jerked his
lines,
And smutted the lid of either eye,
And turned and stared at the busi-
ness signs;
And the street-car driver stopped
and beat
His hands on his shoulders, and
gazed up-street
Till his eye on the long track
reached the sky—
As the little white hearse went
glimmering by.

As the little white hearse went glim-
mering by—
A stranger petted a ragged child
In the crowded walks, and she knew
not why,
But he gave her a coin for the way
she smiled;
And a boot-black thrilled with a
pleasure strange
As a customer put back his change
With a kindly hand and a grate-
ful sigh,
As the little white hearse went
glimmering by.

As the little white hearse went glim-
mering by—
A man looked out of a window dim,
And his cheeks were wet and his heart
was dry,
For a dead child even was dear to
him!

And he thought of his empty life,
and said:—
"Loveless alive, and loveless
dead—
Nor wife nor child in earth or
sky!"
As the little white hearse went
glimmering by.

380

A GLIMPSE OF PAN

I CAUGHT but a glimpse of him.
Summer was here,
And I strayed from the town and
its dust and heat,
And walked in a wood, while the noon
was near,
Where the shadows were cool, and the
atmosphere
Was misty with fragrances stirred
by my feet
From surges of blossoms that billowed
sheer
Of the grasses, green and sweet.

And I peered through a vista of lean-
ing trees,
Tressed with long tangles of vines
that swept
To the face of a river, that answered
these
With vines in the wave like the vines
in the breeze,
Till the yearning lips of the ripples
crept
And kissed them, with quavering
ecstasies,
And wistfully laughed and wept.

And there, like a dream in a swoon,
  I swear
I saw Pan lying,—his limbs in the
  dew
And the shade, and his face in the
  dazzle and glare
Of the glad sunshine; while every-
  where,
Over, across, and around him blew
Filmy dragon-flies hither and there,
  And little white butterflies, two and
  two,
In eddies of odorous air.

381

THE GREAT GOD PAN

What was he doing, the great god Pan!
              —Mrs. Browning.

O PAN is the goodliest god, I wist,
    Of all of the lovable gods that
      be!—
For his two strong hands were the first
    to twist
From the depths of the current,
    through spatter and mist,
The long-hushed reeds that he
    pressed in glee
To his murmurous mouth, as he
    chuckled and kissed
Their souls into melody.

And the wanton winds are in love
    with Pan:
  They loll in the shade with him day
    by day;
And betimes as beast, and betimes as
    man,
  They love him as only the wild winds
    can,—

Or sleeking the coat of his limbs one
    way,
Or brushing his brow with the locks
    they fan
To the airs he loves to play.

And he leans by the river, in gloom
    and gleam,
  Blowing his reeds as the breezes
    blow—
His cheeks puffed out, and his eyes in
    a dream,
And his hoof-tips, over the leaves in
    the stream,
  Tapping the time of the tunes that
    flow
As sweet as the drowning echoes
    seem
  To his rollicking wraith below.

382

HER LIGHT GUITAR

S HE twankled a tune on her light
    guitar—
  A low, sweet jangle of tangled
    sounds,
As blurred as the voices of the fairies
    are,
  Dancing in moondawn dales and
    downs;
  And the tinkling drip of the
    strange refrain
  Ran over the rim of my soul like
    rain.

The great blond moon in the mid-
    night skies
  Paused and poised o'er the trellis
    eaves,
And the stars, in the light of her up-
    turned eyes,

Sifted their love through the rifted
leaves—
Glittered and splintered in crystal
mist
Down the glittering strings that.
her fingers kissed.

O the melody mad! O the tinkle and
thrill
Of the ecstasy of the exquisite
thing!
The red rose dropped from the win-
dow-sill
And lay in a long swoon quivering;
While the dying notes of the strain
divine
Rippled in glee up my spell-bound
spine.

383

THE ALL-GOLDEN

I

THROUGH every happy line I sing
I feel the tonic of the Spring.
The day is like an old-time face
That gleams across some grassy place—
An old-time face—an old-time chum
Who rises from the grave to come
And lure me back along the ways
Of time's all-golden yesterdays.
Sweet day! to thus remind me of
The truant boy I used to love—
To set, once more, his finger-tips
Against the blossom of his lips,
And pipe for me the signal known
By none but him and me alone!

II

I see, across the schoolroom floor,
The shadow of the open door,

And dancing dust and sunshine blent
Slanting the way the morning went,
And beckoning my thoughts afar
Where reeds and running waters are;
Where amber-colored bayous glass
The half-drown'd weeds and wisps of
grass,
Where sprawling frogs, in loveless key,
Sing on and on incessantly.
Against the green wood's dim expanse
The cattail tilts its tufted lance,
While on its tip—one might declare
The white "snake-feeder" blossomed
there!

III

I catch my breath, as children do
In woodland swings when life is new,
And all the blood is warm as wine
And tingles with a tang divine.
My soul soars up the atmosphere
And sings aloud where God can hear,
And all my being leans intent
To mark His smiling wonderment.
O gracious dream, and gracious time,
And gracious theme, and gracious
rhyme—
When buds of Spring begin to blow
In blossoms that we used to know
And lure us back along the ways
Of time's all-golden yesterdays!

384

THE WAY THE BABY CAME

O THIS is the way the baby came:
Out of the night as comes the
dawn
Out of the embers as the flame;
Out of the bud the blossom on

The apple-bough that blooms the same
  As in glad summers dead and
    gone—
With a grace and beauty none could
    name—
O this is the way the baby came!

385

THE WAY THE BABY WOKE

AND this is the way the baby woke:
  As when in deepest drops of
    dew
The shine and shadows sink and
    soak,
  The sweet eyes glimmered through
    and through;
And eddyings and dimples broke
  About the lips, and no one knew
Or could divine the words they
    spoke—
And this is the way the baby woke.

386

THE WAY THE BABY SLEPT

THIS is the way the baby slept:
  A mist of tresses backward
    thrown
By quavering sighs where kisses crept
  With yearnings she had never
    known:
The little hands were closely kept
  About a lily newly blown—
And God was with her. And we
    wept.—
And this is the way the baby slept.

387

WHEN MAIMIE MARRIED

WHEN Maimie married Charley
    Brown,
Joy took possession of the town;
The young folks swarmed in happy
    throngs—
They rang the bells—they caroled
    songs—
They carpeted the steps that led
Into the church where they were wed;
And up and down the altar-stair
They scattered roses everywhere;
When, in her orange-blossom crown,
Queen Maimie married Charley
    Brown.

So beautiful she was, it seemed
Men, looking on her, dreamed they
    dreamed;
And he, the holy man who took
Her hand in his, so thrilled and shook,
The gargoyles round the ceiling's rim
Looked down and leered and grinned
    at him,
Until he half forgot his part
Of sanctity, and felt his heart
Beat worldward through his sacred
    gown—
When Maimie married Charley
    Brown.

The bridesmaids kissed her, left and
    right—
Fond mothers hugged her with de-
    light—
Young men of twenty-seven were seen
To blush like lads of seventeen,
The while they held her hand to quote
Such sentiments as poets wrote.—
Yea, all the heads that Homage bends

Were bowed to her.—But O my
friends,
My hopes went up—*my* heart went
down—
When Maimie married — *Charley
Brown!*

388

HER HAIR

THE beauty of her hair bewilders
  me—
Pouring adown the brow, its cloven
  tide
Swirling about the ears on either
  side
And storming round the neck tumul-
  tuously:
Or like the lights of old antiquity
Through mullioned windows, in
  cathedrals wide,
  Spilled moltenly o'er figures deified
In chastest marble, nude of drapery.
And so I love it.—Either unconfined;
  Or plaited in close braidings mani-
  fold;
Or smoothly drawn; or indolently
  twined
  In careless knots whose coilings
  come unrolled
At any lightest kiss; or by the wind
  Whipped out in flossy ravelings of
  gold.

389

A VISION OF SUMMER

'TWAS a marvelous vision of
  Summer.—
That morning the dawn was late,

And came, like a long dream-ridden
  guest,
Through the gold of the Eastern
  gate.

Languid it came, and halting
  As one that yawned, half roused,
With lifted arms and indolent lids
  And eyes that drowsed and drowsed.

A glimmering haze hung over
  The face of the smiling air;
And the green of the trees and the
  blue of the leas
  And the skies gleamed everywhere.

And the dewdrops' dazzling jewels,
  In garlands and diadems,
Lightened and twinkled and glanced
  and shot
  At the glints of a thousand gems:

Emeralds of dew on the grasses;
  The rose with rubies set;
On the lily, diamonds; and amethysts
  Pale on the violet.

And there were the pinks of the
  fuchsias,
  And the peony's crimson hue,
The lavender of the hollyhocks,
  And the morning-glory's blue:

The purple of the pansy bloom,
  And the passionate flush of the face
Of the velvet-rose; and the thick per-
  fume
  Of the locust every place.

The air and the sun and the shadows
  Were wedded and made as one;
And the winds ran over the meadows
  As little children run:

And the winds poured over the
    meadows
And along the willowy way
The river ran, with its ripples shod
With the sunshine of the day:

O the winds flowed over the meadows
In a tide of eddies and calms,
And the bared brow felt the touch of it
As a sweetheart's tender palms.

And the lark went palpitating
Up through the glorious skies,
His song spilled down from the blue
    profound
As a song from Paradise.

And here was the loitering current—
Stayed by a drift of sedge
And sodden logs—scummed thick
    with the gold
Of the pollen from edge to edge.

The catbird piped in the hazel,
And the harsh kingfisher screamed;
And the crane, in amber and oozy
    swirls,
Dozed in the reeds and dreamed.

And in through the tumbled driftage
And the tangled roots below,
The waters warbled and gurgled and
    lisped
Like the lips of long ago.

And the senses caught, through the
    music,
Twinkles of dabbling feet,
And glimpses of faces in coverts green,
And voices faint and sweet.

And back from the lands enchanted,
Where my earliest mirth was born,

The trill of a laugh was blown to me
Like the blare of an elfin horn.

Again I romped through the clover;
And again I lay supine
On grassy swards, where the skies, like
    eyes,
Looked lovingly back to mine.

And over my vision floated
Misty illusive things—
Trailing strands of the gossamer
On heavenward wanderings:

Figures that veered and wavered,
Luring the sight, and then
Glancing away into nothingness,
And blinked into shape again.

From out far depths of the. forest,
Ineffably sad and lorn,
Like the yearning cry of a long-lost
    love,
The moan of the dove was borne.

And through lush glooms of the
    thicket
The flash of the redbird's wings
On branches of star-white blooms that
    shook
And thrilled with its twitterings.

Through mossy and viny vistas,
Soaked ever with deepest shade,
Dimly the dull owl stared and stared
From his bosky ambuscade.

And up through the rifted tree-tops
That signaled the wayward breeze,
I saw the hulk of the hawk becalmed
Far out on the azure seas.

Then sudden an awe fell on me,
As the hush of the golden day
Rounded to noon, as a May to June
That a lover has dreamed away.

And I heard, in the breathless silence,
And the full, glad light of the sun,
The tinkle and drip of a timorous
    shower—
Ceasing as it begun.

And my thoughts, like the leaves and
    grasses,
In a rapture of joy and pain,
Seemed fondled and petted and beat
    upon
With a tremulous patter of rain.

390

WHILE CIGARETTES TO ASHES TURN

I

"HE smokes—and that's enough,"
    says Ma—
"And cigarettes, at that!" says Pa.

"He must not call again," says she—
"He *shall* not call again!" says he.

They both glare at me as before—
Then quit the room and bang the
    door,—

While I, their wilful daughter, say,
"I guess I'll love him, anyway!"

II

At twilight, in his room, alone,
His careless feet inertly thrown

Across a chair, my fancy can
But worship this most worthless man!

I dream what joy it is to set
His slow lips round a cigarette,

With idle-humored whiff and puff—
Ah! this is innocent enough!

To mark the slender fingers raise
The waxen match's dainty blaze,

Whose chastened light an instant
    glows
On drooping lids and arching nose,

Then, in the sudden gloom, instead,
A tiny ember, dim and red,

Blooms languidly to ripeness, then
Fades slowly, and grows ripe again.

III

I lean back, in my own boudoir—
The door is fast, the sash ajar;

And in the dark, I smiling stare
At one wide window over there,

Where some one, smoking, pinks the
    gloom,
The darling darkness of his room!

I push my shutters wider yet,
And lo! I light a cigarette;

And gleam for gleam, and glow for
    glow,
Each pulse of light a word we know,

We talk of love that still will burn
While cigarettes to ashes turn.

391

THE LITTLE RED RIBBON

THE little red ribbon, the ring and
the rose!
The summer-time comes, and the sum-
mer-time goes—
And never a blossom in all of the land
As white as the gleam of her beckon-
ing hand!

The long winter months, and the glare
of the snows;
The little red ribbon, the ring and the
rose!
And never a glimmer of sun in the
skies
As bright as the light of her glorious
eyes!

Dreams only are true; but they fade
and are gone—
For her face is not here when I waken
at dawn;
The little red ribbon, the ring and the
rose
Mine only; *hers* only the dream and
repose.

I am weary of waiting, and weary of
tears,
And my heart wearies, too, all these
desolate years,
Moaning over the one only song that
it knows,—
The little red ribbon, the ring and
the rose!

392

THE MAN IN THE MOON

SAID The Raggedy Man, on a hot
afternoon:
My!
Sakes!
What a lot o' mistakes
Some little folks makes on The Man
in the Moon!
But people that's be'n up to *see* him,
like *me*,
And calls on him frequent and inti-
muttly,
Might drop a few facts that would in-
terest you
Clean!
Through!—
If you wanted 'em to—
Some *actual* facts that might interest
you!

O The Man in the Moon has a crick
in his back;
Whee!
Whimm!
Ain't you sorry for him?
And a mole on his nose that is purple
and black;
And his eyes are so weak that they
water and run
If he dares to *dream* even he looks
at the sun,—
So he jes' dreams of stars, as the doc-
tors advise—
My!
Eyes!
But isn't he wise—
To jes' dream of stars, as the doc-
tors advise?

And The Man in the Moon has a boil
    on his ear—
Whee!
Whing!
    What a singular thing!
I know! but these facts are authentic,
    my dear,—
There's a boil on his ear; and a corn
    on his chin—
He calls it a dimple—but dimples
    stick in—
Yet it might be a dimple turned over,
    you know!
Whang!
Ho!
    Why, certainly so!—
It might be a dimple turned over,
    you know!

And The Man in the Moon has a rheu-
    matic knee—
Gee!
Whizz!
    What a pity that is!
And his toes have worked round where
    his heels ought to be.—
So whenever he wants to go North he
    goes *South,*
And comes back with porridge-crumbs
    all round his mouth,
And he brushes them off with a Jap-
    anese fan,
Whing!
Whann!
    What a marvelous man!
What a very remarkably marvelous
    man!

And The Man in the Moon, 'sighed
    The Raggedy Man,
Gits!
So!
    Sullonesome, you know,—

Up there by hisse'f sence creation be-
    gan!—
That when I call on him and then
    come away,
He grabs me and holds me and begs
    me to stay,—
Till—*Well!* if it wasn't fer *Jimmy-cum-*
    jim,
Dadd!
Limb!
    I'd go pardners with him—
Jes' jump my job here and be pard-
    ners with *him!*

393

A BAREFOOT BOY

A BAREFOOT boy! I mark him at
    his play—
For May is here once more, and so
    is he,—
His dusty trousers, rolled half to the
    knee,
And his bare ankles grimy, too, as they:
Cross-hatchings of the nettle, in array
    Of feverish stripes, hint vividly to
    me
    Of woody pathways winding end-
    lessly
Along the creek, where even yesterday
He plunged his shrinking body—
    gasped and shook—
    Yet called the water "warm," with
    never lack
Of joy. And so, half enviously I look
Upon this graceless barefoot and his
    track,—
    His toe stubbed—ay, his big toe-nail
    knocked back
Like unto the clasp of an old pocket-
    book.

394

"THE PREACHER'S BOY"

I RICKOLLECT the little tad, back, years and years ago—
"The Preacher's Boy" that every one despised and hated so!
A meek-faced little feller, with white eyes and foxy hair,
And a look like he expected ser'ous trouble everywhere:
A sort o' fixed expression of suspicion in his glance;
His bare feet always scratched with briers; and green stains on his pants;
Molasses-marks along his sleeves; his cap-rim turned behind—
And so it is "The Preacher's Boy" is brought again to mind!

My fancy even brings the sly marauder back so plain,
I see him jump our garden-fence and slip off down the lane;
And I seem to holler at him and git back the old reply:
"Oh, no: your peaches is too green fer such a worm as I!"
Fer he scorned his father's phrases—every holy one he had—
"As good a man," folks put it, "as that boy of his was bad!"
And again from their old buggy-shed, I hear the "rod unspared"—
Of course that never "spoiled the child" for which nobody cared!

If any neighbor ever found his gate without a latch,
Or rines around the edges of his watermelon-patch;
His pasture-bars left open; or his pump-spout chocked with clay,
He'd swear 'twas "that infernal Preacher's Boy," right away!
When strings was stretched acrost the street at night, and some one got
An everlastin' tumble, and his nose broke, like as not,
And laid it on "The Preacher's Boy"—no powers, low ner high,
Could ever quite substantiate that boy's alibi!

And did *nobody* like the boy?—Well, all the *pets* in town
Would eat out of his fingers; and canaries would come down
And leave their swingin' perches and their fish-bone jist to pick
The little warty knuckles that the dogs would leap to lick.—
No little snarlin', snappin' fiste but what would leave his bone
To foller, ef *he* whistled, in that tantalizin' tone
That made a goods-box whittler blasphemeusly protest
"He couldn't tell, 'twixt dog and boy, which one was ornriest!"

'Twas such a little cur as this, onc't, when the crowd was thick
Along the streets, a drunken corner-loafer tried to kick,

When a sudden foot behind him tripped him up, and falling so
He "marked his man," and jerked his gun—drawed up and let 'er go!
And the crowd swarmed round the victim—holding close against his breast
The little dog unharmed, in arms that still, as they caressed,
Grew rigid in their last embrace, as with a smile of joy
He recognized the dog was saved. So died "The Preacher's Boy"!

When it appeared, before the Squire, that fatal pistol-ball
Was fired at "a dangerous beast," and not the boy at all,
And the facts set forth established,—it was like-befittin' then
To order out a possy of the "city councilmen"
To kill *the dog!* But, strange to tell, they searched the country round,
And never hide-ner-hair of that "said" dog was ever found!
And, somehow, *then* I sort o' thought—and half-way think, *to-day*—
The spirit of "The Preacher's Boy" had whistled him away.

395

WE TO SIGH INSTEAD OF SING

"RAIN and rain! and rain and
rain!"
Yesterday we muttered
Grimly as the grim refrain
That the thunders uttered:
All the heavens under cloud—
All the sunshine sleeping;
All the grasses limply bowed
With their weight of weeping.

Sigh and sigh! and sigh and sigh!
Never end of sighing;
Rain and rain for our reply—
Hopes half drowned and dying;
Peering through the window-pane,
Naught but endless raining—
Endless sighing, and, as vain,
Endlessly complaining.

Shine and shine! and shine and shine!
Ah! to-day the splendor!—

All this glory yours and mine—
God! but God is tender!
We to sigh instead of sing,
Yesterday, in sorrow,
While the Lord was fashioning
This for our To-morrow!

396

NOTHIN' TO SAY

NOTHIN' to say, my daughter!
Nothin' at all to say!
Gyrls that's in love, I've noticed, gin-
er'ly has their way!
Yer mother did, afore you, when her
folks objected to me—
Yit here I am and here you air! and
yer mother—where is she?

You look lots like yer mother: purty
much same in size;
And about the same complected; and
favor about the eyes:

Like her, too, about livin' here, because
  she couldn't stay;
It'll 'most seem like you was dead like
  her!—but I hain't got nothin' to
  say!

She left you her little Bible—writ yer
  name acrost the page—
And left her ear-bobs fer you, ef ever
  you come of age;
I've alluz kep' 'em and gyuarded 'em,
  but ef yer goin' away—
Nothin' to say, my daughter! Nothin'
  at all to say!

You don't rickollect her, I reckon?
  No: you wasn't a year old then!
And now yer—how old *air* you? W'y,
  child, not *"twenty"!* When?
And yer nex' birthday's in Aprile? and
  you want to git married that day?
I wisht yer mother was livin'!—but I
  hain't got nothin' to say!

Twenty year! and as good a gyrl as
  parent ever found!
There's a straw ketched on to yer dress
  there—I'll bresh it off—turn round.
(Her mother was jes' twenty when us
  two run away.)
Nothin' to say, my daughter! Noth-
  in' at all to say!

In looking on the gifts that lie
Like broken playthings scattered o'er
Imagination's nursery floor!
Did these old hands once click the key
That let "Jack's" box-lid upward fly,
And that blear-eyed, fur-whiskered elf
Leap, as though frightened at himself,
And quiveringly lean and stare
At me, his jailer, laughing there?

A child then! Now—I only know
They call me very old; and so
They will not let me have my way,—
But uselessly I sit all day
Here by the chimney-jamb, and poke
The lazy fire, and smoke and smoke,
And watch the wreaths swoop up the
  flue,
And chuckle—ay, I often do—
Seeing again, all vividly,
Jack-in-the-box leap, as in glee
To see how much he looks like me!

. . . . They talk. I can't hear what
  they say—
But I am glad, clean through and
  through
Sometimes, in fancying that they
Are saying, "Sweet, that fancy strays
In age back to our childish days!"

397

JACK-IN-THE-BOX

Grandfather, musing

IN childish days! O memory,
  You bring such curious things to
  me!—
Laughs to the lip—tears to the eye,

398

THE OLD TRUNDLE-BED

O THE old trundle-bed where I
  slept when a boy!
What canopied king might not covet
  the joy?
The glory and peace of that slumber
  of mine,

Like a long, gracious rest in the bosom
  divine:
The quaint, homely couch, hidden close
  from the light,
But daintily drawn from its hiding at
  night.
O a nest of delight, from the foot to
  the head,
Was the queer little, dear little, old
  trundle-bed!

O the old trundle-bed, where I wonder-
  ing saw
The stars through the window, and
  listened with awe
To the sigh of the winds as they trem-
  blingly crept
Through the trees where the robin so
  restlessly slept:
Where I heard the low, murmurous
  chirp of the wren,
And the katydid listlessly chirrup again,
Till my fancies grew faint and were
  drowsily led
Through the maze of the dreams of the
  old trundle-bed.

O the old trundle-bed!   O the old
  trundle-bed!
With its plump little pillow, and old-
  fashioned spread;
Its snowy-white sheets, and the blan-
  kets above,
Smoothed down and tucked round with
  the touches of love;
The voice of my mother to lull me to
  sleep
With the old fairy stories my memories
  keep
Still fresh as the lilies that bloom o'er
  the head
Once bowed o'er my own in the old
  trundle-bed.

399

MY MARY

MY Mary, O my Mary!
    The simmer skies are blue:
The dawnin' brings the dazzle,
    An' the gloamin' brings the dew,—
The mirk o' nicht the glory
    O' the moon, an' kindles, too,
The stars that shift aboon the lift.—
    But naething brings me you!

Where is it, O my Mary,
    Ye are biding a' the while?
I ha' wended by your window—
    I ha' waited by the stile,
An' up an' down the river
    I ha' won for mony a mile,
Yet never found, adrift or drown'd,
    Your lang-belated smile.

Is it forgot, my Mary,
    How glad we used to be?—
The simmer-time when bonny bloomed
    The auld trysting-tree,—
How there I carved the name for you,
    An' you the name for me;
An' the gloamin' kenned it only
    When we kissed sae tenderly.

Speek ance to me, my Mary!—
    But whisper in my ear
As light as ony sleeper's breath,
    An' a' my soul will hear;
My heart shall stap its beating,
    An' the soughing atmosphere
Be hushed the while I leaning smile
    An' listen to you, dear!

My Mary, O my Mary!
    The blossoms bring the bees;

The sunshine brings the blossoms,
　An' the leaves on a' the trees;
The simmer brings the sunshine
　An' the fragrance o' the breeze,—
But O wi'out you, Mary,
　I care naething for these!

We were sae happy, Mary!
　O think how ance we said—
Wad ane o' us gae fickle,
　Or ane o' us lie dead,—
To feel anither's kisses
　We wad feign the auld instead,
An' ken the ither's footsteps
　In the green grass owerhead.

My Mary, O my Mary!
　Are ye dochter o' the air,
That ye vanish aye before me
　As I follow everywhere?—
Or is it ye are only
　But a mortal, wan wi' care,
Sin' I search through a' the kirkyird
　An' I dinna find ye there?

400

TWO SONNETS TO THE JUNE-
BUG

I

Y OU make me jes' a little nervouser
　　Than any dog-gone bug I ever
　see!
And you know night's the time to
　pester me—
When any tetch at all 'll rub the fur
Of all my patience back'ards! You're
　the myrrh

And ruburb of my life! A bumble-
　bee
Cain't hold a candle to you; and a he
Bald hornet, with a laminated spur
In his hip-pocket, daresent even cheep
　When you're around! And, dern ye!
　you have made
Me lose whole ricks and stacks and
　piles of sleep,—
And many of a livelong night I've
　laid
And never shut an eye, hearin' you
　keep
Up that eternal buzzin' serenade!

II

And I've got up and lit the lamp, and
　clum
　On cheers and trunks and wash-
　stands and bureaus,
　And all such dangerous articles as
　　those,
And biffed at you with brooms, and
　never come
'In two feet of you,—maybe skeered
　you some,—
　But what does that amount to when
　it throws
A feller out o' balance, and his nose
Gits barked ag'inst the mantel, while
　you hum
Fer joy around the room, and churn
　your head
Ag'inst the ceilin', and draw back
　and butt
The plasterin' loose, and drop—behind
　the bed,
Where never human-bein' ever putt
Harm's hand on you, er ever truthful
　said
He'd choked yer dern infernal wiz-
　zen shut!

401

ONE AFTERNOON

BELOW, cool grasses: over us
The maples waver tremulous.

A slender overture above,
Low breathing as a sigh of love

At first, then gradually strong
And stronger: 'tis the locust's song,

Swoln midway to a pæan of glee,
And lost in silence dwindlingly.

Not utter silence; nay, for hid
In ghosts of it, the katydid

Chirrs a diluted echo of
The loveless song he makes us love.

The low boughs are drugged heavily
With shade; the poem you read to me

Is not more gracious than the trill
Of birds that twitter as they will.

Half consciously, with upturned eyes,
I hear your voice—I see the skies,

Where, o'er bright rifts, the swallows
glance
Like glad thoughts o'er a countenance;

And voices near and far are blent
Like sweet chords of some instrument

Awakened by the trembling touch
Of hands that love it overmuch.

Dear heart, let be the book a while!
I want your face—I want your smile!

Tell me how gladder now are they
Who look on us from Heaven to-day.

402

THE BEAUTIFUL CITY

THE Beautiful City! Forever
Its rapturous praises resound;
We fain would behold it—but never
A glimpse of its glory is found:
We slacken our lips at the tender
White breasts of our mothers to hear
Of its marvelous beauty and splen-
dor;—
We see—but the gleam of a tear!

Yet never the story may tire us—
First graven in symbols of stone—
Rewritten on scrolls of papyrus
And parchment, and scattered and
blown
By the winds of the tongues of all na-
tions,
Like a litter of leaves wildly whirled
Down the rack of a hundred transla-
tions,
From the earliest lisp of the world.

We compass the earth and the ocean,
From the Orient's uttermost light,
To where the last ripple in motion
Lips hem of the skirt of the night,—
But the Beautiful City evades us—
No spire of it glints in the sun—
No glad-bannered battlement shades us
When all our long journey is done.

Where lies it? We question and listen;
We lean from the mountain, or mast,
And see but dull earth, or the glisten
Of seas inconceivably vast:

The dust of the one blurs our vision,
    The glare of the other our brain,
Nor city nor island Elysian
    In all of the land or the main!

We kneel in dim fanes where the thun-
        ders
    Of organs tumultuous roll,
And the longing heart listens and won-
        ders,
    And the eyes look aloft from the
        soul:
But the chanson grows fainter and
        fainter,
    Swoons wholly away and is dead;
And our eyes only reach where the
        painter
    Has dabbled a saint overhead.

The Beautiful City! O mortal,
    Fare hopefully on in thy quest,
Pass down through the green grassy
        portal
    That leads to the Valley of Rest;
There first passed the One who, in pity
    Of all thy great yearning, awaits
To point out the Beautiful City,
    And loosen the trump at the gates.

403

A LIFE TERM

SHE was false, and he was true,—
    Thus their lives were rent apart;
'Twas his dagger driven through
    A mad rival's heart.

He was shut away. The moon
    May not find him; nor the stars—
Nay, nor yet the sun of noon
    Pierce his prison bars.

She was left—again to sin—
    Mistress of all siren arts:
The poor, soulless heroine
    Of a hundred hearts!

Though she dare not think of him
    Who believed her lies, and so
Sent a ghost adown the dim
    Path she dreads to go,—

He, in fancy, smiling, sips
    Of her kisses, purer yet
Than the dew upon the lips
    Of the violet.

404

McFEETERS' FOURTH

IT was needless to say 'twas a glo-
    rious day,
And to boast of it all in that spread-
        eagle way
That our Forefathers had since the
        hour of the birth
Of this most patriotic republic on earth!
But 'twas justice, of course, to admit
        that the sight
Of the old Stars-and-Stripes was a
        thing of delight
In the eyes of a fellow, however he
        tried
To look on the day with a dignified
        pride
That meant not to brook any turbulent
        glee
Or riotous flourish of loud jubilee!

So argued McFeeters, all grim and
        severe,
Who the long night before, with a
        feeling of fear,

Had slumbered but fitfully, hearing the
swish
Of the sky-rocket over his roof, with
the wish
That the boy-fiend who fired it were
fast to the end
Of the stick to forever and ever ascend!
Or to hopelessly ask why the boy with
the horn
And its horrible havoc had ever been
born!
Or to wish, in his wakefulness, staring
aghast,
That this Fourth of July were as dead
as the last!

So yesterday morning, McFeeters arose,
With a fire in his eyes, and a cold in
his nose,
And a guttural voice in appropriate key
With a temper as gruff as a temper
could be.
He growled at the servant he met on
the stair,
Because he was whistling a national
air,
And he growled at the maid on the
balcony, who
Stood enrapt with the tune of "The
Red-White-and-Blue"
That a band was discoursing like mad
in the street,
With drumsticks that banged, and with
cymbals that beat.

And he growled at his wife, as she but-
toned his vest,
And applausively pinned a rosette on
his breast
Of the national colors, and lured from
his purse
Some change for the boys—for fire-
crackers—or worse;

And she pointed with pride to a soldier
in blue
In a frame on the wall, and the colors
there, too;
And he felt, as he looked on the fea-
tures, the glow
The painter found there twenty long
years ago,
And a passionate thrill in his breast,
as he felt
Instinctively round for the sword in his
belt.

What was it that hung like a mist o'er
the room?—
The tumult without—and the music—
the boom
Of the cannon—the blare of the bugle
and fife?—
No matter!—McFeeters was kissing his
wife,
And laughing and crying and waving
his hat
Like a genuine soldier, and crazy, at
that!
—*Was* it needless to say 'twas a glo-
rious day
And to boast of it all in that spread-
eagle way
That our Forefathers had since the
hour of the birth
Of this most patriotic republic on
earth?

405

AT NINETY IN THE SHADE

HOT weather? Yes; but really not,
Compared with weather twice as
hot.
Find comfort, then, in arguing thus,

And you'll pull through victorious!—
For instance, while you gasp and pant
And try to cool yourself—and can't—
With soda, cream and lemonade,
The heat at ninety in the shade,—
Just calmly sit and ponder o'er
These same degrees, with ninety more
On top of them, and so concede
The weather now is cool indeed!
Think—as the perspiration dews
Your fevered brow, and seems to ooze
From out the ends of every hair—
Whole floods of it, with floods to
    spare—
Think, I repeat, the while the sweat
Pours down your spine—how hotter
    yet
Just ninety *more* degrees would be,
And bear *this* ninety patiently!
Think—as you mop your brow and
    hair,
With sticky feelings everywhere—
How ninety more degrees increase
Of heat like this would start the
    grease;
Or, think, as you exhausted stand,
A wilted "palm-leaf" in each hand—
When the thermometer has done
With ease the lap of ninety-one;
O think, I say, what heat might do
At one hundred and eighty-two—
Just twice the heat you now declare,
Complainingly, is hard to bear.
Or, as you watch the mercury
Mount, still elate, one more degree,
And doff your collar and cravat,
And rig a sponge up in your hat,
And ask Tom, Harry, Dick or Jim
If this is hot enough for him—
Consider how the sun would pour
At one hundred and eighty-four—
Just twice the heat that seems to be
Affecting you unpleasantly,

The very hour that you might find
As cool as dew, were you inclined.
But why proceed when none will heed
Advice apportioned to the need?
Hot weather? Yes; but really not,
Compared with weather twice as hot!

406

A SUDDEN SHOWER

BAREFOOTED boys scud up the
    street
  Or skurry under sheltering sheds;
And schoolgirl faces, pale and sweet,
  Gleam from the shawls about their
    heads.

Doors bang; and mother-voices call
  From alien homes; and rusty gates
Are slammed; and high above it all,
  The thunder grim reverberates.

And then, abrupt,—the rain! the rain!
  The earth lies gasping; and the eyes
Behind the streaming window-pane
  Smile at the trouble of the skies.

The highway smokes; sharp echoes
    ring;
  The cattle bawl and cow-bells clank;
And into town comes galloping
  The farmer's horse, with steaming
    flank.

The swallow dips beneath the eaves
  And flirts his plumes and folds his
    wings;
And under the Catawba leaves
  The caterpillar curls and clings.

The bumblebee is pelted down
    The wet stem of the hollyhock;
And sullenly, in spattered brown,
    The cricket leaps the garden-walk.

Within, the baby claps his hands
    And crows with rapture strange and
        vague;
Without, beneath the rose-bush stands
    A dripping rooster on one leg.

407

GOOD-BY ER HOWDY-DO

SAY good-by er howdy-do—
    What's the odds betwixt the two?
Comin'—goin', ev'ry day—
Best friends first to go away—
Grasp of hands you'd ruther hold
Than their weight in solid gold
Slips their grip while greetin' you.—
Say good-by er howdy-do!

Howdy-do, and then, good-by—
Mixes jes' like laugh and cry;
Deaths and births, and worst and best,
Tangled their contrariest;
Ev'ry jinglin' weddin'-bell
Skeerin' up some funer'l knell.—
Here's my song, and there's your
        sigh.—
Howdy-do, and then, good-by!

Say good-by er howdy-do—
Jes' the same to me and you;
'Taint worth while to make no fuss,
'Cause the job's put up on us!
Some One's runnin' this concern
That's got nothin' else to learn:
Ef He's willin', we'll pull through—
Say good-by er howdy-do!

408

WITH THE CURRENT

RAREST mood of all the year!
    Aimless, idle, and content—
Sky and wave and atmosphere
    Wholly indolent.

Little daughter, loose the band
    From your tresses—let them pour
Shadow-like o'er arm and hand
    Idling at the oar.

Low and clear, and pure and deep,
    Ripples of the river sing—
Water-lilies, half asleep,
    Drowsed with listening:

Tremulous reflex of skies—
    Skies above and skies below,—
Paradise and Paradise
    Blending even so!

Blossoms with their leaves unrolled
    Laughingly, as they were lips
Cleft with ruddy beaten gold
    Tongues of pollen-tips.

Rush and reed, and thorn and vine,
    Clumped with grasses lithe and tall—
With a web of summer-shine
    Woven round it all.

Back and forth, and to and fro—
    Flashing scale and wing as one,—
Dragon-flies that come and go,
    Shuttled by the sun.

Fairy lilts and lullabies,
    Fine as fantasy conceives,—
Echoes wrought of cricket-cries
    Sifted through the leaves.

O'er the rose, with drowsy buzz,
  Hangs the bee, and stays his kiss,
Even as my fancy does,
    Gipsy, over this.

Let us both be children—share
  Youth's glad voyage night and day,
Drift adown it, half aware,
    Anywhere we may.—

Drift and curve and deviate,
  Veer and eddy, float and flow,
Waver, swerve and undulate,
    As the bubbles go.

409

WET-WEATHER TALK

IT hain't no use to grumble and com-
      plane;
  It's jest as cheap and easy to re-
      joice.—
When God sorts out the weather and
      sends rain,
  W'y, rain's my choice.

Men ginerly, to all intents—
  Although they're apt to grumble
      some—
Puts most theyr trust in Providence,
  And takes things as they come—
    That is, the commonality
    Of men that's lived as long as me
    Has watched the world enugh to
      learn
    They're not the boss of this con-
      cern.

With *some,* of course, it's different—
  I've saw *young* men that knowed it
      all,

And didn't like the way things went
  On this terrestchul ball;—
    But all the same, the rain, some
      way,
    Rained jest as hard on picnic day;
    Er, when they railly *wanted* it,
    It maybe wouldn't rain a bit!

In this existunce, dry and wet
  Will overtake the best of men—
Some little skift o' clouds'll shet
  The sun off now and then.—
    And mayby, whilse you're wun-
      dern who
    You've fool-like lent your umbrell'
      to,
    And *want* it—out'll pop the sun,
    And you'll be glad you hain't got
      none!

It aggervates the farmers, too—
  They's too much wet, er too much
      sun,
Er work, er waitin' round to do
  Before the plowin' 's done:
    And mayby, like as not, the wheat,
    Jest as it's lookin' hard to beat,
    Will ketch the storm—and jest
      about
    The time the corn's a-jintin' out.

These-here *cy-clones* a-foolin' round—
  And back'ard crops!—and wind and
      rain!—
And yit the corn that's wallerd down
  May elbow up again!—
    They hain't no sense, as I can see,
    Fer mortuls, sich as us, to be
    A-faultin' Natchur's wise intents,
    And lockin' horns with Provi-
      dence!

It hain't no use to grumble and com-
plane;
It's jest as cheap and easy to re-
joice.—
When God sorts out the weather and
sends rain,
W'y, rain's my choice.

410

A POOR MAN'S WEALTH

A POOR man? Yes, I must confess—
No wealth of gold do I possess;
No pastures fine, with grazing kine,
Nor fields of waving grain are mine;
No foot of fat or fallow land
Where rightfully my feet may stand
The while I claim it as my own—
By deed and title, mine alone.

Ah, poor indeed! perhaps you say—
But spare me your compassion, pray!—
When I ride not—with you—I walk
In Nature's company, and talk
With one who will not slight or slur
The child forever dear to her—
And one who answers back, be sure,
With smile for smile, though I am
poor.

And while communing thus, I count
An inner wealth of large amount,—
The wealth of honest purpose blent
With Penury's environment,—
The wealth of owing naught to-day
But debts that I would gladly pay,
With wealth of thanks still unex-
pressed
With cumulative interest.—

A wealth of patience and content—
For all my ways improvident;
A faith still fondly exercised—
For all my plans unrealized;
A wealth of promises that still,
Howe'er I fail, I hope to fill;
A wealth of charity for those
Who pity me my ragged clothes.

A poor man? Yes, I must confess—
No wealth of gold do I possess;
No pastures fine, with grazing kine,
Nor fields of waving grain are mine;
But ah, my friend! I've wealth, no end!
For millionaires might condescend
To bend the knee and envy me
This opulence of poverty.

411

AUTOGRAPHIC

For an Album

I FEEL, if aught I ought to rhyme,
I ought 'a' thought a longer time,
And ought 'a' caught a higher sense,
Of autocratic eloquence.
I ought 'a' sought each haughty Muse
That taught a thought I ought to use,
And fought and fraught, and so de-
vised
A poem *unmonotonized*.—
But since all this was vain, I thought
I ought to simply say,—I ought
To thank you, as I ought to do,
And ought to bow my best to you;
And ought to trust not to intrude
A rudely-wrought-up gratitude,
But ought to smile, and ought to laugh,
And ought to write—an autograph.

412

IN SWIMMING-TIME

CLOUDS above, as white as wool,
    Drifting over skies as blue
As the eyes of beautiful
    Children when they smile at you;
Groves of maple, elm, and beech,
    With the sunshine sifted through
Branches, mingling each with each,
    Dim with shade and bright with
        dew;
Stripling trees, and poplars hoar,
Hickory and sycamore,
And the drowsy dogwood bowed
Where the ripples laugh aloud,
And the crooning creek is stirred
    To a gaiety that now
Mates the warble of the bird
    Teetering on the hazel-bough;
Grasses long and fine and fair
As your schoolboy sweetheart's hair,
Backward roached and twirled and
        twined
By the fingers of the wind.
Vines and mosses, interlinked
    Down dark aisles and deep ravines,
Where the stream runs, willow-
        brinked,
    Round a bend where some one leans
Faint and vague and indistinct
    As the like reflected thing
    In the current shimmering.
Childish voices farther on,
Where the truant stream has gone,
Vex the echoes of the wood
Till no word is understood,
Save that one is well aware
Happiness is hiding there.
There, in leafy coverts, nude
    Little bodies poise and leap,
Spattering the solitude

And the silence everywhere—
    Mimic monsters of the deep!
Wallowing in sandy shoals—
    Plunging headlong out of sight;
And, with spurtings of delight,
Clutching hands, and slippery soles,
    Climbing up the treacherous steep
Over which the spring-board spurns
Each again as he returns.
    Ah! the glorious carnival!
    Purple lips and chattering teeth—
    Eyes that burn—but, in beneath,
    Every care beyond recall,
    Every task forgotten quite—
    And again, in dreams at night,
Dropping, drifting through it all!

413

THE BEST IS GOOD ENOUGH

I QUARREL not with Destiny,
    But make the best of everything—
The best is good enough for me.

Leave Discontent alone, and she
Will shut her mouth and let *you* sing.
I quarrel not with Destiny.

I take some things, or let 'em be—
Good gold has always got the ring;
The best is good enough for me.

Since Fate insists on secrecy,
I have no arguments to bring—
I quarrel not with Destiny.

The fellow that goes "haw" for "gee"
Will find he hasn't got full swing.
The best is good enough for me.

One only knows our needs, and He
Does all of the distributing.
I quarrel not with Destiny:
The best is good enough for me.

414

HE CALLED HER IN

I

HE called her in from me and shut
the door.
And she so loved the sunshine and
the sky!—
She loved them even better yet than I
That ne'er knew dearth of them—my
mother dead,
Nature had nursed me in her lap in-
stead:
And I had grown a dark and eery
child
That rarely smiled,
Save when, shut all alone in grasses
high,
Looking straight up in God's great
lonesome sky
And coaxing Mother to smile back on
me.
'Twas lying thus, this fair girl sud-
denly
Came on me, nestled in the fields
beside
A pleasant-seeming home, with door-
way wide—
The sunshine beating in upon the
floor
Like golden rain.—
O sweet, sweet face above me, turn
again
And leave me! I had cried, but that
an ache

Within my throat so gripped it I could
make
No sound but a thick sobbing.
Cowering so,
I felt her light hand laid
Upon my hair—a touch that ne'er
before
Had tamed me thus, all soothed and
unafraid—
It seemed the touch the children used
to know
When Christ was here, so dear it was
—so dear,—
At once I loved her as the leaves love
dew
In midmost summer when the days
are new.
Barely an hour I knew her, yet a curl
Of silken sunshine did she clip for
me
Out of the bright May-morning of her
hair,
And bound and gave it to me laugh-
ingly,
And caught my hands and called me
"Little girl,"
Tiptoeing, as she spoke, to kiss me
there!
And I stood dazed and dumb for very
stress
Of my great happiness.
She plucked me by the gown, nor saw
how mean
The raiment—drew me with her
everywhere:
Smothered her face in tufts of grasses
green:
Put up her dainty hands and peeped
between
Her fingers at the blossoms—crooned
and talked
To them in strange, glad whispers, as
we walked,—

Said *this* one was her angel mother
—*this,*
Her baby-sister—come back, for a kiss,
Clean from the Good-World!—smiled
    and kissed them, then
Closed her soft eyes and kissed them
    o'er again.
And so did she beguile me—so we
    played,—
She was the dazzling Shine—I, the
    dark Shade—
And we did mingle like to these, and
    thus,
Together, made
The perfect summer, pure and glori-
ous.
So blent we, till a harsh voice broke
    upon
Our happiness.—She, startled as a
    fawn,
Cried, "Oh, 'tis Father!"—all the blos-
    soms gone
From out her cheeks as those from
    out her grasp.—
Harsher the voice came:—She could
    only gasp
Affrightedly, "Good-by! — good-by!
    good-by!"
And lo, I stood alone, with that harsh
    cry
Ringing a new and unknown sense of
    shame
Through soul and frame,
And, with wet eyes, repeating o'er and
    o'er,—
"He called her in from me and shut
    the door!"

II

He called her in from me and shut
    the door!
And I went wandering alone again—

So lonely—O so very lonely then,
I thought no little sallow star, alone
In all a world of twilight, e'er had
    known
Such utter loneliness. But that I wore
Above my heart that gleaming tress
    of hair
To lighten up the night of my despair,
I think I might have groped into my
    grave
Nor cared to wave
The ferns above it with a breath of
    prayer.
And how I hungered for the sweet,
    sweet face
That bent above me in my hiding-
    place
That day amid the grasses there beside
Her pleasant home!—"Her *pleasant*
    home!" I sighed,
Remembering;—then shut my teeth
    and feigned
The harsh voice calling *me,*—then
    clenched my nails
So deeply in my palms, the sharp
    wounds pained,
And tossed my face toward Heaven,
    as one who pales
In splendid martyrdom, with soul
    serene,
As near to God as high the guillotine.
And I had *envied* her? Not that—
    O no!
But I had longed for some sweet haven
    so!—
Wherein the tempest-beaten heart
    might ride
Sometimes at peaceful anchor, and
    abide
Where those that loved me touched
    me with their hands,
And looked upon me with glad eyes,
    and slipped

Smooth fingers o'er my brow, and
    lulled the strands
Of my wild tresses, as they backward
    tipped
My yearning face and kissed it satis-
    fied.
Then bitterly I murmured as before,—
"He called her in from me and shut
    the door!"

III

He called her in from me and shut
    the door!
After long struggling with my pride
    and pain—
A weary while it seemed, in which the
    more
I held myself from her, the greater
    fain
Was I to look upon her face again;—
At last—at last—half conscious where
    my feet
Were faring, I stood waist-deep in the
    sweet
Green grasses there where she
First came to me.—
The very blossoms she had plucked
    that day,
And, at her father's voice, had cast
    away,
Around me lay,
Still bright and blooming in these eyes
    of mine;
And as I gathered each one eagerly,
I pressed it to my lips and drank the
    wine
Her kisses left there for the honey-
    bee.
Then, after I had laid them with the
    tress
Of her bright hair with lingering
    tenderness,

I, turning, crept on to the hedge that
    bound
Her pleasant-seeming home—but all
    around
Was never sign of her!—The windows
    all
Were blinded; and I heard no rippling
    fall
Of her glad laugh, nor any harsh voice
    call;—
But, clutching to the tangled grasses,
    caught
A sound as though a strong man
    bowed his head
And sobbed alone—unloved—uncom-
    forted!—
And then straightway before
My tearless eyes, all vividly, was
    wrought
A vision that is with me evermore:—
A little girl that lies asleep, nor hears
Nor heeds not any voice nor fall of
    tears.—
And I sit singing o'er and o'er and
    o'er,
"God called her in from him and shut
    the door!"

415

GIVE ME THE BABY

GIVE me the baby to hold, my
    dear—
    To hold and hug, and to love and
        kiss.
Ah! he will come to me, never a fear—
    Come to the nest of a breast like this,
As warm for him as his face with
        cheer.
Give me the baby to hold, my dear!

Trustfully yield him to my caress.
"Bother," you say? What! "a
bother" to *me?*—
To fill up my soul with such happi-
ness
As the love of a baby that laughs
to be
Snuggled away where my heart can
hear!
Give me the baby to hold, my dear!

Ah, but his hands are grimed, you say,
And would soil my laces and clutch
my hair.—
Well, what would pleasure me more,
I pray,
Than the touch and tug of the wee
hands there?—
The wee hands there, and the warm
face here—
Give me the baby to hold, my dear!

Give me the baby! (Oh, won't you
see?
. . . Somewhere, out where the
green of the lawn
Is turning to gray, and the maple tree
Is weeping its leaves of gold upon
A little mound, with a dead rose
near. . . .)
Give me the baby to hold, my dear!

416

AN AUTUMNAL TONIC

WHAT mystery is it? The morn-
ing as rare
As the Indian Summer may bring!
A tang in the frost and a spice in the
air
That no city poet can sing!

The crimson and amber and gold of
the leaves,
As they loosen and flutter and fall
In the path of the park, as it rustlingly
weaves
Its way through the maples and under
the eaves
Of the sparrows that chatter and
call.

What hint of delight is it tingles me
through?—
What vague, indefinable joy?
What yearning for something divine
that I knew
When a wayward and wood-roving
boy?
Ah-ha! and Oho! but I have it, I say—
Oh, the mystery brightens at last,—
'Tis the longing and zest of the far, far
away,
For a bountiful, old-fashioned dinner
to-day,
With the hale harvest-hands of the
past.

417

OUT OF THE HITHERWHERE

OUT of the hitherwhere into the
yon—
The land that the Lord's love rests
upon;
Where one may rely on the friends he
meets,
And the smiles that greet him along
the streets:
Where the mother that left you years
ago
Will lift the hands that were folded
so,

And put them about you, with all the love
And tenderness you are dreaming of.

Out of the hitherwhere into the YON—
Where all of the friends of your youth
have gone,—
Where the old schoolmate that laughed
with you,
Will laugh again as he used to do,
Running to meet you, with such a face
As lights like a' moon the wondrous
place
Where God is living, and glad to live,
Since He is the Master and may for-
give.

Out of the hitherwhere into the YON!—
Stay the hopes we are leaning on—
You, Divine, with Your merciful eyes
Looking down from the far-away
skies,—
Smile upon us, and reach and take
Our worn souls Home for the old
home's sake.—
And so Amen,—for our all seems gone
Out of the hitherwhere into the YON.

418

A TINKLE OF BELLS

THE light of the moon on the white
of the snow,
And the answering twinkles along
the street,
And our sleigh flashing by, in the
glamour and glow
Of the glorious nights of the long
ago,
When the laugh of her lips rang
clear and sweet

As the tinkle our horses shook out of
the bells
And flung and tossed back
On our glittering track
In a shower of tremulous, murmuring
swells
Of the echoing, airy, melodious
bells!—
O the mirth of the bells!
And the worth of the bells!
Come tinkle again, in this dearth of
the bells,
The laughter and love that I lack,
yearning back
For the far-away sound of the bells!

Ah! the bells, they were glad in the
long ago!
And the tinkles they had, they have
thrilled me so
I have said: "It is they and her songs
and face
Make summer for me of the wintriest
place!"
And now—but sobbings and sad fare-
wells,
As I peer in the night through the
sleeted pane,
Hearing a clangor and wrangle of bells,
And never a tinkle again!

The snow is a-swoon, and the moon
dead-white,
And the frost is wild in the air to-
night!
Yet still will I linger and listen and
pray
Till the sound of her voice shall
come this way,
With a tinkle of bells,
And the lisp-like tread
Of the hooves of the
sleigh,

And the murmurs and swells
    Of the vows she said.
And oh, I shall listen as madmen
    may,
Till the tinkling bells ring down this
    way!—
Till again the grasp of my hand en-
    twines
The tensioned loops of the quivering
    lines,
And again we ride in the wake of the
    pride
And the strength of the coursers, side
    by side,
With our faces smitten again by the
    spray
Of the froth of our steeds as we gallop
    away
    In affright of the bells,
    And the might of the bells,
And the infinite glee and delight of
    the bells,
As they tinkle and tinkle and tinkle,
    till they
Are heard through the dawn where
    the mists are drawn,
And we canter and gallop and dash
    away
Sheer into The Judgment Day!

419

THE OLD MAN

LO! steadfast and serene,
    In patient pause between
The seen and the unseen,
    What gentle zephyrs fan
Your silken silver hair,—
And what diviner air
Breathes round you like a prayer,
    Old Man?

Can you, in nearer view
Of Glory, pierce the blue
Of happy Heaven through;
    And, listening mutely, can
Your senses, dull to us,
Hear Angel-voices thus,
In chorus glorious—
    Old Man?

In your reposeful gaze
The dusk of Autumn days
Is blent with April haze,
    As when of old began
The bursting of the bud
Of rosy babyhood—
When all the world was good,
    Old Man.

And yet I find a sly
Little twinkle in your eye;
And your whisperingly shy
    Little laugh is simply an
Internal shout of glee
That betrays the fallacy
You'd perpetrate on me,
    Old Man!

So just put up the frown
That your brows are pulling down!
Why, the fleetest boy in town,
    As he bared his feet and ran,
Could read with half a glance—
And of keen rebuke, perchance—
Your secret countenance,
    Old Man!

Now, honestly, confess:
Is an old man any less
Than the little child we bless
    And caress when we can?
Isn't age but just a place
Where you mask the childish face
To preserve its inner grace,
    Old Man?

Hasn't age a truant day,
Just as that you went astray
In the wayward, restless way,
    When, brown with dust and tan,
Your roguish face essayed,
In solemn masquerade,
To hide the smile it made,
    Old Man?

Now, fair, and square, and true,
Don't your old soul tremble through,
As in youth it used to do
    When it brimmed and overran
With the strange, enchanted sights,
And the splendors and delights
Of the old "Arabian Nights,"
    Old Man?

When, haply, you have fared
Where glad Aladdin shared
His lamp with you, and dared
    The Afrite and his clan;
And, with him, clambered through
The trees where jewels grew—
And filled your pockets, too,
    Old Man?

Or, with Sinbad, at sea—
And in veracity
Who has sinned as bad as he,
    Or would, or will, or can?—
Have you listened to his lies,
With open mouth and eyes,
And learned his art likewise,
    Old Man?

And you need not deny
That your eyes were wet as dry,
Reading novels on the sly!
    And review them, if you can
And the same warm tears will fall—
Only faster, that is all—
Over Little Nell and Paul,
    Old Man!

Oh, you were a lucky lad—
Just as good as you were bad!
And the host of friends you had—
    Charley, Tom, and Dick, and
      Dan;
And the old School-Teacher, too,
Though he often censured you;
And the girls in pink and blue,
    Old Man.

And—as often you have leant,
In boyish sentiment,
To kiss the letter sent
    By Nelly, Belle, or Nan—
Wherein the rose's hue
Was red, the violet blue—
And sugar sweet—and you,
    Old Man,—

So, to-day, as lives the bloom,
And the sweetness, and perfume
Of the blossoms, I assume,
    On the same mysterious plan
The Master's love assures,
That the selfsame boy endures
In that hale old heart of yours,
    Old Man.

420

OUR KIND OF A MAN

I

THE kind of a man for you and me!
    He faces the world unflinch-
      ingly,
And smites, as long as the wrong re-
    sists,
With a knuckled faith and force like
    fists:
He lives the life he is preaching of,

And loves where most is the need of
    love;
His voice is clear to the deaf man's
    ears,
And his face sublime through the blind
    man's tears;
The light shines out where the clouds
    were dim,
And the widow's prayer goes up for
    him;
The latch is clicked at the hovel door
And the sick man sees the sun once
    more,
And out o'er the barren fields he sees
Springing blossoms and waving trees,
Feeling as only the dying may,
That God's own servant has come that
    way,
Smoothing the path as it still winds
    on
Through the golden gate where his
    loved have gone.

II

The kind of a man for me and you!
However little of worth we do
He credits full, and abides in trust
That time will teach us how more is
    just.
He walks abroad, and he meets all
    kinds
Of querulous and uneasy minds,
And, sympathizing, he shares the pain
Of the doubts that rack us, heart and
    brain;
And, knowing this, as we grasp his
    hand,
We are surely coming to understand!
He looks on sin with pitying eyes—
E'en as the Lord, since Paradise,—
Else, should we read, Though our
    sins should glow

As scarlet, they shall be white as
    snow?—
And, feeling still, with a grief half
    glad,
That the bad are as good as the good
    are bad,
He strikes straight out for the Right—
    and he
Is the kind of a man for you and me!

421

THE LITTLE COAT

HERE'S his ragged "round-
    about." . . .
Turn the pockets inside out:
See; his penknife, lost to use,
Rusted shut with apple-juice;
Here, with marbles, top and string,
Is his deadly "devil-sling,"
With its rubber, limp at last
As the sparrows of the past!
Beeswax—buckles—leather straps—
Bullets, and a box of caps,—
Not a thing of all, I guess,
But betrays some waywardness—
E'en these tickets, blue and red,
For the Bible-verses said—
Such as this his mem'ry kept,—
                "Jesus wept."

Here's a fishing-hook and -line,
Tangled up with wire and twine,
And dead angleworms, and some
Slugs of lead and chewing-gum,
Blent with scents that can but come
From the oil of rhodium.
Here—a soiled, yet dainty note,
That some little sweetheart wrote,
Dotting—"Vine grows round the
    stump,"

And—"My sweetest sugar-lump!"
Wrapped in this—a padlock key
Where he's filed a touch-hole—see!
And some powder in a quill
Corked up with a liver pill;
And a spongy little chunk
          Of "punk."

Here's the little coat—but O
Where is he we've censured so?
Don't you hear us calling, dear?
Back! come back, and never fear.—
You may wander where you will,
Over orchard, field and hill;
You may kill the birds, or do
Anything that pleases you!
Ah, this empty coat of his!
Every tatter worth a kiss;
Every stain as pure instead
As the white stars overhead:
And the pockets—homes were they
Of the little hands that play
Now no more—but, absent, thus
          Beckon us.

422

AN IMPROMPTU ON ROLLER SKATES

RUMBLE, tumble, growl and grate!
  Skip, and trip, and gravitate!
Lunge, and plunge, and thrash the
    planks
With your blameless, shameless
    shanks:
In excruciating pain,
Stand upon your head again,
And, uncoiling kink by kink,
Kick the roof out of the rink!

In derisive bursts of mirth,
Drop ka-whop and jar the earth!

Jolt your lungs down in your socks,
Oh! tempestuous equinox
Of dismembered legs and arms!
Strew your ways with wild alarms;
Fameward skoot and ricochet
On your glittering vertebrae!

423

ME AND MARY

ALL my feelin's in the Spring
  Gits so blame contrary,
I can't think of anything
    Only me and Mary!
"Me and Mary!" all the time,
"Me and Mary!" like a rhyme,
Keeps a-dingin' on till I'm
    Sick o' "Me and Mary!"

"Me and Mary! Ef us two
  Only was together—
Playin' like we used to do
    In the Aprile weather!"
All the night and all the day
I keep wishin' thataway
Till I'm gittin' old and gray
    Jes' on "Me and Mary!"

Muddy yit along the pike
  Sence the Winter's freezin',
And the orchard's back'ard-like
    Bloomin' out this season;
Only heerd one bluebird yit—
Nary robin ner tomtit;
What's the how and why of it?
    'Spect it's "Me and Mary!"

Me and Mary liked the birds—
  That is, *Mary* sort o'
Liked 'em first, and afterwards,
    W'y, I thought *I'd* ort 'o.

And them birds—ef Mary stood
Right here with me, like she should—
They'd be singin', them birds would,
All fer me and Mary.

Birds er not, I'm hopin' some
I can git to plowin'!
Ef the sun'll only come,
And the Lord allowin',
Guess to-morry I'll turn in
And git down to work ag'in;
This here loaferin' won't win,
Not fer me and Mary!

Fer a man that loves, like me,
And 's afeard to name it,
Till some other feller, he
Gits the girl—dad-shame-it!
Wet er dry, er cloud er sun—
Winter gone er jes' begun—
Outdoor work fer me er none,
No more "Me and Mary!"

424

WRITTEN IN BUNNER'S "AIRS FROM ARCADY"

O EVER gracious Airs from Arcady!
What lack is there of any jocund
thing
In glancing wit or glad imagining
Capricious fancy may not find in
thee?—
The laugh of Momus, tempered
daintily
To lull the ear and lure its listening;
The whistled syllables the birds of
spring
Flaunt ever at our guessings what they
be;

The wood, the seashore, and the clang-
ing town;
The pets of fashion, and the ways of
such;
The *robe de chambre,* and the russet
gown;
The lordling's carriage, and the pil-
grim's crutch—
From hale old Chaucer's wholesome-
ness, clean down
To our artistic Dobson's deftest
touch!

425

A SONG

THERE is ever a song somewhere,
my dear;
There is ever a something sings
alway;
There's the song of the lark when the
skies are clear,
And the song of the thrush when
the skies are gray.
The sunshine showers across the grain,
And the bluebird trills in the or-
chard tree;
And in and out, when the eaves drip
rain,
The swallows are twittering cease-
lessly.

There is ever a song somewhere, my
dear,
Be the skies above or dark or fair,
There is ever a song that our hearts
may hear—
There is ever a song somewhere, my
dear—
There is ever a song somewhere!

There is ever a song somewhere, my
dear,
In the midnight black, or the mid-
day blue:
The robin pipes when the sun is here,
And the cricket chirrups the whole
night through.
The buds may blow, and the fruit may
grow,
And the autumn leaves drop crisp
and sear;
But whether the sun, or the rain, or
the snow,
There is ever a song somewhere, my
dear.

There is ever a song somewhere, my
dear,
Be the skies above or dark or fair,
There is ever a song that our hearts
may hear—
There is ever a song somewhere, my
dear—
There is ever a song somewhere!

426

NEVER TALK BACK

NEVER talk back! sich things is
repperhensible;
A feller only hurts hisse'f that jaws
a man that's hot;
In a quarrel, ef you'll only keep your
mouth shet and act sensible,
The man that does the talkin' 'll git
worsted every shot!

Never talk back to a feller that's
abusin' you—
Jes' let him carry on, and rip, and
snort, and swear;

And when he finds his blamin' and
defamin' 's jes' amusin' you,
You've got him clean kaflummixed,
—and you want to hold him
there!

Never talk back, and wake up the
whole community
And call a man a liar, over Law, er
Politics.—
You can lift and land him furder and
with gracefuller impunity
With one good jolt of silence than a
half a dozen kicks!

427

MY FRIEND

"HE is my friend," I said,—
"Be patient!" Overhead
The skies were drear and dim;
And lo! the thought of him
Smiled on my heart—and then
The sun shone out again!

"He is my friend!" The words
Brought summer and the birds;
And all my winter-time
Thawed into running rhyme
And rippled into song,
Warm, tender, brave, and strong.

And so it sings to-day.—
So may it sing alway!
Though waving grasses grow
Between, and lilies blow
Their trills of perfume clear
As laughter to the ear,
Let each mute measure end
With "Still he is thy friend."

428

THE LITTLE FAT DOCTOR

HE seemed so strange to me, every
    way—
In manner, and form, and size,
From the boy I knew but yesterday,—
    I could hardly believe my eyes!

To hear his name called over there,
    My memory thrilled with glee
And leaped to picture him young and
        fair
    In youth, as he used to be.

But looking, only as glad eyes can,
    For the boy I knew of yore,
I smiled on a portly little man
    I had never seen before!—

Grave as a judge in courtliness—
    Professor-like and bland—
A little fat doctor and nothing less,
    With his hat in his kimboed hand.

But how we talked old times, and
    "chaffed"
    Each other with "Minnie," and
        "Jim"—
And how the little fat doctor laughed,
    And how I laughed with him!

"And it's pleasant," I thought, "though
    I yearn to see
    The face of the youth that was,
To know no boy could smile on me
    As the little fat doctor does!"

429

THE STRANGE YOUNG MAN

'TWAS a strange young man of the
    dreamy times
When bards made money, and bankers
    rhymes;
And drones made honey—and bees
    made naught;
And the bad sung hymns, and the
    good-folk fought;
And the merchants lurked in the shade
    all day
And pitched horseshoes in a listless
    way!
When the ticket-man at the station
    knew
If your trunk would go if you checked
    it through,
And if 2:30 meant half-past two,
And what in-the-name-of-the-land to
    do
If a man got left when he oughtn't to:
When the cabman wept as he took
    your fare,
And the street-car driver led in
    prayer—
And the cuss with the dyed mustache
    was there
That rode in town on a "jumper"-
    sled,
And got whipped twice for the things
    he said
To fellows that told him his hair was
    red.
And the strange young man (of which
    and whom
Our pencil offers to deign presume
To treat of now, in the days like
    these
When young men dress as they please
    to please)

Went round in a coat of pale pink-
blue,
And a snow-white vest of a crimson
hue,
And trousers purple, and gaiters
gray—
All cut, as the French or the Dutch
would say,—
*La—macht nichts aus, oder—décol-
leté,—*
Strange not only in dress, but in
The dimples he wore in cheek and
chin—
All nailed over with scraps of tin,
Where he hadn't been shaved as he'd
ought o' been;—
And his crape cravat, and the shape
of that,
And the ear-tab over his diamond-pin.
And his friends all wondered, and used
to say,—
"What a strange young man! Ah me!
Hooray!
How sad he seems in his wild delight!
And how tickled indeed when he
weeps outright!
What a comical man when he writhes
in pain;
And how grieved he grows when he's
glad again!"
And marveling still to remark new
facts,
They said, "How slender and slim he
acts!
And isn't it odd for a man to wear
A thumb-stall over his nose, and pare
His finger-nails with a carving-knife,
And talk of prunes to the landlord's
wife?
It is patent to us—and, indeed, no
doubt,
Though as safely sealed as an oyster-
can,—

Our interest in him must needs leak
out,—
Namely, that he is a strange young
man!"

430
SCOTTY

SCOTTY'S dead.—Of course he is!
Jes' that same old luck of his!—
Ever sence we went cahoots
He's be'n first, you bet yer boots!
When our schoolin' first begun,
Got two whippin's to my one:
Stold and smoked the first cigar:
Stood up first before the bar,
Takin' whisky-straight—and me
Wastin' time on "blackberry"!
Beat me in the Army, too,
And clean on the whole way
through!—
In more scrapes around the camp,
And more troubles, on the tramp:
Fought and fell there by my side
With more bullets in his hide,
And more glory in the cause,—
That's the kind o' man *he* was!
Luck liked Scotty more'n me.—
I got married: Scotty, he
Never even would *apply*
Fer the pension-money I
Had to beg of "Uncle Sam"—
That's the kind o' cuss *I* am!—
Scotty allus first and best—
Me the last and ornriest!
Yit fer all that's said and done—
All the battles fought and won—
We hain't prospered, him ner me—
Both as pore as pore could be,—
Though we've allus, up tel now,
Stuck together anyhow—
Scotty allus, as I've said,
Luckiest—And now he's *dead!*

431

ON THE SUNNY SIDE

HI and whoop-hooray, boys!
    Sing a song of cheer!
Here's a holiday, boys,
    Lasting half a year!
Round the world, and half is
    Shadow we have tried;
Now we're where the laugh is,—
    On the sunny side!

Pigeons coo and mutter,
    Strutting high aloof
Where the sunbeams flutter
    Through the stable roof.
Hear the chickens cheep, boys,
    And the hen with pride
Clucking them to sleep, boys,
    On the sunny side!

Hear the clacking guinea;
    Hear the cattle moo;
Hear the horses whinny,
    Looking out at you!
On the hitching-block, boys,
    Grandly satisfied,
See the old peacock, boys,
    On the sunny side!

Robins in the peach tree;
    Bluebirds in the pear;
Blossoms over each tree
    In the orchard there!
All the world's in joy, boys,
    Glad and glorified
As a romping boy, boys,
    On the sunny side!

Where's a heart as mellow—
    Where's a soul as free—
Where is any fellow
    We would rather be?

Just ourselves or none, boys,
    World around and wide,
Laughing in the sun, boys,
    On the sunny side!

432

THE HARPER

LIKE a drift of faded blossoms
    Caught in a slanting rain,
His fingers glimpsed down the strings
    of his harp
In a tremulous refrain:

Patter and tinkle, and drip and drip!
    Ah! but the chords were rainy sweet!
And I closed my eyes and I bit my lip,
    As he played there in the street.

Patter, and drip, and tinkle!
    And there was the little bed
In the corner of the garret,
    And the rafters overhead!

And there was the little window—
    Tinkle, and drip, and drip!—
The rain above, and a mother's love,
    And God's companionship!

433

THE BLOSSOMS ON THE TREES

BLOSSOMS   crimson,   white,   or
    blue,
Purple, pink, and every hue,
From sunny skies, to tintings drowned
    In dusky drops of dew,

I praise you all, wherever found,
  And love you through and
    through;—
  But, Blossoms on the Trees,
  With your breath upon the
    breeze,
There's nothing all the world around
As half as sweet as you!

Could the rhymer only wring
  All the sweetness to the lees
Of all the kisses clustering
  In juicy Used-to-bes,
To dip his rhymes therein and sing
  The blossoms on the trees,—
"O Blossoms on the Trees,"
  He would twitter, trill, and coo,
"However sweet, such songs as these
  Are not as sweet as you:—
For you are *blooming* melodies
  The *eyes* may listen to!"

434

LAUGHTER HOLDING BOTH
HIS SIDES

AY, thou varlet! Laugh away!
  All the world's a holiday!
Laugh away, and roar and shout
Till thy hoarse tongue lolleth out!
Bloat thy cheeks, and bulge thine
    eyes
Unto bursting; pelt thy thighs
With thy swollen palms, and roar
As thou never hast before!
Lustier! wilt thou! peal on peal!
Stiflest? Squat and grind thy heel—
Wrestle with thy loins, and then
Wheeze thee whiles, and whoop again!

435

IN STATE

IS it the martins or katydids?—
  Early morning or late at night?
A dream, belike, kneeling down on the
    lids
  Of a dying man's eyesight.

          .   .   .   ,   .   .

Over and over I heard the rain—
  Over and over I waked to see
The blaze of the lamp as again and
    again
  Its stare insulted me.

          .   .   .   .   .   .

It is not the click of the clock I hear—
  It is the *pulse* of the clock,—and lo!
How it throbs and throbs on the
    quickened ear
  Of the dead man listening so!

I heard them whisper *"She* would not
    come;"
  But, being dead, I knew—I
    knew! . . .
Some hearts they love us alive, and
    some
  They love us dead—they do!

And *I* am dead—and I joy to be,— ·
  For here are my folded hands, so
    cold,
And yet blood-warm with the roses
    she
  Has given me to hold.

Dead—yea, dead!—But I hear the beat
  Of her heart, as her warm lips touch
    my brow—

And O how sweet—how *blinding*
  sweet
To know that she loves me *now!*

436

THE DEAD·LOVER

TIME is so long when a man is
  dead!
Some one sews; and the room is
  made
Very clean; and the light is shed
Soft through the window-shade.

Yesterday I thought: "I know
  Just how the bells will sound, and
    how
The friends will talk, and the sermon
    go,
And the hearse-horse bow and bow!"

This is to-day; and I have no thing
  To think of—nothing whatever to
    do
But to hear the throb of the pulse of a
    wing
That wants to fly back to you.

437

THE KIND OLD MAN

THE kind old man—the mild old
  man—
Who smiled on the boys at play,
Dreaming, perchance, of his own glad
    youth
When he was as blithe and gay!

And the larger urchin tossed the ball,
And the lesser held the bat—

Though the kindly old man's eyes
  were blurred
He could even notice that!

But suddenly he was shocked to hear
  Words that I dare not write,
And he hastened, in his kindly way,
  To curb them as he might!

And he said, "Tut! tut! you naughty
    boy
  With the ball! for shame!" and then,
"You boy with the bat, whack him
    over the head
  If he calls you that again!"

The kind old man—the mild old
    man—
Who gazed on the boys at play,
Dreaming, perchance, of his own wild
    youth
When he was as tough as they!

438

A SCRAWL

I WANT to sing something—but
    this is all—
  I try and I try, but the rhymes are
    dull
As though they were damp, and the
    echoes fall
  Limp and unlovable.

Words will not say what I yearn to
    say—
  They will not walk as I want them
    to,
But they stumble and fall in the path
    of the way
  Of my telling my love for you.

Simply take what the scrawl is worth—
Knowing I love you as sun the sod
On the ripening side of the great
round earth
That swings in the smile of
God.

439

AWAY

I CAN not say, and I will not say
That he is dead.—He is just away!

With a cheery smile, and a wave of
the hand,
He has wandered into an unknown
land,

And left us dreaming how very fair
It needs must be, since he lingers
there.

And you—O you, who the wildest
yearn
For the old-time step and the glad
return,—

Think of him faring on, as dear
In the love of There as the love of
Here;

And loyal still, as he gave the blows
Of his warrior-strength to his country's
foes.—

Mild and gentle, as he was brave,—
When the sweetest love of his life he
gave

To simple things:—Where the violets
grew
Blue as the eyes they were likened to,

The touches of his hands have strayed
As reverently as his lips have prayed:

When the little brown thrush that
harshly chirred
Was dear to him as the mocking-bird;

And he pitied as much as a man in
pain
A writhing honey-bee wet with rain.—

Think of him still as the same, I say:
He is not dead—he is just away!

440

A MONUMENT FOR THE SOLDIERS

A MONUMENT for the Soldiers!
And what will ye build it of?
Can ye build it of marble, or brass, or
bronze,
Outlasting the Soldiers' love?
Can ye glorify it with legends
As grand as their blood hath writ
From the inmost shrine of this land of
thine
To the outermost verge of it?

And the answer came: We would build
it
Out of our hopes made sure,
And out of our purest prayers and
tears,
And out of our faith secure:
We would build it out of the great
white truths
Their death hath sanctified,
And the sculptured forms of the men
in arms,
And their faces ere they died.

And what heroic figures
  Can the sculptor carve in stone?
Can the marble breast be made to
    bleed,
  And the marble lips to moan?
Can the marble brow be fevered?
  And the marble eyes be graved
To look their last, as the flag floats
    past,
  On the country they have saved?

And the answer came: The figures
  Shall all be fair and brave,
And, as befitting, as pure and white
  As the stars above their grave!
The marble lips, and breast and brow
  Whereon the laurel lies,
Bequeath us right to guard the flight
  Of the old flag in the skies!

A monument for the Soldiers!
  Built of a people's love,
And blazoned and decked and pano-
    plied
  With the hearts ye build it of!
And see that ye build it stately,
  In pillar and niche and gate,
And high in pose as the souls of those
  It would commemorate!

441

OUT TO OLD AUNT MARY'S

WASN'T it pleasant, O brother
      mine,
In those old days of the lost sunshine
  Of youth—when the Saturday's
      chores were through,
  And the "Sunday's wood" in the
      kitchen, too,

And we went visiting, "me and
      you,"
  Out to Old Aunt Mary's?—

"Me and you"—And the morning fair,
With the dewdrops twinkling every-
      where;
  The scent of the cherry-blossoms
      blown
  After us, in the roadway lone,
  Our capering shadows onward
      thrown—
  Out to Old Aunt Mary's!

It all comes back so clear to-day!
Though I am as bald as you are
      gray,—
  Out by the barn-lot and down the
      lane
  We patter along in the dust again,
  As light as the tips of the drops of
      the rain,
  Out to Old Aunt Mary's.

The few last houses of the town;
Then on, up the high creek-bluffs and
      down;
  Past the squat toll-gate, with its well-
      sweep pole,
  The bridge, and "the old 'babtizin'-
      hole,' "
  Loitering, awed, o'er pool and shoal,
  Out to Old Aunt Mary's.

We cross the pasture, and through the
      wood,
Where the old gray snag of the poplar
      stood,
  Where the hammering "red-heads"
      hopped awry,
  And the buzzard "raised" in the
      "clearing"-sky

And lolled and circled, as we went
    by
    Out to Old Aunt Mary's.

Or, stayed by the glint of the redbird's
    wings,
Or the glitter of song that the bluebird
    sings,
All hushed we feign to strike strange
    trails,
As the "big braves" do in the Indian
    tales,
Till again our real quest lags and
    fails—
    Out to Old Aunt Mary's.—

And the woodland echoes with yells of
    mirth
That make old war-whoops of minor
    worth! . . .
Where such heroes of war as we?—
With bows and arrows of fantasy,
Chasing each other from tree to tree
    Out to Old Aunt Mary's!

And then in the dust of the road again;
And the teams we met, and the coun-
    trymen;
And the long highway, with sun-
    shine spread
As thick as butter on country bread,
Our cares behind, and our hearts
    ahead
    Out to Old Aunt Mary's.—

For only, now, at the road's next bend
To the right we could make out the
    gable-end
Of the fine old Huston homestead
    —not
Half a mile from the sacred spot
Where dwelt our Saint in her simple
    cot—
    Out to Old Aunt Mary's.

Why, I see her now in the open door
Where the little gourds grew up the
    sides and o'er
The clapboard roof!—And her face
    —ah, me!
Wasn't it good for a boy to see—
And wasn't it good for a boy to be
    Out to Old Aunt Mary's?—

The jelly—the jam and the marmalade,
And the cherry and quince "preserves"
    she made!
And the sweet-sour pickles of peach
    and pear,
With cinnamon in 'em, and all
    things rare!—
And the more we ate was the more
    to spare,
    Out to Old Aunt Mary's!

Ah! was there, ever, so kind a face
And gentle as hers, or such a grace
    Of welcoming, as she cut the cake
    Or the juicy pies that she joyed to
      make
Just for the visiting children's sake—
    Out to Old Aunt Mary's!

The honey, too, in its amber comb
One only finds in an old farm-home;
    And the coffee, fragrant and sweet,
      and ho!
So hot that we gloried to drink it so,
With spangles of tears in our eyes,
    you know—
    Out to Old Aunt Mary's.

And the romps we took, in our glad
    unrest!—
Was it the lawn that we loved the best,
    With its swooping swing in the
      locust trees,

Or was it the grove, with its leafy
        breeze,
Or the dim haymow, with its fra-
        grancies—
        Out to Old Aunt Mary's.

Far fields, bottom-lands, creek-banks—
        all,
We ranged at will.—Where the water-
        fall
Laughed all day as it slowly poured
Over the dam by the old mill-ford,
While the tail-race writhed, and the
        mill-wheel roared—
        Out to Old Aunt Mary's.

But home, with Aunty in nearer call,
That was the best place, after all!—
    The talks on the back porch, in the
        low
    Slanting sun and the evening glow,
    With the voice of counsel that
        touched us so,
        Out to Old Aunt Mary's.

And then, in the garden—near the side
Where the beehives were and the path
        was wide,—
    The apple-house—like a fairy cell—
    With the little square door we knew
        so well,
    And the wealth inside but our
        tongues could tell—
        Out to Old Aunt Mary's.

And the old spring-house, in the cool
        green gloom
Of the willow trees,—and the cooler
        room
    Where the swinging shelves and the
        crocks were kept,
    Where the cream in a golden languor
        slept,

While the waters gurgled and
        laughed and wept—
        Out to Old Aunt Mary's.

And as many a time have you and I—
Barefoot boys in the days gone by—
    Knelt, and in tremulous ecstasies
    Dipped our lips into sweets like
        these,—
    Memory now is on her knees
        Out to Old Aunt Mary's.—

For, O my brother so far away,
This is to tell you—she waits *to-day*
    To welcome us:—Aunt Mary fell
    Asleep this morning, whispering,
        "Tell
    The boys to come." . . . And all is
        well
        Out to Old Aunt Mary's.

442

IN THE AFTERNOON

YOU in the hammock; and I, near
    by,
Was trying to read, and to swing
        you, too;
And the green of the sward was so
        kind to the eye,
    And the shade of the maples so cool
        and blue,
    That often I looked from the book to
        you
To say as much, with a sigh.

You in the hammock. The book we'd
        brought
    From the parlor—to read in the open
        air,—

Something of love and of Launcelot
  And Guinevere, I believe, was
    there—
But the afternoon, it was far more
    fair
Than the poem was, I thought.

You in the hammock; and on and on
  I droned and droned through the
    rhythmic stuff—
But, with always a half of my vision
    gone
  Over the top of the page—enough
  To caressingly gaze at you, swathed
    in the fluff
Of your hair and your odorous "lawn."

You in the hammock—and that was a
    year—
Fully a year ago, I guess—
And what do we care for their Guine-
    vere
  And her Launcelot and their lordli-
    ness!—
  You in the hammock still, and—
    Yes—
Kiss me again, my dear!

443

UNINTERPRETED

SUPINELY we lie in the grove's
    shady greenery,
  Gazing, all dreamy-eyed, up through
    the trees,—
And as to the sight is the heavenly
    scenery,
  So to the hearing the sigh of the
    breeze.

We catch but vague rifts of the blue
    through the wavering
  Boughs of the maples; and, alike un-
    defined,
The whispers and lisps of the leaves,
    faint and quavering,
  Meaningless falter and fall on the
    mind.

The vine, with its beauty of blossom,
    goes rioting
Up by the casement, as sweet to the eye
As the trill of the robin is restful and
    quieting
  Heard in a drowse with the dawn in
    the sky.

And yet we yearn on to learn more of
    the mystery—
  We see and we hear, but forever re-
    main
Mute, blind and deaf to the ultimate
    history
  Born of a rose or a patter of rain.

444

BILLY'S ALPHABETICAL
ANIMAL SHOW

A WAS an elegant Ape
    Who tied up his ears with red tape,
    And wore a long veil
    Half revealing his tail
Which was trimmed with jet bugles
    and crape.

B was a boastful old Bear
    Who used to say,—"Hoomh! I de-
    clare
    I can eat—if you'll get me
    The children, and let me—
Ten babies, teeth, toe-nails and hair!"

C was a Codfish who sighed
   When snatched from the home of
      his pride,
   But could he, embrined,
   Guess this fragrance behind,
How glad he would be to have died!

D was a dandified Dog
   Who said,—"Though it's raining
      like fog
   I wear no umbrellah,
   Me boy, for a fellah
Might just as well travel incog!"

E was an elderly Eel
   Who would say,—"Well, I really
      feel—
   As my grandchildren wriggle
   And shout 'I should giggle'—
A trifle run down at the heel!"

F was a Fowl who conceded
   Some hens might hatch more eggs
      than *she* did,—
   But she'd children as plenty
   As eighteen or twenty,
And that was quite all that she needed.

G was a gluttonous Goat
   Who, dining one day, *table d'hôte,*
   Ordered soup-bone, *au fait,*
   And fish, *papier-mâché,*
And a *filet* of Spring overcoat.

H was a high-cultured Hound
   Who could clear forty feet at a
      bound,
   And a coon once averred
   That his howl could be heard
For five   miles   and   three-quarters
      around.

I was an Ibex ambitious
   To dive over chasms auspicious;
   He would leap down a peak
   And not light for a week,
And swear that the jump was deli-
      cious.

J was a Jackass who said
   He had such a bad cold in his head,
   If it wasn't for leaving
   The rest of us grieving,
He'd really rather be dead.

K was a profligate Kite
   Who would haunt the saloons
      every night;
   And often he ust
   To reel back to his roost
Too full to set up on it right.

L was a wary old Lynx
   Who would say,—"Do you know
      wot I thinks?—
   I thinks ef you happen
   To ketch me a-nappin'
I'm ready to set up the drinks!"

M was a merry old Mole,
   Who would snooze all day in his
      hole,
   Then—all night, a-rootin'
   Around and galootin'—
He'd sing "Johnny, Fill up the Bowl!"

N was a caustical Nautilus
   Who sneered, "I suppose, when
      they've *caught* all us,
   Like oysters they'll serve us,
   And can us, preserve us,
And barrel, and pickle, and bottle us!"

O was an autocrat Owl—
  Such a wise—such a wonderful
    fowl!
  Why, for all the night through
  He would hoot and hoo-hoo,
And hoot and hoo-hooter and howl!

P was a Pelican pet,
  Who gobbled up all he could get;
    He could eat on until
    He was full to the bill,
And there he had lodgings to let!

Q was a querulous Quail
  Who said: "It will little avail
    The efforts of those
    Of my foes who propose
To attempt to put salt on my tail!"

R was a ring-tailed Raccoon,
  With eyes of the tinge of the moon,
    And his nose a blue-black,
    And the fur on his back
A sad sort of sallow maroon.

S is a Sculpin—you'll wish
  Very much to have one on your
    dish,
    Since all his bones grow
    On the outside, and so
He's a very desirable fish.

T was a Turtle, of wealth,
  Who went round with particular
    stealth,
    "Why," said he, "I'm afraid
    Of being waylaid
When I even walk out for my health!"

U was a Unicorn curious,
  With one horn, of a growth so
    luxurious,
    He could level and stab it—
    If you didn't grab it—
Clean through you, he was so blamed
    furious!

V was a vagabond Vulture
  Who said: "I don't want to in-
    sult yer,
    But when you intrude
    Where in lone solitude
I'm a-preyin', you're no man o' cul-
    ture!"

W was a wild *Wood*chuck,
  And you just bet that he *could*
    "chuck"—
    He'd eat raw potatoes,
    Green corn, and tomatoes,
And tree roots, and call it all *"good*
    chuck!"

X was a kind of X-cuse
  Of some-sort-o'-thing that got
    loose
    Before we could name it,
    And cage it, and tame it,
And bring it in general use.

Y is a Yellowbird,—bright
  As a petrified lump of starlight,
    Or a handful of lightning-
    Bugs, squeezed in the tight'ning
Pink fist of a boy, at night.

Z is the Zebra, of course!—
  A kind of a clown-of-a-horse,—
    Each other despising,
    Yet neither devising
A way to obtain a divorce!

&. here is the famous—what-is-it?
Walk up, Master Billy, and quiz it:
   You've seen the *rest* of 'em—
   Ain't this the *best* of 'em,
Right at the end of your visit?

445

THE PIXY PEOPLE

IT was just a very
   Merry fairy dream!—
All the woods were airy
   With the gloom and gleam;
Crickets in the clover
   Clattered clear and strong,
And the bees droned over
   Their old honey-song!

In the mossy passes,
   Saucy grasshoppers
Leaped about the grasses
   And the thistle-burs;
And the whispered chuckle
   Of the katydid
Shook the honeysuckle-
   Blossoms where he hid.

Through the breezy mazes
   Of the lazy June,
Drowsy with the hazes
   Of the dreamy noon,
Little Pixy people
   Winged above the walk,
Pouring from the steeple
   Of a mullein-stalk.

One—a gallant fellow—
   Evidently King,—
Wore a plume of yellow
   In a jeweled ring

On a pansy bonnet,
   Gold and white and blue,
With the dew still on it,
   And the fragrance, too.

One—a dainty lady,—
   Evidently Queen—
Wore a gown of shady
   Moonshine and green,
With a lace of gleaming
   Starlight that sent
All the dewdrops dreaming
   Everywhere she went.

One wore a waistcoat
   Of rose-leaves, out and in;
And one wore a faced-coat
   Of tiger-lily-skin;
And one wore a neat coat
   Of palest galingale;
And one a tiny street-coat,
   And one a swallow-tail.

And Ho! sang the King of them,
   And Hey! sang the Queen;
And round and round the ring of them
   Went dancing o'er the green;
And Hey! sang the Queen of them,
   And Ho! sang the King—
And all that I had seen of them
   —Wasn't anything!

It was just a very
   Merry fairy dream!—
All the woods were airy
   With the gloom and gleam;
Crickets in the clover
   Clattered clear and strong,
And the bees droned over
   Their old honey-song!

446

THE TOWN KARNTEEL

THE town Karnteel!—It's who'll
        reveal
Its praises jushtifiable?
For who can sing av anything
So lovely and reliable?
'Whin Summer, Spring, or Winter lies
From Malin's Head to Tipperary,
There's no such town for interprise
Bechuxt Youghal and Londonderry!

There's not its likes in Ireland—
    For twic't the week, be-gorries!
They're playing jigs upon the band,
And joomping there in sacks—and—
        and—
    And racing, wid wheelborries!

Karnteel!—it's there, like any fair,
    The purty gurrls is plinty, sure!—
And, man-alive! at forty-five
    The legs av me air twinty, sure!
I lave me cares, and hoein', too,
    Behint me, as is sinsible,
And it's Karnteel I'm goin' to,
    To cilebrate in principle!

For there's the town av all the land!
    And twic't the week, be-gorries!
They're playing jigs upon the band,
And joomping there in sacks—and—
        and—
    And racing, wid wheelborries!

And whilst I feel for owld Karnteel
    That I've no phrases glorious,
It stands above the need av love
    That boasts in voice uproarious!—
Lave that for Cork, and Dublin, too,
    And Armagh and Killarney, thin,—
And Karnteel won't be troublin' you
    Wid any jilous blarney, thin!

For there's the town av all the land!
    Where twic't the week, be-gorries!
They're playing jigs upon the band,
And joomping there in sacks—and—
        and—
    And racing, wid wheelborries!

447

DONN PIATT OF MAC-O-CHEE

I

DONN PIATT—of Mac-o-chee,—
    Not the one of History,
Who, with flaming tongue and pen,
Scathes the vanities of men;
Not the one whose biting wit
Cuts pretense and etches it
On the brazen brow that dares
Filch the laurel that it wears:
Not the Donn Piatt whose praise
Echoes in the noisy ways
Of the faction, onward led
By the statesman!—But, instead,
Give the simple man to me,—
Donn Piatt of Mac-o-chee!

II

Donn Piatt of Mac-o-chee!
Branches of the old oak tree,
Drape him royally in fine
Purple shade and golden shine!
Emerald plush of sloping lawn
Be the throne he sits upon!
And, O Summer Sunset, thou
Be his crown, and gild a brow
Softly   smoothed   and   soothed   and
        calmed
By the breezes, mellow-palmed
As Erata's white hand agleam
On the forehead of a dream.—

So forever rule o'er me,
Donn Piatt of Mac-o-chee!

III

Donn Piatt of Mac-o-chee!
Through a lilied memory
Plays the wayward little creek
Round thy home at hide-and-seek—
As I see and hear it, still
Romping round the wooded hill,
Till its laugh and babble blends
With the silence while it sends
Glances back to kiss the sight,
In its babyish delight,
Ere it strays amid the gloom
Of the glens that burst in bloom
Of the rarest rhyme for thee,
Donn Piatt of Mac-o-chee!

IV

Donn Piatt of Mac-o-chee!
What a darling destiny
Has been mine—to meet him there—
Lolling in an easy chair
On the terrace, while he told
Reminiscences of old—
Letting my cigar die out,
Hearing poems talked about;
And entranced to hear him say
Gentle things of Thackeray,
Dickens, Hawthorne, and the rest,
Known to him as host and guest—
Known to him as he to me—
Donn Piatt of Mac-o-chee!

448

HERR WEISER

HERR WEISER!—Threescore years
and ten,—
A hale white rose of his countrymen,

Transplanted here in the Hoosier loam,
And blossomy as his German home—
As blossomy and as pure and sweet
As the cool green glen of his calm re-
treat,
Far withdrawn from the noisy town
Where trade goes clamoring up and
down.
Whose fret and fever, and stress and
strife,
May not trouble his tranquil life!

Breath of rest, what a balmy gust!—
Quit of the city's heat and dust,
Jostling down by the winding road,
Through the orchard ways of his
quaint abode.—
Tether the horse, as we onward fare
Under the pear trees trailing there,
And thumping the wooden bridge at
night
With lumps of ripeness and lush de-
light,
Till the stream, as it maunders on till
dawn,
Is powdered and pelted and smiled
upon.

Herr Weiser, with his wholesome
face,
And the gentle blue of his eyes, and
grace
Of unassuming honesty,
Be there to welcome you and me!
And what though the toil of the farm
be stopped
And the tireless plans of the place be
dropped,
While the prayerful master's knees are
set
In beds of pansy and mignonette
And lily and aster and columbine,
Offered in love, as yours and mine?—

What, but a blessing of kindly thought,
Sweet as the breath of forget-me-not!—
What, but a spirit of lustrous love
White as the aster he bends above!—
What, but an odorous memory
Of the dear old man, made known to
    me
In days demanding a help like his,—
As sweet as the life of the lily is—
As sweet as the soul of a babe, bloom-
    wise
Born of a lily in Paradise.

449

FROM DELPHI TO CAMDEN

I

FROM Delphi to Camden—little
    Hoosier towns,—
But here were classic meadows, bloom-
    ing dales and downs;
And here were grassy pastures, dewy
    as the leas
Trampled over by the trains of royal
    pageantries!

And here the winding highway loi-
    tered through the shade
Of the hazel covert, where, in ambus-
    cade,
Loomed the larch and linden, and the
    greenwood-tree
Under which bold Robin Hood loud
    hallooed to me!

Here the stir and riot of the busy
    day
Dwindled to the quiet of the breath of
    May;

Gurgling brooks, and ridges lily-
    marged and spanned
By the rustic bridges found in Won-
    derland!

II

From Delphi to Camden,—from Cam-
    den back again!—
And now the night was on us, and
    the lightning and the rain;
And still the way was wondrous with
    the flash of hill and plain,—
The stars like printed asterisks—the
    moon a murky stain!

And I thought of tragic idyll, and of
    flight and hot pursuit,
And the jingle of the bridle and cuirass
    and spur on boot,
As our horses' hooves struck showers
    from the flinty boulders set
In freshet-ways of writhing reed and
    drowning violet.

And we passed beleaguered castles,
    with their battlements a-frown;
Where a tree fell in the forest was a
    turret toppled down;
While my master and commander—
    the brave knight I galloped with
On this reckless road to ruin or to
    fame was—Dr. Smith!

450

A NOON INTERVAL

A DEEP, delicious hush in earth and
    sky—
A gracious lull—since, from its wak-
    ening,

The morn has been a feverish, rest-
  less thing
In which the pulse of Summer ran too
  high
And riotous, as though its heart went
  nigh
  To bursting with delights past utter-
  ing:
  Now, as an o'erjoyed child may cease
  to sing
All falteringly at play, with drowsy eye
  Draining the pictures of a fairy tale
To brim his dreams with—there comes
  o'er the day
A loathful silence, wherein all sounds
  fail·
Like loitering tones of some faint
  roundelay . . .
No wakeful effort longer may
  avail—
The wand waves, and the dozer sinks
  away.

451

AT MADAME MANICURE'S

DAINTIEST of Manicures!
  What a cunning hand is yours;
And how awkward, rude and great
Mine, as you manipulate!
Wonderfully cool and calm
Are the touches of your palm
To my fingers, as they rest
In their rosy, cozy nest,
While your own, with deftest skill,
Dance and caper as they will,—
Armed with instruments that seem
Gathered from some fairy dream—
Tiny spears and simitars
Such as pixy armorers
Might have made for jocund fays

To parade on holidays,
And flash round in dewy dells,
Lopping down the lily-bells;
Or in tilting, o'er the leas,
At the clumsy bumblebees,
Splintering their stings, perchance,
As the knights in old romance
Snapped the spears of foes that fought
In the jousts at Camelot!
Smiling? Dainty Manicure?—
'Twould delight me, but that you're
Simply smiling, as I see,
At my nails and not at me!
Haply this is why they glow
And light up and twinkle so!

452

JOHN McKEEN

JOHN McKEEN, in his rusty dress,
  His loosened collar, and swarthy
    throat,
His face unshaven, and none the less,
His hearty laugh and his wholesome-
    ness,
  And the wealth of a workman's vote!

Bring him, O Memory, here once more,
  And tilt him back in his Windsor
    chair
By the kitchen stove, when the day is
    o'er
And the light of the hearth is across
    the floor,
  And the crickets everywhere!

And let their voices be gladly blent
  With a watery jingle of pans and
    spoons,
And a motherly chirrup of sweet con-
    tent,

And neighborly gossip and merriment,
And old-time fiddle-tunes!

Tick the clock with a wooden sound,
And fill the hearing with childish
    glee
Of rhyming riddle, or story found
In the Robinson Crusoe, leather-bound
Old book of the Used-to-be!

John McKeen of the Past! Ah, John,
To have grown ambitious in worldly
    ways!—
To have rolled your shirt-sleeves down,
    to don
A broadcloth suit, and, forgetful, gone
Out on election days!

John, ah, John! did it prove your worth
To yield you the office you still main-
    tain?—
To fill your pockets, but leave the
    dearth
Of all the happier things on earth
To the hunger of heart and brain?

Under the dusk of your villa trees,
Edging the drives where your
    blooded span
Paw the pebbles and wait your ease,—
Where are the children about your
    knees,
And the mirth, and the happy man?

The blinds of your mansion are bat-
    tened to;
Your faded wife is a close recluse;
And your "finished" daughters will
    doubtless do
Dutifully all that is willed of you,
And marry as you shall choose!—

But O for the old-home voices, blent
With the watery jingle of pans and
    spoons,
And the motherly chirrup of glad con-
    tent,
And neighborly gossip and merriment,
And the old-time fiddle-tunes!

453

THE BOY-FRIEND

CLARENCE, my boy-friend, hale
    and strong!
O he is as jolly as he is young;
And all of the laughs of the lyre be-
    long
To the boy all unsung:

So I want to sing something in his be-
    half—
To clang some chords, for the good
    it is
To know he is near, and to have the
    laugh
Of that wholesome voice of his.

I want to tell him in gentler ways
Than prose may do, that the arms of
    rhyme,
Warm and tender with tuneful praise,
Are about him all the time.

I want him to know that the quietest
    nights
We have passed together are yet with
    me,
Roistering over the old delights
That were born of his company.

I want him to know how my soul es-
    teems
The fairy stories of Andersen,

And the glad translations of all the
    themes
Of the hearts of boyish men.

Want him to know that my fancy
    flows,
With the lilt of a dear old-fashioned
    tune,
Through "Lewis Carroll's" poemly
    prose,
And the tale of "The Bold Dra-
    goon."

O this is the Prince that I would sing—
    Would drape and garnish in velvet
    line,
Since courtlier far than any king
    Is this brave boy-friend of mine.

454

WHEN BESSIE DIED

"If from your own the dimpled hands
    had slipped,
And ne'er would nestle in your palm
    again;
If the white feet into the grave had
    tripped"——

WHEN Bessie died—
    We braided the brown hair,
    and tied
It just as her own little hands
Had fastened back the silken strands
A thousand times—the crimson bit
Of ribbon woven into it
That she had worn with childish
    pride—
Smoothed down the dainty bow—and
    cried—
        When Bessie died.

When Bessie died—
We drew the nursery blinds aside,
And, as the morning in the room
Burst like a primrose into bloom,
Her pet canary's cage we hung '
Where she might hear him when he
    sung—
And yet not any note he tried
Though she lay listening folded-eyed.

When Bessie died—
We writhed in prayer unsatisfied:
We begged of God, and He did smile
In silence on us all the while;
And we did see Him, through our
    tears,
Enfolding that fair form of hers,
She laughing back against His love
The kisses we had nothing of—
And death to us He still denied,
When Bessie died—
        When Bessie died.

455

THE RIVALS; OR THE SHOW-MAN'S RUSE

A TRAGI-COMEDY, IN ONE ACT

PERSONS REPRESENTED

BILLY MILLER   }
JOHNNY WILLIAMS }   The Rivals
TOMMY WELLS   Conspirator

TIME—Noon. SCENE—Country Town
    —*Rear view of the* Miller Mansion,
    showing Barn, with practical loft-
    window opening on alley-way, with
    colored-crayon poster on wall be-
    neath, announcing:—"BILLY MIL-
    LER's Big Show and Monstur Circus

and Equareum! A shour-bath fer
Each and All fer 20 pins. This
Afternoon! Don't fer git the Date!"
Enter TOMMY WELLS *and* JOHNNY
WILLIAMS, *who gaze a while at
poster,* TOMMY *secretly smiling and
winking at* BILLY MILLER, *concealed
at loft-window above.*

TOMMY [*To* JOHNNY]

Guess 'at Billy hain't got back,—
Can't see nothin' through the crack—
Can't hear nothin' neether—No!
. . . Thinks he's got the dandy show,
Don't he?

JOHNNY [*Scornfully*]

'Course! but what *I* care?—
He hain't got no show in there!—
What's *he* got in there but that
Old hen, cooped up with a cat
An' à turkle, an' that thing
'At he calls his "circus-ring"?
What a "circus-ring"! I'd *quit!*
Bet *mine's* twic't as big as it!

TOMMY

Yes, but *you* got no machine
W'at you bathe with, painted green,
With a string to work it, guess!

JOHNNY [*Contemptuously*]

Folks don't *bathe* in *circuses!*—
Ladies comes to *mine,* you bet!
I' got seats where *girls* can set;
An' a dressin'-room, an' all,
Fixed up in my pony's stall—
Yes, an' I got *carpet,* too,
Fer the tumblers, an' a blue
Center-pole!

TOMMY

Well, Billy, he's
Got a tight-rope an' trapeze,
An' a hoop 'at he jumps through
Head-first!

JOHNNY

Well, what's *that* to do—
Lightin' on a pile o' hay?
Hain't no *actin'* thataway!

TOMMY

Don't care what you say, he draws
Bigger crowds than you do, 'cause
Sence he started up, I know
All the fellers says his show
Is the best-un!

JOHNNY

Yes, an' he
Better not tell things on me!
His old circus hain't no good!—
'Cause he's got the neighborhood
Down on me he thinks 'at I'm
Goin' to stand it all the time;
Thinks ist 'cause my Pa don't 'low
Me to fight, he's got me now,
An' can say I lie, an' call
Me ist anything at all!
Billy Miller thinks I am
'Feard to say 'at he says *"dam"*—
Yes, an' *worser* ones! an' I'm
Goin' to tell his folks sometime!—
An' ef he don't shet his head
I'll tell worse 'an *that* he said
When he fighted Willie King—
An' got licked like ever'thing!—
Billy Miller better shin
Down his Daddy's lane ag'in,

Like a cowardy-calf, an' climb
In fer home another time!
Better—

[*Here* BILLY *leaps down from the loft
upon his unsuspecting victim; and
two minutes later,* JOHNNY, *with the
half of a straw hat, a bleeding nose,
and a straight rent across one trou-
sers-knee, makes his inglorious—
exit.*]

456

THE CHRIST

"FATHER!" (so The Word) He
       cried,—
"Son of Thine, and yet denied;
By my brothers dragged and tried,
Scoffed and scourged, and crucified,
With a thief on either side—
Brothers mine, alike belied,—
Arms of mercy open wide,
Father! Father!" So He died.

457

TO HEAR HER SING

TO hear her sing—to hear her
       sing—
It is to hear the birds of Spring
In dewy groves on blooming sprays
Pour out their blithest roundelays.

It is to hear the robin trill
At morning, or the whippoorwill
At dusk, when stars are blossoming—
To hear her sing—to hear her sing!

To hear her sing—it is to hear
The laugh of childhood ringing clear
In woody path or grassy lane
Our feet may never fare again.

Faint, far away as Memory dwells,
It is to hear the village bells
At twilight, as the truant hears
Them, hastening home, with smiles
       and tears.

Such joy it is to hear her sing,
We fall in love with everything—
The simple things of every day
Grow lovelier than words can say.

The idle brooks that purl across
The gleaming pebbles and the moss
We love no less than classic streams—
The Rhines and Arnos of our dreams.

To hear her sing—with folded eyes,
It is, beneath Venetian skies,
To hear the gondoliers' refrain,
Or troubadours of sunny Spain.—

To hear the bulbul's voice that shook
The throat that trilled for Lalla Rookh:
What wonder we in homage bring
Our hearts to her—to hear her sing!

458

FROM THE HEADBOARD OF A
GRAVE IN PARAGUAY

A TROTH, and a grief, and a bless-
       ing,
Disguised them and came this
       way,—

And one was a promise, and one was
    a doubt,
And one was a rainy day.

And they met betimes with this
    maiden,—
And the promise it spake and lied,
And the doubt it gibbered and hugged
    itself,
And the rainy-day—she died.

459

A CANARY AT THE FARM

FOLKS has be'n to town, and Sahry
    Fetched 'er home a pet canary,—
And of all the blame', contrary,
    Aggervatin' things alive!
I love music—that's I love it
When it's *free*—and plenty of it;—
But I kind o' git above it,
    At a dollar-eighty-five!

Reason's plain as I'm a-sayin',—
Jes' the idy, now, o' layin'
Out yer money, and a-payin'
    Fer a willer-cage and bird,
When the medder-larks is wingin'
Round you, and the woods is ringin'
With the beautifullest singin'
    That a mortal ever heard!

Sahry's sot, tho'.—So I tell her
He's a purty little feller,
With his wings o' creamy-yeller
    And his eyes keen as a cat.
And the twitter o' the critter
'Pears to absolutely glitter!
Guess I'll haf to go and git her
    A high-priceter cage 'n that!

460

SEPTEMBER DARK

I

THE air falls chill;
    The whippoorwill
Pipes lonesomely behind the hill:
The dusk grows dense,
The silence tense;
And, lo, the katydids commence.

II

Through shadowy rifts
Of woodland, lifts
The low, slow moon, and upward
    drifts,
While left and right
The fireflies' light
Swirls eddying in the skirts of Night.

III

O Cloudland, gray
And level, lay
Thy mists across the face of Day!
At foot and head,
Above the dead,
O Dews, weep on uncomforted!

461

ANSELMO

YEARS did I vainly seek the good
    Lord's grace—
    Prayed, fasted, and did penance dire
        and dread;
Did kneel, with bleeding knees and
    rainy face,

And mouth the dust, with ashes on
    my head;
Yea, still with knotted scourge the
    flesh I flayed,
Rent fresh the wounds, and moaned
    and shrieked insanely;
And froth oozed with the pleadings
    that I made,
And yet I prayed on vainly, vainly,
    vainly!

A time, from out of swoon I lifted eye,
    To find a wretched outcast, gray and
        grim,
Bathing my brow, with many a pity-
    ing sigh,
And I did pray God's grace might
    rest on him.—
Then, lo! a gentle voice fell on mine
    ears—
"Thou shalt not sob in suppliance
    hereafter;
Take up thy prayers and wring them
    dry of tears,
And lift them, white and pure with
    love and laughter!"

    So is it now for all men else I
        pray;
    So it is I am blest and glad alway.

                462

        TIME OF CLEARER
           TWITTERINGS

                I

TIME of crisp and tawny leaves,
    And of tarnished harvest sheaves,
And of dusty grasses—weeds—
Thistles, with their tufted seeds

Voyaging the Autumn breeze
Like as fairy argosies:
Time of quicker flash of wings,
And of clearer twitterings
In the grove or deeper shade
Of the tangled everglade,—
Where the spotted water-snake
Coils him in the sunniest brake;
And the bittern, as in fright,
Darts, in sudden, slanting flight,
Southward, while the startled crane
Films his eyes in dreams again.

                II

Down along the dwindled creek
We go loitering. We speak
Only with old questionings
Of the dear remembered things
Of the days of long ago,
When the stream seemed thus and so
In our boyish eyes:—The bank
Greener then, through rank on rank
Of the mottled sycamores,
Touching tops across the shores:
Here, the hazel thicket stood—
There, the almost pathless wood
Where the shellbark hickory tree
Rained its wealth on you and me.
Autumn! as you loved us then,
Take us to your heart again!

                III

Season halest of the year!
How the zestful atmosphere
Nettles blood and brain and smites
Into life the old delights
We have wasted in our youth,
And our graver years, forsooth!
How again the boyish heart
Leaps to see the chipmunk start
From the brush and sleek the sun's

Very beauty, as he runs!
How again a subtle hint
Of crushed pennyroyal or mint
Sends us on our knees, as when
We were truant boys of ten—
Brown marauders of the wood,
Merrier than Robin Hood!

IV

Ah! will any minstrel say,
In his sweetest roundelay,
What is sweeter, after all,
Than black haws, in early Fall?—
Fruit so sweet the frost first sat,
Dainty-toothed, and nibbled at!
And will any poet sing
Of a lusher, richer thing
Than a ripe May-apple, rolled
Like a pulpy lump of gold
Under thumb and finger-tips,
And poured molten through the lips?
Go, ye bards of classic themes,
Pipe your songs by classic streams!
I would twang the redbird's wings
In the thicket while he sings!

463

THE BOYS

WHERE are they?—the friends
of my childhood enchanted—
The clear, laughing eyes looking
back in my own,
And the warm, chubby fingers my
palms have so wanted,
As when we raced over
Pink pastures of clover,
And mocked the quail's whir and the
bumblebee's drone?

Have the breezes of time blown their
blossomy faces
Forever adrift down the years that
are flown?
Am I never to see them romp back to
their places,
Where over the meadow,
In sunshine and shadow,
The meadow-larks trill, and the bum-
blebees drone?

Where are they? Ah! dim in the dust
lies the clover;
The whippoorwill's call has a sor-
rowful tone,
And the dove's—I have wept at it over
and over;—
I want the glad luster
Of youth, and the cluster
Of faces asleep where the bumblebees
drone!

464

LINCOLN

A PEACEFUL life;—just toil and
rest—
All his desire;—
To read the books he liked the best
Beside the cabin fire—
God's word and man's;—to peer some-
times
Above the page, in smoldering
gleams,
And catch, like far heroic rhymes,
The on-march of his dreams.

A peaceful life;—to hear the low
Of pastured herds,
Or woodman's ax that, blow on blow,
Fell sweet as rhythmic words.

And yet there stirred within his breast
A fateful pulse that, like a roll
Of drums, made high above his rest
A tumult in his soul.

A peaceful life! . . . They haled him
    even
As One was haled
Whose open palms were nailed toward
    Heaven
When prayers nor aught availed.
And, lo, he paid the selfsame price
To lull a nation's awful strife
And will us, through the sacrifice
Of self, his peaceful life.

465

THE BLIND GIRL

IF I might see his face to-day!—
    He is so happy now!—To hear
His laugh is like a roundelay—
    So ringing-sweet and clear!
His step—I heard it long before
He bounded through the open door
To tell his marriage.—Ah! so kind—
So good he is!—And I—so blind!

But thus he always came to me—
    Me, first of all, he used to bring
His sorrow to—his ecstasy—
    His hopes and everything;
And if I joyed with him or wept,
It was not long *the music* slept,—
And if he sung, or if I played—
Or both,—we were the braver made.

I grew to know and understand
    His every word at every call,—
The gate-latch hinted, and his hand
    In mine confessed it all:

He need not speak one word to me—
He need not sigh—I need not see,—
But just the one touch of his palm,
And I would answer—song or psalm.

He wanted recognition—name—
    He hungered so for higher things,—
The altitudes of power and fame,
    And all that fortune brings:
Till, with his great heart fevered thus,
And aching as impetuous,
I almost wished sometimes that *he*
Were blind and patient made, like me.

But he has won!—I knew he would.—
    Once in the mighty Eastern mart,
I knew his music only could
    Be sung in every heart!
And when he proudly sent me this
From out the great metropolis,
I bent above the graven score
And, weeping, kissed it o'er and o'er.—

And yet not blither sing the birds
    Than this glad melody,—the tune
As sweetly wedded with the words
    As flowers with middle-June;
Had he not *told* me, I had known
It was composed of love alone—
His love for *her*.—And she can see
His happy face eternally!—

While *I*—O God, forgive, I pray!—
    Forgive me that I did so long
To look upon his face to-day!—
    I know the wish was wrong.—
Yea, I am thankful that my sight
Is shielded safe from such delight:—
I can pray better, with this blur
Of blindness—both for him and her.

466

THE KING

THEY rode right out of the morn-
ing sun—
A glimmering, glittering cavalcade
Of knights and ladies, and every one
In princely sheen arrayed;
And the king of them all, O he rode
ahead,
With a helmet of gold, and a plume of
red
That spurted about in the breeze and
bled
In the bloom of the everglade.

And they rode high over the dewy lawn,
With brave, glad banners of every
hue
That rolled in ripples, as they rode on
In splendor, two and two;
And the tinkling links of the golden
reins
Of the steeds they rode rang such re-
frains
As the castanets in a dream of Spain's
Intensest gold and blue.

And they rode and rode; and the steeds
they neighed
And pranced, and the sun on their
glossy hides
Flickered and lightened and glanced
and played
Like the moon on rippling tides;
And their manes were silken, and thick
and strong,
And their tails were flossy, and fet-
lock-long,
And jostled in time to the teeming
throng,
And their knightly song besides.

Clank of scabbard and jingle of spur,
And the fluttering sash of the queen
went wild
In the wind, and the proud king
glanced at her
As one at a wilful child,—
And as knight and lady away they
flew,
And the banners flapped, and the fal-
con, too,
And the lances flashed and the bugle
blew,
He kissed his hand and smiled.—

And then, like a slanting sunlit
shower,
The pageant glittered across the
plain,
And the turf spun back, and the wild-
weed flower
Was only a crimson stain.
And a dreamer's eyes they are down-
ward cast,
As he blends these words with the
wailing blast:
"It is the King of the Year rides past!"
And Autumn is here again.

467

A LIZ-TOWN HUMORIST

SETTIN' round the stove, last night,
Down at Wess's store, was me
And Mart Strimples, Tunk, and White,
And Doc Bills, and two er three
Fellers o' the Mudsock tribe
No use tryin' to describe!
And says Doc, he says, says he,—
"Talkin' 'bout good things to eat,
Ripe mushmillon's hard to beat!"

I chawed on. And Mart he 'lowed
Wortermillon beat the mush.—
"Red," he says, "and juicy—Hush!—
I'll jes' leave it to the crowd!"
Then a Mudsock chap, says he,—
"Punkin's good enough fer me—
Punkin pies, I mean," he says,—
"Them beats millons!—What say,
    Wess?"

I chawed on. And Wess says,—"Well,
You jes' fetch that wife of mine
All yer wortermillon-*rine,*—
And she'll bile it down a spell—
In with sorghum, I suppose,
And what else, Lord only knows!—
But I'm here to tell all hands
Them p'serves meets my demands!"

I chawed on. And White he says,—
"Well, I'll jes' stand in with Wess—
I'm no hog!" And Tunk says,—"I
Guess I'll pastur' out on pie
With the Mudsock boys!" says he;
"Now what's yourn?" he says to me:
I chawed on—fer—quite a spell—
Then I speaks up, slow and dry,—
"Jes' tobacker!" I-says-I.—
And you'd ort o' heerd 'em yell!

468

LIKE HIS MOTHER USED TO
MAKE

*"Uncle Jake's Place," St. Jo, Missouri,
1874.*

"I WAS born in Indiany," says a
    stranger, lank and slim,
As us fellers in the restarunt was kind
    o' guyin' him,

And Uncle Jake was slidin' him an-
    other punkin pie
And a' extry cup o' coffee, with a
    twinkle in his eye,—
"I was born in Indiany—more'n forty
    year' ago—
And I hain't be'n back in twenty—
    and I'm workin' back'ards slow;
But I've et in ever' restarunt 'twixt
    here and Santy Fee,
And I want to state this coffee tastes
    like gittin' home, to me!

"Pour us out another, Daddy," says the
    feller, warmin' up,
A-speakin' 'crost a saucerful, as Uncle
    tuk his cup,—
"When I seed yer sign out yander," he
    went on, to Uncle Jake,—
" 'Come in and git some coffee like yer
    mother used to make'—
I thought of *my* old mother, and the
    Posey County farm,
And me a little kid ag'in, a-hangin' in
    her arm,
As she set the pot a-bilin', broke the
    eggs and poured 'em in"—
And the feller kind o' halted, with a
    trimble in his chin:

And Uncle Jake he fetched the feller's
    coffee back, and stood
As solemn, fer a minute, as a' under-
    taker would;
Then he sort o' turned and tiptoed
    to'rds the kitchen door—and nex',
Here comes his old wife out with him,
    a-rubbin' of her specs—
And she rushes fer the stranger, and
    she hollers out, "It's him!—
Thank God we've met him comin'!—
    Don't you know yer mother, Jim?"

And the feller, as he grabbed her,
  says,—"You bet I hain't forgot—
But," wipin' of his eyes, says he, "yer
  coffee's mighty hot!"

469

A GOLDEN WEDDING

DECEMBER—1884

YOUR   Golden   Wedding!—fifty
  years
Of comradeship, through smiles and
  tears!
Through summer sun, and winter sleet,
You walked the ways with willing
  feet;
For, journeying together thus,
Each path held something glorious.
No winter wind could blow so chill
But found you even warmer still
In fervor of affection—blest
In knowing all was for the best;
And so, content, you faced the storm
And fared on, smiling, arm in arm.

But why this moralizing strain
Beside a hearth that glows again
As on your *Wooden* wedding-day?—
When butter-prints and paddles lay
Around   in   dough-bowls,   tubs   and
  churns,
And all such "woodenish" concerns;
And "woodenish" they are—for now
Who can afford to keep a cow
And pestle some old churn, when you
Can buy good butter—"golden," too—
Far cheaper than you can afford
To make it and neglect the Lord!

And round your hearth the faces gleam
That may recall, as in a dream,

The brightness of a time when *Tin*
Came glittering and clanging in
And raising noise enough to seize
And settle any swarm of bees!
But those were darling times, no
  doubt,—
To see the mother pouring out
The "tins" of milk, and tilting up
The coffee-pot above each cup;
Or, with the ladle from the wall,
Dipping and serving mush for all.

And *all* the "weddings," as they
  came,—
The *"Glass,"* the *"China,"*—still the
  same
You see them, till the last ere this,—
The *"Silver,"* and your wedded bliss
Abated not!—for love appears
Just silvered over with the years:—
Silver the   grandchild's   laugh   you
  hear—
Silver his hopes, and silver-clear
Your every prayer for him,—and still
Silver your hope, through good and
  ill—
Silver and silver everywhere,
Bright as the silver of your hair!

But on your *Golden* Wedding!—Nay—
What can I give to you to-day
Who am too very poor indeed
To offer what I so much need?
If gold I gave, I fear, alack!
I'd needs provide you gave it back,
To stay me, the long years before
I'd stacked and heaped five dollars
  more!
And so, in lieu—and little worse—
I proffer you this dross of verse—
The merest tinsel, I admit,—
But take it—I have more of it.

470

HIS CHRISTMAS SLED

I

I WATCH him with his Christmas
sled;
He hitches on behind
A passing sleigh, with glad hooray,
And whistles down the wind;
He hears the horses champ their bits,
And bells that jingle-jingle—
You Woolly Cap! you Scarlet Mitts!
You miniature "Kriss Kringle"!

I almost catch your secret joy—
Your chucklings of delight,
The while you whiz where glory is
Eternally in sight!
With you I catch my breath, as swift
Your jaunty sled goes gliding
O'er glassy track and shallow drift,
As I behind were riding!

II

He winks at twinklings of the frost,
And on his airy race,
Its tingles beat to redder heat
The rapture of his face:—
The colder, keener is the air,
The less he cares a feather.
But, there! he's gone! and I gaze on
The wintriest of weather!

Ah, Boy! still speeding o'er the track
Where none returns again,
To sigh for you, or cry for you,
Or die for you were vain.—
And so, speed on! the while I pray
All nipping frosts forsake you—
Ride still ahead of grief, but may
All glad things overtake you!

471

A NEW YEAR'S TIME AT
WILLARDS'S

I

THE HIRED MAN TALKS

THERE'S old man Willards; an' his
wife;
An' Marg'et—S'repty's sister;—an'
There's me—an' I'm the hired man;
An' Tomps McClure, you bet yer life!

Well, now, old Willards hain't so bad,
Considerin' the chance he's had.
Of course, he's rich, an' sleeps an' eats
Whenever he's a mind to: Takes
An' leans back in the Amen-seats
An' thanks the Lord fer all he
makes.—
That's purty much all folks has got
Ag'inst the old man, like as not!
But there's his woman—jes' the turn
Of them-air two wild girls o' hern—
Marg'et an' S'repty—allus in
Fer any cuttin'-up concern—
Church festibals, an' foolishin'
Round Christmas-trees, an' New Year's
sprees—
Set up to watch the Old Year go
An' New Year come—such things as
these;
An' turkey-dinners, don't you know!
S'repty's younger, an' more gay,
An' purtier, an' finer dressed
Than Marg'et is—but, lawsy-day!
She hain't the independentest!—
"Take care!" old Willards used to say,
"Take care!—Let Marg'et have her
way,
An' S'repty, you go off an' play

On your melodeum!"—But, best
Of all, comes Tomps! An' I'll be
bound,
Ef he hain't jes' the beatin'est
Young chap in all the country round!
Ef you know Tomps you'd like
him, shore!
They hain't no man on top o' ground
Walks into my affections more!—
An' all the Settlement'll say
That Tomps was liked jes' thataway
By ever'body, till he tuk
A shine to S'repty Willards.—
Then
You'd ort 'o see the old man buck
An' h'ist hisse'f, an' paw the dirt,
An' hint that "common workin'-
men
That didn't want their feelin's hurt
'Ud better hunt fer 'comp'ny'
where
The folks was pore an' didn't
care!"—
The pine-blank facts is,—the old man,
Last Christmas was a year ago,
Found out some *presents* Tomps
had got
Fer S'repty, an' hit made him
hot—
Set down an' tuk his pen in hand
An' writ to Tomps an' told him so
On legal cap, in white an' black,
An' give him jes' to understand
"No Christmas-gifts o' 'lily-white'
An' bear's-ile could fix matters right,"
An' wropped 'em up an' sent 'em
back!
Well, S'repty cried an' snuffled round
Consid'able. But Marg'et she
Toed out another sock, an' wound
Her knittin' up, an' drawed the tea,
An' then set on the supper-things,
An' went up in the loft an' dressed—

An' through it all you'd never guessed
What she was up to! An' she
brings
Her best hat with her an' her shawl,
An' gloves, an' redicule, an' all,
An' injirubbers, an' comes down
An' tells 'em she's a-goin' to town
To he'p the Christmas goin's-on
Her Church got up. An' go she does—
The best hosswoman ever was!
"An' what'll we do while you're gone?"
The old man says, a-tryin' to be
Agreeable. "Oh! *you?*" says she,—
"*You* kin jaw S'repty, like you did,
An' slander Tomps!" An' off she rid!
Now, this is all *I'm* goin' to tell
Of this-here story—that is, I
Have done my very level best
As fur as this, an' here I "dwell,"
As auctioneers says, winkin' sly:
Hit's old man Willards tells the
rest.

II

THE OLD MAN TALKS

Adzackly jes' one year ago,
This New Year's day, Tomps comes
to me—
In my own house, an' whilse the
folks
Was gittin' dinner,—an' he pokes
His nose right in, an' says, says he:
"I got yer note—an' read it *slow!*
You don't like *me,* ner I don't *you,*"
He says,—"we're even there, you know!
But you've said, furder, that no gal
Of yourn kin marry me, er shall,
An' I'd best shet off *comin',* too!"
An' then he says,—"Well, them's your
views;—
But, havin' talked with S'repty, *we*

Have both agreed to disagree
With your peculiar notions—some;
An', *that's* the reason, I refuse
To quit a-comin' here, but come—
Not fer to threat, ner raise no skeer
An' spile yer turkey-dinner here,—
But, jes' fer *S'repty's* sake, to sheer
Yer New Year's.   Shall I take a
  cheer?"
Well, blame-don! ef I ever see
Sich impidence! I couldn't say
Not nary word! But Mother she
Sot out a cheer fer Tomps, an' they
Shuk hands an' turnt their back on
  me.
Then I riz—mad as mad could be!—
But Marg'et says,—"Now, Pap! you
  set
Right where you're settin'!—Don't
  you fret!
An', Tomps—*you* warm yer feet!" says
  she,
"An' throw yer mitts an' comfert on
The bed there! Where is S'repty
  gone?—
The cabbage is a-scortchin'! Ma,
Stop cryin' there an' stir the slaw!"
Well!—what was *Mother cryin'* fer?—
I half riz up—but Marg'et's chin
Hit squared—an' I set down ag'in—
I allus *was* afeard o' her,
I was, by jucks! So there I set,
Betwixt a sinkin'-chill an' sweat,
An' scuffled with my wrath, an' shet
My teeth to mighty tight, you bet!
  An' yit, fer all that I could do,
I *eeched* to jes' git up an' whet
The carvin'-knife a rasp er two
  On Tomps's ribs—an' so would
  you!—
Fer he had riz an' faced around,
  An' stood there, smilin', as they
  brung

The turkey in, all stuffed an'
  browned—
Too sweet fer nose er tooth er
  tongue!
With sniffs o' sage, an' p'r'aps a
  dash
Of old burnt brandy, steamin'-hot,
  Mixed kind o' in with apple-mash
An' mince-meat, an' the Lord knows
  what!
Nobody was a-talkin' then,
  To 'filiate my awk'ardness—
No noise o' any kind but jes'
The rattle o' the dishes when
They'd fetch 'em in an' set 'em down,
An' fix an' change 'em round an'
  round,
  Like women does—till Mother
  says,—
"Vittels is ready; Abner, call
  Down S'repty—she's up-stairs, I
  guess."—
And Marg'et *she* says, "Ef you bawl
Like that, she'll not come down at
  all!
Besides, we needn't wait till *she*
Gits down! Here, Tomps, set down
  by me,
  An' Pap: say grace!" . . . Well,
  there I was!—
What *could* I do! I drapped my head
Behind my fists an' groaned, an' said:—
  "Indulgent Parent! in Thy cause
  We bow the head an' bend the
  knee,
An' break the bread, an' pour the wine,
  Feelin' "—(The   stair-door   sud-
  dently
  Went bang! an' S'repty flounced
  by me)—
"Feelin'," I says, "this feast is Thine—
  This New Year's feast"—an' *rap-rap-
  rap!*

Went Marg'et's case-knife on her
    plate—
An' next, I heerd a sasser drap,—
    Then I looked up, an', strange to
    state,
There S'repty set in Tomps's lap—
    An' huggin' him, as shore as fate!
An' Mother kissin' him k-slap!—
An' Marg'et—she chips in to drap
    The ruther peert remark to me:—
    "That 'grace' o' yourn," she says,
        "won't 'gee'—
This hain't no *'New Year's* feast,'"
    says she,—
"This is a' INFAIR-Dinner, Pap!"

An' so it was!—be'n married fer
    Purt' nigh a week!—'Twas Marg'et
    planned
    The whole thing fer 'em, through
    an' through
I'm rickonciled; an', understand,
I take things jes' as they occur,—
    Ef *Marg'et* liked Tomps, Tomps
    'ud do!—
But I-says-I, a-holt his hand,—
"I'm glad you didn't marry HER—
'Cause *Marg'et's* my *guardeen*—yes-
    sir!—
An' S'repty's good enough fer you!"

472

WHATEVER THE WEATHER
MAY BE

"WHATEVER the weather may
    be," says he—
    "Whatever the weather may be,
It's plaze, if ye will, an' I'll say me
    say,—
Supposin' to-day was the winterest day,

Wud the weather be changing because
    ye cried,
Or the snow be grass were ye crucified?
The best is to make yer own summer,"
    says he,
"Whatever the weather may be," says
    he—
    "Whatever the weather may be!

"Whatever the weather may be," says
    he—
    "Whatever the weather may be,
It's the songs ye sing, an' the smiles ye
    wear,
That's a-makin' the sun shine every-
    where;
An' the world of gloom is a world of
    glee,
Wid the bird in the bush, an' the bud
    in the tree,
An' the fruit on the stim o' the bough,"
    says he,
"Whatever the weather may be," says
    he—
    "Whatever the weather may be!

"Whatever the weather may be," says
    he—
    "Whatever the weather may be,
Ye can bring the Spring, wid its green
    an' gold,
An' the grass in the grove where the
    snow lies cold;
An' ye'll warm yer back, wid a smiling
    face,
As ye sit at yer heart, like an owld fire-
    place,
An' toast the toes o' yer sowl," says he,
"Whatever the weather may be," says
    he—
    "Whatever the weather may be!"

473

A LEAVE-TAKING

SHE will not smile;
  She will not stir;
I marvel while
  I look on her.
    The lips are chilly
    And will not speak;
    The ghost of a lily
    In either cheek.

Her hair—ah me!
  Her hair—her hair!
How helplessly
  My hands go there!
    But my caresses
      Meet not hers,
    O golden tresses
      That thread my tears!

I kiss the eyes
  On either lid,
Where her love lies
  Forever hid.
    I cease my weeping
    And smile and say:
    I will be sleeping
    Thus, some day!

474

DOWN ON WRIGGLE CRICK

Best time to kill a hog's when he's fat
                              —OLD SAW.

MOSTLY, folks is law-abidin'
  Down on Wriggle Crick,—
Seein' they's no Squire residin'
  In our bailywick;

No grand juries, no suppeenies,
  Ner no vested rights to pick
Out yer man, jerk up and jail ef
  He's outragin' Wriggle Crick!

Wriggle Crick hain't got no lawin',
  Ner no suits to beat;
Ner no court-house gee-and-hawin'
  Like a County-seat;
Hain't no waitin' round fer verdicks,
  Ner non-gittin' witness-fees;
Ner no thiefs 'at gits "new hearin's,"
  By some lawyer slick as grease!

Wriggle Crick's leadin' spirit
  Is old Johnts Culwell,—
Keeps post-office, and right near it
  Owns what's called "The Grand
      Hotel"—
(Warehouse now)—buys wheat and
      ships it;
  Gits out ties, and trades in stock,
And knows all the high-toned drum-
      mers
  'Twixt South Bend and Mishawauk.

Last year comes along a feller—
  Sharper 'an a lance—
Stovepipe-hat and silk umbreller,
  And a boughten all-wool pants,—
Tinkerin' of clocks and watches;
  Says a trial's all he wants—
And rents out the tavern-office
  Next to Uncle Johnts.

Well.—He tacked up his k'dentials,
  And got down to biz.—
Captured Johnts by cuttin' stenchils
  Fer them old wheat-sacks o' his.—

Fixed his clock, in the post-office—
Painted fer him, clean and slick,
'Crost his safe, in gold-leaf letters,
"J. Culwells's, Wriggle Crick."

Any kind o' job you keered to
Resk him with, and bring,
He'd fix fer you—jes' appeared to
Turn his hand to anything!—
Rings, er earbobs, er umbrellers—
Glue a cheer er chany doll,—
W'y, of all the beatin' fellers,
He jes' beat 'em all!

Made his friends, but wouldn't stop
there,—
One mistake he learnt,
That was, sleepin' in his shop there.—
And one Sund'y night it burnt!
Come in one o' jes' a-sweepin'
All the whole town high and dry—
And that feller, when they waked him,
Suffocatin', mighty nigh!

Johnts he drug him from the buildin',
He'pless—'peared to be,—
And the women and the childern
Drenchin' him with sympathy!
But I noticed Johnts helt on him
With a' extry lovin' grip,
And the men-folks gathered round him
In most warmest pardnership!

That's the whole mess, grease-and-
dopin'!
Johnts's safe was saved,—
But the lock was found sprung open,
And the inside caved.
Was no trial—ner no jury—
Ner no jedge ner court-house-click.—
Circumstances alters cases
Down on Wriggle Crick!

475

LORD BACON

WRITTEN AS A JOKE AND ASCRIBED TO A
VERY PRACTICAL BUSINESS MAN, AMOS
J. WALKER

MASTER of masters in the days of
yore,
When art met insult, with no law's
redress;
When Law itself insulted Righteous-
ness,
And Ignorance thine own scholastic
lore,
And thou thine own judicial office
more,—
What master living now canst love
thee less,
Seeing thou didst thy greatest art
repress
And leave the years its riches to re-
store
To us, thy long neglectors. Yield us
grace
To make becoming recompense, and
dawn
On us thy poet-smile; nor let us trace,
In fancy, where the old-world myths
have gone,
The shade of Shakespeare, with averted
face,
Withdrawn to uttermost oblivion.

476

MY FIRST WOMERN

I BURIED my first womern
In the spring; and in the fall
I was married to my second,
And hain't settled yit at all!—

Fer I'm allus thinkin'—thinkin'
Of the first one's peaceful ways,
A-bilin' soap and singin'
Of the Lord's amazin' grace.

And I'm thinkin' of her, constant,
Dyin' carpet-chain and stuff,
And a-makin' up rag carpets,
When the *floor* was good enough!
And I mind her he'p a-feedin'
And I riccollect her now
A-drappin' corn, and keepin'
Clos't behind me and the plow!

And I'm allus thinkin' of her
Reddin' up around the house;
Er cookin' fer the farm-hands;
Er a-drivin' up the cows.—
And there she lays out yander
By the lower medder fence,
Where the cows was barely grazin',
And they're usin' ever sence.

And when I look acrost there—
Say it's when the clover's ripe,
And I'm settin', in the evenin',
On the porch here, with my pipe,
And the *other'n* hollers "Henry!"—
W'y they ain't no sadder thing
Than to think of my first womern
And her funeral last spring
Was a year ago—

477

THE QUEST

I AM looking for Love. Has he
passed this way,
With eyes as blue as the skies of May,

And a face as fair as the summer
dawn?—
You answer back, but I wander on,—
For you say: "Oh, yes; but his eyes
were gray,
And his face as dim as a rainy day."

Good friends, I query, I search for
Love;
His eyes are as blue as the skies above,
And his smile as bright as the midst
of May
When the truce-bird pipes: Has he
passed this way?
And one says: "Ay; but his face,
alack!
Frowned as he passed, and his eyes
were black."

O who will tell me of Love? I cry!
His eyes are as blue as the mid-May
sky,
And his face as bright as the morning
sun;
And you answer and mock me, every
one,
That his eyes were dark, and his face
was wan,
And he passed you frowning and wan-
dered on.

But stout of- heart will I onward fare,
Knowing *my* Love is beyond—some-
where,—
The Love I seek, with the eyes of
blue,
And the bright, sweet smile unknown
of you;
And on from the hour his trail is found
I shall sing sonnets the whole year
round.

478

TO AN IMPORTUNATE GHOST

GET gone, thou most uncomfort-
able ghost!
Thou really dost annoy me with thy
thin
Impalpable transparency of grin;
And the vague, shadowy shape of thee
almost
Hath vexed me beyond boundary and
coast
Of my broad patience. Stay thy
chattering chin,
And reel the tauntings of thy vain
tongue in,
Nor tempt me further with thy vapor-
ish boast
That I am *helpless* to combat thee!
Well,
Have at thee, then! Yet if a doom
most dire
Thou wouldst escape, flee whilst
thou canst!—Revile
Me not, Miasmic Mist!—Rank Air!
Retire!
One instant longer an thou haunt'st
me, I'll
Inhale thee, O thou wraith despicable!

479

WHO BIDES HIS TIME

WHO bides his time, and day by
day
Faces defeat full patiently,
And lifts a mirthful roundelay,
However poor his fortunes be,—
He will not fail in any qualm
Of poverty—the paltry dime

It will grow golden in his palm,
Who bides his time.

Who bides his time—he tastes the
sweet
Of honey in the saltest tear;
And though he fares with slowest feet,
Joy runs to meet him, drawing near:
The birds are heralds of his cause;
And, like a never-ending rhyme,
The roadsides bloom in his applause,
Who bides his time.

Who bides his time, and fevers not
In the hot race that none achieves,
Shall wear cool-wreathen laurel,
wrought
With crimson berries in the leaves;
And he shall reign a goodly king,
And sway his hand o'er every clime,
With peace writ on his signet-ring,
Who bides his time.

480

AS WE READ BURNS

WHO is speaking? Who has
spoken?
Whose voice ceasing thus has broken
The sweet pathos of our dreams?
Sweetest bard of sweetest themes,
Pouring in each poet-heart
Some rare essence of your art
Till it seems your singing lip
Kisses every pencil tip!
Far across the unknown lands—
Reach of heavenly isle and sea—
How we long to touch the hands
You outhold so lovingly!

481

WHEN JUNE IS HERE

WHEN June is here—what art
have we to sing
The whiteness of the lilies 'midst the
green
Of noon-tranced lawns? or flash of
roses seen
Like redbirds' wings? or earliest ripen-
ing
Prince-harvest apples, where the cloyed
bees cling
Round winy juices oozing down be-
tween
The peckings of the robin, while
we lean
In under-grasses, lost in marveling;
Or the cool term of morning, and
the stir
Of odorous breaths from wood and
meadow walks;
The Bob-white's liquid yodel, and
the whir
Of sudden flight; and, where the milk-
maid talks
Across the bars, on tilted barley-stalks
The dewdrops' glint in webs of
gossamer.

482

AT NOON—AND MIDNIGHT

FAR in the night, and yet no rest
for him! The pillow next his
own
The wife's sweet face in slumber
pressed—yet he awake—alone!
alone!

In vain he courted sleep;—one thought
would ever in his heart arise,—
The harsh words that at noon had
brought the tear-drops to her eyes.

Slowly on lifted arm he raised and lis-
tened. All was still as death;
He touched her forehead as he gazed,
and listened yet, with bated
breath:
Still silently, as though he prayed, his
lips moved lightly as she slept—
For God was with him, and he laid
his face with hers and wept.

483

TO JAMES NEWTON
MATTHEWS

IN ANSWER TO A LETTER ON THE
ANATOMY OF THE SONNET

OHO! ye sunny, sonnet-singin'
vagrant,
Flauntin' your simmer sangs in sic
a weather!
Ane maist can straik the bluebells
and the heather
Keekin' aboon the snaw and bloomin'
fragrant!
Whiles you, ye whustlin' brither, sic a
lay grant
O' a' these janglin', wranglin' sweets
thegither,
I weel maun perk my ain doon-
drappin' feather
And pipe a wee: Tho' boisterous and
flagrant
The winds blow whuzzle-whazzle
rhymes that trickle

Fra' aff my tongue less limpid than
    I'd ha'e them,
I in their little music hap a mickle
    O' canty praises, a' asklent to weigh
    them
Agen your pride, and smile to see them
    tickle
The warm nest o' the heart wherein
    I lay them.

484

SPIRITS AT HOME

THE FAMILY

THERE was Father, and Mother,
    and Emmy, and Jane,
And Lou, and Ellen, and John and
    me—
And Father was killed in the war, and
    Lou
She died of consumption, and John
    did too,
And Emmy she went with the
    pleurisy.

THE SPIRITS

Father believed in 'em all his life—
    But Mother, at first, she'd shake her
    head—
Till after the battle of Champion Hill,
When many a flag in the winder-sill
    Had crape mixed in with the white
    and red!

I used to doubt 'em myself till then—
    But me and Mother was satisfied
When Ellen she set, and Father came
And rapped "God Bless You!" and
    Mother's name,
    And "The Flag's up here!" . . .
    And we all just cried.

Used to come often, after that,
    And talk to us—just as he used to do,
Pleasantest kind! And once, for John,
He said he was "lonesome, but
    wouldn't let on—
Fear Mother would worry, and
    Emmy and Lou."

But Lou was the bravest girl on
    earth—
For all she never was hale and
    strong,
She'd have her fun!—With her voice
    clean lost
She'd laugh and joke us that "when
    she crossed
To Father, *we'd* all come taggin'
    along!"

Died—just that way! And the raps
    was thick
That night, as they often since occur,
Extry loud! And when *Lou* got back
She said it was Father and her—and
    "whack!"
She tuk the table—and we knowed
    her!

John and Emmy, in five years more,
    Both had went—And it seemed like
    fate,—
For the old home *it* burnt down.—But
    Jane
And me and Ellen we built again
    The new house, here, on the old
    estate.

And a happier family I don't know
    Of *any*wheres—unless it's *them,*—
Father, with all his love for Lou,
And her there with him, and healthy,
    too,
    And laughin', with John and little
    Em.

And, first we moved in the *new* house
    here,
They all dropped in for a long pow-
    wow:—
"We like your buildin', of course," Lou
    said,—
"But wouldn't swap with you to save
    your head—
    For *we* live in the ghost of the old
    house now!"

485

ART AND LOVE

HE faced his canvas (as a seer
    whose ken
Pierces the crust of this existence
    through)
And smiled beyond on that his
    genius knew
Ere mated with his being. Conscious
    then
Of his high theme alone, he smiled
    again
    Straight back upon himself in many
    a hue
And tint, and light and shade, which
    slowly grew
Enfeatured of a fair girl's face, as
    when
First time she smiles for love's sake
    with no fear.
So wrought he, witless that behind
    him leant
    A woman, with old features, dim
    and sear,
    And glamoured eyes that felt the
    brimming tear,
And with a voice, like some sad in-
    strument,
    That sighing said, "I'm dead there;
    love me here!"

486

SONG

O I would I had a lover!
    A lover! a lover!
O I would I had a lover
    With a twinkering guitar,
    To come beneath my casement
Singing "There is none above her,"
While I, leaning, seemed to hover
    In the scent of his cigar!

Then at morn I'd want to meet him—
    To meet him! to meet him!
O at morn I'd want to meet him,
    When the mist was in the sky,
    And the dew along the path I
    went
To casually greet him,
And to cavalierly treat him,
    And regret it by and by.

And I'd want to meet his brother—
    His brother! his brother!
O I'd want to meet his brother
    At the german or the play,
    To pin a rose on his lapel
And lightly press the other,
And love him like a mother—
    While he thought the other **way.**

O I'd pitilessly test him!
    And test him! and test him!
O I'd pitilessly test him
    Far beyond his own control;
    And every tantalizing lure
With which I could arrest him,
I'd loosen to molest him,
    Till I tried his very soul.

But ah, when I relented!
    Relented, relented!

But ah, when I relented—
  When the stars were blurred and
    dim,
  And the moon above, with cres-
    cent grace,
Looked off as I repented,
And with rapture half demented,
  All my heart went out to him!

487

PAP'S OLD SAYIN'

PAP had one old-fashioned sayin'
  That I'll never quite fergit—
And they's seven growed-up childern
  Of us rickollects it yit!—
Settin' round the dinner-table,
  Talkin' 'bout our friends, perhaps,
Er abusin' of our neghbors,
  I kin hear them words o' Pap's—
  "Shet up, and eat yer vittels!"

Pap he'd never argy with us,
  Ner cut any subject short
Whilse we all kep' clear o' gossip,
  And wuz actin' as we ort:
But ef we'd git out o' order—
  Like sometimes a fambly is,—
Faultin' folks, er one another,
  Then we'd hear that voice o' his—
  "Shet up, and eat yer vittels!"

Wuz no hand hisse'f at talkin'—
  Never hadn't *much* to say,—
Only, as I said, pervidin'
  When we'd rile him thataway:
Then he'd allus lose his temper
  Spite o' fate, and jerk his head
And slam down his case-knife vicious,
  Whilse he glared around and said—
  "Shet up, and eat yer vittels!"

Mind last time 'at Pap was ailin'
  With a misery in his side,
And had hobbled in the kitchen—
  Jes' the day before he died,—
Laury Jane she ups and tells him,
  "Pap, you're pale as pale kin be—
Hain't ye 'feard them-air cowcumbers
  Hain't good fer ye?" And says he,
  "Shet up, and eat yer vittels!"

Well! I've saw a-many a sorrow,—
  Forty year', through thick and thin;
I've got best,—and I've got *worsted,*
  Time and time and time ag'in!—
But I've met a-many a trouble
  That I hain't run on to twice,
Haltin'-like and thinkin' over
  Them-air words o' Pap's advice:
  "Shet up, and eat yer vittels!"

488

GRANNY

GRANNY'S come to our house,
  And ho! my lawzy-daisy!
All the childern round the place
  Is ist a-runnin' crazy!
Fetched a cake fer little Jake,
  And fetched a pie fer Nanny,
And fetched a pear fer all the pack
  That runs to kiss their Granny!

Lucy Ellen's in her lap,
  And Wade and Silas Walker
Both's a-ridin' on her foot,
  And 'Pollos on the rocker;
And Marthy's twins, from   Aunt
    Marinn's,
  And little Orphant Annie,
All's a-eatin' gingerbread
  And giggle-un at Granny!

Tells us all the fairy tales
Ever thought er wundered—
And 'bundance o' other stories—
Bet she knows a hunderd!—
Bob's the one fer "Whittington,"
And "Golden Locks" fer Fanny!
Hear 'em laugh and clap their hands,
Listenin' at Granny!

"Jack the Giant-Killer" 's good;
And "Bean-Stalk" 's another!—
So's the one of "Cinderell'"
And her old godmother;—
That-un's best of all the rest—
Bestest one of any,—
Where the mices scampers home
Like we runs to Granny!

Granny's come to our house,
Ho! my lawzy-daisy!
All the childern round the place
Is ist a-runnin' crazy!
Fetched a cake fer little Jake,
And fetched a pie fer Nanny,
And fetched a pear fer all the pack
That runs to kiss their Granny!

489

BECALMED

I

WOULD that the winds might
only blow
As they blew in the golden long ago!—
Laden with odors of Orient isles
Where ever and ever the sunshine
smiles,
And the bright sands blend with the
shady trees,
And the lotus blooms in the midst of
these.

II

Warm winds won from the midland
vales
To where the tress of the Siren trails
O'er the flossy tip of the mountain
phlox
And the bare limbs twined in the
crested rocks,
High above as the sea-gulls flap
Their lopping wings at the thunder-
clap.

III

Ah! that the winds might rise and
blow
The great surge up from the port
below,
Bloating the sad, lank, silken sails
Of the Argo out with the swift, sweet
gales
That blew from Colchis when Jason
had
His love's full will and his heart was
glad—
When Medea's voice was soft and
low.
Ah! that the winds might rise and
blow!

490

GRIGGSBY'S STATION

PAP'S got his pattent-right, and rich
as all creation;
But where's the peace and comfort
that we all had before?
Le's go a-visitin' back to Griggsby's
Station—
Back where we ust to be so happy
and so pore!

The likes of us a-livin' here! It's jes'
   a mortal pity
To see us in this great big house,
   with cyarpets on the stairs,
And the pump right in the kitchen!
   And the city! city! city!—
And nothin' but the city all around
   us ever'-wheres!

Climb clean above the roof and look
   from the steeple,
And never see a robin, nor a beech
   or ellum tree!
And right here in ear-shot of at least
   a thousan' people,
And none that neighbors with us
   or we want to go and see!

Le's go a-visitin' back to Griggsby's
   Station—
Back where the latch-string's a-hang-
   in' from the door,
And ever' neighbor round the place is
   dear as a relation—
Back where we ust to be so happy
   and so pore!

I want to see the Wiggenses, the whole
   kit-and-bilin',
A-driven' up from Shallor Ford to
   stay the Sunday through;
And I want to see 'em hitchin' at their
   son-in-law's and pilin'
Out there at 'Lizy Ellen's like they
   ust to do!

I want to see the piece-quilts the Jones
   girls is makin';
And I want to pester Laury 'bout
   their freckled hired hand,
And joke her 'bout the widower she
   come purt' nigh a-takin',
Till her Pap got his pension 'lowed
   in time to save his land.

Le's go a-visitin' back to Griggsby's
   Station—
Back where they's nothin' agger-
   vatin' any more,
Shet away safe in the woods around
   the old location—
Back where we ust to be so happy
   and so pore!

I want to see Marindy and he'p her
   with her sewin',
And hear her talk so lovin' of her
   man that's dead and gone,
And stand up with Emanuel to show
   me how he's growin',
And smile as I have saw her 'fore
   she putt her mournin' on.

And I want to see the Samples, on
   the old lower eighty,
Where John, our oldest boy, he was
   tuk and burried—for
His own sake and Katy's,—and I want
   to cry with Katy
As she reads all his letters over,
   writ from The War.

What's in all this grand life and high
   situation,
And nary pink nor hollyhawk
   a-bloomin' at the door?—
Le's go a-visitin' back to Griggsby's
   Station—
Back where we ust to be so happy
   and so pore!

491

FESSLER'S BEES

"TALKIN' 'bout yer bees," says Ike,
   Speakin' slow and ser'ous-like,
"D' ever tell you 'bout old 'Bee'—
Old 'Bee' Fessler?" Ike says-he!

"Might call him a *bee-expert*,
When it come to handlin' bees,—
Roll the sleeves up of his shirt
And wade in amongst the trees
Where a swarm 'u'd settle, and—
Blam'dest man on top of dirt!—
Rake 'em with his naked hand
Right back in the hive ag'in,
Jes' as easy as you please!
Nary bee 'at split the breeze
Ever jabbed a stinger in
Old 'Bee' Fessler—jes' in fun,
Er in *airnest*—nary one!—
Couldn't agg one *on* to, nuther,
Ary one way er the other!

"Old 'Bee' Fessler," Ike says-he,
"Made a speshyality
Jes' o' bees; and built a shed—
Len'th about a half a mild!
Had about a *thousan'* head
O' hives, I reckon—tame and wild!
Durndest buzzin' ever wuz—
Wuss'n telegraph-poles does
When they're sockin' home the news
Tight as they kin let 'er loose!
Visitors rag out and come
Clean from town to hear 'em hum,
And stop at the kivered bridge;
But wuz some 'u'd cross the ridge
Allus, and go clos'ter—so 's
They could *see* 'em hum, I s'pose!
'Peared-like strangers down that track
Allus met folks comin' back
Lookin' extry fat and hearty
Fer a city picnic party!

" 'Fore he went to Floridy,
Old 'Bee' Fessler," Ike says-he—
"Old 'Bee' Fessler couldn't bide
Childern on his place," says Ike.
"Yit, fer all, they'd climb inside

And tromp round there, keerless-like,
In their bare feet. 'Bee' could tell
Ev'ry town-boy by his yell—
So 's 'at when they bounced the fence,
Didn't make no difference!
He'd jes' git down on one knee
In the grass and pat the bee!—
And, ef 't 'adn't stayed stuck in,
Fess' 'u'd set the sting ag'in,
'N' potter off, and wait around
Fer the old famillyer sound.
Allus boys there, more or less,
Scootin' round the premises!
When the buckwheat wuz in bloom,
Lawzy! how them bees 'u'd boom
Round the boys 'at crossed that way
Fer the crick on Saturday!
Never seemed to me su'prisin'
'At the sting o' bees 'uz p'izin!

" 'Fore he went to Floridy,"
Ike says, "nothin' 'bout a bee
'At old Fessler didn't know,—
W'y, it jes' 'peared-like 'at he
Knowed their language, high and low:
Claimed he told jes' by their buzz
What their wants and wishes wuz!
Peek in them-air little holes
Round the porches o' the hive—
Drat their pesky little souls!—
Could 'a' skinned the man alive!
Bore right in there with his thumb,
And squat down and scrape the gum
Outen ev'ry hole, and blow
'N' bresh the crumbs off, don't you
    know!
Take the roof off, and slide back
Them-air glass concerns they pack
Full o' honey, and jes' lean
'N' grabble 'mongst 'em fer the queen!
Fetch her out and *show* you to her—
Jes', you might say, *interview* her!

"Year er two," says Ike, says-he,
" 'Fore he went to Floridy,
Fessler struck the theory,
Honey was the same as *love*—
You could make it day and night:
Said them bees o' his could be
Got jes' twic't the work out of
Ef a feller managed right.
He contended ef bees found
Blossoms all the year around,
He could git 'em down at once
To work all the *winter* months
Same as *summer*. So, one fall,
When their summer's work wuz done,
'Bee' turns in and robs 'em all;
Loads the hives then, one by one,
On the cyars, and 'lowed he'd see
Ef bees loafed in *Floridy!*
Said he bet he'd know the reason
Ef *his* didn't work that season!

"And," says Ike, "it's jes'," says-he,
"Like old Fessler says to me:
'Any man kin fool a *bee,*
Git him down in Floridy!'
'Peared at fust, as old 'Bee' said,
Fer to kind o' turn their head
Fer a spell; but, bless you! they
Didn't lose a half a day
Altogether!—Jes' lit in
Them-air tropics, and them-air
Cacktusses a-ripen-nin',
'N' magnolyers, and sweet peas,
'N' 'simmon and pineapple trees,
'N' ripe bananers, here and there,
'N' dates a-danglin' in the breeze,
'N' figs and reezins ev'rywhere,
All waitin' jes' fer Fessler's bees!
'N' Fessler's bees, with gaumy wings,
A-gittin' down and *whoopin'* things!—
Fessler kind o' overseein'
'Em, and sort o' *'hee-o-heein'!'*

" 'Fore he went to *Floridy,*
Old 'Bee' Fessler," Ike says-he,
"Wuzn't counted, jes' to say,
Mean er or'n'ry anyway;
On'y ev'ry 'tarnel dime
'At 'u'd pass him on the road
He'd ketch up' with, ev'ry time;
And no mortal ever knowed
Him to spend a copper cent—
'Less on some fool-*'speriment*
With them *bees*—like that-un he
Played on 'em in Floridy.
Fess', of course, *he* tuck his ease,
But 'twus *bilious* on the bees!
Sweat, you know, 'u'd jes' stand out
On their *forreds*—pant and groan,
And grunt round and limp about!—
And old 'Bee,' o' course, a-knowin'
'Twuzn't no fair shake to play
On them pore dumb insecks, ner
To abuse 'em thataway.
Bees has rights, I'm here to say,
And that's all they ast him fer!
Man as mean as *that,* jes' 'pears,
Could 'a' worked bees on the sheers!
Cleared big money—well, I guess,
'Bee' shipped honey, more er less,
Into ev'ry state, perhaps,
Ever putt down in the maps!

"But by time he fetched 'em back
In the spring ag'in," says Ike,
"They wuz actin' s'picious-like:
Though they 'peared to lost the track
O' ev'rything they saw er heard,
They'd lay round the porch, and gap'
At their shadders in the sun,
Do-less like, ontel some bird
Suddently 'u'd maybe drap
In a bloomin' churry tree,
Twitterin' a tune 'at run
In their minds familiously!
They'd revive up, kind o', then,

Like they argied: 'Well, it's be'n
The most longest summer we
Ever saw er want to see!
Must be *right,* though, er *old 'Bee'*
'U'd notify us!' they says-ee;
And they'd sort o' square their chin
And git down to work ag'in—
Moanin' round their honey-makin',
Kind o' like their head was achin'.
Tetchin' fer to see how they
Trusted Fessler thataway—
Him a-lazin' round, and smirkin'
To hisse'f to see 'em workin'!

"But old 'Bee,' " says Ike, says-he,—
"*Now* where is he? *Where's* he
        gone?
Where's the head he helt so free?
Where's his pride and vanity?
What's his hopes a-restin' on?—
Never knowed a man," says Ike,
"Take advantage of a bee,
'At affliction didn't strike
Round in that vicinity!
Sinners allus suffers some,
And *old Fessler's* reck'nin' come!
That-air man to-day is jes'
Like the grass 'at Scriptur' says
Cometh up, and then turns in
And jes' gits cut down ag'in!
Old 'Bee' Fessler," Ike says-he,
"Says, last fall, says he to me—
'Ike,' says he, 'them bees has jes'
Ciphered out my or'n'riness!
Nary bee in ary swarm
On the whole endurin' farm
Won't have nothin' more to do
With a man as mean as I've
Be'n to them, last year er two!
Nary bee in ary hive
But'll turn his face away,
Like they ort, whenever they
Hear my footprints drawin' nigh!'

And old 'Bee,' he'd sort o' shy
Round oneasy in his cheer,
Wipe his eyes, and yit the sap,
Spite o' all, 'u'd haf' to drap,
As he wound up: 'Wouldn't keer
Quite so much ef they'd jes' light
In and settle things up right,
Like they ort; but—blame the thing!—
'Pears-like they won't even *sting!*
Pepper me, the way I felt;
And I'd thank 'em, ev'ry welt!'
And as miz'able and mean
As 'Bee' looked, ef you'd 'a' seen
Them-air hungry eyes," says Ike,
"You'd fergive him, more'n like.

"Wisht you had 'a' knowed old 'Bee'
'Fore he went to Floridy!"

492

JONEY

HAD a harelip—Joney had:
    Spiled his looks, and Joney
        knowed it:
Fellers tried to bore him, bad—
    But ef ever he got mad,
    He kep' still and never showed it.
'Druther have his mouth, all pouted
    And split up, and like it wuz,
Than the ones 'at laughed about it.—
    Purty is as purty does!

Had to listen ruther clos't
    'Fore you knowed what he wuz
        givin'
You; and yet, without no boast,
Joney he wuz jes' the most
    Entertainin' talker livin'!
Take the Scriptur's and run through
        'em,
    Might say, like a' auctioneer,

And 'ud argy and review 'em
'At wuz beautiful to hear!

Harelip and impediment,
    Both wuz bad, and both ag'in'
        him—
But the *old folks* where he went,
'Peared like, knowin' his intent,
    'Scused his mouth fer what wuz in
        him.
And *the childern* all loved Joney—
    And he loved 'em back, you bet!—
Putt their arms around him——on'y
    None had ever kissed him yet!

In young company, someway,
    Boys 'ud grin at one another
On the sly; and girls 'ud lay
Low, with nothin' much to say,
    Er leave Joney with their mother.
Many and many a time he's fetched
        'em
    Candy by the paper-sack,
And turned right around and ketched
        'em
    Makin' mouths behind his back!

S'prised, sometimes, the slurs he
        took.—
    Chap said onc't his mouth looked
        sorter
Like a fish's mouth 'ud look
When he'd be'n jerked off the hook
    And plunked back into the worter.—
Same durn feller—it's su'prisin',
    But it's facts—'at stood and cherred
From the bank that big babtizin'
    'Pike-bridge accident occurred!—

Cherred fer Joney while he give
    Life to little childern drowndin'!
Which wuz fittenest to live—
Him 'at cherred, er him 'at div'

And saved thirteen lives? . . . They
        found one
Body, three days later, floated
    Down the by-o, eight mile' south,
All so colored-up and bloated—
    On'y knowed him by his mouth!

Had a harelip—Joney had—
    Folks 'at filed apast all knowed it.—
Them 'at ust to smile looked sad,
But ef *he* thought good er bad,
    He kep' still and never showed it.
'Druther have that mouth, all pouted
    And split up, and like it wuz,
Than the ones 'at laughed about it.—
    Purty is as purty does!

493

KNEE-DEEP IN JUNE

I

TELL you what I like the best—
    'Long about knee-deep in June,
    'Bout the time strawberries melts
On the vine,—some afternoon
Like to jes' git out and rest,
    And not work at nothin' else!

II

Orchard's where I'd ruther be—
Needn't fence it in fer me!—
    Jes' the whole sky overhead,
And the whole airth underneath—
Sort o' so's a man kin breathe
    Like he ort, and kind o' has
Elbow-room to keerlessly
    Sprawl out len'thways on the grass
    Where the shadders thick and soft
    As the kivvers on the bed
    Mother fixes in the loft
Allus, when they's company!

III

Jes' a-sort o' lazin' there—
  S'lazy, 'at you peek and peer
    Through the wavin' leaves above,
    Like a feller 'ats in love
    And don't know it, ner don't keer!
Ever'thing you hear and see
  Got some sort o' interest—
    Maybe find a bluebird's nest
    Tucked up there conveenently
    Fer the boy 'at's ap' to be
    Up some other apple tree!
Watch the swallers skootin' past
Bout as peert as you could ast;
  Er the Bob-white raise and whiz
  Where some other's whistle is.

IV

Ketch a shadder down below,
And look up to find the crow—
  Er a hawk,—away up there,
  'Pearantly *froze* in the air!—
    Hear the old hen squawk, and squat
    Over ever' chick she's got,
Suddent-like!—and she knows where
That-air hawk is, well as you!—
  You jes' bet yer life she do!—
    Eyes a-glitterin' like glass,
    Waitin' till he makes a pass!

V

Pee-wees' singin', to express
  My opinion, 's second-class,
  Yit you'll hear 'em more er less;
    Sapsucks gittin' down to biz,
    Weedin' out the lonesomeness;
    Mr. Bluejay, full o' sass,
      In them baseball clothes o' his,
    Sportin' round the orchard jes'
    Like he owned the premises!
      Sun out in the fields kin sizz,

But flat on yer back, I guess,
  In the shade's where glory is!
That's jes' what I'd like to do
Stiddy fer a year er two!

VI

Plague! ef they ain't somepin' in
Work 'at kind o' goes ag'in'
  My convictions!—'long about
  Here in June especially!—
    Under some old apple tree,
    Jes' a-restin' through   and
      through,
    I could git along without
    Nothin' else at all to do
    Only jes' a-wishin' you
Wuz a-gittin' there like me,
And June wuz eternity!

VII

Lay out there and try to see
Jes' how lazy you kin be!—
  Tumble round and souse yer head
In the clover-bloom, er pull
  Yer straw hat acrost yer eyes
  And peek through it at the
    skies,
  Thinkin' of old chums 'at's dead,
  Maybe, smilin' back at you
In betwixt the beautiful
  Clouds o' gold and white and
    blue!—
Month a man kin railly love—
June, you know, I'm talkin' of!

VIII

March ain't never nothin' new!—
Aprile's altogether too
  Brash fer me! and May—I jes'
  'Bominate its promises,—
  Little hints o' sunshine and

Green around the timber-land—
A few blossoms, and a few
Chip-birds, and a sprout er two,—
Drap asleep, and it turns in
'Fore daylight and *snows* ag'in!—
But when *June* comes—Clear my
th'oat
With wild honey!—Rench my hair
In the dew! and hold my coat!
Whoop out loud! and' th'ow my
hat!—
June wants me, and I'm to spare!
Spread them shadders anywhere,
I'll get down and waller there,
And obleeged to you at that!

494

THE LAW OF THE PERVERSE

WHERE did the custom come
from, anyway—
Sending the boys to "play," at din-
ner-time,
When we have company? What is
there, pray,
About the starched, unmalleable
guest
That, in the host's most genial
interest,
Finds *him* first favor on Thanksgiving
Day
Beside the steaming turkey, with its
wings
Akimbo over all the savory things
It has been stuffed with, yet may
never thus
Make one poor' boy's face glad and
glorious!

Fancy the exiled boy in the back yard,
Ahungered so, that any kind of grub

Were welcome, yet with face set stern
and hard,
Hearing the feasters' mirth and mild
hubbub,
And wanting to kill something with
a club!—
Intuitively arguing the unjust
Distinction, as he naturally must,—
The guest with all the opportunity—
The boy with all the appetite! Ah,
me!

So is it that, when I, a luckless guest,
Am thus arraigned at banquet, I sit
grim
And sullen, eating nothing with a
zest,—
With smirking features, yet a soul dis-
tressed,
Missing the banished boy and envy-
ing him—
Ay, longing for a spatter on my vest
From his deflecting spoon, and yearn-
ing for
The wild swoop of his lips insatiate,
or
His ever-ravenous, marauding eye
Fore-eating everything, from soup to
pie!

495

OUT OF NAZARETH

"HE shall sleep unscathed of thieves
Who loves Allah and believes."
Thus heard one who shared the tent,
In the far-off Orient,
Of the Bedouin ben Ahrzz—
Nobler never loved the stars.
Through the palm-leaves nigh the dim
Dawn his courser neighed to him!

He said: "Let the sands be swarmed
  With such thieves as I, and thou
Shalt at morning rise, unharmed,
  Light as eyelash to the brow
Of thy camel, amber-eyed,
Ever munching either side,
Striding still, with nestled knees,
Through the midnight's oases.

"Who can rob thee an thou hast
More than this that thou hast cast
At my feet—this dust of gold?
Simply this and that, all told!
Hast thou not a treasure of
Such a thing as men call love?

"Can the dusky band I lead
Rob thee of thy daily need
Of a whiter soul, or steal
What thy lordly prayers reveal?
Who could be enriched of thee
By such hoard of poverty
As thy niggard hand pretends
To dole me—thy worst of friends?
  Therefore shouldst thou pause to
    bless
One indeed who blesses thee:
  Robbing thee, I dispossess
But myself.—Pray thou for me!"

"He shall sleep unscathed of thieves
Who loves Allah and believes."

496

TIME

I

THE ticking—ticking—ticking of
  the clock!—
That vexed me so last night!—"For
  though Time keeps

Such drowsy watch," I moaned, "he
  never sleeps,
But only nods above the world to
  mock
Its restless occupant, then rudely rock
  It as the cradle of a babe that weeps!"
I seemed to see the seconds piled in
  heaps
Like sand about me; and at every
  shock
O' the bell, the pilèd sands were
  swirled away
As by a desert-storm that swept the
  earth
Stark as a granary floor, whereon the
  gray
And mist-bedrizzled moon amidst the
  dearth
Came crawling, like a sickly child,
  to lay
Its pale face next mine own and weep
  for day.

II

Wait for the morning! Ah! we wait
  indeed
For daylight, we who toss about
  through stress
Of vacant-armed desires and empti-
  ness
Of all the warm, warm touches that we
  need,
And the warm kisses upon which we
  feed
Our famished lips in fancy! May
  God bless
The starved lips of us with but one
  caress
Warm as the yearning blood our poor
  hearts bleed!
. . . A wild prayer!—bite thy pillow,
  praying so—

Toss this side, and whirl that, and
    moan for dawn;
Let the clock's seconds dribble out their
    woe
And Time be drained of sorrow!
    Long ago
We heard the crowing cock, with
    answer drawn
As hoarsely sad at throat as sobs.
    . . . Pray on!

497

IKE WALTON'S PRAYER

I CRAVE, dear Lord,
    No boundless hoard
Of gold and gear,
    Nor jewels fine,
    Nor lands, nor kine,
Nor treasure-heaps of anything.—
    Let but a little hut be mine
Where at the hearthstone I may
    hear
    The cricket sing,
    And have the shine
Of one glad woman's eyes to make,
    For my poor sake,
    Our simple home a place divine;—
Just the wee cot—the cricket's chirr—
Love, and the smiling face of her.

    I pray not for
    Great riches, nor
For vast estates and castle halls,—
Give me to hear the bare footfalls
    Of children o'er
    An oaken floor
New-rinsed with sunshine, or be-
    spread

With but the tiny coverlet
And pillow for the baby's head;
And, pray Thou,' may
The door stand open and the day
    Send ever in a gentle breeze,
    With fragrance from the locust
      trees,
    And drowsy moan of doves, and
      blur
Of robin-chirps, and drone of bees,
    With after-hushes of the stir
Of interminging sounds, and then
    The goodwife and the smile of
      her
Filling the silences again—
    The cricket's call
    And the wee cot,
    Dear Lord of all,
    Deny me not!

    I pray not that
    Men tremble at
My power of place
    And lordly sway,—
I only pray for simple grace
To look my neighbor in the face
    Full honestly from day to day—
Yield me his horny palm to hold,
    And I'll not pray
    For gold;—
The tanned face, garlanded with mirth,
It hath the kingliest smile on earth;
The swart brow, diamonded with
    sweat,
Hath never need of coronet.
    And so I reach,
    Dear Lord, to Thee,
    And do beseech
    Thou givest me
The wee cot, and the cricket's chirr,
Love, and the glad sweet face of
    her!

498

THE WAY IT WUZ

LAS' July—and, I persume,
    'Bout as hot
As the old Gran'-jury room
    Whare they sot!—
Fight 'twixt Mike and Dock Mc-
        Greff. . . .
'Pears to me jes' like as ef
    I'd a-dremp' the whole blame thing—
    Allus ha'nts me roun' the gizzard
When they's nightmares on the wing
    And a feller's blood's jes' friz!
    Seed the row from A to Izzard—
'Cause I wuz a-standin' as clos't to
        'em
    As me and you is!

Tell you the way it wuz—
    And I don't *want* to see,
Like *some* fellers does,
    When they's goern to be
Any kind o' fuss—
On'y makes a rumpus wuss
    Fer to *interfere*
        When theyr dander's riz—
    Might as lif to *cheer!*
But I wuz a-standin' as clos't to 'em
    As me and you is!

I wuz kind o' strayin'
    Past the blame saloon—
Heerd some fiddler playin'
    That old "Hee-cup tune!"
I'd *stopped*-like, you know,
Fer a minit er so,
    And wuz jes' about
Settin' down, when—*Jeemses-whizz!*—
    Whole durn winder-sash fell out!
And thare laid Dock McGreff, and
        Mike

A-straddlin' him, all bloody-like,
    And both a-gittin' down to biz!—
And I wuz a-standin' as clos't to 'em
    As me and you is!

I wuz the on'y man aroun'—
    (Durn old-fogey town!
    'Peared more like, to me,
    Sund'y than *Saturd'y!*)
Dog come 'crost the road
    And tuk a smell
        And putt right back:
Mishler driv by 'ith a load
    O' cantalo'pes he couldn't sell—
        Too mad, 'i jack!
To even ast
    What wuz up, as he went past!
Weather most outrageous hot!—
    Fairly hear it sizz
Roun' Dock and Mike—tel Dock he
        shot,—
    And Mike he slacked that grip o'
        his
    And fell, all spraddled out. Dock
        riz
'Bout half up, a-spittin' red,
    And shuck his head. . . .
And I wuz a-standin' as clos't to 'em
    As me and you is!

And Dock he says,
    A-whisperin'-like,—
    "It hain't no use
A-tryin'!—Mike
    He's jes' ripped my daylights
        loose!—
Git that blame-don fiddler to
Let up, and come out here—You
Got some burryin' to do,—
    Mike makes *one,* and, I expects,
'Bout ten seconds, I'll make *two!"*
    And he drapped back, whare he'd
        riz,

'Crost Mike's body, black and blue,
Like a great big letter X!—
And I wuz a-standin' as clos't to 'em
As me and you is!

499

CURLY LOCKS

C URLY Lock̦s! Curly Lock̦s! wilt
thou be mine?
Thou shalt not wash the dishes, nor yet
feed the swine,—
But sit on a cushion and sew a fine
seam,
And feast upon strawberries, sugar and
cream.

Curly Locks! Curly Locks! wilt thou
be mine?
The throb of my heart is in every line,
And the pulse of a passion as airy and
glad
In its musical beat as the little Prince
had!

Thou shalt not wash the dishes, nor
yet feed the swine!—
O I'll dapple thy hands with these
kisses of mine
Till the pink of the nail of each finger
shall be
As a little pet blush in full blossom for
me.

But sit on a cushion and sew a fine
seam,
And thou shalt have fabric as fair as a
dream,—
The red of my veins, and ·the white of
my love,
And the gold of my joy for the braid-
ing thereof.

And feast upon strawberries, sugar and
cream
From a service of silver, with jewels
agleam,—
At thy feet will I bide, at thy beck will
I rise,
And twinkle my soul in the night of
thine eyes!

Curly Lock̦s! Curly Lock̦s! wilt thou be
mine?
Thou shalt not wash the dishes, nor
yet feed the swine,—
But sit on a cushion and sew a fine
seam,
And feast upon strawberries, sugar and
cream.

500

WHAT "OLD SANTA" OVER-
HEARD

'Tis said old Santa Claus one time
Told this joke on himself in rime:

O NE Christmas in the early din
That ever leads the morning in,
I heard the happy children shout
In rapture at the toys turned out
Of bulging little socks and shoes—
A joy at which I could but choose
To listen enviously, because
I'm always just "Old Santa Claus."
But ere my rising sigh had got
To its first quaver of the thought,
It broke in laughter as I heard
A little voice chirp like a bird—
"Old Santa's mighty good, I kno'w,
And awful rich—and he can go
Down ever' chimbly anywhere
In all the world!—But I don't care.

I wouldn't trade with *him,* and be
Old Santa Claus, and him be me,
Fer all his toys and things—and *I*
Know why and bet you *he* knows
    why!—
They wuz no Santa Claus when *he*
Wuz ist a little boy like me!"

501

GRANT

AT REST—AUGUST 8, 1885

Sir Launcelot rode overthwart and
endlong in a wide forest, and held no
path but as wild adventure led him.
. . . And he returned and came again
to his horse, and took off his saddle
and his bridle, and let him pasture; and
unlaced his helm, and ungirdled his
sword, and laid him down to sleep
upon his shield before the cross.—AGE
OF CHIVALRY.

WHAT shall we say of the soldier,
    Grant,
    His sword put by and his great soul
        free
How shall we cheer him now or chant
    His requiem befittingly?
The fields of his conquest now are seen
    Ranged no more with his armèd
        men—
But the rank and file of the gold and
        green
    Of the waving grain is there again.

Though his valiant life is a nation's
        pride,
    And his death heroic and half di-
        vine,

And our grief as great as the world is
        wide,
    There breaks in speech but a single
        line:—
We loved him living, revere him
        dead!—
A silence then on our lips is laid:
We can say no thing that has not been
        said,
    Nor pray one prayer that has not
        been prayed.

But a spirit within us speaks: and lo,
    We lean and listen to wondrous
        words
That have a sound as of winds that
        blow,
    And the voice of waters and low of
        herds;
And we hear, as the song flows on
        serene,
    The neigh of horses, and then the
        beat
Of hooves that scurry o'er pastures
        green,
    And the patter and pad of a boy's
        bare feet.

A brave lad, wearing a manly brow,
    Knit as with problems of grave dis-
        pute,
And a face, like the bloom of the or-
        chard bough,
    Pink and pallid, but resolute;
And flushed it grows as the clover-
        bloom,
    And fresh it gleams as the morning
        dew,
As he reins his steed where the quick
        quails boom
    Up from the grasses he races
        through.

And ho! as he rides what dreams are
    his?
And what have the breezes to sug-
    gest?—
Do they whisper to him of shells that
    whiz
O'er fields made ruddy with wrongs
    redressed?
Does the hawk above him an Eagle
    float?
Does he thrill and his boyish heart
    beat high,
Hearing the ribbon about his throat
Flap as a Flag as the winds go by?

And does he dream of the Warrior's
    fame—
This western boy in his rustic dress?
For, in miniature, this is the man that
    came
Riding out of the Wilderness!—
The selfsame figure—the knitted
    brow—
The eyes full steady—the lips full
    mute—
And the face, like the bloom of the
    orchard bough,
Pink and pallid, but resolute.

Ay, this is the man, with features grim
And stoical as the Sphinx's own,
That heard the harsh guns calling him,
As musical as the bugle blown,
When the sweet spring heavens were
    clouded o'er
With a tempest, glowering and wild,
And our country's flag bowed down be-
    fore
Its bursting wrath as a stricken child.

Thus, ready mounted and booted and
    spurred,

He loosed his bridle and dashed
    away!—
Like a roll of drums were his hoof-
    beats heard,
Like the shriek of the fife his
    charger's neigh!
And over his shoulder and backward
    blown,
We heard his voice, and we saw the
    sod
Reel, as our wild steeds chased his
    own
As though hurled on by the hand of
    God!

And still, in fancy, we see him ride
    In the blood-red front of a hundred
    frays,
His face set stolid, but glorified
    As a knight's of the old Arthurian
    days:
And victor ever as courtly, too,
    Gently lifting the vanquished foe,
And staying him with a hand as true
    As dealt the deadly avenging blow.

So, brighter than all of the cluster of
    stars
    Of the flag enshrouding his form to-
    day,
His face shines forth from the grime
    of wars
    With a glory that shall not pass
    away:
He rests at last: he has borne his
    part
    Of salutes and salvos and cheers on
    cheers—
But O the sobs of his country's heart,
    And the driving rain of a nation's
    tears!

502

ON THE BANKS O' DEER CRICK

ON the banks o' Deer Crick!
    There's the place fer me!—
Worter slidin' past ye jes' as clair as it
    kin be:—
See yer shadder in it, and the shadder
    o' the sky,
And the shadder o' the buzzard as he
    goes a-lazin' by;
Shadder o' the pizen-vines, and shadder
    o' the trees—
And I purt' nigh said the shadder o'
    the sunshine and the breeze!
Well!—I never seen the ocean ner I
    never seen the sea.—
On the banks o' Deer Crick's grand
    enough fer me!

On the banks o' Deer Crick—mil'd er
    two from town—
'Long up where the mill-race comes
    a-loafin' down,—
Like to git up in there—'mongst the
    sycamores—
And watch the worter at the dam,
    a-frothin' as she pours:
Crawl out on some old log, with my
    hook and line,
Where the fish is jes' so thick you kin
    see 'em shine
As they flicker round yer bait, *coaxin'*
    you to jerk,
Tel yer tired ketchin' of 'em, mighty
    nigh, as *work!*

On the banks o' Deer Crick!—Allus
    my delight
Jes' to be around there—take it day er
    night!—

Watch the snipes and killdees foolin'
    half the day—
Er these-'ere little worter-bugs skootin'
    ever' way!—
Snake-feeders glancin' round, er dartin'
    out o' sight;
And dewfall, and bullfrogs, and light-
    nin'-bugs at night—
Stars up through the tree-tops—er in
    the crick below,—
And smell o' mussrat through the dark
    clean from the old by-o!

Er take a tromp, some Sund'y, say,
    'way up to "Johnson's Hole,"
And find where he's had a fire, and
    hid his fishin'-pole:
Have yer "dog-leg" with ye, and yer
    pipe and "cut-and-dry"—
Pocketful o' corn-bread, and slug er
    two o' rye. . . .
Soak yer hide in sunshine and waller
    in the shade—
Like the Good Book tells us—"where
    there're none to make afraid!"
Well!—I never seen the ocean ner I
    never seen the sea.—
On the banks o' Deer Crick's grand
    enough fer me!

503

BILLY COULD RIDE

I

O THE way that Billy could ride!
    You should hear Grandfather
    tell of the lad—
For Grandfather was a horseman too,
Though he couldn't ride now as he
    used to do,

It yet was his glory and boast and
pride,
That he'd "back" Billy for all he had—
And that's a cool million, I'll say to
you!—
And you should hear him, with all his
praise
Of this boy Billy, and his wild ways;—
The way that he handled a horse, and
the way
He rode in town on election day—
The way he bantered, and gaffed, and
guyed,
And the ways he swapped, and the
ways he lied,
And the way he'd laugh at his victims
grim,
Till half of the time they would laugh
with him,
Forgetting their anger, and pacified—
Seeing the way that Billy could ride!

II

Billy was born for a horse's back!—
That's what Grandfather used to say:—
He'd seen him in dresses, a-many a
day,
On a two-year-old, in the old barn-
lot,
Prancing around, with the bridle slack,
And his two little sunburnt legs out-
shot
So straight from the saddle-seat you'd
swear
A spirit-level had plumbed him there!
And all the neighbors that passed the
place
Would just haul up in the road and
stare
To see the little chap's father boost
The boy up there on his favorite roost,
To canter off, with a laughing face.—

Put him up there, he was satisfied—
And O' the way that Billy could ride!

III

At celebration or barbecue—
And Billy, a boy of fifteen years—
Couldn't he cut his didoes there?—
What else would you expect him to,
On his little mettlesome chestnut mare,
With her slender neck, and her pointed
ears,
And the four little devilish hooves of
hers?
The "delegation" moved too slow
For the time that Billy wanted to go!
And to see him dashing out of the line
At the edge of the road and down the
side
Of the long procession, all laws de-
fied,
And the fife and drums, was a sight
divine,
To the girls, in their white-and-span-
gled pride
Wearily waving their scarfs about
In the great "Big Wagon," all gilt
without
And jolt within, as they lumbered on
Into the town where Billy had gone
An hour ahead, like a knightly guide—
O but the way that Billy could ride!

IV

"Billy can ride! Oh, Billy can ride!
But what on earth can he do beside?"
That's what the farmers used to say,
As time went by a year at a stride,
And Billy was twenty if he was a day!
And many a wise old father's foot
Was put right down where it should be
put,

While many a dutiful daughter sighed
In vain for one more glorious ride
With the gallant Billy, who none the
less
Smiled at the old man's selfishness
And kissed his daughter, and rode
away,—
Till one especially rich old chap—
Noted for driving a famous bay—
Gave poor Billy so sharp a rap
Regarding HIS daughter, that Billy re-
plied
By noising it over the country wide,
That the old curmudgeon was simply
mad
Because he (Billy) undoubtedly had
A faster horse than the famous bay,
And that was all that he had to say!—
Touched his horse in the flank—and
zipp!—
Talk about horses and horsemanship!—
Folks stared after him just wild-
eyed. . . .
Oomh! the way that Billy could ride!

V

Bang the cymbals! and thump the
drum!
Stun the guineas! and pound the gong!
Mr. Bull, git up and come!
And beller and paw for five days long!
Whoop and howl till you drown the
band
That hoots and toots in the "Judges'
Stand!"
For this is the term of the county fair,
And you bet Billy will be there!—
And watch him there, old horsemen,
all!
And judges, you, in your lifted stall!
And gamblers, you, as you clap and
clack,

As the order is heard to clear the
track!
And watch him, you, by the "Floral
Hall;"
With sweet face, pink as the parasol
You wave as you stand on the buggy-
seat!—
And you, young man, as you feel her
hand
Tremble in yours, as there you stand!
And watch him, too, you old man gray,
With your houses, lands, and your
wealth complete—
Not forgetting the famous bay
You ride with him in the race to-
day!—
And lash, as you start there side by
side!
Lash! for the sake of your bay de-
fied!
Lash! for the proof of your boasted
pride!
Lash! as you'd lash a cur that lied!
Lash! but watch him with both eyes
wide—
For O the way that Billy can ride.—

VI

Side by side in the open track
The horses stood—such a glossy pair!—
Trim as sparrows about to fly—
Plumage of mane and song of eye!
Ho! They were beautiful!—bay and
black—
The sunshine glittered along each
back—
Glanced at the shoulders, and flickered
and run
In dapples of light that would daze the
sun!—
The veins of their limbs like tremulous
vines

The breeze blows through, and the vi-
brant lines
Of their nostrils like to the lips of the
cups
Of the gods, brimmed over with rose-
ate sups—
From swish of tail to the toss of mane,
Pharaoh's favorites lived again!—
Lived, and served, and as nobly, too,
As they sprang to the race, and onward
flew!
Ho! but the sight of them side by
side!—
Their masters' faces seemed glorified
As they flashed from view—in an in-
stant gone,
And you saw but their shoulders, as
they rode on,
Narrowing—narrowing—less and less—
As you gazed after in breathlessness.

VII

Shoulder to shoulder, and neck to
neck—
And the hearts of the crowd spun
round with them
As they dwindled away to the selfsame
speck—
When sudden—a flash—like the flash
of a gem
That had dropped in the dust, while
onward came
But one wild rider, who homeward
led,
So mad with delight that he shrieked
his name—
And it was not "Billy"—but all the
same,
Though far behind, he was far
ahead!—
As the one rode in on "his famous
bay,"

His gray hair streaming beneath his
hat,
And the wind-blown, upturned brim
of that
Flat on his forehead—was no ac-
claim,—
The crowd was looking the other way!
Where, far in the distance, and through
the mist
Of the dust, you saw where a hand
was kissed
As in hasty adieu—nor was that all,
But, fairly and clearly and sharply de-
fined,
You saw the black horse, with Billy
astride,
With a sweet little witch of a woman
behind,
Gaily waving a pink parasol,
And the crowd answered roundly with
cheer upon cheer,
As the horse lightly wheeled with their
manifold weight,
And dashed from your gaze through
the big lower gate,
While back down the track, midst a
tumult of jeers,
Was seen to rack out, on a "winded"
bay,
An aged parent—amazed—irate—
On a race that might not end for
years.—
But end it did. . . . " 'Who won the
race!' "
Grandfather paused, with a graver
face,—
"Well, Billy won—but the reason why,
Was the bay was 'blowed'—and so was
I!

"Fizzles in everything else he's tried—
But O the way that Billy can ride!"

504

DAVE FIELD

LET me write you a rune of a rhyme,
    Dave Field,
For the sake of the past we knew,
When we were vagrants along the
    road,
Yet glad as the skies were blue;
When we struck hands, as in alien
    lands
Old friend to old friend is revealed,
And each hears a tongue that he un-
    derstands
    And a laugh that he loves, Dave
    Field.

Ho! let me chant you a stave, Dave
    Field,
Of those indolent days of ours,
With our chairs atilt at the wayside
    inn
Or our backs in the woodland
    flowers;
With your pipe alit, and the breath of
    it
Like a nimbus about your head,
While I sipped, like a monk, of your
    winy wit,
    With my matins all unsaid.

Let me drone you a dream of the
    world, Dave Field,
And the glory it held for us—
You with your pencil-and-canvas
    dreams,
And I with my pencil thus;
Yet with never a thought of the prize
    we sought,
Being at best but a pain,

As we looked from the heights and our
    blurred eyes caught
The scenes of our youth again.

Oh, let me sing you a song, Dave
    Field,
Jolly and hale, but yet
With a quaver of pathos along the
    lines,
And the throb of a vain regret;—
A sigh for the dawn long dead and
    gone,
But a laugh for the dawn concealed,
As bravely a while we still toil on
    Toward the topmost heights, Dave
    Field.

505

WHEN WE THREE MEET

WHEN we three meet?   Ah!
    friend of mine
Whose verses well and flow as wine,—
My thirsting fancy thou dost fill
With draughts delicious, sweeter still
Since tasted by those lips of thine.

I pledge thee, through the chill sun-
    shine
Of autumn, with a warmth divine,
    Thrilled through as only I shall thrill
    When we three meet.

I pledge thee, if we fast or dine,
We yet shall loosen, line by line,
    Old ballads, and the blither trill
Of our-time singers—for there will
Be with us all the Muses nine
    When we three meet.

JOSH BILLINGS

DEAD IN CALIFORNIA, OCTOBER 15, 1885

JOLLY-HEARTED old Josh Bill-
   ings,
With his wisdom and his wit,
And his gravity of presence,
   And the drollery of it!—
Has he left us, and forever?—
   When so many merry years
He has only left us laughing—
   And he leaves us now in tears?

Has he turned from his "Deer Pub-
   lik,"
With his slyly twinkling eyes
Now grown dim and heavy-lidded
   In despite of sunny skies?—
Yet with rugged brow uplifted,
   And the long hair tossed away,
Like an old heroic lion,
   With a mane of iron-gray.

Though we lose him, still we find him
   In the mirth of every lip,
And we fare through all his pages
   In his glad companionship:
His voice is wed with Nature's,
   Laughing in each woody nook
With the chirrup of the robin
   And the chuckle of the brook.

But the children—O the children!—
   They who leaped to his caress,
And felt his arms about them,
   And his love and tenderness,—
Where—where will they find comfort
   As their tears fall like the rain,
And they swarm his face with kisses
   That he answers not again?

THE LAND OF THUS-AND-SO

"HOW would Willie like to go
   To the Land of Thus-and-So?
Everything is proper there—
All the children comb their hair
Smoother than the fur of cats,
Or the nap of high silk hats;
Every face is clean and white
As a lily washed in light;
Never vaguest soil or speck
Found on forehead, throat or neck;
Every little crimpled ear,
In and out, as pure and clear
As the cherry-blossom's blow
In the Land of Thus-and-So.

"Little boys that never fall
Down the stairs, or cry at all—
Doing nothing to repent,
Watchful and obedient;
Never hungry, nor in haste—
Tidy shoe-strings always laced,
Never button rudely torn
From its fellows all unworn;
Knickerbockers always new—
Ribbon, tie, and collar, too;
Little watches, worn like men,
Always promptly half past ten—
Just precisely right, you know,
For the Land of Thus-and-So!

"And the little babies there
Give no one the slightest care—
Nurse has not a thing to do
But be happy and sigh 'Boo!'
While Mamma just nods, and knows
Nothing but to doze and doze:
Never litter round the grate;
Never lunch or dinner late;
Never any household din

Peals without or rings within—
Baby coos nor laughing calls
On the stairs or through the halls—
Just Great Hushes to and fro
Pace the Land of Thus-and-So!

"Oh! the Land of Thus-and-So!
Isn't it delightful, though?"
"Yes," lisped Willie, answering me
Somewhat slow and doubtfully—
"Must be awful nice, but I
Ruther wait till by and by
'Fore I go there—maybe when
I be dead I'll go there *then*.—
But"—the troubled little face
Closer pressed in my embrace—
"Le's don't never *ever* go
To the Land of Thus-and-So!"

508

THE HOSS

THE hoss he is a splendud beast;
    He is man's friend, as heaven
        desined,
And, search the world from west to
        east,
    No honester you'll ever find!

Some calls the hoss "a pore dumb
        brute,"
    And yit, like Him who died fer you,
I say, as I theyr charge refute,
    " 'Fergive; they know not what they
        do!' "

No wiser animal makes tracks
    Upon these earthly shores, and
        hence
Arose the axium, true as facts,
    Extoled by all, as "Good hoss-
        sense!"

The hoss is strong, and knows his
        stren'th,—
    You hitch him up a time er two
And lash him, and he'll go his len'th
    And kick the dashboard out fer you!

But, treat him allus good and kind,
    And never strike him with a stick,
Ner aggervate him, and you'll find
    He'll never do a hostile trick.

A hoss whose master tends him right
    And worters him with daily care,
Will do your biddin' with delight,
    And act as docile as *you* air.

He'll paw and prance to hear your
        praise,
    Because he's learnt to love you well;
And, though you can't tell what he
        says,
    He'll nicker all he wants to tell.

He knows you when you slam the
        gate
    At early dawn, upon your way
Unto the barn, and snorts elate,
    To git his corn, er oats, er hay.

He knows you, as the orphant knows
    The folks that loves her like theyr
        own,
And raises her and "finds" her clothes,
    And "schools" her tel a womern-
        grown!

I claim no hoss will harm a man,
    Ner kick, ner run away, cavort,
Stump-suck, er balk, er "catamaran,"
    Ef you'll jes' treat him as you ort.

But when I see the beast abused,
    And clubbed around as I've saw
        some,

I want to see his owner noosed,
And jes' yanked up like Absolum!

Of course they's differunce in stock,—
A hoss that has a little yeer,
And slender build, and shaller hock,
Can beat his shadder, mighty near!

Whilse one that's thick in neck and
chist
And big in leg and full in flank,
That tries to race, I still insist
He'll have to take the second rank.

And I have jes' laid back and laughed,
And rolled and wallered in the grass
At fairs, to see some heavy-draft
Lead out at *first,* yit come in *last!*

Each hoss has his appinted place,—
The heavy hoss should plow the
soil;—
The blooded racer, he must race,
And win big wages fer his toil.

I never bet—ner never wrought
Upon my feller man to bet—
And yit, at times, I've often thought
Of my convictions with regret.

I bless the hoss from hoof to head—
From head to hoof, and tale to
mane!—
I bless the hoss, as I have said,
From head to hoof, and back again!

I love my God the first of all,
Then Him that perished on the
cross,
And next, my wife,—and then I fall
Down on my knees and love the
hoss.

509

A OLD PLAYED-OUT SONG

IT'S the curiousest thing in creation,
Whenever I hear that old song
"Do They Miss Me at Home," I'm so
bothered,
My life seems as short as it's long!—
Fer ev'rything 'pears like adzackly
It 'peared in the years past and
gone,—
When I started out sparkin', at twenty,
And had my first neckercher on!

Though I'm wrinkelder, older and
grayer
Right now than my parents was
then,
You strike up that song "Do They
Miss Me,"
And I'm jes' a youngster again!—
I'm a-standin' back thare in the furries
A-wishin' fer evening to come,
And a-whisperin' over and over
Them words "Do They Miss Me at
Home?"

You see, *Marthy Ellen she* sung it
The first time I heerd it; and so,
As she was my very first sweethart,
It reminds me of her, don't you
know;—
How her face ust to look, in the twi-
light,
As I tuck her to Spellin'; and she
Kep' a-hummin' that song tel I ast
her,
Pine-blank, ef she ever missed *me!*

I can shet my eyes now, as you sing it,
And hear her low answerin' words;
And then the glad chirp of the crickets,
As clear as the twitter of birds;

And the dust in the road is like
velvet,
And the ragweed and fennel and
grass
Is as sweet as the scene of the lilies
Of Eden of old, as we pass.

"*Do They Miss Me at Home?*" Sing
it lower—
And softer—and sweet as the breeze
That powdered our path with the
snowy
White bloom of the old locus' trees!
Let the whipperwills he'p you to sing
it,
And the echoes 'way over the hill,

Tel the moon boolges out, in a chorus
Of stars, and our voices is still.

But, oh! "They's a chord in the music
That's missed when *her* voice is
away!"
Though I listen from midnight tel
morning,
And dawn tel the dusk of the day!
And I grope through the dark, lookin'
up'ards
And on through the heavenly dome,
With my longin' soul singin' and
sobbin'
The words "Do They Miss Me at
Home?"

510

LITTLE ORPHANT ANNIE

INSCRIBED

WITH ALL FAITH AND AFFECTION

To all the little children:—The happy ones; and sad ones;
The sober and the silent ones; the boisterous and glad ones;
The good ones—Yes, the good ones, too; and all the lovely bad ones.

LITTLE Orphant Annie's come to our house to stay,
An' wash the cups an' saucers up, an' brush the crumbs away,
An' shoo the chickens off the porch, an' dust the hearth, an' sweep,
An' make the fire, an' bake the bread, an' earn her board-an'-keep;
An' all us other childern, when the supper-things is done,
We set around the kitchen fire an' has the mostest fun
A-list'nin' to the witch-tales 'at Annie tells about,
An' the Gobble-uns 'at gits you
                    Ef you
                 Don't
              Watch
           Out!

Wunst they wuz a little boy wouldn't say his prayers,—
An' when he went to bed at night, away up-stairs,
His Mammy heerd him holler, an' his Daddy heerd him bawl,
An' when they turn't the kivvers down, he wuzn't there at all!
An' they seeked him in the rafter-room, an' cubby-hole, an' press,
An' seeked him up the chimbly-flue, an' ever'-wheres, I guess;
But all they ever found wuz thist his pants an' roundabout:—
An' the Gobble-uns 'll git you
      Ef you
        Don't
          Watch
          Out!

An' one time a little girl 'ud allus laugh an' grin,
An' make fun of ever' one, an' all her blood-an'-kin;
An' wunst, when they was "company," an' ole folks wuz there,
She mocked 'em an' shocked 'em, an' said she didn't care!
An' thist as she kicked her heels, an' turn't to run an' hide,
They wuz two great big Black Things a-standin' by her side,
An' they snatched her through the ceilin' 'fore she knowed what she's about!
An' the Gobble-uns 'll git you
      Ef you
        Don't
          Watch
          Out!

An' little Orphant Annie says, when the blaze is blue,
An' the lamp-wick sputters, an' the wind goes *woo-oo!*
An' you hear the crickets quit, an' the moon is gray,
An' the lightnin'-bugs in dew is all squenched away,—
You better mind yer parunts, an' yer teachurs fond an' dear,
An' churish them 'at loves you, an' dry the orphant's tear,
An' he'p the pore an' needy ones 'at clusters all about,
Er the Gobble-uns 'll git you
      Ef you
        Don't
          Watch
          Out!

511

A DOS'T O' BLUES

I GOT no patience with blues at all!
    And I ust to kind o' talk
Ag'inst 'em, and claim, tel along last
        Fall,
    They wuz none in the fambly stock;
But a nephew of mine, from Eelinoy,
    That visitud us last year,
He kind o' convinct me differunt
    Whilse he wuz a-stayin' here.

From ev'ry-which-way that blues is
        from,
    They'd pester him ev'ry-ways;
They'd come to him in the night, and
        come
    On Sund'ys, and rainy days;
They'd tackle him in corn-plantin'
        time,
    And in harvest, and airly Fall,—
But a dos't o' blues in the *Winter*-time,
    He 'lowed, wuz the worst of all!

Said "All diseases that ever *he* had—
    The mumps, er the rhumatiz—
Er ev'ry-other-day-aigger—bad
    As ever the blame thing is!—
Er a cyarbuncle, say, on the back of his
        neck,
    Er a felon on his thumb,—
But you keep *the blues* away from
        him,
    And all o' the rest could come!"

And he'd moan, "They's nary a leaf
        below!
    Ner a spear o' grass in sight!
And the whole wood-pile's clean under
        snow!
    And the days is dark as night!

You can't go out—ner you can't stay
        in—
    Lay down—stand up—ner set!"
And a tetch o' regular tyfoid-blues
    Would double him jes' clean shet!

I writ his parunts a postal-kyard
    He could stay tel Spring-time come;
And Aprile—*first,* as I rickollect—
    Wuz the day we shipped him home!
Most o' his *relatives,* sence then,
    Has eether give up, er quit,
Er jes' died off; but I understand
    He's the same old color yit!

512

THE TRAIN-MISSER

At Union Station

'LL where in the world my eyes has
        bin—
    Ef I hain't missed that train ag'in!
Chuff! and whistle! and toot! and
        ring!
But blast and blister the dasted train!—
How it does it I can't explain!
Git here thirty-five minutes before
The durn thing's due!—and, drat the
        thing!
It'll manage to git past—shore!

The more I travel around, the more
I got no sense!—To stand right here
And let it beat me! 'Ll ding my melts!
I got no gumption, ner nothin' else!
Ticket Agent's a dad-burned bore!
Sell you a ticket's all they keer!—
Ticket Agents ort to all be
Prosecuted—and that's jes' what!—

How'd I know which train's fer me?
And how'd I know which train was
    not?
Goern and comin' and gone astray,
And backin' and switchin' ever'-which-
    way!
Ef I could jes' sneak round behind
Myse'f, where I could git full swing,
I'd lift my coat, and kick, by jing!
Till I jes' got jerked up and fined!—
Fer here I stood, as a durn fool's apt
To, and let that train jes' chuff and
    choo
Right   apast   me—and   mouth   jes'
    gapped
Like a blamed old sandwitch warped
    in two!

513

THE PLAINT HUMAN

SEASON of snows, and season of
    flowers,
  Seasons of loss and gain!—
Since grief and joy must alike be ours,
  Why do we still complain?

Ever our failing, from sun to sun,
  O my intolerant brother:—
We want just a little too little of one,
  And much too much of the other.

514

WHICH ANE

WHICH ane, an' which ane,
  An' which ane for thee?—
Here thou hast thy vera choice
  An' which sall it be?—

Ye hae the Holy Brither,
  An' ye hae the Scholarly;
An', last, ye hae the butt o' baith—
  Which sall it be?

Ane's oot o' Edinborough,
  Wi' the Beuk an' Gown;
An' ane's came frae Cambridge;
  An' ane frae scaur an' down:
An' Deil tak the hindmaist!
  Sae the test gaes roun':
An' here ye hae the lairdly twa,
  An' ane frae scaur an' down.

Yon's Melancholy—
  An' the pipes a-skirlin'—
Gangs limp an' droopet,
  Like a coof at hirlin',—
Droopet ayc his lang skirts
  I' the wins unfurlin';
Yon's Melancholy—
  An' the pipes a-skirlin'!

Which ane, an' which ane,
  An' which ane for thee?—
Here thou hast thy vera choice:
  An' which sall it be?—
Ye hae the Holy Brither,
  An' ye hae the Scholarly;
An', last, ye hae the butt o' baith—
  Which sall it be?

Elbuck ye'r bag, mon!
  An' pipe as ye'd burst!
Can ye gie's a waur mon
  E'en than the first?—
Be it Meister Wisemon,
  I' the classics ver'sed,
An' a slawer gait yet
  E'en than the first?

Then gie us Merriment:
  Loose him like a linnet

Teeterin' on a bloomin' spray—
　We ken him i' the minute,—
Twinklin' is ane ee asklent,
　Wi' auld Clootie in it—
Auld Sawney Lintwhite,
　We ken him i' the minute!

An' which ane, an' which ane,
　An' which ane for thee?—
For thou shalt hae thy vera choice,
　An' which sall it be?—
Ye hae the Holy Brither,
　An' ye hae the Scholarly;
A' last, ye hae the butt o' baith—
　Which sall it be?

515

REGARDIN' TERRY HUT

SENCE I tuk holt o' Gibbses' Churn
　And be'n a-handlin' the concern,
I've traveled round the grand old State
Of Indiany, lots, o' late!—
I've canvassed Crawferdsville and
　sweat
Around the town o' Layfayette;
I've saw a many a County-seat
I *ust* to think was hard to beat:
At constant dreenage and expense
I've worked Greencastle and Vin-
　cennes—
Drapped out o' Putnam into Clay,
Owen, and on down thataway
Plum into Knox, on the back-track
Fer home ag'in—and glad I'm back!—
I've saw these towns, as I say—but
They's none 'at beats old Terry Hut!

It's more'n likely you'll insist
I claim this 'cause I'm predjudist,

Bein' born'd here in ole Vygo
In sight o' Terry Hut;—but no,
Yer clean dead wrong!—and I main-
　tain
They's nary drap in ary vein
O' mine but what's as free as air
To jes' take issue with you there!—
'Cause, boy and man, fer forty year,
I've argied *ag'inst* livin' here,
And jawed around and traded lies
About our lack o' enterprise,
And tuk and turned in and agreed
All other towns was in the lead,
When—drat my melts!—they couldn't
　cut
No shine a-tall with Terry Hut!

Take, even, statesmanship, and wit,
And ginerel git-up-and-git,
Old Terry Hut is sound clean
　through!—
Turn old Dick Thompson loose, er
　Dan
*Vore*hees—and where's they any man
Kin even hold a. candle to
Their eloquence?—And where's as
　clean
A fi-nan-seer as Rile' McKeen—
Er puorer, in his daily walk,
In railroad er in racin' stock!
And there's 'Gene Debs—a man 'at
　stands
And jes' holds out in his two hands
As warm a heart as ever beat
Betwixt here and the Jedgment Seat!—
All these is reasons why I putt
Sich bulk o' faith in Terry Hut.

So I've come back, with eyes 'at sees
My faults, at last,—to make my peace
With this old place, and truthful'
　swear—

Like Gineral Tom Nelson does,—
"They hain't no city anywhere
On God's green earth lays over us!"
Our city govament is *grand*—
"Ner is they better farmin'-land
Sun-kissed"—as Tom goes on and
    says—
"Er dower'd with sich advantages!"
And I've come back, with welcome
    tread,
From journeyin's vain, as I have said,
To settle down in ca'm content,
And cuss the towns where I have went,
And brag on ourn, and boast and strut
Around the streets o' Terry Hut!

516

A TALE OF THE AIRLY DAYS

OH! tell me a tale of the airly
    days—
Of the times as they ust to be;
"Piller of Fi-er" and "Shakespeare's
    Plays"
Is a'most too deep fer me!
I want plane facts, and I want plane
    words,
Of the good old-fashioned ways,
When speech run free as the songs of
    birds
'Way back in the airly days.

Tell me a tale of the timber-lands—
Of the old-time pioneers;
Somepin' a pore man understands
With his feelin's 's well as ears.
Tell of the old log house,—about
The loft, and the puncheon flore—

The old fi-er-place, with the crane
    swung out,
And the latch-string thrugh the
    door.

Tell of the things jest as they was—
They don't need no excuse!—
Don't tetch 'em up like the poets
    does,
Tel theyr all too fine fer use!—
Say they was 'leven in the fambily—
Two beds, and the chist, below,
And the trundle-beds that each helt
    three,
And the clock and the old bureau.

Then blow the horn at the old back-
    door
Tel the echoes all halloo,
And the childern gethers home onc't
    more,
Jest as they ust to do:
Blow fer Pap tel he hears and comes,
With Tomps and Elias, too,
A-marchin' home, with the fife and
    drums
And the old Red White and Blue!

Blow and blow tel the sound draps
    low
As the moan of the whipperwill,
And wake up Mother, and Ruth and
    Jo,
All sleepin' at Bethel Hill:
Blow and call tel the faces all
    Shine out in the back-log's blaze,
And the shadders dance on the old
    hewed wall
As they did in the airly days.

517

THE ROSSVILLE LECTUR' COURSE

[*Set down from the real facts of the case that come under notice of the author whilse visitun far distunt relatives who wuz then residin' at Rossville, Mich.*]

FOLKS up here at Rossville got up a Lectur' Course:—
 All the leadin' citizens they wuz out in force;
Met and talked at Williamses', and 'greed to meet ag'in;
And helt another corkus when the next reports wuz in:
Met ag'in at Samuelses'; and met ag'in at Moore's
And Johnts putt the shutters up and jest barr'd the doors!—
And yit, I'll jest be dagg-don'd! ef't didn't take a week
'Fore we'd settled whare to write to git a man to speak!

Found out whare the *"Bureau"* wuz; and then and thare agreed
To strike whilse the iron's hot and foller up the lead.—
Simp wuz Secatary; so he tuk his pen in hand,
And ast 'em what they'd tax us fer the one on "Holy Land"—
"One of Colonel J. De-Koombs's Abelust and Best
Lectur's," the circ'lar stated, "Give East er West!"
Wanted fifty dollars and his kyar-fare to and from,
And Simp wuz hence instructed fer to write him not to come.

Then we talked and jawed around another week er so,
And writ the *"Bureau"* 'bout the town a-bein' sorto' slow—
Old-fogey-like, and pore as dirt, and lackin' interprise,
And ignornter'n any other, 'cordin' to its size:
Tel finully the *"Bureau"* said they'd send a cheaper man
Fer forty dollars, who would give "A Talk About Japan"—
"A reg'lar Japanee hise'f," the pamphlet claimed; and so,
Nobody knowed his languige, and of course we let him go!

Kindo' then let up a spell—but rallied onc't ag'in,
And writ to price a feller on what's called the "violin"—
A Swede, er Pole, er somepin'—but no matter what he wuz,
Doc Cooper said he'd heerd him, and he wuzn't wuth a kuss!
And then we ast fer *Swingse's* terms; and *Cook,* and *Ingersoll*—
And blame! ef forty dollars looked like anything at all!
And then *Burdette,* we tried fer *him;* and Bob he writ to say
He wuz busy writin' ortographts and couldn't git away.

At last—along in Aprile—we signed to take this-here
Bill Nye of Californy, 'at wuz posted to appear
"The Comicalest Funny Man 'at Ever Jammed a Hall!"
So we made big preperations, and swep' out the church and all!
And night he wuz to lectur', and the neghbors all wuz thare,
And strangers packed along the aisles 'at come from ev'rywhare,
Committee got a telegrapht the preacher read, 'at run—
"Got off at Rossville, *Indiany,* 'stid of Michigun."

518

HER BEAUTIFUL EYES

O HER beautiful eyes! they are as
blue as the dew
On the violet's bloom when the morn-
ing is new,
And the light of their love is the gleam
of the sun
O'er the meadows of Spring where the
quick shadows run:
As the morn shifts the mists and the
clouds from the skies—
So I stand in the dawn of her beautiful
eyes.

And her beautiful eyes are as midday
to me,
When the lily-bell bends with the
weight of the bee,
And the throat of the thrush is apulse
in the heat,
And the senses are drugged with the
subtle and sweet
And delirious breaths of the air's lulla-
bies—
So I swoon in the noon of her beauti-
ful eyes.

O her beautiful eyes! they have smit-
ten mine own
As a glory glanced down from the
glare of The Throne;

And I reel, and I falter and fall, as
afar
Fell the shepherds that looked on the
mystical Star,
And yet dazed in the tidings that bade
them arise—
So I grope through the night of her
beautiful eyes.

519

WANT TO BE WHUR
MOTHER IS

"WANT to be whur mother is!
Want to be whur mother
is!"
Jeemses Rivers! won't some one ever
shet that howl o' his?
That-air yellin' drives me wild!
Cain't none of ye stop the child?
Want yer Daddy? "Naw." Gee
whizz!
"Want to be whur mother is!"

"Want to be whur mother is! Want
to be whur mother is!"
Coax him, Sairy! Mary, sing somepin'
fer him! Lift him, Liz—
Bang the clock-bell with the key—
Er the *meat-ax!* Gee-mun-nee!
Listen to them lungs o' his!
"Want to be whur mother is!"

"Want to be whur mother is! Want
   to be whur mother is!"
Preacher guess 'll pound all night on
   that old pulpit o' his;
'Pears to me some wimmin jest
Shows religious interest
Mostly 'fore their fambly's riz!
"Want to be whur mother is!"

. . . .

"Want to be whur mother is! Want
   to be whur mother is!"
Nights like these and whipperwills
   allus brings that voice of
   his!
Sairy; Mary; 'Lizabeth;
Don't set there and ketch yer
   death
In the dew—er rheumatiz—
Want to be whur mother is?

520

BABE HERRICK

AS a rosebud might, in dreams,
   'Mid some lilies lie, meseems
Thou, pink youngling, on the breast
Of thy mother slumberest.

521

TO A JILTED SWAIN

GET thee back neglected friends;
   And repay, as each one lends,
Tithes of shallow-sounding glee
Or keen-ringing raillery:
Get thee from lone vigils; be

But in jocund company,
Where is laughter and acclaim
Boisterous above the name.—
Get where sulking husbands sip
Ale-house cheer, with pipe at lip;
And where Mol the barmaid saith
Curst is she that marrieth.

522

KNEELING WITH HERRICK

DEAR Lord, to Thee my knee is
   bent.—
   Give me content—
Full-pleasured with what comes to me,
   Whate'er it be:
An humble roof—a frugal board,
   And simple hoard;
The wintry fagot piled beside
   The chimney wide,
While the enwreathing flames up-
   sprout
   And twine about
The brazen dogs that guard my hearth
   And household worth:
Tinge with the embers' ruddy glow
   The rafters low;
And let the sparks snap with delight,
   As fingers might
That mark deft measures of some tune
   The children croon:
Then, with good friends, the rarest
   few
   Thou holdest true,
Ranged round about the blaze, to share
   My comfort there,—
Give me to claim the service meet
   That makes each seat
A place of honor, and each guest
   Loved as the rest.

523

IN THE SOUTH

THERE is a princess in the South
About whose beauty rumors hum
Like honey-bees about the mouth
Of roses dewdrops falter from;
And O her hair is like the fine
Clear amber of a jostled wine
In tropic revels; and her eyes
Are blue as rifts of Paradise.

Such beauty as may none before
Kneel daringly, to kiss the tips
Of fingers such as knights of yore
Had died to lift against their lips:
Such eyes as might the eyes of
gold
Of all the stars of night behold
With glittering envy, and so glare
In dazzling splendor of despair.

So, were I but a minstrel, deft
At weaving, with the trembling
strings
Of my glad harp, the warp and weft
Of rondels such as rapture sings,—
I'd loop my lyre across my breast,
Nor stay me till my knee found rest
In midnight banks of bud and
flower
Beneath my lady's lattice-bower.

And there, drenched with the teary
dews,
I'd woo her with such wondrous art
As well might stanch the songs that ooze
Out of the mockbird's breaking heart;
So light, so tender, and so sweet
Should be the words I would re-
peat,
Her casement, on my gradual
sight,
Would blossom as a lily might.

524

THE HAPPY LITTLE CRIPPLE

I'M thist a little crippled boy, an' never goin' to grow
An' git a great big man at all!—'cause Aunty told me so.
When I was thist a baby onc't I falled out of the bed
An' got "The Curv'ture of the Spine"—'at's what the Doctor said.
I never had no Mother nen—fer my Pa runned away
An' dassn't come back here no more—'cause he was drunk one day
An' stobbed a man in thish-ere town, an' couldn't pay his fine!
An' nen my Ma she died—an' I got "Curv'ture of the Spine"!

I'm nine years old! An' you can't guess how much I weigh, I bet!—
Last birthday I weighed thirty-three!—An' I weigh thirty yet!
I'm awful little fer my size—I'm purt' nigh littler nan
Some babies is!—an' neighbors all calls me "The Little Man"!

An' Doc one time he laughed an' said: "I s'pect, first think you know,
You'll have a little spike-tail coat an' travel with a show!"
An' nen I laughed—till I looked round an' Aunty was a-cryin'—
Sometimes she acts like that, 'cause I got "Curv'ture of the Spine"!

I set—while Aunty's washin'—on my little long-leg stool,
An' watch the little boys an' girls a-skippin' by to school;
An' I peck on the winder, an' holler out an' say:
"Who wants to fight The Little Man 'at dares you all to-day?"
An' nen the boys climbs on the fence, an' little girls peeks through,
An' they all says: " 'Cause you're so big, you think we're 'feard o' you!"
An' nen they yell, an' shake their fist at me, like I shake mine—
They're thist in fun, you know, 'cause I got "Curv'-ture of the Spine"!

At evening, when the ironin' 's done, an' Aunty's fixed the fire,
An' filled an' lit the lamp, an' trimmed the wick an' turned it higher,
An' fetched the wood all in fer night, an' locked the kitchen door,
An' stuffed the old crack where the wind blows in up through the floor—
She sets the kittle on the coals, an' biles an' makes the tea,
An' fries the liver an' the mush, an' cooks a egg fer me;
An' sometimes—when I cough so hard—her elderberry wine
Don't go so bad fer little boys with "Curv'ture of the Spine"!

An' nen when she putts me to bed—an' 'fore she does she's got
My blanket-nighty, 'at she maked, all good an' warm an' hot,
Hunged on the rocker by the fire—she sings me hymns, an' tells
Me 'bout The Good Man—yes, an' Elves, an' Old Enchanter spells;
An' tells me more—an' more—an' more!—tel I'm *asleep,* purt' nigh—
Only I thist set up ag'in an' kiss her when she cry,
A-tellin' on 'bout *some* boy's Angel-mother—an' it's *mine!* . . .
My *Ma's a Angel*—but *I'm* got "The Curv'ture of the Spine"!

But Aunty's all so childish-like on my account, you see,
I'm most afeard she'll be took down—an' 'at's what bothers *me!*—
'Cause ef my good old Aunty ever would git sick an' die,
I don't know what she'd do in Heaven—till *I* come, by an' by:—
Fer she's so ust to all my ways, an' ever'thing, you know,
An' no one there like me, to nurse an' worry over so!—
'Cause all the little childerns there's so straight an' strong an' fine,
They's nary angel 'bout the place with "Curv'ture of the Spine"!

525

HAS SHE FORGOTTEN?

I

HAS she forgotten?   On this very
   May
We were to meet here, with the birds
   and bees,
As on that Sabbath, underneath the
   trees
We strayed among the tombs, and
   stripped away
The vines from these old granites, cold
   and gray—
And yet, indeed, not grim enough were
   they
To stay our kisses, smiles and ecstasies,
Or closer voice-lost vows and rhapso-
   dies.
Has she forgotten—that the May has
   won
Its promise?—that the bird-songs from
   the tree
Are sprayed above the grasses as the
   sun
Might jar the dazzling dew down
   showeringly?
Has she forgotten life—love—every
   one—
Has she forgotten me—forgotten me?

II

Low, low down in the violets I
   press
My lips and whisper to her.   Does she
   hear,
And yet hold silence, though I call her
   dear,
Just as of old, save for the tearful-
   ness

Of the clenched eyes, and the soul's
   vast distress?
Has she forgotten thus the old caress
That made our breath a quickened at-
   mosphere
That failed nigh unto swooning with
   the sheer
Delight?   Mine arms clutch now this
   earthen heap
Sodden with tears that flow on cease-
   lessly
As autumn rains the long, long, long
   nights weep
In memory of days that used to be,—
Has she forgotten these?   And, in her
   sleep,
Has she forgotten me—forgotten me?

III

To-night, against my pillow, with shut
   eyes,
I mean to weld our faces—through the
   dense
Incalculable darkness make pretense
That she has risen from her reveries
To mate her dreams with mine in
   marriages
Of mellow palms, smooth faces, and
   tense ease
Of every longing nerve of indolence,—
Lift from the grave her quiet lips, and
   stun
My senses with her kisses—draw the
   glee
Of her glad mouth, full blithe and
   tenderly,
Across mine own, forgetful if is done
The old love's awful dawn-time when
   said we,
"To-day is ours!" . . . Ah, Heaven!
   can it be
She has forgotten me—forgotten me!

526

ILLILEO

ILLILEO, the moonlight seemed lost
  across the vales—
The stars but strewed the azure as an
  armor's scattered scales;
The airs of night were quiet as the
  breath of silken sails,
And all your words were sweeter than
  the notes of nightingales.

Illileo Legardi, in the garden there
  alone,
With your figure carved of fervor, as
  the Psyche carved of stone,
There came to me no murmur of the
  fountain's undertone
So mystically, musically mellow as your
  own.

You whispered low, Illileo—so low the
  leaves were mute,
And the echoes faltered breathless in
  your voice's vain pursuit;
And there died the distant dalliance of
  the serenader's lute:
And I held you in my bosom as the
  husk may hold the fruit.

Illileo, I listened. I believed you. In
  my bliss,
What were all the worlds above me
  since I found you thus in this?—
Let them reeling reach to win me—
  even Heaven I would miss,
Grasping earthward!—I would cling
  here, though I clung by just a
  kiss.

And blossoms should grow odorless—
  and lilies all aghast—

And I said the stars should slacken in
  their paces through the vast,
Ere yet my loyalty should fail endur-
  ing to the last.—
So vowed I. It is written.   It is
  changeless as the past.

Illileo Legardi, in the shade your palace
  throws
Like a cowl about the singer at your
  gilded porticoes,
A moan goes with the music that may
  vex the high repose
Of a heart that fades and crumbles as
  the crimson of a rose.

527

THE JOLLY MILLER

RESTORED ROMAUNT

IT was a Jolly Miller lived on the
  River Dee;
He looked upon his piller, and there
  he found a flea:
"O Mr. Flea! you have bit me,
  And you shall shorely die!"
So he scrunched his bones ag'inst the
  stones—
  And there he let him lie!

'Twas then the Jolly Miller he laughed
  and told his wife,
And *she* laughed fit to kill her, and
  dropped her carving knife!—
"O Mr. Flea!" "Ho-ho!" "Tee-hee!"
  They *both* laughed fit to kill,
Until the sound did almost drownd
  The rumble of the mill!

*"Laugh on, my Jolly Miller! and
  Missus Miller, too!—*

*But there's a weeping-willer will soon
    wave over you!"*
The voice was all so awful small—
So very small and slim!—
He durst' infer that it was her,
Ner her infer 'twas him!

That night the Jolly Miller, says he,
    "It's, Wifey dear,
That cat o' yourn, I'd kill her!—her
    actions is so queer,—
She's rubbin' 'g'inst the grindstone-
    legs,
And yowlin' at the sky—
And I 'low the moon hain't greener
Than the yaller of her eye!"

And as the Jolly Miller went chuckle-
    un to bed,
Was *Somepin'* jerked his piller from
    underneath his head!
"O Wife," says he, on-easi-lee,
    "Fetch here that lantern there!"
But *Somepin'* moans in thunder-tones,
    "You tetch it ef you dare!"

'Twas then the Jolly Miller he trimbled
    and he quailed—
And his wife choked until her breath
    come back, 'n' she *wailed!*
And *"Oh!"* cried she, "it is *the Flea,*
    All white and pale and wann—
He's got you in his clutches, and
    He's bigger than a man!"

"Ho! ho! my Jolly Miller" (*fer 'twas
    the Flea, fer shore!*),
*"I reckon you'll not rack my bones ner
    scrunch 'em any more!"*
Then *the Flea-Ghost* he grabbed him
    clos't,
    With many a ghastly smile,

And from the door-step stooped and
    hopped
    About four hunderd mile!

528

HE COMETH IN SWEET SENSE

HE cometh in sweet sense to thee,
    Be it or dawn, or noon, or
        night,—
No deepest pain, nor halest glee,
    But He discerneth it aright.

If there be tears bedim thine eyes,
    His sympathy thou findest plain,—
The darkest midnight of the skies
    He weepeth with the tears of rain.

If thou art joyful, He hath had
    His gracious will, and lo, 'tis well,—
As thou art glad, so He is glad,
    Nor mercy strained one syllable.

Wild vows are words, as prayers are
        words.—
    God's mercy is not measured by
Our poor deservings: He affords
    To listen, if we laugh or cry.

529

KINGRY'S MILL

ON old Brandywine—about
    Where White's Lots is now laid
        out,
And the old crick narries down
To the ditch that splits the town,—
Kingry's Mill stood. Hardly see
Where the old dam ust to be;

Shallor, long, dry trought o' grass
Where the old race ust to pass!

That's be'n forty years ago—
Forty years o' frost and snow—
Forty years o' shade and shine
Sence them boyhood-days o' mine!—
All the old landmarks o' town
Changed about, er rotted down!
Where's the Tanyard?   Where's the
        Still?
Tell me where's old Kingry's Mill?

Don't seem furder back, to me,
I'll be dogg'd! than yisterd'y,
Sence us fellers, in bare feet
And straw hats, went through the
        wheat,
Cuttin' 'crost the shortest shoot
Fer that-air old ellum-root
Jest above the mill-dam—where
The blame' cars now crosses there!

Through the willers down the crick
We could see the old mill stick
Its red gable up, as if
It jest knowed we'd stol'd the skiff!
See the winders in the sun
Blink like they wuz wunderun'
What the miller ort to do
With sich boys as me and you!

But old Kingry!—who could fear
That old chap, with all his cheer?—
Leanin' at the winder-sill,
Er the half-door o' the mill,
Swappin'' lies, and pokin' fun,
'N' jigglin' like his hoppers done—
Laughin' grists o' gold and red
Right out o' the wagon-bed!

What did *he* keer where we went?—
"Jest keep out o' devilment,

And don't fool around the belts,
Bolts, ner burrs, ner nothin' else
'Bout the blame *machinery,*
And that's all I ast!" says-ee.
Then we'd climb the stairs, and play
In the bran-bins half the day!

Rickollect the dusty wall,
And the spider-webs, and all!
Rickollect the trimblin' spout
Where the meal come josslin' out—
Stand and comb yer fingers through
The fool-truck an hour er two—
Felt so sort o' warm-like and
Soothin' to a feller's hand!

Climb, high up above the stream,
And "coon" out the wobbly beam
And peek down from out the lof'
Where the weather-boards was off—
Gee-mun-*nee!* w'y, it takes grit
Even jest to think of it!—
Lookin' way down there below
On the worter roarin' so!

Rickollect the flume, and wheel,
And the worter slosh and reel
And jest ravel out in froth
Flossier'n satin cloth!
Rickollect them paddles jest
Knock the bubbles galley-west,
And plunge under, and come up,
Drippin' like a worter-pup!

And, to see them old things gone
That I onc't was bettin' on,
In rale p'int o' fact, I feel
Kind o' like that worter-wheel,—-
Sort o' drippy-like and wet
Round the eyes—but paddlin' yet,
And, in mem'ry, loafin' still
Down around old Kingry's Mill!

530

THE EARTHQUAKE

CHARLESTON, SEPTEMBER 1, 1886

AN hour ago the lulling twilight
    leant
Above us like a gentle nurse who
    slips
A slow palm o'er our eyes, in soft
    eclipse
Of feigned slumber of most sweet con-
    tent.
The fragrant zephyrs of the tropic
    went
And came across the senses, like to
    sips
Of lovers' kisses, when upon her
    lips
Silence sets finger in grave merriment.
Then—sudden—did the earth moan as
    it slept,
And start as one in evil dreams, and
    toss
Its peopled arms up, as the horror
    crept,
And with vast breast upheaved and
    rent across,
Fling down the storied citadel where
    wept,
And still shall weep, a world above
    its loss.

531

A FALL-CRICK VIEW OF THE EARTHQUAKE

I KIN hump my back and take the
    rain,
And I don't keer how she pours;

I kin keep kind o' ca'm in a thunder-
    storm,
    No matter how loud she roars;
I hain't much skeered o' the light-
    nin',
    Ner I hain't sich awful shakes
Afeard o' *cyclones*—but I don't want
    none
    O' yer dad-burned old earthquakes!

As long as my legs keeps stiddy,
    And long as my head keeps plum',
And the buildin' stays in the front
    lot,
    I still kin whistle, *some!*
But about the time the old clock
    Flops off'n the mantel-shelf,
And the bureau skoots fer the kitchen,
    I'm a-goin' to skoot, myself!

Plague-take! ef you keep me stabled
    While any earthquakes is around!—
I'm jes' like the stock,—I'll beller
    And break fer the open ground!
And I 'low you'd be as nervous
    And in jes' about my fix,
When yer whole farm slides from
    inunder you,
    And on'y the mor'gage sticks!

Now cars hain't a-goin' to kill you
    Ef you don't drive 'crost the track;
Crediters never'll jerk you up
    Ef you go and pay 'em back;
You kin stand all moral and mundane
    storms
    Ef you'll on'y jes' behave—
But a' EARTHQUAKE:—Well, ef it
    wanted you
    It 'ud husk you out o' yer grave!

532

WHEN THE WORLD BU'STS THROUGH

Casually Suggested by an Earthquake

WHERE'S a boy a-goin',
     An' what's he goin' to do,
An' how's he goin' to do it,
   When the world bu'sts through?
Ma she says "she can't tell
   What we're comin' to!"
An' Pop says "he's ist skeered
   Clean—plum—through!"

S'pose we'd be a-playin'
   Out in the street,
An' the ground 'ud split up
   'Bout forty feet!—
Ma says "she ist knows
   We 'ud tumble in";
An' Pop says "he bets you
   Nen we wouldn't grin!"

S'pose we'd ist be 'tendin'
   Like we had a show,
Down in the stable
   Where we mustn't go,—
Ma says, "The earthquake
   Might make it fall";
An' Pop says, "More'n like
   Swaller barn an' all!"

Landy! ef we both wuz
   Runnin' 'way from school,
Out in the shady woods
   Where it's all so cool!—
Ma says "a big tree
   Might sqush our head";
An' Pop says, "Chop 'em out
   Both—killed—dead!"

But where's a boy goin',
   An' what's he goin' to do,
An' how's he goin' to do it,
   Ef the world bu'sts through?
Ma she says "she can't tell
   What we're comin' to!"
An' Pop says "he's ist skeered
   Clean—plum—through!"

533

THE OLD RETIRED SEA-CAPTAIN

THE old sea-captain has sailed the
     seas
So long, that the waves at mirth,
Or the waves gone wild, and the crests
   of these,
   Were as near playmates from birth:
He has loved both the storm and the
   calm, because
   They seemed as his brothers twain,—
The flapping sail was his soul's ap-
     plause,
   And his rapture, the roaring main.

But now—like a battered hulk seems
   he,
   Cast high on a foreign strand,
Though he feels "in port," as it need
   must be,
   And the stay of a daughter's hand—
Yet ever the round of the listless
   hours,—
   His pipe, in the languid air—
The grass, the trees, and the garden
   flowers,
   And the strange earth everywhere!

And so betimes he is restless here
   In this little inland town,

With never a wing in the atmosphere
But the windmill's, up and down;
His daughter's home in this peaceful
vale,
And his grandchild 'twixt his
knees—
But never the hail of a passing sail,
Nor the surge of the angry seas!

He quits his pipe, and he snaps its
neck—
Would speak, though he coughs in-
stead,
Then paces the porch like a quarter-
deck
With a reeling mast o'erhead!
Ho! the old sea-captain's cheeks glow
warm,
And his eyes gleam grim and weird,
As he mutters about, like a thunder-
storm,
In the cloud of his beetling beard.

534

JIM

HE was jes' a plain, ever'-day, all-
round kind of a jour.,
Consumpted-lookin'—but la!
The jokeiest, wittiest, story-tellin',
song-singin', laughin'est,
jolliest
Feller you ever saw!
Worked at jes' coarse work, but you
kin bet he was fine enough
in his talk,
And his feelin's too!
Lordy! ef he was on'y back on his
bench ag'in to-day, a-carry-
in' on
Like he ust to do!

Any shopmate'll tell you there never
was, on top o' dirt,
A better feller'n Jim!
You want a favor, and couldn't git it
anywheres else—
You could git it o' him!
Most free-heartedest man thataway in
the world, I guess!
Give up ever' nickel he's
worth—
And, ef you'd a-wanted it, and named
it to him, and it was his,
He'd 'a' give you the earth!

Allus a-reachin' out, Jim was, and
a-he'ppin' some
Pore feller on to his feet—
He'd 'a' never 'a' keered how hungry
he was hisse'f,
So's *the feller* got somepin' to
eat!
Didn't make no differ'nce at all to him
how *he* was dressed,
He ust to say to me.—
"You togg out a tramp purty comfort-
able in winter-time, a-hunt-
in' a job,
And he'll git along!" says he.

Jim didn't have, ner never could git
ahead, so overly much
O' this world's goods at a
time.—
'Fore now I've saw him, more'n onc't,
lend a dollar, and haf to,
more'n likely,
Turn round and borry a dime!
Mebby laugh and joke about it hisse'f
fer a while—then jerk his
coat,
And kind o' square his chin,
Tie on his apern, and squat hisse'f on
his old shoe-bench,
And go to peggin' ag'in!

Patientest feller, too, I reckon, 'at ever
    jes' natchurly
Coughed hisse'f to death!
Long enough after his voice was lost
    he'd laugh in a whisper and
    say
He could git ever'thing but his
    breath—
"*You* fellers," he'd sort o' twinkle his
    eyes and say,
"Is a-pilin' on to me
A mighty big debt fer that-air little
    weak-chested ghost o' mine
    to pack
Through all Eternity!"

Now there was a man 'at jes' 'peared-
    like, to me,
'At ortn't '*a*' *never* 'a' died!
"But death hain't a-showin' no favors,"
    the old boss said—
"On'y to *Jim!*" and cried:
And Wigger, who puts up the best
    sewed-work in the shop—
    Er the whole blame neighber-
    hood,—
He says, "When God made Jim, I bet
    you He didn't do anything
    else that day
    But jes' set around and feel
    good!"

Back from green to gray and red,
Brown and yeller, with their stems
Loosenin' on the oaks and e'ms;
And the balance of the trees
Gittin' balder every breeze—
Like the heads we're scratchin' on!
Old October's purt' nigh gone.

I love Old October so,
I can't bear to see her go—
Seems to me like losin' some
Old home relative er chum—
'Pears like sort o' settin' by
Some old friend 'at sigh by sigh
Was a-passin' out o' sight
Into everlastin' night!
Hickernuts a feller hears
Rattlin' down is more like tears
Drappin' on the leaves below—
I love Old October so!

Can't tell what it is about
Old October knocks me out!—
I sleep well enough at night—
And the blamedest appetite
Ever mortal man possessed,—
Last thing et, it tastes the best!—
Warnuts, butternuts, pawpaws,
'Iles and limbers up my jaws
Fer raal service, sich as new
Pork, spareribs, and sausage, too.—
Yit, fer all, they's somepin' 'bout
Old October knocks me out!

535

OLD OCTOBER

OLD October's purt' nigh gone,
    And the frosts is comin' on
Little *heavier* every day—
Like our hearts is thataway!
Leaves is changin' overhead

536

JUDITH

O HER eyes are amber-fine—
    Dark and deep as wells of wine;
While her smile is like the noon
Splendor of a day of June.

If she sorrow—lo! her face
It is like a flowery space
In bright meadows, overlaid
With light clouds and lulled with
    shade.
If she laugh—it is the trill
Of the wayward whippoorwill
Over upland pastures, heard
Echoed by the mocking-bird
In dim thickets dense with bloom
And blurred cloyings of perfume.
If she sigh—a zephyr swells
Over odorous asphodels
And wan lilies in lush plots
Of moon-drown'd forget-me-nots.
Then, the soft touch of her hand—
Takes all breath to understand
What to liken it thereto!—
Never rose-leaf rinsed with dew
Might slip soother-suave than slips
Her slow palm, the while her lips
Swoon through mine, with kiss on kiss
Sweet as heated honey is.

537

THE LEGEND GLORIFIED

"I DEEM that God is not dis-
    quieted"—
This in a mighty poet's rhymes I
    read;
And blazoned so forever doth abide
Within my soul the legend glorified.

Though awful tempests thunder over-
    head,
I deem that God is not disquieted,—
The faith that trembles somewhat yet
    is sure
Through storm and darkness of a
    way secure.

Bleak winters, when the naked spirit
    hears
The break of hearts, through stinging
    sleet of tears,
I deem that God is not disquieted;
Against all stresses am I clothed and
    fed.

Nay, even with fixed eyes and broken
    breath,
My feet dip down into the tides of
    death,
Nor any friend be left, nor prayer be
    said,
I deem that God is not disquieted.

538

ON A FLY-LEAF

IN JOHN BOYLE O'REILLY'S POEMS

SINGERS there are of courtly
    themes—
    Drapers in verse—who would dress
        their rhymes
In robes of ermine; and singers of
    dreams
    Of gods high-throned in the classic
        times;
Singers of nymphs, in their dim re-
    treats,
    Satyrs, with scepter and diadem;
But the singer who sings as a man's
    heart beats
    Well may blush for the rest of them.

I like the thrill of such poems as
    these,—
    All spirit and fervor of splendid
        fact—
Pulse, and muscle, and arteries
    Of living, heroic thought and act!—

Where every line is a vein of red
And rapturous blood all unconfined
As it leaps from a heart that has joyed
    and bled
With the rights and the wrongs of
    all mankind.

539

OLD MAN'S NURSERY RHYME

IN the jolly winters
    Of the long-ago,
It was not so cold as now—
    Oh! No! No!
Then, as I remember,
    Snowballs to eat
Were as good as apples now,
    And every bit as sweet!

In the jolly winters
    Of the dead-and-gone,
Bub was warm as summer,
    With his red mitts on,—
Just in his little waist-
    And-pants all together,
Who ever heard him growl
    About cold weather?

In the jolly winters
    Of the long-ago—
Was it *half* so cold as now?
    Oh! No! No!
Who caught his death o' cold,
    Making prints of men
Flat-backed in snow that now's
    Twice as cold again?

In the jolly winters
    Of the dead-and-gone,
Startin' out rabbit-huntin'
    Early as the dawn,—

Who ever froze his fingers,
    Ears, heels, or toes,—
Or'd 'a' cared if he had?
    Nobody knows!

Nights by the kitchen stove,
    Shellin' white and red
Corn in the skillet, and
    Sleepin' four abed!
Ah! the jolly winters
    Of the long-ago!
We were not as old as now—
    Oh! No! No!

540

LEWIS D. HAYES

OBIT DECEMBER 28, 1886

IN the midmost glee of the Christ-
    mas
    And the mirth of the glad New
        Year,
A guest has turned from the revel,
    And we sit in silence here.

The band chimes on, yet we listen
    Not to the air's refrain,
But over it ever we strive to catch
    The sound of his voice again—

For the sound of his voice was music,
    Dearer than any note
Shook from the strands of harp-
        strings,
    Or poured from the bugle's throat.—

A voice of such various ranges,
    His utterance rang from the height
Of every rapture, down to the sobs
    Of every lost delight.

Though he knew Man's force and his
    purpose,
As strong as his strongest peers,
He knew, as well, the kindly heart,
And the tenderness of tears.

So is it the face we remember
    Shall be always as a child's
That, grieved some way to the very
    soul,
    Looks bravely up and smiles.

O brave it shall look, as it looked its
    last
On the little daughter's face—
Pictured only—against the wall,
    In its old accustomed place—

Where the last gleam of the lamplight
Out of the midnight dim
Yielded its grace, and the earliest dawn
Gave it again to him.

541

A LOCAL POLITICIAN FROM AWAY BACK

JEDGE is good at argyin'—
    No mistake in that!
Most folks 'at tackles *him*
    He'll skin 'em like a cat!
You see, the Jedge is read up,
    And b'en in politics,
Hand-in-glove, you might say,
    Sence back in '56.

Elected to the Shurrif, first,
    Then elected Clerk;
Went into lawin' then,
    And buckled down to work;
Practised three or four terms,
    Then he run for jedge—

Speechified a little 'round,
    And went in like a wedge!

Run fer Legislatur' twic't—
    Made her, ever' pop!
Keeps on the way he's doin',
    Don't know where he'll stop!
Some thinks he's got his eye
    On the gov'nership;—
Well, ef he tuk the track,
    Guess he'd make the trip.

But I started out to tell ye—
    (Now I allus liked *the man*—
Not fer his politics,
    But *social'*, understan'!—
Fer, 's regards to *my* views,
    Political and sich.—
When we come together there
    We're purty ap' to hitch)—

Ketched him in at Knox's shop
    On'y t'other day—
Gittin' shaved, the Jedge was,
    Er somepin' thataway.—
Well, I tetched him up some
    On the silver bill:—
Jedge says, "I won't discuss it;"
    I says, "You *will!*"

I-says-ee, "I reckon
    You'll concede with me,
Coin's the on'y ginuine
    Money," I-says-ee;
Says I, "What's a dollar-bill?"
Says I, "What's a ten—
Er forty-'leven hunderd of 'em?—
    Give us *specie*, then!"

I seed I was a-gittin'
    The Jedge kind o' red
Around the gills. He hawked some
    And cle'red his throat and said—

"Facts is too complicated
    'Bout the bill in view,"
Squirmed and told the barber then
    He wisht he'd hurry through.

'Ll, then, I knowed I had him,—
    And the crowd around the fire
Was all a-winkin' at me,
    As the barber raised him higher—
Says I, "Jedge, what's a dollar?—
    Er a half-un," I-says-ee—
"What's a *quarter?*—What's a *dime?*"
    "What's *cents?*" says he.

W'y, I had him fairly b'ilin'!
    "You needn't comb my hair,"
He says to the barber—
    "I want fresh air;"
And you'd 'a' died a-laughin'
    To 'a' seed him grab his hat,
As I-says-ee, says I, "Judge,
    Where you goin' at!"

'edge is good at argyin',
    By-and-large; and yit
Beat him at his own game
    And he's going' to git!
And yit the Jedge is read up,
    And b'en in politics,
Hand-in-glove, you might say,
    Sence back in '56.

542

THE MUTE SINGER

I

THE morning sun seemed fair as
        though
It were a great red rose ablow
    In lavish bloom,

With all the air for its perfume,—
    Yet he who had been wont to
        sing,
Could trill no thing.

II

Supine, at noon, as he looked up
Into the vast inverted cup
    Of heavenly gold,
Brimmed with its marvels manifold,
    And his eye kindled, and his
        cheek—
Song could not speak.

III

Night fell forebodingly; he knew
Soon must the rain be falling, too,—
    And, home, heartsore,
A missive met him at the door—
    —Then Song lit on his lips, and he
Sang gloriously.

543

THE CYCLONE

SO lone I stood, the very trees
    seemed drawn
In conference with themselves.—In-
    tense—intense
Seemed everything; — the summer
    splendor on
The sight,—magnificence!

A babe's life might not lighter fail and
    die
Than failed the sunlight.—Though
    the hour was noon,
The palm of midnight might not
    lighter lie
Upon the brow of June.

With eyes upraised, I saw the under-
    wings
Of swallows—gone the instant after-
    ward—
While from the elms there came
    strange twitterings,
Stilled scarce ere they were heard.

The river seemed to shiver; and, far
    down
Its darkened length, I saw the syca-
    mores
Lean inward closer, under the vast
    frown
That weighed above the shores.

Then was a roar, born of some awful
    burst! . . .
And one lay, shrieking, chattering,
    in my path—
Flung—he or I—out of some space
    accurst
As of Jehovah's wrath:

Nor barely had he wreaked his latest
    prayer,
Ere back the noon flashed o'er the
    ruin done,
And, o'er uprooted forests tousled
    there,
The birds sang in the sun.

544

IN DAYS TO COME

IN days to come—whatever ache
    Of age shall rack our bones, or
      quake
Our slackened thews—whatever grip
Rheumatic catch us i' the hip,—

We, each one, for the other's sake,
Will of our very wailings make
Such quips of song as well may shake
    The spasm'd corners from the lip—
      In days to come.

Ho! ho! how our old hearts shall rake
The past up!—how our dry eyes slake
    Their sight upon the dewy drip
    Of juicy-ripe companionship,
And blink stars from the blind
    opaque—
      In days to come.

545

THE STEPMOTHER

FIRST she come to our house,
    Tommy run and hid;
And Emily and Bob and me
    We cried jus' like we did
When Mother died,—and we all said
'At we all wisht 'at we was dead!

And Nurse she couldn't stop us;
    And Pa he tried and tried,—
We sobbed and shook and wouldn't
    look,
    But only cried and cried;
And nen some one—we couldn't jus'
Tell who—was cryin' same as us!

Our Stepmother! Yes, it was her,
    Her arms around us all—
'Cause Tom slid down the banister
    And peeked in from the hall.—
And we all love her, too, because
She's purt' nigh good as Mother was!

546

WHEN MY DREAMS COME TRUE

I

WHEN my dreams come true—
when my dreams come true—
Shall I lean from out my casement, in
the starlight and the dew,
To listen—smile and listen to the
tinkle of the strings
Of the sweet guitar my lover's fingers
fondle, as he sings?
And as the nude moon slowly, slowly
shoulders into view,
Shall I vanish from his vision—when
my dreams come true?

When my dreams come true—shall the
simple gown I wear
Be changed to softest satin, and my
maiden-braided hair
Be raveled into flossy mists of rarest,
fairest gold,
To be minted into kisses, more than
any heart can hold?—
Or "the summer of my tresses" shall
my lover liken to
"The fervor of his passion"—when my
dreams come true?

II

When my dreams come true—I shall
bide among the sheaves
Of happy harvest meadows; and the
grasses and the leaves
Shall lift and lean between me and
the splendor of the sun,
Till the noon swoons into twilight,
and the gleaners' work is done—

Save that yet an arm shall bind me,
even as the reapers do
The meanest sheaf of harvest—when
my dreams come true.

When my dreams come true! when
my dreams come true!
True love in all simplicity is fresh and
pure as dew;—
The blossom in the blackest mold is
kindlier to the eye
Than any lily born of pride that looms
against the sky:
And so it is I know my heart will
gladly welcome you,
My lowliest of lovers, when my dreams
come true.

547

THE CHANT OF THE CROSS-
BEARING CHILD

I BEAR dis cross dis many a mile.
O de cross-bearin' chile—
De cross-bearin' chile!

I bear dis cross 'long many a road
Wha' de pink ain't bloom' an' de grass
done mowed.
O de cross-bearin' chile—
De cross-bearin' chile!

Hit's on my conscience all dese days
Fo' ter bear de cross 'ut de good Lord
lays
On my po' soul, an' ter lif my praise
O de cross-bearin' chile—
De cross-bearin' chile!

I's nigh 'bout weak ez I mos' kin be,
Yit de Marstah call an' He say,—
"You's free

Fo' ter 'cept dis cross, an' ter cringe yo'
       knee
To no n'er man in de worl' but Me!"
   O de cross-bearin' chile—
     De cross-bearin' chile!

Says you guess wrong, ef I let you
       guess—
Says you 'spec' mo', an'-a you git
       less:—
Says you go eas', says you go wes',
An' whense you fine de road 'ut you
       like bes'
You betteh take chice er any er de res'!
   O de cross-bearin' chile—
     De cross-bearin' chile!

He build my feet, an' He fix de signs
Dat de shoe hit pinch an' de shoe hit
       bines
Ef I on'y w'ah eights an'-a wanter w'ah
       nines;
I hone fo' de rain, an' de sun hit
       shines,
An' whilse I hunt de sun, hit's de rain
       I fines.—
O-a trim my lamp, an'-a gyrd my lines!
   O de cross-bearin' chile—
     De cross-bearin' chile!

I wade de wet, an' I walk de dry:
I done tromp long, an' I done clim'
       high;
An' I pilgrim on ter de jasper sky,
An' I taken de resk fo' ter cas' my eye
Wha' de Gate swing wide an' de Lord
       draw nigh,
An' de Trump hit blow, an' I hear de
       cry,—
"You lay dat cross down by an' by!—
   O de Cross-bearin' Chile—
     De Cross-bearin' Chile!"

548

THREE DEAD FRIENDS

ALWAYS suddenly they are gone—
   The friends we trusted and held
     secure—
Suddenly we are gazing on,
  Not a *smiling* face, but the marble-
     pure
Dead mask of a face that nevermore
   To a smile of ours will make reply—
    The lips close-locked as the eyelids
     are,—
Gone—swift as the flash of the molten
     ore
  A meteor pours through a midnight
     sky,
    Leaving it blind of a single star.

Tell us, O Death, Remorseless Might!
  What is this old, unescapable ire
You wreak on us?—from the birth of
     light
  Till the world be charred to a core
     of fire!
We do no evil thing to you—
  We seek to evade you—that is all—
    That is your will—you will not
     be known
Of men. What, then, would you have
     us do?—
  Cringe, and wait till your vengeance
     fall,
    And your graves be fed, and the
     trumpet blown?

You desire no friends; but *we*—O we
  Need them so, as we falter here,
Fumbling through each new vacancy,
  As each is stricken that we hold
     dear.

One you struck but a year ago;
  And one not a month ago; and
    one—
    (God's vast pity!)—and one lies
      now
Where the widow wails, in her name-
    less woe,
  And the soldiers pace, with the
    sword and gun,
    Where the comrade sleeps, with
      the laureled brow.

And what did the first?—that way-
    ward soul,
  Clothed of sorrow, yet nude of sin,
And with all hearts bowed in the
    strange control
Of the heavenly voice of his violin.
Why, it was music the way he *stood,*
  So grand was the poise of the head
    and so
  Full was the figure of majesty!—
One heard with the eyes, as a deaf
    man would,
  And with all sense brimmed to the
    overflow
    With tears of anguish and ecstasy.

And what did the girl, with the great
    warm light
  Of genius sunning her eyes of blue,
With her heart so pure, and her soul
    so white—
What, O Death, did she do to you?
Through field and wood as a child
    she strayed,
  As Nature, the dear sweet mother
    led;
    While from her canvas, mirrored
      back,
Glimmered the stream through the
    everglade

Where the grape-vine trailed from
    the trees to wed
  Its likeness of emerald, blue and
    black.

And what did he, who, the last of
    these,
  Faced you, with never a fear, O
    Death?
Did you hate *him* that he loved the
    breeze,
  And the morning dews, and the
    rose's breath?
Did you hate him that he answered
    not
  Your hate again—but turned, in-
    stead,
    His only hate on his country's
      wrongs?
Well—you possess him, dead!—but
    what
  Of the good he wrought?   With
    laureled head
    He bides with us in his deeds and
      songs.

Laureled, first, that he bravely fought,
  And forged a way to our flag's re-
    lease;
Laureled, next, for the harp he taught
  To wake glad songs in the days of
    peace—
Songs of the woodland haunts he held
  As close in his love as they held
    their bloom
    In their inmost bosoms of leaf and
      vine—
Songs that echoed and pulsed and
    welled
  Through the town's pent streets, and
    the sick child's room,
    Pure as a shower in soft sunshine.

Claim them, Death; yet their fame en-
dures.
What friend next will you rend from
us
In that cold, pitiless way of yours,
And leave us a grief more dolorous?
Speak to us!—tell us, O Dreadful
Power!—
Are we to have not a lone friend
left?—
Since, frozen, sodden, or green the
sod,
In every second of every hour,
Some one, Death, you have thus bereft,
Half inaudibly shrieks to God.

549

WHEN SHE COMES HOME

WHEN she comes home again! A thousand ways
I fashion, to myself, the tenderness
Of my glad welcome: I shall tremble
—yes;
And touch her, as when first in the old
days
I touched her girlish hand, nor dared
upraise
Mine eyes, such was my faint heart's
sweet distress
Then silence: and the perfume of
her dress:
The room will sway a little, and a haze
Cloy eyesight—soul-sight, even—for
a space;
And tears—yes; and the ache here in
the throat,
To know that I so ill deserve the place
Her arms make for me; and the sob-
bing note
I stay with kisses, ere the tearful face
Again is hidden in the old embrace.

550

LUTHER A. TODD

OBIT JULY 27, 1887, KANSAS CITY,
MISSOURI

GIFTED, and loved and praised
By every friend;
Never a murmur raised
Against him, to the end!
With tireless interest
He wrought as he thought best,—
And—lo, we bend
Where now he takes his rest!

His heart was loyal, to
Its latest thrill,
To the home-loves he knew—
And now forever will,—
Mother and brother—they
The first to pass away,—
And, lingering still,
The sister bowed to-day.

Pure as a rose might be,
And sweet, and white,
His father's memory
Was with him day and night:—
He spoke of him, as one
May now speak of the son,—
Sadly and tenderly,
Yet as a trump had done.

Say, then, of him: He knew
Full depths of care
And stress of pain, and you
Do him scant justice there,—
Yet in the lifted face
Grief left not any trace,
Nor mark unfair,
To mar its manly grace.

It was as if each day
  Some new hope dawned—
Each blessing in delay,
  To him, was just beyond;
Between whiles, waiting, he
Drew pictures cunningly—
  Fantastic—fond—
Things that we laughed to see.

Sometimes, as we looked on
  His crayon's work,
Some angel-face would dawn
  Out radiant, from the mirk
Of features old and thin,
Or jowled with double-chin,
  And eyes asmirk,
And gaping mouths agrin.

That humor in his art,
  Of genius born,
Welled warmly from a heart
  That could not but adorn
All things it touched with love—
The eagle, as the dove—
  The burst of morn—
The night—the stars above.

Sometimes, amid the wild
  Of faces queer,
A mother, with her child
  Pressed warm and close to her;
This, I have thought, somehow,
The wife, with head abow,
  Unreconciled,
In the great shadow now.

.   .   .   .

O ye of sobbing breath,
  Put by all sighs
Of anguish at his death—
  Turn—as he turned *his* eyes,

In that last hour, unknown
In strange lands, all alone—
  Turn thine eyes toward the skies,
And, smiling, cease thy moan.

551

WHEN OLD JACK DIED

WHEN Old Jack died, we stayed
    from school (they said,
At home, we needn't go that day), and
  none
Of us ate any breakfast—only one,
And that was Papa—and his eyes were
  red
When he came round where we were,
  by the shed
Where Jack was lying, half-way in the
  sun
And half-way in the shade. When we
  begun
To cry out loud, Pa turned and
  dropped his head
And went away; and Mamma, she
  went back
Into the kitchen. Then, for a long while,
All to ourselves, like, we stood there
  and cried.
We thought so many good things of
  Old Jack,
And funny things—although we didn't
  smile—
We couldn't only cry when Old Jack
  died.

When Old Jack died, it seemed a hu-
  man friend
Had suddenly gone from us; that some
  face
That we had loved to fondle and em-
  brace

From babyhood, no more would con-
descend
To smile on us forever. We might
bend
With tearful eyes above him, inter-
lace
Our chubby fingers o'er him, romp and
race,
Plead with him, call and coax—aye,
we might send
The old halloo up for him, whistle,
hist,
(If sobs had let us) or, as wildly
vain,
Snapped thumbs, called "Speak," and
he had not replied;
We might have gone down on our
knees and kissed
The tousled ears, and yet they must
remain
Deaf, motionless, we knew—when Old
Jack died.

When Old Jack died, it seemed to us,
some way,

That all the other dogs in town were
pained
With our bereavement, and some that
were chained,
Even, unslipped their collars on that
day
To visit Jack in state, as though to pay
A last, sad tribute there, while neigh-
bors craned
Their heads above the high board
fence, and deigned
To sigh "Poor Dog!" remembering
how they
Had cuffed him, when alive, perchance,
because,
For love of them he leaped to lick
their hands—
Now, that he could not, were they sat-
isfied?
We children thought that, as we crossed
his paws,
And o'er his grave, 'way down the
bottom-lands,
Wrote "Our First Love Lies Here,"
when Old Jack died.

552

WHEN THE HEARSE COMES BACK

A THING 'at's 'bout as tryin' as a healthy man kin meet
Is some poor feller's funeral a-joggin' 'long the street:
The slow hearse and the hosses—slow enough, to say the least,
Fer to even tax the patience of the gentleman deceased!
The low scrunch of the gravel—and the slow grind of the wheels,—
The low, slow go of ev'ry woe 'at ev'rybody feels!
So I ruther like the contrast when I hear the whiplash crack
A quickstep fer the hosses,
   When the
    Hearse
     Comes
      Back!

Meet it goin' to'rds the cimet'ry, you'll want to drap yer eyes—
But ef the plumes don't fetch you, it'll ketch you otherwise—
You'll haf to see the caskit, though you'd ort to look away
And 'conomize and save yer sighs fer any other day!
Yer sympathizin' won't wake up the sleeper from his rest—
Yer tears won't thaw them hands o' his 'at's froze acrost his breast!
And this is why—when airth and sky's a-gittin' blurred and black—
I like the flash and hurry
                When the
                    Hearse
                        Comes
                            Back!

It's not 'cause I don't 'preciate it ain't no time fer jokes,
Ner 'cause I' got no common human feelin' fer the folks;—
I've went to funerals myse'f, and tuk on some, perhaps—
Fer my heart's 'bout as mal'able as any other chap's,—
I've buried father, mother—but I'll haf to jes' git *you*
To "excuse *me*," as the feller says.—The p'int I'm drivin' to
Is, simply, when we're plum broke down and all knocked out o' whack,
It he'ps to shape us up, like,
                When the
                    Hearse
                        Comes
                            Back!

The idy! wadin' round here over shoe-mouth deep in woe,
When they's a graded 'pike o' joy and sunshine, don't you know!
When evening strikes the pastur', cows'll pull out fer the bars,
And skittish-like from out the night'll prance the happy stars.
And so when *my* time comes to die, and I've got ary friend
'At wants expressed my last request—I'll, mebby, rickommend
To drive slow, ef they haf to, goin' 'long the *out'ard* track,
But I'll smile and say, "You speed 'em
                When the
                    Hearse
                        Comes
                            Back!"

553

NESSMUK

I HAIL thee, Nessmuk, for the lofty
tone
Yet simple grace that marks thy
poetry!
True forester thou art, and still to
be,
Even in happier fields than thou hast
known.
Thus, in glad visions, glimpses am I
shown
Of groves delectable—"preserves" for
thee—
Ranged but by friends of thine—I
name thee three:—
First, Chaucer, with his bald old pate
new-grown
With changeless laurel; next, in Lin-
coln-green,
Gold belted, bowed and bugled,
Robin Hood;
And next, Ike Walton, patient and
serene:
These three, O Nessmuk, gathered
hunter-wise,
Are camped on hither slopes of Para-
dise,
To hail thee first and greet thee, as
they should.

554

BACK FROM A TWO-YEARS'
SENTENCE

BACK from a two-years' sentence!
And though it had been ten,
You think, I were scarred no deeper
In the eyes of my fellow men.

"My fellow men"?—sounds like a satire,
You think—and I so allow,
Here in my home since childhood,
Yet more than a stranger now!

Pardon!—Not wholly a stranger,—
For I have a wife and child:
That woman has wept for two long
years,
And yet last night she smiled!—
Smiled, as I leapt from the platform
Of the midnight train, and then—
All that I knew was that smile of hers,
And our babe in my arms again!

Back from a two-years' sentence—
But I've thought the whole thing
through,—
A hint of it came when the bars swung
back
And I looked straight up in the blue
Of the blessed skies with my hat off!
Oho! I've a wife and child:
That woman has wept for two long
years,
And yet last night she smiled!

555

TO ROBERT LOUIS STEVENSON

ON HIS FIRST VISIT TO AMERICA

ROBERT LOUIS STEVENSON!
Blue the lift and braw the dawn
O' yer comin' here amang
Strangers wha hae luved ye lang!
Strangers tae ye we maun be,
Yet tae us ye're kenned a wee
By the writin's ye hae done,
Robert Louis Stevenson.

Syne ye've pit yer pen tae sic'
Tales it stabbt us tae the quick—
Whiles o' tropic isles an' seas
An' o' gowden treesuries—
Tales o' deid men's banes; an' tales
Swete as sangs o' nightingales
When the nune o' mirk's begun—
Robert Louis Stevenson.

Sae we hail thee! nane the less
For the "burr" that ye caress
Wi' yer denty tongue o' Scots,
Makin' words forget-me-nots
O' yer bonnie braes that were
Sung o' Burns the Poemer—
And that later lavrock, one
Robert Louis Stevenson.

556

THEM FLOWERS

TAKE a feller 'at's sick and laid up
    on the shelf,
All shaky, and ga'nted, and pore—
Jes' all so knocked out he can't handle
    hisself
    With a stiff upper-lip any more;
Shet him up all alone in the gloom of
    a room
As dark as the tomb, and as grim,
And then take and send him some
    roses in bloom,
    And you can have fun out o' him!

You've ketched him 'fore now—when
    his liver was sound
    And his appetite notched like a
    saw—
A-mockin' you, maybe, fer romancin'
    round
    With a big posy-bunch in yer paw;

But you ketch him, say, when his
    health is away,
And he's flat on his back in distress,
And *then* you kin trot out yer little
    bokay
    And not be insulted, I guess!

You see, it's like this, what his weak-
    nesses is,—
    Them flowers makes him think of
    the days
Of his innocent youth, and that mother
    o' his,
    And the roses that *she* us't to raise:—
So here, all alone with the roses you
    send—
    Bein' sick and all trimbly and
    faint,—
My eyes is—my eyes is—my eyes is—
    old friend—
    Is a-leakin'—I'm blamed ef they
    ain't!

557

THE ROBINS' OTHER NAME

IN the Orchard-Days, when you
    Children look like blossoms, too;
Bessie, with her jaunty ways
And trim poise of head and face,
Must have looked superior
Even to the blossoms,—for
Little Winnie once averred
Bessie looked just like the bird
Tilted on the topmost spray
Of the apple boughs in May,
With the redbreast, and the strong,
Clear, sweet warble of his song.—
"I don't know their *name*," Win said—
"I ist *maked* a name instead."—
So forever afterwards
We called robins "Bessie-birds."

558

THE RAIN

I

THE rain! the rain! the rain!
   It gushed from the skies and
     streamed
Like awful tears; and the sick man
     thought
   How pitiful it seemed!
And he turned his face away
   And stared at the wall again,
His hopes nigh dead and his heart
     worn out.
   O the rain! the rain! the rain!

II

The rain! the rain! the rain!
   And the broad stream brimmed the
     shores;
And ever the river crept over the
     reeds
   And the roots of the sycamores:
A corpse swirled by in a drift
   Where the boat had snapt its chain—
And a hoarse-voiced mother shrieked
     and raved.
   O the rain! the rain! the rain!

III

The rain! the rain! the rain!—
   Pouring, with never a pause,
Over the fields and the green byways—
   How beautiful it was!
And the new-made man and wife
   Stood at the window-pane
Like two glad children kept from
     school.
   O the rain! the rain! the rain!

559

TO EDGAR WILSON NYE

O "WILLIAM," in thy blithe com-
    panionship
  What liberty is mine—what sweet re-
    lease
  From clamorous strife, and yet what
    boisterous peace!
Ho! ho! it is thy fancy's finger-tip
That dints the dimple now, and kinks
    the lip
That scarce may sing, in all this glad
    increase
  Of merriment! So, pray-thee, do not
    cease
To cheer me thus;—for, underneath the
    quip
Of thy droll sorcery, the wrangling fret
  Of all distress is stilled—no syllable
Of sorrow vexeth me—no tear-drops
    wet
  My teeming lids save those that leap
    to tell
Thee thou'st a guest that overweepeth,
    yet
  Only because thou jokest overwell.

560

A DISCOURAGING MODEL

JUST the airiest, fairiest slip of a
    thing,
With a Gainsborough hat, like a but-
    terfly's wing,
Tilted up at one side with the jauntiest
    air,
And a knot of red roses sewn in under
    there
  Where the shadows are lost in her
    hair.

Then a cameo face, carven in on a
    ground
Of that shadowy hair where the roses
    are wound;
And the gleam of a smile, O as fair
    and as faint
And as sweet as the masters of old used
    to paint
    Round the lips of their favorite
    saint!

And that lace at her throat—and the
    fluttering hands
Snowing there, with a grace that no
    art understands,
The flakes of their touches—first flut-
    tering at
The bow—then the roses—the hair—
    and then that
    Little tilt of the Gainsborough hat.

Ah, what artist on earth with a model
    like this,
Holding not on his palette the tint of
    a kiss,
Nor a pigment to hint of the hue of
    her hair
Nor the gold of her smile—O what
    artist could dare
    To expect a result half so fair?

561

THE SERENADE

THE midnight is not more bewil-
    dering
    To her drowsed eyes, than, to her
    ears, the sound
    Of dim, sweet singing voices, inter-
    wound
With purl of flute and subtle twang of
    string,
Strained through the lattice, where the
    roses cling
    And, with their fragrance, waft the
    notes around
    Her haunted senses. Thirsting be-
    yond bound
Of her slow-yielding dreams, the lilt
    and swing
    Of the mysterious, delirious tune,
She drains like some strange opiate,
    with awed eyes
    Upraised against her casement,
    where, aswoon,
The stars fail from her sight, and up
    the skies
    Of alien azure rolls the full round
    moon
    Like some vast bubble blown of
    summer noon.

562

DOC SIFERS

OF all the doctors I could cite you to in this-'ere town
    Doc Sifers is my favorite, jes' take him up and down!
Count in the Bethel Neighberhood, and Rollins, and Big Bear,
And Sifers' standin' jes' as good as ary doctor's there!

There's old Doc Wick, and Glenn, and Hall, and Wurgler, and McVeigh,
But I'll buck Sifers 'g'inst 'em all and down 'em any day!

Most old Wick ever knowed, I s'pose, was *whisky!* Wurgler—well,
He et morphine—ef actions shows, and facts' reliable!

But Sifers—though he ain't no sot, he's got his faults; and yit
When you *git* Sifers onc't, you've got *a doctor,* don't fergit!
He ain't much at his office, er his house, er anywhere
You'd natchurly think certain fer to ketch the feller there.—

But don't blame Doc: he's got all sorts o' cur'ous notions—as
The feller says, his odd-come-shorts, like smart men mostly has.
He'll more'n like be potter'n' 'round the Blacksmith Shop; er in
Some back lot, spadin' up the ground, er gradin' it ag'in.

Er at the work bench, planin' things; er buildin' little traps
To ketch birds; galvenizin' rings; er graftin' plums, perhaps.
Make anything! good as the best!—a gun-stock—er a flute;
He whittled out a set o' chesstmen onc't o' laurel root.

Durin' the Army—got his trade o' surgeon there—I own
To-day a finger-ring Doc made out of a Sesesh bone!
An' glued a fiddle onc't fer me—jes' all so busted you
'D 'a' throwed the thing away, but he fixed her as good as new!

And take Doc, now, in *ager,* say, er *biles,* er *rheumatiz,*
And all afflictions thataway, and he's the best they is!
Er janders—milksick—I don't keer—k-yore anything he tries—
A abscess; getherin' in yer yeer; er granilated eyes!

There was the Widder Daubenspeck they all give up fer dead;
A blame cowbuncle on her neck, and clean out of her head!
First had this doctor, what's-his-name, from "Pudblesburg," and then
This little red-head, "Burnin' Shame" they call him—Dr. Glenn.

And they "consulted" on the case, and claimed she'd haf to die,—
I jes' was joggin' by the place, and heerd her dorter cry,
And stops and calls her to the fence; and I-says-I, "Let me
Send Sifers—bet you fifteen cents he'll k-yore her!" "Well," says she,

"Light out!" she says: And, lipp-tee-cut, I loped in town, and rid
'Bout two hours more to find him, but I kussed him when I did!
He was down at the Gunsmith Shop a-stuffin' birds! Says he,
"My sulky's broke." Says I, "You hop right on and ride with me!"

I got him there.—"Well, Aunty, ten days k'yores you," Sifers said,
"But what's yer idy livin' when yer jes' as good as dead?"
And there's Dave Banks—jes' back from war without a scratch—one day
Got ketched up in a sickle-bar, a reaper runaway.—

His shoulders, arms, and hands and legs jes' sawed in strips! And Jake
Dunn starts fer Sifers—feller begs to shoot him fer God-sake.
Doc, 'course, was gone, but he had penned the notice, "At Big Bear—
Be back to-morry; Gone to 'tend the Bee Convention there."

But Jake, he tracked him—rid and rode the whole endurin' night!
And 'bout the time the roosters crowed they both hove into sight.
Doc had to ampitate, but 'greed to save Dave's arms, and swore
He could 'a' saved his legs ef he'd be'n there the day before.

Like when his wife's own mother died 'fore Sifers could be found,
And all the neighbors fer and wide a' all jes' chasin' round;
Tel finally—I had to laugh—it's jes' like Doc, you know,—
Was learnin' fer to telegraph, down at the old deepo.

But all they're faultin' Sifers fer, there's none of 'em kin say
He's biggoty, er keerless, er not posted any way;
He ain't built on the common plan of doctors nowadays,
He's jes' a great, big, brainy man—that's where the trouble lays!

563

AFTERWHILES

W HERE are they—the After-
whiles—
Luring us the lengthening miles
Of our lives? Where is the dawn
With the dew across the lawn
Stroked with eager feet the far
Way the hills and valleys are?
Where the sun that smites the frown
Of the eastward-gazer down?
Where the rifted wreaths of mist
O'er us, tinged with amethyst,
Round the mountain's steep defiles?
Where are all the afterwhiles?

Afterwhile—and we will go
Thither, yon, and to and fro—
From the stifling city streets
To the country's cool retreats—
From the riot to the rest
Where hearts beat the placidest:
Afterwhile, and we will fall
Under breezy trees, and loll
In the shade, with thirsty sight
Drinking deep the blue delight
Of the skies that will beguile
Us as children—afterwhile.

Afterwhile—and one intends
To be gentler to his friends,—
To walk with them, in the hush
Of still evenings, o'er the plush

Of home-leading fields, and stand
Long at parting, hand in hand:
One, in time, will joy to take
New resolves for some one's sake,
And wear then the look that lies
Clear and pure in other eyes—
He will soothe and reconcile
His own conscience—afterwhile.

Afterwhile—we have in view
A far scene to journey to,—
Where the old home is, and where
The old mother waits us there,
Peering, as the time grows late,
Down the old path to the gate.—
How we'll click the latch that locks
In the pinks and hollyhocks,
And leap up the path once more
Where she waits us at the door!—
How we'll greet the dear old smile,
And the warm tears—afterwhile!

Ah, the endless afterwhiles!—
Leagues on leagues, and miles on miles,
In the distance far withdrawn,
Stretching on, and on, and on,
Till the fancy is footsore
And faints in the dust before
The last milestone's granite face,
Hacked with: Here Beginneth Space.
O far glimmering worlds and wings,
Mystic smiles and beckonings,
Lead us through the shadowy aisles,
Out into the afterwhiles.

564

A HOME-MADE FAIRY TALE

BUD, come here to your uncle a
spell,
And I'll tell you something you mustn't
tell—

For it's a secret and shore-'nuf true,
And maybe I oughtn't to tell it to
you!—
But out in the garden, under the shade
Of the apple trees, where we romped
and played
Till the moon was up, and you thought
I'd gone
Fast asleep,—That was all put on!
For I was a-watchin' something queer
Goin' on there in the grass, my dear!—
'Way down deep in it, there I see
A little dude-Fairy who winked at me,
And snapped his fingers, and laughed
as low
And fine as the whine of a mus-kee-to!
I kept still—watchin' him closer—and
I noticed a little guitar in his hand,
Which he leant 'g'inst a little dead bee
—and laid
His cigarette down on a clean grass-
blade,
And then climbed up on the shell of
a snail—
Carefully dusting his swallowtail—
And pulling up, by a waxed web-
thread,
This little guitar, you remember, I
said!
And there he trinkled and trilled a
tune,—
"My Love, so Fair, Tans in the Moon!"
Till, presently, out of the clover-top
He seemed to be singing to, came,
k'pop!
The purtiest, daintiest Fairy face
In all this world, or any place!
Then the little ser'nader waved his
hand,
As much as to say, "We'll excuse *you!*"
and
I heard, as I squinted my eyelids to,
A kiss like the drip of a drop of dew!

565

A VOICE FROM THE FARM

IT is my dream to have you here
with me,
Out of the heated city's dust and
din—
Here where the colts have room to
gambol in,
And kine to graze, in clover to the
knee.
I want to see your wan face happily
Lit with the wholesome smiles that
have not been
In use since the old games you used
to win
When we pitched horseshoes: And I
want to be
At utter loaf with you in this dim
land
Of grove and meadow, while the
crickets make
Our own talk tedious, and the bat
wields
His bulky flight, as we cease converse
and
In a dusk like velvet smoothly take
Our way toward home across the
dewy fields.

566

THE OLD HOME BY THE MILL

THIS is "The Old Home by the Mill"—fer we still call it so,
Although the *old mill*, roof and sill, is all gone long ago,
The old home, though, and the old folks—the old spring, and a few
Old cattails, weeds and hartychokes, is left to welcome you!

Here, Marg'et!—fetch the man a *tin* to drink out of! Our spring
Keeps kindo'-sorto' cavin' in, but don't *"taste"* anything!
She's kindo' *agin'*, Marg'et is—"the *old* process"—like me,
All ham-stringed up with rhumatiz, and on in seventy-three.

Jest me and Marg'et lives alone here—like in long ago;
The childern all putt off and gone, and married, don't you know?
One's millin' 'way out West somewhare; two other miller-boys
In Minnyopolis they air; and one's in Illinoise.

The *oldest* gyrl—the first that went—married and died right here;
The next lives in Winn's Settlement—fer purt' nigh thirty year!
And youngest one—was allus fer the old home here—but no!—
Her man turns in and he packs *her* 'way off to Idyho!

I don't miss them like *Marg'et* does—'cause I got *her*, you see;
And when she pines for them—that's 'cause *she's* only jest got *me!*

I laugh, and joke her 'bout it all.—But talkin' sense, I'll say,
When she was tuk so bad last Fall, I laughed then t'other way!

I hain't so favor'ble impressed 'bout *dyin'*; but ef I
Found I was only second-best when *us two* come to die,
I'd 'dopt the "new process," in full, ef *Marg'et* died, you see,—
I'd jest crawl in my grave and pull the green grass over me!

567

THE OLD MAN AND JIM

OLD man never had much to say—
    'Ceptin' to Jim,—
And Jim was the wildest boy he had—
    And the old man jes' wrapped up in
        him!
Never heerd him speak but once
Er twice in my life,—and first time
        was
When the army broke out, and Jim he
        went,
The old man backin' him, fer three
        months;
And all 'at I heerd the old man say
Was, jes' as we turned to start away,—
    "Well, good-by, Jim:
        Take keer of yourse'f!"

'Peared-like, he was more satisfied
Jes' *lookin'* at Jim
And likin' him all to hisse'f-like, see?—
    'Cause he was jes' wrapped up in
        him!
And over and over I mind the day
The old man come and stood round in
        the way
While we was drillin', a-watchin' Jim—
And down at the deepot a-heerin' him
        say,
    "Well, good-by, Jim:
        Take keer of yourse'f!"

Never was nothin' about the *farm*
    Disting'ished Jim;
Neighbors all ust to wonder why
    The old man 'peared wrapped up in
        him:
But when Cap. Biggler he writ back
'At Jim was the bravest boy we had
In the whole dern rigiment, white er
        black,
And his fightin' good as his farmin'
        bad—
'At he had led, with a bullet clean
Bored through his thigh, and carried
        the flag
Through the bloodiest battle you ever
        seen.—
The old man wound up a letter to him
'At Cap. read to us, 'at said: "Tell Jim
        Good-by,
    And take keer of hisse'f!"

Jim come home jes' long enough
    To take the whim
'At he'd like to go back in the calvery—
    And the old man jes' wrapped up in
        him!
Jim 'lowed 'at he'd had sich luck afore,
Guessed he'd tackle her three years
        more.
And the old man give him a colt he'd
        raised,
And follered him over to Camp Ben
        Wade,
And laid around fer a week er so,

Watchin' Jim on dress-parade—
Tel finally he rid away,
And last he heerd was the old man
    say,—
  "Well, good-by, Jim:
    Take keer of yourse'f!"

Tuk the papers, the old man did,
  A-watchin' fer Jim—
Fully believin' he'd make his mark
  Some way—jes' wrapped up in
    him!—
And many a time the word 'u'd come
'At stirred him up like the tap of a
    drum—
At Petersburg, fer instunce, where
Jim rid right into their cannons there,
And *tuk* 'em, and p'inted 'em t'other
    way,
And socked it home to the boys in
    gray,
As they scooted fer timber, and on and
    on—
Jim a lieutenant and one arm gone,
And the old man's words in his mind
    all day,—
  "Well, good-by, Jim:
    Take keer of yourse'f!"

Think of a private, now, perhaps,
  We'll say like Jim,
'At's clumb clean up to the shoulder-
    straps—
  And the old man jes' wrapped up in
    him!
Think of him—with the war plum'
    through,
And the glorious old Red-White-and-
    Blue
A-laughin' the news down over Jim,
And the old man, bendin' over him—
The surgeon turnin' away with tears
'At hadn't leaked fer years and years,

As the hand of the dyin' boy clung to
His father's, the old voice in his ears,—
  "Well, good-by, Jim:
    Take keer of yourse'f!"

568

OUR OLD FRIEND NEVERFAIL

O IT'S good to ketch a relative 'at's
    richer and don't run
When you holler out to hold up, and'll
    joke and have his fun;
It's good to hear a man called bad and
    then find out he's not,
Er strike some chap they call luke-
    warm 'at's really red-hot;
It's good to know the Devil's painted
    jes' a leetle black,
And it's good to have most anybody
    pat you on the back;—
But jes' the best thing in the world's
    our old friend Neverfail,
When he wags yer hand as honest as
    an old dog wags his tail!

I like to strike the man I owe the
    same time I can pay,
And take back things I've borried, and
    su'prise folks thataway;
I like to find out that the man I voted
    fer last fall,
That didn't git elected, was a scoun-
    drel after all;
I like the man that likes the pore and
    he'ps 'em when he can;
I like to meet a ragged tramp 'at's still
    a gentleman;
But most I like—with you, my boy—
    our old friend Neverfail,
When he wags yer hand as honest as
    an old dog wags his tail!

569

DAN O'SULLIVAN

DAN O'SULLIVAN: It's your
Lips have kissed "The Blarney,"
sure!—
To be trillin' praise av me,
Dhrippin' swhate wid poethry!—
Not that I'd not have ye sing—
Don't lave off for anything—
Jusht be aisy whilst the fit
Av me head shwells up to it!

Dade and thrue, I'm not the man,
Whilst yer singin', loike ye can,
To cry shtop because ye've blesht
My songs more than all the resht:—
I'll not be the b'y to ax
Any shtar to wane or wax,
Or ax any clock that's woun'
To run up inshtid av down!

Whist yez! Dan O'Sullivan!—
Him that made the Irishman
Mixt the birds in wid the dough,
And the dew and mistletoe
Wid the whusky in the quare
Muggs av us—and here we air,
Three parts right, and three parts
wrong,
Shpiked wid beauty, wit and song!

570

AT "THE LITERARY"

FOLKS in town, I reckon, thinks
They git all the fun they air
Runnin' loose 'round!—but, 'y jinks!
We' got fun, and fun to spare,
Right out here amongst the ash

And oak timber ever'where!
Some folks else kin cut a dash
'Sides town-people, don't fergit!—
'Specially in *winter*-time,
When they's snow, and roads is fit.
In them circumstances I'm
Resig-nated to my lot—
Which putts me in mind o' what
'S called "The Literary."

Us folks in the country sees
Lots o' fun!—Take spellin'-school;
Er ole hoe-down jamborees;
Er revivals; er ef you'll
Tackle taffy-pullin's you
Kin git fun, and quite a few!—
Same with huskin's. But all these
Kind o' frolics they hain't new
By a hunderd year' er two
Cipher on it as you please!
But I'll tell you what I jest
Think walks over all the rest—
Anyway it suits *me* best,—
That's "The Literary."

First they started it—" 'y gee!"
Thinks-says I, "this settle-ment
'S gittin' too high toned fer me!"
But when all begin to jine,
And I heerd *Izory* went,
I jest kind o' drapped in line,
Like you've seen some sandy, thin,
Scrawny shoat putt fer the crick
Down some pig-trail through the thick
Spice-bresh, where the whole drove's
been
'Bout six weeks 'fore he gits in!—
"Can't tell nothin'," I-says-ee,
" 'Bout it tel you go and see
Their blame 'Literary'!"

Very first night I was there
I was 'p'inted to be what

They call "Critic"—so's a fair
And square jedgment could be got
On the pieces 'at was read,
And on the debate,—"Which air
Most destructive element,
Fire er worter?" Then they hed
Compositions on "Content,"
"Death," and "Botany"; and Tomps
He read one on "Dreenin' Swamps"
I p'nounced the boss, and said,
"*So* fur, 'at's the best thing read
        In yer 'Literary'!"

Then they *sung* some—tel I called
Order, and got back ag'in
In the critic's cheer, and hauled
All o' the p'formers in:—
Mandy Brizendine read one
I fergit; and Doc's was "Thought";
And Sarepty's, hern was "None
Air Denied 'at Knocks"; and Daut—
Fayette Strawnse's little niece—
She got up and spoke a piece:
Then Izory she read hern—
"Best thing in the whole concern,"
I-says-ee; "now le' 's adjourn
        This-here 'Literary'!"

They was some contendin'—yit
We broke up in harmony.
Road outside as white as grit,
And as slick as slick could be!—
I'd fetched 'Zory in my sleigh,—
And I had a heap to say,
Drivin' back—in fact, I driv
'Way around the old north way,
Where the Daubenspeckses live.
'Zory allus—'fore that night—
Never 'peared to feel jest right
In my company.—You see,
On'y thing on earth saved me
        Was that "Literary"!

571

SHE "DISPLAINS" IT

"HAD, too!"
        "Hadn't, neither!"
So contended Bess and May—
    Neighbor children, who were boast-
        ing
Of their grandmammas, one day.

    "Had, too!"
        "Hadn't, neither!"
All the difference begun
    By May's saying she'd *two* grand-
        mas—
While poor Bess had only one.

    "Had, too!"
        "Hadn't, neither!"
Tossing curls, and kinks of friz!—
    "How could you have *two* gran'-
        muvvers
When ist *one* is all they is?"

    "Had, too!"
        "Hadn't, neither!—
'Cause ef you had *two*," said Bess,
    "You'd *displain* it!" Then May an-
        swered,
"My gran'mas wuz *twins,* I guess!"

572

DEAD, MY LORDS

DEAD, my lords and gentlemen!—
        Stilled the tongue, and stayed
            the pen;
Cheek unflushed and eye unlit—
Done with life, and glad of it.

Curb your praises now as then:
Dead, my lords and gentlemen.—
What he wrought found its reward
In the tolerance of the Lord.

Ye who fain had barred his path,
Dread ye now this look he hath?—

Dead, my lords and gentlemen—
Dare ye not smile back again?

Low he lies, yet high and great
Looms he, lying thus in state.—
How exalted o'er ye when
Dead, my lords and gentlemen!

573

A MAN BY THE NAME OF BOLUS

A MAN by the name of Bolus—(all 'at we'll ever know
Of the stranger's name, I reckon—and I'm kind o' glad it's so!)—
Got off here, Christmas morning, looked 'round the town, and then
Kind o' sized up the folks, I guess, and—went away again!

The fac's is, this man Bolus got "run in," Christmas-day;
The town turned out to see it, and cheered, and blocked the way;
And they dragged him 'fore the Mayor—fer he couldn't er *wouldn't* **walk—**
And socked him down fer trial—though he couldn't er *wouldn't* **talk!**

Drunk? They was no doubt of it!—W'y, the marshal of the town
Laughed and testified 'at he fell *up*-stairs 'stid o' *down!*
This man by the name of Bolus?—W'y, he even drapped his jaw
And snored on through his "hearin' "—drunk as you ever saw!

One feller spit in his boot-leg, and another 'n' drapped a small
Little chunk o' ice down his collar,—but he didn't wake at all!
And they all nearly split when his Honor said, in one of his witty **ways,**
To "chalk it down fer him, 'Called away—be back in thirty days!' "

That's where this man named Bolus slid, kind o' like in a fit,
Flat on the floor; and—drat my ears! I hear 'em a-laughin' yit!
Somebody fetched Doc Sifers from jes' acrost the hall—
And all Doc said was, "Morphine! We're too late!" and that's **all!**

That's how they found his name out—piece of a letter 'at read:
"Your wife has lost her reason, and little Nathan's dead—
Come ef you kin,—fergive *her*—but, Bolus, as fer *me,*
This hour I send a bullet through where my heart *ort* to be!"

Man by the name of Bolus!—As his revilers broke
Fer the open air, 'peared-like, to me, I heerd a voice 'at spoke—
Man by the name of Bolus! git up from where you lay—
Git up and smile white at 'em, with your hands crossed thataway!

574

THE TRAVELING MAN

I

COULD I pour out the nectar the
    gods only can,
I would fill up my glass to the brim
And drink the success of the Travel-
    ing Man,
And the house represented by him;
And could I but tincture the glorious
    draught
With his smiles, as I drank to him
    then,
And the jokes he has to'd and the
    laughs he has laughed,
I would fill up the goblet again—

And drink to the sweetheart who gave
    him good-by
With a tenderness thrilling him this
Very hour, as he thinks of the tear in
    her eye
That salted the sweet of her kiss;
To her truest of hearts and her fairest
    of hands
I would drink, with all serious
    prayers,
Since the heart she must trust is a
    Traveling Man's,
And as warm as the ulster he wears.

II

I would drink to the wife, with the
    babe on her knee,
Who awaits his returning in vain—
Who breaks his brave letters so tremu-
    lously
And reads them again and again!
And I'd drink to the feeble old mother
    who sits

At the warm fireside of her son
And murmurs and weeps o'er the
    stocking she knits,
As she thinks of the wandering one.

I would drink a long life and a health
    to the friends
Who have met him with smiles an l
    with cheer—
To the generous hand that the land
    lord extends
To the wayfarer journeying here:
And I pledge, when he turns from this
    earthly abode
And pays the last fare that he can,
Mine Host of the Inn at the End of
    the Road
Will welcome the Traveling Man!

575

THE ABSENCE OF LITTLE
WESLEY

SENCE little Wesley went, the place
    seems all so strange and still—
W'y, I miss his yell o' "Gran-pap!" as
    I'd miss the whipperwill!
And to think I ust to *scold* him fer his
    everlastin' noise,
When I on'y rickollect him as the best
    o' little boys!
I wisht a hunderd times a day 'at he'd
    come trompin' in,
And all the noise he ever made was
    twic't as loud ag'in!—
It 'u'd seem like some soft music
    played on some fine insturment,
'Longside o' this loud lonesomeness,
    sence little Wesley went!

Of course the clock don't tick no louder
    than it ust to do—

Yit now they's times it 'pears like it
  'u'd bu'st itse'f in two!
And let a rooster, suddent-like, crow
  som'ers clos't around,
And seems's ef, mighty nigh it, it 'u'd
  lift me off the ground!
And same with all the cattle when they
  bawl around the bars,
In the red o' airly morning, er the
  dusk and dew and stars,
When the neighbers' boys 'at passes
  never stop, but jes' go on,
A-whistlin' kind o' to theirse'v's—sence
  little Wesley's gone!

And then, o' nights, when Mother's
  settin' up oncommon late,
A-bilin' pears er somepin', and I set
  and smoke and wait,
Tel the moon out through the winder
  don't look bigger'n a dime,
And things keeps gittin' stiller—stiller
  —stiller all the time,—
I've ketched myse'f a-wishin' like—as
  I clumb on the cheer
To wind the clock, as I hev done fer
  more'n fifty year—
A-wishin' 'at the time hed come fer
  us to go to bed,
With our last prayers, and our last
  tears, sence little Wesley's dead!

576

WHEN THE GREEN GITS BACK
IN THE TREES

IN spring, when the green gits back
  in the trees,
And the sun comes out and *stays,*
And yer boots pulls on with a good
  tight squeeze,

And you think of yer barefoot days;
When you *ort* to work and you want
  to *not,*
And you and yer wife agrees
It's time to spade up the garden-lot,
  When the green gits back in the
    trees—
    Well! work is the least o' *my*
      idees
    When the green, you know, gits
      back in the trees!

When the green gits back in the trees,
  and bees
  Is a-buzzin' aroun' ag'in
In that kind of a lazy go-as-you-please
  Old gait they bum roun' in;
When the groun's all bald whare the
  hay rick stood,
  And the crick's riz, and the breeze
Coaxes the bloom in the old dogwood,
  And the green gits back in the
    trees,—
    I like, as I say, in sich scenes as
      these,
    The time when the green gits back
      in the trees!

When the whole tail-fethers o' Winter-
  time
  Is all pulled out and gone!
And the sap it thaws and begins to
  climb,
  And the swet it starts out on
A feller's forred, a-gittin' down
  At the old spring on his knees—
I kindo' like jest a-loaferin' roun'.
  When the green gits back in the
    trees—
    Jest a-potterin' roun' as I—durn—
      please—
    When the green, you know, gits
      back in the trees!

577

HOW IT HAPPENED

I 'GOT to *thinkin'* of her—both her parunts dead and gone—
And all her sisters married off, and none but her and John
A-livin' all alone thare in that lonesome sorto' way,
And him a blame' old bachelor, confirm'der ev'ry day!
I'd knowed 'em all, from childern, and theyr daddy from the time
He settled in the neghborhood, and hadn't ary a dime
Er dollar, when he married, fer to start housekeepin' on!—
So I got to *thinkin'* of her—both her parunts dead and gone!

I got to *thinkin'* of her; and a-wundern what *she* done
That all *her sisters* kep' a-gittin' married, one by one,
And her without *no* chances—and the best girl of the pack—
A' old maid, with her hands, you might say, tied behind her back!
And *Mother,* too, afore she died,—*she* ust to jest take on,
When none of 'em wuz left, you know, but Evaline and John,
And jest declare to goodness 'at the young men must be bline
To not see what a wife they'd git ef they got Evaline!

I got to *thinkin'* of her: In my great affliction she
Wuz sich a comfort to us, and so kind and neghborly,—
She'd come, and leave her housework, fer to he'p out little Jane,
And talk of *her own* mother 'at she'd never see again—
They'd sometimes *cry* together—though, fer the most part, she
Would have the child so rickonciled and happy-like 'at we
Felt lonesomer'n ever when she'd putt her bonnet on
And say she'd railly *haf* to be a-gittin' back to John!

I got to *thinkin'* of her, as I say,—and more and more
I'd think of her dependence, and the burdens 'at she bore,—
Her parunts both a-bein' dead, and all her sisters gone
And married off, and her a-livin' thare alone with John—
You might say jest a-toilin' and a-slavin' out her life
Fer a man 'at hadn't pride enugh to git hisse'f a wife—
'Less some one married *Evaline* and packed her off some day!—
So I got to *thinkin'* of her—and—It happened *thataway.*

578

GLADNESS

MY ole man named Silas: he
Dead long 'fo' ole Gin'l Lee
S'rendah, whense de wah wuz done.
Yanks dey tuk de plantation—
Mos' high-handed evah you see!—
Das rack round', an' fiah an' bu'n,
An' jab de beds wid deir bay-net-gun,
An' sweah we niggahs all scotch-free,—
An' Massah John C. Pemberton
Das tuk an' run!

"Gord Armighty, marm," he 'low,
"He'p you an' de chillen now!"
Blaze crack out 'n de roof inside
Tel de big house all das charified!
Smoke roll out 'n de ole haymow
An' de wa'house do'—an' de fiah das
roah—
An' all dat 'backer, 'bout half dried,
Hit smell das fried!

Nelse, my ol'est boy, an' John,—
Atter de baby das wuz bo'n,
Erlongse dem times, an' lak ter 'a'
died,
An' Silas he be'n slip an' gone
'Bout eight weeks ter de Union side,—
Dem two boys dey start fo' ter fine
An' jine deir fader acrost de line.
Ovahseeah he wade an' tromp
Eveh-which-way fo' to track 'em
down—
Sic de bloodhoun' fro' de swamp—
An' bring de news dat John he
drown'—
But dey save de houn'!

Someway ner Nelse git fru'
An' fight fo' de ole Red, White, an'
Blue,

Lak his fader is, ter er heart's delight—
An' nen crope back wid de news, one
night—
Sayes, "Fader's killed in a scrimmage-
fight,
An' saunt farewell ter ye all, an' sayes
Fo' ter name de baby 'Gladness,' 'caze
Mighty nigh she 'uz be'n borned free!"
An' de boy he smile so strange at me
I sayes, "Yo' 's hurt *yo'se'f!*" an' he
Sayes, "I's killed, too—an' dat's all
else!"
An' dah lay Nelse!

Hope an' Angrish, de twins, be'n sole
'Fo' dey mo' 'n twelve year ole:
An' Mary Magdaline sole too.
An' dah I's lef', wid Knox-Andrew,
An' Lily, an' Maje, an' Margaret,
An' little gal-babe, 'at's borned dat new
She scaisely ole fo' ter be named yet—
Less'n de name 'at Si say to—
An' co'se hit *do.*

An' I taken dem chillen, evah one
(An' a-oh my Mastah's will be done!),
An' I break fo' de Norf, whah dey all
raised free
(An' a-oh good Mastah, come git me!).
Knox-Andrew, on de day he died,
Lef' his fambly er shop an' er lot ber-
side;
An' Maje die ownin' er team—an' he
Lef' all ter me.

Lily she work at de Gran' Hotel—
(Mastah! Mastah! take me—do!)—
An' Lily she ain' married well:
He stob a man—an' she die too;
An' Margaret she too full er pride

Ter own her kin tel er day she died!
But Gladness!—'t ain' soun' sho'-nuff
   true,—
But she teached school!—an' er white
   folks, too,
Ruspec' dat gal 'mos' high ez I do!—
'Caze she 'uz de bes' an' de mos' high
   bred—
De las' chile bo'n, an' de las chile dead,
   O' all ten head!

. . . .

Gladness! Gladness! a-oh my chile!
Wa'm my soul in yo' sweet smile!
Daughter o' Silas! o-rise an' sing
Tel er heart-beat pat lak er pigeon-
   wing!
Sayes, O Gladness! wake dem eyes—
Sayes, a-lif' dem folded han's, an' rise—
Sayes, a-coax me erlong ter Paradise,
   An' a-hail de King,
      O Gladness!

579

THE WIFE-BLESSED

IN youth he wrought, with eyes ablur,
   Lorn-faced and long of hair—
In youth—in youth he painted her
   A sister of the air—
Could clasp her not, but felt the stir
   Of pinions everywhere.

She lured his gaze, in braver days,
   And tranced him siren-wise;
And he did paint her, through a haze
   Of sullen paradise,

With scars of kisses on her face
   And embers in her eyes.

And now—nor dream nor wild con-
   ceit—
Though faltering, as before—
Through tears he paints her, as is meet,
   Tracing the dear face o'er
With lilied patience meek and sweet
   As Mother Mary wore.

580

ROBERT BURNS WILSON

WHAT intuition named thee?—
   Through what thrill
Of the awed soul came the command
   divine
Into the mother-heart, foretelling
   thine
Should palpitate with his whose rap-
   tures will
Sing on while daisies bloom and lav-
   rocks trill
   Their undulating ways up through
      the fine
   Fair mists of heavenly reaches? Thy
      pure line
Falls as the dew of anthems, quiring
   still
The sweeter since the Scottish singer
   raised
   His voice therein, and, quit of every
      stress
   Of earthly ache and longing and
      despair,
Knew certainly each simple thing he
   praised
   Was no less worthy, for its lowliness,
      Than any joy of all the glory
         There.

COMPLETE POETICAL WORKS 419

581

'MONGST THE HILLS O' SOMERSET

'MONGST the Hills o' Somerset
Wisht I was a-roamin' yet!
My feet won't get usen to
These low lands I'm trompin' through.
Wisht I could go back there, and
Stroke the long grass with my hand,
Kind o' like my sweetheart's hair
Smoothed out underneath it there!
Wisht I could set eyes once more
On our shadders, on before,
Climbin', in the airly dawn,
Up the slopes 'at love growed on
Natchurl as the violet
'Mongst the Hills o' Somerset!

How 't 'u'd rest a man like me
Jes' fer 'bout an hour to be
Up there where the morning air
Could reach out and ketch me there!—
Snatch my breath away, and then
Rensh and give it back again
Fresh as dew, and smellin' of
The old pinks I ust to love,
And a-flavor'n' ever' breeze
With mixt hints o' mulberries
And May-apples, from the thick
Bottom-lands along the crick
Where the fish bit, dry er wet,
'Mongst the Hills o' Somerset!

Like a livin' pictur' things
All comes back: the bluebird swings
In the maple, tongue and bill
Trillin' glory fit to kill!
In the orchard, jay and bee
Ripens the first pears fer me,
And the "Prince's Harvest" they
Tumble to me where I lay

In the clover, provin' still
"A boy's will is the wind's will."
Clean fergot is time, and care,
And thick hearin', and gray hair—
But they's nothin' I ferget
'Mongst the Hills o' Somerset!

Middle-aged—to be edzact
Very middle-aged, in fact,
Yet a-thinkin' back to then,
I'm the same wild boy again!
There's the dear old home once more,
And there's Mother at the door—
Dead, I know, fer thirty year',
Yet she's singin', and I hear;
And there's Jo, and Mary Jane,
And Pap, comin' up the lane!
Dusk's a-fallin'; and the dew,
'Pears like, it's a-fallin' too—
Dreamin' we're all livin' yet
'Mongst the Hills o' Somerset!

582

A PASSING HAIL

LET us rest ourselves a bit!
Worry?—Wave your hand to it—
Kiss your finger-tips and smile
It farewell a little while.

Weary of the weary way
We have come from Yesterday,
Let us fret us not, instead,
Of the weary way ahead.

Let us pause and catch our breath
On the hither side of death,
While we see the tender shoots
Of the grasses—not the roots,—

While we yet look down—not up—
To seek out the buttercup

And the daisy where they wave
O'er the green home of the grave.

Let us launch us smoothly on
The soft billows of the lawn,
And drift out across the main
Of our childish dreams again:

Voyage off, beneath the trees,
O'er the field's enchanted seas,
Where the lilies are our sails,
And our sea-gulls, nightingales:

Where no wilder storm shall beat
Than the wind that waves the wheat,
And no tempest-burst above
The old laughs we used to love:

Lose all troubles—gain release,
Languor, and exceeding peace,
Cruising idly o'er the vast,
Calm mid-ocean of the Past.

Let us rest ourselves a bit!
Worry?—wave your hand to it—
Kiss your finger-tips, and smile
It farewell a little while.

583

"LAST CHRISTMAS WAS A YEAR AGO"

The Old Lady Speaks

LAST Christmas was a year ago,
   Says I to David, I-says-I,
"We're goin' to morning-service, so
You hitch up right away: I'll try
To tell the girls jes' what to do
Fer dinner.—We'll be back by two."

I didn't wait to hear what he
Would more'n like say back to me,
But banged the stable door and flew
Back to the house, jes' plumb chilled
   through.

Cold! *Wooh!* how cold it was! My-oh!
Frost flyin', and the air, you know,
"Jes' sharp enough," heerd David
   swear,
"To shave a man and cut his hair!"
And blow and blow! and snow and
   snow!—
Where it had drifted 'long the fence
And 'crost the road,—some places,
   though,
Jes' swep' clean to the gravel, so
The goin' was as bad fer sleighs
As 'twas fer wagons,—and both ways,
'Twixt snow-drifts and the bare
   ground, I've
Jes' wundered we got through alive;
I hain't saw nothin', 'fore er sence,
'At beat it anywheres, I know—
Last Christmas was a year ago.

And David said, as we set out,
'At Christmas services was 'bout
As cold and wuthless kind o' love
To offer up as he knowed of;
And as fer him, he railly thought
'At the Good Bein' up above
Would think more of us—as He
   ought—
A-stayin' home on sich a day,
And thankin' of Him thataway!
And jawed on, in a' undertone,
'Bout leavin' Lide and Jane alone
There on the place, and me not there
To oversee 'em, and p'are
The stuffin' fer the turkey, and
The sass and all, you understand.

I've allus managed David by
Jes' sayin' *nothin'*. That was why
He'd chased Lide's beau away—'cause
  Lide
She'd allus take up Perry's side
When David tackled him; and so,
Last Christmas was a year ago,—
Er ruther, 'bout *a week afore,*—
David and Perry'd quarr'l'd about
Some tom-fool argyment, you know,
And Pap told him to "Jes' git out
O' there, and not to come no more,
And, when he went, to shet the door!"
And as he passed the winder, we
Saw Perry, white as white could be,
March past, onhitch his hoss, and light
A see-gyar, and lope out o' sight.
Then Lide she come to me and cried!
And I said nothin'—was no need.
And yit, you know, that man jes' got
Right out o' there's ef he'd be'n shot,
P'tendin' he must go and feed
The stock er somepin'. Then I tried
To git the pore girl pacified.

But, gittin' back to—where was we?—
Oh, yes!—where David lectered me
All way to meetin', high and low,
Last Christmas was a year ago:
Fer all the awful cold, they was
A fair attendunce; mostly, though,
The crowd was round the stoves, you
  see,
Thawin' their heels and scrougin' us.
Ef 't 'adn't be'n fer the old Squire
Givin' *his* seat to us, as in
We stomped, a-fairly perishin',
And David could 'a' got no fire,
He'd jes' 'a' drapped there in his
  tracks:
And Squire, as I was tryin' to yit
Make room fer him, says, "No; the
  fac's

Is, *I* got to git up and git
'Ithout no preachin'. Jes' got word—
Trial fer life—can't be deferred!"
And out he putt!

. . . . . . And all way through
The sermont—and a long one, too—
I couldn't he'p but think o' Squire
And us changed round so, and admire
His gintle ways,—to give his warm
Bench up, and have to face the storm.
And when I noticed David he
Was needin' jabbin'—I thought best
To kind o' sort o' let him rest:
'Peared-like he slep' so peacefully!
And then I thought o' home, and how
And what the gyrls was doin' now,
And kind o' prayed, 'way in my breast,
And breshed away a tear er two
As David waked, and church was
  through.

By time we'd "howdyed" round and
  shuck
Hands with the neighbors, must 'a
  tuck
A half-hour longer: ever' one
A-sayin' "Christmas gift!" afore
David er me—so we got none!
But David warmed up, more and more,
And got so jokey-like, and had
His sperits up, and 'peared so glad,
I whispered to him, "S'pose you ast
A passel of 'em come and eat
Their dinners with us. Gyrls's got
A full-and-plenty fer the lot
And all their kin!" So David passed
The invite round: and ever' seat
In ever' wagon-bed and sleigh
Was jes' packed, as we rode away,—
The young folks, mil'd er so along,
A-strikin' up a sleighin'-song,

Tel David laughed and yelled, you
    know,
And jes' whirped up and sent the
    snow
And gravel flyin' thick and fast—
Last Christmas was a year ago.
W'y, that-air seven-mil'd ja'nt we
    come—
Jes' seven mil'd scant from church to
    home—
It didn't 'pear, *that* day, to be
Much furder railly 'n 'bout *three!*

But I was purty squeamish by
The time home hove in sight and I
See two vehickles standin' there
Already. So says I, *"Prepare!"*
All to myse'f. And presently
David he sobered; and says he,
"Hain't that-air Squire Hanch's old
Buggy," he says, "and claybank mare?"
Says I, "Le' 's git in out the cold—
Your company's nigh 'bout froze!" He
    says,
"Whose sleigh's that-air, a-standin'
    there?"
Says I, "It's no odds *whose—you* jes'
Drive to the house and let us out,
'Cause we're jes' *freezin',* nigh about!"

Well, David swung up to the door,
And out we piled. And first I heerd
Jane's voice, then *Lide's,*—I thought
    afore

I reached that gyrl I'd jes' die, shore;
And *when* I reached her, wouldn't
    keered
Much ef I had, I was so glad,
A-kissin' her through my green veil,
And jes' excitin' her so bad,
'At *she* broke down *herse'f*—and Jane,
She cried—and we all hugged again.
And *David?*—David jes' turned pale!—
Looked at the gyrls, and then at me,
Then at the open door—and then—
"Is old Squire Hanch in there?" says he.
The old Squire suddenly stood in
The doorway, with a sneakin' grin.
"Is Perry Anders in there, too?"
Says David, limberin' all through,
As Lide and me both grabbed him, and
Perry stepped out and waved his hand
And says, "Yes, Pap." And David jes'
Stooped and kissed Lide, and says, "I
    guess
Yer *mother's* much to blame as you.
Ef *she* kin resk him, I kin too!"

The dinner we had then hain't no
Bit better'n the one to-day
'At we'll have fer 'em! Hear some sleigh
A-jinglin' now. David, fer *me,*
I wish you'd jes' go out and see
Ef they're in sight yit. It jes' does
Me good to think, in times like these,
Lide's done so well. And David he's
More tractabler'n what he was,
Last Christmas was a year ago.

584

LITTLE JOHNTS'S CHRIS'MUS

WE got it up a-purpose, jes' fer little Johnts, you know;
    His mother was so pore an' all, an' had to manage so.—
Jes' bein' a War-widder, an' her pension mighty slim,
She'd take in weavin', er work out, er anything fer him!

An' little Johnts was puny-like—but law, the *nerve* he had!—
You'd want to kind o' pity him, but couldn't, very bad,—
His pants o' army-blanket an' his coat o' faded blue
Kep' hintin' of his father like, an' pity wouldn't do!

So we collogued together onc't, one winter-time, 'at we—
Jes' me an' Mother an' the girls, and Wilse, John-Jack an' Free—
Would jine and git up little Johnts, by time 'at Chris'mus come,
Some sort o' doin's, don't you know, 'at would su'prise him some.

An' so, all on the quiet, Mother she turns in an' gits
Some blue-janes—cuts an' makes a suit; an' then sets down and knits
A pair o' little galluses to go 'long with the rest—
An' putts in a red-flannen back an' buckle on the vest.—

The little feller'd be'n so much around our house, you see,
An' be'n sich he'p to her an' all, an' handy as could be,
'At Mother couldn't do too much fer little Johnts—No, *sir!*
She ust to jes' declare 'at "he was meat-an'-drink to her!"

An' Piney, Lide, an' Madeline they watch their chance an' rid
To Fountaintown with Lijey's folks; an' bought a book, they did,
O' fairy tales, with pictur's in; an' got a little pair
O' red-top boots 'at John-Jack said he'd be'n a-pricin' there.

An' Lide got him a little sword, an' Madeline, a drum;
An' shootin'-crackers—Lawzy-day! an' they're so danger-some!
An' Piney, ever' time the rest 'ud buy some other toy,
She'd take an' turn in then an' buy more candy fer the boy!

"Well," thinks-says-I, when they got back, "*your* pocketbooks is dry!"—
But little Johnts was there hisse'f that afternoon, so I—
Well, *all* of us kep' mighty mum, tel we got him away
By tellin' him to be shore an' come to-morry—Chris'mus Day—

An' fetch *his mother* 'long with him! An' how he scud acrost
The fields—his towhead, in the dusk, jes' like a streak o' frost!—
His comfert flutter'n' as he run—an' old Tige, don't you know,
A-jumpin' high fer rabbits an' a plowin' up the snow!

It must 'a' be'n 'most *ten* that night afore we got to bed—
With Wilse an' John-Jack he'ppin' us; an' Freeman in the shed,
An' Lide out with the lantern while he trimmed the Chris'mus Tree
Out of a little scrub-oak-top 'at suited to a "T"!

All night I dreamp' o' hearin' things a-skulkin' round the place—
An' "Old Kriss," with his whiskers off, an' freckles on his face—
An' reindeers, shaped like shavin'-hosses at the cooper-shop,
A-stickin' down the chimbly, with their heels out at the top!

By time 'at Mother got me up 'twas plum daylight an' more—
The front yard full o' neighbors all a-crowdin' round the door,
With Johnts's mother leadin'; yes—an' little Johnts hisse'f,
Set up on Freeman's shoulder, like a jug up on the she'f!

Of course I can't describe it when they all got in to where
We'd conjered up the Chris'mus Tree an' all the fixin's there!—
Fer all the shouts o' laughture—clappin' hands, an' crackin' jokes,
Was heap o' kissin' goin' on amongst the women-folks:—

Fer, lo-behold-ye! there they had that young-un!—An' his chin
A-wobblin'-like;—an', shore enough, at last he started in—
An'—sich another bellerin', in all my mortal days,
I never heerd, er 'spect to hear, in woe's app'inted ways!

An' Mother grabs him up an' says: "It's more'n he can bear—
It's all too *suddent* fer the child, an' too su'prisin'!—*There!*"
"Oh, no it ain't"—sobbed little Johnts—"I ain't su'prised—but I'm
A-cryin' 'cause I watched you all, an' knowed it all the time!"

585

THAT-AIR YOUNG-UN

THAT-AIR young-un ust to set
By the crick here day by day.—
Watch the swallers dip and wet
Their slim wings and skoot away;
Watch these little snipes along
The low banks tilt up and down
'Mongst the reeds, and hear the song
Of the bullfrogs croakin' roun':
Ust to set here in the sun
Watchin' things, and listenun,
'Peared-like, mostly to the roar
Of the dam below, er to
That-air riffle nigh the shore

Jes' acrost from me and you.
Ust to watch him from the door
Of the mill.—'Ud rigg him out
With a fishin'-pole and line—
Dig worms fer him—nigh about
Jes' spit on his bait!—but he
Never keered much, 'pearantly,
To ketch fish!—He'd ruther fine
Out some sunny place, and set
Watchin' things, with droopy head,
And "a-listenun," he said—
"Kind o' listenun above
The old crick to what the wet
Warter was a-talkin' of!"

Jevver hear sich talk as that?
Bothered *Mother* more'n me

What the child was cipher'n' at.—
Come home onc't and said 'at he
Knowed what the snake-feeders
    thought
When they grit their wings; and
    knowed
Turkle-talk, when bubbles riz
Over where the old roots growed
Where he th'owed them pets o' his—
Little turripuns he caught
In the County Ditch and packed
In his pockets days and days!—
Said he knowed what goslin's
    quacked—
Could tell what the killdees sayes,
And grasshoppers, when they lit
In the crick and "minnies" bit
Off their legs—"But, *blame!*" sayes
    he,
Sort o' lookin' clean above
Mother's head and on through me—
(And them eyes!—I see 'em yet!)—
"*Blame!*" he sayes, "ef I kin see,
Er make *out,* jes' what the wet
Warter is a-talkin' of!"

Made me *nervous!* Mother, though,
Said best not to scold the child—
The Good Bein' knowed.—And so
We was only rickonciled
When he'd be asleep.—And then,
Time, and time, and time again,
We've watched over him, you know—
Her a-sayin' nothin'—jes'
Kind o' smoothin' back his hair,
And, all to herse'f, I guess,
Studyin' up some kind o' prayer
She ain't tried yet.—Onc't she said,
Cotin' Scriptur', " 'He,' " says she,
In a solemn whisper, " 'He
Givuth His beloved sleep!' "
And jes' then I heerd the rain
Strike the shingles, as I turned

Res'less to'rds the wall again.
Pity strong men dast to weep!—
Specially when up above
Thrash! the storm comes down, and
    you
Feel the midnight plum soaked
    through
Heart and soul, and wunder, too,
What the warter's talkin' of!

.   .   .   .

Found his hat 'way down below
Hinchman's Ford.—'Ves' Anders he
Rid and fetched it. Mother she
Went *wild* over that, you know—
Hugged it! kissed it!—*Turribul!*
My hopes then was all gone too. . . .
Brung him in, with both hands full
O' warter-lilies—'peared-like new-
Bloomed fer him—renched whiter still
In the clear rain, mixin' fine
And finer in the noon sunshine. . . .
Winders of the old mill looked
On him where the hill-road crooked
In on through the open gate. . . .
Laid him on the old settee
On the porch there. Heerd the great
Roarin' dam acrost—and we
Heerd a crane cry in amongst
The sycamores—and then a dove
Cutterin' on the mill-roof—then
Heerd the crick, and thought again,
"*Now* what's it a-talkin' of?"

586

THE PIPES OF PAN

THE Pipes of Pan! Not idler now
    are they
Than when their cunning fashiono
    first blew

The pith of music from them: Yet
  for you
And me their notes are blown in many
  a way
Lost in our murmurings for that old
  day
That fared so well without us.—
  Waken to
The pipings here at hand:—The
  clear halloo
Of truant voices, and the roundelay
The waters warble in the solitude
  Of blooming thickets, where the
  robin's breast
  Sends up such ecstasy o'er dale
  and dell
Each tree top answers, till in all the
  wood
  There lingers not one squirrel in his
  nest
  Whetting his hunger on an empty
  shell.

587

DOWN AROUND THE RIVER

NOON-TIME and June-time, down
    around the river!
Have to furse with Lizey Ann—but
  lawzy! I fergive her!
Drives me off the place, and says 'at
  all 'at she's a-wishin',
Land o' gracious! time'll come I'll git
  enough o' fishin'!
Little Dave, a-choppin' wood, never
  'pears to notice;
Don't know where she's hid his hat,
  er keerin' where his coat is,—
Specalatin', more'n like, he hain't
  a-goin' to mind me,
And guessin' where, say twelve o'clock,
  a feller'd likely find me.

Noon-time   and   June-time,   down
    around the river!
Clean out o' sight o' home, and skulk-
  in' under kivver
Of the sycamores, jack-oaks, and
  swamp-ash and ellum—
Idies all so jumbled up, you kin hardly
  tell 'em!—
Tired, you know, but *lovin'* it, and
  smilin' jes' to think 'at
Any sweeter tiredness you'd fairly
  want to *drink* it.
Tired o' fishin'—tired o' fun—line out
  slack and slacker—
All you want in all the world's a little
  more tobacker!

Hungry, but *a-hidin'* it, er jes' a-not
  a-keerin':—
Kingfisher gittin' up and skootin' out
  o' hearin';
Snipes on the t'other side, where the
  County Ditch is,
Wadin' up and down the aidge like
  they'd rolled their britches!
Old turkle on the root kind o' sort o'
  drappin'
Intoo th' worter like he don't know
  how it happen!
Worter, shade and all so mixed, don't
  know which you'd orter
Say, th' *worter* in the shadder—*shad-
  der* in the *worter!*

Somebody hollerin'—'way around the
  bend in
Upper Fork—where yer eye kin jes'
  ketch the endin'
Of the shiney wedge o' wake some
  muss-rat's a-makin'
With that pesky nose o' his! Then a
  sniff o' bacon,

Corn-bread and 'dock-greens—and lit-
tle Dave a-shinnin'
'Crost the rocks and mussel-shells,
a-limpin' and a-grinnin',
With yer dinner fer ye, and a blessin'
from the giver.
Noon-time and June-time down around
the river!

588

HIS MOTHER

DEAD! my wayward boy—*my
own*—
Not *the Law's!* but *mine*—the good
God's free gift to me alone,
Sanctified by motherhood.

"Bad," you say: Well, who is not?
"Brutal"—"with a heart of stone"—
And "red-handed."—Ah! the hot
Blood upon your own!

I come not, with downward eyes,
To plead for him shamedly,—
God did not apologize
When he gave the boy to me.

Simply, I make ready now
For *His* verdict.—*You* prepare—
You have killed us both—and how
Will you face us There?

589

IN BOHEMIA

HA! My dear! I'm back again—
Vender of Bohemia's wares!
Lordy! How it pants a man

Climbing up those awful stairs!
Well, I've made the dealer say
Your sketch *might* sell, anyway!
And I've made a publisher
Hear my poem, Kate, my dear.

In Bohemia, Kate, my dear—
Ledgers in a musty flat
On the top floor—living here
Neighborless, and used to that,—
Like a nest beneath the eaves,
So our little home receives
Only guests of chirping cheer—
We'll be happy, Kate, my dear!

Under your north light there, you
At your easel, with a stain
On your nose of Prussian blue,
Paint your bits of shine and rain;
With my feet thrown up at will
O'er my littered window-sill,
I write rhymes that ring as clear
As your laughter, Kate, my dear.

Puff my pipe, and stroke my hair—
Bite my pencil-tip and gaze
At you, mutely mooning there
O'er your "Aprils" and your "Mays"!
Equal inspiration in
Dimples of your cheek and chin,
And the golden atmosphere
Of your paintings, Kate, my dear!

Trying! Yes, at times it is,
To clink happy rhymes, and fling
On the canvas scenes of bliss,
When we are half famishing!—
When your "jersey" rips in spots,
And your hat's "forget-me-nots"
Have grown tousled, old and
sear—
It is trying, Kate, my dear!

But—as sure—*some* picture sells,
And—sometimes—the poetry—
Bless us! How the parrot yells
His acclaims at you and me!
How we revel then in scenes
Or high banqueting!—sardines—
Salads—olives—and a sheer
Pint of sherry, Kate, my dear!

Even now I cross your palm
With this great round world of
gold!—
"Talking wild?" Perhaps I am—
Then, this little five-year-old!—
Call it anything you will,
So it lifts your face until
I may kiss away that tear
Ere it drowns me, Kate, my dear.

590

MOON-DROWNED

'TWAS the height of the fête when
we quitted the riot,
And quietly stole to the terrace
alone,
Where, pale as the lovers that ever
swear by it,
The moon it gazed down as a god
from his throne.
We stood there enchanted.—And O
the delight of
The sight of the stars and the moon
and the sea,
And the infinite skies of that opulent
night of
Purple and gold and ivory!

The lisp of the lip of the ripple just
under—
The half-awake nightingale's dream
in the yews—

Came up from the water, and down
from the wonder
Of shadowy foliage, drowsed with
the dews,—
Unsteady the firefly's taper—unsteady
The poise of the stars, and their
light in the tide,
As it struggled and writhed in caress
of the eddy,
As love in the billowy breast of a
bride.

The far-away lilt of the waltz rippled
to us,
And through us the exquisite thrill
of the air:
Like the scent of bruised bloom was
her breath, and its dew was
Not honier-sweet than her warm
kisses were.
We stood there enchanted.—And O
the delight of
The sight of the stars and the moon
and the sea,
And the infinite skies of that opulent
night of
Purple and gold and ivory!

591

WHO SANTY CLAUS WUZ

JES' a little bit o' feller—I remember
still,—
Ust to almost *cry* fer Christmas, like
a youngster will.
Fourth o' July's nothin' to it!—New-
Year's ain't a smell:
Easter-Sunday — Circus-Day — jes' all
dead in the shell!
Lordy, though! at night, you know, to
set around and hear

The old folks work the story off about
 the sledge and deer,
And "Santy" skootin' round the roof,
 all wrapped in fur and fuzz—
Long afore
 I knowed who
 "Santy Claus" wuz!

Ust to wait, and set up late, a week or
 two ahead:
Couldn't hardly keep awake, ner
 wouldn't go to bed:
Kittle stewin' on the fire, and Mother
 settin' here
Darnin' socks, and rockin' in the
 skreeky rockin'-cheer;
Pap gap', and wunder where it wuz
 the money went,
And quar'l with his frosted heels, and
 spill his liniment:
And me a-dreamin' sleigh-bells when
 the clock 'ud whir and buzz,
Long afore
 I knowed who
 "Santy Claus" wuz!

Size the fireplace up, and figger how
 "Old Santy" could
Manage to come down the chimbly,
 like they said he would:
Wisht that I could hide and see him
 —wundered what he'd say
Ef he ketched a feller layin' fer him
 thataway!
But I bet on him, and liked him, same
 as ef he had
Turned to pat me on the back and
 say, "Look here, my lad,
Here's my pack,—jes' he'p yourse'f,
 like all good boys does!"
Long afore
 I knowed who
 "Santy Claus" wuz!

Wisht that yarn wuz true about him,
 as it 'peared to be—
Truth made out o' lies like that 'un's
 good enough fer me!—
Wisht I still wuz so confidin' I could
 jes' go wild
Over hangin' up my stockin's, like the
 little child
Climbin' in my lap to-night, and beg-
 gin' me to tell
'Bout them reindeers, and "Old Santy"
 that she loves so well
I'm half sorry fer this little-girl-sweet-
 heart of his—
Long afore
 She knows who
 "Santy Claus" is!

592

TO MY GOOD MASTER

IN fancy, always, at thy desk, thrown
 wide,
 Thy most betreasured books ranged
 neighborly—
 The rarest rhymes of every land and
 sea
And curious tongue—thine old face
 glorified,—
Thou haltest thy glib quill, and,
 laughing-eyed,
 Givest hale welcome even unto me,
 Profaning thus thine attic's sanctity,
Briefly to visit, yet to still abide
Enthralled there of thy sorcery of wit
 And thy songs' most exceeding dear
 conceits.
O lips, cleft to the ripe core of all
 sweets,
 With poems, like nectar, issuing
 therefrom,

Thy gentle utterances do overcome
My listening heart and all the love
  of it!

593

CHAIRLEY BURKE'S IN TOWN

IT'S Chairley Burke's in town, b'ys!
  He's down til "Jamesy's Place,"
Wid a bran'-new shave upon 'um, an'
  the fhwhuskers aff his face;
He's quit the Section-Gang last night,
  an' yez can chalk it down
There's goin' to be the divil's toime,
  since Chairley Burke's in town.

Ye'll know 'um by the neck av 'um
  behind—the tan an' fair
The barber left he overfilled before he
  mowed a hair;
Ye'll know 'um by the ja'nty hat juist
  bought he's wearin' now—
But Chairley—He'll not miss it in the
  mornin' onyhow!

It's treatin' iv'ry b'y he is, an' poundin'
  on the bar
Till iv'ry man he's dhrinkin' wid
  musht shmoke a foine cigar;
An' Missus Murphy's little Kate, that's
  coomin' there for beer,
Can't pay wan cint the bucketful, the
  whilst that Chairley's here!

He's joompin' oor the tops av shtools,
  the both forninsht an' back!
He'll lave yez pick the blessed flure,
  an' walk the straightest crack!
He's liftin' barrels wid his teeth, an'
  singin' "Garry Owen,"
Till all the house be shtrikin' hands,
  since Chairley Burke's in town.

He'll sink the glitther av his eye
  a-dancin' deep an' dim
The toime yez tie his hands behind
  an' thin lave go av him!—
An' fwhat's the knots av mortal man
  ag'insht the nimble twisht
An' shlim an' shlender soopleness that
  he have in his wrisht!

The Road-Yaird hands coomes dhrop-
  pin' in, an' niver goin' back;
An' there's two freights upon the
  switch—the wan on aither track—
An' Mr. Gearry, from The Shops, he's
  mad enough to shwear,
An' durstn't spake a word but grin,
  the whilst that Chairley's there!

Och! Chairley! Chairley! Chairley
  Burke! ye divil, wid yer ways
Av dhrivin' all the throubles aff, these
  dhark an' ghloomy days!
Ohone! that it's meself, wid all the
  graifs I have to dhrown,
Must lave me pick to resht a bit, since
  Chairley Burke's in town.

594

WAIT FOR THE MORNING

WAIT for the morning:—it will
  come, indeed,
As surely as the night hath given
  need.
The yearning eyes, at last, will strain
  their sight
No more unanswered by the morning
  light;
No longer will they vainly strive,
  through tears,

To pierce the darkness of thy doubts
and fears,
But, bathed in balmy dews and rays
of dawn,
Will smile with rapture o'er the dark-
ness drawn.

Wait for the morning, O thou smitten
child,
Scorned, scourged and persecuted and
reviled—
Athirst and famishing, none pitying
thee,
Crowned with the twisted thorns of
agony—
No faintest gleam of sunlight through
the dense
Infinity of gloom to lead thee thence.—
Wait for the morning:—It will come,
indeed,
As surely as the night hath given
need.

595

YOUTH AND AGE

WHEN in our blithest youth we
sing,
We sing our saddest—slack the string
Of music into saddest key,
And sob, with voices quavering
In pangs of melody.

When in maturer years—
When grown acquaint with sighs and
tears—
Our voices ring a lighter tone,
Our perverse harp peals o'er the
moan—
A pæan of hope that lifts and cheers.

And last, in age's bleak extreme,
With youth, life, love, all—all a dream,
What glad songs leap
To our glad lips—what raptures gleam
In the old eyes—too glad to weep.

596

THE POET OF. THE FUTURE

O THE Poet of the Future! He
will come to us as comes
The beauty of the bugle's voice above
the roar of drums—
The beauty of the bugle's voice above
the roar and din
Of battle-drums that pulse the time
the victor marches in.
His hands will hold no harp, in sooth;
his lifted brow will bear
No coronet of laurel—nay, nor symbol
anywhere,
Save that his palms are brothers to the
toiler's at the plow,
His face to heaven, and the dew of
duty on his brow.

He will sing across the meadow,—
and the woman at the well
Will stay the dripping bucket, with
a smile ineffable;
And the children in the orchard will
gaze wistfully the way
The happy songs come to them, with
the fragrance of the hay;
The barn will neigh in answer, and
the pasture-lands behind
Will chime with bells, and send re-
sponsive lowings down the wind;
And all the echoes of the wood will
jubilantly call
In sweetest mimicry of that one sweet
voice of all.

O the Poet of the Future! He will
  come as man to man,
With the honest arm of labor, and the
  honest face of tan,
The honest heart of lowliness, the hon-
  est soul of love
For human-kind   and   nature-kind
  about him and above.
His hands will hold no harp, in sooth;
  his lifted brow will bear
No coronet of laurel—nay, nor symbol
  anywhere,
Save that his palms are brothers to the
  toiler's at the plow,
His face to heaven, and the dew of
  duty on his brow.

597

NAUGHTY CLAUDE

WHEN Little Claude was naughty
  wunst
At dinner-time, an' said
He won't say "Thank you" to his Ma,
  She maked him go to bed
An' stay two hours an' not git up,—
  So when the clock struck Two,
Nen Claude says,—"Thank you, Mr.
  Clock,
  I'm much obleeged to you!"

598

THE ARTEMUS OF MICHIGAN

GRAND HAVEN is in Michigan,
  and in possession, too,
Of as many rare attractions as our
  party ever knew:—

The fine hotel, the landlord, and the
  lordly bill of fare,
And the dainty-neat completeness of
  the pretty waiters there;
The touch on the piano in the parlor,
  and the trill
Of the exquisite soprano—in our fancy
  singing still;
Our cozy room, its comfort, and our
  thousand grateful thoughts,
And at our door the gentle face
        Of
          H.
            Y.
              Potts!

His artless observations, and his droll-
  ery of style,
Bewildered with that sorrowful seren-
  ity of smile—
The eye's elusive twinkle, and the
  twitching of the lid,
Like he didn't go to say it and was
  sorry that he did.
O Artemus of Michigan! so worthy of
  the name,
Our manager indorses it, and Bill Nye
  does the same,—
You tickled our affection in so many
  tender spots
That even Recollection laughs
        At
          H.
            Y.
              Potts!

And hark ye! O Grand Haven! count
  your rare attractions o'er—
The commerce of your ships at sea,
  and ships along the shore;
Your railroads, and your industries,
  and interests untold,

Your Opera-house—our lecture, and
the gate-receipts in gold!—
Ay, Banner Town of Michigan! count
all your treasures through—
Your crowds of summer tourists, and
your Sanitarium, too;
Your lake, your beach, your drives,
your breezy groves and grassy
plots,
But head the list of all of these
With
H.
Y.
Potts!

599

WAITIN' FER THE CAT TO DIE

LAWZY! don't I rickollect
That-air old swing in the lane!
Right and proper, I expect,
Old times *can't* come back again;
But I want to state, ef they
Could come back, and I could say
What *my* pick 'ud be, i jing!
I'd say, Gimme the old swing
'Nunder the old locus' trees
On the old place, ef you please!—
Danglin' there with half-shet eye,
Waitin' fer the cat to die!

I'd say, Gimme the old gang
O' barefooted, hungry, lean,
Ornry boys you want to hang
When you're growed up twic't as
mean!
The old gyarden-patch, the old
Truants, and the stuff we stol'd!
The old stompin'-groun', where we
Wore the grass off, wild and free
As the swoop o' the old swing,

Where we ust to climb and cling,
And twist roun', and fight, and lie—
Waitin' fer the cat to die!

'Pears like I most allus could
Swing the highest of the crowd—
Jes' sail up there tel I stood
Down-side up, and screech out
loud,—
Ketch my breath, and jes' drap back
Fer to let the old swing slack,
Yit my towhead dippin' still
In the green boughs, and the chill
Up my backbone taperin' down,
With my shadder on the groun'
Slow and slower trailin' by—
Waitin' fer the cat to die!

Now my daughter's little Jane's
Got a kind o' baby-swing
On the porch, so's when it rains
She kin play there—little thing!
And I'd limped out t'other day
With my old cheer thisaway,
Swingin' *her* and rockin' too,
Thinkin' how *I* ust to do
At *her* age, when suddenly,
"Hey, Gran'pap!" she says to me,
"Why you rock so slow?" . . . Says I,
"Waitin' fer the cat to die!"

600

THE ALL-KIND MOTHER

LO, whatever is at hand
Is full meet for the demand:
Nature ofttimes giveth best
When she seemeth chariest.
She hath shapen shower and sun
To the need of every one—
Summer bland and winter drear,
Dimpled pool and frozen mere.

All thou lackest she hath still
Near thy finding and thy fill.
Yield her fullest faith, and she
Will endow thee royally.

Loveless weed and lily fair
She attendeth here and there—
Kindly to the weed as to
The lorn lily teared with dew.
Each to her hath use as dear
As the other; an thou clear
Thy cloyed senses thou may'st see
Haply all the mystery.
Thou shalt see the lily get
Its divinest blossom; yet
Shall the weed's tip bloom no less
With the song-bird's gleefulness.

Thou art poor, or thou art rich—
Never lightest matter which;
All the glad gold of the noon,
All the silver of the moon,
She doth lavish on thee, while
Thou withholdest any smile
Of thy gratitude to her,

Baser used than usurer.
Shame be on thee an thou seek
Not her pardon, with hot cheek,
And bowed head, and brimming eyes
At her merciful "Arise!"

601

TO HATTIE—ON HER BIRTHDAY

WRITTEN IN "A CHILD'S GARDEN OF
VERSES"

WHEN your "Uncle Jim" was
younger,
In the days of childish hunger
For the honey of such verses
As this little book rehearses
     In such sweet simplicity,—
Just the simple gift that this is
Would have brimmed his heart with
     blisses
Sweet as Hattie's sweetest kisses,
     On her anniversary.

602

DOWN TO THE CAPITAL

I'BE'N down to the Capital at Washington, D. C.,
     Where Congerss meets and passes on the pensions ort to be
Allowed to old one-legged chaps, like me, 'at sence the war
Don't wear their pants in pairs at all—and yit how proud we are!

Old Flukens, from our deestrick, jes' turned in and tuck and made
Me stay with him whilse I was there; and longer 'at I stayed
The more I kep' a-wantin' jes' to kind o' git away,
And yit a-feelin' sociabler with Flukens ever' day.

You see I'd got the idy—and I guess most folks agrees—
'At men as rich as him, you know, kin do jes' what they please;

A man worth stacks o' money, and a Congerssman and all,
And livin' in a buildin' bigger'n Masonic Hall!

Now mind, I'm not a-faultin' Fluke—he made his money square:
We both was Forty-niners, and both bu'sted gittin' there;
I weakened and onwindlassed, and he stuck and stayed and made
His millions; don't know what *I'm* worth untel my pension's paid.

But I was goin' to tell you—er a-ruther goin' to try
To tell you how he's livin' now: gas burnin' mighty nigh
In ever' room about the house; and ever' night, about,
Some blame reception goin' on, and money goin' out.

They's people there from all the world—jes' ever' kind 'at lives,
Injuns and all! and Senaters, and Ripresentatives;
And girls, you know, jes' dressed in gauze and roses, I *de*clare,
And even old men shamblin' round and a-waltzin' with 'em there!

And bands a-tootin' circus-tunes, 'way in some other room
Jes' chokin' full o' hothouse plants and pinies and perfume;
And fountains, squirtin' stiddy all the time; and statutes, made
Out o' puore marble, 'peared-like, sneakin' round there in the shade.

And Fluke he coaxed and begged and pled with *me* to take a hand
And sashay in amongst 'em—crutch and all, you understand;
But when I said how tired I was, and made fer open air,
He follered, and tel five o'clock we set a-talkin' there.

"My God!" says he—Fluke says to me, "I'm tireder'n you;
Don't putt up yer tobacker tel you give a man a chew.
Set back a leetle furder in the shadder—that'll do;
I'm tireder'n you, old man; I'm tireder'n you.

"You see that-air old dome," says he, "humped up ag'inst the sky?
It's grand, first time you see it; but it changes, by and by,
And then it stays jes' thataway—jes' anchored high and dry
Betwixt the sky up yender and the achin' of yer eye.

"Night's purty; not so purty, though, as what it ust to be
When my first wife was livin'. You remember her?" says he.
I nodded-like, and Fluke went on, "I wonder now ef she
Knows where I am—and what I am—and what I ust to be?

"That band in there!—I ust to think 'at music couldn't wear
A feller out the way it does; but that ain't music there—
That's jes' a' *imitation,* and like ever'thing, I swear,
I hear, er see, er tetch, er taste, er tackle anywhere!

"It's all jes' *artificial,* this-'ere high-priced life of ours;
The theory, *it's* sweet enough, tel it saps down and sours.
They's no *home* left, ner *ties* o' home about it.   By the powers,
The whole thing's artificialer'n artificial flowers!

"And all I want, and could lay down and *sob* fer, is to know
The homely things of homely life; fer instance, jes' to go
And set down by the kitchen stove—Lord! that 'u'd rest me so,—
Jes' set there, like I ust to do, and laugh and joke, you know.

"Jes' set there, like I ust to do," says Fluke, a-startin' in,
'Peared-like, to say the whole thing over to hisse'f ag'in;
Then stopped and turned, and kind o' coughed, and stooped and fumbled fer
Somepin' o' 'nuther in the grass—I guess his handkercher.

Well, sence I'm back from Washington, where I left Fluke a-still
A-leggin' fer me, heart and soul, on that-air pension bill,
I've half-way struck the notion, when I think o' wealth and sich,
They's nothin' much patheticker'n jes' a-bein' rich!

603

JAP MILLER

JAP MILLER down at Martins-
ville's the blamedest feller yit!
When *he* starts in a-talkin' other folks
is apt to quit!—
'Pears like that mouth o' his'n wuzn't
made fer nothin' else
But jes' to argify 'em down and gether
in their pelts:
He'll talk you down on tariff; er he'll
talk you down on tax,
And prove the pore man pays 'em all
—and them's about the fac's!—

Religen, law, er politics, prize-fightin'
er baseball—
Jes' tetch Jap up a little and he'll post
you 'bout 'em all.

And the comicalist feller ever tilted
back a cheer
And tuk a chaw tobacker kind o' like
he didn't keer.—
There's where the feller's stren'th
lays,—he's so common-like and
plain,—
They hain't no dude about old Jap,
you bet you—nary grain!
They 'lected him to Council and it
never turned his head,

And didn't make no differunce what
anybody said,—
He didn't dress no finer, ner rag out
in fancy clothes;
But his voice in Council-meetin's is a
turrer to his foes.

He's fer the pore man ever' time!
And in the last campaign
He stumped old Morgan County,
through the sunshine and the
rain,
And helt the banner up'ards from
a-trailin' in the dust,
And cut loose on monopolies and
cuss'd and cuss'd and cuss'd!
He'd tell some funny story ever' now
and then, you know,
Tel, blame it! it wuz better'n a Jack-
o'-lantern show!
And I'd go furder, yit, to-day, to hear
old Jap norate
Than any high-toned orater 'at ever
stumped the State!

W'y, that-air blame Jap Miller, with
his keen sircastic fun,
Has got more friends than ary candi-
date 'at ever run!
Don't matter what *his* views is, when
he states the same to you,
They allus coincide with yourn, the
same as two and two:
You *can't* take issue with him—er, at
least, they hain't no sense
In startin' in to down him, so you bet-
ter not commence.—
The best way's jes' to listen, like your
humble servant does,
And jes' concede Jap Miller is the best
man ever wuz!

604

JOHN TARKINGTON JAMESON

JOHN JAMESON, my jo John!
  Ye're bonnie wee an' sma';
Your ee's the morning violet,
  Wi' tremblin' dew an' a';
Your smile's the gowden simmer-
    sheen,
  Wi' glintin' pearls aglow
Atween the posies o' your lips,
  John Jameson, my jo!

Ye hae the faither's braidth o brow,
  An' synes his look benign
Whiles he hings musin' ower the burn,
  Wi' leestless hook an' line;
Ye hae the mither's mou' an' cheek
  An' denty chin—but O!
It's maist ye're like your ain braw sel',
  John Jameson, my jo!

John Jameson, my jo John,
  Though, wi' sic luvers twain,
Ye dance far yont your whustlin' frien'
  Wha laggart walks his lane,—
Be mindet, though he naps his last
  Whaur kirkyird thistles grow,
His ghaist shall caper on wi' you,
  John Jameson, my jo!

605

HENRY W. GRADY

ATLANTA, DECEMBER 23, 1889

TRUE-HEARTED friend of all
  true friendliness!—
Brother of all true brotherhoods!—
  Thy hand

And its late pressure now we under-
　　stand
Most fully, as it falls thus gestureless
And Silence lulls thee into sweet ex-
　　cess
Of sleep.　Sleep thou content!—Thy
　　loved Southland
　Is swept with tears, as rain in sun-
　　shine; and
Through all the frozen North our eyes
　　confess
　Like sorrow—seeing still the princely
　　sign
Set on thy lifted brow, and the rapt
　　light
　Of the dark, tender, melancholy
　　eyes—
　Thrilled with the music of those lips
　　of thine,
And yet the fire thereof that lights the
　　night
　With the white splendor of thy
　　prophecies.

606

IN THE EVENING

I

IN the evening of our days,
　When the first far stars above
Glimmer dimmer, through the haze,
　Than the dewy eyes of love,
Shall we mournfully revert
　To the vanished morns and Mays
Of our youth, with hearts that hurt,—
　In the evening of our days?

II

Shall the hand that holds your own
　Till the twain are thrilled as now,—

Be withheld, or colder grown?
　Shall my kiss upon your brow
Falter from its high estate?
　And, in all forgetful ways,
Shall we sit apart and wait—
　In the evening of our days?

III

Nay, my wife—my life!—the gloom
　Shall enfold us velvet-wise,
And my smile shall be the groom
　Of the gladness of your eyes:
Gently, gently as the dew
　Mingles with the darkening maze,
I shall fall asleep with you—
　In the evening of our days.

607

THOUGHTS ON THE LATE WAR

I WAS for Union—you, ag'in' it.
　'Pears like, to me, each side was
　　winner,
Lookin' at now and all 'at's in it.
　Le' 's go to dinner.

Le' 's kind o' jes' set down together
And do some pardnership forgittin'—
Talk, say, for instunce, 'bout the
　weather,
　Or somepin' fittin'.

The war, you know, 's all done and
　ended,
And ain't changed no p'ints o' the
　compass;
Both North and South the health's jes'
　splendid
　　As 'fore the rumpus.

The old farms and the old plantations
Still ockipies the'r old positions.
Le' 's git back to old situations
    And old ambitions.

Le' 's let up on this blame', infernal
Tongue-lashin' and lap-jacket vauntin',
And git back home to the eternal
    Ca'm we're a-wantin'.

Peace kind o' sort o' suits my diet—
When women does my cookin' for me;
Ther' wasn't overly much pie et
    Durin' the army.

608

THE OLD BAND

IT'S mighty good to git back to the
    old town, shore,
Considerin' I've b'en away twenty year
    and more.
Sence I moved then to Kansas, of
    course I see a change,
A-comin' back, and notice things that's
    new to me and strange;
Especially at evening when yer new
    band-fellers meet,
In fancy uniforms and all, and play out
    on the street—
. . . What's come of old Bill Lindsey
    and the Saxhorn fellers—say?
    I want to hear the *old* band play.

What's come of Eastman, and Nat
    Snow? And where's War Bar-
    nett at?
And Nate and Bony Meek; Bill Hart;
    Tom Richa'son and that
Air brother of him played the drum
    as twic't as big as Jim;

And old Hi Kerns, the carpenter—
    say, what's become o' him?
I make no doubt yer *new band* now's
    a *competenter* band,
And plays their music more by note
    than what they play by hand,
And stylisher and grander tunes; but
    somehow—*any*way,
    I want to hear the *old* band play.

Sich tunes as "John Brown's Body"
    and "Sweet Alice," don't you
    know;
And "The Camels Is A-Comin'," and
    "John Anderson, My Jo";
And a dozent others of 'em—"Num-
    ber Nine" and "Number 'Leven"
Was favo-*rites* that fairly made a feller
    dream o' Heaven.
And when the boys 'u'd saranade, I've
    laid so still in bed
I've even heerd the locus'-blossoms
    droppin' on the shed
When "Lilly Dale," er "Hazel Dell,"
    had sobbed and died away—
    . . . I want to hear the *old*
    band play.

Yer *new* band ma'by beats it, but the
    old band's what I said—
It allus 'peared to kind o' chord with
    somepin' in my head;
And, whilse I'm no musicianer, when
    my blame' eyes is jes'
Nigh drownded out, and Mem'ry
    squares her jaws and sort o' says
She *won't* ner *never will* fergit, I want
    to jes' turn in
And take and light right out o' here
    and git back West ag'in
And *stay* there, when I git there,
    where I never haf' to say
    I want to hear the *old* band play.

609

BY ANY OTHER NAME

FIRST the teacher called the roll,
　　Clos't to the beginnin',
"Addeliney Bowersox!"
　　Set the school a-grinnin'.
Winter-time, and stingin' cold
　　When the session took up—
Cold as *we* all looked at *her,*
　　Though *she* couldn't look up!

Total stranger to us, too—
　　Country folks ain't allus
Nigh so shameful unpolite
　　As some people call us!—
But the honest facts is, *then,*
　　Addeliney Bower-
Sox's feelin's was so hurt
　　She cried half an hour!

My dest was acrost from hern:
　　Set and watched her tryin'
To p'tend she didn't keer,
　　And a kind o' dryin'
Up her tears with smiles—tel I
　　Thought, "Well, *'Addeliney
Bowersox'* is plain, but *she's*
　　Purty as a piney!"

.　　.　　.　　.　　.　　.　　.

It's be'n many of a year
　　Sence that most oncommon
Cur'ous name o' *Bowersox*
　　Struck me so abomin-
Nubble and outlandish-like!—
　　I changed it to Adde-
Liney *Daubenspeck*—and *that*
　　Nearly killed her Daddy!

610

LINES FER ISAAC BRADWELL, OF INDANOPLIS, IND., COUN-TY-SEAT OF MARION

[*Writ on the fly-leaf of a volume of
the author's poems that come in one
of gittin' burnt up in the great Bowen-
Merrill's fire of March 17, 1890.*]

THROUGH fire and flood this book
　　has passed.—
Fer what?—I hardly dare to ast—
Less'n it's still to pamper me
With extry food fer vanity;—
Fer, sence it's fell in hands as true
As *yourn* is—and a *Hoosier* too,—
I'm prouder of the book, I jing!
Than 'fore they tried to burn the
　　thing! ·

611

"THE LITTLE MAN IN THE TIN-SHOP"

WHEN I was a little boy, long
　　ago,
And spoke of the theater as the
　　"show,"
The first one that I went to see,
Mother's brother it was took me—
(My uncle, of course, though he
　　seemed to be
Only a boy—I loved him so!)
And ah, how pleasant he made it all!
And the things he knew that *I* should
　　know!—
The stage, the "drop," and the fres-
　　coed wall;
The sudden flash of the lights; and oh,

The orchestra, with its melody,
And the lilt and jingle and jubilee
    Of "The Little Man in the Tin-
        shop"!

For Uncle showed me the "Leader"
    there,
With his pale, bleak forehead and
    long, black hair;
Showed me the "Second," and
    " 'Cello," and "Bass,"
And the "B-Flat," pouting and puffing
    his face
At the little end of the horn he
    blew
Silvery bubbles of music through;
And he coined me names of them,
    each in turn,
Some comical name that I laughed to
    learn,
Clean on down to the last and best,—
The lively little man, never at rest,
Who hides away at the end of the
    string,
And tinkers and plays on everything,—
    That's "The Little Man in the
        Tin-shop"!

Raking a drum like a rattle of hail,
Clinking a cymbal or castanet;
Chirping a twitter or sending a wail
Through a piccolo that thrills me
    yet;
Reeling ripples of riotous bells,
And tipsy tinkles of triangles—
Wrangled and tangled in skeins of
    sound
Till it seemed that my very soul spun
    round,
As I leaned, in a breathless joy, toward
    my

Radiant uncle, who snapped his eye
And said, with the courtliest wave of
    his hand,
"Why, that little master of all the band
    Is 'The Little Man in the Tin-
        shop'!

"And I've heard Verdi the Wonderful,
And Paganini, and Ole Bull,
Mozart, Handel, and Mendelssohn,
And fair Parepa, whose matchless tone
Karl, her master, with magic bow,
Blent with the angels', and held her
    so
Tranced till the rapturous Infinite—
And I've heard arias, faint and low,
From many an operatic light
Glimmering on my swimming sight
Dimmer and dimmer, until, at last,
I still sit, holding my roses fast
    For 'The Little Man in the Tin-
        Shop.' "

Oho! my Little Man, joy to you—
And *yours*—and *theirs*—your lifetime
    through!
Though *I've* heard melodies, boy and
    man,
Since first "the show" of my life began,
Never yet have I listened to
Sadder, madder or gladder glees
Than your unharmonied harmonies;
For yours is the music that appeals
To all the fervor the boy's heart feels—
All his glories, his wildest cheers,
His bravest hopes, and his brightest
    tears;
And so, with his first bouquet, he
    kneels
    To "The Little Man in the Tin-
        shop."

612

A SOUTHERN SINGER

WRITTEN IN MADISON CAWEIN'S "LYRICS
AND IDYLS"

HEREIN are blown from out the
South
Songs blithe as those of Pan's pursed
mouth—
As sweet in voice as, in perfume,
The night-breath of magnolia-bloom.

Such sumptuous languor lures the
sense—
Such luxury of indolence—
The eyes blur as a nymph's might blur,
With water-lilies watching her.

You waken, thrilling at the trill
Of some wild bird that seems to spill
The silence full of winy drips
Of song that Fancy sips and sips.

Betimes, in brambled lanes where-
through
The chipmunk stripes himself from
view,
You pause to lop a creamy spray
Of elder-blossoms by the way.

Or where the morning dew is yet
Gray on the topmost rail, you set
A sudden palm and, vaulting, meet
Your vaulting shadow in the wheat.

On lordly swards, of suave incline,
Entessellate with shade and shine,
You shall misdoubt your lowly birth,
Clad on as one of princely worth:

The falcon on your wrist shall ride—
Your milk-white Arab side by side

With one of raven-black.—You fain
Would kiss the hand that holds the
rein.

Nay, nay, Romancer! Poet! Seer
Sing us back home—from there to
here:
Grant your high grace and wit, but we
Most honor your simplicity.—

Herein are blown from out the South
Songs blithe as those of Pan's pursed
mouth—
As sweet in voice as, in perfume,
The night-breath of magnolia-bloom.

613

JUNE AT WOODRUFF

OUT at Woodruff Place—afar
From the city's glare and jar,
With the leafy trees, instead
Of the awnings, overhead;
With the shadows cool and sweet,
For the fever of the street;
With the silence, like a prayer,
Breathing round us everywhere.

Gracious anchorage, at last,
From the billows of the vast
Tide of life that comes and goes,
Whence and where nobody knows—
Moving, like a skeptic's thought,
Out of nowhere into naught.
Touch and tame us with thy grace,
Placid calm of Woodruff Place!

Weave a wreath of beechen leaves
For the brow that throbs and grieves
O'er the ledger, bloody-lined,
'Neath the sunstruck window-blind!

Send the breath of woodland bloom
Through the sick man's prison-room,
Till his old farm-home shall swim
Sweet in mind to hearten him!

Out at Woodruff Place the Muse
Dips her sandal in the dews,
Sacredly as night and dawn
Baptize lilied grove and lawn:
Woody path, or paven way—
She doth haunt them night and day,—
Sun or moonlight through the trees,
To her eyes, are melodies.

Swinging lanterns, twinkling clear
Through night-scenes, are songs to
    her—
Tinted lilts and choiring hues,
Blent with children's glad halloos;
Then belated lays that fade
Into midnight's serenade—
Vine-like words and zithern-strings
Twined through all her slumberings.

Blessèd be each hearthstone set
Neighboring the violet!
Blessèd every roof-tree prayed
Over by the beech's shade!
Blessèd doorway, opening where
We may look on Nature—there
Hand to hand and face to face—
Storied realm, or Woodruff Place.

614

IRY AND BILLY AND JO

A TINTYPE

IRY an' Billy an' Jo!—
    Iry an' Billy's *the boys,*
An' *Jo's* their *dog,* you know,—

Their pictur's took all in a row.
    Bet they kin kick up a noise—
    Iry an' Billy, the boys,
An' that-air little dog Jo!

Iry's the one 'at stands
    Up there a-lookin' so mild
An' meek—with his hat in his hands,
    Like such a *'bediant* child—
(*Sakes-alive!*)—An' *Billy* he sets
In the cheer an' holds on to Jo an'
        sweats
Hisse'f, a-lookin' so good! Ho-ho!
Iry an' Billy an' Jo!

Yit the way them boys, you know,
    Usen to jes' turn in
An' fight over that dog Jo
        Wuz   a   burnin'-shame-an'-a-
            sin!—
Iry *he'd* argy 'at, by gee-whizz!
That-air little Jo-dog wuz *his!*—
An' Billy *he'd* claim it wuzn't so—
    'Cause the dog wuz *hisn!*—An' at it
        they'd go,
Nip-an'-tugg,   tooth-an'-toe-nail,   you
    know—
Iry an' Billy an' Jo!

But their Pa—(He wuz the marshal
        then)—
    He 'tended-like 'at he *jerked 'em*
        up;
An' got a jury o' Brick-yard men
    An' helt *a trial* about the pup:
An' *he* says *he* jes' like to 'a' died
When the rest o' us town-boys *testi-*
        fied—
    Regardin', you know,
    Iry an' Billy an' Jo.—

'Cause we all knowed, when *the
Gipsies* they
Camped down here by the crick last
Fall,
They brung Jo with 'em, 'an' give him
away
To Iry an' Billy fer nothin' at all!—
So the jury fetched in the *verdick* so
Jo he ain't *neether* o' theirn fer
shore—
He's *both* their dog, an' jes' no
more!
An' so
They've quit quarrelin' long
ago,
Iry an' Billy an' Jo.

615

UNCLE SIDNEY'S VIEWS

I HOLD that the true age of wis-
dom is when
We are boys and girls, and not women
and men,—
When as credulous children we *know*
things because
We *believe* them—however averse to
the laws.
It is *faith,* then, not science and rea-
son, I say,
That is genuine wisdom.—And would
that to-day
We, as then, were as wise and ineffably
blest
As to live, love and die, and trust God
for the rest!

So I simply deny the old notion, you
know,
That the wiser we get as the older we
grow!—

For *in youth* all we know we are *cer-
tain* of.—*Now*
The greater our knowledge, the more
we allow
For skeptical margin.—And hence I
regret
That the world isn't flat, and the sun
doesn't set,
And we may not go creeping up home,
when we die,
Through the moon, like a round yel-
low hole in the sky.

616

BEREAVED

LET me come in where you sit weep-
ing,—ay,
Let me, who have not any child to die,
Weep with you for the little one whose
love
I have known nothing of.

The little arms that slowly, slowly
loosed
Their pressure round your neck; the
hands you used
To kiss.—Such arms—such hands I
never knew.
May I not weep with you?

Fain would I be of service—say some
thing,
Between the tears, that would be com-
forting,—
But ah! so sadder than yourselves
am I,
Who have no child to die.

617

THE RIDER OF THE KNEE

KNIGHTLY Rider of the Knee
Of Proud-prancing Unclery!
Gaily mount, and wave the sign
Of that mastery of thine.

Pat thy steed and turn him free,
Knightly Rider of the Knee!
Sit thy charger as a throne—
Lash him with thy laugh alone:

Sting him only with the spur
Of such wit as may occur,
Knightly Rider of the Knee,
In thy shriek of ecstasy.

Would, as now, we might endure,
Twain as one—thou miniature
Ruler, at the rein of me—
Knightly Rider of the Knee!

618

THE LITTLE-RED-APPLE TREE

THE Little-red-apple Tree!—
O the Little-red-apple Tree!
When I was the little-est bit of a boy
And you were a boy with me!
The bluebird's flight from the topmost
boughs,
And the boys up there—so high
That we rocked over the roof of the
house
And whooped as the winds went
by!

Hey! The Little-red-apple Tree!
With the garden-beds below,
And the old grape-arbor so welcomely
Hiding the rake and hoe!
Hiding, too, as the sun dripped
through
In spatters of wasted gold,
Frank and Amy away from you
And me in the days of old!

The Little-red-apple Tree!—
In the edge of the garden-spot,
Where the apples fell so lavishly
Into the neighbor's lot;—
So do I think of you alway,
Brother of mine, as the tree,—
Giving the ripest wealth of your love
To the world as well as me.

Ho! The Little-red-apple Tree!
Sweet as its juiciest fruit
Spanged on the palate spicily,
And rolled o'er the tongue to boot,
Is the memory still and the joy
Of the Little-red-apple Tree,
When I was the little-est bit of a boy
And you were a boy with me!

619

UNCLE SIDNEY

SOMETIMES, when I bin bad,
An' Pa "currecks" me nen,
An' Uncle Sidney he comes here,
I'm allus good again;

'Cause Uncle Sidney says,
An' takes me up an' smiles,—
*The goodest mens they is ain't good
As baddest little childs!*

620

IN THE NIGHT

WHEN it's night, and no light,
        too,
Wakin' by yourse'f,
With the old clock mockin' you
    On the mantel-she'f;
In the dark—so still and black,
    You're afeard you'll hear
Somepin' awful pop and crack,—
    "Go to sleep, my dear!"

That's what *Mother* says.—And *then's*
    When we ain't *afeard!*
Wunder, when we be big mens,
    Then 'ul we be skeerd?—
Some night Mother's goned away,
    And ist *us* is here,
Will The Good Man wake and say,
    "Go to sleep, my dear"?

621

THE DREAM OF THE
LITTLE PRINCESS

'TWAS a curious dream, good
        sooth!—
    The dream of The Little Princess,
It seemed a dream, yet a truth,
Long years ago in her youth.—
    It *came* as a dream—no less
    It was *not* a dream, she says.

(She is singing and saying things
    Musical as the wile
Of the eery quaverings
That drip from the grievèd strings
    Of her lute.—We weep or smile
    Even as she, meanwhile.)

In a day, long dead and gone,
    When her castle-turrets threw
Their long, sharp shadows on
The sward like lances,—wan
    And lone, she strayed into
    Strange grounds where lilies grew.

There, late in the afternoon,
    As she sate in the terrace shade,
Rav'ling a half-spun tune
From a lute like a wee new-moon,—
    High off was a bugle played,
    And a sound as of steeds that
        neighed.

And the lute fell from her hands,
    As her eyes raised, half in doubt,
To the arch of the azure lands
Where lo! with the fluttering strands
    Of a rainbow reined about
    His wrist, rode a horseman out.

And The Little Princess was stirred
    No less at his steeds than him;—
A jet-black span of them gird
In advance, he bestrode the third;
    And the troop of them seemed to
        swim
    The skies as the Seraphim.

Wingless they were, yet so
    Upborne   in   their   wondrous
        flight—
As their master bade them go,
They dwindled on high; or lo!
    They curved from their heaven-
        most height
    And swooped to her level sight.

And the eyes of The Little Princess
    Grow O so bright as the chants
Of the horseman's courtliness,—

Saluting her low—Ah, yes!
   And lifting a voice that haunts
   Her own song's weird romance.

For (she sings) at last he swept
   As near to her as the tips
Of the lilies, that whitely slept,
As he leaned o'er one and wept
   And touched it with his lips—
   Sweeter than honey-drips!

And she keeps the lily yet—
   As the horseman bade (she says)
As he launched, with a wild curvet,
His steeds toward the far sunset,
   Till gulfed in its gorgeousness
   And lost to The Little Princess:

But O my master sweet!
   He is coming again! (*she sings*)
My Prince of the Coursers fleet,
   With his bugle's echoings,
   And the breath of his voice for
      the wings
Of the sandals of his feet!

622

THE SQUIRT-GUN UNCLE
MAKED ME

UNCLE SIDNEY, when he was
   here,
   Maked me a squirt-gun out o'
      some
Elder-bushes 'at growed out near
Where wuz the brick-yard—'way out
   clear
   To where the Toll-Gate come!

So when we walked back home again,
   He maked it, out in our wood-
      house where

Wuz the old work-bench, an' the old
   jack-plane,
An' the old 'poke-shave, an' the tools
   all lay'n'
   Ist like he wants 'em there.

He sawed it first with the old hand-
   saw;
An' nen he peeled off the bark,
   an' got
Some glass an' scraped it; an' told
   'bout Pa,
When *he* wuz a boy an' fooled his
   Ma,
   An' the whippin' 'at he caught.

Nen Uncle Sidney, he took an' filed
   A' old arn ramrod; an' one o' the
      ends
He screwed fast into the vise; an'
   smiled,
Thinkin', he said, o' when he wuz a
   child,
   'Fore him an' Pa wuz mens.

He punched out the peth, an' nen he
   putt
   A plug in the end with a hole
      notched through;
Nen took the old drawey-knife an' cut
An' maked a hande 'at shoved clean
   shut
   But ist where yer hand held to.

An' he wropt th'uther end with some
   string an' white
   Piece o' the sleeve of a' old tored
      shirt;
An' nen he showed me to hold it tight,
An' suck in the water an' work it
   right.—
   An' it 'ud ist squirt an' squirt!

623

THE YOUTHFUL PRESS

LITTLE Georgie Tompers, he
        Printed some fine cards for me;
But his press hád "J" for *James*—
By no means the choice of names.—

Yet it's proper, none the less,
That his little printing-press
Should be taught that *James* for "J"
Always is the better way.

For, if left to its own whim,
Next time it might call me "Jim,"—
Then THE CULTURED PRESS would be
Shocked at such a liberty.

Therefore, little presses all
Should be trained, while they are
        small,
To develop *taste* in these
Truths that shape our destinies.

624

MAX AND JIM

MAX an' Jim,
        They're each other's
Fat an' slim
        Little brothers.

Max is thin,
        An' Jim, the fac's is,
Fat ag'in
        As little Max is!

Their Pa 'lowed
        He don't know whuther
He's most proud
        Of one er th'other!

Their Ma says
        They're both so sweet—'*m!*—
That she guess
        She'll haf to eat 'em!

625

THE OLD HAYMOW

THE Old Haymow's the place to
        play
Fer boys, when it's a rainy day!
I good 'eal ruther be up there
Than down in town, er anywhere!

When I play in our stable-loft,
The good old hay's so dry an' soft,
An' feels so fine, an' smells so sweet,
I 'most ferget to go an' eat.

An' one time onc't I *did* ferget
To go tel dinner was all et,—
An' they had shortcake—an'—Bud he
Hogged up the piece Ma saved fer me!

Nen I won't let him play no more
In our haymow where I keep store
An' got hen-eggs to sell,—an' shoo
The cackle-un old hen out, too!

An' nen, when Aunty she was here
A-visitun from Rensselaer,
An' bringed my little cousin,—*he*
Can come up there an' play with me.

But, after while—when Bud he bets
'At I can't turn no summersetts,
I let him come up, ef he can
Ac' ha'f-way like a gentleman!

626

GUINEY-PIGS

GUINEY-PIGS is awful cute,
   With their little trimbly snoot
Sniffin' at the pussly that
We bring 'em to nibble at.
   Looks like they're so clean an' white,
   An' so dainty an' polite,
   They could eat like you an' me
   When they's company!

Tiltin' down the clover-tops
Till they spill, an' overdrops
The sweet morning dew—Don't you
Think they might have napkins, too?
   Ef a guiney-pig was big
   As a *shore-an'-certain* pig,
   Nen he wouldn't ac' so fine
   When he come to dine.

Nen he'd chomp his jaws an' eat
Things out in the dirty street,
Dirt an' all! An' nen lay down
In mud-holes an' waller roun'!
   So the *guiney-pigs* is best,
   'Cause they're nice an' tidiest;
   They eat 'most like you an' me
   When they's company!

627

BUSCH AND TOMMY

LITTLE Busch and Tommy Hays—
   Small the theme, but large the
      praise,—
For two braver brothers,
Of such toddling years and size,
Bloom of face, and blue of eyes,
Never trampled soldier-wise
   On the rights of mothers!

Even boldly facing their
Therapeutic father's air
   Of complex abstraction,
But to kindle—kindlier gaze,
Wake more smiles and gracious ways—
Ay, nor find in all their days
   Ampler satisfaction!

Hail ye, then, with chirp and cheer,
All wan patients, waiting here
   Bitterer medications!—
Busch and Tommy, *tone* us, too.—
How our life-blood leaps anew,
Under loving touch of you
   And your ministrations!

628

THE LUGUBRIOUS WHING-WHANG

THE rhyme o' The Raggedy Man's
      'at's best
   Is Tickle me, Love, in these
      Lonesome Ribs,
'Cause that-un's the strangest of all o'
      the rest,
An' the worst to learn, an' the last one
      guessed,
An' the funniest one, an' the foolish-
      est.—
   Tickle me, Love, in these Lone-
      some Ribs!

I don't know what in the world it
      means—
   Tickle me, Love, in these Lone-
      some Ribs!—
An' nen when I *tell* him I don't, he
      leans
Like he was a-grindin' on some ma-
      chines

An' says: Ef I *don't,* w'y, I don't
    know *beans!*
  Tickle me, Love, in these Lone-
    some Ribs!

Out on the margin of Moonshine
    Land,
  Tickle me, Love, in these Lone-
    some Ribs!
Out where the Whing-Whang loves
    to stand,
Writing his name with his tail in the
    sand,
And swiping it out with his oogerish
    hand;
  Tickle me, Love, in these Lone-
    some Ribs!

Is it the gibber of Gungs or Keeks?
  Tickle me, Love, in these Lone-
    some Ribs!
Or what *is* the sound that the Whing-
    Whang seeks?—
Crouching low by the winding creeks,
And holding his breath for weeks and
    weeks!
  Tickle me, Love, in these Lone-
    some Ribs!

Aroint him the wraithest of wraithly
    things!
  Tickle me, Love, in these Lone-
    some Ribs!
'Tis a fair Whing-Whangess, with
    phosphor rings,
And bridal-jewels of fangs and stings;
And she sits and as sadly and softly
    sings
As the mildewed whir of her own dead
    wings,—
    Tickle me, Dear,
      Tickle me here,
  Tickle me, Love, in me Lonesome
    Ribs!

629

LITTLE MANDY'S CHRISTMAS-TREE

LITTLE Mandy and her Ma
    'S porest folks you ever saw!—
Lived in porest house in town,
Where the fence 'uz all tore down.

And no front-door steps at all—
Ist a' old box 'g'inst the wall;
And no door-knob on the door
Outside.—*My!* but they 'uz pore!

Wuz no winder-shutters on,
And some of the *winders* gone,
And where they 'uz broke they'd pas'e
Ist brown paper 'crost the place.

Tell you! when it's *winter there,*
And the snow ist ever'where,
Little Mandy's Ma she say
'Spec' they'll freeze to death some day.

Wunst my Ma and me—when we
Be'n to church, and's goin' to be
Chris'mus purty soon,—we went
There—like the Committee sent.

And-sir! when we're in the door,
Wuz no carpet on the floor,
And no fire—and heels-and-head
Little Mandy's tucked in bed!

And her Ma told *my* Ma she
Got no coffee but ist tea,
And fried mush—and's all they had
Sence her health broke down so bad.

Nen Ma hug and hold me where
Little Mandy's layin' there;
And she kiss her, too, and nen
Mandy kiss my Ma again.

And my Ma she telled her *we*
Goin' to have a Chris'mus-Tree,
At the Sund'y-School, 'at's fer
ALL the childern, and fer *her.*

Little Mandy *think*—nen she
Say, "What *is* a Chris'mus-Tree?"
Nen my Ma she give *her* Ma
Somepin' 'at I never saw.

And say she *must* take it,—and
She ist maked her keep her hand
Wite close shut,—and nen she *kiss*
Her hand—shut ist like it is.

Nen we comed away. . . . And nen
When it's Chris'mus Eve again,
And all of us childerns be
At the Church and Chris'mus-Tree—

And all git toys and things
'At old Santy Claus he brings
And puts on the Tree;—wite where
The *big* Tree 'uz standin' there,

And the things 'uz all tooked down,
And the childerns, all in town,
Got their presents—nen we see
They's a *little* Chris'mus-Tree

Wite *behind* the *big* Tree—so
We can't see till *nen,* you know,—
And it's all ist loaded down
With the purtiest things in town!

And the teacher smile and say:
"This-here Tree 'at's hid away
It's marked *'Little Mandy's Tree.'*—
Little Mandy! Where is she?"

Nen nobody say a word.—
Stillest place you ever heard!—
Till a man tiptoe up where
Teacher's still a-waitin' there.

Nen the man he whispers, so
Ist the *Teacher* hears, you know.
Nen he tiptoe back and go
Out the big door—ist so slow!

. . . .

Little Mandy, though, *she* don't
Answer—and Ma say "she won't
Never, though each year they'll be
'Little Mandy's Chris'mus-Tree'

Fer pore childern"—my Ma says—
And *Committee* say they guess
"Little Mandy's Tree" 'ull be
Bigger than the *other* Tree!

630

THE FUNNIEST THING IN
THE WORLD

THE funniest thing in the world,
  I know,
Is watchin' the monkeys 'at's in the
    show!—
Jumpin' an' runnin' an' racin' roun',
'Way up the top o' the pole; nen
    down!
First they're here, an' nen they're
    there,
An' ist a'most any an' ever'where!—
Screechin' an' scratchin' wherever they
    go,
They're the funniest thing in the
    world, I know!

They're the funniest thing in the
    world, I think:—
Funny to watch 'em eat an' drink;
Funny to watch 'em a-watchin' us,
An' actin' 'most like grown folks
    does!—

Funny to watch 'em p'tend to be
Skeered at their tail 'at they happen
    to see;—
But the funniest thing in the world
    they do
Is never to laugh, like me an' you!

631

A FRUIT-PIECE

THE afternoon of summer folds
    Its warm arms round the mari-
golds,

And, with its gleaming fingers, pets
The watered pinks and violets

That from the casement vases spill,
Over the cottage window-sill,

Their fragrance down the garden
    walks
Where droop the dry-mouthed holly-
    hocks.

How vividly the sunshine scrawls
The grape-vine shadows on the walls!

How like a truant swings the breeze
In high boughs of the apple-trees!

The slender "free-stone" lifts aloof,
Full languidly above the roof,

A hoard of fruitage, stamped with gold
And precious mintings manifold.

High up, through curled green leaves,
    a pear
Hangs hot with ripeness here and
    there.

Beneath the sagging trellisings,
In lush, lack-luster clusterings,

Great torpid grapes, all fattened
    through
With moon and sunshine, shade and
    dew,

Until their swollen girths express
But forms of limp deliciousness—

Drugged to an indolence divine
With heaven's own sacramental wine.

632

THE BUMBLEBEE

YOU better not fool with a Bum-
    blebee!—
Ef you don't think they can sting—
    you'll see!
They're lazy to look at, an' kind o' go
Buzzin' an' bummin' aroun' so slow,
An' ac' so slouchy an' all fagged out,
Danglin' their legs as they drone about
The hollyhawks 'at they can't climb in
'Ithout ist a-tumble-un out ag'in!
Wunst I watched one climb clean 'way
In a jimson-blossom, I did, one day,—
An' I ist grabbed it—an' nen let go—
An' "Ooh-ooh! Honey! I told ye so!"
Says The Raggedy Man; an' he ist run
An' pullt out the stinger, an' don't
    laugh none,
An' says: "They *has* be'n folks, I guess,
'At thought I wuz predjudust, more
    er less,—
Yit I still muntain 'at a Bumblebee
Wears out his welcome too quick fer
    me!"

633

A PROSPECTIVE GLIMPSE

JANEY PETTIBONE'S the best
  Little girl an' purtiest
In this town! an' lives next door,
Up-stairs over their old store.

Little Janey Pettibone
An' her Ma lives all alone,—
'Cause her Pa broke up, an' nen
Died 'cause they ain't rich again.

Little Janey's Ma she sews
Fer my Ma sometimes, an' goes
An' gives music-lessuns—where
People's got pianers there.

But when Janey Pettibone
Grows an' grows, like I'm a-growin',
Nen *I'm* go' to keep a store,
An' sell things—an' sell some more—

Till I'm ist as rich!—An' nen
Her Ma can be rich again,—
Ef *I'm* rich enough to own
Little Janey Pettibone!

634

THE OLD TRAMP

A' OLD Tramp slep' in our stable
  wunst,
  An' The Raggedy Man he caught
An' roust him up, an' chased him off
  ˙ Clean out through our back lot!

An' th' old Tramp hollered back an'
  said,—
  "You're a *purty* man!—*You* air!—
With a pair o' eyes like two fried eggs,
An' a nose like a Bartlutt pear!"

635

THE PET COON

NOEY BIXLER ketched him, an'
  fetched him in to me
When he's ist a little teenty-weenty
  baby-coon
'Bout as big as little pups, an' tied
  him to a tree;
An' Pa gived Noey fifty cents, when
  he come home at noon.
Nen he buyed a chain fer him, an'
  little collar, too,
An' sawed a hole in a' old tub an'
  turnt it upside down;
An' little feller'd stay in there and
  won't come out fer you—
'Tendin' like he's kind o' skeered o'
  boys 'at lives in town.

Now he ain't afeard a bit! he's ist so
  fat an' tame,
We on'y chain him up at night, to
  save the little chicks.
Holler "Greedy! Greedy!" to him, an'
  he knows his name,
An' here he'll come a-waddle-un, up
  fer any tricks!
He'll climb up my leg, he will, an'
  waller in my lap,
An' poke his little black paws 'way
  in my pockets where
They's beechnuts, er chinkypins, er
  any little scrap
Of anything 'at's good to eat—an'
  he don't care!

An' he's as spunky as you please, an'
  don't like dogs at all,—
Billy Miller's black-an'-tan tackled
  him one day,
An' "Greedy" he ist kind o' doubled
  all up like a ball,

An' Billy's dog he gived a yelp er
    two an' runned away!
An' nen when Billy fighted me, an'
    hit me with a bone,
An' Ma she purt' nigh ketched him
    as he dodged an' skooted
    through
The fence, she says, "You better let
    my little boy alone,
Er 'Greedy,' next he whips yer dog,
    shall whip you, too!"

636

AN IMPETUOUS RESOLVE

WHEN little Dickie Swope's a
    man,
He's go' to be a Sailor;
An' little Hamey Tincher, he's
    A-go' to be a Tailor:
Bud Mitchell, he's a-go' to be
    A stylish Carriage-Maker;
An' when *I* grow a grea'-big man,
    I'm go' to be a Baker!

An' Dick'll buy his sailor-suit
    O' Hame; an' Hame'll take it
An' buy as fine a double-rig
    As ever Bud kin make it:
An' nen all three'll drive roun' fer me,
    An' we'll drive off togevver,
A-slingin' pie-crust 'long the road
    Ferever an' ferever!

637

THE HUNTER BOY

HUNTER Boy of Hazelwood—
    Happier than Robin Hood!
Dance across the green, and stand

Suddenly, with lifted hand
Shading eager eyes, and be
Thus content to capture me!—
Cease thy quest for wilder prey
Than my willing heart to-day!

Hunter Boy! with belt and bow,
Bide with me, or let me go,
An thou wilt, in wake of thee,
Questing for mine infancy!
With thy glad face in the sun,
Let thy laughter overrun
Thy ripe lips, until mine own
Answer, ringing, tone for tone!

O my Hunter! tilt the cup
Of thy silver bugle up,
And like wine pour out for me
All its limpid melody!
Pout thy happy lips and blare
Music's kisses everywhere—
Whiff o'er forest, field and town,
Tufts of tune like thistle-down!
    O to go, as once I could,
    Hunter Boy of Hazelwood!

638

BILLY GOODIN'

A big piece o' pie, and a big piece o'
    puddin'—
I laid it all by fer little Billy Goodin'!
                            —BOY POET.

LOOK so neat an' sweet in all yer
    frills an' fancy pleatin'!
Better shet yer kitchen, though, afore
    you go to Meetin'!—
Better hide yer mince-meat an'
    stewed fruit an' plums!

Better hide yer pound-cake an' bresh
away the crumbs!
Better hide yer cubbord-key when
Billy Goodin' comes,
A-eatin'! an' a-eatin'! an'
a-eatin'!

Sight o' Sund'y-doin's done 'at ain't
done in Meetin'!
Sun acrost yer garden-patch a-pourin'
an' a-beatin';
Meller apples drappin' in the weeds
an' roun' the groun'—
Clingstones an' sugar-pears a-ist
a-plunkin' down!—
Better kind o' comb the grass 'fore
Billy comes aroun',
A-eatin'! an' a-eatin'! an'
a-eatin'!

Billy Goodin' ain't a-go' to go to any
Meetin'!
We 'ull watch an' ketch an' give the
little sneak a beatin'!—
Better hint *we* want'o stay 'n' snoop
yer grapes an' plums!
Better eat 'em all yerse'f an' suck
yer stingy thumbs!—
Won't be nothin' anyhow when
Billy Goodin' comes!—
A-eatin'! an' a-eatin'! an'
a-eatin'!

639

SONG—FOR NOVEMBER

WHILE skies glint bright with
bluest light
Through clouds that race o'er field
and town,
And leaves go dancing left and right,
And orchard apples tumble down;

While schoolgirls sweet, in lane or
street,
Lean 'gainst the wind and feel and
hear
Its glad heart like a lover's beat,—
So reigns the rapture of the year.

*Then ho! and hey! and whoop-
hooray!*
Though winter clouds be looming,
Remember a November day
Is merrier than mildest May
With all her blossoms blooming.

While birds in scattered flight are
blown
Aloft and lost in bosky mist,
And truant boys scud home alone
'Neath skies of gold and amethyst;
While twilight falls, and echo calls
Across the haunted atmosphere,
With low, sweet laughs at intervals,—
So reigns the rapture of the year.

*Then ho! and hey! and whoop-
hooray!*
Though winter clouds be looming,
Remember a November day
Is merrier than mildest May
With all her blossoms blooming.

640

AT AUNTY'S HOUSE

ONE time, when we'z at Aunty's
house—
'Way in the country!—where
They's ist but woods—an' pigs, an'
cows—
An' all's outdoors an' air!—
An' orchurd-swing; an' churry trees—

An' *churries* in 'em!—Yes, an' these-
Here redhead birds steals all they
　　please,
An' tetch 'em ef you dare!—
W'y, wunst, one time, when we wuz
　　there,
　　We et out on the porch!

Wite where the cellar door wuz shut
　　The table wuz; an' I
Let Aunty set by me an' cut
　　My vittuls up—an' pie.
'Tuz awful funny!—I could see
The redheads in the churry tree;
An' beehives, where you got to be
　　So keerful, goin' by;—
An' "Comp'ny" there an' all!—an'
　　we—
　　We et out .on the porch!

An' I ist et *p'surves* an' things
　　'At Ma don't 'low me to—
An' *chickun-gizzurds*—(don't　like
　　wings
Like *Parunts* does! do *you?*)
An' all the time the wind blowed
　　there,
An' I could feel it in my hair,
An' ist smell clover *ever*'where!—
　　An' a old redhead flew
Purt' nigh wite over my high-chair,
　　When we et on the porch!

641

LIFE AT THE LAKE

THE green below and the blue
　　above!—
The waves caressing the shores they
　　love:
Sails in haven, and sails afar
And faint as the water-lilies are

In inlets haunted of willow wands,
Listless lovers, and trailing hands
With spray to gem them and tan to
　　glove.—
The green below and the blue above.

The blue above and the green below!
Would that the world were always
　　so!—
Always summer and warmth and
　　light,
With mirth and melody day and
　　night!
Birds in the boughs of the beckoning
　　trees,
Chirr of locusts and whiff of breeze—
World-old roses that bud and blow.—
The blue above and the green below.

The green below and the blue above!
Heigh! young hearts and the hopes
　　thereof!—
Kate in the hammock, and Tom
　　sprawled on
The sward—like a lover's picture,
　　drawn
By the lucky dog himself, with Kate
To moon o'er his shoulder and medi-
　　tate
On a fat old purse or a lank young
　　love.—
The green below and the blue above.

The blue above and the green below!
Shadow and sunshine to and fro.—
Season for dreams—whate'er befall
Hero, heroine, hearts and all!
Wave or wildwood—the blithe bird
　　sings,
And the leaf-hid locust whets his
　　wings—
Just as a thousand years ago—
The blue above and the green below.

642

JOHN BOYLE O'REILLY

SEPULTURE—BOSTON, AUGUST 13, 1890

DEAD? this peerless man of men—
Patriot, Poet, Citizen!—
Dead? and ye weep where he lies
Mute, with folded eyes!

Courage! All his tears are done;
Mark him, dauntless, face the sun!
He hath led you.—Still, as true,
He is leading you.

Folded eyes and folded hands
Typify divine commands
He is hearkening to, intent
Beyond wonderment.

'Tis promotion that has come
Thus upon him. Stricken dumb
Be your moanings dolorous!
God knows what He does.

Rather, as your chief, *aspire!*—
Rise and seize his toppling lyre,
And sing Freedom, Home and Love,
And the rights thereof!

Ere in selfish grief ye sink,
Come! catch rapturous breath and
think—
Think what sweep of wing hath he,
Loosed in endless liberty.

643

THE BOY'S CANDIDATE

LAS' time 'at Uncle Sidney come,
He bringed a watermelon home—
An' half the boys in town

Come taggin' after him.—An' he
Says, when we et it,—*"Gracious me!
'S the boy-house fell down?"*

644

CHRISTINE

*Two strangers meeting at a festival;
Two lovers whispering by an orchard
wall.*
—TENNYSON.

MOST quaintly touching, in her
German tongue—
Haply, had he but mastered that as
well
As she his English, this were not to
tell:—
Touring through her dear Fatherland,
the young
American first found her, as she
sung
*"Du bist mir nah' und doch so
fern,"* while fell
Their eyes together, and the mira-
cle
Of love and doom was wrought. Her
father wrung
The lovers from each other's arms for-
ever—
Forgive him, all forgiving souls that
can!
She died that selfsame hour—just
paused to write
Her broken heart's confession thus: "I
never
Was O so loving in a young gentle-
man
Than yet I am to you. So ist
Good night."

645

OLD JOHN CLEVENGER
ON BUCKEYES

OLD John Clevenger lets on,
    Allus, like he's purty rough
Timber.—He's a grate old John!—
    "Rough?"—don't swaller no sich
        stuff!
Moved here, sence the war was
        through,
    From Ohio—somers near
Old Bucyrus,—loyal, too,
    As us "Hoosiers" is to *here!*
Git old John stirred up a bit
    On his old home stompin'-ground—
Talks same as he lived thare yit,
    When some subject brings it round—
Like, fer instunce, Sund'y last,
    Fetched his wife, and et and stayed
All night with us.—Set and gassed
    Tel plum midnight—'cause I made
Some remark 'bout "buckeyes" and
    "What was buckeyes good fer?"—
        So,
Like I 'lowed, he waved his hand
    And lit in and let me know:—

" 'What   is   Buckeyes good fer?—
        What's
Pineys and *fergit-me-nots?*—
Honeysuckles, and sweet peas,
And sweet-williamsuz and these
Johnny-jump-ups ev'rywhare,
Growin' round the roots o' trees
In Spring-weather?—what air *they*
Good fer?—kin you tell me—*Hey?*
'Good to look at?' Well they air!
'Specially when *Winter's* gone,
Clean *dead-cert'in!* and the wood's
Green again, and sun feels good's
June!—and shed your blame boots on

The back porch, and lit out to
Roam round like you ust to do,
Bare-foot, up and down the crick,
Whare the buckeyes growed so thick,
And witch-hazel and pop-paws,
And hackberries and black-haws—
With wild pizen-vines jist knit
Over and *en-nunder* it,
And wove round it all, I jing!
Tel you couldn't hardly stick
A durn *case-knife* through the thing!
Wriggle round through *that;* and
        then—
All het-up, and scratched and tanned,
And muskeeter-bit and mean-
Feelin'—all at onc't again,
Come out suddent on a clean
Slopin' little hump o' green
Dry soft grass, as fine and grand
As a pollor-sofy!—And
Jis pile down thare!—and tell *me*
Anywhares you'd ruther be—
'Ceptin' *right thare,* with the wild-
Flowrs all round ye, and your eyes
Smilin' with 'em at the skies,
Happy as a little child!
Well!—right here, *I* want to say,
Poets kin talk all they please
'Bout 'wild-flowrs, in colors gay,'
And 'sweet blossoms flauntin' theyr
Beauteous fragrunce on the breeze'—
But the sight o' *buckeyes* jis
Sweet to me as *blossoms* is!

"I'm *Ohio-born*—right whare
People's *all* called 'Buckeyes' *thare*—
'Cause, I s'pose, our buckeye crap's
Biggest in the world, perhaps!—
Ner my head don't stretch my hat
Too much on account o' *that!*—
'Cause it's Natchur's ginerus hand
Sows 'em broadcast ore the land,
With eye-single fer man's good

And the gineral neghborhood!
So *buckeyes* jis natchurly
'Pears like *kith-and-kin* to *me!*
'S like the good old sayin' wuz,
'Purty *is* as purty *does!'*—
We can't *eat* 'em, cookd er raw—
Yit, I mind, *tomattusuz*
Wuz considerd pizenus
Onc't—and dasen't eat 'em!—*Pshaw*—
'Twouldn't take *me* by supprise,
Some day, ef we et *buckeyes!*
That, though, 's nuther here ner
   thare!—
Jis the Buckeye, whare we air,
In the present times, is what
Ockuppies my lovin' care
And my most perfoundest thought!
. . . Guess, this minute, what I got
In my pocket, 'at I've packed
Purt' nigh forty year.—A dry,
Slick and shiny, warped and cracked,
Wilted, weazened old *buckeye!*
What's it *thare* fer? What's my hart
In my *brest* fer?—'Cause it's part
Of my *life*—and 'tends to biz—
Like this *buckeye's* bound to act—
'Cause *it* tends to *Rhumatiz!*

". . . Ketched more *rhumatiz* than
   fish,
Seinen', onc't—and pants froze on
My blame legs!—And ust to wish
I wuz well er *dead and gone!*
Doc give up the case, and shod
His old hoss again and stayed
On good roads!—*And thare I laid!*
Pap he tuck some bluegrass sod
Steeped in whisky, bilin'-hot,
And socked *that* on! Then I got
Sorto' holt o' him, *somehow*—
Kindo' crazy-like, they say—
And I'd *killed* him, like as not,
Ef I hadn't swooned away!

Smell my scortcht pelt purt' nigh now!
Well—to make a long tale short—
I hung on the blame disease
Like a shavin'-hoss! and sort
O' wore it out by slow degrees—
Tel my legs wuz straight enugh
To poke through my pants again
And kick all the doctor-stuff
In the fi-er-place! Then turned in
And tuck Daddy Craig's old cuore—
Jis a buckeye—and that's *shore.*—
Hain't no case o' rhumatiz
Kin subsist whare buckeyes is!"

646

MEREDITH NICHOLSON

KEATS, and Kirk White, David
   Gray and the rest of you
Heavened and blest of you young
   singers gone,—
Slender in sooth though the theme un-
   expressed of you,
Leave us this like of you yet to sing
   on!

Let your Muse mother him and your
   souls brother him,
Even as now, or in fancy, you do:
Still let him sing to us ever, and bring
   to us
Musical musings of glory and—you.

Never a note to do evil or wrong to
   us—
Beauty of melody—beauty of
   words,—
Sweet and yet strong to us comes his
   young song to us,
Rippled along to us clear as the
   bird's.
No fame elating him falsely, nor
   sating him—

Feasting and fêting him faint of her
    joys,
But singing on where the laurels are
    waiting him,
Young yet in art, and his heart yet
    a boy's.

647

MY RUTHERS

[*Writ durin' State Fair at Indanop-
lis, whilse visitin' a Soninlaw then re-
sidin' thare, who has sence got back
to the country whare he says a man
that's raised there ort to a-stayed in
the first place.*]

I TELL you what I'd ruther do—
    Ef I only had my ruthers,—
I'd ruther work when I wanted to
    Than be bossed round by others;—
    I'd ruther kindo' git the swing
    O' what was *needed*, first, I jing!
    Afore I *swet* at anything!—
Ef I only had my ruthers;—
In fact I'd aim to be the same
    With all men as my brothers;
And they'd all be the same with *me*—
    Ef I only had my ruthers.

I wouldn't likely know it all—
    Ef I only had my ruthers;—
I'd know *some* sense, and some base-
    ball—
    Some *old* jokes, and—some others:
    I'd know *some politics*, and 'low
    Some tarif-speeches same as now,
    Then go hear Nye on "Branes and
        How
    To Detect Theyr Presence." *T'others*,
That stayed away, I'd *let* 'em stay—
    All my dissentin' brothers

Could chuse as shore a kill er cuore,
    Ef I only had my ruthers.

The pore 'ud git theyr dues *some-
        times*—
    Ef I only had my ruthers,—
And be paid *dollars* 'stid o' *dimes,*
    Fer childern, wives and mothers:
    Theyr boy that slaves; theyr girl
        that sews—
    Fer *others*—not   herself,   God
        knows!—
    The grave's *her* only change of
        clothes!
    . . . Ef I only had my ruthers,
They'd all have "stuff" and time enugh
    To answer one-another's
Appealin' prayer fer "lovin' care"—
    Ef I only had my ruthers.

They'd be few folks 'ud ast fer trust,
    Ef I only had my ruthers,
And blame few business men to bu'st
    Theyrselves, er harts of others:
    Big Guns that come here durin'
        Fair-
    Week could put up jest anywhare,
    And find a full-and-plenty thare,
    Ef I only had my ruthers:
The rich and great 'ud 'sociate
    With all theyr lowly brothers,
Feelin' *we* done the honorun—
    Ef I only had my ruthers.

648

GOD'S MERCY

BEHOLD, one faith endureth still—
    Let factions rail and creeds con-
        tend—
God's mercy *was*, and *is*, and *will*
Be with us, foe and friend.

649

THE WHITHERAWAYS

SET SAIL OCTOBER 15, 1890

THE Whitheraways!—That's what
I'll have to call
You—sailing off, with never word at
all
Of parting!—sailing 'way across the
sea,
With never one good-by to *me*—to ME!

Sailing away from me, with no fare-
well!—
Ah, Parker Hitt and sister Muriel—
And Rodney, too, and little Laurance
—all
Sailing away—just as the leaves, this
Fall!

Well, then, *I* too shall sail on cheerily
As now you all go sailing o'er the sea:
I've *other* little friends with me on
shore—
Though they but make me yearn for
you the more!

And so, sometime, dear little friends
afar,
When this faint voice shall reach you,
and you are
All just a little homesick, you must be
As brave as I am now, and think of
me!

Or, haply, if your eyes, as mine, droop
low,
And would be humored with a tear
or so,—
Go to your *Parents,* Children! let *them*
do
The *crying*—'twill be easier for them
to!

650

A BOY'S MOTHER

MY mother she's so good to me,
Ef I was good as I could be,
I couldn't be as good—no, sir!—
Can't any boy be good as her!

She loves me when I'm glad er sad;
She loves me when I'm good er bad;
An', what's a funniest thing, she says
She loves me when she punishes.

I don't like her to punish me.—
That don't hurt,—but it hurts to see
Her cryin'.—Nen *I* cry; an' nen
We both cry an' be good again.

She loves me when she cuts an' sews
My little cloak an' Sund'y clothes;
An' when my Pa comes home to tea,
She loves him most as much as me.

She laughs an' tells him all I said,
An' grabs me up an' pats my head;
An' I hug *her,* an' hug my Pa
An' love him purt' nigh as much as
Ma.

651

THE RUNAWAY BOY

WUNST I sassed my Pa, an' he
Won't stand that, an' pun-
ished me,—
Nen when he wuz gone that day,
I slipped out an' runned away.

I tooked all my copper-cents,
An' clumbed over our back fence

In the jimpson-weeds 'at growed
Ever'where all down the road.

Nen I got out there, an' nen
I runned some—an' runned again,
When I met a man 'at led
A big cow 'at shooked her head.

I went down a long, long lane
Where wuz little pigs a-playin';
An' a grea'-big pig went *"Booh!"*
An' jumped up, an' skeered me too.

Nen I scampered past, an' they
Was somebody hollered *"Hey!"*
An' I ist looked ever'where,
An' they wuz nobody there.

I *want* to, but I'm 'fraid to try
To go back. . . . An' by an' by
Somepin' hurts my th'oat inside—
An' I want my Ma—an' cried.

Nen a grea'-big girl come through
Where's a gate, an' telled me who
Am I? an' ef I tell where
My home's at she'll show me there.

But I couldn't ist but tell
What's my *name;* an' she says "well,"
An' ist tooked me up an' says
"She know where I live, she guess."

Nen she telled me hug wite close
Round her neck!—an' off she goes
Skippin' up the street! An' nen
Purty soon I'm home again.

An' my Ma, when she kissed me,
Kissed the big girl too, an' *she*
Kissed me—ef I p'omise shore
I won't run away no more!

652

THE FISHING PARTY

WUNST we went a-fishin'—Me
    An' my Pa an' Ma, all three,
When they wuz a picnic, 'way
Out to Hanch's Woods, one day.

An' they wuz a crick out there,
Where the fishes is, an' where
Little boys 'taint big an' strong
Better have their folks along!

My Pa he ist fished an' fished!
An' my Ma she said she wished
Me an' her was home; an' Pa
Said he wished so worse'n Ma.

Pa said ef you talk, er say
Anything, er sneeze, er play,
Hain't no fish, alive er dead,
Ever go' to bite! he said.

Purt' nigh dark in town when we
Got back home; an' Ma, says she,
Now she'll have a fish fer shore!
An' she buyed one at the store.

Nen at supper, Pa he won't
Eat no fish, an' says he don't
Like 'em.—An' he pounded me
When I choked! . . . Ma, didn't he?

653

THE RAGGEDY MAN

O THE Raggedy Man! He works
    fer Pa;
An' he's the goodest man ever you saw!
He comes to our house every day,

An' waters the horses, an' feeds 'em
hay;
An' he opens the shed—an' we all ist
laugh
When he drives out our little old wob-
ble-ly calf;
An' nen—ef our hired girl says he
can—
He milks the cow fer 'Lizabuth Ann.—
Ain't he a' awful good Raggedy
Man?
Raggedy! Raggedy! Raggedy
Man!

W'y, The Raggedy Man—he's ist so
good,
He splits the kindlin' an' chops the
wood;
An' nen he spades in our garden, too,
An' does most , things 'at *boys* can't
do.—
He clumbed clean up in our big tree
An' shooked a' apple down fer me—
An' 'nother 'n', too, fer 'Lizabuth
Ann—
An' 'nother 'n', too, fer The Raggedy
Man.—
Ain't he a' awful kind Raggedy
Man?
Raggedy! Raggedy! Raggedy
Man!

An' The Raggedy Man one time say
he
Pick' roast' rambos from a' orchurd-
tree,
An' et 'em—all ist roast' an' hot!—
An' it's so, too!—'cause a corn-crib got
Afire one time an' all burn' down
On "The Smoot Farm," 'bout four mile
from town—
On "The Smoot Farm"! Yes—an' the
hired han'

'At worked there nen 'uz The Rag-
gedy Man!—
Ain't he the beatin'est Raggedy
Man?
Raggedy! Raggedy! Raggedy
Man!

The Raggedy Man's so good an' kind
He'll be our "horsey," an' "haw" an'
mind
Ever'thing 'at you make him do—
An' won't run off—'less you want him
to!
I drived him wunst way down our
lane
An' he got skeered, when it 'menced to
rain,
An' ist rared up an' squealed and run
Purt' nigh away!—an' it's all in fun!
Nen he skeered *ag'in* at a' old tin
can . . .
Whoa! y' old runaway Raggedy
Man!
Raggedy! Raggedy! Raggedy
Man!

An' The Raggedy Man, he knows most
rhymes,
An' tells 'em, ef I be good, sometimes:
Knows 'bout Giunts, an' Griffuns, an'
Elves,
An' the Squidgicum-Squees 'at swallers
the'rselves:
An', wite by the pump in our pasture-
lot,
He showed me the hole 'at the Wunks
is got,
'At lives 'way deep in the ground, an'
can
Turn into me, er 'Lizabuth Ann!
Er Ma, er Pa, er The Raggedy Man!
Ain't he a funny old Raggedy Man?
Raggedy! Raggedy! Raggedy
Man!

An' wunst, when The Raggedy Man
      come late,
An' pigs ist root' thue the garden-gate,
He 'tend like the pigs 'uz *bears* an'
      said,
"Old Bear-shooter'll shoot 'em dead!"
An' race' an' chase' 'em, an' they'd ist
      run
When he pint his hoe at 'em like it's a
      gun
An' go "Bang!—Bang!" nen 'tend he
      stan'
An' load up his gun ag'in! Raggedy
      Man!
   He's an old Bear-Shooter Raggedy
      Man!
      Raggedy!   Raggedy!   Raggedy
      Man!

An' sometimes The Raggedy Man lets
      on
We're little *prince*-children, an' old
      King's gone
To git more money, an' lef' us there—
And *Robbers* is ist thick ever'where;
An' nen—ef we all won't cry, fer
      shore—
The Raggedy Man he'll come and
      "splore
The Castul-Halls," an' steal the
      "gold"—
An' steal *us,* too, an' grab an' hold
An' pack us off to his old "Cave"!—
      An'
   Haymow's the "cave" o' The Rag-
      gedy Man!—
      Raggedy!   Raggedy!   Raggedy
      Man!

The Raggedy Man—one time, when
      he
Wuz makin' a little bow-'n'-orry fer
      me,

Says "When you're big like your Pa
      is,
Air *you* go' to keep a fine store like
      his—
An' be a rich merchunt—an' wear fine
      clothes?—
Er what *air* you go' to be, goodness
      knows?"
An' nen he laughed at 'Lizabuth
      Ann,
An' I says "'M go' to be a Raggedy
      Man!—
   I'm ist go' to be a nice Raggedy
      Man!"
      Raggedy!   Raggedy!   Raggedy
      Man!

654

OUR HIRED GIRL

OUR hired girl, she's 'Lizabuth
      Ann;
   An' she can cook best things to eat!
She ist puts dough in our pie-pan,
   An' pours in somepin' 'at's good an'
      sweet;
An' nen she salts it all on top
   With cinnamon; an' nen she'll stop
   An' stoop an' slide it, ist as slow,
In th' old cook-stove, so's 'twon't slop
   An' git all spilled; nen bakes it, so
   It's custard-pie, first thing you
      know!
         An' nen she'll say,
         "Clear out o' my way!
They's time fer work, an' time fer
      play!
   Take yer dough, an' run, child,
      run!
   Er I cain't git no cookin' done!"

When our hired girl 'tends like she's
    mad,
An' says folks got to walk the chalk
When *she's* around, er wisht they had!
I play out on our porch an' talk
To Th' Raggedy Man 'at mows our
    lawn;
An' he says, *"Whew!"* an' nen leans
    on
His old crook-scythe, and blinks his
    eyes,
An' sniffs all 'round an' says, "I
    swawn!
Ef my old nose don't tell me lies,
It 'pears like I smell custard-pies!"
      An' nen *he'll* say,
      "Clear out o' my way!
They's time fer work, an' time fer
    play!
Take yer dough, an' run, child,
    run!
Er she caint' git no cookin' done!"

Wunst our hired girl, when she
    Got the supper, an' we all et,
An' it wuz night, an' Ma an' me
    An' Pa went wher' the "Social"
      met,—
An' nen when we come home, an' see
A light in the kitchen door, an' we
    Heerd a maccordeun, Pa says, "Lan'-
O'-Gracious! who can *her* beau be?"
      An' I marched in, an' 'Lizabuth
      Ann
    Wuz parchin' corn fer The Raggedy
    Man!
      Better say,
      "Clear out o' the way!
They's time fer work, an' time fer
    play!
Take the hint, an' run, child, run!
Er we cain't git no courtin' done!"

THE BOY LIVES ON OUR FARM

THE Boy lives on our Farm, he's
    not
Afeard o' horses none!
An' he can make 'em lope, er trot,
    Er rack, er pace, er run.
Sometimes he drives *two* horses, when
    He comes to town an' brings
A wagonful o' 'taters nen,
    An' roastin'-ears an' things.

Two horses is "a team," he says,—
    An' when you drive er hitch,
The *right* un's a "near horse," I guess,
    Er "off"—I don't know which.—
The Boy lives on our Farm, he told
    Me, too, 'at he can see,
By looking at their teeth, how old
    A horse is, to a T!

I'd be the gladdest boy alive
    Ef I knowed much as that,
An' could stand up like him an' drive,
    An' ist push back my hat,
Like he comes skallyhootin' through
    Our alley, with one arm
A-wavin' Fare-ye-well! to you—
    The Boy lives on our Farm!

SONG OF THE BULLET

IT whizzed and whistled along the
    blurred
And red-blent ranks; and it nicked
    the star
Of an epaulette, as it snarled the
    word—
      War!

On it sped—and the lifted wrist
  Of the ensign-bearer stung, and
    straight
Dropped at his side as the word was
    hissed—
        Hate!

On went the missile—smoothed the
    blue
  Of a jaunty cap and the curls there-
    of,
Cooing, soft as a dove might do—
        Love!

Sang!—sang on!—sang hate—sang
    war—
  Sang love, in sooth, till it needs must
    cease,
Hushed in the heart it was questing
    for.—
        Peace!

657

CHRISTMAS GREETING

A WORD of Godspeed and good
      cheer
To all on earth, or far or near,
Or friend or foe, or thine or mine—
In echo of the voice divine,
Heard when the Star bloomed forth
    and lit
The world's face, with God's smile on
    it.

658

UNCLE WILLIAM'S PICTURE

UNCLE WILLIAM, last July,
      Had his picture took.
"Have it done, of course," says I,
  "Jes' the way you look!"

(All dressed up, he was, fer the
Barbecue and jubilee
The old settlers helt.) So he—
  Last he had it took.

Lide she'd coaxed and begged and
    pled,
  Sence her mother went;
But he'd cough and shake his head
  At all argyment;
Mebby clear his th'oat and say,
"What's *my* likeness 'mount to, hey,
Now with *Mother* gone away
  From us, like she went?"

But we projicked round, tel we
  Got it figgered down
How we'd git him, Lide and me,
  Drivin' into town;
Bragged how well he looked and
    fleshed
Up around the face, and freshed
With the morning air; and breshed
  His coat-collar down.

All so providential! W'y,
  Now he's dead and gone,
Picture 'pears so lifelike I
  Want to start him on
Them old tales he ust to tell,
And old talks so sociable,
And old songs he sung so well—
  'Fore his voice was gone!

Face is sad to *Lide,* and they's
  Sorrow in the eyes—
Kisses it sometimes, and lays
  It away and cries.
I smooth down her hair, and 'low
He is happy, anyhow,
Bein' there with Mother now,—
  Smile, and wipe my eyes.

659

ERASMUS WILSON

'RAS WILSON, I respect you,
'cause
You're common, like you allus was
Afore you went to town and s'prised
The world by gittin' "reckonized,"
And yit perservin', as I say,
Your common hoss-sense ev'ryway!
And when that name o'·yourn occurs
On hand-bills, er in newspapers,
Er letters writ by friends 'at ast
About you, same as in the past,·
And neghbors and relations 'low
You're out o' the tall timber now,
And "gittin' thare" about as spry's
The next!—as *I say,* when my eyes,
Er ears, lights on your name, I mind
The first time 'at I come to find
You—and my Rickollection yells,
Jest jubilunt as old sleigh-bells—
" 'Ras Wilson! Say! Hold up! and
shake
A paw, fer old acquaintance sake!"

My *Rickollection,* more'n like,
Hain't overly too apt to strike
The what's-called "cultchurd public
eye"
As wisdum of the deepest dye,—
And yit my *Rickollection* makes
So blame lots fewer bad mistakes,
Regardin' human-natur' and
The fellers 'at I've shook theyr hand,
Than my *best jedgemunt's* done, the
day
I've met 'em—'fore I got away,—
'At—Well, 'Ras Wilson, let me grip
Your hand in warmest pardnership!

Dad-burn ye!—Like to jest haul back
A' old flat-hander, jest che-whack!

And take you 'twixt the shoulders,
say,
Sometime you're lookin' t'other way!—
Er, maybe whilse you're speakin' to
A whole blame Court-house-full o' 'thu-
Syastic friends, I'd like to jest
Come in-like and break up the nest
Afore you hatched another cheer,
And say: " 'Ras, *I* can't stand hitched
here
All night—ner wouldn't ef I could!—
But Little Bethel Neghborhood,
You ust to live at, 's sent some word
Fer you, ef ary chance occurred
To git it to ye,—so ef you
Kin stop, I'm waitin' fer ye to!"

You're common, as I said afore—
You're common, yit oncommon *more.*—
You allus kindo' 'pear, to me,
What all mankind had ort to be—
Jest *natchurl,* and the more hurraws
You git, the less you know the cause—
Like as ef God Hisse'f stood by,
Where best on earth hain't half knee-
high,
And *seein'* like, and knowin' *He*
'S the Only Grate Man really,
You're jest content to size your hight
With any feller man's in sight.—
And even then they's scrubs, like me,
Feels stuck-up, in your company!

Like now:—I want to go with you
Plum out o' town a mile er two
Clean past the Fair-ground whare's
some hint
O' pennyrile er peppermint,
And bottom-lands, and timber thick
Enugh to sorto' shade the crick!
I want to *see* you—want to set
Down somers, whare the grass hain't
wet,

And kindo' *breathe* you, like puore
    air—
And taste o' your tobacker thare,
And talk and chaw! Talk o' the birds
We've knocked with cross-bows.—
    Afterwards
Drop, mayby, into some dispute
'Bout "pomgrannies," er cal'mus-root—
And how *they* growed, and *whare?*—
    on tree
Er vine?—Who's best boy-memory!—
And wasn't it *gingsang,* insted
O' cal'mus-root, growed like you
    said?—
Er how to tell a coon-track from
A mussrat's;—er how milksick come—
Er ef *cows* brung it?—Er why now
We never see no "muley"-cow—
Ner "frizzly"-chicken—ner no "clay-
Bank" mare—ner nothin' thataway!—
And what's come o' the *yeller-*core
Old wortermelons?—hain't no more.—
Tomattusus, the same—all *red-*
Uns nowadays—All past joys fled—
Each and all jest gone k-whizz!
Like our days o' childhood is!

Dag-gone it, 'Ras! they hain't no friend,
It 'pears-like, left to comperhend
Sich things as these but you, and see
How dratted sweet they air to me!
But you, 'at's loved 'em allus, and
Kin sort 'em out and understand
'Em, same as the fine books you've
    read,
And all fine thoughts you've writ, er
    said,
Er worked out, through long nights o'
    rain,
And doubts and fears, and hopes,
    again,
As bright as morning when she
    broke,—

You know a tear-drop from a joke!
    And so, 'Ras Wilson, stop and shake
    A paw, fer old acquaintance sake!

660

BACK FROM TOWN

OLD friends allus is the best,
    Halest-like and heartiest:
Knowed us first, and don't allow
We're so blame much better now!
They was standin' at the bars
When we grabbed "the kivvered kyars"
And lit out fer town, to make
Money—and that old mistake!

We thought then the world we went
Into beat "The Settlement,"
And the friends 'at we'd make there
Would beat any anywhere!—
And they *do*—fer that's their biz:
They beat all the friends they is—
'Cept the raal old friends like you
'At staid at home, like *I'd* ort to!

W'y, of all the good things yit
I ain't shet of, is to quit
Business, and git back to sheer
These old comforts waitin' here—
These old friends; and these old hands
'At a feller understands;
These old winter nights, and old
Young-folks chased in out the cold!

Sing "Hard Times'll come ag'in
No More!" and neighbers all jine in!
Here's a feller come from town
Wants that-air old fiddle down
From the chimbly!—Git the floor

Cleared fer one cowtillion more!—
It's poke the kitchen fire, says he,
And shake a friendly leg with me!

661

TUGG MARTIN

I

TUGG MARTIN'S tough.—No
doubt o' that!
And down there at
The camp he come from word's bin
sent
Advisin' this-here Settle-ment
To kind o' *humor* Tugg, and not
To git him hot.—
Jest pass his imperfections by,
And he's as good as pie!

II

They claim he's *wanted* back there.—
Yit
The officers they mostly quit
Insistin' when
They notice Tugg's so *back'ard,* and
Sort o' gives 'em to understand
He'd ruther not!—A Deputy
(The slickest one you ever see!)
Tackled him *last*—"disguisin' then,"
As Tugg says, "as *a gentleman"!*—
You'd ort o' hear *Tugg* tell it—*My!*
I thought I'd *die!*

III

The way it wuz:—Tugg and the rest
The boys wuz jest
A-kind o' gittin' thawed out, down
At "Guss's Place," fur-end o' town,
One night,—when, first we knowed,
Some feller rode

Up in a buggy at the door,
And hollered fer some one to come
And fetch him some
Red-licker out—And whirped and
swore
That colt he drove wuz *"Thompson's"*
—shore!

IV

Guss went out, and come in ag'in
And filled a pint and tuk it out—
Stayed quite a spell—then peeked back
in,
Half-hid-like where the light wuz
dim,
And jieuked his head
At Tugg and said,—
"Come out a minute—here's a gent
Wants you to take a drink with
him."

V

Well—Tugg laid down his cards and
went—
In fact, *we all*
Got up, you know,
Startin' to go—
When in reels Guss ag'inst the wall,
As white as snow,
Gaspin',—*"He's tuk Tugg!—Wher' 's
my gun?"*
And-sir, outside we heerd
The hoss snort and kick up his heels
Like he wuz skeerd,
And then the buggy-wheels
Scrape—and then *Tugg's* voice hol-
lerun,—
"I'm bested!—Good-by, fellers!" . . .
'Peared
S' all-fired suddent,
Nobody couldn't

Jest git it fixed,—tel hoss and man,
  Buggy and Tugg, off through the
      dark
Went like the devil beatin' tan-
    Bark!

VI

What *could* we do? . . . We filed
      back to
  The bar: And Guss jest *looked* at
      us,
And we looked back "The same as
      you,"
Still *sayin'* nothin'—And the sap
      It stood in every eye,
And every hat and cap
Went off, as we teched glasses solemnly,
      And Guss says-he:
"Ef it's 'good-by' with Tugg, fer *shore,*
      —I say
  God bless him!—Er ef they
Ain't railly no *need* to pray,
I'm not *reniggin'*—board's the play,
And here's God bless him, anyway!"

VII

It must 'a' bin an hour er so
      We all set there,
  Talkin' o' pore
      Old Tugg, you know,
'At never wuz ketched up before,—
When—all slow-like—the door-
Knob turned—and Tugg come sham-
      blin' in
Handcuffed!—'at's what he wuz, I
      swear!—
      Yit smilin', like he hadn't
          bin
Away at all! And when we ast him
      where

The *Deputy* wuz at,—"I don't know
      where,"
  Tugg said,—
"All *I* know is—he's dead."

662

TO RUDYARD KIPLING

TO do some worthy deed of charity
    In secret and then have it found
        out by
Sheer accident, held gentle Elia—
    That—that was the best thing be-
        neath the sky!
Confirmed in part, yet somewhat dif-
      fering—
    (Grant that his gracious wraith will
        pardon me
If impious!)—I think a better thing
    Is: being found out when one strives
        to be.

So, Poet and Romancer—old as young,
    And wise as artless—masterful as
        mild,—
If there be sweet in any song I've sung,
    'Twas savored for thy palate, O my
        Child!
For thee the lisping of the children
      all—
    For thee the youthful voices of old
        years—
For thee all chords untamed or musi-
      cal—
    For thee the laughter, and for thee
        the tears.

And thus, borne to me o'er the seas
      between
    Thy land and mine, thy Song of cer-
        tain wing

Circles above me in the "pure serene"
Of our high heaven's vast o'er-wel-
  coming;
While, packeted with joy and thankful-
  ness,
And fair hopes many as the stars
  that shine,
And bearing all love's loyal messages,
  Mine own goes homing back to thee
  and thine.

663

DECORATION DAY ON THE PLACE

IT'S lonesome—sorto' lonesome,—it's
  a *Sund'y-day,* to me,
It 'pears-like—more'n any day I
  nearly ever see!—
Yit, with the Stars and Stripes above,
  a-flutterin' in the air,
On ev'ry Soldier's grave I'd love to lay
  a lily thare.

They say, though, Decoration Days is
  giner'ly observed
'Most *ev'rywheres*—espeshally by sol-
  dier-boys that's served.—
But me and Mother's never went—
  we seldom git away,—
In p'int o' fact, we're *allus* home on
  Decoration Day.

They say the old boys marches through
  the streets in colum's grand,
A-follerin' the old war-tunes they're
  playin' on the band—
And citizuns all jinin' in—and little
  childern, too—
All marchin', under shelter of the old
  Red White and Blue.—

With roses! roses! roses!—ev'rybody in
  the town!—
And crowds o' little girls in white, jest
  fairly loaded down!—
Oh! don't THE BOYS know it, from
  theyr camp acrost the hill?—
Don't they see theyr com'ards comin'
  and the old flag wavin' still?

Oh! can't they hear the bugul and the
  rattle of the drum?—
Ain't they no way under heavens they
  can rickollect us some?
Ain't they no way we can coax 'em,
  through the roses, jest to say
They know that ev'ry day on earth's
  theyr Decoration Day?

We've tried that—me and Mother,—
  whare Elias takes his rest,
In the orchurd—in his uniform, and
  hands acrost his brest,
And the flag he died fer, smilin' and
  a-ripplin' in the breeze
Above his grave—and over that,—*the
  robin in the trees!*

And *yit* it's lonesome—lonesome!—It's
  a *Sund'y-day,* to *me,*
It 'pears-like—more'n any day I nearly
  ever see!—
Still, with the Stars and Stripes above,
  a-flutterin' in the air,
On ev'ry soldier's grave I'd love to lay
  a lily thare.

664

TOWN AND COUNTRY

THEY'S a predjudice allus 'twixt
  country and town
Which I wisht in my hart wasent so.

You take *city* people, jest square up
    and down,
  And they're mighty good people to
    know:
And whare's better people a-livin', to-
    day,
  Than us in the *country?*—Yit good
As both of us is, we're divorsed, you
    might say,
  And won't compermise when we
    could!

Now as nigh into town fer yer Pap,
    ef you please,
  Is what's called the sooburbs.—Fer
    thare
You'll at least ketch a whiff of the
    breeze and a sniff
  Of the breth of wild-flowrs ev'ry-
    whare.
They's room fer the childern to play,
    and grow, too—
  And to roll in the grass, er to climb
Up a tree and rob nests, like they
    ortent to do,
  But they'll do *anyhow* ev'ry time!

My Son-in-law said, when he lived in
    the town,
  He jest natchurly pined, night and
    day,
Fer a sight of the woods, er a acre of
    ground
  Whare the trees wasent all cleared
    away!
And he says to me onc't, whilse a-visit-
    in' us
  On the farm, "It's not strange, I
    declare,
That we can't coax you folks, without
    raisin' a fuss,
  To come to town, visitin' thare!"

And says I, "Then git back whare you
    sorto' *belong*—
  And *Madaline,* too,—and yer three
Little childern," says I, "that don't
    know a bird-song,
  Ner a hawk from a chicky-dee-dee!
Git back," I-says-I, "to the blue of the
    sky
  And the green of the fields, and the
    shine
Of the sun, with a laugh in yer voice
    and yer eye
  As harty as Mother's and mine!"

Well—long-and-short of it,—he's com-
    permised *some*—
  He's moved in the sooburbs.—And
    now
They don't haf to coax, when they
    want us to come,
  'Cause we turn in and go *anyhow!*
Fer thare—well, they's room fer the
    songs and purfume
  Of the grove and the old orchurd-
    ground,
And they's room fer the childern out
    thare, and they's room
  Fer theyr Gran'pap to waller 'em
    round!

665

THE FIRST BLUEBIRD

JEST rain and snow! and rain again!
  And dribble! drip! and blow!
Then snow! and thaw! and slush! and
    then—
  Some more rain and snow!

This morning I was 'most afeard
  To *wake* up—when, I jing!

I seen the sun shine out and heerd
The first bluebird of Spring!—
Mother she'd raised the winder
some;—
And in acrost the orchurd come,
Soft as a' angel's wing,
A breezy, treesy, beesy hum,
Too sweet for anything!

The winter's shroud was rent apart—
The sun bu'st forth in glee,—
And when *that bluebird* sung, my hart
Hopped out o' bed with me!

666

LINES TO PERFESSER JOHN
CLARK RIDPATH

A. M., LL. D. T-Y-TY

[*Composed by A Old Friend of the
Fambily sence 'way back in the Forties,
when they Settled nigh Fillmore, Put-
nam County, this State, whare John
was borned and growed up, you might
say, like the wayside flower.*]

YOUR neghbors in the country,
whare you come from, hain't fer-
got!—
We knowed you even better than your
own-self, like as not.
We profissied your runnin'-geers 'ud
stand a soggy load
And pull her, purty stiddy, up a
mighty rocky road:
We been a-watchin' your career sence
you could write your name—
But way you writ it *first*, I'll say, was
jest a burnin' shame!—
Your "J. C." in the copy-book, and
"Ridpath"—mercy-sakes!—

Quiled up and tide in dubble bows,
lookt like a nest o' snakes!—
But *you* could read it, I *suppose,* and
kindo' gloted on
A-bein' *"J. C. Ridpath"* when *we*
only called you *"John."*

But you'd work's well as fool, and
what you had to do was *done:*
We've watched you at the wood-pile
—not the *wood-shed*—wasent
none,—
And snow and sleet, and haulin', too,
and lookin' after stock,
And milkin', nights, and feedin' pigs,
—then turnin' back the clock,
So's you could set up studyin' your
'Rethmatic, and fool
Your Parents, whilse a-piratin' your
way through winter school!
And I've heerd tell—from your own
folks—you've set and baked your
face
A-readin' Plutark Slives all night by
that old fi-er-place.—
Yit, 'bout them times, the blackboard,
onc't, had on it, I *de*-clare,
"Yours truly, *J. Clark* Ridpath."—
And the teacher—left it thare!

And they was other symptums, too,
that pinted, plane as day,
To nothin' short of *College!*—and *one*
was the lovin' way
Your mother had of cheerin' you to
efforts brave and strong,
And puttin' more faith in you, as you
needed it along:
She'd pat you on the shoulder, er she'd
grab you by the hands,
And *laugh* sometimes, er *cry* some-
times.—They's few that under-
stands

Jest *what* theyr mother's drivin at
　　when they act thataway;—
But I'll say this fer *you,* John-Clark,—
　　you answered, night and day,
To ev'ry trust and hope of hers—
　　and half your College fame
Was battled fer and won fer her and
　　glory of her name.

The likes of *you* at *College!* But you
　　went thare. How you paid
Your way nobody's astin'—but you
　　worked,—you hain't afraid,—
Your *clothes* was, more'n likely, kindo'
　　out o' style, perhaps,
And not as snug and warm as some
　　'at hid the other chaps;—
But when it come to *Intullect*—they
　　tell me yourn was dressed
A *leetle* mite *superber*-like than any of
　　the rest!
And thare you *stayed*—and thare
　　you've made your rickord, fare
　　and square—
Tel *now* it's *Fame* 'at writes your
　　name, approvin', *ev'rywhare*—
Not *jibblets* of it, nuther,—but all
　　John Clark Ridpath, set
Plum at the dashboard of the whole-
　　endurin' Alfabet!

667

ELIZABETH

MAY 1, 1891

I

ELIZABETH! Elizabeth!
　　The first May-morning whispereth
Thy gentle name in every breeze
That lispeth through the young-leaved
　　trees,
New raimented in white and green

Of bloom and leaf to crown thee
　　queen;—
And, as in odorous chorus, all
The orchard-blossoms sweetly call
Even as a singing voice that saith,
　　Elizabeth! Elizabeth!

II

Elizabeth! Lo, lily-fair,
In deep, cool shadows of thy hair,
Thy face maintaineth its repose.—
Is it, O sister of the rose,
So better, sweeter, blooming thus
Than in this briery world with us?—
　　Where frost o'ertaketh, and the
　　　breath
　　Of biting winter harrieth
With sleeted rains and blighting snows
　　All fairest blooms—Elizabeth!

III

Nay, then!—So reign, Elizabeth,
Crowned, in thy May-day realm of
　　death!
Put forth the scepter of thy love
In every star-tipped blossom of
The grassy dais of thy throne!
Sadder are we, thus left alone,
But gladder they that thrill to see
Thy mother's rapture, greeting thee.
　　Bereaved are we by life—not death—
　　Elizabeth! Elizabeth!

668

SONGS OF A LIFE-TIME

MRS. SARAH T. BOLTON'S POEMS

SONGS of a Life-Time—with the
　　Singer's head
　　A silvery glory shining midst the
　　green

Of laurel-leaves that bind a brow
  serene.
And godlike as was ever garlanded.—
So seems *her* glory who herein has
  wed
Melodious Beauty to the strong of
  mien
And kingly Speech—made kinglier
  by this queen
In lilied cadence voiced and raimented.
Songs of a Life-Time: by your own
  sweet stress
Of singing were ye loved of bygone
  years—
  As through our day ye are, and
    shall be hence,
Till *fame divine* marks your melodi-
  ousness
And on the Singer's lips, with smiles
  and tears,
  Seals there the kiss of love and
    reverence.

669

AN OLD MAN'S MEMORY

THE delights of our childhood is
  soon passed away,
And our gloryus youth it departs,—
And yit, dead and burried, they's blos-
  soms of May
  Ore theyr medderland graves in our
    harts.
So, friends of my barefooted days on
  the farm,
  Whether truant in city er not,
God prosper you same as He's pros-
  perin' me,
  Whilse your past hain't despised er
    fergot.

Oh! they's nothin', at morn, that's as
  grand unto me
As the glorys of Natchur so fare,—
With the Spring in the breeze, and the
  bloom in the trees,
  And the hum of the bees ev'rywhare!
The green in the woods, and the birds
  in the boughs,
  And the dew spangled over the
    fields;
And the bah of the sheep and the bawl
  of the cows
  And the call from the house to your
    meals!

Then ho! fer your brekfast! and ho!
  fer the toil
  That waiteth alike man and beast!
Oh! it's soon with my team I'll be
  turnin' up soil,
  Whilse the sun shoulders up in the
    East
Ore the tops of the ellums and beeches
  and oaks,
  To smile his Godspeed on the plow,
And the furry and seed, and the Man
  in his need,
  And the joy of the swet of his brow!

670

US FARMERS IN THE COUNTRY

US farmers in the country, as the
  seasons go and come,
Is purty much like other folks,—we're
  apt to grumble some!
The Spring's too back'ard fer us, er
  too for'ard—ary one—
We'll jaw about it anyhow, and have
  our way er none!
The thaw's set in too suddent; er the
  frost's stayed in the soil

Too long to give the wheat a chance,
and crops is bound to spoil!
The weather's eether most too mild, er
too outrageous rough,
And altogether too much rain, er not
half rain enugh!

Now what I'd like and what you'd
like is plane enugh to see:
It's jest to have old Providence drop
round on you and me
And ast us what our views is first, re-
gardin' shine er rain,
And post 'em when to shet her off, er
let her on again!
And yit I'd ruther, after all—consid-
er'n other chores
I' got on hands, a-tendin' both to my
affares and yours—
I'd ruther miss the blame I'd git,
a-rulin' things up thare,
And spend my extry time in praise
and gratitude and prayer.

671

ON A DEAD BABE

FLY away! thou heavenly one!—
I do hail thee on thy flight!
Sorrow? thou hath tasted none—
Perfect joy is yourn by right.
Fly away! and bear our love
To thy kith and kin above!

I can tetch thy finger-tips
Ca'mly, and bresh back the hair
From thy forr'ed with my lips,
And not leave a tear-drop thare.—
Weep fer *Tomps and Ruth*—and
me—
But I can not weep fer *thee*.

672

"MYLO JONES'S WIFE"

"MYLO JONES'S wife" was all
I heerd, mighty near, last Fall—
Visitun relations down
T'other side of Morgantown!
Mylo Jones's wife she does
This and that, and "those" and
"thus"!—
Can't bide babies in her sight—
Ner no childern, day and night,
Whoopin' round the premises—
Ner no nothin' else, I guess!

Mylo Jones's wife she 'lows
She's the boss of her own house!—
Mylo—consequences is—
Stays whare things seem *some* like
his,—
Uses, mostly, with the stock—
Coaxin' "Old Kate" not to balk,
Ner kick hoss-flies' branes out, ner
Act, I s'pose, so much like *her!*
Yit the wimern-folks tells you
She's *perfection.*—Yes they do!

Mylo's wife she says she's found
Home hain't home with *men-folks*
round
When they's work like *hern* to do—
Picklin' pears and *butcher'n',* too,
And a-render'n' lard, and then
Cookin' fer a pack o' men
To come trackin' up the flore
She's scrubbed *tel* she'll scrub no
more!—
Yit she'd keep things clean ef they
Made her scrub tel Jedgmunt Day!

Mylo Jones's wife she sews
Carpet-rags and patches clothes

Jest year *in* and *out!*—and yit
Whare's the livin' use of it?
She asts Mylo that.—And he
Gits back whare he'd ruther be,
With his team;—jest *plows*—and don't
Never sware—like some folks won't!
Think ef *he'd cut loose,* I gum!
'D he'p his heavenly chances some!

Mylo's wife don't see no use,
Ner no reason ner excuse
Fer his pore relations to
Hang round like they allus do!
Thare 'bout onc't a year—and *she*—
She jest *ga'nts* 'em, folks tells me,
On spiced pears!—Pass Mylo one,
He says "No, he don't chuse none!"
Workin' men like Mylo they
'D ort to have *meat* ev'ry day!

Dad-burn Mylo Jones's wife!
Ruther rake a blame case-knife
'Crost my wizzen than to see
Sich a womern rulin' *me!*—
Ruther take and turn in and
Raise a fool mule-colt by hand!
Mylo, though—od-rot the man!—
Jest keeps ca'm—like some folks *can*—
And 'lows such as her, I s'pose,
Is *Man's he'pmeet!*—Mercy knows!

673

A PEN-PICTUR' OF A CERT'IN
FRIVVOLUS OLD MAN

MOST ontimely old man yit!
'Pear-like sometimes he jest *tries*
His fool-self, and takes the bitt
In his teeth and jest de-fies
All perpryties!—Lay and swet
Doin' *nothin'*—only jest

Sorto' speckillatun on
Whare old summer-times is gone,
And 'bout things that he loved best
When a youngster! Heerd him say
Spring-times made him thataway—
Speshully on *Sund'ys*—when
Sun shines out and in again,
And the lonesome old hens they
Git off under the old kern-
Bushes, and in deep concern
Talk-like to theyrselves, and scratch
Kindo' absunt-minded, jest
Like theyr thoughts was fur away
In some neghbor's gyarden-patch
Folks has tended keerfulest!
Heerd the old man dwell on these
Idys time and time again!—
Heerd him claim that orchurd-trees
Bloomin', put the mischief in
His old hart sometimes that bad
And owdacious that he *"had
To break loose some*way," says he,
"Ornry as I ust to be!"

Heerd him say one time—when I
Was a sorto' standin' by,
And the air so still and clear,
Heerd the bell fer church clean
here!—
Said: "Ef I could climb and set
On the old three-cornerd rail
Old home-place, nigh Maryette',
Swap my soul off, hide and tale!"
And-sir! blame ef tear and laugh
Didn't ketch him half and half!
"Oh!" he says, "to wake and be
Barefoot, in the airly dawn
In the pastur'!—thare," says he,
"Standin' whare the cow's slep' or
The cold, dewy grass that's got
Print of her jest steamy hot
Fer to warm a feller's heels

In a while!—How good it feels!
Sund'y!—Country!—Morning!—
Hear
Nothin' but the *silunce*—see
Nothin' but green woods and clear
Skies and unwrit poetry
By the acre! . . . Oh!" says he,
"What's this voice of mine?—to seek
To speak out, and yit *can't* speak!
"*Think!*—the lazyest of days"—
Takin' his contrairyest leap,
He went on,—"git up, er sleep—
Er whilse feedin', watch the haze
Dancin' crost the wheat,—and keep
My pipe goin' leisurely—
Puff and whiff as pleases me,—
Er I'll leave a trail of smoke
Through *the house!*—no one'll say
'*Throw that nasty thing away!*'
'Pear-like nothin' sacerd's broke,
Goin' barefoot ef I chuse!—
I *have fiddled;*—and dug bait
And *went fishin';*—pitched hoss-
shoes—
Whare they couldn't see us from
The main road.—And I've *beat* some.
I've set round and had my joke
With the thrashers at the barn—
And I've swapped 'em yarn fer
yarn!—
Er I've he'pped the childern poke
Fer hens'-nests—agged on a match
'Twixt the boys, to watch 'em scratch
And paw round and rip and tare,
And bu'st buttons and pull hair
To theyr rompin' harts' content—
And me jest a-settin' thare
Hatchin' out more devilment!

"What you s'pose now ort to be
Done with sich a man?" says he—
"Sich a fool-old-man as me!"

674

THOUGHTS ON A PORE JOKE

I LIKE fun—and I like jokes
'Bout as well as most o' folks!—
Like my joke, and like my fun;—
But a joke, I'll state right here,
'S got some p'int—er I don't keer
Fer no joke that hain't got none.—
I hain't got no use, I'll say,
Fer a *pore* joke, anyway!

F'r instunce, now, when *some* folks gits
To relyin' on theyr wits,
Ten to one they git too smart
And *spile* it all, right at the start!
Feller wants to jest go slow
And do his *thinkin'* first, you know.
'F I can't think up somepin' good,
I set still and chaw my cood!
'F you *think* nothin'—jest keep on,
But don't *say* it—er you're gone!

675

EVAGENE BAKER

Who Was Dyin' of Dred Consum-
tion as These Lines Was Penned by
a True Friend

PORE afflicted Evagene!
Whilse the woods is fresh and
green,
And the birds on ev'ry hand
Sings in rapture sweet and grand,—
Thou, of all the joyus train,
Art bedridden, and in pain
Sich as only them can cherish
Who, like flowrs, is first to perish!

When the neghbors brought the word
She was down, the folks inferred
It was jest a cold she'd caught,
Dressin' thinner than she'd ort
Fer the frolics and the fun
Of the dancin' that she'd done
   'Fore the Spring was flush er ary
   Blossom on the peach er cherry.

But, last Sund'y, her request
Fer the Church's prayers was jest
Rail hart-renderin' to hear!—
Many was the silunt tear
And the tremblin' sigh, to show
She was dear to us below
   On this earth—and *dearer,* even,
   When we thought of her a-leavin'!

Sisters prayed, and coted from
Genesis to Kingdom-come
Provin' of her title clear
To the mansions.—"Even *her,"*
They claimed, "might be saved, *some-*
     way,
Though she'd danced, and played
     crowkay,
   And wrought on her folks to git her
   Fancy shoes that never fit her!"

Us to pray fer *Evagene!*—
With her hart as puore and clean
As a rose is after rain
When the sun comes out again!—
What's the use to pray fer *her?*
She don't need no prayin' fer!—
   Needed, all her life, more *playin'*
   Than she ever needed prayin'!

I jest thought of all she'd been
Sence her *mother* died, and when
She turned in and done *her* part—
All *her* cares on that child-hart!—

Thought of years she'd slaved—and
   had
Saved the farm—danced and was
   glad . . .
Mayby Him who marks the sporry
Will smooth down her wings to-
   morry!

676

ON ANY ORDENARY MAN IN A HIGH STATE OF LAUGH-TURE AND DELIGHT

AS it's give' me to perceive,
   I most cert'in'y believe
When a man's jest glad plum through,
God's pleased with him, same as you.

677

THE HOODOO

OWNED a pair o' skates onc't.—
   Traded
   Fer 'em,—stropped 'em on and
     waded
Up and down the crick, a-waitin'
Tel she'd freeze up fit fer skatin'.
Mildest winter I remember—
   More like Spring- than Winter-
     weather!—
Didn't *frost* tel 'bout December—
   Git up airly, ketch a feather
Of it, mayby, 'crost the winder—
Sunshine swinge it like a cinder!

Well—I *waited*—and *kep'* waitin'!
   Couldn't see my money's wo'th in
Them-air skates, and was no skatin'
   Ner no hint o' ice ner nothin'!

So, one day—along in airly
Spring—I swapped 'em off—and barely
Closed the dicker, 'fore the weather
 Natchurly jes' slipped the ratchet,
And crick—tail-race—all together,
 Froze so tight, cat couldn't scratch
   it!

678

CUORED O' SKEERIN'

'LISH, you rickollect that-air
 Dad-burn skittish old bay mare
Was no livin' with!—'at skeerd
'T ever'thing she seed er heerd!—
Th'owed 'Ves' Anders, and th'owed
   Pap,
First he straddled her—k-slap!—
And Izory—well!—th'owed her
Hain't no tellin' jest how fur!—
Broke her collar-bone—and might
Jes 'a' kilt the gyrl outright!

Course I'd heerd 'em make their boast
She th'ow any feller, 'most,
Ever topped her! S' I, "I know
One man 'at she'll never th'ow!"
So I rid her in to mill,
And, jest comin' round the hill,
Met a traction-engine!—Ort
Jest 'a' heerd that old mare snort,
And lay back her yeers, and see
Her a-tryin' to th'ow me!
Course I never said a word,
But thinks I, "My ladybird,
You'll git cuored, right here and now,
Of yer dy-does anyhow!"

So I stuck her—tel she'd jest
Done her very level best;
Then I slides off—strips the lines
Over her fool-head, and finds

Me a little saplin'-gad,
'Side the road:—And there we had
Our own fun!—jest wore her out!
Mounted her, and faced about,
And jest made her nose that-air
Little traction-engine there!

679

OLD WINTERS ON THE FARM

I HAVE jest about decided
  It'd keep a town-boy hoppin'
Fer to work all winter, choppin'
Fer a' old fireplace, like I did!
Lawz! them old times wuz contrary!—
 Blame' backbone o' winter, 'peared-
   like,
 Wouldn't break!—and I wuz skeerd-
   like
Clean on into Feb'uary!
 Nothin' ever made me madder
Than fer Pap to stomp in, layin'
On a' extry forestick, sayin',
 "Groun'-hog's out and seed his shad-
   der!"

680

"COON-DOG WESS"

"COON-DOG WESS"—he allus
  went
'Mongst us here by that-air name.
Moved in this-here Settlement
 From next county—he laid claim,—
Lived down in the bottoms—whare
Ust to be some coons in thare!—

In nigh Clayton's, next the crick,—
 Mind old Billy ust to say

Coons in thare was jest that thick,
  He'p him corn-plant any day!—
And, in rostneer-time, be then
Aggin' him to plant again!

Well,—In Spring o' '67,
  This-here "Coon-dog Wess" he
    come—
Fetchin' 'long 'bout forty-'leven
Ornriest-lookin' hounds, I gum!
Ever mortul-man laid eyes
On sence dawn o' Christian skies!

Wife come traipsin' at the rag-
Tag-and-bobtail of the crowd,
Dogs and childern, with a bag
  Corn-meal and some side-meat,—
    Proud
And as *independunt*—*My!*
Yit a mild look in her eye.

Well—this "Coon-dog Wess" he jest
  Moved in that-air little pen
Of a pole-shed, aidgin' west
  On "The Slues o' Death," called
    then.—
Otter- and mink-hunters ust
To camp thare 'fore game vam-
    moosed.

Abul-bodied man,—and lots
  Call fer *choppers*—and fer hands
To git *cross-ties out.*—But what's
  Work to sich as understands
Ways appinted and is hence
Under special providence?—

"Coon-dog Wess's" holts was *hounds*
  And *coon-huntin';* and he knowed
His own range, and stayed in bounds
  And left work fer them 'at showed
Talents fer it—same as his
Gifts regardin' coon-dogs is.

Hounds of ev'ry mungerl breed
  Ever whelped on earth!—Had these
Yeller kind, with punkin-seed
Marks above theyr eyes—and fleas
Both to sell and keep!—Also
These-here *lop-yeerd* hounds, you
    know.—

Yes-and *brindle* hounds—and long,
  Ga'nt hounds, with them eyes they'
    got
So blame *sorry,* it seems wrong,
  'Most, to kick 'em as to not!
Man, though, wouldn't dast, I guess,
Kick a hound fer "Coon-dog Wess"!

'Tended to his own affairs
  Stric'ly;—made no brags,—and yit
You could see 'at them hounds' cares
  'Peared like *his,*—and he'd 'a' fit
Fer 'em, same as wife er child!—
Them facts made folks rickonciled,

Sorto', fer to let him be
  And not pester him. And then
Word begin to spread 'at he
  Had brung in as high as ten
Coon-pelts in one night—and yit
Didn't 'pear to boast of it!

Neghborhood made some complaints
  'Bout them plague-gone hounds at
    night
Howlin' fit to wake the saints,
  Clean from dusk tel plum daylight!
But to "Coon-dog Wess" them-thare
Howls was "music in the air"!

Fetched his pelts to Gilson's Store—
  Newt he shipped fer him, and said,
Sence *he'd* cooned thare, he'd shipped
    more
  Than three hundred pelts!—"By
    Ned!

Git shet of my *store,*" Newt says,
"I'd go in with 'Coon-dog Wess'!"

And the feller 'peared to be
  Makin' best and most he could
Of his rale prospairity:—
  Bought some household things—and
    good,—
Likewise, wagon-load onc't come
From wherever he'd moved from.

But pore feller's huntin'-days,
  'Bout them times, was glidin' past!—
Goes out onc't one night and *stays!*
  . . . Neghbors they turned out, at
    last,
Headed by his wife and one
Half-starved hound—and search be-
    gun.

Boys said, that blame hound, he led
  Searchin' party, 'bout a half-
Mile ahead, and bellerin', said,
  Worse'n ary yearlin' calf!—
Tel, at last, come fur-off sounds
Like the howl of other hounds.

And-sir, shore enugh, them signs
  Fetched 'em—in a' hour er two—
Whare the *pack* was;—and they finds
  "Coon-dog Wess" *right thare;*—
    And you
Would admitted he was right
Stayin', as he had, *all night!*

Facts is, cuttin' down a tree,
  The blame thing had sorto' fell
In a twist-like—*mercy me!*
  And had ketched him.—Couldn't
    tell,
Wess said, *how* he'd managed—yit
He'd got both legs under it!

Fainted and come to, I s'pose,
  'Bout a dozen times whilse they
Chopped him out!—And wife she
    froze
To him!—bresh his hair away
And smile cheerful'—only when
He'd faint.—Cry and kiss him *then.*

Had *his* nerve!—And nussed him
    through,—
  Neghbors he'pped her—all she'd
    stand.—
Had a loom, and she could do
  Carpet-weavin' railly grand!—
" 'Sides," she ust to laugh and say,
  "She'd have Wess, now, *night* and
    day!"

As fer *him,* he'd say, says-ee,
  "I'm resigned to bein' lame:—
They was four coons up that tree,
  And hounds got 'em, jest the same!"
'Peared like, one er two legs less
Never worried "Coon-Dog Wess"!

681

GOIN' TO THE FAIR

OLD STYLE

WHEN Me an' · my Ma an' Pa
    went to the Fair,
Ma borried Mizz Rollins-uz rigg to go
    there,
'Cause *our* buggy's *new,* an' Ma says,
  "Mercy-sake!
It wouldn't hold *half* the folks *she's*
    go' to take!"
An' she took Marindy, an' Jane's
    twins, an' Jo,

An' Aunty Van Meters-uz girls—an'
  old Slo'
Magee, 'at's so fat, come a-scrougin' in
  there,
When me an' my Ma an' Pa went to
  the Fair!

The road's full o' loads-full 'ist ready
  to bu'st,
An' all hot, an' smokin' an' chokin'
  with dust;
The Wolffs an' their wagon, an'
  Brizentines, too—
An' horses 'ist r'ared when the toot-
  cars come through!
An' 'way from fur off we could hear
  the band play,
An' peoples all there 'u'd 'ist whoop
  an' hooray!
An' I stood on the dashboard, an' Pa
  boost' me there
'Most high as the fence, when we went
  to the Fair.

An' when we 'uz there an' inside, we
  could see
Wher' the flag's on a pole wher' a
  show's go' to be;
An' boys up in trees, an' the grea'-big
  balloon
'At didn't goned up a-tall, all after-
  noon!
An' a man in the crowd there gived
  money away—
An' Pa says "he'd ruther earn his by
  the day!"—
An' he gim-me some, an' says "ain't
  nothin' there
Too good fer his boy," when we went
  to the Fair!

Wisht The Raggedy Man wuz there,
  too!—but he says,

"Don't talk fairs to me, child! I went
  to one;—yes,—
An' they wuz a swing there ye rode—
  an' I rode,
An' a thing-um-a-jing 'at ye blowed—
  an' I blowed;
An' they wuz a game 'at ye played—
  an' I played,
An' a hitch in the same wher' ye paid
  —an' I paid;
An' they wuz two bad to one good
  peoples there—
Like you an' your Pa an' Ma went to
  the Fair!"

682

THE WATCHES OF THE NIGHT

O THE waiting in the watches of
  the night!
In the darkness, desolation, and con-
  trition and affright;
The awful hush that holds us shut
  away from all delight:
  The ever-weary memory that ever
    weary goes
  Recounting ever over every aching
    loss it knows—
  The ever-weary eyelids gasping ever
    for repose—
    In the dreary, weary watches of
      the night!

Dark—stifling dark—the watches of the
  night!
With tingling nerves at tension, how
  the blackness flashes white
With spectral visitations smitten past
  the inner sight!—

What shuddering sense of wrongs
    we've wrought that may not
    be redressed—
Of tears we did not brush away—
    of lips we left unpressed,
And hands that we let fall, with all
    their loyalty unguessed!
    Ah! the empty, empty watches of
    the night!

What solace in the watches of the
    night?—
What frailest staff of hope to stay—
    what faintest shaft of light?
Do we *dream,* and dare *believe* it,
    that by never weight of right
Of our own poor weak deservings,
    we shall win the dawn at
    last—
Our famished souls find freedom
    from this penance for the past,
In a faith that leaps and lightens
    from the gloom that flees
    aghast—
    Shall we survive the watches of
    the night?

ONE leads us through the watches of
    the night—
By the ceaseless intercession of our
    loved ones lost to sight
He is with us through all trials, in His
    mercy and His might;—
With our mothers there about Him,
    all our sorrow disappears,
Till the silence of our sobbing is the
    prayer the Master hears,
And His hand is laid upon us with
    the tenderness of tears
    In the waning of the watches of
    the night.

683

OSCAR C. McCULLOCH

INDIANAPOLIS, DECEMBER 12, 1891

WHAT would best please our
    friend, in token of
The sense of our great loss?—Our
    sighs and tears?
Nay, these he fought against through
    all his years,
Heroically voicing, high above
Grief's ceaseless minor, moaning like a
    dove,
    The pæan triumphant that the sol-
    dier hears,
    Scaling the walls of death, midst
    shouts and cheers,
    The old Flag laughing in his eyes'
    last love.

Nay, then, to pleasure him were it not
    meet
    To yield him bravely, as his fate
    arrives?—
Drape him in radiant roses, head and
    feet,
    And be partakers, while his work
    survives,
Of his fair fame,—paying the tribute
    sweet
    To all humanity—our nobler lives.

684

WHAT CHRIS'MAS FETCHED
THE WIGGINSES

WINTER-TIME, er Summer-
    time,
Of late years I notice I'm,

Kind o' like, more subjec' to
What the *weather* is. Now, *you*
Folks 'at lives in *town,* I s'pose,
Thinks it's bully when it snows;
But the chap 'at chops and hauls
Yer wood fer ye, and then stalls,
And snapps tuggs and swingletrees,
And then has to walk er freeze,
Hain't so much "stuck *on*" the snow
As stuck *in* it—Bless ye, no!—
When it's packed, and sleighin' 's
   good,
And *church* in the neighberhood,
Them 'at's *got* their girls, I guess,
Takes 'em, likely, more er less.
Tell the plain fac's o' the case,
No men-folks about our place
On'y me and Pap—and he
'Lows 'at young folks' company
Allus made him sick! So I
Jes' don't want, and jes' don't try!
Chinkypin, the dad-burn town,
'S too fur off to loaf aroun'
Eether day er night—and no
Law compellin' me to go!—
'Less'n some Old-Settlers' Day,
Er big-doin's thataway—
Then, to tell the p'inted fac',
I've went more so's to come back
By old Guthrie's still-house, where
Minors *has* got licker there—
That's pervidin' we could show 'em
Old folks sent fer it from home!
Visit roun' the neighbors some,
When the *boys* wants me to come.—
Coon-hunt with 'em; er set traps
Fer mussrats; er jes', perhaps,
Lay in roun' the stove, you know,
And parch corn, and let her snow!
Mostly, nights like these, you'll be
(Ef you' got a writ fer *me*)
Ap' to skeer me up, I guess,
In about the Wigginses'.

Nothin' roun' *our* place to keep
Me at home—with Pap asleep
'Fore it's dark; and Mother in
Mango pickles to her chin;
And the girls, all still as death,
Piecin' quilts.—Sence I drawed breath
Twenty year' ago, and heerd
Some girls whisper'n' so's it 'peared
Like they had a row o' pins
In their mouth—right there begins
My first rickollections, built
On that-air blame' old piece-quilt!

Summer-time, it's jes' the same—
'Cause I've noticed,—and I claim,
As I said afore, I'm more
Subjec' to the weather, *shore,*
'Proachin' my majority,
Than I ever ust to be!
Callin' back *last* Summer, say,—
Don't seem hardly past away—
With night closin' in, and all
S' lonesome-like in the dewfall:
Bats—ad-drat their ugly muggs!—
Flicker'n' by; and lightnin'-bugs
Huckster'n' roun' the airly night
Little sickly gasps o' light;—
Whippoorwills, like all possess'd,
Moanin' out their mournfullest;—
Frogs and katydids and things
Jes' *clubs* in and sings and sings
Their *ding-dangdest!*—Stock's all fed,
And Pap's warshed his feet fer bed;—
Mother and the girls all down
At the milk-shed, foolin' roun'—
No wunder 'at I git blue,
And lite out—and so would you!
I cain't stay aroun' no place
Whur they hain't no livin' face:—
'Crost the fields and thue the gaps
Of the hills they's friends, perhaps,
Waitin' somers, 'at kin be
Kind o' comfertin' to me!

Neighbers all is plenty good,
Scattered thue this neighberhood;
Yit, of all, I like to jes'
Drap in on the Wigginses.—
Old man, and old lady too,
'Pear-like, makes so much o' you—
Least, they've allus pampered me
Like one of the fambily.—
The boys, too, 's all thataway—
Want you jes' to come and stay;—
Price, and Chape, and Mandaville,
Poke, Chasteen, and "Catfish Bill"—
Poke's the runt of all the rest,
But he's jes' the beatin'est
Little schemer, fer fourteen,
Anybody ever seen!—
"Like his namesake," old man claims,
"Jeems K. Poke, the first o' names!
Full o' tricks and jokes—and you
Never know what *Poke's* go' do!"
Genius, too, that-air boy is,
With them awk'ard hands o' his:
Gits this blame' pokeberry-juice,
Er some stuff, fer ink—and goose-
Quill pen-p'ints: And then he'll draw
Dogdest pictures yevver saw!—
Jes' make deers and eagles good
As a writin' teacher could!
Then they's two twin boys they've
        riz
Of old Coonrod Wigginses
'At's deceast—and glad of it,
'Cause his widder's livin' yit!
'Course *the boys* is mostly jes'
Why I go to Wigginses'.—
Though *Melviney,* sometimes, *she*
Gits her slate and algebry
And jes' sets there cipher'n' thue
Sums old Ray hisse'f cain't do!—
Jes' sets there, and tilts her chair
Forreds tel, 'pear-like, her hair
Jes' *spills* in her lap—and then
She jes' dips it up again

With her hands, as white, I swan,
As the apern she's got on!

Talk o' hospitality!—
Go to Wigginses' with me—
Overhet, or froze plum thue,
You'll find welcome waitin' you:—
Th'ow out yer tobacker 'fore
You set foot acrost that floor,—
"Got to eat whatever's set—
Got to drink whatever's wet!"
Old man's sentimuns—them's his—
And means jes' the best they is!
Then he lights his pipe; and she,
The old lady, presen'ly
She lights hern; and Chape and
        Poke.—
I hain't got none, ner don't smoke,—
(In the crick afore their door—
Sort o' so's 'at I'd be shore—
Drownded mine one night and says
"I won't smoke at *Wiggenses'*!")
Price he's mostly talkin' 'bout
Politics, and "thieves turned out"—
What he's go' to be, ef he
Ever "gits there"—and "we'll see!"—
Poke he 'lows they's blame' few
        men
Go' to hold their breath tel then!
Then Melviney smiles, as she
Goes on with her algebry,
And the clouds clear, and the room's
Sweeter'n crabapple-blooms!
(That Melviney, she's got some
Most surprisin' ways, i gum!—
Don't 'pear-like she ever *says*
Nothin', yit you'll *listen* jes'
Like she *was* a-talkin', and
Half-way seem to understand,
But not quite,—*Poke* does, I know,
'Cause he good as told me so,—
Poke's *her* favo-rite; and he—
That is, confidentially—

He's *my* favo-rite—and I
Got my whurfore and my why!)

I hain't never be'n no hand
Much at talkin', understand,
But they's *thoughts* o' mine 'at's jes'
Jealous o' them Wigginses!—
Gift o' talkin' 's what they' got,
Whuther they want to er not.—
F'r instunce, start the old man on
Huntin'-scrapes, 'fore game was gone,
'Way back in the Forties, when
Bears stold pigs right out the pen,
Er went waltzin' 'crost the farm
With a beehive on their arm!—
And—sir, *ping!* the old man's gun
Has plumped over many a one,
Firin' at him from afore
That-air very cabin door!
Yes—and *painters,* prowlin' 'bout,
Allus darkest nights.—Lay out
Clost yer cattle.—Great, big red
Eyes a-blazin' in their head,
Glitter'n' 'long the timber-line—
Shine out some and then *un-shine,*
And shine back—Then, stiddy! *whizz!*
'N' there yer Mr. Painter is
With a hole bored spang between
Them-air eyes! . . . Er start Chasteen,
Say, on blooded racin'-stock,
Ef you want to hear him talk;
Er tobacker—how to raise,
Store, and k-yore it, so's she pays. . . .
The old lady—and she'll cote
Scriptur' tel she'll git yer vote!
Prove to you 'at wrong is right,
Jes' as plain as black is white:
Prove when you're asleep in bed
You're a-standin' on yer head,
And yer train 'at's goin' West,
'S goin' East its level best;
And when bees dies, it's their wings
Wears out—And a thousan' things!

And the boys is "chips," you know,
"Off the old block"—So I go
To the Wigginses', 'cause—jes'
'Cause I *like* the Wigginses—
Even ef Melviney *she*
Hardly 'pears to notice me!

Rid to Chinkypin this week—
Yisterd'y.—No snow to speak
Of, and didn't have no sleigh
Anyhow; so, as I say,
I rid in—and froze one ear
And both heels—and I don't keer!—
"Mother and the girls kin jes'
Bother 'bout their Chris'mases
Next time fer *theirse'v's,* i jack!"
Thinks-says-I, a-startin' back,—
Whole durn meal-bag full of things
Wropped in paper sacks, and strings
Liable to snap their holt
Jes' at any little jolt!
That in front o' me, and *wind*
With *nicks* in it, 'at jes' skinned
Me alive!—I'm here to say
Nine mile' hossback thataway
Would 'a' walked my log! But, as
Somepin' allus comes to pass,
As I topped old Guthrie's hill,
Saw a buggy, front the Still,
P'inted home'ards, and a thin
Little chap jes' climbin' in.
Six more minutes I were there
On the groun's!—And 'course it were—
It were little Poke—and he
Nearly fainted to see *me!*—
"You be'n in to Chinky, too?"
"Yes; and go' ride back with you,"
I-says-I. He he'pped me find
Room fer my things in behind—
Stript my hoss's reins down, and
Putt his mitt' on the right hand
So's to lead—"Pile in!" says he,
"But you've struck pore company!"

Noticed he was pale—looked sick,
Kind o' like, and had a quick
Way o' flickin' them-air eyes
O' his roun' 'at didn't size
Up right with his usual style—
S' I, "You *well?*" He tried to smile,
But his chin shuck and tears come.—
"I've run 'Viney 'way from home!"
Don't know jes' what all occurred
Next ten seconds—Nary word,
But my heart jes' drapt, stobbed thue,
And whirlt over and come to.—
Wrenched a big quart-bottle from
That fool-boy!—and cut my thumb
On his little fiste-teeth—helt
Him snug in one arm, and felt
That-air little heart o' his
Churn the blood o' Wigginses
Into that old bead 'at spun
Roun' her, spilt at Lexington!
His k'niptions, like enough,
He'pped us both,—though it was rough—
Rough on him, and rougher on
Me when, last his nerve was gone
And he laid there still, his face
Fishin' fer some hidin'-place
Jes' a leetle lower down
In my breast than he'd yit foun'!
Last I kind o' soothed him, so's
He could talk.—And what you s'pose
Them-air revelations of
Poke's was? . . . He'd be'n writin'
love-
Letters to Melviney, and
Givin' her to understand
They was from "a young man who
Loved her," and—"the violet's blue
'N' sugar's sweet"—and Lord knows
what!
Tel, 'peared-like, Melviney got
S'interested in "the young
Man," Poke *he* says, 'at she brung

A' answer onc't fer him to take,
Statin' "she'd die fer his sake,"
And writ fifty *x*'s "fer
Love-kisses fer him from her!" . . .
I was standin' in the road
By the buggy, all I knowed
When Poke got that fur.—"That's
why,"
Poke says, "I 'fessed up the lie—
Had to—'cause I see," says he,
" 'Viney was in *airnest*—she
Cried, too, when I told her.—Then
She swore me, and smiled again,
And got Pap and Mother to
Let me hitch and drive her thue
Into Chinkypin, to be
At Aunt 'Rindy's Chris'mas-tree—
That's to-night." Says I, "Poke—durn
Your lyin' soul!—'s that beau o' hern—
That—*she*—loves—Does *he* live in
That hell-hole o' Chinkypin?"
"No," says Poke, "er 'Viney would
Went some *other* neighberhood."
"Who *is* the blame' whelp?" says I.
"Promised 'Viney, hope I'd die
Ef I ever told!" says Poke,
Pittiful and jes' heartbroke'—
" 'Sides that's why she left the place,—
She cain't look him in the face
Now no more on earth!' she says."—
And the child broke down and jes'
Sobbed! . . . Says I, "Poke, I p'tend
T' be *your* friend, and your *Pap's*
friend,
And your *Mother's* friend, and all
The *boys'* friend, little, large and
small—
The *whole fambily's* friend—and you
Know that means *Melviney,* too.—
Now—you hursh yer troublin'!—I'm
Go' to he'p friends ever' time—
On'y in *this* case, *you* got
To he'p *me*—and, like as not,

I kin he'p *Melviney* then,
And we'll have her home again.
And now, Poke, with your consent,
I'm go' go to that-air gent
She's in love with, and confer
With *him* on his views o' *her!*—
Blast him! give the man *some* show.—
Who *is* he?—*I'm go' to know!"*
Somepin' struck the little chap
Funny, 'peared-like.—Give a slap
On his leg—laughed thue the dew
In his eyes, and says: *"It's you!"*

Yes, and—'cordin' to the last
Love-letters of ours 'at passed
Thue his hands—we was to be
Married Chris'mas.—"Gee-mun-*nee!*
Poke," says I, "it's *suddent*—yit
We *kin* make it! You're to git
Up to-morry, say, 'bout *three*—
Tell your folks you're go' with me:—
We'll hitch up, and jes' drive in
'N' *take* the town o' Chinkypin!"

685

THE GUDEWIFE

MY gudewife—she that is tae be—
O she sall seeme sang-sweete tae
me
As her ain croon tuned wi' the chiel's
Or spinnin'-wheel's.
An' faire she'll be, an' saft, an' light,
An' muslin-bright
As her spick apron, jimpy laced
The-round her waiste.—
Yet aye as rosy sall she bloome
Intil the roome
(The where alike baith bake an' dine)
As a full-fine
Ripe rose, lang rinset wi' the raine,
Sun-kist againe,

Sall seate me at her table-spread,
White as her bread.—
Where I, sae kissen her for *grace,*
Sall see her face
Smudged, yet aye sweeter, for the bit
O' floure on it,
Whiles, witless, she sall sip wi' me
Luve's tapmaist-bubblin' ecstasy.

686

RIGHT HERE AT HOME

RIGHT here at home, boys, in old
Hoosierdom,
Where strangers allus joke us when
they come,
And brag o' *their* old States and inter-
prize—
Yit *settle* here; and 'fore they realize,
They're "hoosier" as the rest of us, and
live
Right here at home, boys, with their
past fergive'!

Right here at home, boys, is the place,
I guess,
Fer me and you and plain old happi-
ness:
We hear the World's lots grander—
likely so,—
We'll take the World's word fer it and
not go.—
We know *its* ways ain't *our* ways—so
we'll stay
Right here at home, boys, where we
know the way.

Right here at home, boys, where a
well-to-do
Man's plenty rich enough—and knows
it, too,

And's got a' extry dollar, any time,
To boost a feller up 'at *wants* to
    climb
And's got the git-up in him to go in
And *git there,* like he purt' nigh allus
    kin!

Right here at home, boys, is the place
    fer us!—
Where folks' heart's bigger'n their
    money-pu's';
And where a *common* feller's jes' as
    good
As ary other in the neighberhood:
The World at large don't worry you
    and me
Right here at home, boys, where we
    ort to be!

Right here at home, boys—jes' right
    where we air!—
Birds don't sing any sweeter anywhere:
Grass don't grow any greener'n she
    grows
Acrost the pastur' where the old path
    goes,—
All things in ear-shot's purty, er in
    sight,
Right here at home, boys, ef we *size*
    'em right.

Right here at home, boys, where the
    old home-place
Is sacerd to us as our mother's face,
Jes' as we rickollect her, last she smiled
And kissed us—dyin' so and rickon-
    ciled,
Seein' us all at home here—none
    astray—
Right here at home, boys, where she
    sleeps to-day.

687

LITTLE MARJORIE

"WHERE is little Marjorie?"
        There's the robin in the tree,
With his gallant call once more
From the boughs above the door!
There's the bluebird's note, and there
Are spring-voices everywhere
Calling, calling ceaselessly—
"Where is little Marjorie?"

And her old playmate, the rain,
Calling at the window-pane
In soft syllables that win
Not her answer from within—
"Where is little Marjorie?"—
Or is it the rain, ah me!
Or wild gusts of tears that were
Calling us—not calling her!

"Where is little Marjorie?"
Oh, in high security
She is hidden from the reach
Of all voices that beseech:
She is where no troubled word,
Sob or sigh is ever heard,
Since God whispered tenderly—
"Where is little Marjorie?"

688

KATHLEEN MAVOURNEEN

1892

*[Frederick Nicholls Crouch, the
Musical Genius and Composer of the
world-known air "Kathleen Mavour-
neen," was, at above date, living, in*

helpless age, in his adopted country,
America—a citizen since 1849.]

KATHLEEN   MAVOURNEEN!
     The song is still ringing
As fresh and as clear as the trill of
     the birds;
In world-weary hearts it is throbbing
     and singing
In pathos too sweet for the tenderest
     words.
Oh, have we forgotten the one who
     first breathed it?
Oh, have we forgotten his rapturous
     art—
Our meed to the master whose genius
     bequeathed it?
Oh, why art thou silent, thou Voice
     of the Heart?—
Our need to the master whose genius
     bequeathed it—
     Oh, why are we silent, Kathleen
     Mavourneen!

Kathleen Mavourneen! Thy lover still
     lingers;
The long night is waning, the stars
     pale and few;
Thy sad serenader, with tremulous
     fingers,
Is bowed with his tears as the lily
     with dew;
The old harp-strings quaver, the old
     voice is shaking;
In sighs and in sobs moans the
     yearning refrain;
The old vision dims, and the old heart
     is breaking . . .
Kathleen Mavourneen, inspire us
     again!
The old vision dims, and the old heart
     is breaking:
     Oh, why are we silent, Kathleen
     Mavourneen!

689

OLD JOHN HENRY

OLD John's jes' made o' the com-
       monest stuff—
     Old John Henry—
He's tough, I reckon,—but none too
     tough—
Too tough though's better than not
     enough!
     Says old John Henry.
He does his best, and when his best's
     bad,
He don't fret none, ner he don't git
     sad—
He simply 'lows it's the best he had:
     Old John Henry!

His doctern's jes' o' the plainest
     brand—
     Old John Henry—
A smilin' face and a hearty hand
'S religen 'at all folks understand,
     Says old John Henry.
He's stove up some with the rhumatiz,
And they hain't no shine on them
     shoes o' his,
And his hair hain't cut—but his eye-
     teeth is:
     Old John Henry!

He feeds hisse'f when the stock's all
     fed—
     Old John Henry—
And sleeps like a babe when he goes
     to bed—
And dreams o' Heaven and home-
     made bread,
     Says old John Henry.
He hain't refined as he'd ort to be
To fit the statutes o' poetry,

Ner his clothes don't fit him—but *he*
   fits *me:*
     Old John Henry!

690

BEING HIS MOTHER

BEING his mother,—when he goes
   away
I would not hold him overlong, and
   so
Sometimes my yielding sight of him
   grows O
So quick of tears, I joy he did not stay
To catch the faintest rumor of them!
   Nay,
Leave always his eyes clear and glad,
   although
Mine own, dear Lord, do fill to
   overflow;
Let his remembered features, as I
   pray,
Smile ever on me! Ah! what stress of
   love
Thou givest me to guard with Thee
   thiswise:
Its fullest speech ever to be denied
Mine own—being his mother! All
   thereof
Thou knowest only, looking from
   the skies
   As when not Christ alone was
   crucified.

691

GREEN FIELDS AND RUNNING
BROOKS

HO! green fields and running
   brooks!
Knotted strings and fishing-hooks

Of the truant, stealing down
Weedy back-ways of the town.

Where the sunshine overlooks,
By green fields and running brooks,
All intruding guests of chance
With a golden tolerance.

Cooing doves, or pensive pair
Of picnickers, straying there—
By green fields and running brooks,
Sylvan shades and mossy nooks!

And—O Dreamer of the Days,
Murmurer of roundelays
All unsung of words or books,
Sing green fields and running brooks!

692

SOME SCATTERING REMARKS
OF BUB'S

WUNST I tooked our pepper-box
   lid
An' cut little pie-dough biscuits, I did,
An' cooked 'em on our stove one day
When our hired girl she said I may.

Honey's the *goodest* thing—Oo-*ooh!*
An' blackburry-pies is goodest, too!
But wite hot biscuits, ist soakin' wet
Wiv tree-mullasus, is goodest yet!

Miss Maimie she's my Ma's friend,—
   an'
She's purtiest girl in all the lan'!—
An' sweetest smile an' voice an' face—
An' eyes ist looks like p'serves tas'e'!

I *ruther* go to the Circus-show;
But, 'cause my *parunts* told me so,

I ruther go to the Sund'y-school,
'Cause there I learn the goldun rule.

Say, Pa,—what *is* the goldun rule
'At's allus at the Sund'y-school?

693

BY HER WHITE BED

BY her white bed I muse a little
space:
She fell asleep—not very long ago,—
And yet the grass was here and not
the snow—
The leaf, the bud, the blossom, and—
her face!—

Midsummer's heaven above us, and
the grace
Of Love's own day, from dawn to
afterglow;
The fireflies' glimmering, and the
sweet and low
Plaint of the whippoorwills, and every
place
In thicker twilight for the roses' scent.
Then *night.*—She slept—in such
tranquillity,
I walk atiptoe still, nor *dare* to
weep,
Feeling, in all this hush, she rests
content—
That though God stood to wake her
for me, she
Would mutely plead: "Nay, Lord!
Let *him* so sleep."

694

HOW JOHN QUIT THE FARM

NOBODY on the old farm here but Mother, me and John,
Except, of course, the extry he'p when harvest-time come on,—
And *then,* I want to say to you, we *needed* he'p about,
As you'd admit, ef you'd 'a' seen the way the crops turned out!

A better quarter-section ner a richer soil warn't found
Than this-here old-home place o' ourn fer fifty miles around!—
The house was small—but plenty-big we found it from the day
That John—our only livin' son—packed up and went away.

You see, we tuk sich pride in John—his mother more'n me—
That's natchurul; but *both* of us was proud as proud could be;
Fer the boy, from a little chap, was most oncommon bright,
And seemed in work as well as play to take the same delight.

He allus went a-whistlin' round the place, as glad at heart
As robins up at five o'clock to git an airly start;
And many a time 'fore daylight Mother's waked me up to say—
"Jes' listen, David!—listen!—Johnny's beat the birds to-day!"

High-sperited from boyhood, with a most inquirin' turn,—
He wanted to learn ever'thing on earth they was to learn:
He'd ast more plaguy questions in a mortal-minute here
Than his grandpap in Paradise could answer in a year!

And *read!* w'y, his own mother learnt him how to read and spell;
And "The Childern of the Abbey"—w'y, he knowed that book as well
At fifteen as his parents!—and "The Pilgrim's Progress," too—
Jes' knuckled down, the shaver did, and read 'em through and through!

At eighteen, Mother 'lowed the boy must have a better chance—
That we ort to educate him, under any circumstance;
And John he j'ned his mother, and they ding-donged and kep' on,
Tel I sent him off to school in town, half glad that he was gone.

But—I missed him—w'y of course I did!—The Fall and Winter through
I never built the kitchen fire, er split a stick in two,
Er fed the stock, er butchered, er swung up a gambrel-pin,
But what I thought o' John, and wished that he was home ag'in.

He'd come, sometimes—on Sund'ys most—and stay the Sund'y out;
And on Thanksgivin'-Day he 'peared to like to be about:
But a change was workin' on him—he was stiller than before,
And didn't joke, ner laugh, ner sing and whistle any more.

And his talk was all so proper; and I noticed, with a sigh,
He was tryin' to raise side-whiskers, and had on a stripèd tie,
And a standin'-collar, ironed up as stiff and slick as bone;
And a breastpin, and a watch and chain and plug-hat of his own.

But when Spring-weather opened out, and John was to come home
And he'p me through the season, I was glad to see him come;
But my happiness, that evening, with the settin' sun went down,
When he bragged of "a position" that was offered him in town.

"But," says I, "you'll not accept it?" "W'y, of course I will," says he.—
"This drudgin' on a farm," he says, "is not the life fer me;
I've set my stakes up higher," he continued, light and gay,
"And town's the place fer *me,* and I'm a-goin' right away!"

And go he did!—his mother clingin' to him at the gate,
A-pleadin' and a-cryin'; but it hadn't any weight.
I was tranquiller, and told her 'twarn't no use to worry so,
And onclasped her arms from round his neck round mine—and let him go!

I felt a little bitter feelin' foolin' round about
The aidges of my conscience; but I didn't let it out;—
I simply retch out, trimbly-like, and tuk the boy's hand,
And though I didn't say a word, I knowed he'd understand.

And—well!—sence then the old home here was mighty lonesome, shore!
With we a-workin' in the field, and Mother at the door,
Her face ferever to'rds the town, and fadin' more and more—
Her only son nine miles away, a-clerkin' in a store!

The weeks and months dragged by us; and sometimes the boy would write
A letter to his mother, sayin' that his work was light,
And not to feel oneasy about his health a bit—
Though his business was confinin', he was gittin' used to it.

And sometimes he would write and ast how *I* was gittin' on,
And ef I had to pay out much fer he'p sence he was gone;
And how the hogs was doin', and the balance of the stock,
And talk on fer a page er two jes' like he used to talk.

And he wrote, along 'fore harvest, that he guessed he would git home,
Fer business would, of course, be dull in town.—But *didn't* come:—
We got a postal later, sayin' when they had no trade
They filled the time "invoicin' goods," and that was why he stayed.

And then he quit a-writin' altogether: Not a word—
Exceptin' what the neighbers brung who'd been to town and heard
What store John was clerkin' in, and went round to inquire
If they could buy their goods there less and sell their produce higher.

And so the Summer faded out, and Autumn wore away,
And a keener Winter never fetched around Thanksgivin'-Day!
The night before that day of thanks I'll never quite fergit,
The wind a-howlin' round the house—it makes me creepy yit!

And there set me and Mother—me a-twistin' at the prongs
Of a green scrub-ellum forestick with a vicious pair of tongs,
And Mother sayin', *"David! David!"* in a' undertone,
As though she thought that I was thinkin' bad-words unbeknown.

"I've dressed the turkey, David, fer to-morrow," Mother said,
A-tryin' to wedge some pleasant subject in my stubborn head,—
"And the mince-meat I'm a-mixin' is perfection mighty nigh;
And the pound-cake is delicious-rich—" "Who'll eat 'em?" I-says-I.

"The cramberries is drippin'-sweet," says Mother, runnin' on,
P'tendin' not to hear me;—"and somehow I thought of John
All the time they was a-jellin'—fer you know they allus was
His *favorite*—he likes 'em so!"   Says I, "Well, s'pose he does?"

"Oh, nothin' much!" says Mother, with a quiet sort o' smile—
"This gentleman behind my cheer may tell you after while!"
And as I turnt and looked around, some one riz up and leant
And putt his arms round Mother's neck, and laughed in low content.

"It's *me*," he says—"your fool-boy John, come back to shake your hand;
Set down with you, and talk with you, and make you understand
How dearer yit than all the world is this old home that we
Will spend Thanksgivin' in fer life—jes' Mother, you and me!"

. . . .

Nobody on the old farm here but Mother, me and John,
Except, of course, the extry he'p when harvest-time comes on;
And then, I want to say to you, we *need* sich he'p about,
As you'd admit, ef you could see the way the crops turns out!

695

HIS MOTHER'S WAY

TOMPS 'ud allus haf to say
    Somepin' 'bout "his Mother's
        way."—
He lived hard-like—never j'ined
Any church of any kind.—
"It was Mother's way," says he,
"To be good enough fer *me*
And her too,—and cert'inly
    Lord has heerd *her* pray!"
Propped up on his dyin' bed,—
"Shore as Heaven's overhead,
I'm a-goin' there," he said—
    "It was Mother's way."

696

THE HOOSIER FOLK-CHILD

THE Hoosier Folk-Child—all un-
    sung—
Unlettered all of mind and tongue;
Unmastered, unmolested—made
Most wholly frank and unafraid:
Untaught of any school—unvexed
Of law or creed—all unperplexed—
Unsermoned, ay, and undefiled,
An all imperfect-perfect child—
A type which (Heaven forgive us!) you
And I do tardy honor to,
And so profane the sanctities
Of our most sacred memories.

Who, growing thus from boy to man,
That dares not be American?
Go, Pride, with prudent underbuzz—
Go *whistle!* as the Folk-Child does.

The Hoosier Folk-Child's world is not
Much wider than the stable-lot
Between the house and highway fence
That bounds the home his father rents.
His playmates mostly are the ducks
And chickens, and the boy that
    "shucks
Corn by the shock," and talks of town,
And whether eggs are "up" or "down,"
And prophesies in boastful tone
Of "owning horses of his own,"
And "being his own man," and "when
He gets to be, what he'll do then."—
Takes out his jack-knife dreamily
And makes the Folk-Child two or
    three
Crude corn-stalk figures,—a wee span
Of horses and a little man.

The Hoosier Folk-Child's eyes are wise
And wide and round as brownies' eyes:
The smile they wear is ever blent
With all-expectant wonderment,—
On homeliest things they bend a look
As rapt as o'er a picture-book,
And seem to ask, whate'er befall,
The happy reason of it all:—
Why grass is all so glad a green,
And leaves—and what their lispings
    mean;—
Why buds grow on the boughs, and
    why
They burst in blossom by and by—
As though the orchard in the breeze
Had shook and popped its *pop-corn*
    trees,
To lure and whet, as well they might,
Some seven-league giant's appetite!

The Hoosier Folk-Child's chubby face
Has scant refinement, caste or grace,—
From crown to chin, and cheek to
    cheek,
It bears the grimy water-streak
Of rinsings such as some long rain
Might drool across the window-pane
Wherethrough he peers, with troubled
    frown,
As some lorn team drives by for town.
His brow is elfed with wispish hair,
With tangles in it here and there,
As though the warlocks snarled it so
At midmirk when the moon sagged
    low,
And boughs did toss and skreek and
    shake,
And children moaned themselves
    awake,
With fingers clutched, and starting
    sight
Blind as the blackness of the night!

The Hoosier Folk-Child!—Rich is he
In all the wealth of poverty!
He owns nor title nor estate,
Nor speech but half articulate,—
He owns nor princely robe nor
    crown;—
Yet, draped in patched and faded
    brown,
He owns the bird-songs of the hills—
The laughter of the April rills;
And his are all the diamonds set
In Morning's dewy coronet,—
And his the Dusk's first minted
    stars
That twinkle through the pasture-bars
And litter all the skies at night
With glittering scraps of silver light;—
The rainbow's bar, from rim to rim,
In beaten gold, belongs to him.

697
THEIR SWEET SORROW

THEY meet to say farewell: Their
    way
Of saying this is hard to say—
    He holds her hand an instant, wholly
    Distressed — and she unclasps it
        slowly.

He bends *his* gaze evasively
Over the printed page that she
    Recurs to, with a new-moon shoulder
    Glimpsed from the lace-mists that
        infold her.

The clock, beneath its crystal cup,
Discreetly clicks—"*Quick! Act! Speak
    up!*"
    A tension circles both her slender
    Wrists—and her raised eyes flash in
        splendor,

Even as he feels his dazzled own.—
Then, blindingly, round either thrown,
    They feel a stress of arms that ever
    Strain   tremblingly—and   "*Never!
        Never!*"

Is whispered brokenly, with half
A sob, like a belated laugh,—
    While cloyingly their blurred kiss
        closes,—
    Sweet as the dew's lip to the rose's.

698
DAWN, NOON AND DEWFALL

I

DAWN, noon and dewfall! Blue-
    bird and robin
Up and at it airly, and the orchard-
    blossoms bobbin'!

Peekin' from the winder, half awake,
    and wishin'
I could go to sleep ag'in as well as go
    a-fishin'!

II

On the apern o' the dam, legs a-dan-
    glin' over,
Drowsy-like with sound o' worter and
    the smell o' clover:
Fish all out a-visitin'—'cept some
    dratted minnor!
Yes, and mill shet down at last and
    hands is gone to dinner.

III

Trompin' home acrost the fields: Light-
    nin'-bugs a-blinkin'
In the wheat like sparks o' things feller keeps a-thinkin':—
Mother waitin' supper, and the chil-
    dern there to cherr me;
And fiddle on the kitchen wall a-jes'
    a-eechin' fer me!

699
LONGFELLOW

THE winds have talked with him
    confidingly;
    The trees have whispered to him;
        and the night
    Hath held him gently as a mother
        might,
And taught him all sad tones of mel-
    ody:
    The mountains have bowed to him;
        and the sea,
    In clamorous waves, and murmurs
        exquisite,

Hath told him all her sorrow and
    delight—
Her legends fair—her darkest mystery.
His verse blooms like a flower, night
    and day;
Bees cluster round his rhymes; and
    twitterings
Of lark and swallow, in an endless
    May,
Are mingling with the tender songs
    he sings.—
Nor shall he cease to sing—in every
    lay
Of Nature's voice he sings—and will
    alway.

700

HIS VIGIL

CLOSE the book and dim the light,
    I shall read no more to-night.
No—I am not sleepy, dear—
Do not go: sit by me here
In the darkness and the deep
Silence of the watch I keep.
Something in your presence so
Soothes me—as in long ago
I first felt your hand—as now—
In the darkness touch my brow:
I've no other wish than you
Thus should fold mine eyelids to,
Saying naught of sigh or tear—
Just as God were sitting here.

701

THE QUARREL

THEY faced each other: Topaz-
    brown
And lambent burned her eyes and shot

Sharp flame at his of amethyst.—
"I hate you! Go, and be forgot
As death forgets!" their glitter *hissed*
(So *seemed* it) in their hatred. Ho!
Dared any mortal front her so?—
Tempestuous eyebrows knitted down—
Tense nostril, mouth—no muscle
    slack,—
And black—the suffocating black—
The stifling blackness of her frown!

Ah! but the lifted face of her!
And the twitched lip and tilted head!
Yet he did neither wince nor stir,—
Only—his hands clenched; and, in-
    stead
Of words, he answered with a stare
That stammered not in aught it said,
As might his voice if trusted there.

And what—what spake his steady
    gaze?—
Was there a look that harshly fell
To scoff her?—or a syllable
Of anger?—or the bitter phrase
That myrrhs the honey of love's lips,
Or curdles blood as poison-drips?
What made their breasts to heave and
    swell
As billows under bows of ships
In broken seas on stormy days?
We may not know—nor *they* indeed—
What mercy found them in their
    need.

A sudden sunlight smote the gloom;
And round about them swept a breeze,
With faint breaths as of clover-bloom;
A bird was heard, through drone of
    bees,—

Then, far and clear and eerily,
A child's voice from an orchard-tree—
Then laughter, sweet as the perfume
Of lilacs, could the hearing see.
And he—O Love! he fed thy name
On bruisèd kisses, while her dim
Deep eyes, with all their inner flame,
Like drowning gems were turned on
    him.

702

JOHN BROWN

WRIT in between the lines of his
    life-deed
We trace the sacred service of a heart
Answering the Divine command, in
    every part
Bearing on human weal: His love did
    feed
The loveless; and his gentle hands did
    lead
    The blind, and lift the weak, and
        balm the smart
    Of other wounds than rankled at the
        dart
In his own breast, that gloried thus to
    bleed.
He served the lowliest first—nay, then
    alone—
    The most despisèd that e'er wreaked
        vain breath
        In cries of suppliance in the reign
            whereat
Red Guilt sate squat upon her spat-
    tered throne.—
    For these doomed there it was he
        went to death.
    God! how the merest man loves
        one like that!

703

GO, WINTER!

GO, Winter! Go thy ways! We
    want again
The twitter of the bluebird and the
    wren;
Leaves ever greener growing, and the
    shine
    Of Summer's sun—not thine.—

Thy sun, which mocks our need of
    warmth and love
And all the heartening fervencies
    thereof,
It scarce hath heat enow to warm our
    thin
    Pathetic yearnings in.

So get thee from us! We are cold, God
    wot,
Even as *thou* art.—We remember not
How blithe we hailed thy coming.—
    That was O
    Too long—too long ago!

Get from us utterly! Ho! Summer
    then
Shall spread her grasses where thy
    snows have been,
And thy last icy footprint melt and
    mold
    In her first marigold.

704

THANKSGIVING

LET us be thankful—not alone be-
    cause
Since last our universal thanks were
    told

We have grown greater in the world's
     applause,
And fortune's newer smiles surpass
     the old—

But thankful for all things that come
     as alms
From out the open hand of Provi-
     dence:—
The winter clouds and storms—the
     summer calms—
The sleepless dread—the drowse of
     indolence.

Let us be thankful—thankful for the
     prayers
Whose gracious answers were long,
     long delayed,
That they might fall upon us una-
     wares,
And bless us, as in greater need we
     prayed.

Let us be thankful for the loyal hand
     That love held out in welcome to
     our own,
When love and *only* love could under-
     stand
     The need of touches we had never
     known.

Let us be thankful for the longing eyes
     That gave their secret to us as they
     wept,
Yet in return found, with a sweet sur-
     prise,
     Love's touch upon their lids, and,
     smiling, slept.

And let us, too, be thankful that the
     tears
Of sorrow have not all been drained
     away,

That through them still, for all the
     coming years,
We may look on the dead face of
     To-day.

705

AUTUMN

AS a harvester, at dusk,
     Faring down some wooded trail
Leading homeward through the musk
Of May-apple and papaw,
Hazel-bush and spice and haw,—
So comes Autumn, swart and hale,
Drooped of frame and slow of stride,
But withal an air of pride
Looming up in stature far
Higher than his shoulders are;
Weary both in arm and limb,
Yet the wholesome heart of him
Sheer at rest and satisfied.

Greet him as with glee of drums
And glad cymbals, as he comes!
Robe him fair, O Rain and Shine!
He the Emperor—the King—
Royal lord of everything
Sagging Plenty's granary floors
And out-bulging all her doors;
He the god of corn and wine,
Honey, milk, and fruit and oil—
Lord of feast, as lord of toil—
Jocund host of yours and mine!

Ho! the revel of his laugh!—
Half is sound of winds, and half
Roar of ruddy blazes drawn
Up the throats of chimneys wide,
Circling which, from side to side,
Faces—lit as by the Dawn,
With her highest tintings on

Tip of nose, and cheek, and chin—
Smile at some old fairy tale
Of enchanted lovers, in
Silken gown and coat of mail,
With a retinue of elves
Merry as their very selves,
Trooping ever, hand in hand,
Down the dales of Wonderland.

Then the glory of his song!—
Lifting up his dreamy eyes—
Singing haze across the skies;
Singing clouds that trail along
Towering tops of trees that seize
Tufts of them to stanch the breeze;
Singing slanted strands of rain
In between the sky and earth,
For the lyre to mate the mirth
And the might of his refrain:
Singing southward-flying birds
Down to us, and afterwards
Singing them to flight again:
Singing blushes to the cheeks
Of the leaves upon the trees—
Singing on and changing these
Into pallor, slowly wrought,
Till the little, moaning creeks
Bear them to their last farewell,
As Elaine, the lovable,
Was borne down to Lancelot.—
Singing drip of tears, and then
Drying them with smiles again.

Singing apple, peach and grape,
Into roundest, plumpest shape;
Rosy ripeness to the face
Of the pippin; and the grace
Of the dainty stamen-tip
To the huge bulk of the pear,
Pendent in the green caress
Of the leaves, and glowing through
With the tawny laziness

Of the gold that Ophir knew,—
Haply, too, within its rind
Such a cleft as bees may find,
Bungling on it half aware,
And wherein to see them sip,
Fancy lifts an oozy lip,
And the singer's falter there.

Sweet as swallows swimming through
Eddyings of dusk and dew,
Singing happy scenes of home
Back to sight of eager eyes
That have longed for them to come,
Till their coming is surprise
Uttered only by the rush
Of quick tears and prayerful hush:
Singing on, in clearer key,
Hearty palms of you and me
Into grasps that tingle still
Rapturous, and ever will!
Singing twank and twang of strings—
Trill of flute and clarinet
In a melody that rings
Like the tunes we used to play,
And our dreams are playing yet!
Singing lovers, long astray,
Each to each; and, sweeter things,—
Singing in their marriage-day,
And a banquet holding all
These delights for festival.

706

JOHN ALDEN AND PERCILLY

WE got up a Christmas-doin's
    Last Christmas Eve—
Kind o' dimonstration
    'At I railly believe
Give more satisfaction—
    Take it up and down—
Than airy intertainment
    Ever come to town!

Railly was a *theater*—
That's what it was,—
But, bein' in the church, you know,
We had a *"Santy Claus"*—
So's to git the *old folks*
To patternize, you see,
And *back* the institootion up
Kind o' *morally.*

School-teacher writ the thing—
(Was a friend o' mine)
Got it out o' Longfeller's
Pome "Evangeline"—
Er somers—'bout the *Purituns.*—
*Any*way, the part
"John Alden" fell to *me*—
And learnt it all by heart!

Claircy was *"Percilly"*—
(School-teacher 'lowed
Me and her could act them **two**
Best of all the crowd)—
Then—blame' ef he didn't
Git her Pap, i jing!—
To take the part o' *"Santy Claus,"*
To wind up the thing.

Law! the fun o' practisun!—
Was a week er two
Me and Claircy didn't have
Nothin' else to do!—
Kep' us jes' a-meetin' round,
Kind o' here and there,
Ever' night rehearsin'-like,
And gaddin' ever'where!

Game was wo'th the candle, though!—
Christmas Eve at last
Rolled around.—And 'tendance jes'
Couldn't been su'passed!—
Neighbors from the country
Come from Clay and Rush—
Yes, and 'crost the county-line
Clean from Puckerbrush!

Meetin'-house jes' trimbled
As "Old Santy" went
Round amongst the childern,
With their pepperment
And sassafrac and wintergreen
Candy, and "a ball
O' pop-corn," the preacher 'nounced,
"Free fer each and all!"

School-teacher suddently
Whispered in my ear,—
"Guess I got you:—*Christmas-gift!*—
Christmas is here!"
I give *him* a gold pen,
And case to hold the thing.—
And *Claircy* whispered, *"Christmas-gift!"*
And I give her *a ring.*

"And now," says I, "jes' watch *me*—
Christmas-gift," says I,
"I'm a-goin' to git one—
'Santy's' comin' by!"—
Then I rech' and grabbed him:
And, as you'll infer,
'Course I got the old man's,
And *he* gimme *her!*

707

THE RHYMES OF IRONQUILL

I'VE allus held—till jest of late—
That *Poetry* and me
Got on best, not to 'sociate—
That is, *most* poetry;
But t'other day my *son-in-law,*
Milt—be'n in town to mill—
Fetched home a present-like, fer Ma,—
The Rhymes of Ironquill.

Milt ust to teach; and, 'course, *his*
    views
Ranks over *common* sense;—
That's *biased* me, till I refuse
'Most all he rickommends.—
But Ma *she* read and read along
And cried, like women will,
About that "Washerwoman's Song"
In Rhymes of Ironquill.

And then she made *me* read the thing,
    And found my specs and all:
And I jest leant back there—i jing!—
    My cheer ag'inst the wall—
And read and *read,* and read and *read,*
    All to myse'f—ontil
I lit the lamp and went to bed
    With Rhymes of Ironquill!

I propped myse'f up there, and—
        durn!—
    I never shet an eye
Till daylight!—hogged the whole con-
        cern
    Tee-total, mighty nigh!—
I'd sigh sometimes, and cry sometimes,
    Er laugh jest fit to kill—
Clean *captured*-like with them-air
        rhymes
    O' that-air Ironquill!

Read that-un 'bout old "Marmaton"
    'At hain't be'n ever "sized"
In Song before—and yit's rolled on
    Jest same as 'postrophized!—
Putt me in mind o' *our* old crick
    At *Freeport*—and the *mill*—
And Hinchman's Ford—till jest *home-*
        sick—
    Them Rhymes of Ironquill!

Read that-un, too, 'bout "Game o'
        Whist,"
    And likenin' Life to fun

Like *that*—and playin' out yer fist,
    However cards is run:
And them "Tobacker-Stemmers' Song"
    They sung with sich a will
Down 'mongst the misery and wrong—
    In Rhymes of Ironquill.

And old John Brown, who broke the
        sod
    Of freedom's faller field
And sowed his *heart* there, thankin'
        God
    Pore slaves would git the yield—
Rained his last tears fer them and *us*
    To irrigate and till
A crop of Song as glorious
    As Rhymes of Ironquill.

And—sergeant, died there in the War,
    'At talked, out of his head . . .
He went "back to the Violet Star,"
    I'll bet—jest like he said!—
Yer Wars kin riddle bone and flesh,
    And blow out brains, and spill
Life-blood,—but *Somepin'* lives on,
        fresh
    As Rhymes of Ironquill!

708

THE CURSE OF THE WANDER-
ING FOOT

ALL hope of rest withdrawn me!—
    What dread command hath put
This awful curse upon me—
    The curse of the wandering foot?
Forward and backward and thither,
    And hither and yon again—
Wandering ever! And whither?
    Answer them, God! Amen.

The blue skies are far o'er me—
The bleak fields near below:
Where the mother that bore me?—
Where her grave in the snow?—
Glad in her trough of a coffin—
The sad eyes frozen shut
That wept so often, often,
The curse of the wandering foot!

Here in your marts I care not
Whatsoever ye think.
Good folk many who dare not
Give me to eat and drink:
Give me to sup of your pity—
Feast me on prayers!—O ye,
Met I your Christ in the city,
He would fare forth with me—

Forward and onward and thither,
And hither again and yon,
With milk for our drink together
And honey to feed upon—
Nor hope of rest withdrawn us,
Since the one Father put
The blessèd curse upon us—
The curse of the wandering foot.

709

AS MY UNCLE UST TO SAY

I'VE thought a power on men and
things—
As my uncle ust to say,—
And ef folks don't work as they pray,
i jings!
W'y, they ain't no use to pray!
Ef you want somepin', and jes' dead-
set
A-pleadin' fer it with both eyes wet,

And *tears* won't bring it, w'y, you try
sweat,
As my uncle ust to say.

They's some don't know their A, B,
C's—
As my uncle ust to say—
And yit don't waste no candle-grease,
Ner whistle their lives away!
But ef they can't write no book, ner
rhyme
No ringin' song fer to last all time,
They can blaze the way fer "the march
sublime,"
As my uncle ust to say.

Whoever's Foreman of all things here,
As my uncle ust to say,
He knows each job 'at we're best fit fer,
And our round-up, night and day:
And a-sizin' *His* work, east and west,
And north and south, and worst and
best,
I ain't got nothin' to suggest,
As my uncle ust to say.

710

WHITTIER—AT NEWBURYPORT

SEPTEMBER 7, 1892

HAIL to thee, with all good cheer!
Though men say thou liest here
Dead,
And mourn, all uncomforted.

By thy faith refining mine,
Life still lights those eyes of thine,
Clear
As the Autumn atmosphere.

Ever still thy smile appears
As the rainbow of thy tears
                    Bent
O'er thy love's vast firmament.

Thou endurest—shalt endure,
Purely, as thy song is pure.
                    Hear
Thus my hail: Good cheer! good cheer!

711

ROSAMOND C. BAILEY

THOU brave, good woman! Loved
    of every one;
  Not only that in singing thou didst
  fill
  Our thirsty hearts with sweetness,
  trill on trill,
  Even as a wild bird singing in the
  sun—
Not only that in all thy carols none
  But held some tincturing of tears to
  thrill
  Our gentler natures, and to quicken
  still
Our human sympathies; but thou hast
  won
Our equal love and reverence because
  That thou wast ever mindful of the
  poor,
    And thou wast ever faithful to thy
    friends.
So, loving all, serving all, thy best ap-
  plause
  Thy requiem—the vast throng at the
  door
    Of the old church, with mute
    prayers and amens.

712

TENNYSON

ENGLAND, OCTOBER 5, 1892

WE of the New World clasp
    hands with the Old
In newer fervor and with firmer hold
  And nobler fellowship,—
O Master Singer, with the finger-tip
Of Death laid thus on thy melodious
    lip!

All ages thou hast honored with thine
    art,
And ages yet unborn thou wilt be part
  Of all songs pure and true!
Thine now the universal homage due
From Old and New World—ay, and
    still The New!

713

MRS. BENJAMIN HARRISON

WASHINGTON, OCTOBER 25, 1892

NOW utter calm and rest;
    Hands folded o'er the breast
In peace the placidest,
    All trials past;
All fever soothed—all pain
Annulled in heart and brain
Never to vex again—
    She sleeps at last.

She sleeps; but O most dear
And best beloved of her
Ye sleep not—nay, nor stir,
    Save but to bow
The closer each to each,

With sobs and broken speech,
That all in vain beseech
   Her answer now.

And lo! we weep with you,
One grief the wide world through:
Yet with the faith she knew
   We see her still,
Even as here she stood—
All that was pure and good
And sweet in womanhood—
   God's will her will.

714

THE POEMS HERE AT HOME

THE Poems here at Home!—Who'll
   write 'em down,
Jes' as they air—in Country and in
   Town?—
Sowed thick as clods is 'crost the fields
   and lanes,
Er these-'ere little hop-toads when it
   rains!—
Who'll "voice" 'em?· as I heerd a feller
   say
'At speechified on Freedom, t'other
   day,
And soared the Eagle tel, it 'peared to
   me,
She wasn't bigger'n a bumblebee!

Who'll sort 'em out and set 'em down,
   says I,
'At's got a stiddy hand enough to try
To do 'em justice 'thout a-foolin' some,
And headin' facts off when they want
   to come?—
Who's got the lovin' eye, and heart,
   and brain

To reco'nize 'at nothin's made in
   vain—
'At the Good Bein' made the bees and
   birds
And brutes first choice, and us-folks
   afterwards?

What We want, as I sense it, in the
   line
O' poetry is somepin' Yours and
   Mine—
Somepin' with live stock in it, and
   out-doors,
And old crick-bottoms, snags, and syca-
   mores:
Putt weeds in—pizen-vines, and under-
   bresh,
As well as johnny-jump-ups, all so
   fresh
And sassy-like!—and groun'-squir'ls,—
   yes, and "We,"
As sayin' is,—"We, Us and Com-
   pany!"

Putt in old Nature's sermonts,—them's
   the best,—
And 'casion'ly hang up a hornets' nest
'At boys 'at's run away from school
   can git
At handy-like—and let 'em tackle it!
Let us be wrought on, of a truth, to
   feel
Our proneness fer to hurt more than
   we heal,
In ministratin' to our vain delights—
Fergittin' even insec's has their rights!

No "Ladies' Amaranth," ner "Treas-
   ury" book—
Ner "Night Thoughts," nuther—ner
   no "Lally Rook"!
We want some poetry 'at's to Our
   taste,

Made out o' truck 'at's jes' a-goin' to
    waste
'Cause smart folks thinks it's alto-
    gether too
Outrageous common—'cept fer me and
    you!—
Which goes to argy, all sich poetry
Is 'bliged to rest its hopes on You and
    Me.

715

LITTLE COUSIN JASPER

LITTLE Cousin Jasper, he
    Don't live in this town, like me,—
He lives 'way to Rensselaer,
An' ist comes to visit here.

He says 'at our court-house square
Ain't nigh big as theirn is there!—
He says their town's big as four
Er five towns like this, an' more!

He says ef his folks moved here
He'd cry to leave Rensselaer—
'Cause they's prairies there, an' lakes,
An' wile-ducks an' rattlesnakes!

Yes, 'n' little Jasper's Pa
Shoots most things you ever saw!—
Wunst he shot a deer, one day,
'At swummed off an' got away.

Little Cousin Jasper went
An' camped out wunst in a tent
Wiv his Pa, an' helt his gun
While he kilt a turrapun.

An' when his Ma heerd o' that,
An' more things his Pa's bin at,
She says, "Yes, 'n' he'll git shot
'Fore he's man-grown, like as not!"

An' they's mussrats there, an' minks,
An' di-dippers, an' chee-winks,—
Yes, 'n' cal'mus-root you chew
All up an' 't 'on't pizen you!

An', in town, 's a flag-pole there—
Highest one 'at's anywhere
In this world!—wite in the street
Where the big mass-meetin's meet.

Yes, 'n' Jasper he says they
Got a brass band there, an' play
On it, an' march up an' down
An' all over round the town!

Wisht our town ain't like it is!—
Wisht it's ist as big as his!
Wisht 'at *his* folks they'd move *here*,
An' *we'd* move to Rensselaer!

716

THE DOODLE-BUGS'S CHARM

WHEN Uncle Sidney he comes
    here—
    An' Fred an' me' an' Min,—
My Ma she says she bet you yet
    The roof'll tumble in!
Fer Uncle he ist *romps* with us:
    An' wunst, out in our shed,
He told us 'bout the Doodle-Bugs,
    An' what they'll do, he said,
Ef you'll ist holler "Doodle-Bugs!"—
    Out by our garden-bed—
"Doodle-Bugs! Doodle-Bugs!
    Come up an' git some bread!"

Ain't Uncle Sidney funny man?—
    "He's childish 'most as me"—
My Ma sometimes she tells him that—
    "He ac's so foolishly!"

W'y, wunst, out in our garden-path,
  Wite by the pie-plant bed,
He all sprawled out there in the dirt
  An' ist scrooched down his head,
An' "Doodle! Doodle! Doodle-Bugs!"
  My Uncle Sidney said,—
"Doodle-Bugs! Doodle-Bugs!
  Come up an' git some bread!"

An' nen he showed us little holes
  All bored there in the ground,
An' little weenty heaps o' dust
  'At's piled there all around:
An' Uncle said, when he's like us,
  Er purt' nigh big as Fred,
That wuz the Doodle-Bugs's Charm—
  To call 'em up, he said:—
"Doodle! Doodle! Doodle-Bugs!"
  An' they'd poke out their head—
"Doodle-Bugs! Doodle-Bugs!
  Come up an' git some bread!"

717

"HOME AG'IN"

I'M a-feelin' ruther sad,
  Fer a father proud and glad
As *I* am—my only child
Home, and all so rickonciled!
Feel so strange-like, and don't know
What the mischief ails me so!
'Stid o' bad, I ort to be
Feelin' good pertickerly—
Yes, and extry thankful, too,
'Cause my nearest kith-and-kin,
My Elviry's schoolin' 's through,
And I' got her home ag'in—
  Home ag'in with me!

Same as ef her mother'd been
Livin', I have done my best

By the girl, and watchfulest;
Nussed her—keerful' as I could—
From a baby, day and night,—
Drawin' on the neighborhood
And the women-folks as light
As needsessity 'ud 'low—
'Cept in "teethin'," onc't, and fight
Through black-measles. Don't know
    now
How we ever saved the child!
Doc *he'd* give her up, and said,
As I stood there by the bed
Sort o' foolin' with her hair
On the hot, wet pillar there,
"Wuz no use!"—And at them-air
Very words she waked and smiled—
Yes, and *knowed* me. And that's where
I broke down, and simply jes'
Bellered like a boy—I guess!—
Women claim I did, but I
Allus helt I didn't cry,
But wuz laughin',—and I *wuz,*—
Men don't cry like *women* does!
Well, right then and there I felt
'T'uz her mother's doin's, and,
Jes' like to myse'f, I knelt
Whisperin', "I understand." . . .
So I've raised her, you might say,
Stric'ly in the narrer way
'At her mother walked therein—
Not so quite religiously,
Yit still strivin'-like to do
Ever'thing a father *could*
Do he knowed the *mother* would
Ef she'd lived—And now all's through
And I' got her home ag'in—
  Home ag'in with me!

And I' been so lonesome, too,
Here o' late, especially,—
"Old Aunt Abigail," you know,
Ain't no company;—and so
Jes' the hired hand, you see—

Jonas—like a relative
More—sence he come here to live
With us, nigh ten year' ago.
Still he don't count much, you know,
In the way o' company—
Lonesome, 'peared-like, 'most as me!
So, as *I* say, I' been so
Special lonesome-like and blue,
With Elviry, like she's been,
'Way so much, last two or three
Year'—But now she's home ag'in—
Home ag'in with me!

Driv in fer her yisterday,
Me and Jonas—gay and spry,—
We jes' cut up, all the way!—
Yes, and sung!—tel, blame it! I
Keyed my voice up 'bout as high
As when—days 'at I wuz young—
"Buckwheat-notes" wuz all they sung.
Jonas bantered me, and 'greed
To sing one 'at town-folks sing
Down at Split Stump 'er High-Low—
Some new "ballet," said, 'at he'd
Learnt — about   "The   Grape - vine
                Swing."
And when *he* quit, *I* begun
To chune up my voice and run
Through the what's-called "scales" and
                "do-
Sol-me-fa's" I *ust* to know—
Then let loose old favor*ite* one,
"Hunters o' Kentucky!" *My!*
Tel I thought the boy would *die!*
And we *both* laughed—Yes, and still
Heerd more laughin', top the hill;
Fer we'd missed Elviry's train,
And she'd lit out 'crost the fields,—
Dewdrops dancin' at her heels,
And cut up old Smoots's lane
So's to meet us. And there in
Shadder o' the chinkypin,
With a dangl:n' dogwood-bough

Bloomin' 'bove her—See her now!—
Sunshine sort o' flickerin' down
And a kind o' laughin' all
Round her new red parasol,
Tryin' to git at *her!*—well—like
I jumped out and showed 'em how—
Yes, and jes' the place to strike
That-air mouth o' hern—as sweet
As the blossoms breshed her brow
Er sweet-williams round her feet—
White and blushy, too, as she
"Howdied" up to Jonas, and
Jieuked her head, and waved her hand.
"Hey!" says I, as she bounced in
The spring-wagon, reachin' back
To give *me* a lift, "whoop-ee!"
I-says-ee, "you're home ag'in—
                Home ag'in with me!"

Lord! how *wild* she wuz, and glad,
Gittin' home!—and things she had
To inquire about, and talk—
Plowin', plantin', and the stock—
News o' neighborhood; and how
Wuz the Deem-girls doin' now,
Sence that-air young chicken-hawk
They was "tamin' " soared away
With their settin'-hen, one day?—
(Said she'd got Mame's postal-card
'Bout it, very day 'at she
Started home from Bethany.)
How wuz produce—eggs, and lard?—
Er wuz stores still claimin' "hard
Times," as usual? And, says she,
Troubled-like, "How's Deedie—say?
Sence pore child e-loped away
And got back, and goin' to 'ply
Fer school-license by and by—
And where's 'Lijy workin' at?
And how's 'Aunt' and 'Uncle Jake'?
How wuz 'Old Maje'—and the cat?
And wuz Marthy's baby fat
As his 'Humpty-Dumpty' ma?—

Sweetest thing she ever saw!—
Must run 'crost and see her, too,
Soon as she turned in and got
Supper fer us—smokin'-hot—
And the 'dishes' all wuz through.—"
Sich a supper! W'y, I set
There and et, and et, and et!—
Jes' et on, tel Jonas he
Pushed his chair back, laughed, and
       says,
"I could walk *his* log!" and we
All laughed then, tel 'Viry she
Lit the lamp—and I give in!—
Riz and kissed her: "Heaven bless
You!" says I—"you're home ag'in—
Same old dimple in your chin,
Same white apern," I-says-ee,
"Same sweet girl, and good to see
As your *mother* ust to be,—
And I' got you home ag'in—
       Home ag'in with me!"

I turns then to go on by her
Through the door—and see her eyes
Both wuz swimmin', and she tries
To say somepin'—can't—and so
Grabs and hugs and lets me go.
Noticed Aunty'd made a fire
In the settin'-room and gone
Back where her p'serves wuz on
Bilin' in the kitchen. I
Went out on the porch and set,
Thinkin'-like. And by and by
Heerd Elviry, soft and low,
At the organ, kind o' go
A mi-anderin' up and down
With her fingers 'mongst the keys—
"Vacant Chair" and "Old Camp-
       Groun'." . . .
Dusk was moist-like, with a breeze
Lazin' round the locus' trees—
Heerd the hosses champin', and
Jonas feedin', and the hogs—

Yes, and katydids and frogs—
And a tree-toad, somers. Heerd
Also whipperwills.—*My land!*—
All so mournful ever'where—
Them out here, and her in there,—
'Most like 'tendin' *services!*
Anyway, I must 'a' jes'
Kind o' drapped asleep, I guess;
'Cause when Jonas must 'a' passed
Me, a-comin' in, I knowed
Nothin' of it—yit it seemed
Sort o' like I kind o' dreamed
'Bout him, too, a-slippin' in,
And a-watchin' back to see
Ef I *wuz* asleep, and then
Passin' in where 'Viry wuz;
And where I declare it does
'Pear to me I heerd him say,
Wild and glad and whisperin'—
'Peared-like heerd him say, says-ee,
"Ah! I' got you home ag'in—
       Home ag'in with me!"

718

THE SPOILED CHILD

'CAUSE Herbert Graham's a' only
       child—
       "Wuz I there, Ma?"
His parunts uz got him purt' nigh
       spiled—
       "Wuz I there, Ma?"
Allus ever'where his Ma tells
Where *she's* bin at, little Herbert yells,
       "Wuz I there, Ma?"
An' when she telled us wunst when
       she
Wuz ist 'bout big as him an' me,
       W'y, little Herbert he says,
       says-ee,
       "Wuz I there, Ma?"

Foolishest young-un you ever saw.—
"Wuz I there, Ma? Wuz I there,
      Ma?"

719

THE BEE-BAG

WHEN I was ist a Brownie—a
      weenty-teenty Brownie—
Long afore I got to be like Chil-
      derns is to-day,—
My good old Brownie granny gimme
      sweeter thing 'an can'y—
An' 'at's my little bee-bag the Fairies
      stold away!
      O my little bee-bag—
      My little funny bee-bag—
      My little honey bee-bag
      The Fairies stold away!

One time when I bin swung in wiv
      annuver Brownie young-un
An' lef' sleepin' in a pea-pod while
      our parunts went to play,
I waked up ist a-cryin' an' a-sobbin' an'
      a-sighin'
Fer my little funny bee-bag the
      Fairies stold away!
      O my little bee-bag—
      My little funny bee-bag—
      My little honey bee-bag
      The Fairies stold away!

It's awful much bewilder'n', but 'at's
      why I'm *a Childern,*
      Ner goin' to git to be no more a
      Brownie sence that day!
My parunts, so imprudent, lef' me
      sleepin' when they shouldn't!

An' I want my little bee-bag the
      Fairies stold away!
      O my little bee-bag—
      My little funny bee-bag—
      My little honey bee-bag
      The Fairies stold away!

720

THE TRULY MARVELOUS

GIUNTS is the biggest mens they
      air
In all this world er anywhere!—
An' Tom Thumb he's the most little-
      est man,
'Cause wunst he lived in a oyshture-
      can!

721

OLD CHUMS

"IF I die first," my old chum paused
      to say,
"Mind! not a whimper of regret:—
      instead,
Laugh and be glad, as I shall.—
      Being dead,
I shall not lodge so very far away
But that our mirth shall mingle.—So,
      the day
The word comes, joy with me." "I'll
      try," I said,
Though, even speaking, sighed and
      shook my head
And turned, with misted eyes. His
      roundelay
Rang gaily on the stair; and then the
      door

Opened and—closed. . . . Yet some-
    thing of the clear,
Hale hope, and force of whole-
    some faith he had
Abided with me—strengthened more
    and more.—
Then—then they brought his broken
    body here:
And I laughed—whisperingly—
    and we were glad.

722

"THIS DEAR CHILD-HEARTED WOMAN THAT IS DEAD"

I

THIS woman, with the dear child-
    heart,
Ye mourn as dead, is—where and
    what?
With faith as artless as her Art,
    I question not,—

But dare divine, and feel, and know
    Her blessedness—as hath been writ
In allegory.—Even so
    I fashion it:—

II

A stately figure, rapt and awed
    In her new guise of Angelhood,
Still lingered, wistful—knowing God
    Was very good.—

Her thought's fine whisper filled the
    pause;
And, listening, the Master smiled,
And lo! the stately angel was
    —A little child.

723

"HOW DID YOU REST, LAST NIGHT?"

"HOW did you rest, last night?"—
    I've heard my gran'pap say
Them words a thousand times—that's
    right—
Jes' them words thataway!
As punctchul-like as morning dast
    To ever heave in sight
Gran'pap 'ud allus haf to ast—
    "How did you rest, last night?"

Us young-uns used to grin,
    At breakfast, on the sly,
And mock the wobble of his chin
    And eyebrows helt so high
And kind: *"How did you rest, last
    night?"*
We'd mumble and let on
Our voices trimbled, and our sight
    Wuz dim, and hearin' gone.

.   .   .   .   .   .

Bad as I ust to be,
    All I'm a-wantin' is
As puore and ca'm a sleep fer me
    And sweet a sleep as his!
And so I pray, on Jedgment Day
    To wake, and with its light
See *his* face dawn, and hear him say—
    "How did you rest, last night?"

724

TO—"THE J. W. R. LITERARY CLUB"

WELL, it's enough to turn his
    head to have a feller's name
Swiped with a *Literary* Club!—But
    you're the ones to blame!—

I call the World to witness that I never
  agged ye to it
By ever writin' *Classic-like—because I
  couldn't* do it:
I never run to "Hellicon," ner writ
  about "Per-nas-sus,"
Ner ever tried to rack er ride around
  on old "P-*gass*us"!
When "Tuneful Nines" has cross'd my
  lines, the ink 'ud blot and blur it,
And pen 'ud jest putt back fer home,
  and take the short-way fer it!
And so, as I'm a-sayin',—when you
  name your LITERARY
In honor o' this name o' mine, it's
  railly nessessary—
Whilse I'm *a-thankin'* you and all—
  to *warn* you, ef you do it,
I'll haf to jine the thing myse'f 'fore I
  can live up to it!

725

OUT OF THE DARK AND THE DEARTH

HO! but the darkness was densely
    black!
  And young feet faltered and groped
    their way,
With never the gleam of a star, alack!
  Nor a moonbeam's lamest ray!—
    Blind of light as the blind of
      sight.—
    And that was the night—the
      night!

And out of the blackness, vague and
    vast,
  And out of the dark and the dearth,
    behold!—

A great ripe radiance grew at last
  And burst like a bubble of gold,
    Gilding the way that the feet
      danced on.—
    And that was the dawn—The
      Dawn!

726

LITTLE DAVID

THE mother of the little boy that
    sleeps
Has blest assurance, even as she weeps:
She knows her little boy has now no
  pain—
No further ache, in body, heart or
  brain;
All sorrow is lulled for him—all dis-
  tress
Passed into utter peace and restful-
  ness.—
All health that heretofore has been
  denied—
All happiness, all hope, and all beside
Of childish longing, now he clasps and
  keeps
In voiceless joy—the little boy that
  sleeps.

727

HOME AGAIN

I'M bin a-visitun 'bout a week
  To my little Cousin's at Nameless
    Creek;
An' I'm got the hives an' a new straw
  hat,
An' I'm come back home where my
  beau lives at.

728

A SEA-SONG FROM THE SHORE

HAIL! Ho!
   Sail! Ho!
Ahoy! Ahoy! Ahoy!
   Who calls to me,
   So far at sea?
Only a little boy!

Sail! Ho!
Hail! Ho!
The sailor he sails the sea:
   I wish he would capture
   A little sea-horse
And send him home to me.

I wish, as he sails
Through the tropical gales,
He would catch me a sea-bird, too,
   With its silver wings
   And the song it sings,
And its breast of down and dew!

I wish he would catch me a
Little mermaid,
Some island where he lands,
   With her dripping curls,
   And her crown of pearls,
And the looking-glass in her hands!

Hail! Ho!
Sail! Ho!
Sail far o'er the fabulous main!
   And if I were a sailor,
   I'd sail with you,
Though I never sailed back again.

729

THE DEAD WIFE

ALWAYS I see her in a saintly guise
   Of lilied raiment, white as her
      own brow
When first I kissed the tear-drops to
      the eyes
   That smile forever now.

Those gentle eyes! They seem the
      same to me,
   As, looking through the warm dews
      of mine own,
I see them gazing downward patiently
      Where, lost and all alone   ·

In the great emptiness of night, I bow
   And sob aloud for one returning
      touch
Of the dear hands that, Heaven having
      now,
   I need so much—so much!

730

TO ELIZABETH

OBIT JULY 8, 1893

O NOBLE, true and pure and
   lovable
   As thine own blessed name, ELIZA-
      BETH!—
Aye, even as its cadence lingereth
Upon the lips that speak it, so the spell
Of thy sweep memory shall ever dwell
   As music in our hearts. Smiling at
      Death
As on some later guest that tarrieth,

Too gratefully o'erjoyed to say fare-
    well,
Thou hast turned from us but a little
    space—
We miss thy presence but a little
    while,
Thy voice of sympathy, thy word
    of cheer,
The radiant glory of thine eyes and face,
The glad midsummer morning of
    thy smile,—
For still we feel and know that
    thou art here.

731

ARMAZINDY

ARMAZINDY;—fambily name
    Ballenger,—you'll find the same,
As her Daddy answered it,
In the old War-rickords yit,—
And, like him, she's airnt the good
Will o' all the neighberhood.—
Name ain't down in *History,*—
But, i jucks! it *ort* to be!
Folks is got respec' fer *her*—
Armazindy Ballenger!—
'Specially the ones 'at knows
Fac's o' how her story goes
From the start:—Her father blowed
Up—eternally furloughed—
When the old "Sultana" bu'st,
And sich men wuz needed wusst.—
Armazindy, 'bout fourteen-
Year-old then—and thin and lean
As a killdee,—but—*my la!*—
Blamedest nerve you ever saw!
The girl's mother'd *allus* be'n
Sickly—wuz consumpted when
Word came 'bout her husband.—So
Folks perdicted *she'd* soon go—

(Kind o' grief *I* understand,
Losin' *my* companion,—and
Still a widower—and still
Hinted at, like neighbors will!)
So, app'inted, as folks said,
Ballenger a-bein' dead,
Widder, 'peared-like, gradjully,
Jes' grieved after him tel *she*
Died, nex' Aprile wuz a year,—
And in Armazindy's keer
Leavin' the two twins, as well
As her pore old miz'able
Old-maid aunty 'at had be'n
Struck with palsy, and wuz then
Jes' a he'pless charge on *her*—
Armazindy Ballenger.

Jevver watch a primrose 'bout
Minute 'fore it blossoms out—
Kind o' loosen-like, and blow
Up its muscles, don't you know,
And, all suddent, bu'st and bloom
Out life-size?—Well, I persume
'At's the only measure I
Kin size Armazindy by!—
Jes' a *child, one* minute,—nex',
Woman-grown, in all respec's
And intents and purposuz—
'At's what Armazindy wuz!
Jes' a *child,* I tell ye! Yit
She made things git up and git
Round that little farm o' hern!—
Shouldered all the whole concern;—
Feed the stock, and milk the cows—
Run the *farm* and run the *house!*—
Only thing she didn't do
Wuz to plough and harvest too—
But the house and childern took
Lots o' keer—and had to look
After her old fittified
Grand-aunt.—Lord! ye could 'a' cried,
Seein' Armazindy smile,
'Peared-like, sweeter all the while!

And I've heerd her laugh and say:—
"Jes' afore Pap marched away,
He says, 'I depend on *you,*
Armazindy, come what may—
You must be a Soldier, too!' "

Neighbers, from the fust, 'ud come—
And she'd *let* 'em help her *some,*—
"Thanky, ma'am!" and "Thanky, sir!"
But no charity fer *her!*—
"*She* could raise the means to pay
Fer her farm-hands ever' day
Sich wuz needed!"—And she *could*—
In cash-money jes' as good
As farm-produc's ever brung
Their perducer, *old* er young!
So folks humored her and smiled,
And at last wuz rickonciled
Fer to let her have her own
Way about it.—But a-goin'
Past to town, they'd stop and see
"Armazindy's fambily,"
As they'd allus laugh and say,
And look sorry right away,
Thinkin' of her Pap, and how
He'd indorse his "Soldier" now!

'Course *she* couldn't never be
Much in *young-folks'* company—
Plenty of *in*-vites to go,
But das't leave the house, you know—
'Less'n *Sund'ys* sometimes, when
Some old *Granny*'d come and 'ten'
Things, while Armazindy *has*
Got away fer Church er "Class."
Most the youngsters *liked* her—and
'Twuzn't hard to understand,—
Fer, by time she wuz sixteen,
Purtier girl you never seen—
'Ceptin' she lacked schoolin', ner
Couldn't rag out stylisher—
Like some *neighber*-girls, ner thumb
On their blame' melodium,

Whilse their pore old mothers sloshed
Round the old back-porch and washed
Their clothes fer 'em—rubbed and
scrubbed
Fer girls'd ort to jes' be'n clubbed!
—And jes' sich a girl wuz Jule
Reddinhouse.—*She'd* be'n to school
At *New Thessaly,* i gum!—
Fool before, but that he'pped *some*—
'Stablished-like more confidence
'At she *never* had no sense.
But she wuz a cunnin', sly,
Meek and lowly sort o' lie,
'At men-folks like me and you
B'lieves jes' 'cause we ortn't to.—
Jes' as purty as a snake,
And as *pizen*—mercy sake!
Well, about them times it wuz,
Young Sol Stephens th'ashed fer us;
And we sent him over to
Armazindy's place to do
Her work fer her.—And-sir! Well—
Mighty little else to tell,—
Sol he fell in love with her—
Armazindy Ballenger!

Bless ye!—'Ll, of all the love
'At I've ever yit knowed of,
That-air case o' theirn beat all!
W'y, she *worshiped* him!—And Sol,
'Peared-like, could 'a' kissed the sod
(Sayin' is) where that girl trod!
Went to town, she did, and bought
Lot o' things 'at neighbers thought
Mighty strange fer *her* to buy,—
Raal chintz dress-goods—and 'way
high!—
Cut long in the skyrt,—also
Gaiter-pair o' shoes, you know;
And lace collar;—yes, and fine
Stylish hat, with ivy-vine
And red ribbons, and these-'ere
Artificial flowers and queer

Little beads and spangles, and
Oysturch-feathers round the band!
Wore 'em, Sund'ys, fer a while—
Kind o' went to Church in style,
Sol and Armazindy!—Tel
It was noised round purty well
They wuz *promised.*—And they wuz—
Sich news travels—well it does!—
Pity 'at *that* did!—Fer jes'
That-air fac' and nothin' less
Must 'a' putt it in the mind
O' Jule Reddinhouse to find
Out some dratted way to hatch
Out *some* plan to break the match—
'Cause she *done* it!—*How?* they's none
Knows adzac'ly *what* she done;
Some claims she writ letters to
Sol's folks, up nigh Pleasant View
Somers—and described, you see,
"Armazindy's fambily"—
Hintin' "ef Sol married *her,*
He'd jes' be pervidin' fer
Them-air twins o' hern, and old
Palsied aunt 'at couldn't hold
Spoon to mouth, and layin' near
Bedrid' on to eighteen year',
And still likely, 'pearantly,
To live out the century!"
Well—whatever plan Jule laid
Out to reach the p'int she made,
It wuz *desper't.*—And she won,
Finully, by marryun
Sol herse'f—*e-lopin',* too,
With him, like she *had* to do,—
'Cause her folks 'ud allus swore
"Jule should never marry pore!"

This-here part the story I
Allus haf to hurry by,—
Way 'at Armazindy jes'
Drapped back in her linsey dress,
And grabbed holt her loom, and shet
Her jaws square.—And ef she fret

Any 'bout it—never 'peared
Sign 'at *neighbers* seed er heerd;—
Most folks liked her all the more—
I know *I* did—certain-shore!—
('Course *I'd* knowed her *Pap,* and
     what
Stock she come of.—Yes, and thought,
And think *yit,* no man on earth
'S worth as much as that girl's worth!)

As fer Jule and Sol, they had
Their sheer!—less o' good than bad!—
Her folks let her go.—They said,
"Spite o' them she'd made her bed
And must sleep in it!"—But she,
'Peared-like, didn't sleep so free
As she ust to—ner so *late,*
Ner so *fine,* I'm here to state!—
Sol wuz pore, of course, and she
Wuzn't ust to poverty—
Ner she didn't 'pear to jes'
'Filiate with lonesomeness,—
'Cause Sol *he* wuz off and out
With his th'asher nigh about
Half the time; er, season done,
He'd be off mi-anderun
Round the country, here and there,
Swappin' hosses. Well, that-air
Kind o' livin' didn't suit
Jule a bit!—and then, to boot,
She had now the keer o' two
Her own childern—and to do
Her own work and cookin'—yes,
And sometimes fer *hands,* I guess,
Well as fambily of her own.—
Cut her pride clean to the bone!
So how *could* the whole thing end?—
She set down, one night, and penned
A short note, like—'at she sewed
On the childern's blanket—blowed
Out the candle—pulled the door
To close after her—and, shore-
Footed as a cat is, clumb

In a rigg there and left home,
With a man a-drivin' who
"Loved her ever fond and true,"
As her note went on to say,
When Sol read the thing next day.

Raaly didn't 'pear to be
Extry waste o' sympathy
Over Sol—pore feller!—Yit,
Sake o' them-air little bit
O' two *orphants*—as you might
Call 'em *then,* by law and right,—
Sol's old friends wuz sorry, and
Tried to hold him out their hand
Same as allus: But he'd flinch—
Tel, jes' 'peared-like, inch by inch,
He let *all* holts go; and so
Took to drinkin', don't you know,—
Tel, to make a long tale short,
He wuz fuller than he ort
To 'a' be'n, at work one day
'Bout his th'asher, and give way,
Kind o' like and fell and ketched
In the beltin'.
. . . Rid and fetched
Armazindy to him.—He
Begged me to.—But time 'at she
Reached his side, he smiled and *tried*
To speak.—Couldn't. So he died. . . .
Hands all turned and left her there
And went somers else—*some*where.
Last, she called us back—in clear
Voice as man'll ever hear—
Clear and stiddy, 'peared to me,
As her old Pap's ust to be.—
Give us orders what to do
'Bout the body—he'pped us, too.
So it wuz, Sol Stephens passed
In Armazindy's hands at last.
More'n that, she claimed 'at she
Had consent from him to be
Mother to his childern—now
'Thout no parents anyhow.

Yes-sir! and she's *got* 'em, too,—
Folks saw nothin' else 'ud do—
So they let her have *her way*—
Like she's doin' yit to-day!
Years now, I've be'n coaxin' her—
Armazindy Ballenger—
To in-large her fambily
Jes' *one* more by takin' *me*—
Which I'm feared she never will,
Though I'm 'lectioneerin' still.

732

THREE SINGING FRIENDS

I

LEE O. HARRIS

SCHOOLMASTER and Songmaster!
Memory
Enshrines thee with an equal love,
for thy
Duality of gifts,—thy pure and high
Endowments — Learning rare, and
Poesy.
These were as mutual handmaids, serv-
ing thee,
Throughout all seasons of the years
gone by,
With all enduring joys 'twixt earth
and sky—
In turn shared nobly with thy friends
and me.
Thus is it that thy clear song, ringing
on,
Is endless inspiration, fresh and free
As the old Mays at verge of June
sunshine;
And musical as then, at dewy dawn,
The robin hailed us, and all
twinklingly
Our one path wandered under
wood and vine.

II

BENJ. S. PARKER

Thy rapt song makes of Earth a realm
    of light
And shadow mystical as some
    dreamland
Arched with unfathomed azure—
    vast and grand
With splendor of the morn; or daz-
    zling bright
With orient noon; or strewn with stars
    of night
Thick as the daisies blown in grasses
    fanned
By odorous midsummer breezes and
Showered over by all bird-songs ex-
    quisite.
This is thy voice's beatific art—
    To make melodious all things be-
        low,
    Calling through them, from far,
        diviner space,
Thy clearer hail to us.—The faltering
    heart
Thou cheerest; and thy fellow mor-
    tal so
Fares onward under Heaven with
    lifted face.

III

JAMES NEWTON MATTHEWS

Bard of our Western world!—its
    prairies wide,
    With edging woods, lost creeks and
        hidden ways;
Its isolated farms, with roundelays
Of orchard warblers heard on every
    side;
Its cross-road schoolhouse, wherein still
    abide

Thy fondest memories,—since there
    thy gaze
First fell on classic verse; and thou,
    in praise
Of that, didst find thine own song
    glorified.
So singing, smite the strings and coun-
    terchange
    The lucently melodious drippings of
        Thy happy harp, from airs of
            "Tempe Vale,"
To chirp and trill of lowliest flight
    and range,
    In praise of our To-day and home
        and love—
    Thou meadow-lark no less than
        nightingale.

733

AT HIS WINTRY TENT

SAMUEL RICHARDS—ARTIST—DENVER,
COLORADO

NOT only master of his art was he,
    But master of his spirit—
        winged indeed
For lordliest height, yet poised for
    lowliest need
Of those, alas! upheld less buoyantly.
He gloried even in adversity,
    And won his country's plaudits, and
        the meed
    Of Old World praise, as one loath to
        succeed
While others were denied like victory.
Though passed, I count him still my
    master-friend,
    Invincible as through his mortal
        fight,—
    The laughing light of faith still
        in his eye

As, at his wintry tent, pitched at the
end
Of life, he gaily called to me "Good
night,
Old friend, good night—for
there is no good-by."

734

UP AND DOWN OLD BRANDY-
WINE

UP and down old Brandywine,
In the days 'at's past and gone—
With a dad-burn hook-and-line
And a saplin'-pole—i swawn!
I've had more fun, to the square
Inch, than ever *any*where!
Heaven to come can't discount
mine,
Up and down old Brandywine!

Hain't no sense in *wishin'*—yit
Wisht to goodness I *could* jes'
"Gee" the blame' world round and git
Back to that old happiness!—
Kind o' drive back in the shade
"The old Covered Bridge" there
laid
'Crosst the crick, and sort o' soak
My soul over, hub and spoke!

Honest, now!—it hain't no *dream*
'At I'm wantin',—but *the fac's*
As they wuz; the same old stream,
And the same old times, i jacks!—
Gimme back my bare feet—and
Stonebruise too!—And scratched
and tanned!—
And let hottest dog-days shine
Up and down old Brandywine!

In and on betwixt the trees
'Long the banks, pour down yer
noon,
Kind o' curdled with the breeze
And the yallerhammer's tune;
And the smokin', chokin' dust
O' the turnpike at its wusst—
Saturd'ys, say, when it seems
Road's jes' jammed with country
teams!

Whilse the old town, fur away
'Crosst the hazy pastur'-land,
Dozed-like in the heat o' day
Peaceful' as a hired hand.
Jolt the gravel th'ough the floor
O' the old bridge!—grind and
roar
With yer blame' percession-line—
Up and down old Brandywine!

Souse me and my new straw hat
Off the foot-log!—what *I* care?—
Fist shoved in the crown o' that—
Like the old Clown ust to wear.—
Wouldn't swap it fer a' old
Gin-u-wine raal crown o' gold!—
Keep yer *King* ef you'll gim-me
Jes' the boy I ust to be!

Spill my fishin'-worms! er steal
My best "goggle-eye!"—but you
Can't lay hands on joys I feel
Nibblin' like they ust to do!
So, in memory, to-day
Same old ripple lips away
At my "cork" and saggin' line,
Up and down old Brandywine!

There the logs is, round the hill,
Where "Old Irvin" ust to lift

Out sunfish from daylight till
   Dewfall—'fore he'd leave "The
      Drift"
And give *us* a chance—and then
Kind o' fish back home again,
Ketchin' 'em jes' left and right
Where *we* hadn't got "a bite"!

Er, 'way windin' out and in,—
Old path th'ough the iurnweeds
And dog-fennel to yer chin—
   Then come suddent, th'ough the
      reeds
   And cattails, smack into where
   Them-air woods-hogs ust to scare
   Us clean 'crosst the County-line,
   Up and down old Brandywine!

But the dim roar o' the dam
It 'ud coax us furder still
To'rds the old race, slow and ca'm,
   Slidin' on to Huston's mill—
   Where, I 'spect, "the Freeport
      crowd"
   Never *warmed* to us er 'lowed
   We wuz quite so overly
   Welcome as we aimed to be.

Still it 'peared-like ever'thing—
Fur away from home as *there*—
Had more *relish*-like, i jing!—
   Fish in stream, er bird in air!
   O them rich old bottom-lands,
   Past where Cowden's Schoolhouse
      stands!
   Wortermelons—*master-mine!*
   Up and down old Brandywine!

And sich pop-paws!—Lumps o' raw
Gold and green,—jes' oozy th'ough
With ripe yaller—like you've saw
   Custard-pie with no crust to:
   And jes' *gorges* o' wild plums,

Till a feller'd suck his thumbs
Clean up to his elbows! *My!—*
Me some more er lem me die!

Up and down old Brandywine!
   Stripe me with pokeberry-juice!—
Flick me with a pizen-vine
   And yell *"Yip!"* and lem me loose!
   —Old now as I then wuz young,
   'F I could sing as I *have* sung,
   Song 'ud shorely ring *dee-vine*
   Up and down old Brandywine!

735

WRITIN' BACK TO THE HOME-
FOLKS

MY dear old friends—It jes' beats
      all,
The way you write a letter
So's ever' *last* line beats the *first,*
And ever' *next*-un's better!—
W'y, ever' fool-thing you putt down
   You make so inte*rest*in',
A feller, readin' of 'em all,
   Can't tell which is the *best*-un.

It's all so comfortin' and good,
   'Pears-like I almost *hear* ye
And git more sociabler, you know,
   And hitch my cheer up near ye
And jes' smile on ye like the sun
Acrosst the whole per-rairies
In Aprile when the thaw's begun
And country couples marries.

It's all so good-old-fashioned like
   To *talk* jes' like we're *thinkin'*,
Without no hidin' back o' fans
   And giggle-un and winkin',

Ner sizin' how each other's dressed—
  Like some is allus. doin',—
"*Is* Marthy Ellen's basque be'n *turned*
  Er shore-enough a new-un!"—

Er "ef Steve's city-friend hain't jes'
  'A *lee*tle kind o' sort o'' "—
Er "wears them-air blame' eye-glasses
  Jes' 'cause he hadn't ort to?'"—
And so straight on, *dad-libitum,*
  Tel all of us feels, *some*way,
Jes' like our "comp'ny" wuz the best
  When we git up to come 'way!

That's why I like *old* friends like
  you,—
Jes' 'cause you're so *abidin'.*—
Ef I wuz built to live *"fer keeps,"*
  My principul residin'
Would be amongst the folks 'at kep'
  Me allus *thinkin'* of 'em,
And sort o' eechin' all the time
  To tell 'em how I love 'em.—

Sich folks, you know, I jes' love so
  I wouldn't live without 'em,
Er couldn't even drap asleep
  But what I *dreamp'* about 'em,—
And ef we minded God, I guess
  We'd *all* love one another
Jes' like one famb'ly,—me and Pap
  And Madaline and Mother.

736

WE DEFER THINGS

WE say and we say and we say,
    We promise, engage and
      declare,
Till a year from to-morrow is yester-
  day,
And yesterday is—Where?

737

FOR THIS CHRISTMAS

YE old-time stave that pealeth out
   To Christmas revelers all,
At tavern-tap and wassail bout,
  And in ye banquet hall,—
Whiles ye old burden rings again,
  Add yet ye verse, as due:
"God bless you, merry gentlemen"—
  And gentlewomen, too!

738

TO A POET-CRITIC

YES,—the bee sings—I confess it—
   Sweet as honey—Heaven bless
    it!—
Yit he'd be a *sweeter* singer
Ef he didn't have no stinger.

739

A NOON LULL

'POSSUM in de 'tater-patch;
   Chicken-hawk a-hangin'
Stiddy 'bove de stable-lot,
  An' cyarpet-loom a-bangin'!
Hi! Mr. Hoppergrass, chawin' yo' ter-
  backer,
Flick ye wid er buggy-whirp yer spit
  er little blacker!

Niggah in de roas'in'-yeers,
  Whiskers in de shuckin';
Weasel croppin' mighty shy,
  But ole hen a-cluckin'!

—What's got de matter er de mule-
    colt now?
Drapt in de turnip-hole, chasin' f'um
    de cow!

740

RABBIT IN THE CROSS-TIES

RABBIT in the cross-ties.—
    Punch him out—quick!
Git a twister on him
    With a long prong stick.
Watch him on the south side—
    Watch him on the—Hi!—
There he goes! Sic him, Tige!
    Yi! Yi!! Yi!!!

741

WHEN LIDE MARRIED *HIM*

WHEN Lide married *him*—w'y,
    she had to jes' dee-fy
The whole popilation!—But she never
    bat' an eye!
Her parents begged, and *threatened*—
    she must give him up—that *he*
Wuz jes' "a common drunkard!"—
    And he *wuz,* appearantly.—
        Swore they'd chase him off
          the place
        Ef he ever showed his face—
Long after she'd *eloped* with him and
    married him fer shore!—
When Lide married *him,* it wuz
    "Katy, bar the door!"

When Lide married *him*—Well! she
    had to go and be
A *hired girl* in town somewheres—
    while he tromped round to see

What *he* could git that *he* could do,
    —you might say, jes' sawed wood
From door to door!—that's what he
    done—'cause that wuz best he
    could!
        And the strangest thing, i
          jing!
        Wuz, he didn't *drink* a
          thing,—
But jes' got down to bizness, like he
    someway *wanted* to,
When Lide married *him,* like they
    warned her *not* to do!

When Lide married *him*—er, ruther,
    had be'n married
A little up'ards of a year—some feller
    come and carried
That *hired girl* away with him—a
    ruther *stylish* feller
In a bran-new green spring-wagon, with
    the wheels striped red and yeller:
        And he whispered, as they driv
        To'rds the country, *"Now*
        we'll live!"—
And *somepin' else* she *laughed* to
    hear, though both her eyes wuz
    dim,
'Bout *"trustin' Love and Heav'n above,*
    sence Lide married *him!"*

742

"RINGWORM FRANK"

JEST Frank Reed's his *real* name—
    though
    Boys all calls him "Ringworm
    Frank,"
'Cause he allus *runs round* so.—
    No man can't tell where to bank
    Frank'll be,
    Next you see

Er *hear* of him!—Drat his melts!—
That man's allus *somers else!*

We're old pards.—But Frank he jest
Can't stay still!—Wuz *prosper'n'*
here,
But lit out on furder West
Somers on a ranch, last year:
Never heard
Nary a word
How he liked it, tel to-day,
Got this card, reads thisaway:—

"Dad-burn climate out here makes
Me homesick all Winter long,
And when Spring-time *comes,* it takes
Two pee-wees to sing one song,—
One sings *'pee,'*
And the other one *'wee!'*
Stay right where you air, old pard.—
Wisht *I* wuz this postal card!"

743

THE YOUTHFUL PATRIOT

O WHAT did the little boy do
'At nobody wanted him to?
Didn't do nothin' but romp an' run,
An' whoop an' holler an' bang his gun
An' bu'st fire-crackers, an' ist have
fun—
An' *'at's* all the little boy done!

744

PONCHUS PILUT

PONCHUS PILUT *ust* to be
Ist a *Slave,* an' now he's *free.*
Slaves wuz on'y ist before
The War wuz—an' *ain't* no more.

He works on our place fer us,—
An' comes here—*sometimes* he does.
He shocks corn an' shucks it.—An'
He makes hominy "by han'"!—

Wunst he bringed us some, one trip,
Tied up in a piller-slip:
Pa says, when Ma cooked it, "My!
This-here's gooder'n you *buy!"*

Ponchus *pats* fer me an' sings;
An' he says most *funny* things!
Ponchus calls a dish a *"deesh"*—
Yes, an' *he* calls fishes *"feesh"!*

When Ma want him eat wiv us
He says, " 'Skuse me—'deed you mus'!
Ponchus know' good manners, Miss.—
He ain' eat wher' White-folks is!"

'Lindy takes *his* dinner out
Wher' he's workin'—roun' about.—
Wunst he et his dinner spread
In our ole wheelborry-bed.

Ponchus Pilut says " *'at's* not
His *right* name,—an' done fergot
What his *sho'-'nuff* name is now—
An' don' matter none *no*how!"

Yes, an' Ponchus he'ps Pa, too,
When our *butcherin' 's* to do,
An' scalds hogs—an' says, "Take care
'Bout it, er you'll *set the hair!"*

Yes, an' out in our back yard
He he'ps 'Lindy rendur lard;
An', wite in the fire there, he
Roast' a pigtail wunst fer me.—

An' ist nen th'ole tavurn bell
Rung, down-town, an' he says,
"Well!—

Hear dat! *Lan' o' Caanan,* Son,
Ain't dat bell say '*Pigtail done!*'

—'*Pigtail done!*
Go call Son!—
Tell dat
Chile dat
Pigtail done!' "

745
SLUMBER-SONG

SLEEP, little one! The Twilight
folds her gloom
Full tenderly about the drowsy Day,
And all his tinseled hours of light and
bloom
Like toys are laid away.

Sleep! sleep! The noon-sky's airy
cloud of white
Has deepened wide o'er all the
azure plain;
And, trailing through the leaves, the
skirts of Night
Are wet with dews as rain.

But rest thou sweetly, smiling in thy
dreams,
With round fists tossed like roses
o'er thy head,
And thy tranc'd lips and eyelids kissed
with gleams
Of rapture perfected.

746
THE CIRCUS PARADE

THE Circus!—The Circus!—The
throb of the drums,
And the blare of the horns, as the
Band-wagon comes;

The clash and the clang of the cymbals
that beat,
As the glittering pageant winds down
the long street!

In the Circus parade there is glory
clean down
From the first spangled horse to the
mule of the Clown,
With the gleam and the glint and the
glamour and glare
Of the days of enchantment all glim-
mering there!

And there are the banners of silvery
fold
Caressing the winds with their fringes
of gold,
And their high-lifted standards, with
spear-tips aglow,
And the helmeted knights that go
riding below.

There's the Chariot, wrought of some
marvelous shell
The Sea gave to Neptune, first wash-
ing it well
With its fabulous waters of gold, till
it gleams
Like the galleon rare of an Argonaut's
dreams.

And the Elephant, too, (with his un-
dulant stride
That rocks the high throne of a king
in his pride),
That in jungles of India shook from
his flanks
The tigers that leapt from the Jujubee-
banks.

Here's the long, ever-changing, mys-
terious line
Of the Cages, with hints of their
glories divine

From the barred little windows, cut
　high in the rear
Where the close-hidden animals' noses
　appear.

Here's the Pyramid-car, with its splen-
　dor and flash,
And the Goddess on high, in a hot-
　scarlet sash
And a pen-wiper skirt!—O the rarest
　of sights
Is this "Queen of the Air" in cerulean
　tights!

Then the far-away clash of the cym-
　bals, and then
The swoon of the tune ere it wakens
　again
With the capering tones of the gallant
　cornet
That go dancing away in a mad
　minuet.

The Circus!—The Circus!—The throb
　of the drums,
And the blare of the horns, as the
　Band-wagon comes;
The clash and the clang of the cymbals
　that beat,
As the glittering pageant winds down
　the long street.

747

FOLKS AT LONESOMEVILLE

PORE-FOLKS lives at Lonesome-
　　ville—
　Lawzy! but they're pore
Houses with no winders in,
　And hardly any door:

Chimbly all tore down, and no
　Smoke in that at all—
Ist a stovepipe through a hole
　In the kitchen wall!

Pump 'at's got no handle on;
　And no wood-shed—And, *wooh!*—
Mighty cold there, choppin' wood,
　Like pore-folks has to do!—
Winter-time, and snow and sleet
　Ist fairly fit to kill!—
Hope to goodness *Santy Claus*
　Goes to Lonesomeville!

748

THE THREE JOLLY HUNTERS

O THERE were three jolly hunters;
　　And a-hunting they did go,
With a spaniel-dog, and a pointer-dog,
　And a setter-dog also.
　　　　　Looky there!

And they hunted and they hal-looed;
　And the first thing they did find
Was a dingling-dangling hornet's-nest
　A-swinging in the wind.
　　　　　Looky there!

And the first one said—"What is it?"
　Said the next, "We'll punch and
　　　　see":
And the next one said, a mile from
　　　　there,
　"I wish we'd let it be!"
　　　　　Looky there!

And they hunted and they hal-looed;
　And the next thing they did raise
Was a bobbin' bunny cottontail
　That vanished from their gaze.
　　　　　Looky there!

One said it was a hot baseball,
  Zipped through the brambly thatch,
But the others said 'twas a note by
    post,
  Or a telegraph-despatch.
            Looky there!

So they hunted and they hal-looed;
  And the next thing they did sight
Was a great big bulldog chasing them,
  And a farmer, hollerin' "Skite!"
            Looky there!

And the first one said, "Hi-jinktum!"
  And the next, "Hi-jinktum-jee!"
And the last one said, "Them very
    words
  Had just occurred to me!"
            Looky there!

749

THE LITTLE DOG-WOGGY

A LITTLE Dog-Woggy
    Once walked round the World:
So he shut up his house; and, forget-
    ting
  His two puppy-children
  Locked in there, he curled
Up his tail in pink bombazine netting,
    And set out
    To walk round
    The World.

He walked to Chicago,
  And heard of the Fair—
Walked on to New York, where he
  never,—
    In fact, he discovered
    That many folks there

Thought less of Chicago than ever,
    As he musing-
    Ly walked round
    The World.

He walked on to Boston,
  And round Bunker Hill,
Bow-wowed, but no citizen heerd
    him—
  Till he ordered his baggage
  And called for his bill,
And then, bless their souls! how they
    cheered him,
    As he gladly
    Walked on round
    The World.

He walked and walked on
  For a year and a day—
Dropped down at his own door and
    panted,
  Till a teamster came driving
  Along the highway
And told him that house there was
    ha'nted
    By the two starve-
    Dest pups in
    The World.

750

CHARMS

I

FOR CORNS AND THINGS

PRUNE your corn in the gray of the
    morn
  With a blade that's shaved the dead,
And barefoot go and hide it so
  The rain will rust it red:
Dip your foot in the dew and put
  A print of it on the floor,

And stew the fat of a brindle cat,
And say this o'er and o'er:—
Corny! morny! blady! dead!
Gory! sory! rusty! red!
Footsy! putsy! floory! stew!
Fatsy! catsy!
    Mew!
    Mew!
Come grease my corn
In the gray of the morn!
Mew! Mew! Mew!

II

TO REMOVE FRECKLES—SCOTCH ONES

Gae the mirkest night an' stan'
'Twixt twa graves, ane either han';
Wi' the right han' fumblin' ken
Wha the deid mon's name's ance
    be'n,—
Wi' the ither han' sae read
Wha's neist neebor o' the deid;
An it be or wife or lass,
Smoor tha twa han's i' the grass,
Weshin' either wi' the ither,
Then tha faice wi baith thegither;
Syne ye'll seeket at cockcraw—
Ilka freckle's gang awa!

751

A FEW OF THE BIRD-FAMILY

THE Old Bob-white and Chipbird;
    The Flicker, and Chewink,
And little hopty-skip bird
    Along the river-brink.

The Blackbird, and Snowbird,
    The Chicken-hawk, and Crane;
The glossy old black Crow-bird,
    And Buzzard down the lane.

The Yellowbird, and Redbird,
    The Tomtit, and the Cat;
The Thrush, and that Red*head*-bird
    The rest's all pickin' at!

The Jay-bird, and the Bluebird,
    The Sapsuck, and the Wren—
The Cockadoodle-doo-bird,
    And our old Settin'-hen!

752

THROUGH SLEEPY-LAND

WHERE do you go when you go
    to sleep,
Little Boy! Little Boy! where?
'Way—'way in where's Little Bo-Peep,
And Little Boy Blue, and the Cows
    and Sheep
A-wandering 'way in there—in
    there—
A-wandering 'way in there!

And what do you see when lost in
    dreams,
Little Boy, 'way in there?
Firefly-glimmers and glowworm
    gleams,
And silvery, low, slow-sliding streams,
And mermaids, smiling out—'way in
    where
They're a-hiding—'way in there!

Where do you go when the Fairies call,
Little Boy! Little Boy! where?
Wade through the dews of the grasses
    tall,
Hearing the weir and the waterfall
And the Wee Folk—'way in there—
    in there—
And the Kelpies—'way in there!

And what do you do when you wake
    at dawn,
Little Boy! Little Boy! what?
Hug my Mommy and kiss her on
Her smiling eyelids, sweet and wan,
And tell her everything I've forgot,
A-wandering 'way in there—in
    there—
Through the blind-world 'way in
    there!

753
THE TRESTLE AND THE BUCK-SAW

THE Trestle and the Buck-Saw
    Went out a-walking once,
And stayed away and stayed away
For days and weeks and months:
And when they got back home again,
Of all that had occurred,
The neighbors said the gossips said
They never said a word.

754
THE KING OF OO-RINKTUM-JING

DAINTY Baby Austin!
    Your Daddy's gone to Boston
To see the King
Of Oo-Rinktum-Jing
And the whale he rode acrost on!

Boston Town's a city:
But O it's such a pity!—
They'll greet the King
Of Oo-Rinktum-Jing
With never a nursery ditty!

But me and you and Mother
Can stay with Baby-brother,
And sing of the King
Of Oo-Rinktum-Jing
And laugh at one another!

So what cares Baby Austin
If Daddy *has* gone to Boston
To see the King
Of Oo-Rinktum-Jing
And the whale he rode acrost on?

755
THE TOY PENNY-DOG

MA put my Penny-Dog
    Safe on the shelf,
An' left no one home but him,
    Me an' myself;
So I clumbed a big chair
    I pushed to the wall—
But the Toy Penny-Dog
    Ain't there at all!
I went back to Dolly—
    An' *she* 'uz gone too,
An' little Switch 'uz layin' there;—
    An' Ma says *"Boo!"*—
An' there she wuz a-peepin'
    Through the front-room door:
An' I ain't goin' to be a bad
    Little girl no more!

756
JARGON-JINGLE

TAWDERY!—faddery! Feathers
    and fuss!
Mummery!—flummery! Wusser and
    wuss!
All o' Humanity—Vanity Fair!—
Heaven for nothin', and—nobody
    there!

757

THE GREAT EXPLORER

HE sailed o'er the weltery watery
    miles
For a tabular year-and-a-day,
To the kindless, kinkable Cannibal Isles
He sailed and he sailed away!
He captured a loon in a wild lagoon,
    And a yak that weeps and smiles,
And a bustard-bird, and a blue baboon,
    In the kindless Cannibal Isles
        And wilds
            Of the kinkable Cannibal Isles.

He swiped in bats with his butterfly-
        net,
    In the kindless Cannibal Isles
And got short-waisted and over-het
    In the haunts of the crocodiles;
And nine or ten little Pigmy Men
    Of the quaintest shapes and styles
He shipped back home to his old Aunt
        Jenn,
    From the kindless Cannibal Isles
        And wilds
            Of the kinkable Cannibal Isles.

758

THE SCHOOLBOY'S FAVORITE

*Over the river and through the wood
    Now Grandmother's cap I spy:
Hurrah for the fun!—Is the pudding
        done?
    Hurrah for the pumpkin-pie!*
                        –School Reader.

FER any boy 'at's little as me,
    Er any little girl,
That-un's the goodest poetry piece
In any book in the worl'!

An' ef grown-peoples wuz little ag'in
    I bet they'd say so, too,
Ef *they'd* go see *their* ole Gran'ma,
    Like our Pa lets *us* do!

*Over the river an' through the wood
    Now Gran'mother's cap I spy:
Hurrah fer the fun!—Is the puddin'
        done?—
    Hurrah fer the punkin-pie!*

An' 'll tell *you* why 'at's the goodest
        piece:—
    'Cause it's ist like *we* go
To *our* Gran'ma's, a-visitun there,
    When our Pa he says so;
An' Ma she fixes my little cape-coat
    An' little fuzz-cap; an' Pa
He tucks me away—an' yells *"Hoo-
        ray!"*—
An' whacks Ole Gray, an' drives the
        sleigh
    Fastest you ever saw!

*Over the river an' through the wood
    Now Gran'mother's cap I spy:
Hurrah fer the fun!—Is the puddin'
        done?—
    Hurrah fer the punkin-pie!*

An' Pa ist snuggles me 'tween his
        knees—
    An' I he'p hold the lines,
An' peek out over the buffalo-robe;—
An' the wind ist *blows!*—an' the snow
        ist *snows!*—
An' the sun ist shines! an' shines!—
An' th' ole horse tosses his head an'
        coughs
    The frost back in our face.—
An' I' ruther go to my Gran'ma's
    Than any other place!

Over the river an' through the wood
Now Gran'mother's cap I spy:
Hurrah fer the fun!—Is the puddin'
done?—
Hurrah fer the punkin-pie!

An' all the peoples they is in town
Watches us whizzin' past
To go a-visitun *our* Gran'ma's,
Like we all went there last;—
But *they* can't go, like ist *our* folks
An' Johnny an' Lotty, and three
Er four neighber-childerns, an' Rober-
ut Volney,
An' Charley an' Maggy an' me!

Over the river an' through the wood
Now Gran'mother's cap I spy:
Hurrah fer the fun!—Is the puddin'
done?—
Hurrah fer the punkin-pie!

759

ALBUMANIA

Some certain misty yet tenable signs
Of the oracular Raggedy Man,
Happily found in these fugitive lines
Culled from the Album of 'Lizabuth
Ann.

FRIENDSHIP

O FRIENDSHIP, when I muse on
you,
As thoughtful minds, O Friendship,
do,
I muse, O Friendship, o'er and o'er,
O Friendship—as I said before.

LIFE

"What is Life?" If the *Dead* might
say,
'Spect they'd answer, under breath,
Sorry-like yet a-laughin':—A
Poor pale yesterday of Death!

LIFE'S HAPPIEST HOURS

Best, I guess,
Was the old *"Recess."*—
'Way back there's where I'd love to
be—
Shet of each lesson and hateful rule,
When the whole round World was as
sweet to me
As the big ripe apple I brung to
School.

MARION-COUNTY MAN HOMESICK ABROAD

I, who had hobnobbed with the shades
of kings,
And canvassed grasses from old mas-
ters' graves,
And in cathedrals stood and looked at
things
In niches, crypts and naves;—
My heavy heart was sagging with its
woe,
Nor Hope to prop it up, nor Prom-
ise, nor
One woman's hands—and O I wanted
so
To be felt sorry for!

BIRDY! BIRDY!

The Redbreast loves the blooming
bough—
The Bluebird loves it same as he;—
And as they sit and sing there now,
So do I sing to thee—

Only, dear heart, unlike the birds,
 I do not climb a tree
  To sing—
 I do not climb a tree.

When o'er this page, in happy years to
  come,
 Thou jokest on these lines and on
  my name,
Doubt not my love and say, "Though
  he lies dumb,
 He's lying, just the same!"

760

THE LITTLE MOCK-MAN

THE Little Mock-man on the
  Stairs—
He mocks the lady's horse 'at rares
 At bi-sickles an' things,—
He mocks the mens 'at rides 'em, too;
An' mocks the Movers, drivin' through,
An' hollers, "Here's the way *you* do
 With them-air hitchin'-strings!"
  "Ho! ho!" he'll say,
  Ole Settlers' Day,
When they're all jogglin' by,—
  "You look like *this*,"
 He'll say, an' twis'
His mouth an' squint his eye
An' 'tend-like *he* wuz beat the bass
 Drum at both ends—an' toots an'
  blares
Ole dinner-horn an' puffs his face—
 The Little Mock-man on the Stairs!

The Little Mock-man on the Stairs
Mocks all the peoples all he cares
 At passes up an' down!

He mocks the chickens round the door,
An' mocks the girl 'at scrubs the floor,
An' mocks the rich, an' mocks the pore,
 An' ever'thing in town!
  "Ho! ho!" says he,
  To you er me;
 An' ef w.e turns an' looks,
  He's all cross-eyed
  An' mouth all wide
 Like Giunts is, in books.—
"Ho! ho!" he yells, "look here at *me*,"
 An' rolls his fat eyes roun' an'
  glares,—
"You look like *this!"* he says, says he—
 The Little Mock-man on the Stairs!

The Little Mock—
  The Little Mock—
  The Little Mock-man on the Stairs,
He mocks the music-box an' clock,
 An' roller-sofy an' the chairs;
He mocks his Pa, an' specs he wears;
He mocks the man 'at picks the pears
 An' plums an' peaches on the shares;
He mocks the monkeys an' the bears
 On picture-bills, an' rips an' tears
 'Em down,—an' mocks ist all he
  cares,
 An' EVER'body EVER'wheres!

761

SUMMER-TIME AND WINTER-
TIME

IN the golden noon-shine,
 Or in the pink of dawn;
In the silver moonshine,
 Or when the moon is gone;
Open eyes, or drowsy lids,
 'Wake or 'most asleep,
I can hear the katydids,—
 "Cheep! Cheep! Cheep!"

Only in the winter-time
    Do they ever stop,
In the chip-and-splinter-time,
    When the backlogs pop,—
Then it is, the kettle-lids,
    While the sparkles leap,
Lisp like the katydids,—
    "Cheep! Cheep! Cheep!"

762

HOME-MADE RIDDLES

ALL BUT THE ANSWERS

I

NO one ever saw it
        Till I dug it from the ground;
I found it when I lost it,
    And lost it when I found:
I washed it, and dressed it,
    And buried it once more—
Dug it up, and loved it then
    Better than before.
I was paid for finding it—
    I don't know why or how,—
But I lost, found, and kept it,
    And haven't got it now.

II

Sometimes it's all alone—
    Sometimes in a crowd;
It says a thousand bright things,
    But never talks aloud.
Everybody loves it,
    And likes to have it call.
But if you shouldn't happen to,
    It wouldn't care at all.
First you see or hear of it,
    It's a-singing,—then
You may look and listen,
    But it never sings again.

763

THE LOVELY CHILD

LILIES are both pure and fair,
        Growing 'midst the roses there—
Roses, too, both red and pink,
Are quite beautiful, I think.

But of all bright blossoms—best—
Purest—fairest—loveliest,—
Could there be a sweeter thing
Than a primrose, blossoming?

764

THE YELLOWBIRD

HEY! my little Yellowbird,
        What you doing there?
Like a flashing sun-ray,
    Flitting everywhere:
Dangling down the tall weeds
    And the hollyhocks,
And the lordly sunflowers
    Along the garden-walks.

Ho! my gallant Golden-bill,
    Pecking 'mongst the weeds,
You must have for breakfast
    Golden flower-seeds:
Won't you tell a little fellow
    What you have for *tea*?—
'Spect a peck o' yellow, mellow
    Pippin on the tree.

765

SAD PERVERSITY

WHEN but a little boy, it seemed
        My dearest rapture ran
In fancy ever, when I dreamed
    I was a man—a man!

Now—sad perversity!—my theme
Of rarest, purest joy
Is when, in fancy blest, I dream
I am a little boy.

766

A FEEL IN THE CHRIS'MAS-AIR

THEY'S a kind o' *feel* in the air, to
me,
When the Chris'mas-times sets in
That's about as much of a mystery
As ever I've run ag'in'!—
Fer instunce, now, whilse I gain in
weight
And gineral health, I swear
They's a *goneness* somers I can't quite
state—
A kind o' *feel* in the air!

They's a feel in the Chris'mas-air goes
right
To the spot where a man *lives* at!—
It gives a feller a' appetite—
They ain't no doubt about *that!*—
And yit they's *somepin'*—I don't know
what—
That follers me, here and there,
And ha'nts and worries and spares me
not—
A kind o' feel in the air!

They's a *feel,* as I say, in the air that's
jest
As blame-don sad as sweet!—
In the same ra-sho as I feel the best
And am spryest on my feet,
They's allus a kind o' sort of a *ache*
That I can't lo-cate no-where;—
But it comes with *Chris'mas,* and no
mistake!—
A kind o' feel in the air.

Is it the racket the childern raise?—
W'y, *no!*—God bless 'em!—*no!*—
Is it the eyes and the cheeks ablaze—
Like my *own* wuz, long ago?—
Is it the bleat o' the whistle and beat
O' the little toy-drum and blare
O' the horn?—*No! no!*—it is jest the
sweet—
The sad-sweet feel in the air.

767

MISTER HOP-TOAD

HOWDY, Mister Hop-Toad! Glad
to see you out!
Bin a month o' Sund'ys sense I seen
you hereabout.
Kind o' biu a-layin' in, from the frost
and snow?
Good to see you out ag'in, it's bin so
long ago!
Plow's like slicin' cheese, and sod's
loppin' over even;
Loam's like gingerbread, and clods's
softer'n deceivin'—
Mister Hop-Toad, honest-true—Spring-
time—don't you love it?
You old rusty rascal you, at the bot-
tom of it!

Oh! oh! oh!
I grabs up my old hoe;
But I sees *you,*
And s' I, "Ooh-ooh!
Howdy, Mister Hop-Toad! How-
dee-do!"

Make yourse'f more comfo'bler—square
'round at your ease—
Don't set saggin' slanchwise, with your
nose below your knees.

Swell that fat old throat o' yourn and
    lemme see you swaller;
Straighten up and h'ist your head!—
    You don't owe a dollar!—
Hain't no mor'gage on your land—ner
    no taxes, nuther;
You don't haf to work no roads, even
    ef you'd ruther.
'F I was you, and *fixed* like you, I
    railly wouldn't keer
To swap fer life and hop right in the
    presidential cheer!

    Oh! oh! oh!
    I hauls back my old hoe;
    But I sees *you,*
    And s' I, "Ooh-ooh!
    Howdy, Mister Hop-Toad! How-
    dee-do!"

'Long about next Aprile, hoppin' down
    the furry,
Won't you mind I ast you what 'peared
    to be the hurry?—
Won't you mind I hooked my hoe and
    hauled you back and smiled?—
W'y, bless you, Mister Hop-Toad, I
    love you like a child!
S'pose I'd want to 'flict you any more'n
    what you air?—
S'pose I think you got no rights 'cept
    the warts you wear?
Hulk, sulk, and blink away, you old
    bloat-eyed rowdy!—
Hain't you got a word to say?—Won't
    you tell me "Howdy"?

    Oh! oh! oh!
    I swish round my old
    hoe;
    But I sees *you,*
    And s' I, "Ooh-ooh!
    Howdy, Mister Hop-Toad! How-
    dee-do!"

768

THE SILENT SINGER

MRS. D. M. JORDAN, APRIL 29, 1895

ALL sudden she hath ceased to sing,
    Hushed in eternal slumbering,
And we make moan that she is
    dead.—
    Nay; peace! be comforted.

Between her singing and her tears
She pauses, listening—and she hears
    The Song we can not hear.—And
        thus
    She mutely pities us.

Could she speak out, we doubt not she
Would turn to us full tenderly,
    And in the old melodious voice
    Say: "Weep not, but rejoice."

Ay, musical as waters run
In woodland rills through shade and
        sun,
    The sweet voice would flow on and
        say,—
    "Be glad with me to-day.—

"Your Earth was very dear and fair
To me—the groves and grasses there;
    The bursting buds and blossoms—O
    I always loved them so!—

"The very dews within them seemed
Reflected by mine eyes and gleamed
    Adown my cheeks in what you knew
    As 'tears,' and not as dew.

"Your birds, too, in the orchard-
        boughs—
I could not hear them from the house,
    But I must leave my work and stray
    Out in the open day

"And the illimitable range
Of their vast freedom—always strange
And new to me—It pierced my heart
With sweetness as a dart!—

"The singing! singing! singing!—All
The trees bloomed blossoms musical
That chirped and trilled in colors till
My whole soul seemed to fill

"To overflow with music, so
That I have found me kneeling low
Midst the lush grass, with murmur-
ous words
Thanking the flowers and birds.

"So with the ones to me most dear—
I loved them, as I love them Here:
Bear with my memory, therefore,
As when in days of yore,

"O friends of mine, ye praised the note
Of some song, quavering from my
throat
Out of the overstress of love
And all the pain thereof.

"And ye, too, do I love with this
Same love—and Heaven knows all it
is,—
The birds' song in it—bud and
bloom—
The turf, but not the tomb."

Between her singing and her tears
She pauses, listening—and she hears
The Song we can not hear.—And
thus
She mutely pities us.

769

THE GREEN GRASS OF OLD IRELAND

THE green grass av owld Ireland!
Whilst I be far away,
All fresh an' clean an' jewel-green
It's growin' there to-day.
Oh, it's cleaner, greener growin'—
All the grassy worrld around,
It's greener yet nor any grass
That grows on top o' ground!

The green grass av owld Ireland,
Indade, an' balm 't'ud be
To eyes like mine that drip wid brine
As salty as the sea!
For still the more I'm stoppin' here,
The more I'm sore to see
The glory av the green grass av owld
Ireland.

Ten years ye've paid my airnin's—
I've the l'avin's on the shelf,
Though I be here widout a queen
An' own meself meself:
I'm comin' over steerage,
But I'm goin' back firrst-class,
Patrollin' av the foremost deck
For firrst sight av the grass.

God bless yez, free Ameriky!
I love yez, dock an' shore!
I kem to yez in poverty
That's worstin' me no more
But most I'm lovin' Erin yet,
Wid all her graves, d'ye see,
By reason av the green grass av owld
Ireland.

770

A PEACE-HYMN OF THE REPUBLIC

LOUISVILLE, KENTUCKY, SEPTEMBER 12, 1895: TWENTY-NINTH ENCAMPMENT, G. A. R.

THERE'S a Voice across the Nation like a mighty ocean-hail,
   Borne up from out the Southward as the seas before the gale;
Its breath is in the streaming Flag and in the flying sail—
     As we go sailing on.

'Tis a Voice that we remember—ere its summons soothed as now—
When it rang in battle-challenge, and we answered vow with vow,—
With roar of gun and hiss of sword and crash of prow and prow,
     As we went sailing on.

Our hope sank, even as we saw the sun sink faint and far,—
The Ship of State went groping through the blinding smoke of War—
Through blackest midnight lurching, all uncheered of moon or star,
     Yet sailing—sailing on.

As One who spake the dead awake, with life-blood leaping warm—
Who walked the troubled waters, all unscathed, in mortal form,—
We felt our Pilot's presence with His hand upon the storm,
     As we went sailing on.

O Voice of passion lulled to peace, this dawning of To-day—
O Voices twain now blent as one, ye sing all fears away,
Since foe and foe are friends, and lo! the Lord, as glad as they.—
     He sends us sailing on.

771

MY DANCIN'-DAYS IS OVER

WHAT is it in old fiddle-chunes
   'at makes me ketch my breath
And ripples up my backbone tel I'm
   tickled most to death?—
Kind o' like that sweet-sick feelin', in
   the long sweep of a swing,
The first you ever swung in, with
   yer first sweetheart, i jing!—

Yer first picnic—yer first ice-cream—
   yer first o' *ever'thing*
'At happened 'fore yer dancin'-
   days wuz over!

I never understood it—and I s'pose I
   never can,—
But right in town here, yisterd'y I
   heard a pore blind man
A-fiddlin' old "Gray Eagle"—*And*-
   sir! I jes' stopped my load

O' hay and listened at him—yes,
and watched the way be
"bow'd,"—
And back I went, plum forty year',
with boys and girls I knowed
And loved, long 'fore my dancin'-
days wuz over!—

At high noon in yer city,—with yer
blame' Magnetic-Cars
A-hummin' and a-screetchin' past—and
bands and G. A. R.'s
A-marchin'—and   fire-ingines.—*All*
the noise, the whole street
through,
Wuz lost on me!—I only heard a
whipperwill er two,
It 'peared-like, kind o' callin' 'crost
the darkness and the dew,
Them nights afore my dancin'-
days wuz over.

'T'uz Chused'y-night at Wetherell's, er
We'n'sd'y-night at Strawn's,
Er Fourth - o - July - night at uther
Tomps's house er John's!—
With old Lew Church from Sugar
Crick, with that old fiddle he
Had sawed clean through the Army,
from Atlanty to the sea—
And yit he'd fetched her home ag'in,
so's he could play fer me
Onc't more afore my dancin'-days
wuz over!

The woods 'at's all be'n cut away wuz
growin' same as then;
The youngsters all wuz boys ag'in 'at's
now all oldish men;
And all the girls 'at *then* wuz girls—
I saw 'em, one and all,
As *plain* as then—the middle-sized,
the short-and-fat, and tall—

And 'peared-like, I danced "Tucker"
fer 'em up and down the wall
Jes' like afore my dancin'-days wuz
over!

.   .   .   .

The facts is, I wuz *dazed* so 'at I clean
fergot jes' where
I railly wuz,—a-blockin' streets, and
still a-standin' there:
I heard the *po*-leece yellin', but my
ears wuz kind o' *blurred*—
My *eyes*, too, fer the odds o' that,—
bekase I thought I heard
My wife 'at's dead a-laughin'-like,
and jokin', word-fer-word
Jes' like afore her dancin'-days wuz
over.

772

EUGENE FIELD

WITH gentlest tears, no less than
jubilee
Of blithest joy, we heard him, and
still hear
Him singing on, with full voice, pure
and clear,
Uplifted, as some classic melody
In sweetest legends of old minstrelsy;
Or, swarming Elfin-like upon the ear,
His airy notes make all the atmos-
phere
One blur of bird and bee and lullaby.
His tribute:—Luster in the faded bloom
Of checks of old, old mothers; and
the fall
Of gracious dews in eyes long dry
and dim;
And hope in lover's pathways midst
rerfume

Of woodland haunts; and—meed ex-
ceeding all,—
The love of little children laurels
him.

773

DREAM-MARCH

WASN'T it a funny dream!—per-
fectly bewild'rin'!—
Last night, and night before, and
night before that,
Seemed like I saw the march o' regi-
ments o' children,
Marching to the robin's fife and
cricket's rat-ta-tat!
Lily-banners overhead, with the dew
upon 'em,
On flashed the little army, as with
sword and flame;
Like the buzz o' bumble-wings, with
the honey on 'em,
Came an eery, cheery chant, chim-
ing as it came:—

Where go the children?   Traveling!
Traveling!
Where go the children, traveling
ahead?
Some go to kindergarten; some go to
day-school;
Some go to night-school; and some
go to bed!

Smooth roads or rough roads, warm or
winter weather,
On go the children, towhead and
brown,
Brave boys and brave girls, rank and
file together,
Marching out of Morning-Land, over
dale and down:

Some go a-gipsying out in country
places—
Out through the orchards, with blos-
soms on the boughs
Wild, sweet, and pink and white as
their own glad faces;
And some go, at evening, calling
home the cows.

Where go the children?   Traveling!
Traveling!
Where go the children, traveling
ahead?
Some go to foreign wars, and camps
by the fire-light—
Some go to glory so; and some go
to bed!

Some go through grassy lanes leading
to the city—
Thinner grow the green trees and
thicker grows the dust;
Ever, though, to little people any path
is pretty
So it leads to newer lands, as they
know it must.
Some go to singing less; some go to
list'ning;
Some go to thinking over ever-nobler
themes;
Some go anhungered, but ever bravely
whistling,
Turning never home again only in
their dreams.

Where go the children?   Traveling!
Traveling!
Where go the children, traveling
ahead?
Some go to conquer things; some go to
try them;
Some go to dream them; and some
go to bed!

774

A CHRISTMAS MEMORY

PA he bringed me here to stay
   'Til my Ma she's well.—An' nen
He's go' hitch up, Chris'mus-day,
   An' come take me back again
Wher' my Ma's at! Won't I be
Tickled when he comes fer me!

My Ma an' my A'nty they
   'Uz each-uvver's sisters. Pa—
A'nty telled me, th' other day,—
   He comed here an' married Ma. . . .
A'nty said nen, "Go run play,
   I must work now!" . . . An' I saw,
When she turn' her face away,
   She 'uz cryin'.—An' nen I
'Tend-like I "run play"—an' cry.

This-here house o' A'nty's wher'
They 'uz borned—my Ma an' her!—
An' her Ma 'uz my Ma's Ma,
An' her Pa 'uz my Ma's Pa—
Ain't that funny?—An' they're dead:
An' this-here's "th' ole Homestead."—
An' my A'nty said, an' cried,
It's mine, too, ef my Ma died—
Don't know what she mean—'cause my
Ma she's nuvver go' to die!

When Pa bringed me here 't'uz night—
   'Way dark night! An' A'nty spread
Me a piece—an' light the light
   An' say I must go to bed.—
I cry not to—but Pa said,
"Be good boy now, like you telled
   Mommy 'at you're go' to be!"
An', when he 'uz kissin' me
   My good night, his cheek's all wet
An' taste salty.—An' he held
   Wite close to me an' rocked some

An' laughed-like—'til A'nty come
   Git me while he's rockin' yet.

A'nty he'p me, 'til I be
Purt' nigh strip-pud—nen hug me
In bofe arms an' lif' me 'way
Up in her high bed—an' pray
   Wiv me,—'bout my Ma—an' Pa—
An' ole Santy Claus—an' Sleigh—
   An' Reindeers an' little Drum—
   Yes, an' Picture-books, "Tom
      Thumb,"
An' "Three Bears," an' ole "Fee-
      Faw"—
   Yes, an' "Tweedle-Dee" an'
      "Dum,"
   An' "White Knight" an' "Squid-
      jicum,"
An' most things you ever saw!—
   An' when A'nty kissed me, she
   'Uz all cryin' over me!

Don't want Santy Claus—ner things
Any kind he ever brings!—
Don't want A'nty!—Don't want Pa!—
I ist only want my Ma!

775

TO ALMON KEEFER

INSCRIBED IN "TALES OF THE OCEAN"

THIS first book that I ever knew
   Was read aloud to me by you—
Friend of my boyhood, therefore take
It back from me, for old times' sake—
The selfsame "Tales" first read to me,
Under "the old sweet apple tree,"
Ere I myself could read such great
Big words,—but listening all elate,
At your interpreting, until

Brain, heart and soul were all athrill
With wonder, awe, and sheer excess
Of wildest childish happiness.

So take the book again—forget
All else,—long years, lost hopes, re-
    gret;
Sighs for the joys we ne'er attain,
Prayers we have lifted all in vain;
Tears for the faces seen no more,
Once as the roses at the door!
Take the enchanted book—And lo,
On grassy swards of long ago,
Sprawl out again, beneath the shade
The breezy old-home orchard made,
The veriest barefoot boy indeed—
And I will listen as you read.

776

LITTLE MAID-O'-DREAMS

LITTLE Maid-o'-Dreams, with your
    Eery eyes so clear and pure
Gazing, where we fain would see
Into far futurity,—
Tell us what you there behold,
In your visions manifold!
What is on beyond our sight,
Biding till the morrow's light,
Fairer than we see to-day,
As our dull eyes only may?

Little Maid-o'-Dreams, with face
Like as in some woodland place
Lifts a lily, chaste and white,
From the shadow to the light;—
Tell us, by your subtler glance,
What strange sorcery enchants
You as now,—here, yet afar
As the realms of moon and star?—
Have you magic lamp and ring,
And genii for vassaling?

Little Maid-o'-Dreams, confess
You're divine and nothing less,—
For with mortal palms, we fear,
Yet must pet you, dreaming here—
Yearning, too, to lift the tips
Of your fingers to our lips;
Fearful still you may rebel,
High and heav'nly oracle!
Thus, though all unmeet our kiss,
Pardon this!—and this!—and this!

Little Maid-o'-Dreams, we call
Truce and favor, knowing all!—
All your magic is, in truth,
Pure foresight and faith of youth—
You're a child, yet even so,
You're a sage, in embryo—
Prescient poet—artist—great
As your dreams anticipate.—
Trusting God and Man, you do
Just as Heaven inspires you to.

777

EDGAR WILSON NYE

FEBRUARY 22, 1896

THE saddest silence falls when
    Laughter lays
Finger on lip, and falteringly breaks
The glad voice into dying minor
    shakes
And quavers, lorn as airs the wind-harp
    plays
At urge of drearest Winter's bleakest
    days:
    A troubled hush, in which all hope
        forsakes
    Us, and the yearning upstrained vi-
        sion aches
With tears that drown e'en heaven
    from our gaze.

Such silence—after such glad merri-
ment!
O prince of halest humor, wit and
cheer!
Could you yet speak to us, I doubt
not we

Should catch your voice, still blithely
eloquent
Above all murmurings of sorrow
here,
Calling your love back to us laugh-
ingly.

778

CASSANDER

"CASSANDER! O Cassander!"—her mother's voice seems cle'r
As ever, from the old back-porch, a-hollerin' fer her—
Especially in airly Spring—like May, two year' ago—
Last time she hollered fer her,—and Cassander didn't hear!

Cassander was so chirpy-like and sociable and free,
And good to ever'body, and wuz even good to me
Though *I* wuz jes' a common—well, a farm-hand, don't you know,
A-workin' on her father's place, as pore as pore could be!

Her bein' jes' a' only child, Cassander had her way
A good-'eal more'n other girls; and neighbors ust to say
She looked most like her Mother, but wuz turned most like her Pap,—
Except *he* had no use fer *town*-folks then—ner *yit to-day!*

I can't claim she incouraged *me:* She'd let me drive her in
To town sometimes, on Saturd'ys, and fetch her home ag'in,
Tel onc't she 'scused "Old Moll" and me,—and some blame' city-chap,
He driv her home, two-forty style, in face o' kith-and-kin.

She even tried to make him stay fer supper, but I 'low
He must 'a' kind o' 'spicioned some objections.—Anyhow,
Her mother callin' at her, whilst her father stood and shook
His fist,—the town-chap turnt his team and made his partin' bow.

"Cassander! *You,* Cassander!"—hear her mother jes' as plain,
And see Cassander blushin' like the peach tree down the lane,
Whilse I sneaked on apast her, with a sort o' hang-dog look,
A-feelin' cheap as sorghum and as green as sugar-cane!

(You see, I'd *skooted* when she met her *town*-beau—when, in fact,
Ef I'd had sense I'd *stayed* fer her.—But sense wuz what I lacked!

So I'd cut home ahead o' her, so's I could tell 'em what
Wuz keepin' her. And—*you* know how a jealous fool'll act!)

I past her, I wuz sayin',—but she never turnt her head;
I swallered-like and cle'red my th'oat—but that wuz all I said;
   And whilse I hoped fer some word back, it wuzn't what I got.—
That girl'll not stay stiller on the day she's layin' dead!

Well, that-air silence *lasted!*—Ust to listen ever' day
I'd be at work and hear her mother callin' thataway;
   I'd *sight* Cassander, mayby, cuttin' home acrost the blue
And drizzly fields; but nary answer—nary word to say!

Putt in about two weeks o' that—two weeks o' rain and mud,
Er mostly so: I couldn't plow. The old crick like a flood:
   And, lonesome as a borried dog, I'd wade them old woods through—
The dogwood blossoms white as snow, and redbuds red as blood.

Last time her mother called her—sich a morning like as now:
The robins and the bluebirds, and the blossoms on the bough—
   And this wuz yit 'fore brekfust, with the sun out at his best,
And hosses kickin' in the barn—and dry enough to plow.

"Cassander! *O* Cassander!" . . . And her only answer—What?—
A letter, twisted round the cook-stove damper, smokin'-hot,
   A-statin': "I wuz married on that day of all the rest,
The day my husband fetched me home—ef you ain't all fergot!"

"Cassander! *O* Cassander!" seems, allus, 'long in May,
I hear her mother callin' her—a-callin', night and day—
   "Cassander! *O* Cassander!" allus callin', as I say,
"Cassander! *O* Cassander!" jes' a-callin' thataway.

A CHILD-WORLD

779

PROEM

*T*HE *Child-World—long and long since lost to view—*
   A Fairy Paradise!—
How always fair it was and fresh and new—
   How every affluent hour heaped heart and eyes
     With treasures of surprise!

Enchantments tangible: The under-brink
Of dawns that launched the sight
Up seas of gold: The dewdrop on the pink,
With all the green earth in it and blue height
Of heavens infinite:

The liquid, dripping songs of orchard-birds—
The wee bass of the bees,—
With lucent deeps of silence afterwards;
The gay, clandestine whisperings of the breeze
And glad leaves of the trees.

. . . .

O Child-World: After this world—just as when
I found you first sufficed
My soulmost need—if I found you again,
With all my childish dream so realized,
I should not be surprised.

780

THE CHILD-WORLD

A CHILD-WORLD, yet a wondrous
world no less,
To those who knew its boundless hap-
piness.
A simple old frame house—eight
rooms in all—
Set just one side the center of a small
But very hopeful Indiana town,—
The upper story looking squarely
down
Upon the main street, and the main
highway
From East to West,—historic in its
day,
Known as The National Road—old-
timers, all
Who linger yet, will happily recall
It as the scheme and handiwork, as
well

As property, of "Uncle Sam," and tell
Of its importance, "long and long afore
*Rail*roads wuz ever *dreamp'* of!"—
Furthermore,
The reminiscent first inhabitants
Will make that old road blossom with
romance
Of snowy caravans, in long parade
Of covered vehicles, of every grade
From ox-cart of most primitive design,
To Conestoga wagons, with their fine
Deep-chested six-horse teams, in heavy
gear,
High hames and chiming bells—to
childish ear
And eye entrancing as the glittering
train
Of some sun-smitten pageant of old
Spain.
And, in like spirit, haply they will
tell
You of the roadside forests, and the
yell

But dropped, *k'whop!* and scraped the
  buggy-shed,
Leaving a tuft of woolly, foxy hair
Under the sharp end of a gate-hinge
  there.
Then, all ignobly scrambling to his
  feet
And whinnying a whinny like a bleat,
He would pursue himself around the
  lot
And—do the whole thing over, like
  as not! . . .
Ah! what a life of constant fear and
  dread
And flop and squawk and flight the
  chickens led!

Above the fences, either side, were
  seen
The neighbor-houses, set in plots of
  green
Dooryards and greener gardens, tree
  and wall
Alike whitewashed, an order in it all:
The scythe hooked in the tree-fork;
  and the spade
And hoe and rake and shovel all,
  when laid
Aside, were in their places, ready for
The hand of either the possessor or
Of any neighbor, welcome to the loan
Of any tool he might not chance to
  own.

781

THE OLD HOME-FOLKS

SUCH was the Child-World of the
    long ago—
The little world these children used to
  know:—

Johnty, the oldest, and the best, per-
  haps,
Of the five happy little Hoosier
  chaps
Inhabiting this wee world all their
  own.—
Johnty, the leader, with his native
  tone
Of grave command—a general on pa-
  rade
Whose each punctilious order was
  obeyed
By his proud followers.

                    But Johnty yet—
After all serious duties—could forget
The gravity of life to the extent,
At times, of kindling much astonish-
  ment
About him: With a quick, observant
  eye,
And mind and memory, he could sup-
  ply
The tamest incident with liveliest
  mirth;
And at the most unlooked-for times on
  earth
Was wont to break into some travesty
On those around him—feats of mim-
  icry
Of this one's trick of gesture—that
  one's walk—
Or this one's laugh—or that one's
  funny talk,—
The way "the watermelon-man" would
  try
His humor on town-folks that wouldn't
  buy;—
How he drove into town at morning—
  then
At dusk (alas!) how he drove out
  again.

Though these divertisements of Johnty's
were
Hailed with a hearty glee and relish,
there
Appeared a sense, on his part, of re-
gret—
A spirit of remorse that would not
let
Him rest for days thereafter.—Such
times he,
As some boy said, "jist got too overly
Blame' good fer common boys like us,
you know
To 'sociate with—'less'n we 'ud go
And jine his church!"

Next after Johnty came
His little towhead brother, Bud by
name.—
And O how white his hair was—and
how thick
His face with freckles,—and his ears,
how quick
And curious and intrusive!—And how
pale
The blue of his big eyes;—and how a
tale
Of Giants, Trolls or Fairies, bulged
them still
Bigger and bigger!—And when "Jack"
would kill
The old "Four-headed Giant," Bud's
big eyes
Were swollen truly into giant-size.
And Bud was apt in make-believes—
would hear
His Grandma talk or read, with such
an ear
And memory of both subject and big
words,
That he would take the book up after-
wards

And feign to "read aloud," with such
success
As caused his truthful elders real dis-
tress.
But he *must* have *big words*—they
seemed to give
Extremer range to the superlative—
That was his passion. "My Gran'ma,"
he said,
One evening, after listening as she read
Some heavy old historical review—
With copious explanations thereunto
Drawn out by his inquiring turn of
mind,—
"My Gran'ma she's read *all* books—
ever' kind
They is, 'at tells all 'bout the land an'
sea
An' Nations of the Earth!—An' she is
the
Historicul-est woman ever wuz!"
(Forgive the verse's chuckling as it
does
In its erratic current.—Oftentimes
The little willowy water-brook of
rhymes
Must falter in its music, listening to
The children laughing as they used to
do.)

Who shall sing a simple ditty all about the
Willow,
Dainty-fine and delicate as any bending
spray
That dandles high the happy bird that flut-
ters there to trill a
Tremulously tender song of greeting to
the May.

Bravest, too, of all the trees!—none to
match your daring,—
First of greens to greet the Spring and
lead in leafy sheen;—
Ay, and you're the last—almost into winter
wearing
Still the leaf of loyalty—still the badge of
green.

Ah, my lovely Willow!—Let the Waters lilt
    your graces,—
They alone with limpid kisses lave your
    leaves above,
Flashing back your sylvan beauty, and in
    shady places
Peering up with glimmering pebbles, like
    the eyes of love.

Next, Maymie, with her hazy cloud of
    hair,
And the blue skies of eyes beneath it
    there.
Her dignified and "little lady" airs
Of never either romping up the stairs
Or falling down them; thoughtful
    every way
Of others first—The kind of child at
    play
That "gave up," for the rest, the ripest
    pear
Or peach or apple in the garden there
Beneath the trees where swooped the
    airy swing—
She pushing it, too glad for anything!
Or, in the character of hostess, she
Would entertain her friends delight-
    fully
In her playhouse,—with strips of carpet
    laid
Along the garden-fence within the
    shade
Of the old apple trees—where from
    next yard
Came the two dearest friends in her
    regard,
The little Crawford girls, Ella and
    Lu—
As shy and lovely as the lilies grew
In their idyllic home,—yet sometimes
    they
Admitted Bud and Alex to their play,
Who did their heavier work and
    helped them fix

To have a "Festibul"—and brought the
    bricks
And built the "stove," with a real fire
    and all,
And stovepipe-joint for chimney, loom-
    ing tall
And wonderfully smoky—even to
Their childish aspirations, as it blew
And swooped and swirled about them
    till their sight
Was feverish even as their high de-
    light.

Then Alex, with his freckles, and his
    freaks
Of temper, and the peach-bloom of his
    cheeks,
And "amber-colored hair"—his mother
    said
'Twas that, when others laughed and
    called it "red"
And Alex threw things at them—till
    they'd call
A truce, agreeing " 't'uzn't red ut-tall!"
But Alex was affectionate beyond
The average child, and was extremely
    fond
Of the paternal relatives of his,
Of whom he once made estimate like
    this:—
"I'm only got two brothers,—but my
    Pa
He's got most brothers'n you ever
    saw!—
He's got seben brothers!—Yes, an'
    they're all my
Seben Uncles!—Uncle John, an' Jim,
    —an' I
Got Uncle George, an' Uncle Andy,
    too,
An' Uncle Frank, an' Uncle Joe.—An'
    you

Know Uncle *Mart.*—An', all but *him,*
    they're great
Big mens!—An' nen's Aunt Sarah—she
    makes eight!—
I'm got *eight* uncles!—'cept Aunt Sarah
    can't
Be ist my *uncle* 'cause she's ist my
    a'nt!"

Then, next to Alex—and the last in-
    deed
Of these five little ones of whom you
    read—
Was baby Lizzie, with her velvet
    lisp,—
As though her elfin lips had caught
    some wisp
Of floss between them as they strove
    with speech,
Which ever seemed just in, yet out of,
    reach—
Though what her lips missed, her dark
    eyes could say
With looks that made her meaning
    clear as day.
And, knowing now the children, you
    must know
The father and the mother they loved
    so:—
The father was a swarthy man, black-
    eyed,
Black-haired, and high of forehead;
    and, beside
The slender little mother, seemed in
    truth
A very king of men—since, from his
    youth,
To his hale manhood *now*—(worthy
    as then,—
A lawyer and a leading citizen
Of the proud little town and county-
    seat—

His hopes his neighbors', and their
    fealty sweet)—
He had known outdoor labor—rain
    and shine—
Bleak Winter, and bland Summer—
    foul and fine.
So Nature had ennobled him and set
Her symbol on him like a coronet:
His lifted brow, and frank, reliant
    face—
Superior of stature as of grace,—
Even the children by the spell were
    wrought
Up to heroics of their simple thought,
And saw him, trim of build, and lithe
    and straight
And tall, almost, as at the pasture-gate
The towering ironweed the scythe had
    spared
For their sakes, when The Hired Man
    declared
It would grow on till it became a *tree,*
With cocoanuts and monkeys in—may-
    be!

Yet, though the children, in their pride
    and awe
And admiration of the father, saw
A being so exalted—even more
Like adoration was the love they bore
The gentle mother.—Her mild, plain-
    tive face
Was purely fair, and haloed with a
    grace
And sweetness luminous when joy
    made glad
Her features with a smile; or saintly sad
As twilight, fell the sympathetic gloom
Of any childish grief, or as a room
Were darkened suddenly, the curtain
    drawn
Across the window and the sunshine
    gone.

Her brow, below her fair hair's glim-
mering strands,
Seemed meetest resting-place for bless-
ing hands
Or holiest touches of soft finger-tips
And little rose-leaf cheeks and dewy
lips.

Though heavy household tasks were
pitiless,
No little waist or coat or checkered
dress
But knew her needle's deftness; and no
skill
Matched hers in shaping plait or
flounce or frill;
Or fashioning, in complicate design,
All rich embroideries of leaf and vine,
With tiniest twining tendril,—bud and
bloom
And fruit, so like, one's fancy caught
perfume
And dainty touch and taste of them, to
see
Their semblance wrought in such rare
verity.

Shrined in her sanctity of home and
love,
And love's fond service and reward
thereof,
Restore her thus, O blessed Memory!—
Throned in her rocking-chair, and on
her knee
Her sewing—her work-basket on the
floor
Beside her,—Spring-time through the
open door
Balmily stealing in and all about
The room; the bees' dim hum, and the
far shout
And laughter of the children at their
play

And neighbor children from across the
way
Calling in gleeful challenge—save alone
One boy whose voice sends back no
answering tone—
The boy, prone on the floor, above a
book
Of pictures, with a rapt, ecstatic look—
Even as the mother's, by the selfsame
spell,
Is lifted, with a light ineffable—
As though her senses caught no mortal
cry,
But heard, instead, some poem going
by.

The Child-heart is so strange a little
thing—
So mild—so timorously shy and small,—
When *grown-up* hearts throb, it goes scam-
pering
Behind the wall, nor dares peer out at
all!—
It is the veriest mouse
That hides in any house—
So wild a little thing is any Child-heart!

Child-heart!—mild heart!—
Ho, my little wild heart!—
Come up here to me out o' the dark,
Or let me come to you!

So lorn at times the Child-heart needs
must be
With never one maturer heart for friend
And comrade, whose tear-ripened sympathy
And love might lend it comfort to the
end,—
Whose yearnings, aches and stings,
Over poor little things
Were pitiful as ever any Child-heart.

Child-heart!—mild heart!—
Ho, my little wild heart!—
Come up here to me out o' the dark,
Or let me come to you!

Times, too, the little Child-heart must be
glad—
Being so young, nor knowing, as *we*
know,

The fact from fantasy, the good from bad,
The joy from woe, the—*all* that hurts us
    so!
What wonder then that thus
    It hides away from us?—
So weak a little thing is any Child-heart!

    Child-heart!—mild heart!—
    Ho, my little wild heart!—
    Come up here to me in o' the dark,
    Or let me come to you!

Nay, little Child-heart, you have never need
    To fear *us;*—we are weaker far than
    you—
'Tis *we* who should be fearful—we indeed
    Should hide us, too, as darkly as you
    do,—
    Safe, as yourself, withdrawn,
    Hearing the World roar on
Too wilful, woeful, awful for the Child-
    heart!

    Child-heart!—mild heart!—
    Ho, my little wild heart!—
    Come up here to me out o' the dark,
    Or let me come to you!

The clock chats on confidingly; a rose
Taps at the window, as the sunlight
    throws
A brilliant, jostling checkerwork of
    shine
And shadow, like a Persian-loom de-
    sign,
Across the home-made carpet—fades,—
    and then
The dear old colors are themselves
    again.
Sounds drop in visiting from every-
    where—
The bluebird's and the robin's trill are
    there,
Their sweet liquidity diluted some
By dewy orchard-spaces they have
    come:
Sounds of the town, too, and the great
    highway—

The Mover-wagons' rumble, and the
    neigh
Of over-traveled horses, and the bleat
Of sheep and low of cattle through the
    street—
A Nation's thoroughfare of hopes and
    fears,
First blazed by the heroic pioneers
Who gave up old-home idols and set
    face
Toward the unbroken West, to found
    a race
And tame a wilderness now mightier
    than
All peoples and all tracts American.

Blent with all outer sounds, the sounds
    within:—
In mild remoteness falls the household
    din
Of porch and kitchen: the dull jar and
    thump
Of churning; and the "glung-glung"
    of the pump,
With sudden pad and skurry of bare
    feet
Of little outlaws, in from field or
    street:
The clang of kettle,—rasp of damper-
    ring
And bang of cook-stove door—and
    everything
That jingles in a busy kitchen lifts
Its individual wrangling voice and
    drifts
In sweetest tinny, coppery, pewtery
    tone
Of music hungry ear has ever known
In wildest famished yearning and con-
    ceit
Of youth, to just cut loose and eat and
    eat!—
The zest of hunger still incited on

To childish desperation by long-drawn
Breaths of hot, steaming, wholesome
 things that stew
And blubber, and uptilt the pot-lids, too,
Filling the sense with zestful rumors of
The dear old-fashioned dinners chil-
 dren love:
Redolent savorings of home-cured
 meats,
Potatoes, beans and cabbage; turnips,
 beets
And parsnips—rarest composite entire
That ever pushed a mortal child's de-
 sire
To madness by new-grated fresh, keen,
 sharp
Horseradish—tang that sets the lips
 awarp
And watery, anticipating all
The cloyed sweets of the glorious fes-
 tival.—
Still add the cinnamony, spicy scents
Of clove, nutmeg, and myriad condi-
 ments
In like-alluring whiffs that prophesy
Of sweltering pudding, cake, and cus-
 tard-pie—
The swooning-sweet aroma haunting
 all
The house—up-stairs and down—
 porch, parlor, hall
And sitting-room — invading even
 where
The Hired Man sniffs it in the orchard-
 air,
And pauses in his pruning of the trees
To note the sun minutely and to—
 sneeze.

Then Cousin Rufus comes—the chil-
 dren hear
His hale voice in the old hall, ringing
 clear

As any bell. Always he came with
 song
Upon his lips and all the happy throng
Of echoes following him, even as the
 crowd
Of his admiring little kinsmen—proud
To have a cousin *grown*—and yet as
 young
Of soul and cheery as the songs he
 sung.

He was a student of the law—intent
Soundly to win success, with all it
 meant;
And so he studied—even as he
 played,—
With all his heart: And so it was he
 made
His gallant fight for fortune—through
 all stress
Of battle bearing him with cheeriness
And wholesome valor.

 And the children had
Another relative who kept them glad
And joyous by his very merry ways—
As blithe and sunny as the summer
 days,—
Their father's youngest brother—Uncle
 Mart.
The old "Arabian Nights" he knew by
 heart—
"Baron Munchausen," too; and like-
 wise "The
Swiss Family Robinson."—And when
 these three
Gave out, as he rehearsed them, he
 could go
Straight on in the same line—a steady
 flow
Of arabesque invention that his good
Old mother never clearly understood.

He *was* to be a *printer*—wanted,
though,
To be an *actor.*—But the world was
"show"
Enough for *him,*—theatric, airy, gay,—
Each day to him was jolly as a play.
And some poetic symptoms, too, in
sooth,
Were certain.—And, from his appren-
tice youth,
He joyed in verse-quotations—which he
took
Out of the old "Type Foundry Speci-
men Book."
He craved and courted most the favor
of
The children.—They were foremost in
his love;
And pleasing *them,* he pleased his own
boy-heart
And kept it young and fresh in every
part.
So was it he devised for them and
wrought
To life his quaintest, most romantic
thought:—
Like some lone castaway in alien
seas,
He built a house up in the apple trees,
Out in the corner of the garden, where
No man-devouring native, prowling
there,
Might pounce upon them in the dead
o' night—
For lo, their little ladder, slim and
light,
They drew up after them. And it was
known
That Uncle Mart slipped up some-
times alone
And drew the ladder in, to lie and
moon
Over some novel all the afternoon.

And one time Johnty, from the crowd
below,—
Outraged to find themselves deserted
so—
Threw bodily their old black cat up in
The airy fastness, with much yowl and
din
Resulting, while a wild periphery
Of cat went circling to another tree,
And, in impassioned outburst, Uncle
Mart
Loomed up, and thus relieved his tragic
heart:

" *'Hence, long-tailed, ebon-eyed, noc-*
turnal ranger!
What led thee hither 'mongst the
types and cases?
Didst thou not know that running
midnight races
O'er standing types was fraught with
imminent danger?
Did hunger lead thee—didst thou think
to find
Some rich old cheese to fill thy hun-
gry maw?
Vain hope! for none but literary jaw
Can masticate our cookery for the
mind!' "

So likewise when, with lordly air and
grace,
He strode to dinner, with a tragic face
With ink-spots on it from the office,
he
Would aptly quote more "Specimen-
poetry"—
Perchance like " 'Labor's bread is
sweet to eat,
(*Ahem!*) And toothsome is the toiler's
meat.' "

Ah, could you see them *all,* at lull of
   noon!—
A sort of *boisterous* lull, with clink of
   spoon
And clatter of deflecting knife, and
   plate
Dropped saggingly, with its all-bounte-
   ous weight,
And dragged in place voraciously; and
   then
Pent exclamations, and the lull again.—
The garland of glad faces round the
   board—
Each member of the family restored
To his or her place, with an extra chair
Or two for the chance guests so often
   there.—
The father's farmer-client, brought
   home from
The court room, though he "didn't
   want to come
Tel he jist saw he *hat* to!" he'd ex-
   plain,
Invariably, time and time again,
To the pleased wife and hostess, as she
   pressed
Another cup of coffee on the guest.—
Or there was Johnty's special chum,
   perchance,
Or Bud's, or both—each childish coun-
   tenance
Lit with a higher glow of youthful
   glee,
To be together thus unbrokenly,—
Jim Offutt, or Eck Skinner, or George
   Carr—
The very nearest chums of Bud's these
   are,—
So, very probably, *one* of the three,
At least, is there with Bud, or *ought*
   to be.
Like interchange the town-boys each
   had known—

His playmate's dinner better than his
   own—
Yet blest that he was ever made to
   stay
At *Almon Keefer's any* blessed day,
For *any* meal! . . . Visions of biscuits,
   hot
And flaky-perfect, with the golden blot
Of molten butter for the center, clear,
Through pools of clover-honey—*dear-
   o-dear!*—
With creamy milk for its divine "fare-
   well":
And then, if any one delectable
Might yet exceed in sweetness, O re-
   store
The cherry-cobbler of the days of
   yore
Made only by Al Keefer's mother!—
   Why,
The very thought of it ignites the eye
Of memory with rapture—cloys the
   lip
Of longing, till it seems to ooze and
   drip
With veriest juice and stain and over-
   waste
Of that most sweet delirium of taste
That ever visited the childish tongue,
Or proved, as now, the sweetest thing
   unsung.
Ah, Almon Keefer! what a boy you
   were,
With your back-tilted hat and careless
   hair,
And open, honest, fresh, fair face and
   eyes
With their all-varying looks of pleased
   surprise
And joyous interest in flower and
   tree,
And poising humming-bird, and maun-
   dering bee.

The fields and woods he knew; the
tireless tramp
With gun and dog; and the night-
fisher's camp—
No other boy, save Bee Lineback, had
won
Such brilliant mastery of rod and gun.
Even in his earliest childhood had he
shown
These traits that marked him as his
father's own.
Dogs all paid Almon honor and bow-
wowed
Allegiance, let him come in any crowd
Of rabbit-hunting town-boys, even
though
His own dog "Sleuth" rebuked their
acting so
With jealous snarls and growlings.

But the best
Of Almon's virtues—leading all the
rest—
Was his great love of books, and skill
as well
In reading them aloud, and by the
spell
Thereof enthralling his mute listeners,
as
They grouped about him in the or-
chard-grass,
Hinging their bare shins in the mot-
tled shine
And shade, as they lay prone, or
stretched supine
Beneath their favorite tree, with
dreamy eyes
And Argo-fancies voyaging the skies.
"Tales of the Ocean" was the name of
one
Old dog's-eared book that was sur-
passed by none

Of all the glorious list.—Its back was
gone,
But its vitality went bravely on
In such delicious tales of land and sea
As may not ever perish utterly.
Of still more dubious caste, "Jack Shep-
pard" drew
Full admiration; and "Dick Turpin,"
too.
And, painful as the fact is to convey,
In certain lurid tales of their own
day,
These boys found thieving heroes and
outlaws
They hailed with equal fervor of ap-
plause:
"The League of the Miami"—why, the
name
Alone was fascinating—is the same,
In memory, this venerable hour
Of moral wisdom shorn of all its
power,
As it unblushingly reverts to when
The old barn was "the Cave," and
hears again
The signal blown, outside the buggy-
shed—
The drowsy guard within uplifts his
head,
And " 'Who goes there?' " is called, in
bated breath—
The challenge answered in a hush of
death,—
"Sh! — 'Barney Gray!' " And then
" 'What do you seek?' "
" 'Stables of The League!' " the voice
comes spent and weak,
For, ha! the Law is on the "Chieftain's"
trail—
Tracked to his very lair!—Well, what
avail?
The "secret entrance" opens—closes.—
So

The "Robber-Captain" thus outwits his
   foe;
And, safe once more within his "cav-
   ern-halls,"
He shakes his clenched fist at the
   warped plank-walls
And mutters his defiance through the
   cracks
At the balked Enemy's retreating backs
As the loud horde flees pell-mell down
   the lane,
And—*Almon Keefer* is himself again!

Excepting few, they were not books in-
   deed
Of deep import that Almon chose to
   read;—
Less fact than fiction.—Much he fa-
   vored those—
If not in poetry, in hectic prose—
That made our native Indian a wild,
Feathered and fine-preened hero that
   a child
Could recommend as just about the
   thing
To make a god of, or at least a king.

Aside from Almon's own books—two
   or three—
His store of lore The Township Li-
   brary
Supplied him weekly: All the books
   with "or's"
Subtitled—lured him—after "Indian
   Wars,"
And "Life of Daniel Boone,"—not to
   include
Some few books spiced with humor,—
   "Robin Hood"
And rare "Don Quixote."—And one
   time he took
"Dadd's Cattle Doctor." . . . How he
   hugged the book

And hurried homeward, with internal
   glee
And humorous spasms of expectancy!—
All this confession—as he promptly
   made
It, the day later, writhing in the shade
Of the old apple tree with Johnty and
Bud, Noey Bixler, and The Hired
   Hand—
Was quite as funny as the book was
   not. . . .
O Wonderland of wayward Childhood!
   what
An easy, breezy realm of summer calm
And dreamy gleam and gloom and
   bloom and balm
Thou art!—The Lotus-Land the poet
   sung,
It is the Child-World while the heart
   beats young. . . .

While the heart beats young!—O the splendor
   of the Spring,
With all her dewy jewels on, is not so fair
   a thing!
The fairest, rarest morning of the blossom-
   time of May
Is not so sweet a season as the season of
   to-day
While Youth's diviner climate folds and holds
   us, close caressed
As we feel our mothers with us by the touch
   of face and breast;—
Our bare feet in the meadows, and our fan-
   cies up among
The airy clouds of morning—while the heart
   beats young.

While the heart beats young and our pulses
   leap and dance,
With every day a holiday and life a glad ro-
   mance,—
We hear the birds with wonder, and with
   wonder watch their flight—
Standing still the more enchanted, both of
   hearing and of sight,
When they have vanished wholly,—for, in
   fancy, wing-to-wing

We fly to Heaven with them; and, returning,
still we sing
The praises of this *lower* Heaven with tireless
voice and tongue,
Even as the Master sanctions—while the heart
beats young.

While the heart beats young!—While the
heart beats young!
O green and gold old Earth of ours, with
azure overhung
And looped with rainbows!—grant us yet this
grassy lap of thine—
We would be still thy children, through the
shower and the shine!
So pray we, lisping, whispering, in childish
love and trust,
With our beseeching hands and faces lifted
from the dust
By fervor of the poem, all unwritten and un-
sung,
Thou givest us in answer, while the heart
beats young.

Another hero of those youthful years
Returns, as Noey Bixler's name ap-
pears.
And Noey—if in any special way—
Was notably good-natured.—Work or
play
He entered into with selfsame de-
light—
A wholesome interest that made him
quite
As many friends among the old as
young,—
So everywhere were Noey's praises
sung.

And he was awkward, fat and over-
grown,
With a round full-moon face, that
fairly shone
As though to meet the simile's demand.
And, cumbrous though he seemed, both eye and hand
Were dowered with the discernment
and deft skill

Of the true artisan: He shaped at will,
In his old father's shop, on rainy days,
Little toy-wagons, and curved-runner
sleighs;
The trimmest bows and arrows—fash-
ioned, too,
Of "seasoned timber," such as Noey
knew
How to select, prepare, and then com-
plete,
And call his little friends in from the
street.
"The very *best* bow," Noey used to
say,
"Hain't made o' ash ner hick'ry thata-
way!—
But you git *mulberry*—the *bearin'*-tree,
Now mind ye! and you fetch the piece
to me,
And lemme git it *seasoned;* then, i
gum!
I'll make a bow 'at you kin brag on
some!
Er—ef you can't git *mulberry,*—you
bring
Me a' old *locus'* hitch-post, and, i jing!
I'll make a bow o' *that* 'at *common*
bows
Won't dast to pick on ner turn up
their nose!"

And Noey knew the woods, and all
the trees
And thickets, plants and myriad mys-
teries
Of swamp and bottom-land. And he
knew where
The ground-hog hid, and why located
there.—
He knew all animals that burrowed,
swam,
Or lived in tree-tops: And, by race and
dam,

He knew the choicest, safest deeps
wherein
Fish-traps might flourish nor provoke
the sin
Of theft in some chance peeking, pry-
ing sneak,
Or town-boy, prowling up and down
the creek.
All four-pawed creatures tamable—he
knew
Their outer and their inner natures
too;
While they, in turn, were drawn to
him as by
Some subtle recognition of a tie
Of love, as true as truth from end to
end,
Between themselves and this strange
human friend.
The same with birds—he knew them
every one
And he could "name them, too, with-
out a gun."
No wonder *Johnty* loved him, even to
The verge of worship.—Noey led him
through
The art of trapping redbirds—yes, and
taught
Him how to keep them when he had
them caught—
What food they needed, and just where
to swing
The cage, if he expected them to *sing*.

And *Bud* loved Noey, for the little
pair
Of stilts he made him; or the stout old
hair
Trunk Noey put on wheels, and laid a
track
Of scantling-railroad for it in the back
Part of the barn-lot; or the crossbow,
made

Just like a gun, which deadly weapon
laid
Against his shoulder as he aimed, and
—"*Sping!*"
He'd hear the rusty old nail zoon and
sing—
And *zip!* your Mr. Bluejay's wing
would drop
A farewell-feather from the old tree-
top!

And *Maymie* loved him, for the very
small
But perfect carriage for her favorite
doll—
A *lady's* carriage—not a *baby*-cab,—
But oil-cloth top, and two seats, lined
with drab
And trimmed with white lace-paper
from a case
Of shaving-soap his uncle bought some
place
At auction once.

And *Alex* loved him yet
The best, when Noey brought him, for
a pet,
A little flying-squirrel, with great
eyes—
Big as a child's: And, childlike other-
wise,
It was at first a timid, tremulous, coy,
Retiring little thing that dodged the
boy
And tried to keep in Noey's pocket;—
till,
In time responsive to his patient will,
It became wholly docile, and content
With its new master, as he came and
went,—
The squirrel clinging flatly to his
breast,
Or sometimes scampering its craziest

Around his body spirally, and then
Down to his very heels and up again.

And *Little Lizzie* loved him, as a bee
Loves a great ripe red apple—utterly.
For Noey's ruddy morning-face she
   drew
The window-blind, and tapped the
   window, too;
Afar she hailed his coming, as she
   heard
His tuneless whistling—sweet as any
   bird
It seemed to her, the one lame bar or so
Of old "Wait for the Wagon"—hoarse
   and low   .
The sound was,—so that, all about the
   place,
Folks joked and said that Noey "whis-
   tled bass"—
The light remark originally made
By Cousin Rufus, who knew notes,
   and played
The flute with nimble skill, and taste
   as well,
And, critical as he was musical,
Regarded Noey's constant whistling
   thus
"Phenomenally unmelodious."
Likewise when Uncle Mart, who shared
   the love
Of jest with Cousin Rufus hand-in-
   glove,
Said "Noey couldn't whistle *'Bonny
   Doon'*
Even! and, *he'd* bet, couldn't carry a tune
If it had handles to it!"

                          —But forgive
The deviations here so fugitive,
And turn again to Little Lizzie, whose
High estimate of Noey we shall choose
Above all others.—And to her he was
Particularly lovable because

He laid the woodland's harvest at her
   feet.—
He brought her wild strawberries,
   honey-sweet
And dewy-cool, in mats of greenest
   moss
And leaves, all woven over and across
With tender, biting "tongue-grass," and
   "sheep-sour,"
And twin-leaved beech-mast, pranked
   with bud and flower
Of every gipsy-blossom of the wild,
Dark, tangled forest, dear. to any
   child.—
All these in season. Nor could barren,
   drear,
White and stark-featured Winter in-
   terfere
With Noey's rare resources: Still the
   same
He blithely whistled through the snow
   and came
Beneath the window with a Fairy sled;
And Little Lizzie, bundled heels-and-
   head,
He took on such excursions of delight
As even "Old Santy" with his reindeer
   might
Have envied her! And, later, when the
   snow
Was softening toward Spring-time and
   the glow
Of steady sunshine smote upon it,—
   then
Came the magician Noey yet again—
While all the children were away a
   day
Or two at Grandma's!—and behold
   when they
Got home once more;—there, tower-
   ing taller than
The doorway—stood a mighty, old
   Snow-Man!

A thing of peerless art—a masterpiece
Doubtless unmatched by even classic
   Greece
In heyday of Praxiteles.—Alone
It loomed in lordly grandeur all its own.
And steadfast, too, for weeks and weeks
   it stood,
The admiration of the neighborhood
As well as of the children Noey sought
Only to honor in the work he wrought.
The traveler paid it tribute, as he
   passed
Along the highway—paused and, turn-
   ing, cast
A lingering, last look—as though to
   take
A vivid print of it, for memory's sake,
To lighten all the empty, aching miles
Beyond with brighter fancies, hopes
   and smiles.
The cynic put aside his biting wit
And tacitly declared in praise of it;
And even the apprentice-poet of the
   town
Rose to impassioned heights, and then
   sat down
And penned a panegyric scroll of
   rhyme
That made the Snow-Man famous for
   all time.

And though, as now, the ever warmer
   sun
Of summer had so melted and undone
The perishable figure that—alas!—
Not even in dwindled white against
   the grass
Was left its latest and minutest ghost,
The children yet—*materially,* almost—
Beheld it—circled round it hand-in-
   hand—
(Or rather round the place it used to
   stand)—

With "Ring-a-round-a-rosy! Bottle full
O' posy!" and, with shriek and laugh,
   would pull
From seeming contact with it—just as
   when
It was the *real-est* of old Snow-Men!

Even in such a scene of senseless play
The children were surprised one sum-
   mer day
By a strange man who called across
   the fence,
Inquiring for their father's residence;
And, being answered that this was the
   place,
Opened the gate, and, with a radiant
   face,
Came in and sat down with them in
   the shade
And waited—till the absent father
   made
His noon appearance, with a warmth
   and zest
That told he had no ordinary guest
In this man whose low-spoken name
   he knew
At once, demurring as the stranger
   drew
A stuffy note-book out, and turned and
   set
A big fat finger on a page, and let
The writing thereon testify instead
Of further speech. And as the father
   read
All silently, the curious children took
Exacting inventory both of book
And man:—He wore a long-napped
   white fur hat
Pulled firmly on his head, and under
   that
Rather long silvery hair, or iron-gray—
For he was not an old man,—anyway,
Not beyond sixty. And he wore a pair

Of square-framed spectacles—or rather
    there
Were two more than a pair,—the extra
    two
Flared at the corners, at the eyes' side-
    view,
In as redundant vision as the eyes
Of grasshoppers or bees or dragon-flies.
Later the children heard the father say
He was "A Noted Traveler," and
    would stay
Some days with them.—In which time
    host and guest
Discussed, alone, in deepest interest,
Some vague, mysterious matter that
    defied
The wistful children, loitering outside
The spare-room door. There Bud ac-
    quired a quite
New list of big words—such as "Dis-
    unite,"
And "Shibboleth," and "Aristocracy,"
And "Juggernaut," and "Squatter Sov-
    ereignty,"
And "Antislavery," "Emancipate,"
"Irrepressible Conflict," and "The
    Great
Battle of Armageddon"—obviously
A pamphlet brought from Washington,
    D. C.,
And spread among such friends as
    might occur
Of like views with "The Noted Trav-
    eler."

782

A PROSPECTIVE VISIT

WHILE *any* day was notable and
    dear
That gave the children Noey, history
    here

Records his advent emphasized indeed
With sharp italics, as he came to feed
The stock one special morning, fair
    and bright,
When Johnty and Bud met him, with
    delight
Unusual even as their extra dress—
Garbed as for holiday, with much ex-
    cess
Of proud self-consciousness and vain
    conceit
In their new finery.—Far up the street
They called to Noey, as he came, that
    they,
As promised, both were going back
    that day
To *his* house with him!

                    And by time that each
Had one of Noey's hands—ceasing
    their speech
And coyly anxious, in their new attire,
To wake the comment of their mute
    desire,—
Noey seemed rendered voiceless. Quite
    a while
They watched him furtively.—He
    seemed to smile
As though he would conceal it; and
    they saw
Him look away, and his lips purse
    and draw
In curious, twitching spasms, as though
    he might
Be whispering,—while in his eye the
    white
Predominated strangely.—Then the
    spell
Gave way, and his pent speech burst
    audible:
"They wuz two stylish little boys, and
    they wuz mighty bold ones,

Had two new pairs o' britches made
    out o' their Daddy's old ones!"
And at the inspirational outbreak,
Both joker and his victims seemed to
    take
An equal share of laughter,—and all
    through
Their morning visit kept recurring to
The funny words and jingle of the
    rhyme
That just kept getting funnier all the
    time.

783

AT NOEY'S HOUSE

AT Noey's house—when they arrived
    with him—
How snug seemed everything, and
    neat and trim:
The little picket-fence, and little gate—
Its little pulley, and its little weight,—
All glib as clockwork, as it clicked be-
    hind
Them, on the little red-brick pathway,
    lined
With little paint-keg vases and tea-
    pots
Of wee moss-blossoms and forget-me-
    nots:
And in the windows, either side the
    door,
Were ranged as many little boxes more
Of like old-fashioned larkspurs, pinks
    and moss
And fern and phlox; while up and
    down across
Them rioted the morning-glory vines
On taut-set cotton strings, whose snowy
    lines
Whipped in and out and under the
    bright green

Like basting-threads; and, here and
    there between,
A showy, shiny hollyhock would flare
Its pink among the white and purple
    there.—
And still behind the vines, the children
    saw
A strange, bleached, wistful face that
    seemed to draw
A vague, indefinite sympathy. A face
It was of some newcomer to the
    place.—
In explanation, Noey, briefly, said
That it was "Jason," as he turned and
    led
The little fellows round the house to
    show
Them his menagerie of pets. And so
For quite a time the face of the strange
    guest
Was partially forgotten, as they pressed
About the squirrel-cage and rousted
    both
The lazy inmates out, though wholly
    loath
To whirl the wheel for them.—And
    then with awe
They walked round Noey's big pet
    owl, and saw
Him film his great, clear, liquid eyes
    and stare
And turn and turn and turn his head
    round there
The same way they kept circling—as
    though he
Could turn it one way thus eternally.

Behind the kitchen, then, with special
    pride
Noey stirred up a terrapin inside
The rain-barrel where he lived, with
    three or four
Little mud-turtles of a size not more

In neat circumference than the tiny tòy
Dumb-watches worn by every little
    boy.

Then, back of the old shop, beneath
    the tree
Of "rusty-coats," as Noey called them,
    he
Next took the boys, to show his fa-
    vorite new
Pet coon—pulled rather coyly into view
Up through a square hole in the bot-
    tom of
An old inverted tub he bent above,
Yanking a little chain, with "Hey! you,
    sir!
Here's *comp'ny* come to see you, Boli-
    vur!"
Explanatory, he went on to say,
"I named him *Bolivur* jes' thisaway,—
He looks so *round* and *ovalish* and *fat,*
'Peared-like no other name 'ud fit but
    that."

Here Noey's father called and sent him
    on
Some errand. "Wait," he said—"I
    won't be gone
A half a' hour.—Take Bud, and go
    on in
Where Jason is, tel I git back ag'in."

Whoever *Jason* was, they found him
    there
Still at the front-room window.—By
    his chair
Leaned a new pair of crutches; and
    from one
Knee down, a leg was bandaged.—
    "Jason done
That-air with one o' these-'ere tools *we*
    call
A *'shin-hoe'*—but a *foot-adze* mostly
    all

Hardware-store-keepers calls 'em."—
    (*Noey* made
This explanation later.)
                Jason paid
But little notice to the boys as they
Came in the room:—An idle volume
    lay
Upon his lap—the only book in sight—
And Johnty read the title,—"Light,
    More Light,
There's Danger in the Dark,"—though
    first and best—
In fact, the *whole* of Jason's interest
Seemed centered on a little *dog*—one
    pet
Of Noey's all uncelebrated yet—
Though *Jason,* certainly, avowed his
    worth,
And niched him over all the pets on
    earth—
As the observant Johnty would relate
The *Jason*-episode, and imitate
The all-enthusiastic speech and àir
Of Noey's kinsman and his tribute
    there:—

"That little dog 'ud scratch at that
    door
And go on a-whinin' two hours before
He'd ever let up! *There!*—Jane: Let
    him in.—
(Hah, there, you little rat!) Look at
    him grin!
        Come down off o' that!—
        W'y, look at him! (*Drat
You! you-rascal-you!*)—bring me that
    hat!
Look *out!*—He'll snap *you!*—*He*
    wouldn't let
You take it away from him, now you
    kin bet!
That little rascal's jist natchurly
    mean.—

I tell you, I *never* (*Git out!!*), never seen
A *spunkier* little rip! (*Scratch to git in,*
And *now* yer a-scratchin' to git *out*
  ag'in!
Jane: Let him out.) Now, watch him
  from here
Out through the winder!—You notice
  one ear
Kind o' *in*side-*out,* like he holds it?—
  Well,
He's got a *tick* in it—*I* kin tell!
  Yes, and he's cunnin'—
  Jist watch him a-runnin',
Sidelin'—see!—like he ain't *'plum'd*
  true'
And legs don't 'track' as they'd ort to
  do!—
Ploughin' his nose through the weeds
  —i jing!
Ain't he jist cuter'n anything!

"W'y, that little dog's got *grown*-peo-
  ple's sense;—
See how he gits out under the fence?—
And watch him a-whettin' his hind
  legs 'fore
His dead square run of a mile'd er
  more—
'Cause *Noey's* a-comin', and Trip allus
  knows
When *Noey's* a-comin'—and off he
  goes!—
Putts out to meet him and—*There they*
  come now!
Well-sir! it's raially singalar how
  That dog kin *tell,*—
  But he knows as well
When Noey's a-comin' home!—Reckon
  his *smell*
'Ud carry two mile'd?—You needn't to
  smile—
He runs to meet *him,* ever'-once-'n-a-
  while,

Two mile'd and over—when he's
  slipped away
And left him at home here, as he's
  done to-day—
'Thout ever knowin' where Noey wuz
  goin'—
But that little dog allus hits the right
  way!
Hear him a-whinin' and scratchin'
  ag'in?—
(*Little tormentin' fice!*) Jane: Let him
  in.

"—You say he ain't *there?*—
  Well now, I declare!—
Lem*me* limp out and look! . . . I
  wunder where—
Heuh, Trip!—*Heuh,* Trip!—*Heuh,*
  Trip! . . . *There*—
There he is!—Little sneak!—What-a'-
  you-'bout?—
There he is—quiled up as meek as a
  mouse,
His tail turnt up like a tea-kittle spout,
A-sunnin' hiss'f at the side o' the
  house!
Next time you scratch, sir, you'll half
  to git in,
My fine little feller, the best way you
  kin!
—Noey *he* learns him sich capers!—
  And they—
Both of 'em's ornrier every day!—
Both tantalizin' and meaner'n sin—
Allus a—(*Listen there!*)—Jane: Let
  him in.

"—Oh! yer so *innocent!* hangin' yer
  head!—
(Drat ye! you'd *better* git under the
  bed!)
  . . . Listen at that!—
  He's tackled the cat!—

Hah, there! you little rip! come out o'
　that!—
Git yer blame' little eyes scratched out
'Fore you know what yer talkin'
　about!—
Here! come away from there!—(Let
　him alone—
He'll snap *you,* I tell ye, as quick as
　a bone!)
Hi, Trip!—Hey, here!—What-a'-you-
　'bout!—
Oo! ouch! 'Ll, I'll be blamed!—*Blast
　ye!* GIT OUT!
. . . Oh, it ain't nothin'—jist *scratched*
　me, you see.—
Hadn't no idy he'd try to bite *me!*
*Plague take him!—*Bet he'll not try
　that ag'in!—
Hear him yelp.—(*Pore feller!*) Jane:
　Let him in."

784

THE LOEHRS AND THE
HAMMONDS

"HEY, Bud! *O* Bud!" rang out a
　　gleeful call,—
"The Loehrs is come to your house!"
And a small
But very much elated little chap,
In snowy linen suit and tasseled cap,
Leaped from the back fence just across
　the street
From Bixlers', and came galloping to
　meet
His equally delighted little pair
Of playmates, hurrying out to join him
　there—
*"The Loehrs is come!—The Loehrs is
　come!"* his glee

Augmented to a pitch of ecstasy
Communicated wildly, till the cry
"The Loehrs is come!" in chorus
　quavered high
And thrilling as some pæan of chal-
　lenge or
Soul-stirring chant of armied con-
　queror.
And who this *avant-courier* of "the
　Loehrs"?—
This happiest of all boys out o' doors—
Who but Will Pierson, with his heart's
　excess
Of summer warmth and light and
　breeziness!
"From our front winder I 'uz first to
　see
'Em all a-drivin' into town!" bragged
　he—
"An' seen 'em turnin' up the alley
　where
Your folks lives at. An' John an' Jake
　wuz there
Both in the wagon;—yes, an' Willy,
　too;
An' Mary—yes, an' Edith—with bran-
　new
An' purtiest-trimmed hats 'at ever
　wuz!—
An' Susan, an' Janey.—An' the *Ham-
　mond-uz*
In their fine buggy 'at they're ridin'
　roun'
So much, all over an' aroun' the town
An' *ever'*wheres,—them *city* people
　who's
A-visitin' at Loehrs-uz!"
　　　　　　Glorious news!—
Even more glorious when verified
In the boys' welcoming eyes of love
　and pride,
As one by one they greeted their old
　friends

And neighbors.—Nor until their earth-
life ends
Will that bright memory become less
bright
Or dimmed indeed.

    . . . Again, at candle-light,
The faces all are gathered. And how
glad
The Mother's features, knowing that
she had
Her dear, sweet Mary Loehr back
again.—
She always was so proud of her; and
then
The dear girl, in return, was happy,
too,
And with a heart as loving, kind and
true
As that maturer one which seemed to
blend
As one the love of mother and of
friend.
From time to time, as hand in hand
they sat,
The fair girl whispered something low,
whereat
A tender, wistful look would gather
in
The mother-eyes; and then there would
begin
A sudden cheerier talk, directed to
The stranger guests—the man and
woman who,
It was explained, were coming now to
make
Their temporary home in town for
sake
Of the wife's somewhat failing health.
Yes, they
Were city people, seeking rest this
way,

The man said, answering a query
made
By some well-meaning neighbor—with
a shade
Of apprehension in the answer. . . .
No,—
They had no *children*. As he an-
swered so,
The man's arm went about his wife,
and she
Leaned toward him, with her eyes lit
prayerfully:
Then she arose—he following—and
bent
Above the little sleeping innocent
Within the cradle at the mother's
side—
He patting her, all silent, as she
cried.—
Though, haply, in the silence that en-
sued,
His musing made melodious interlude.

In the warm, health-giving weather
    My poor pale wife and I
Drive up and down the little town
    And the pleasant roads thereby:
Out in the wholesome country
    We wind, from the main highway,
In through the wood's green solitudes—
    Fair as the Lord's own Day.

We have lived so long together,
    And joyed and mourned as one,
That each with each, with a look for
    speech,
    Or a touch, may talk as none
But Love's elect may comprehend—
    Why, the touch of her hand on mine
Speaks volume-wise, and the smile of her
    eyes,
    To me, is a song divine.

There are many places that lure us:—
    "The Old Wood Bridge" just west
Of town we know—and the creek below,
    And the banks the boys love best:

And "Beech Grove," too, on the hilltop;
And "The Haunted House" beyond,
With its roof half off, and its old pump-
trough
Adrift in the roadside pond.

We find our way to "The Marshes"—
At least where they used to be;
And "The Old Camp Grounds"; and "The
Indian Mounds,"
And the trunk of "The Council Tree":
We have crunched and splashed through
"Flint-bed Ford";
And at "Old Big Bee-gum Spring"
We have stayed the cup, half lifted up,
Hearing the redbird sing.

And then, there is "Wesley Chapel,"
With its little graveyard, lone
At the crossroads there, though the sun sets
fair
On wild rose, mound and stone. . . .
A wee bed under the willows—
My wife's hand on my own—
And our horse stops, too. . . . And we
hear the coo
Of a dove in undertone.

The dusk, the dew, and the silence!
"Old Charley" turns his head
Homeward then by the pike again,
Though never a word is said—
One more stop, and a lingering one—
After the fields and farms,—
At the old Toll-Gate, with the woman
await
With a little girl in her arms.

The silence sank—Floretty came to call
The children in the kitchen, where
they all
Went helter-skeltering with shout and
din
Enough to drown most sanguine si-
lence in,—
For well indeed they knew that sum-
mons meant
Taffy and pop-corn—so with cheers
they went.

785

THE HIRED MAN AND FLORETTY

THE Hired Man's supper, which he
sat before,
In near reach of the wood-box, the
stove-door
And one leaf of the kitchen-table, was
Somewhat belated, and in lifted pause
His dexterous knife was balancing a
bit
Of fried mush near the port awaiting
it.

At the glad children's advent—gladder
still
To find *him* there—"Jest tickled fit to
kill
To see ye all!" he said, with unctuous
cheer.—
"I'm tryin'-like to he'p Floretty here
To git things cleared away and give
ye room
Accordin' to yer stren'th.   But I
p'sume
It's a pore boarder, as the poet says,
That quarrels with his victuals, so I
guess
I'll take another wedge o' that-air cake,
Florett', that you're a-*learnin'* how to
bake."
He winked and feigned to swallow
painfully.—
"Jest 'fore ye all come in, Floretty she
Was boastin' 'bout her *biscuits*—and
they *air*
As good—sometimes—as you'll find
anywhere.—
But, women gits to braggin' on their
bread,

I'm s'picious 'bout their *pie*—as Danty
  said."
This raillery Floretty strangely seemed
To take as compliment, and fairly
  beamed
With pleasure at it all.
          —"Speakin' o' *bread*—
When she come here to live," The
  Hired Man said,—
"Never be'n out o' *Freeport* 'fore she
  come
Up here,—of course she needed *'speri-
  ence* some.—
So, one day, when yer Ma was goin' to
  set
The risin' fer some bread, she sent
  Florett'
To borry *leaven,* 'crost at Ryans'.—
  So,
She went and asked fer *twelve.*—She
  didn't *know,*
But thought, *whatever* 'twuz, that she
  could keep
One fer *herse'f* she said. O she wuz
  deep!"

Some little evidence of favor hailed
The Hired Man's humor; but it wholly
  failed
To touch the serious Susan Loehr,
  whose air
And thought rebuked them all to
  listening there
To her brief history of the *city* man
And his pale wife—"A sweeter woman
  than
She ever saw!"—So Susan testified,—
And so attested all the Loehrs beside.—
So entertaining was the history, that
The Hired Man, in the corner where
  he sat
In quiet sequestration, shelling corn,

Ceased wholly, listening, with a face
  forlorn
As Sorrow's own, while Susan, John
  and Jake
Told of these strangers who had come
  to make
Some weeks' stay in the town, in hopes
  to gain
Once more the health the wife had
  sought in vain:
Their doctor, in the city, used to know
The Loehrs—Dan and Rachel—years
  ago,—
And so had sent a letter and request
For them to take a kindly interest
In favoring the couple all they could—
To find some home-place for them, if
  they would,
Among their friends in town. He
  ended by
A dozen further lines, explaining why
His patient must have change of scene
  and air—
New faces, and the simple friendships
  there
With *them,* which might, in time,
  make her forget
A grief that kept her ever brooding
  yet
And wholly melancholy and de-
  pressed,—
Nor yet could she find sleep by night
  nor rest
By day, for thinking—thinking—
  thinking still
Upon a grief beyond the doctor's
  skill,—
The death of her one little girl.
                    "Pore thing!"
Floretty sighed, and with the turkey-
  wing
Brushed off the stove-hearth softly, and
  peered in

The kettle of molasses, with her thin
Voice wandering into. song uncon-
sciously—
In purest, if most witless, sympathy.—

" 'Then sleep no more:
Around thy heart
Some ten-der dream may i-dlee play,
But mid-night song,
With mad-jick art,
Will chase that dree muh-way!' "

"That-air besetment of Floretty's," said
The Hired Man,—"*singin'*—she *in-
hairited*,—
Her *father* wuz addicted—same as
her—
To singin'—yes, and played the dulci-
mer!
But—gittin' back,—I s'pose yer talkin'
'bout
Them *Hammondses*. Well, Ham-
mond he gits out
Pattents on things—inventions-like,
I'm told—
And's got more money'n a house could
hold!
And yit he can't git up no pattent-
right
To do away with *dyin'*.—And he
might
Be worth a *million*, but he couldn't
find
Nobody sellin' *health* of any kind! . . .
But they's no thing onhandier fer
me
To use than other people's misery.—
Floretty, hand me that-air skillet there
And lemme git 'er het up, so's them-
air
Childern kin have their pop-corn."
It was good
To hear him now, and so the children
stood

Closer about him, waiting.
"Things to *eat*,"
The Hired Man went on, " 'smighty
hard to beat!
Now, when *I* wuz a boy, we wuz so
pore,
My parunts couldn't 'ford pop-corn no
more
To pamper *me* with;—so, I hat to
go
Without pop-corn—sometimes a *year*
er so!—
And *suffer'n' saints!* how hungry I
would git
Fer jest one other chance—like this—
at it!
Many and many a time I've *dreamp'*,
at night,
About pop-corn,—all bu'sted open
white,
And hot, you know—and jest enough
o' salt
And butter on it fer to find no
fault—
Oomh!—Well! as I was goin' on to
say,—
After a-*dreamin'* of it thataway,
Then havin' to wake up and find it's
all
A *dream*, and hain't got no pop-corn
at-tall,
Ner hain't *had* none—I'd think, '*Well,
where's the use!*'
And jest lay back and sob the plaster'n'
loose!
And I have *prayed*, what*ever* hap-
pened, it
'Ud eether be pop-corn er death! . . .
And yit
I've noticed—more'n likely so have
you—
That things don't happen when you
want 'em to."

And thus he ran on artlessly, with
    speech
And work in equal exercise, till each
Tureen and bowl brimmed white.
    And then he greased
The saucers ready for the wax, and
    seized
The fragrant-steaming kettle, at a sign
Made by Floretty; and, each child in
    line,
He led out to the pump—where, in the
    dim
New coolness of the night, quite near
    to him
He felt Floretty's presence, fresh and
    sweet
As . . . dewy night-air after kitchen-
    heat.

There, still, with loud delight of laugh
    and jest,
They plied their subtle alchemy with
    zest—
Till, sudden, high above their tumult,
    welled
Out of the sitting-room a song which
    held
Them stilled in some strange rapture,
    listening
To the sweet blur of voices chorus-
    ing:—

. . . .

" 'When twilight approaches the season
    That ever is sacred to song,
Does some one repeat my name over,
    And sigh that I tarry so long?
And is there a chord in the music
    That's missed when my voice is away?—
And a chord in each heart that awakens
    Regret at my wearisome stay-ay—
    Regret at my wearisome stay.' "

All   to   himself,   The   Hired   Man
    thought—"Of course

They'll sing *Floretty* homesick!"
              . . . O strange source
Of ecstasy! O mystery of Song!—
To hear the dear old utterance flow
    along:—

    " 'Do they set me a chair near the table
        When   evening's   home-pleasures   are
            nigh?—
    When the candles are lit in the parlor,
        And the stars in the calm azure sky.' ". . .

Just then the moonlight sliced the
    porch slantwise,
And flashed in misty spangles in the
    eyes
Floretty clenched, while through the
    dark—"I jing!"
A voice asked, "Where's that song
    'you'd learn to sing
Ef I sent you the *ballat?'*—which I done
Last I was home at Freeport.—S'pose
    you run
And git it—and we'll all go in to where
They'll know the notes and sing it fer
    ye there."
And up the darkness of the old stair-
    way
Floretty fled, without a word to say—
Save to herself some whisper muffled by
Her apron, as she wiped her lashes
    dry.

Returning, with a letter, which she laid
Upon the kitchen-table while she made
A hasty crock of "float,"—poured
    thence into
A deep glass dish of iridescent hue
And glint and sparkle, with an over-
    flow
Of froth to crown it, foaming white as
    snow.—
And then—pound-cake, and jelly-cake
    as rare,
For its delicious complement,—with air

Of Hebe mortalized, she led her van
Of votaries, rounded by The Hired Man.

786

THE EVENING COMPANY

WITHIN the sitting-room, the
company
Had been increased in number. Two
or three
Young couples had been added: Emma
King,
Ella and Mary Mathers—all could sing
Like veritable angels—Lydia Martin,
too,
And Nelly Millikan.—What songs they
knew!—

" 'Ever of thee—wherever I may be,
Fondly I'm drea-m-ing ever of thee!'"

And with their gracious voices blend
the grace
Of Warsaw Barnett's tenor; and the bass
Unfathomed of Wick Chapman—
Fancy still
Can *feel,* as well as *hear* it, thrill on
thrill,
Vibrating plainly down the backs of
chairs
And through the wall and up the old
hall-stairs.—
Indeed, young Chapman's voice espe-
cially
Attracted *Mr. Hammond.*—For, said he,
Waiving the most Elysian sweetness of
The *ladies'* voices—altitudes above
The *man's* for sweetness;—*but*—as
contrast, would
Not Mr. Chapman be so very good
As, just now, to oblige *all* with—in fact,
Some sort of *jolly* song,—to counteract

In part, at least, the sad, pathetic trend
Of music *generally.* Which wish our
friend
"The Noted Traveler" made second to
With heartiness—and so each, in re-
view,
Joined in—until the radiant *basso*
cleared
His wholly unobstructed throat and
peered
Intently at the ceiling—voice and eye
As opposite indeed as earth and sky.—
Thus he uplifted his vast bass and let
It roam at large the memories booming
yet:

" 'Old Simon the Cellarer keeps a rare store
Of Malmsey and Malvoi-sie,
Of Cyprus, and who can say how many
more?—
But a chary old soul is he-e-ee—
A chary old so-u-l is he!
Of hock and Canary he never doth fail;
And all the year round, there is brewing of
ale;—
Yet he never aileth, he quaintly doth say,
While he keeps to his sober six flagons a
day.' "

. . . And then the chorus—the men's
voices all
Warred in it—like a German Carni-
val.—
Even *Mrs.* Hammond smiled, as in her
youth,
Hearing her husband.—And in veriest
truth
"The Noted Traveler's" ever-present hat
Seemed just relaxed a little, after that,
As at conclusion of the Bacchic song
He stirred his "float" vehemently and
long.
Then Cousin Rufus with his flute, and
art
Blown blithely through it from both
soul and heart—

Inspired to heights of mastery by the
glad,
Enthusiastic audience he had
In the young ladies of a town that
knew
No other flutist,—nay, nor *wanted* to,
Since they had heard *his* "Polly
Hopkins Waltz,"
Or "Rickett's Hornpipe," with its
faultless faults,
As rendered solely, he explained, "by
ear,"
Having but heard it once, Commence-
ment Year,
At "Old Ann Arbor."
⠀⠀⠀⠀⠀⠀⠀⠀⠀⠀Little Maymie now
Seemed "friends" with *Mr. Ham-
mond*—anyhow,
Was lifted to his lap—where settled, she,
Enthroned thus, in her dainty majesty,
Gained *universal* audience—although
Addressing him alone:—"I'm come to
show
You my new Red-blue pencil; and *she*
says"—
(Pointing to *Mrs.* Hammond)—"that
she guess'
You'll make a *picture* fer me."
⠀⠀⠀⠀⠀⠀⠀⠀⠀⠀"And what *kind*
Of picture?" Mr. Hammond asked, in-
clined
To serve the child as bidden, folding
square
The piece of paper she had brought
him there,—
"I don't know," Maymie said—"only
ist make
A *little dirl*, like me!"
⠀⠀⠀⠀⠀⠀⠀⠀⠀⠀He paused to take
A sharp view of the child, and then he
drew—
A while with red, and then a while
with blue—

The outline of a little girl that stood
In converse with a wolf in a great
wood;
And she had on a hood and cloak of
red—
As Maymie watched—"*Red Riding-
Hood!*" she said.
"And who's *'Red Riding-Hood'?*"
⠀⠀⠀⠀⠀⠀⠀⠀"W'y, don't *you* know?"
Asked little Maymie—
⠀⠀⠀⠀⠀⠀⠀⠀⠀⠀But the man looked so
All uninformed, that little Maymie
could
But tell him *all about* Red Riding-
Hood.

787

MAYMIE'S STORY OF RED RIDING-HOOD

W'Y, one time wuz a little-weenty
⠀⠀⠀dirl,
An' she wuz named Red Riding-Hood,
'cause her—
Her *Ma* she maked a little red cloak
fer her
'At turnt up over her head.—An' it
'uz all
Ist one piece o' red cardinul 'at's like
The drate-long stockin's the store-
keepers has.—
Oh! it 'uz purtiest cloak in all the
world
An' *all* this town er anywheres they is!
An' so, one day, her Ma she put it on
Red Riding-Hood, she did—one day,
she did—
An' it 'uz *Sund'y*—'cause the little
cloak
It 'uz too nice to wear ist *ever'* day
An' *all* the time!—An' so her Ma, she
put

It on Red Riding-Hood—an' telled her
    not
To dit no dirt on it ner dit it mussed
Ner nothin'! An'—an'—nen her Ma
    she dot
Her little basket out, 'at Old Kriss
    bringed
Her wunst—one time, he did. An'
    nen she fill'
It full o' whole lots an' 'bundance o'
    dood things t' eat
(Allus my Dran'ma *she* says ' 'bun-
    dance,' too.)
An' so her Ma fill' little Red Riding-
    Hood's
Nice basket all ist full o' dood things
    t' eat,
An' tell her take 'em to her old
    Dran'ma—
An' not to *spill* 'em, neever—'cause ef
    she
'Ud stump her toe an' spill 'em, her
    Dran'ma
She'll haf to *punish* her!
                 An' nen—An' so
Little Red Riding-Hood she p'omised
    she
'Ud be all careful nen, an' cross' her
    heart
'At she won't run an' spill 'em all fer
    six—
Five — ten — two-hundred-bushel-dol-
    lars-gold!
An' nen she kiss' her Ma doo'-by an'
    went
A-skippin' off—away fur off frough
    the
Big woods, where her Dran'ma she
    live at—No!—
She didn't do *a-skippin'*, like I said:—
She ist went *walkin'*—careful-like an'
    slow—
Ist like a little lady—walkin' 'long

As all polite an' nice—an' slow—an'
    straight—
An' turn her toes—ist like she's
    marchin' in
The Sund'y-School k-session!
                 An'—an'—so
She 'uz a-doin' along—an' doin'
    along—
On frough the drate-big woods—'cause
    her Dran'ma
She live 'way, 'way fur off frough the
    big woods
From *her* Ma's house. So when Red
    Riding-Hood
Dit to do there, she allus have most
    fun—
When she do frough the drate-big
    woods, you know.—
'Cause she ain't feard a bit o' any-
    thing!
An' so she sees the little hoppty-
    birds
'At's in the trees, an' flyin' all around,
An' singin' dlad as ef their parunts
    said
They'll take 'em to the magic-lantern
    show!
An' she 'ud pull the purty flowers an'
    things
A-growin' round the stumps.—An' she
    'ud ketch
The purty butterflies, an' drasshoppers,
An' stick pins frough 'em—No!—I ist
    said that!—
'Cause she's too dood an' kind an'
    'bedient
To *hurt* things thataway.—She'd *ketch*
    'em, though,
An' ist *play* wiv 'em ist a little while,
An' nen she'd let 'em fly away, she
    would,
An' ist skip on ad'in to her Dran'ma's.

An' so, while she 'uz doin' 'long an'
    'long,
First thing you know they 'uz a drate-
    big old
Mean wicked Wolf jumped out 'at
    wanted t' eat
Her up, but *dassent* to—'cause wite
    clos't there
They wuz a Man a-choppin' wood, an'
    you
Could *hear* him.—So the old Wolf he
    'uz *feard*
Only to ist be *kind* to her.—So he
Ist 'tended-like he wuz dood friends
    to her
An' says, "Dood morning, little Red
    Riding-Hood!"—
All ist as kind!
                An' nen Riding-Hood
She say "Dood morning," too—all
    kind an' nice—
Ist like her Ma she learn'—No!—
    mustn't say
"Learn'," 'cause *"learn' "* it's unproper.
    —So she say
It like her *Ma* she *"teached"* her.—
    An'—so she
Ist says "Dood morning" to the Wolf
    —'cause she
Don't know ut-tall 'at he's a *wicked*
    Wolf
An' want to eat her up!
                Nen old Wolf smile
An' say, so kind: "Where air you doin'
    at?"
Nen little Red Riding-Hood she say:
    "I'm doin'
To my Dran'ma's, 'cause my Ma say I
    might."
Nen, when she tell him that, the old
    Wolf he
Ist turn an' light out frough the big
    thick woods,

Where she can't see him any more.
    An' so
She think he's went to *his* house—but
    he hain't,—
He's went to her Dran'ma's, to be there
    first—
An' *ketch* her, ef she don't watch
    mighty sharp
What she's about!
                An' nen when the old Wolf
Dit to her Dran'ma's house, he's purty
    smart,—
An' so he 'tend-like *he's* Red Riding-
    Hood,
An' knock at th' door. An' Riding-
    Hood's Dran'ma
She's sick in bed an' can't come to the
    door
An' open it. So th' old Wolf knock'
    two times.
An' nen Red Riding-Hood's Dran'ma
    she says,
"Who's there?" she says. An' old
    Wolf 'tends-like he's
Little Red Riding-Hood, you know,
    an' make'
His voice soun' ist like hers, an' says:
    "It's me,
Dran'ma—an' I'm Red Riding-Hood
    an' I'm
Ist come to *see* you."
                Nen her old Dran'ma
She think it *is* little Red Riding-
    Hood,
An' so she say: "Well, come in nen an'
    make
You'se'f at home," she says, " 'cause
    I'm down sick
In bed, an' got the 'ralgia, so's I can't
Dit up an' let ye in."
                An' so th' old Wolf
Ist march' in nen an' shet the door
    ad'in,

An' *drowl'*, he did, an' *splunge'* up on
the bed
An' et up old Miz Riding-Hood 'fore she
Could put her specs on an' see who it
wuz.—
An' so she never knowed *who* et her
up!

An' nen the wicked Wolf he ist put on
Her nightcap, an' all covered up in
bed—
Like he wuz *her*, you know.
Nen, purty soon
Here come along little Red Riding-
Hood,
An' *she* knock' at the door. An' old
Wolf 'tend-
Like *he's* her Dran'ma; an' he say,
"Who's there?"
Ist like her Dran'ma say, you know.
An' so
Little Red Riding-Hood she say: "It's
me,
Dran'ma—an' I'm Red Riding-Hood
an' I'm
Ist come to *see* you."
An' nen old Wolf nen
He cough an' say: "Well, come in nen
an' make
You'se'f at home," he says, " 'cause I'm
down sick
In bed, an' got the 'ralgia, so's I can't
Dit up an' let ye in."
An' so she think
It's her Dran'ma a-talkin'.—So she ist
Open' the door an' come in, an' set
down
Her basket, an' taked off her things,
an' bringed
A chair an' clumbed up on the bed,
wite bv
The old big Wolf she thinks is her
Dran'ma—

Only she thinks the old Wolf's dot
whole lots
More bigger ears, an' lots more
whiskers, too,
Than her Dran'ma; an' so Red Rid-
ing-Hood
She's kind o' skeered a little. So she
says,
"Oh, Dran'ma, what *big eyes* you dot!"
An' nen
The old Wolf says: "They're ist big
thataway
'Cause I'm so dlad to see you!"
Nen she says,
"Oh, Dran'ma, what a drate-big nose
you dot!"
Nen th' old Wolf says: "It's ist big
thataway
Ist 'cause I smell the dood things 'at
you bringed
Me in the basket!"
An' nen Riding-Hood
She says, "Oh-me-oh-*my!* Dran'ma!
what big
White long sharp teeth you dot!"
Nen old Wolf says:
"Yes — an' they're thataway"—an'
drowled—
"They're thataway," he says, "to *eat*
you wiv!"
An' nen he ist *jump'* at her.—
But she *scream'*—
An' *scream'*, she did.—So's 'at the Man
'At wuz a-choppin' wood, you know,
—*he* hear,
An' come a-runnin' in there wiv his
ax;
An', 'fore the old Wolf know' what
he's about,
He split his old brains out an' killed
him s' quick
It make' his head swim!—An' Red
Riding-Hood

She wuzn't hurt at all!
             An' the big Man
He tooked her all safe home, he did,
    an' tell
Her Ma she's all right an' ain't hurt
    at all
An' old Wolf's dead an' killed—an'
    ever'thing!—
So her Ma wuz so tickled an' so proud,
She gived *him* all the good things t'
    eat they wuz
'At's in the basket, an' she tell' him 'at
She's much oblige', an' say to "call
    ad'in."
An' story's honest *truth*—an' all *so,* too!

788

LIMITATIONS OF GENIUS

THE audience entire seemed pleased
             —indeed,
Extremely pleased. And little Maymie,
    freed
From her task of instructing, ran to
    show
Her wondrous colored picture to and
    fro
Among the company.
             "And how comes it," said
Some one to Mr. Hammond, "that,
    instead
Of the inventor's life, you did not
    choose
The *artist's?*—since the world can bet-
    ter lose
A cutting-box or reaper than it can
A noble picture painted by a man
Endowed with gifts this drawing
    would suggest"—
Holding the picture up to show the
    rest.

"There now!" chimed in the wife, her
    pale face lit
Like winter snow with sunrise over
    it,—
"That's what *I'm* always asking him.
    —But *he*—
Well, as he's answering *you,* he an-
    swers *me,*—
With that same silent, suffocating
    smile
He's wearing now!"
             For quite a little while
No further speech from any one, al-
    though
All looked at Mr. Hammond and that
    slow,
Immutable, mild smile of his. And
    then
The encouraged querist asked him yet
    again
Why was it, and et cetera—with all
The rest, expectant, waiting round the
    wall,—
Until the gentle Mr. Hammond said
He'd answer with a *"parable,"* in-
    stead—
About "a dreamer" that he used to
    know—
"An artist" — "master" — *all* — in *em-
    bryo.*

789

MR. HAMMOND'S PARABLE

THE DREAMER

I

HE was a Dreamer of the Days:
         Indolent as a lazy breeze
Of midsummer, in idlest ways
    Lolling about in the shade of trees.

The farmer turned—as he passed him
  by
Under the hillside where he kneeled
Plucking a flower—with scornful eye
And rode ahead in the harvest-field
Muttering—"Lawz! ef that-air shirk
Of a boy wuz mine fer a week er so,
He'd quit *dreamin'* and git to work
And *airn* his livin'—er—Well! *I*
  know!"
And even kindlier rumor said,
Tapping with finger a shaking head,—
"Got such a curious kind o' way—
Wouldn't surprise me much, I say!"

Lying limp, with upturned gaze
Idly dreaming away his days.
No companions? Yes, a book
Sometimes under his arm he took
To read aloud to a lonesome brook.
  And schoolboys, truant, once had
  heard
A strange voice chanting, faint and
  dim—
Followed the echoes, and found it him,
  Perched in a tree-top like a bird,
Singing, clean from the highest limb;
And, fearful and awed, they all slipped
  by
To wonder in whispers if he could fly.

"Let him alone!" his father said
  When the old schoolmaster came to
  say,
  "He took no part in his books to-
  day—
Only the lesson the readers read.—
  His mind seems sadly going astray!"
"Let him alone!" came the mournful
  tone,
And the father's grief in his sad eyes
  shone—

Hiding his face in his trembling hand,
Moaning, "Would I could understand!
But as Heaven wills it I accept
Uncomplainingly!" So he wept.

Then went "The Dreamer" as he
  willed,
As uncontrolled as a light sail filled
Flutters about with an empty boat
Loosed from its moorings and afloat:
Drifted out from the busy quay
Of dull school-moorings listlessly;
Drifted off on the talking breeze,
All alone with his reveries;
Drifted on, as his fancies wrought—
Out on the mighty gulfs of thought.

II

The farmer came in the evening gray
  And took the bars of the pasture
  down;
Called to the cows in a coaxing way,
  "Bess" and "Lady" and "Spot" and
  "Brown,"
While each gazed with a wide-eyed
  stare,
As though surprised at his coming
  there—
Till another tone, in a higher key,
Brought their obeyance loathfully.

Then, as he slowly turned and
  swung
The topmost bar to its proper rest,
  Something fluttered along and clung
An instant, shivering at his breast—
  A wind-scared fragment of legal cap
Which darted again, as he struck his
  hand
  On his sounding chest with a sudden
  slap,

And hurried sailing across the land.
But as it clung he had caught the
    glance
Of a little penciled countenance,
And a glamour of written words; and
    hence,
A minute later, over the fence,
"Here and there and gone astray
Over the hills and far away,"
He chased it into a thicket of trees
And took it away from the captious
    breeze.

A scrap of paper with a rhyme
Scrawled upon it of summer-time:
A pencil-sketch of a dairymaid,
Under a farmhouse porch's shade,
Working merrily; and was blent
With her glad features such sweet con-
    tent,
That a song she sang in the lines be-
    low
Seemed delightfully apropos:—

            SONG
    "Why do I sing—Tra-la-la-la-la!
    Glad as a King?—Tra-la-la-la-la!
      Well, since you ask,—
      I have such a pleasant task,
    I can not help but sing!

    "Why do I smile—Tra-la-la-la-la!
    Working the while?—Tra-la-la-la-la!
      Work like this is play,—
      So I'm playing all the day—
    I can not help but smile!

    "So, if you please—Tra-la-la-la-la!
    Live at your ease!—Tra-la-la-la-la!
      You've only got to turn,
      And, you see, it's bound to churn—
    It can not help but please!"

The farmer pondered and scratched
    his head,
Reading over each mystic word.—

"Some o' The Dreamer's work!" he
    said—
"Ah, here's more—and name and
    date
In his handwrite'!"—And the good
    man read,—
" 'Patent applied for, July third,
Eighteen hundred and forty-eight'!"
The fragment fell from his nerveless
    grasp—
His awed lips thrilled with the joyous
    gasp:
"I see the p'int to the whole con-
    cern,—
He's studied out a patent churn!"

            790

FLORETTY'S MUSICAL CON-
        TRIBUTION

ALL seemed delighted, though the
    elders more,
Of course, than were the children.—
    Thus, before
Much interchange of mirthful compli-
    ment,
The story-teller said *his* stories "went"
(Like a bad candle) *best* when they
    went *out,*—
And that some sprightly music, dashed
    about,
Would *wholly* quench his "glimmer,"
    and inspire
Far brighter lights.
        And, answering this desire,
The flutist opened, in a rapturous
    strain
Of rippling notes—a perfect April-
    rain
Of melody that drenched the senses
    through;—

Then—gentler—gentler—as the dusk
    sheds dew,
It fell, by velvety, staccatoed halts,
Swooning away in old "Von Weber's
    Waltz."
Then the young ladies sang "Isle of
    the Sea"—
In ebb and flow and wave so bil-
    lowy,—
Only with quavering breath and folded
    eyes
The listeners heard, buoyed on the fall
    and rise
Of its insistent and exceeding stress
Of sweetness and ecstatic tender-
    ness. . . .
With lifted finger *yet,* Remembrance
    —List!—
"Beautiful isle of the sea!" wells in a
    mist
Of tremulous. . . .
            . . . After much whispering
Among the children, Alex came to
    bring
Some kind of *letter*—as it seemed to
    be—
To Cousin Rufus. This he carelessly
Unfolded—reading to himself alone,—
But, since its contents became, later,
    known,
And no one *"played* so *awful* bad," the
    same
May here be given—of course without
    full name,
Facsimile, or written kink or curl
Or clue. It read:—

    "Wild Roved an indian Girl
    Brite al Floretty"
                deer freind
            i now take
    this These means to send that *Song* to you &
        make
    my Promus good to you in the Regards
    Of doing What i Promust afterwards.

the *notes* & *Words* is both here *Printed* sos
    you kin can git *uncle Mart* to read you them
    those
& cousin Rufus you can git to *Play*
the *notes* fur you on eny Plezunt day
His Legul Work aint Presein Pressing.
                Ever thine
        As shore as the Vine
        doth the Stump intwine
        thou art my Lump of Sackkerrine
            Rinaldo Rinaldine
            the Pirut in Captivity.

                . . . There dropped
Another square scrap.—But the hand
    was stopped
That reached for it—Floretty suddenly
Had set a firm foot on her property—
Thinking it was the *letter,* not the
    song,—
But blushing to discover she was
    wrong,
When, with all gravity of face and air,
Her precious letter *handed* to her there
By Cousin Rufus left her even more
In apprehension than she was before.
But, testing his unwavering, kindly
    eye,
She seemed to put her last suspicion
    by,
And, in exchange, handed the song to
    him.—

A page torn from a song-book: Small
    and dim
Both notes and words were—but as
    plain as day
They seemed to him, as he began to
    play—
And plain to *all* the singers,—as he
    ran
An airy, warbling prelude, then began
Singing and swinging in so blithe a
    strain,
That every voice rang in the old re-
    frain:

MOUNTAIN MAID'S INVITATION

ARRANGED BY J. E. GOULD.

1. Come! come! come! O'er the hills, free from care, In my home true pleas-ure share; Blos-soms sweet, flow'rs most rare, Come where joys are found! Here the spar-kling dews of morn Tree and shrub with gems a-dorn, Jew-els bright, gay-ly worn, Beau-ty all a-round! Tra la la la,

tra la la! Tra la la la, tra la la la! Jew - els bright,

gay - ly worn, Beau - ty all a - round!

II	III
Come! come! come!	Come! come! come!
Not a sigh, not a tear,	When the day's gently gone,
E'er is found in sadness here;	Evening shadows coming on,
Music soft, breathing near,	Then, by love, kindly won,
Charms away each care!	Truest bliss be thine!
Birds, in joyous hours among	Ne'er was found a bliss so pure
Hill and dell, with grateful song,	Never joys so long endure;
Dearest strains here prolong,	Who would not love secure?
Vocal all the air!	Who would joys decline?
Tra la la la, tra la la!	Tra la la la, tra la la!
Tra la la la, tra la la!	Tra la la la, tra la la!
Dearest strains here prolong,	Who would not love secure?
Vocal all the air!	Who would joys decline?

From the beginning of the song, clean
    through,
Floretty's features were a study to
The flutist who "read *notes*" so readily,
Yet read so little of the mystery
Of that face of the girl's.—Indeed, *one*
    thing
Bewildered him quite into worrying,
And that was, noticing, throughout it
    all,
The Hired Man shrinking closer to the
    wall,
She ever backing toward him through
    the throng
Of barricading children—till the song
Was ended, and at last he saw her near
Enough to reach and take him by the
    ear
And pinch it just a pang's worth of
    her ire
And leave it burning like a coal of
    fire.
He noticed, too, in subtle pantomime
She seemed to dust him off, from time
    to time;
And when somebody, later, asked if she
Had never heard the song before—
    "What! *me?*"
She said—then blushed again and
    smiled,—
"I've knowed that song sence *Adam*
    wuz a child!—
It's jes' a joke o' this-here man's.—He's
    learned
To *read* and *write* a little, and it's turned
His fool-head some—That's all!"
             And then some one
Of the loud-wrangling boys said—
    " '*Course* they's none
No more, *these* days!—They's Fairies
    ust to be,
But they're all dead, a hundred years!"
    said he.

"Well, there's where you're *mustak-
    ened!*"—in reply
They heard Bud's voice, pitched sharp
    and thin and high.—

"An' how you goin' to *prove* it?"

             "Well, I *kin!*"
Said Bud, with emphasis.—"They's one
    lives in
Our garden—and I *see* 'im wunst, wiv
    my
Own eyes—*one* time I did."

             "*Oh, what a lie!*"
—" '*Sh!*"

      "Well, nen," said the skeptic
    —seeing there
The older folks attracted—"tell us *where*
You saw him, an' all '*bout* him!"

           "Yes, my son.—
If you tell 'stories,' you may tell us one,"
The smiling father said, while Uncle
    Mart,
Behind him, winked at Bud, and pulled
    apart
His nose and chin with comical gri-
    mace—
Then sighed aloud, with sanctimonious
    face,—
    " '*How good and comely it is to see
    Children and parents in friendship
    agree!'*—
You fire away, Bud, on your Fairy
    tale—
Your *Uncle's* here to back you!"
             Somewhat pale,
And breathless as to speech, the little
    man
Gathered himself. And thus his story
    ran.

791

BUD'S FAIRY TALE

SOME peoples thinks they ain't no
Fairies *now*
No more yet!—But they *is,* I bet!
'Cause ef
They *wuzn't* Fairies, nen I' like to know
Who'd w'ite 'bout Fairies in the books,
an' tell
What Fairies *does,* an' how their *pic-
ture* looks,
An' all an' ever'thing! W'y, ef they don't
Be Fairies any more, nen little boys
'Ud ist *sleep* when they go to sleep an'
won't
Have ist no dweams at all,—'cause
Fairies—*good*
Fairies—they're a-purpose to make
dweams!
But they *is* Fairies—an' I *know* they is!
'Cause one time wunst, when it's all
Summer-time,
An' don't haf to be no fires in the stove
Er fireplace to keep warm wiv—ner
don't haf
To wear old scwatchy flannen shirts at
all,
An' ain't no fweeze—ner cold—ner
snow!—An'—an'
Old skweeky twees got all the gween
leaves on
An' ist keeps noddin', noddin' all the
time,
Like they 'uz lazy an' a-twyin' to go
To sleep an' couldn't, 'cause the wind
won't quit
A-blowin' in 'em, an' the birds won't stop
A-singin', so's they *kin.*—But twees
don't sleep,
I guess! But *little boys* sleeps—an'
dweams, too.—

An' that's a sign they's Fairies.
So, one time,
When I be'n playin' "Store" wunst over in
The shed of their old stable, an' Ed
Howard
He maked me quit a-bein' pardners,
'cause
I dwinked the 'tend-like sody-water up
An' et the shore-'nuff crackers,—w'y,
nen I
Clumbed over in our garden where the
gwapes
Wuz purt' nigh ripe: An' I wuz ist
a-layin'
There on th' old cwooked seat 'at Pa
maked in
Our arber,—an' so I 'uz layin' there
A-whittlin' beets wiv my new dog-
knife, an'
A-lookin' wite up thue the twimbly
leaves—
An' wuzn't 'sleep at all!—An'-sir!—
first thing
You know, a little *Fairy* hopped out
there!—
A *leetle-teenty Fairy!*—hope-may-die!
An' he look' down at me, he did—an' he
Ain't bigger'n a *yellerbird!*—an' he
Say "Howdy-do!" he did—an' I could
hear
Him—ist as *plain!*
Nen *I* say "Howdy-do!"
An' he say *"I'm* all hunky, Nibsey; how
Is *your* folks comin' on?"
An' nen I say
"My name ain't *'Nibsey,'* neever—my
name's *Bud.*—
An' what's *your* name?" I says to him.
An' he
Ist laugh an' say, " *'Bud's* awful *funny*
name!"
An' he ist laid back on a big bunch o'
gwapes

An' laugh' an' laugh', he did—like
   somebody
'Uz tick-el-un his feet!
                        An' nen I say—
"What's *your* name," nen I say, "afore
   you bu'st
Yo-se'f a-laughin' bout *my* name?" I says.
An' nen he dwy up laughin'—kind o'
   mad—
An' say, "W'y, *my* name's *Squid-
jicum*," he says.
An' nen *I* laugh an' say—"*Gee!* what
   a name!"
An' when I make fun of his name, like
   that,
He ist git awful mad an' spunky, an'
'Fore you know, he gwabbed holt of a
   vine—
A big long vine 'at's danglin' up there, an'
He ist helt on wite tight to that, an'
   down
He swung quick past my face, he did,
   an' ist
Kicked at me hard's he could!
                        But I'm too quick
Fer *Mr. Squidjicum!* I ist weached out
An' ketched him, in my hand—an' helt
   him, too,
An' *squeezed* him, ist like little wobins
   when
They can't fly yet an' git flopped out
   their nest.
An' nen I turn him all wound over, an'
Look at him clos't, you know—wite
   clos't—cause ef
He *is* a Fairy, w'y, I want to see
The *wings* he's got.—But he's dwessed
   up so fine
'At I can't *see* no wings.—An' all the
   time
He's twyin' to kick me yet: An' so I take
F'esh holts an' *squeeze* ag'in—an'
   harder, too;

An' I says, "*Hold up, Mr. Squidjicum!*—
You're kickin' the w'ong man!" I says;
   an' nen
I ist *squeeze'* him, purt' nigh my *best,*
   I did—
An' I heerd somepin' bu'st!—An' nen
   he cwied
An' says, "You better look out what
   you're doin'!—
You' bu'st my spider-web suspenners,
   an'
You' got my wose-leaf coat all cwinkled
   up
So's I can't go to old Miss Hoodjicum's
Tea-party, 's afternoon!"
                        An' nen I says—
"Who's 'old Miss Hoodjicum'?" I says.
                        An' he
Says, "Ef you lemme loose I'll tell you."
                        So
I helt the little skeezics 'way fur out
In one hand—so's he can't jump down
   t' th' ground
Wivout a-gittin' all stove up: an' nen
I says, "You're loose now.—Go ahead
   an' tell
'Bout the 'tea-party' where you're goin' at
So awful fast!" I says.
                        An' nen he say.—
"No use to *tell* you 'bout it, 'cause you
   won't
Believe it, 'less you go there your own se'f
An' see it wiv your own two eyes!" he
   says.
An' *he* says: "Ef you lemme *shore-'nuff*
   loose,
An' p'omise 'at you'll keep wite still,
   an' won't
Tetch nothin' 'at you see—an' never tell
Nobody in the world—n' lemme loose—
W'y, nen I'll *take* you there!"
                        But I says, "Yes
An' ef I let you loose, you'll *run!*" I says.

An' he says, "No, I won't!—I hope-
may-die!"
Nen I says, "Cwoss your heart you
won't!"
          An' he
Ist cwoss his heart; an' nen I reach an'
set
The little feller up on a long vine—
An' he 'uz so tickled to git lose ag'in,
He gwab the vine wiv boff his little
hands
An' ist take an' turn in, he did, an' skin
'Bout forty-'leben cats!
        Nen when he git
Thue whirlin' wound the vine, an' set
on top
Of it ag'in, w'y, nen his "wose-leaf coat"
He bwag so much about, it's ist all tored
Up, an' ist hangin' strips an' rags—so he
Look like his Pa's a dwunkard. An'
so nen
When he see what he's done—a-actin' up
So smart,—he's awful mad, I guess;
an' ist
Pout out his lips an' twis' his little face
Ist ugly as he kin, an' set an' tear
His whole coat off—an' sleeves an' all.
—An' nen
He wad it all togevver an' ist *th'ow*
It at me ist as hard as he kin dwive!

An' when I weach to ketch him, an' 'uz
goin'
To give him 'nuvver squeezin', *he ist
flewed
Clean up on top the arbor!*—'Cause,
you know,
They *wuz* wings on him—when he
tored his *coat*
Clean off—they *wuz* wings *under there.*
But they
Wuz purty wobbly-like an' wouldn't
work

Hardly at all—'cause purty soon, when I
Th'owed clods at him, an' sticks, an'
got him shooed
Down off o' there, he come a-floppin'
down
An' lit k-bang! on our old chicken-coop,
An' ist laid there a-whimper'n' like a
child!
An' I tiptoed up wite clos't, an' I says,
"What's
The matter wiv ye, Squidjicum?"
           An' he
Says: "Dog-gone! when my wings gits
stwaight ag'in,
Where you all *crumpled* 'em," he says,
"I bet
I'll ist fly clean away, an' won't take you
To old Miss Hoodjicum's at all!" he
says.
An' nen I ist weach out wite quick, I
did,
An' gwab the sassy little snipe ag'in—
Nen tooked my top-stwing an' tie down
his wings
So's he *can't* fly, 'less'n I want him to!
An' nen I says: "Now, Mr. Squid-
jicum,
You better ist light out," I says, "to old
Miss Hoodjicum's, an' show *me* how
to git
There, too," I says; "er ef you don't,"
I says,
"I'll climb up wiv you on our buggy-
shed
An' push you off!" I says.
          An' nen he say
All wite, he'll show me there; an' tell
me nen
To set him down wite easy on his
feet,
An' loosen up the stwing a little where
It cut him under th' arms. An' nen he
says,

"Come on!" he says; an' went a-limpin'
   'long
The garden-paph—an' limpin' 'long an'
   'long
Tel—purty soon he come on 'long to
   where's
A grea'-big cabbage-leaf. An' he stoop
   down
An' say, "Come on inunder here wiv
   me!"
So *I* stoop down an' crawl inunder there,
   Like he say.
         An' inunder there's a grea'-
Big clod, they is—a' awful grea'-big
   clod!
An' nen he says, *"Woll this-here clod
   away!"*
An' so I woll' the clod away. An' nen
It's all wet, where the dew'z inunder
   where
The old clod wuz.—An' nen the Fairy
   he
Git on the wet-place: Nen he say to me,
"Git on the wet-place, too!" An' nen
   he say,
"Now hold yer breff an' shet yer eyes!"
   he says,
"Tel I say *Squinchy-winchy!"* Nen he
   say—
Somepin' *in Dutch,* I guess.—An' nen
   I felt
Like we 'uz sinkin' down—an' sinkin'
   down!—
Tel purty soon the little Fairy weach
An' pinch my nose an' yell at me an' say,
*"Squinchy-winchy! Look wherever you
   please!"*
Nen when I looked—Oh! they 'uz
   purtiest place
Down there you ever saw in all the
   World!—
They 'uz ist *flowers* an' *woses*—yes,
   an' *twees*

Wiv *blossoms* on an' *big wipe apples*
   boff!
An' butterflies, they wuz—an' hum-
   min'-birds—
An' *yeller*birds an' *blue*birds—yes, an'
   wed!—
An' ever'wheres an' all awound 'uz vines
Wiv wipe p'serve-pears on 'em!—Yes,
   an' all
An' ever'thing 'at's ever growin' in
A garden—er canned up—all wipe at
   wunst!—
It wuz ist like a garden—only it
'Uz ist a *little bit* o' garden—'bout big
   wound
As ist our twun'el-bed is.—An' all
   wound
An' wound the little garden's a gold
   fence—
An' little gold gate, too—an' ash-hopper
'At's all gold, too—an' ist full o' gold
   ashes!
An' wite in th' middle o' the garden wuz
A little gold house, 'at's ist 'bout as big
As ist a bird-cage is: An' *in* the house
They 'uz whole-lots *more* Fairies there
   —'cause I
Picked up the little house, an' peeked
   in at
The winders, an' I see 'em all in there
Ist *buggin'* round! An' Mr. Squidjicum
He twy to make me quit, but I gwab
   him
An' poke him down the chimbly, too,
   I did!—
An' y'ort to see *him* hop out 'mongst
   'em there!—
Ist like he 'uz the boss an' ist got back!—
*"Hain't ye got on them-air dew-dump-
   lin's yet?"*
He says.
        An' they says no.
           An' nen he says—

"Better git at 'em nen!" he says, *"wite
    quick—*
*'Cause old Miss Hoodjicum's a-com-
    in'!"*
        Nen
They all set wound a little gold tub—
    an'
All 'menced a-peelin' dewdwops, ist
    like they
'Uz *peaches.*—An', it looked so funny,
    I
Ist laugh' out loud, an' *dwopped* the
    little house,
An' 't bu'sted like a soap-bubble!—
    an' 't skeered
Me so, I—I—I—I,—it skeered me so,—
I—ist *waked* up.—No! I *ain't* be'n
    asleep
An' *dweam* it all, like *you* think,—but
    it's shore
Fer-certain *fact* an' cwoss my heart it
    is!

792

A DELICIOUS INTERRUPTION

ALL were quite gracious in their
    plaudits of
Bud's Fairy; but another stir above
That murmur was occasioned by a
    sweet
Young lady-caller, from a neighboring
    street,
Who rose reluctantly to say good night
To all the pleasant friends and the de-
    light
Experienced,—as she had promised
    sure
To be back home by nine. Then
    paused, demure,
And wondered was it *very* dark.—Oh,
    no!—

She had *come* by herself and she could
    go
Without an *escort.* Ah, you sweet girls
    all!
What young gallant but comes at such
    a call,
Your most abject slaves! Why, there
    were three
Young men, and several men of fam-
    ily,
Contesting for the honor—which at
    last
Was given to Cousin Rufus; and· he
    cast
A kingly look behind him, as the pair
Vanished with laughter in the dark-
    ness there.
As order was restored, with everything
Suggestive, in its way, of "romancing,"
Some one observed that *now* would be
    the chance
For *Noey* to relate a circumstance
That *he*—the very specious rumor
    went—
Had been eye-witness of, by accident.
Noey turned   pippin-crimson; then
    turned pale
As death; then turned to flee, without
    avail.—
"There! head him off! *Now!* hold
    him in his chair!—
Tell us the Serenade-tale, now, Noey.
    —*There!"*

793

NOEY'S NIGHT-PIECE

"THEY ain't much 'tale' about it!"
    Noey said.—
"K'tawby grapes wuz gittin' good-'n'-
    red
I rickollect; and Tubb Kingry and me

'Ud kind o' browse round town, day-
time, to see
What neighbers 'peared to have the
most to spare
'At wuz git-at-able and no dog there
When we come round to git 'em, say
'bout ten
O'clock at night, when mostly old folks
then
Wuz snorin' at each other like they yit
Helt some old grudge 'at never slep' a
bit.
Well, at the *Pars'nige*—ef ye'll call to
mind,—
They's 'bout the biggest grape-arber
you'll find
'Most anywheres.—And mostly there,
we knowed
They wuz *k'tawbies* thick as ever
growed—
And more'n they'd *p'serve.*—Besides
I've heerd
Ma say k'tawby-grape p'serves jes'
'peared
A waste o' sugar, anyhow!—And so
My conscience stayed outside and
lemme go
With Tubb, one night, the back-way,
clean up through
That long black arber to the end next
to
The house, where the k'tawbies, don't
you know,
Wuz thickest. And 't'uz lucky we
went *slow,*—
Fer jes' as we wuz cropin' to'rds the
gray-
End, like, of the old arber—heerd
Tubb say
In a skeered whisper, 'Hold up!
They's some one
Jes' slippin' in here!—and *looks like a
gun*

He's carryin'!" I *golly!* we both
spread
Out flat ag'inst the ground!
               'What's that?' Tubb said.—
And jes' then—'*plink! plink! plink!*'
we heerd something
Under the back-porch winder.—Then,
i jing!
Of course we rickollected 'bout the
young
School-mam 'at wuz a-boardin' there,
and sung,
And played on the melodium in the
choir.—
And she 'uz 'bout as purty to admire
As any girl in town!—the fac's is, she
Jes' *wuz,* them times, to a dead cer-
tainty,
The belle o' this-here bailywick!—But
—Well,—
I'd best git back to what I'm tryin' to
tell:—
It wuz some feller come to serenade
Miss Wetherell: And there he plunked
and played
His old guitar, and sung, and kep' his
eye
Set on her winder, blacker'n the sky!—
And black it *stayed.*—But mayby she
wuz 'way
From home, er wore out—bein' *Satur-
day!*

"It *seemed* a good 'eal *longer,* but I
know
He sung and plunked there half a'
hour er so
Afore, it 'peared-like, he could ever git
His own free qualified consents to quit
And go off 'bout his business. When
he went
I bet you could 'a' bought him fer a
cent!

"And now, behold ye all!—as Tubb
and me
Wuz 'bout to raise up,—right in front
we see
A feller slippin' out the arber, square
Smack under that-air little winder
where
The *other* feller had been standin'.—
And
The thing he wuz a-carryin' in his
hand
Wuzn't no *gun* at all!—it wuz a
flute,—
And *whoop-ee!* how it did git up and
toot
And chirp and warble, tel a mockin'-
bird
'Ud dast to never let hisse'f be heerd
Ferever, after such miracalous, high
Jimcracks and grand skyrootics played
there by
Yer Cousin Rufus!—Yes-sir; it wuz
him!—
And what's more,—all a-suddent that-
air dim
Dark winder o' Miss Wetherell's wuz
lit
Up like a' oyshture-sign, and under
it
We see him sort o' wet his lips and
smile
Down 'long his row o' dancin' fingers,
while
He kind o' stiffened up and kinked his
breath
And everlastin'ly jes' blowed the peth
Out o' that-air old one-keyed flute o'
his.
And, bless their hearts, that's all the
'tale' they is!"

And even as Noey closed, all radiantly
The unconscious hero of the history,

Returning, met a perfect driving
storm
Of welcome—a reception strangely
warm
And *unaccountable,* to *him,* although
Most *gratifying,*—and he told them so.
"I only urge," he said, "my right to be
Enlightened." And a voice said:
"Certainly:—
During your absence we agreed that
you
Should tell us all a story, old or new,
Just in the immediate happy frame of
mind
We knew you would return in."
So, resigned,
The ready flutist tossed his hat aside—
Glanced at the children, smiled, and
thus complied.

794

COUSIN RUFUS' STORY

MY little story, Cousin Rufus said,
Is not so much a story as a
fact.
It is about a certain wilful boy—
An aggrieved, unappreciated boy,
Grown to dislike his own home very
much,
By reason of his parents being not
At all up to his rigid standard and
Requirements and exactions as a son
And disciplinarian.
So, sullenly
He brooded over his disheartening
Environments and limitations, till,
At last, well knowing that the outside
world
Would yield him favors never found
at home,

He rose determinedly one July dawn—
Even before the call for breakfast—
and,
Climbing the alley-fence, and bitterly
Shaking his clenched fist at the wood-
pile, he
Evanished down the turnpike.—Yes:
he had,
Once and for all, put into execution
His long low-muttered threatenings—
He had
Run off!—He had—had run away
from home!
His parents, at discovery of his flight,
Bore up first-rate—especially his Pa,—
Quite possibly recalling his own youth,
And therefrom predicating, by high
noon,
The absent one was very probably
Disporting his nude self in the delights
Of the old swimmin'-hole, some hun-
dred yards
Below the slaughter-house, just east
of town.
The stoic father, too, in his surmise
Was accurate—For, lo! the boy was
there!

And there, too, he remained through-
out the day—
Save at one starving interval in which
He clad his sunburnt shoulders long
enough
To shy across a wheat-field, shadow-
like,
And raid a neighboring orchard—bit-
terly,
And with spasmodic twitchings of the
lip,
Bethinking him how all the other boys
Had *homes* to go to at the dinner-
hour—

While *he*—alas!—*he had no home!*—
At least
These very words seemed rising mock-
ingly,
Until his every thought smacked raw
and sour
And green and bitter as the apples he
In vain essayed to stay his hunger
with.
Nor did he join the glad shouts when
the boys
Returned rejuvenated for the long
Wet revel of the feverish afternoon.—
Yet, bravely, as his comrades splashed
and swam
And spluttered, in their weltering
merriment,
He tried to laugh, too,—but his voice
was hoarse
And sounded to him like some other
boy's.
And then he felt a sudden, poking
sort
Of sickness at the heart, as though
some cold
And scaly pain were blindly nosing it
Down in the dreggy darkness of his
breast.
The tensioned pucker of his purple lips
Grew ever chillier and yet more
tense—
The central hurt of it slow spreading
till
It did possess the little face entire.
And then there grew to be a knuckled
knot—
An aching kind of core within his
throat—
An ache, all dry and swallowless,
which seemed
To ache on just as bad when he'd
pretend
He didn't notice it as when he did.

It was a kind of a conceited pain—
An overbearing, self-assertive and
Barbaric sort of pain that clean out-
   hurt
A boy's capacity for suffering—
So, many times, the little martyr
   needs
Must turn himself all suddenly and
   dive
From sight of his hilarious playmates
   and
Surreptitiously weep under water.
                              Thus
He wrestled with his awful agony
Till almost dark; and then, at last—
   then, with
The very latest lingering group of his
Companions, he moved turgidly to-
   ward home—
Nay, rather *oozed* that way, so slow
   he went,—
With loathful, hesitating, loitering,
Reluctant late-election-returns air,
Heightened somewhat by the con-
   science-made resolve
Of chopping a double armful of wood
As he went in by rear way of the
   kitchen.
And this resolve he executed;—yet
The hired girl made no comment
   whatsoever
But went on washing up the supper-
   things,
Crooning the unutterably sad song,
   "Then think,
Oh, think how lonely this heart must
   ever be!"
Still, with affected carelessness, the
   boy
Ranged through the pantry; but the
   cupboard-door
Was locked. He sighed then like a
   wet forestick

And went out on the porch.—At least
   the pump,
He prophesied, would meet him kindly
   and
Shake hands with him and welcome
   his return!
And long he held the old tin dipper
   up—
And oh, how fresh and pure and
   sweet the draught!
Over the upturned brim, with grate-
   ful eyes
He saw the back-yard, in the gathering
   night,
Vague, dim and lonesome; but it all
   looked good:
The lightning-bugs, against the grape-
   vines, blinked
A sort of sallow gladness over his
Home-coming, with this softening of
   the heart.
He did not leave the dipper carelessly
In the milk-trough.—No: he hung it
   back upon
Its old nail thoughtfully—even ten-
   derly.
All slowly then he turned and saun-
   tered toward
The rain-barrel at the corner of the
   house,
And, pausing, peered into it at the few
Faint stars reflected there.   Then—
   moved by some
Strange impulse new to him—he
   washed his feet.
He then went in the house—straight
   on into
The very room where sat his parents
   by
The evening lamp.—The father all in-
   tent
Reading his paper, and the mother
   quite

As intent with her sewing. Neither
looked
Up at his entrance—even reproach-
fully,—
And neither spoke.
        The wistful runaway
Drew a long, quavering breath, and
then sat down
Upon the extreme edge of a chair.
And all
Was very still there for a long, long
while.—
Yet everything, someway, seemed *rest-
ful*-like
And *homy* and old-fashioned, good
and kind,
And sort of *kin* to him!—Only too
still!
If somebody would *say* something—
just *speak*—
Or even rise up suddenly and come
And lift him by the ear sheer off his
chair—
Or box his jaws—Lord bless 'em!—
*any*thing!—
Was he not there to thankfully ac-
cept
Any reception from parental source
Save this incomprehensible *voiceless-
ness?*
O but the silence held its very breath!
If but the ticking clock would only
strike
And for an instant drown the whisper-
ing,
Lisping, sifting sound the katydids
Made outside in the grassy nowhere!
                        Far
Down some back street he heard the
faint halloo
Of boys at their night-game of "Town-
fox,"
But now with no desire at all to be

Participating in their sport.—No;
no;—
Never again in this world would he
want
To join them there!—he only wanted
just
To stay in home of nights—Always—
always—
Forever and a day!
            He moved; and coughed—
Coughed hoarsely, too, through his
rolled tongue; and yet
No vaguest of parental notice or
Solicitude in answer—no response—
No word—no look. O it was deathly
still!—
So still it was that really he could not
Remember any prior silence that
At all approached it in profundity
And depth and density of utter hush.
He felt that he himself must break it:
So,
Summoning every subtle artifice
Of seeming nonchalance and native
ease
And naturalness of utterance to his aid,
And gazing raptly at the house-cat
where
She lay curled in her wonted corner of
The hearth-rug, dozing, he spoke airily
And said: "I see you've got the same
old cat!"

795

BEWILDERING EMOTIONS

THE merriment that followed was
    subdued—
As though the story-teller's attitude
Were dual, in a sense, appealing quite
As much to sorrow as to mere delight,

According, haply, to the listener's bent
Either of sad or merry temperament.—
"And of your two appeals I much pre-
     fer
The pathos," said "The Noted Trav-
     eler,"—
"For should I live to twice my present
     years,
I know I could not quite forget the
     tears
That child-eyes bleed, the little palms
     nailed wide,
And quivering soul and body cruci-
     fied. . . .
But, bless them! there are no such
     children here
To-night, thank God!—Come here to
     me, my dear!"
He said to little Alex, in a tone
So winning that the sound of it alone
Had drawn a child more loathful to
     his knee:—
"And, now-sir, *I'll* agree if *you'll*
     agree,—
You tell us all a story, and then *I*
Will tell one."
          "But I can't."
               "Well, can't you *try?*"
"Yes, Mister: he *kin* tell *one*. Alex,
     tell
The one, you know, 'at you made up
     so well,
About the *Bear*. He allus tells that one,"
Said *Bud*,—"He gits it mixed some
     'bout the *gun*
An' *ax* the Little Boy had, an' *apples*,
     too."—
Then Uncle Mart said—"There, now!
     that'll do!—
Let *Alex* tell his story his own way!"
And Alex, prompted thus, without de-
     lay
Began.

796

THE BEAR STORY

THAT ALEX "IST MAKED UP HIS-OWN-
     SE'F"

W'Y, wunst they wuz a Little Boy
          went out
In the woods to shoot a Bear. So, he
     went out
'Way in the grea'-big woods—he did.
     —An' he
Wuz goin' along—an' goin' along, you
     know,
An' purty soon he heerd somepin' go
     "Wooh!"
Ist thataway—*"Woo-ooh!"* An' he wuz
     skeered,
He wuz. An' so he runned an' clumbed
     a tree—
A grea'-big tree, he did,—a sicka-*more*
     tree.
An' nen he heerd it ag'in: an' he
     looked round,
An' *'t'uz a Bear—a grea'-big shore-*
     'nuff Bear!—
No: 't'uz *two* Bears, it wuz—two
     grea'-big Bears—
One of 'em wuz—ist *one's* a *grea'-big*
     Bear.—
But they ist *boff* went *"Wooh!"*—An'
     here *they* come
To climb the tree an' git the Little
     Boy
An' eat him up!
               An' nen the Little Boy
He 'uz skeered worse'n ever! An' here
     come
The grea'big Bear a-climbin' th' tree to
     git
The Little Boy an' eat him up—Oh,
     no!—

It 'uzn't the *Big* Bear 'at clumb the
tree—
It 'uz the *Little* Bear. So here *he* come
Climbin' the tree—an' climbin' the
tree! Nen when
He git wite *clos't* to the Little Boy,
w'y, nen
The Little Boy he ist pulled up his gun
An' *shot* the Bear, he did, an' killed
him dead!
An' nen the Bear he falled clean on
down out
The tree—away clean to the ground,
he did—
Spling-splung! he falled *plum* down,
an' killed him, too!
An' lit wite side o' where the *Big*
Bear's at.

An' nen the Big Bear's awful mad,
you bet!—
'Cause—'cause the Little Boy he shot
his gun
An' killed the *Little* Bear.—'Cause the
Big Bear
He—he 'uz the Little Bear's Papa.—
An' so here
He come to climb the big old tree an'
git
The Little Boy an' eat him up! An'
when
The Little Boy he saw the *grea'-big*
Bear
A-comin', he 'uz badder skeered, he
wuz,
Than *any* time! An' so he think he'll
climb
Up *higher*—'way up higher in the tree
Than the old *Bear* kin climb, you
know.—But he—
He *can't* climb higher 'an old *Bears* kin
climb,—

'Cause Bears kin climb up higher in
the trees
Than any little Boys in all the
Wo-r-r-ld!

An' so here come the grea'-big Bear,
he did,—
A'climbin' up—an' up the tree, to git
The Little Boy an' eat him up! An' so
The Little Boy he clumbed on higher,
an' higher,
An' higher up the tree—an' higher—
an' higher—
An' higher'n iss-here *house* is!—An'
here come
The old Bear—clos'ter to him all the
time!—
An' nen—first thing you know,—when
th' old Big Bear
Wuz wite clos't to him—nen the Little
Boy
Ist jabbed his gun wite in the old
Bear's mouf
An' shot an' killed him dead!—No; I
fergot,—
He didn't shoot the grea'-big Bear at
all—
'Cause *they 'uz no load in the gun,*
you know—
'Cause when he shot the *Little* Bear,
w'y, nen
No load 'uz any more nen *in* the gun!

But th' Little Boy clumbed *higher* up,
he did—
He clumbed *lots* higher—an' on up
higher—an' higher
An' *higher*—tel he ist *can't* climb no
higher,
'Cause nen the limbs 'uz all so little,
'way
Up in the teeny-weeny tip-top of

The tree, they'd break down wiv him
  ef he don't
Be keerful! So he stop an' think: An'
  nen
He look around—An' here come the
  old Bear!
An' so the Little Boy make up his
  mind
He's got to ist git out o' there *some-
  way*!—
'Cause here come the old Bear!—so
  clos't, his bref's
Purt' nigh so's he kin feel how hot it
  is
Ag'inst his bare feet—ist like old
  "Ring's" bref
When he's be'n out a-huntin' an' 's all
  tired.
So when th' old Bear's so clos't—the
  Little Boy
Ist gives a grea'-big jump fer *'nother*
  tree—
No!—no, he don't do that!—I tell you
  what
The Little Boy does:—W'y, nen—w'y,
  he—Oh, *yes*!—
The Little Boy *he finds a hole up there*
'At's in the tree—an' climbs in there
  an' *hides*—
An' *nen* th' old Bear can't find the
  Little Boy
At all!—but purty soon the old Bear
  finds
The Little Boy's *gun* 'at's up there—
  'cause the *gun*
It's too *tall* to tooked wiv him in the
  hole.
So, when the old Bear find' the *gun*,
  he knows
The Little Boy's ist *hid* round *somers*
  there,—
An' th' old Bear 'gins to snuff and
  sniff around,

An' sniff an' snuff around—so's he kin
  find
Out where the Little Boy's hid at.—
  An' nen—nen—
Oh, *yes*!—W'y, purty soon the old Bear
  climbs
'Way out on a big limb—a grea'-long
  limb,—
An' nen the Little Boy climbs out the
  hole
An' takes his ax an' chops the limb
  off! . . . Nen
The old Bear falls *ḳ-splunge!* clean to
  the ground,
An' bu'st an' kill hisse'f plum dead, he
  did!

An' nen the Little Boy he git his gun
An' 'menced a-climbin' down the tree
  ag'in—
No!—no, he *didn't* git his *gun*—'cause
  when
The *Bear* falled, nen the *gun* falled, too
  —An' broked
It all to pieces, too!—An' *nicest* gun!—
His Pa ist buyed it!—An' the Little
  Boy
Ist cried, he did; an' went on climbin'
  down
The tree—an' climbin' down—an'
  climbin' down!—
An'-sir! when he 'uz purt' nigh down,
  —w'y, nen
The old Bear he jumped up ag'in!—
  an' he
Ain't dead at all—*ist* 'tendin' thata-
  way,
So he kin git the Little Boy an' eat
Him up! But the Little Boy he 'uz too
  smart
To climb clean *down* the tree.—An'
  the old Bear

He can't climb *up* the tree no more—
  'cause when
He fell, he broke one of his—He broke
  all
His legs!—an' nen he *couldn't* climb!
  But he
Ist won't go 'way an' let the Little Boy
Come down out of the tree. An' the
  old Bear
Ist growls round there, he does—ist
  growls an' goes
"*Wooh!—woo-ooh!*" all the time! An'
  Little Boy
He haf to stay up in the tree—all
  night—
An' 'thout no *supper* neever!—Only
  they
Wuz *apples* on the tree!—An' Little
  Boy
Et apples—ist all night—an' cried—an'
  cried!
Nen when 't'uz morning the old Bear
  went "*Wooh!*"
Ag'in, an' try to climb up in the tree
An' git the Little Boy—But he *can't*
Climb t' save his *soul*, he can't!—An'
  oh! he's *mad!*—
He ist tear up the ground! an' go
  "*Woo-ooh!*"
An'—*Oh, yes!*—purty soon, when
  morning's come
All *light*—so's you kin *see*, you know,
  w'y, nen
The old Bear finds the Little Boy's
  gun, you know,
'At's on the ground.—(An' it ain't
  broke at all—
I ist *said* that!) An' so the old Bear
  think
He'll take the gun an' *shoot* the Little
  Boy:—
But *Bears they* don't know much 'bout
  shootin' guns:

So when he go to shoot the Little Boy,
The old Bear got the *other* end the gun
Ag'in' his shoulder, 'stid o' *th' other*
  end—
So when he try to shoot the Little Boy,
It shot *the Bear*, it did—an' killed him
  dead!
An' nen the Little Boy clumb down the
  tree
An' chopped his old woolly head off.
  —Yes, an' killed
The *other* Bear ag'in, he did—an' killed
All *boff* the bears, he did—an' tuk 'em
  home
An' *cooked* 'em, too, an' *et* 'em!
      —An' that's all.

797

THE PATHOS OF APPLAUSE

THE greeting of the company
    throughout
Was like a jubilee,—the children's
  shout
And fusillading hand-claps, with great
  guns
And detonations of the older ones,
Raged to such tumult of tempestuous
  joy,
It even more alarmed than pleased the
  boy;
Till, with a sudden twitching lip, he
  slid
Down to the floor and dodged across
  and hid
His face against his mother as she
  raised
Him to the shelter of her heart, and
  praised
His story in low whisperings, and
  smoothed

The "amber-colored hair," and kissed
and soothed
And lulled him back to sweet tran-
quillity—
"An' 'at's a sign 'at you're the Ma fer
me!"
He lisped, with gurgling ecstasy, and
drew
Her closer, with shut eyes; and feeling,
too,
If he could only *purr* now like a cat,
He would undoubtedly be doing that!

"And now"—the serious host said,
lifting there
A hand entreating silence;—"now,
aware
Of the good promise of our Traveler
guest
To add some story with and for the
rest,
I think I favor you, and him as well,
Asking a story I have heard him tell,
And know its truth, in each minute
detail:"
Then leaning on his guest's chair, with
a hale
Hand-pat by way of full endorsement,
he
Said, "Yes—the Free-Slave story—cer-
tainly."

The old man, with his waddy note-
book out,
And glittering spectacles, glanced
round about
The expectant circle, and still firmer
drew
His hat on, with a nervous cough or
two;
And, save at times the big hard words,
and tone

Of gathering passion—all the speaker's
own,—
The tale that set each childish heart
astir
Was thus told by "The Noted
Traveler."

798

TOLD BY "THE NOTED
TRAVELER"

COMING, clean from the Mary-
land-end
Of this great National Road of ours,
Through your vast West; with the
time to spend,
Stopping for days in the main towns,
where
Every citizen seemed a friend,
And friends grew thick as the wayside
flowers,—
I found no thing that I might narrate
More singularly strange or queer
Than a thing I found in your sister-
State
Ohio,—at a river-town—down here
In my note-book: *Zanesville—situate
On the stream Muskingum—broad
and clear,
And navigable, through half the year,
North, to Coshocton; south, as far
As Marietta.*—But these facts are
Not of the *story,* but the *scene*
Of the simple little tale I mean
To tell *directly*—from this, straight
through
To the *end* that is best worth listening
to:

Eastward of Zanesville, two or three
Miles from the town, as our stage
drove in,

I on the driver's seat, and he
Pointing out this and that to me,—
On beyond us—among the rest—
A grovy slope, and a fluttering throng
Of little children, which he "guessed"
Was a picnic, as we caught their thin
High laughter, as we drove along,
Clearer and clearer. Then suddenly
He turned and asked, with a curious
    grin,
What were my views on *Slavery?*
    "Why?"
I asked, in return, with a wary eye.
"Because," he answered, pointing his
    whip
At a little, whitewashed house and
    shed
On the edge of the road by the grove
    ahead,—
"Because there are two slaves *there,"*
    he said—
"Two Black slaves that I've passed
    each trip
For eighteen years.—Though they've
    been set free,
They have been slaves ever since!"
    said he.
And, as our horses slowly drew
Nearer the little house in view,
All briefly I heard the history
Of this little old Negro woman and
Her husband, house, and scrap of
    land;
How they were slaves and had been
    made free
By their dying master, years ago
In old Virginia; and then had come
North here into a *free* State—so,
Safe forever, to found a home—
For themselves alone?—for they left
    South there
Five strong sons, who had, alas!
All been sold ere it came to pass

This first old master with his last
    breath
Had freed the *parents.*—(He went to
    death
Agonized and in dire despair
That the poor slave *children* might not
    share
Their parents' freedom. And wildly
    then
He moaned for pardon and died.
    Amen!)

Thus, with their freedom, and little
    sum
Of money left them, these two had
    come
North, full twenty long years ago;
And, settling there, they had hope-
    fully
Gone to work, in their simple way,
Hauling—gardening—raising sweet
Corn, and pop-corn.—Bird and bee
In the garden-blooms and the apple
    tree
Singing with them throughout the
    slow
Summer's day, with its dust and
    heat—
The crops that thirst and the rains that
    fail;
Or in Autumn chill, when the clouds
    hung low,
And hand-made hominy might find
    sale
In the near town-market; or baking
    pies
And cakes, to range in alluring show
At the little window, where the eyes
Of the Movers' children, driving past,
Grew fixed, till the big white wagons
    drew
Into a halt that would sometimes last
Even the space of an hour or two—

As the dusty, thirsty travelers made
Their noonings there in the beeches'
    shade
By the old black Aunty's spring-house,
    where,
Along with its cooling draughts, were
    found
Jugs of her famous sweet spruce-beer,
Served with her gingerbread horses
    there,
While Aunty's snow-white cap bobbed
    round
Till · the children's rapture knew no
    bound,
As she sang and danced for them,
    quavering clear
And high the chant of her old slave-
    days—

    "Oh, Lo'd, Jimmy! my toes is so',
    Dancin' on yo' sandy flo'!"

Even so had they wrought all ways
To earn the pennies, and hoard them,
    too,—
And with what ultimate end in
    view?—
They were saving up money enough
    to be
Able, in time, to buy their own
Five children back.
        Ah! the toil gone through!
And the long delays and the heart-
    aches, too,
And self-denials that they had known!
But the pride and glory that was theirs
When they first hitched up their
    shackly cart
For the long, long journey South!—
    The start
In the first drear light of the chilly
    dawn,
With no friends gathered in grieving
    throng,—

With no farewells and favoring
    prayers;
But, as they creaked and jolted on,
Their chiming voices broke in song—

    " 'Hail, all hail! don't you see the stars a-
        fallin'?
    Hail, all hail! I'm on my way.
      Gideon am
        A healin' ba'm—
    I belong to the blood-washed army.
      Gideon am
        A healin' ba'm—
          On my way!' "

And their *return!*—with their oldest
    boy
Along with them! Why, their happi-
    ness
Spread abroad till it grew a joy
Universal—It even reached
And thrilled the town till the *Church*
    was stirred
Into suspecting that wrong was
    wrong!—
And it stayed awake as the preacher
    preached
A *Real* "Love"-text that he had not
    long
To ransack for in the Holy Word.
And the son, restored, and welcomed
    so,
Found service readily in the town;
And, with the parents, sure and slow,
He went "saltin' de cole cash down."

So with the *next* boy—and each one
In turn, till *four* of the five at last
Had been brought back; and, in each
    case,
With steady work and good homes
    not
Far from the parents, *they* chipped in
To the family fund, with an equal
    grace.

Thus they managed and planned and
wrought,
And the old folks throve—Till the
night before
They were to start for the lone last son
In the rainy dawn—their money fast
Hid away in the house,—two mean,
Murderous robbers burst the door.
. . . Then, in the dark, was a scuffle—
a fall—
An old man's gasping cry—and then
A woman's fife-like shriek.
            . . . Three men
Splashing by on horseback heard
The summons: And in an instant all
Sprang to their duty, with scarce a
word.
And they were *in time*—not only to
save
The lives of the old folks, but to
bag
Both the robbers, and buck-and-gag
And land them safe in the county
jail—
Or, as Aunty said, with a blended awe
And subtlety,—"Safe in de calaboose
whah
De dawgs cain't bite 'em!"
                —So prevail
The faithful!—So had the Lord upheld
His servants of both deed and prayer,—
His the glory unparalleled—
Theirs the reward,—their every son
Free, at last, as the parents were!
And, as the driver ended there
In front of the little house, I said,
All fervently, "Well done! well done!"
At which he smiled, and turned his
head,
And pulled on the leader's lines, and—
"See!"
He said,—"you can read old Aunty's
sign?"

And, peering down through these
specs of mine
On a little, square board-sign, I read:

"Stop, traveler, if you think it fit,
And quench your thirst, for a-fi'-penny-
bit—
The rocky spring is very clear,
And soon converted into beer."

And, though I read aloud, I could
Scarce hear myself for laugh and shout
Of children—a glad multitude
Of little people, swarming out
Of the picnic-grounds I spoke about.—
And in their rapturous midst, I see
Again—through mists of memory—
An old black Negress laughing up
At the driver, with her broad lips
rolled
Back from her teeth, chalk-white, and
gums
Redder than reddest red-ripe plums.
He took from her hand the lifted cup
Of clear spring-water, pure and cold,
And passed it to me: And I raised my
hat
And drank to her with a reverence
that
My conscience knew was justly due
The old black face, and the old eyes,
too—
The old black head, with its mossy mat
Of hair, set under its cap and frills
White as the snows on Alpine hills;
Drank to the old *black* smile, but yet
Bright as the sun on the violet,—
Drank to the gnarled and knuckled old
Black hands whose palms had ached
and bled
And pitilessly been worn pale
And white almost as the palms that
hold
Slavery's lash while the victim's wail

Fails as a crippled prayer might fail.—
Ay, with a reverence infinite,
I drank to the old black face and
head—
The old black breast with its life of
light—
The old black hide with its heart of
gold.

799

HEAT-LIGHTNING

THERE was a curious quiet for a
space
Directly following: and in the face
Of one rapt listener pulsed the flush
and glow
Of the heat-lightning that pent pas-
sions throw
Long ere the crash of speech.—He
broke the spell—
The host:—The Traveler's story, told
so well,
He said, had wakened there within his
breast
A yearning, as it were, to know *the*
rest—
That all unwritten sequence that the
Lord
Of Righteousness must write with
flame and sword,
Some awful session of His patient
thought.
Just then it was, his good old mother
caught
His blazing eye—so that its fire be-
came
But as an ember—though it burned
the same.
It seemed to her, she said, that she
had heard

It was the *Heavenly* Parent never
erred,
And not the *earthly* one that had such
grace:
"Therefore, my son," she said, with
lifted face
And eyes, "let no one dare anticipate
The Lord's intent. While *He* waits, *we*
will wait."
And with a gust of reverence genuine
Then Uncle Mart was aptly ringing
in—
" '*If the darkened heavens lower,*
Wrap thy cloak around thy
form;
Though the tempest rise in power,
God is mightier than the
storm!' "
Which utterance reached the restive
children all
As something humorous. And then a
call
For *him* to tell a story, or to "say
A funny piece." His face fell right
away:
He knew no story worthy. Then he
must
Declaim for them: In that, he could
not trust
His memory. And then a happy
thought
Struck some one, who reached in his
vest and brought
Some scrappy clippings into light and
said
There was a poem of Uncle Mart's he
read
Last April in "The Sentinel." He had
It there in print, and knew all would
be glad
To hear it rendered by the author.
And,
All reasons for declining at command

Exhausted, the now helpless poet rose
And said: "I am discovered, I suppose.
Though I have taken all precautions
    not
To sign my name to any verses
    wrought
By my transcendent genius, yet, you see,
Fame wrests my secret from me bodily;
So I must needs confess I did this deed
Of poetry red-handed, nor can plead
One whit of unintention in my crime—
My guilt of rhythm and my glut of
    rhyme.—

" 'Mæonides rehearsed a tale of arms,
    And Naso told of curious meta*mur*-
        phoses;
    Unnumbered pens have pictured woman's
        charms,
    While crazy *I*'ve made poetry *on pur-
        poses!*'

In other words, I stand convicted—
    need
I say—by my own doing, as I read."

800

UNCLE MART'S POEM

THE OLD SNOW-MAN

HO! the old Snow-Man
    That Noey Bixler made!
He looked as fierce and sassy
    As a soldier on parade!—
'Cause Noey, when he made him,
    While we all wuz gone, you see,
He made him, jist a-purpose,
    Jist as fierce as he could be!—
        But when we all got *ust* to him,
            Nobody wuz afraid
        Of the old Snow-Man
            That Noey Bixler made!

'Cause Noey told us 'bout him
    And what he made him fer:—
He'd come to feed, that morning
    He found we wuzn't here;
And so the notion struck him,
    When we all come taggin' home
'T'ud *s'prise* us ef a' old Snow-Man
    'Ud meet us when we come!
So, when he'd fed the stock, and
        milked,
    And be'n back home, and chopped
His wood, and et his breakfast, he
    Jist grabbed his mitts and hopped
Right in on that-air old Snow-Man
    That he laid out he'd make
Er bu'st a trace *a-tryin'*—jist
    Fer old-acquaintance-sake!—
        But work like that wuz lots more
            fun,
        He said, than when he played!
        Ho! the old Snow-Man
            That Noey Bixler made!

He started with a big snowball,
    And rolled it all around;
And as he rolled, more snow 'ud stick
    And pull up off the ground.—
He rolled and rolled all round the
        yard—
    'Cause we could see the *track*,
All wher' the snow come off, you
        know,
    And left it wet and black.
He got the Snow-Man's *legs-part*
        rolled—
    In front the kitchen-door,—
And then he hat to turn in then
    And roll and roll some more!—
He rolled the yard all round ag'in,
    And round the house, at that—
Clean round the house and back to
        wher'

The blame legs-half wuz at!
  He said he missed his dinner,
      too—
  Jist clean fergot and stayed
  There workin'. Oh! the old Snow-
      Man
    That Noey Bixler made!

And Noey said he hat to *hump*
  To git the *top-half* on
The *legs-half!*—When he *did,* he said,
  His wind wuz purt' nigh gone.—
He said, i jucks! he jist drapped down
  There on the old porch-floor
And panted like a dog!—And then
  He up! and rolled some more!—
The *last* batch—that wuz fer his
    head,—
  And—time he'd got it right
And clumb and fixed it on, he said—
  He hat to quit fer night!—
And *then,* he said, he'd kep' right on
  Ef they'd be'n any *moon*
To work by! So he crawled in bed—
  And *could* 'a' slep' tel *noon,*
    He wuz so plum wore out! he
      said,—
    But it wuz washin'-day,
  And hat to cut a cord o' wood
  'Fore he could git away!

But, last, he got to work ag'in,—
  With spade, and gouge, and hoe,
And trowel, too—(All tools 'ud do
  What *Noey* said, you know!)
He cut his eyebrows out like cliffs—
  And his cheek-bones and chin
Stuck *furder* out—and his old *nose*
  Stuck out as fur-ag'in!
He made his eyes o' walnuts,
  And his whiskers out o' this-
Here buggy-cushion stuffin'—*moss,*
  The teacher says it is.

And then he made a' old wood' **gun,**
  Set keerless-like, you know,
Acrost one shoulder—kind o' like
  Big Foot, er Adam Poe—
    Er, mayby, Simon Girty,
    The dinged old Renegade!
  Wooh! the old Snow-Man
    That Noey Bixler made!

And there he stood, all fierce and **grim,**
  A stern, heroic form:
What was the winter blast to him,
  And what the driving storm?—
What wonder that the children pressed
  Their faces at the pane
And scratched away the frost, in pride
  To look on him again?—
    What wonder that, with yearning
      bold,
    Their all of love and care
  Went warmest through the keen-
      est cold
    To that Snow-Man out there!

But the old Snow-Man—
  What a dubious delight
He grew at last when Spring came **on**
  And days waxed warm and bright!—
Alone he stood—all kith and kin
  Of snow and ice were gone;—
Alone, with constant tear-drops in
  His eyes and glittering on
His thin, pathetic beard of black—
  Grief in a hopeless cause!—
Hope—hope is for the man that *dies*—
  What for the man that *thaws!*
  O Hero of a hero's make!—
    Let *marble* melt and fade,
  But never *you*—you old Snow-
    Man
    That Noey Bixler made!

801

"LITTLE JACK JANITOR"

AND there, in that ripe Summer
night, once more
A wintry coolness through the open door
And window seemed to touch each
glowing face
Refreshingly; and, for a fleeting space,
The quickened fancy, through the fra-
grant air,
Saw snowflakes whirling where the
rose-leaves were,
And sounds of veriest jingling bells
again
Were heard in tinkling spoons and
glasses then.

Thus Uncle Mart's old poem sounded
young
And crisp and fresh and clear as when
first sung,
Away back in the wakening of Spring,
When his rhyme and the robin,
chorusing,
Rumored, in duo-fanfare, of the soon
Invading Johnny-jump-ups, with pla-
toon
On platoon of sweet-williams, mar-
shaled fine
To bloomèd blarings of the trumpet-
vine.

The poet turned to whisperingly confer
A moment with "The Noted Traveler,"
Then left the room, tripped up the
stairs, and then
An instant later reappeared again,
Bearing a little, lacquered box, or
chest,
Which, as all marked with curious in-
terest,

He gave to the old Traveler, who in
One hand upheld it, pulling back his
thin
Black luster coat-sleeves, saying he had
sent
Up for his "Magic Box," and that he
meant
To test it there—especially to show
The Children. "It is *empty now,* you
know."—
He thumped it with his knuckles, so
they heard
The hollow sound—"But lest it be in-
ferred
It is not *really* empty, I will ask
Little Jack Janitor, whose pleasant task
It is to keep it ship-shape."
                    Then he tried
And rapped the little drawer in the
side,
And called out sharply, "Are you in
there, Jack?"
And then a little, squeaky voice came
back,—
*"Of course I'm in here—ain't you got
the key*
Turned on me!"
                    Then the Traveler leisurely
Felt through his pockets, and at last
took out
The smallest key they ever heard
about!—
It wasn't any longer than a pin:
And this at last he managed to fit in
The little keyhole, turned it, and then
cried,
"Is everything swept out clean there
inside?"
*"Open the drawer and see! Don't talk
so much;*
Or else," the little voice squeaked,
"talk in Dutch—
You age me, asking questions!"

Then the man
Looked hurt, so that the little folks
began
To feel so sorry for him, he put down
His face against the box and had to
frown.—
"Come, sir!" he called,—"no impudence
to *me!*—
You've swept out clean?"
"Open the drawer and see!"
And so he drew the drawer out: Noth-
ing there
But just the empty drawer, stark and
bare.
He shoved it back again, with a sharp
click.—

"Ouch!" yelled the little voice—*"un-
snap it—quick!—
You've got my nose pinched in the
crack!"*
And then
The frightened man drew out the
drawer again,
The little voice exclaiming, *"Jee-mun-
nee!—
Say what you want, but please don't
murder me!"*
"Well, then," the man said, as he
closed the drawer
With care, "I want some cotton-batting
for
My supper! Have you got it?"
And inside,
All muffled-like, the little voice replied,
"Open the drawer and see!"
And, sure enough,
He drew it out, filled with the cotton
stuff.
He then asked for a candle to be
brought
And held for him; and tuft by tuft he
caught

And lit the cotton, and, while blazing,
took
It in his mouth and ate it, with a look
Of purest satisfaction.
"Now," said he,
"I've eaten the drawer empty, let me
see
What this is in my mouth:" And with
both hands
He began drawing from his lips long
strands
Of narrow silken ribbons, every hue
And tint;—and crisp they were and
bright and new
As if just purchased at some Fancy-
Store.
"And now, Bub, bring your cap," he
said, "before
Something might happen!" And he
stuffed the cap
Full of the ribbons. *"There,* my little
chap,
Hold *tight* to them," he said, "and take
them to
The ladies there, for they know what
to do
With all such rainbow finery!"
He smiled
Half sadly, as it seemed, to see the
child
Open his cap first to his mother. . . .
There
Was not a ribbon in it anywhere!
"Jack Janitor!" the man said sternly
through
The Magic Box—"Jack Janitor, did
you
Conceal those ribbons anywhere?"
"Well, yes,"
The little voice piped—*"but you'd
never guess
The place I hid 'em if you'd guess a
year!"*

"Well, won't you *tell* me?"
                    "Not until you clear
Your mean old conscience," said the
    voice, *"and make*
Me first do something for the Chil-
    dren's sake."
"Well, then, fill up the drawer," the
    Traveler said,
"With whitest white on earth and red-
    dest red!—
Your terms accepted—Are you satis-
    fied?"

"Open the drawer and see!" the voice
    replied.

"Why, bless my soul!"—the man said,
    as he drew
The contents of the drawer into view—
"It's   level-full   of   *candy!*—Pass   it
    round—
Jack Janitor shan't steal *that,* I'll be
    bound!"—
He raised and crunched a stick of it,
    and smacked
His lips.—"Yes, that *is* candy, for a
    fact!—
And it's all *yours!"*
                    And how the children there
Lit into it!—O never anywhere
Was such a feast of sweetness!
                    "And now, then,"
The man said, as the empty drawer
    again
Slid to its place, he bending over it,—
"Now, then, Jack Janitor, before we quit
Our entertainment for the evening, tell
Us where you hid the ribbons—can't
    you?"
            "Well,"
The squeaky little voice drawled
    sleepily—
"Under your old hat, maybe.—Look
    and see!"

All carefully the man took off his hat:
But there was not a ribbon under
    that.—
He shook his heavy hair, and all in
    vain
The old white hat—then put it on
    again:
"Now, tell me, *honest,* Jack, where *did*
    you hide
The ribbons?"
                    "Under your hat," the
    voice replied.—
"Mind! I said 'under' and not 'in' it.
    —*Won't*
You ever take the hint on earth?—or
    don't
You want to show folks where the
    ribbon's at?—
Law! but I'm sleepy!—Under—unner
    yer hat!"

Again the old man carefully took off
The empty hat, with an embarrassed
    cough,
Saying, all gravely, to the children:
    "You
Must promise not to *laugh*—you'll all
    want to—
When you see where Jack Janitor has
    dared
To hide those ribbons—when he might
    have spared
My feelings.—But no matter!—Know
    the worst—
Here are the ribbons, as I feared at
    first."—
And, quick as snap of thumb and fin-
    ger, there
The old man's head had not a sign of
    hair,
And in his lap a wig of iron-gray
Lay, stuffed with all that glittering
    array

Of ribbons. . . . "Take 'em to the
  ladies—Yes.
Good night to everybody, and God
  bless
The Children."
        In a whisper no one missed
The Hired Man yawned: "He's a van-
  trilloquist."

. . . .

So gloried all the night. Each trundle-
  bed
And pallet was enchanted—each child-
  head
Was packed with happy dreams. And
  long before
The dawn's first far-off rooster crowed,
  the snore
Of Uncle Mart was stilled, as round
  him pressed
The bare arms of the wakeful little
  guest
That he had carried home with him. . . .
                            "I think,"
An awed voice said—"(No: I don't
  want a *dwink.*—
Lay still.)—I think 'The Noted Trav-
  eler' he
'S the inscrutibul-est man I ever see!"

803

"THEM OLD CHEERY WORDS"

PAP he allus ust to say,
    "Chris'mus comes but onc't a year!"
Liked to hear him thataway,
    In his old split-bottomed cheer
By the fireplace here at night—
Wood all in,—and room all bright,
Warm and snug, and folks all here:
"Chris'mus comes but onc't a year!"

Me and 'Lize, and Warr'n and Jess
    And Eldory home fer two
Weeks' vacation; and, I guess,
    Old folks tickled through and
      through,
Same as *we* was,—"Home onc't more
Fer another Chris'mus—shore!"
Pap 'ud say, and tilt his cheer,—
"Chris'mus comes but onc't a year!"

And front of kindliest humanity—
With *"Jemmy Jackman, m'am,"* full
  courteously
Saluting *"After you, m'am"*; and *"Our
  boy"*—
The *Junior* Jemmy, with the zest and
  joy
So strangely born out of the hopeless
  state
Of sacred motherhood made violate,
Yet glorified by the compassion of
The mortal, answering the Immortal
  love.
Writing like this must be, not from
  the wrist,
But from the heart no reader may re-
  sist.

————◆————

802

ST. LIRRIPER

WHEN Dickens first dawned on
    us. . . . Hey! to wake
On such a morning *now,* to rise and
  break
Brain-fast on such an appetizing
  spread
As Mrs. Lirriper, the unconscious head

Mostly Pap was ap' to be
    Ser'ous in his "daily walk,"
As he called it; giner'ly
    Was no hand to joke er talk.
Fac's is, Pap had never be'n
Rugged-like at all—and then
Three years in the army had
Hepped to break him purty bad.

Never *flinched!* but frost and snow
    Hurt his wownd in winter. But
You bet *Mother* knowed it, though!—
    Watched his feet, and made him putt
On his flannen; and his knee,
Where it never healed up, he
Claimed was "well now—mighty
    near—
Chris'mus comes but onc't a year!"

"Chris'mus comes but onc't a year!"
    Pap 'ud say, and snap his eyes . . . .
Row o' apples sputter'n' here
    Round the hearth, and me and 'Lize
Crackin' hicker'-nuts; and Warr'n
And Eldory parchin' corn;
And whole raft o' young folks here.
"Chris'mus comes but onc't a year!"

Mother tuk most comfort in
Jes' a-he'ppin' Pap: She'd fill
His pipe fer him, er his tin
    O' hard cider; er set still
And read fer him out the pile
O' newspapers putt on file
Whilse he was with Sherman—(She
Knowed the whole war-history!)

Sometimes he'd git het up some.—
    "Boys," he'd say, "and you girls, too,
Chris'mus is about to come;
    So, as you've a right to do,
Celebrate it! Lots has died,

Same as Him they crucified,
That you might be happy here.
Chris'mus comes but onc't a year!"

Missed his voice last Chris'mus—missed
    Them old cheery words, you know!
Mother helt up tel she kissed
    All of us—then had to go
And break down! And I laughs,
    "Here!
'Chris'mus comes but onc't a year!' "
"Them's his very words," sobbed she,
"When he asked to marry me."

"Chris'mus comes but onc't a year!"—
    "Chris'mus comes but onc't a year!"
Over, over, still I hear,
    "Chris'mus comes but onc't a year!"
Yit, like him, I'm goin' to smile
And keep cheerful all the while:
Allus Chris'mus *There*—And here
"Chris'mus comes but onc't a year!"

804

A DUBIOUS "OLD KRISS"

US-FOLKS is purty pore—but Ma
    She's waitin'—two years more—
    tel Pa
He serves his term out. Our Pa he—
He's in the Penitenchurrie!

Now don't you tell!—'cause *Sis,*
The baby, *she* don't know he is.—
'Cause she wuz only four, you know,
He kissed her last an' hat to go!

Pa alluz liked Sis best of all
Us childern.—'Spect it's 'cause she fall
When she 'uz ist a *child,* one day—
An' make her back look thataway.

Pa—'fore he be a burglar—he's
A locksmiff, an' maked locks, an' keys,
An' knobs you pull fer bells to ring,
An' he could ist make *anything!*—

'Cause our Ma *say* he can!—*An'* this
Here little pair of crutches Sis
Skips round on—Pa maked *them*—yes-
   sir!—
An' silivur-plate-name here fer her!

Pa's out o' work when Chris'mus come
One time, an' stay away from home,
An' 's drunk an' 'buse our Ma, an'
   swear
They ain't no "Old Kriss" anywhere!

An' Sis she alluz say they *wuz*
A' Old Kriss—an' she alluz does.
But ef they *is* a' Old Kriss, why,
When's Chris'mus, Ma she alluz *cry?*

This Chris'mus *now,* we live here in
Where Ma's rent's alluz due ag'in—
An' she "ist slaves"—I heerd her say
She did—ist them words thataway!

An' th'other night, when all's so cold
An' stove's 'most out—our Ma she
   rolled
Us in th' old feather-bed an' said,
"To-morry's Chris'mus—go to bed,

"An' thank yer blessed stars fer this—
We don't *'spect* nothin' from old
   Kriss!"
An' cried, an' locked the door, an'
   prayed,
An' turned the lamp down. . . . An'
   I laid

There, thinkin' in the dark ag'in,
"Ef *wuz* Old Kriss, he can't git in,

'Cause ain't no chimbly here at all—
Ist old stovepipe struck frue the wall!"

I sleeped nen.—An' wuz dreamin'
   some
When I waked up an' mornin' 's
   come,—
Fer our Ma she wuz settin' square
Straight up in bed, a-readin' there

Some letter 'at she'd read, an' quit,
An' nen hold like she's huggin' it.—
An' diamon' ear-rings she don't *know*
Wuz in her ears tel I say so—

An' wake the rest up. An' the sun
In frue the winder dazzle-un
Them eyes o' Sis's, wiv a sure-
Enough gold chain Old Kriss bringed
   to 'er!

An' *all* of us git gold things!—Sis,
Though, say she know it *"ain't* Old
   Kriss—
He kissed her, so she waked an' saw
Him skite out—an' it wuz her Pa."

805

YOUR HEIGHT IS OURS

TO RICHARD HENRY STODDARD, AT THE
STODDARD BANQUET BY THE AUTHORS
CLUB, NEW YORK, MARCH 25, 1897

O PRINCELY poet!—kingly heir
   Of gifts divinely sent,—
Your own!—nor envy anywhere,
   Nor voice of discontent.

Though, of ourselves, all poor are we,
   And frail and weak of wing,
Your height is ours—your ecstasy—
   Your glory, when you sing.

Most favored of the gods, and great
    In gifts beyond our store,
We covet not your rich estate,
    But prize our own the more.—

The gods give as but gods may do—
    We count *our* riches thus,—
They gave their richest gifts to you,
    And then gave you to us.

806

HYMN EXULTANT

FOR EASTER

VOICE of Mankind, sing over
        land and sea—
Sing, in this glorious morn!
The long, long night is gone from Cal-
        vary—
    The cross, the thong and thorn;
The sealed tomb yields up its saintly
        guest,
No longer to be burdened and op-
        pressed.

Heart of Mankind, thrill answer to
        His own,
    So human, yet divine!
For earthly love He left His heavenly
        throne—
    For love like thine and mine—
For love of us, as one might kiss a
        bride,
His lifted lips touched death's, all sat-
        isfied.

Soul of Mankind, He wakes—He lives
        once more!
    O soul, with heart and voice

Sing! sing!—the stone rolls chorus
        from the door—
    Our Lord stands forth.—Rejoice!
Rejoice, O garden-land of song and
        flowers;
Our King returns to us, forever ours!

807

"O LIFE! O BEYOND!"

STRANGE—strange, O mortal Life,
    The perverse gifts that came to me
        from you!
From childhood I have wanted *all* good
        things:
            You gave me few.

You gave me faith in One—
    Divine—above your own imperious
        might,
O mortal Life, while I but wanted you
            And your delight.

I wanted dancing feet,
    And flowery, grassy paths by laugh-
        ing streams;
You gave me loitering steps, and eyes
        all blurred
            With tears and dreams.

I wanted love,—and, lo!
    As though in mockery, you gave me
        loss.
O'erburdened sore, I wanted rest: you
        gave
            The heavier cross.

I wanted one poor hut
    For mine own home, to creep away
        into:
You gave me only lonelier desert lands
            To journey through.

Now, at the last vast verge
Of barren age, I stumble, reel, and
fling
Me down, with strength all spent and
heart athirst
And famishing.

Yea, now, Life, deal me death,—
Your worst—your vaunted worst!
. . . Across my breast
With numb and fumbling hands I gird
me for
The best.

808

OUR QUEER OLD WORLD

*Fer them 'at's here in airliest infant
stages,
It's a hard world:
Fer them 'at gits the knocks of boy-
hood's ages,
It's a mean world:
Fer them 'at nothin's good enough
they're gittin',
It's a bad world:
Fer them 'at learns at last what's right
and fittin',
It's a good world.*
—THE HIRED MAN

IT'S a purty hard world you find, my
child—
It's a purty hard world you find!
You fight, little rascal! and kick and
squall,
And snort out medicine, spoon and all!
When you're here longer you'll
change your mind

And simmer down sort o' half-rickon-
ciled.
But *now*—Jee!-
My!-mun-nee!
It's a purty hard world, my child!

It's a purty mean world you're in, my
lad—
It's a purty mean world you're in!
We know, of course, in your school-
boy-days
It's a world of too many troublesome
ways
Of tryin' things over and startin'
ag'in,—
Yit *your* chance beats what your
parents had.
But *now*—Oh!
Fire-and-tow!
It's a purty mean world, my lad!

It's a purty bad world you've struck,
young chap—
It's a purty bad world you've
struck—
But *study* the cards that you hold, you
know,
And your hopes will sprout and your
mustache grow,
And your store-clothes likely will
change your luck,
And you'll rake a rich ladybird into
your lap!
But *now*—Doubt
All things out.—
It's a purty bad world, young chap!

It's a purty good world this is, old
man—
It's a purty good world this is!
For all its follies and shows and lies—

Its rainy weather, and cheeks likewise,
   And age, hard-hearin' and rheuma-
      tiz.—
We're not a-faultin' the Lord's own
      plan—
         All things 's jest
         At their best.—
It's a purty good world, old man!

809

ON A YOUTHFUL PORTRAIT
OF STEVENSON

A FACE of youth mature; a mouth
      of tender,
Sad, human sympathy, yet some-
      thing stoic
In clasp of lip: wide eyes of calmest
      splendor,
And brow serenely ample and heroic:

The features—all—lit with a soul
      ideal . . .
O visionary boy! what were you see-
      ing,
What hearing, as you stood thus midst
      the real
Ere yet one master-work of yours had
      being?

Is it a foolish fancy that we humor—
   Investing daringly with life and spirit
This youthful portrait of you ere one
      rumor
   Of your great future spoke that men
      might hear it?—
Is it a fancy, or your first of glories,
   That you were listening, and the
      camera drew you
Hearing the voices of your untold
      stories
   And all your lovely poems calling to
      you?

810

PROEM

W E *found him in that Far-away that yet to us seems near—*
      We vagrants of but yesterday when idlest youth was here,—
When lightest song and laziest mirth possessed us through and through,
And all the dreamy summer-earth seemed drugged with morning dew:

When our ambition scarce had shot a stalk or blade indeed:
Yours,—choked as in the garden-spot you still deferred to "weed":
Mine,—but a pipe half-cleared of pith—as now it flats and whines
In sympathetic cadence with a hiccough in the lines.

Ay, even then—O timely hour!—the High Gods did confer
In our behalf:—And, clothed in power, lo, came their Courier—
Not winged with flame nor shod with wind,—but ambling down the pike,
Horseback, with saddle-bags behind, and guise all human-like.

And it was given us to see, beneath his rustic rind,
A native force and mastery of such inspiring kind,
That half unconsciously we made obeisance.—Smiling, thus
His soul shone from his eyes and laid its glory over us.

.   .   .   .

Though, faring still that Far-away that yet to us seems near,
His form, through mists of yesterday, fades from the vision here,
Forever as he rides, it is in retinue divine,—
The hearts of all his time are his, with your hale heart and mine.

811

RUBÁIYÁT OF DOC SIFERS

I

IF you don't know Doc Sifers I'll jes' argy, here and now,
You've bin a mighty little while about here, anyhow,
'Cause Doc he's rid these roads and woods—er *swum* 'em, now and then—
And practised in this neighberhood sence hain't no tellin' when!

II

In radius o' fifteen mil'd, all p'ints o' compass round,
No man er woman, chick er child, er team, on top o' ground,
But knows *him*—yes, and got respects and likin' fer him, too,
Fer all his so-to-speak dee-fects o' genius showin' through!

III

Some claims he's absent-minded; some has said they wuz afeard
To take his powders when he come and dosed 'em out, and 'peared
To have his mind on somepin' else—like County Ditch, er some
New way o' tannin' mussrat-pelts, er makin' butter come.

IV

He's cur'ous—they hain't no mistake about it!—but he's got
Enough o' extry brains to make a *jury*—like as not.
They's no *describin'* Sifers,—fer, when all is said and done,
He's jes' *hisse'f* Doc Sifers—ner they hain't no other one!

V

Doc's allus sociable, polite, and 'greeable, you'll find—
Pervidin' ef you strike him right and nothin' on his mind,—
Like in some *hurry,* when they've sent fer Sifers *quick,* you see,
To 'tend some sawmill-accident, er picnic jamboree;

VI

Er when the lightin' 's struck some harebrained harvest-hand; er in
Some 'tempt o' suicidin'—where they'd ort to try ag'in!
I've *knowed* Doc haul up from a trot and talk a' hour er two
When railly he'd a-ort o' not a-stopped fer *"Howdy-do!"*

VII

And then, I've met him 'long the road, *a-lopin',*—starin' straight
Ahead,—and yit he never knowed me when I hollered *"Yate,
Old Saddlebags!"* all hearty-like, er *"Who you goin' to kill?"*
And he'd say nothin'—only hike on faster, starin' still!

VIII

I'd bin insulted, many a time, ef I jes' wuzn't shore
Doc didn't mean a thing. And I'm not tetchy any more
Sence that-air day, ef he'd a-jes' a-stopped to jaw with *me,*
They'd bin a little dorter less in my own fambily!

IX

Times *now,* at home, when Sifers' name comes up, I jes' *let on,*
You know, 'at *I* think Doc's to *blame,* the way he's bin and gone
And disapp'inted folks—'Ll-*jee*-mun-*nee!* you'd ort to then
Jes' hear my wife light into me—*"ongratefulest o' men!"*

X

'Mongst *all* the women—mild er rough, splendiferous er plain,
Er them *with* sense, er not enough to come in out the rain,—
Jes' ever' shape and build and style o' women, fat er slim—
They all like Doc, and got a smile and pleasant word fer *him!*

XI

Ner hain't no horse I've ever saw but what'll neigh and try
To sidle up to him, and paw, and sense him, ear-and-eye:
Then jes' a tetch o' Doc's old pa'm, to pat 'em, er to shove
Along their nose—and they're as ca'm as any cooin' dove!

XII

And same with *dogs,*—take any breed, er strain, er pedigree,
Er racial caste 'at can't concede no use fer you er me,—
They'll putt all predju-dice aside in *Doc's* case and go in
Kahoots with him, as satisfied as he wuz kith-and-kin!

XIII

And Doc's a wonder, trainin' pets!—He's got a chicken-hawk,
In kind o' half-cage, where he sets out in the gyarden-walk,
And got that wild bird trained so tame, he'll loose him, and he'll fly
Clean to the woods!—Doc calls his name—and he'll come, by and by!

XIV

Same says no money down 'ud buy that bird o' Doc.—Ner no
Inducement to the *bird,* says I, 'at *he'd* let *Sifers* go!
And Doc *he* say 'at *he's* content—long as a bird o' prey
Kin 'bide *him,* it's a *compliment,* and takes it thataway.

XV

But, gittin' back to *docterin'*—all the sick and in distress,
And old and pore, and weak and small, and lone and motherless,—
I jes' tell *you* I 'preciate the man 'at's got the love
To "go ye forth and ministrate!" as Scriptur' tells us of.

XVI

Dull times, Doc jes' *mi*anders round, in that old rig o' his:
And hain't no tellin' where he's bound ner guessin' where he is;
He'll drive, they tell, jes' thataway fer maybe six er eight
Days at a stretch; and neighbers say he's bin clean round the State.

XVII

He picked a' old tramp up, one trip, 'bout eighty mil'd from here,
And fetched him home and k-yored his hip, and kep' him 'bout a year;
And feller said—in all *his* ja'nts round this terreschul ball
'At no man wuz a *circumstance* to *Doc!*—he topped 'em all!—

XVIII

Said, bark o' trees 's a' open book to Doc, and vines and moss
He read like writin'—with a look knowed ever' dot and cross:
Said, stars at night wuz jes' as good's a compass: said, he s'pose
You couldn't lose Doc in the woods the darkest night that blows!

XIX

Said, Doc'll tell you, purty clos't, by underbresh and plants,
How fur off *warter* is,—and 'most perdict the sort o' chance
You'll have o' findin' *fish;* and how they're liable to *bite,*
And whether they're a-bitin' now, er only after night.

XX

And, whilse we're talkin' *fish,*—I mind they formed a fishin'-crowd
(When folks *could* fish 'thout gittin' *fined,* and seinin' wuz allowed!)
O' leadin' citizens, you know, to go and seine "Old Blue"—
But hadn't no big seine, and so—w'y, what wuz they to do? . . .

XXI

And Doc he say he thought 'at *he* could *knit* a stitch or two—
"Bring the *materials* to me—'at's all I'm astin' you!"
And down he sets—six weeks, i jing! and knits that seine plum done—
Made corks too, brails and ever'thing—good as a boughten one!

XXII

Doc's *public* sperit—when the sick's not takin' *all* his time
And he's got *some* fer politics—is simple yit sublime:—
He'll *talk* his *principles*—and they air *honest;*—but the sly
Friend strikes him first, election-day, he'd 'commode, er die!

XXIII

And yit, though Doc, as all men knows, is square straight up and down,
That vote o' his is—well, I s'pose—the cheapest one in town;—
A fact 'at's sad to verify, as could be done on oath—
I've voted Doc myse'f—*And I was criminal fer both!*

XXIV

You kin corrupt the *ballot-box*—corrupt *yourse'f,* as well—
Corrupt *some* neighbers,—but old Doc's as oncorruptible
As Holy Writ. So putt a pin right there!—Let *Sifers* be,
I jucks! he wouldn't vote ag'in' his own worst inimy!

XXV

When Cynthy Eubanks laid so low with fever, and Doc Glenn
Told Euby Cynth 'ud haf to go—they sends fer *Sifers* then! . . .
Doc sized the case: "She's starved," says he, "fer *warter*—yes, and *meat!*
The treatment 'at she'll git from *me's* all she kin drink and eat!"

XXVI

He orders Euby then to split some wood, and take and build
A fire in kitchen-stove, and git a young spring-chicken killed;
And jes' whirled in and th'owed his hat and coat there on the bed,
And warshed his hands and sailed in that-air kitchen, Euby said,

XXVII

And biled that chicken-broth, and got that dinner—all complete
And clean and crisp and good and 'hot as mortal ever eat!
And Cynth and Euby both'll say 'at Doc'll git as good
Meals-vittles up, jes' any day, as any *woman* could!

XXVIII

Time Sister Abbick tuk so bad with striffen o' the lung,
P'tracted Meetin', where she had jes' shouted, prayed, and sung
All winter long, through snow and thaw,—when Sifers come, says he:
"No, M'lissy; don't poke out your raw and cloven tongue at me!—

XXIX

"I know, without no symptoms but them *injarubber-shoes*
You promised me to never putt a fool-foot in ner use
At purril o' your life!" he said.   "And I won't save you *now,*
Onless—here on your dyin' bed—you consecrate your vow!"

XXX

Without a-claimin' *any creed,* Doc's rail religious views
Nobody knows—ner got no *need* o' knowin' whilse he choose
To be heerd not of man, ner raise no loud, vain-glorious prayers
In crowded marts, er public ways, er—i jucks, *any*wheres!—

XXXI

'Less'n it *is* away deep down in his own heart, at night,
Facin' the storm, when all the town's a-sleepin' snug and tight—
Him splashin' hence from scenes o' pride and sloth and gilded show,
To some pore sufferer's bedside o' anguish, don't you know!

XXXII

Er maybe dead o' *winter*—makes no odds to *Doc,*—he's got
To face the weather ef it takes the hide off! 'cause he'll not
Lie out o' goin' and p'tend he's sick hisse'f—like *some*
'At I could name 'at folks might send fer and they'd *never* come!

XXXIII

Like pore Phin Hoover—when he goes to that last dance o' his!
That Chris'mus when his feet wuz froze—and Doc saved all they is
Left of 'em—" 'Nough," as Phin say now, "to *track* me by, and be
A adver*tise*ment, anyhow, o' what Doc's done fer me!—

XXXIV

"When *he* come—knife-and-saw"—Phin say, "I knowed, ef I'd the spunk,
'At Doc 'ud fix me up *some* way, ef nothin' but my *trunk*
Wuz left, he'd fasten *casters* in, and have me, spick-and-span,
A-skootin' round the streets ag'in as spry as any man!"

XXXV

Doc sees a patient's *got* to quit—he'll ease him down serene
As dozin' off to sleep, and yit not dope him with mor*pheen*.—
He won't tell *what*—jes' 'lows 'at he has "airnt the right to sing
'O grave, where is thy victory! O death, where is thy sting!'"

XXXVI

And, mind ye now!—it's not in scoff and scorn, by long degree,
'At Doc gits things like that-un off: it's jes' his *shority*
And total faith in Life to Come,—w'y, "from that *Land o' Bliss*,"
He says, "we'll haf to chuckle some, a-lookin' back at this!"

XXXVII

And, still in p'int, I mind, one *night o' 'nitiation* at
Some secert lodge, 'at Doc set right down on 'em, square and flat,
When they mixed up some Scriptur' and wuz *funnin'*-like—w'y, he
Lit in 'em with a rep'imand 'at ripped 'em, A to Z!

XXXVIII

And onc't—when gineral loafin'-place wuz old Shoe-Shop—and all
The gang 'ud git in there and brace their backs ag'inst the wall
And *settle* questions that had went onsettled long enough,—
Like "wuz no Heav'n—ner no torment"—*jes' talkin' awful rough!*

XXXIX

There wuz Sloke Haines and old Ike Knight and Coonrod Simmes—all three
Ag'inst the Bible and the Light, and scoutin' Deity.
"*Science*," says Ike, "it DIM*onstrates*—it takes nobody's word—
Scriptur' er not,—it *'vestigates* ef sich things could occurred!"

XL

Well, Doc he heerd this,—he'd drapped in a minute, fer to git
A tore-off heel pegged on ag'in,—and, as he stood on it
And stomped and grinned, he says to Ike, "I s'pose now, purty soon
Some lightin'-bug, indignant-like, 'll 'vestigate the moon! . . .

XLI

"No, Ike," says Doc, "this world hain't saw no brains like yourn and mine
With sense enough to grasp a law 'at takes a brain divine.—
I've bared the thoughts of brains in doubt, and felt their finest pulse,—
And mortal brains jes' won't turn out omnipotent results!"

XLII

And Doc he's got respects to spare the *rich* as well as *pore*—
Says he, "I'd turn no *millionnaire* onsheltered from my door."—
Says he, "What's wealth to him in quest o' *honest* friends to back
And love him fer *hisse'f?*—not jes' because he's made his jack!"

XLIII

And childern.—*Childern?* Lawzy-day! Doc *worships* 'em!—You call
Round at his house and *ast* 'em—they're a-*swarmin'* there—that's all!—
They're in his *Li*b'ry—in best room—in kitchen—fur and near,—
In office too, and, I p'sume, his operatin'-cheer!

XLIV

You know they's men 'at *bees* won't sting?—They's plaguy *few,*—But Doc
He's one o' *them.*—And same, i jing! with *childern;*—they jes' flock
Round Sifers *natchurl!*—in his lap, and in his pockets, too,
And in his old fur mitts and cap, and *heart* as warm and true!

XLV

It's cur'ous, too,—'cause Doc hain't got no childern of his own—
'Ceptin' the ones he's tuk and brought up, 'at's bin left alone
And orphans when their father died, er mother,—and Doc he
Has he'pped their dyin' satisfied.—"The child shall live with me

XLVI

"And Winniferd, my wife," he'd say, and stop right there, and cle'r
His th'oat, and go on thinkin' way *some* mother-hearts down here
Can't never feel *their own* babe's face a-pressin' 'em, ner make
Their naked breasts a restin'-place fer any baby's sake.

XLVII

Doc's *Lib*'ry—as he calls it,—well, they's ha'f-a-dozen she'ves
Jam-full o' books—I couldn't tell *how* many—count yourse'ves!
One whole she'f's Works on Medicine! and most the rest's about
First Settlement, and Indians in here,—'fore we driv 'em out.—

XLVIII

And Plutarch's Lives—and life also o' Dan'el Boone, and this-
Here Mungo Park, and Adam Poe—jes' all the *lives* they is!
And Doc's got all the *novels* out,—by Scott and Dickison
And Cooper.—And, I make no doubt, he's read 'em ever' one!

XLIX

Onc't, in his office, settin' there, with crowd o' eight er nine
Old neighbers with the time to spare, and Doc a-feelin' fine,
A man rid up from Rollins, jes' fer Doc to write him out
Some blame' p'scription—done, I guess, in minute, nigh about.—

L

And *I* says, "Doc, you 'pear so spry, jes' write me that recei't
You have fer bein' *happy* by,—fer that 'ud shorely beat
Your *medicine!*" says I.—And quick as *s'cat!* Doc turned and writ
And handed me: "Go he'p the sick, and putt your heart in it."

LI

And then, "A-talkin' furder 'bout that line o' thought," says he,
"Ef we'll jes' do the work cut out and give' to you and me,
We'll lack no joy, ner appetite, ner all we'd ort to eat,
And sleep like childern ever' night—as puore and ca'm and sweet."

LII

Doc *has* bin 'cused o' *offishness* and lack o' talkin' free
And extry friendly; but he says, "I'm *'feard* o' talk," says he,—
"I've got," he says, "a natchurl turn fer talkin' fit to kill.—
The best and hardest thing to learn is trick o' keepin' still."

LIII

Doc *kin* smoke, and I s'pose he *might* drink licker—jes' fer fun.
He says, *"You* smoke, *you* drink all right; but *I* don't—neether one"—
Says, "I *like* whisky—'good old rye'—but like it in its place,
Like that-air warter in your eye, er nose there on your face."

LIV

Doc's bound to have his joke! The day he got that off on me
I jes' had sold a load o' hay at "Scofield's Livery,"
And tolled Doc in the shed they kep' the hears't in, where I'd hid
The stuff 'at got me "out o' step," as Sifers said it did.

LV

Doc hain't, to say, no *"rollin' stone,"* and yit he hain't no hand
Fer *'cumulatin'.*—Home's his own, and scrap o' farmin'-land—
Enough to keep him out the way when folks is tuk down sick
The suddentest—'most any day they want him 'special quick.

LVI

And yit Doc loves his practise; ner don't, wilful, want to slight
No call—no matter who—how fur away—er day er night.—
He loves his work—he loves his friends—June, Winter, Fall, and Spring:
His *lovin'*—facts is—never ends; he loves jes' *ever*'thing. . . .

LVII

'Cept—*keepin' books.* He never sets down no accounts.—He hates,
The worst of all, collectin' debts—the worst, the more he waits.—
I've knowed him, when at last he *had* to dun a man, to end
By makin' him a loan—and mad he hadn't more to lend.

LVIII

When Pence's Drug Store ust to be in full blast, they wuz some
Doc's patients got things frekantly there, charged to *him,* i gum!—
Doc run a bill there, don't you know, and allus when he squared,
He never questioned nothin',—so he had his feelin's spared.

LIX

Now sich as that, I hold and claim, hain't *'scusable*—it's not
Perfessional!—It's jes' a shame 'at Doc hisse'f hain't got
No better *business*-sense! That's why lots 'd respect him more,
And not give him the clean go-by fer *other* doctors. Shore!

LX

This-here Doc *Glenn,* fer instance; er this little jack-leg *Hall;*—
They're *business*—folks respects 'em fer their *business* more'n all
They ever knowed, er ever *will,* 'bout *medicine.*—Yit they
Collect their money, k-yore er kill.—They're *business,* anyway!

LXI

You ast Jake Dunn:—he's worked it out in *figgers.*—He kin show
Stastistics how Doc's airnt about *three* fortunes in a row,—
Ever' ten-year' hand-runnin' straight—*three* of 'em—*thirty* year'
'At Jake kin count and 'lucidate o' Sifer's practise here.

LXII

Yit—"Praise the Lord," says Doc, "we've got our little home!" says he—
"(It's railly *Winniferd's,* but what she owns, she sheers with me.)
We' got our little gyarden-spot, and peach and apple trees,
And stable, too, and chicken-lot, and eighteen hive' o' bees."

LXIII

You call it anything you please, but it's *witchcraft*—the power
'At Sifers has o' handlin' bees!—He'll watch 'em by the hour—
Mix right amongst 'em, mad and hot and swarmin'!—yit they won't
Sting *him,* er *want* to—*'pear* to not,—at least I know they *don't.*

LXIV

With *me* and bees they's no *p'tense* o' socialbility—
A dad-burn bee 'ud climb a fence to git a whack at *me!*
I s'pose no thing 'at's *got* a sting is railly satisfied
It's *sharp* enough, ontel, i jing! he's honed it on my hide!

LXV

And Doc he's allus had a knack *inventin'* things.—Dee-vised
A windlass wound its own se'f back as it run down: and s'prised
Their new hired girl with *clothes-line,* too, and *clothes-pins,* all in *one:*
Purt' nigh all left fer *her* to do wuz git her *primpin'* done!

LXVI

And onc't, I mind, in airly Spring, and tappin' sugar trees,
Doc made a dad-burn little thing to sharpen *spiles* with—these-
Here wood'-spouts 'at the peth's punched out, and driv' in where they bore
The auger-holes. He sharpened 'bout a *million* spiles er more!

LXVII

And Doc's the first man ever swung a *bucket* on a tree
Instid o' *troughs;* and first man brung *grained* sugar—so's 'at he
Could use it fer his coffee, and fer cookin', don't you know.—
Folks come clean up from Pleasantland 'fore they'd *believe* it, though!

LXVIII

And all Doc's stable-doors *onlocks* and locks *theirse'ves*—and gates
The same way;—all rigged up like clocks, with pulleys, wheels, and weights,—
So, 's Doc says, "Drivin' *out,* er *in,* they'll *open;* and they'll *then,*
All quiet-like, shet up ag'in like little gentlemen!"

LXIX

And Doc 'ud made a mighty good *detective.*—Neighbers all
Will testify to *that*—er *could,* ef they wuz legal call:
His theories on any crime is worth your listenin' to.—
And he has hit 'em, many a time, long 'fore established true.

LXX

At this young druggist Wenfield Pence's trial fer his life,
On *primy faishy* evidence o' pizonin' his wife,
Doc's testimony saved and cle'red and 'quitted him and freed
Him so's he never even 'peared cog-*ni*zant of the deed!

LXXI

The facts wuz—Sifers testified,—at inquest he had found
The stummick showed the woman *died* o' pizon, but had downed
The dos't *herse'f*,—because *amount* and *cost* o' drug imployed
No *druggist* would, on *no* account, 'a' lavished and distroyed!

LXXII

Doc tracked a blame-don burglar down, and *nailed* the scamp, to boot,
But told him ef he'd leave the town he wouldn't prosecute.
He traced him by a tied-up thumb-print in fresh putty, where
Doc glazed it. Jes' *that's* how he come to track him to his lair!

LXXIII

Doc's jes' a *leetle* too inclined, *some* thinks, to overlook
The criminal and vicious kind we'd ort to bring to book
And punish, 'thout no extry show o' *sympathizin'*, where
They hain't showed none fer *us*, you know. But he takes issue there:

LXXIV

Doc argies 'at "The Red-eyed Law," as *he* says, "ort to learn
To lay a mighty leenient paw on deeds o' sich concern
As only the Good Bein' knows the wherefore of, and spreads
His hands above accused and sows His mercies on their heads."

LXXV

Doc even holds 'at *murder* hain't no crime we got a right
To *hang* a man fer—claims it's *taint* o' *lunacy,* er *quite.*—
'Hold *sich* a man responsibul fer murder," Doc says,—"then,
When *he's* hung, where's the rope to pull them *sound-mind* jurymen?

LXXVI

'It's in a nutshell—*all* kin see," says Doc,—"it's cle'r the *Law's*
As ap' to err as you er me, and kill without a cause:
The man most innocent o' sin *I've* saw, er *'spect* to see,
Wuz servin' a life-sentence in the penitentchury."

LXXVII

And Doc's a whole hand at a *fire!*—directin' how and where
To set your ladders, low er higher, and what first duties air,—
Like formin' warter-bucket-line; and best man in the town
To chop holes in old roofs, and mine defective chimblies down:

LXXVIII

Er durin' any public crowd, mass-meetin', er big day,
Where ladies ortn't be allowed, as I've heerd Sifers say,—
When they's a suddent rush somewhere, it's Doc's voice, ca'm and cle'r,
Says, "Fall back, men, and give her air!—that's all she's faintin' fer."

LXXIX

The sorriest I ever feel fer Doc is when some show
Er circus comes to town and he'll not git a chance to go.
'Cause he jes' natchurly *de*lights in circuses—clean down
From tumblers, in their spangled tights, to trick-mule and Old Clown.

LXXX

And ever'body *knows* it, too, how Doc is, thataway! . . .
I mind a circus onc't come through—wuz there myse'f that day.—
Ring-master cracked his whip, you know, to start the ridin'—when
In runs Old Clown and hollers *"Whoa!*—Ladies and gentlemen

LXXXI

"Of this vast audience, I fain would make in*qui*ry cle'r,
And learn, find out, and ascertain—*Is Doctor Sifers here?"*
And when some fool-voice bellers down: "He is! He's settin' in
Full view o' ye!" *"Then,"* says the Clown, *"the circus may begin!"*

LXXXII

Doc's got a *temper;* but, he says, he's learnt it which is boss,
Yit has to *watch* it, more er less. . . . I never seen him cross
But onc't, enough to make him swear;—milch-cow stepped on his toe,
And Doc ripped out *"I doggies!"*—There's the only case I know.

LXXXIII

Doc says that's what your temper's fer—to hold back out o' view,
And learn it never to occur on out ahead o' *you*.—
"You lead the way," says Sifers—"git your *temper* back in line—
And *furdest* back the *best,* ef it's as mean a one as mine!"

LXXXIV

He hates contentions—can't abide a wrangle er dispute
O' any kind; and he 'ull slide out of a crowd and skoot
Up some back-alley 'fore he'll stand and listen to a furse
When ary one's got upper-hand and t'other one's got worse.

LXXXV

Doc says: "I 'spise, when pore and weak and awk'ard talkers fails,
To see it's them with hardest cheek and loudest mouth pervails.—
A' all-one-sided quarr'l 'll make me *biassed,* mighty near,—
'Cause ginerly the side I take's the one I never hear."

LXXXVI

What 'peals to Doc the most and best is "seein' folks *agreed,*
And takin' ekal interest and universal heed
O' ever'body *else's* words and idies—same as we
Wuz glad and chirpy as the birds—jes' as we'd *ort* to be!"

LXXXVII

And *paterotic!* Like to git Doc started, full and fair,
About the war, and why 't'uz fit, and what wuz 'complished there;
"And who wuz *wrong,*" says Doc, "er *right,* 't'uz waste o' blood and tears,
All prophesied in *Black* and *White* fer years and years and years!"

LXXXVIII

And then he'll likely kind o' tetch on old John Brown, and dwell
On what *his* warnin's wuz; and ketch his breath and cough, and tell
On down to Lincoln's death. And *then*—well, he jes' chokes and quits
With "I must go now, gentlemen!" and grabs his hat, and *gits!*

LXXXIX

Doc's own war-rickord wuzn't won so much in line o' fight
As line o' work and nussin' done the wownded, day and night.—
His wuz the hand, through dark and dawn, 'at bound their wownds, and laid
As soft as their own mother's on their forreds when they prayed. . . .

XC

His wuz the face they saw the first—all dim, but smilin' bright,
As they come to and knowed the worst, yit saw the old *Red-White-
And-Blue* where Doc had fixed it where they'd see it *wavin'* still,
Out through the open tent-flap there, er 'crost the winder-sill.

XCI

And some's a-limpin' round here yit—a-waitin' Last Review,—
'Ud give the pensions 'at they git, and pawn their crutches, too,
To he'p Doc out, ef he wuz pressed financial'—same as he
Has *allus* he'pped them when distressed—ner never tuk a fee.

XCII

Doc never wuz much hand to pay attention to *p'tense*
And fuss-and-feathers and display in men o' prominence:
"A railly *great* man," Sifers 'lows, "is not the out'ard dressed—
All uniform, salutes and bows, and swellin' out his chest.

XCIII

"I *met* a great man onc't," Doc says, "and shuk his hand," says he,
"And *he* come 'bout in *one,* I guess, o' disapp'intin' *me*—
He talked so common-like, and brought his mind so cle'r in view
And simple-like, I purt' nigh thought, *'I'm* best man o' the two!' "

XCIV

Yes-*sir!* Doc's got convictions and old-fashioned kind o' ways
And idies 'bout this glorious Land o' Freedom; and he'll raise
His hat clean off, no matter where, jes' ever' time he sees
The Stars and Stripes a-floatin' there and flappin' in the breeze.

XCV

And tunes like old "Red-White-and-Blue" 'll fairly drive him wild,
Played on the brass band, marchin' through the streets! Jes' like a child
I've saw that man, his smile jes' set, all kind o' pale and white,
Bareheaded, and his eyes all wet, yit dancin' with delight!

XCVI

And yit, that very man we see all trimbly, pale and wann,
Give him a case o' *surgery,* we'll see another man!—
We'll do the trimblin' then, and *we'll* git white around the gills—
He'll show us *nerve* o' nerves, and he 'ull show us *skill* o' skills!

XCVII

Then you could toot your horns and beat your drums and bang your guns,
And wave your flags and march the street, and charge, all Freedom's sons!—
And Sifers *then,* I bet my hat, 'ud never flinch a hair,
But, stiddy-handed, 'tend to that pore patient layin' there.

XCVIII

And Sifers' *eye's* as stiddy as that hand o' his!—He'll shoot
A' old-style rifle, like he has, and smallest bore, to boot,
With any fancy rifles made to-day, er expert shot
'At works at shootin' like a *trade*—and all *some* of 'em's got!

XCIX

Let 'em go right out in the *woods* with Doc, and leave their "traps"
And blame' glass-balls and queensware-goods, and see how Sifers draps
A squirrel out the tallest tree.—And 'fore he fires he'll say
Jes' where he'll hit him—yes, sir-*ee!* And he's hit thataway!

C

Let 'em go out with him, i jucks! with fishin'-pole and gun,—
And ekal chances, fish and ducks, and take the *rain,* er *sun,*
Jes' as it pours, er as it blinds the eyesight; *then* I guess
'At they'd acknowledge, in their minds, their disadvantages.

CI

And yit *he'd* be the last man out to flop his wings and crow
Insultin'-like, and strut about above his fallen foe!—
No-*sir!* the hand 'at tuk the wind out o' their sails 'ud be
The very first they grabbed, and grinned to feel sich sympathy.

CII

Doc gits off now and then and takes a huntin'-trip somewhere
'Bout Kankakee, up 'mongst the lakes—sometimes'll drift round there
In his canoe a week er two; then paddle clean on back
By way o' old Wabash and Blue, with fish—all he kin pack,—

CIII

And wild ducks—some with feathers on 'em yit, and stuffed with grass.
And neighbers—all knows he's bin *gone*—comes round and gits a bass—
A great big double-breasted "rock," er "black," er maybe *pair*
Half fills a' ordinary crock. . . . Doc's *fish'll* give out there

CIV

Long 'fore his *ducks!*—But folks'll smile and blandish him, and make
Him tell and *tell* things!—all the while enjoy 'em jes' fer sake
O' pleasin' *him;* and then turn in and la'nch him from the start
A-tellin' all the things ag'in they railly know by heart.

CV

He's jes' a *child,* 's what Sifers is! And-sir, I'd ruther see
That happy, childish face o' his, and puore simplicity,
Than any shape er style er plan o' mortals otherwise—
With perfect faith in God and man a-shinin' in his eyes.

TAMÁM

812

WHERE THE CHILDREN USED TO PLAY

THE old farm-home is Mother's yet
and mine,
And filled it is with plenty and
to spare,—
But we are lonely here in life's decline,
Though fortune smiles around us
everywhere:
We look across the gold
Of the harvests, as of old—
The corn, the fragrant clover, and the
hay;
But most we turn our gaze,
As with eyes of other days,
To the orchard where the children
used to play.

O from our life's full measure
And rich hoard of worldly treasure
We often turn our weary eyes
away,
And hand in hand we wander
Down the old path winding yon-
der
To the orchard where the chil-
dren used to play.

Our sloping pasture-lands are filled
with herds;
The barn and granary-bins are bulg-
ing o'er;
The grove's a paradise of singing
birds—
The woodland brook leaps laughing
by the door;
Yet lonely, lonely still,
Let us prosper as we will,

Our old hearts seem so empty every
way—
We can only through a mist
See the faces we have kissed
In the orchard where the children
used to play.

O from our life's full measure
And rich hoard of worldly treasure
We often turn our weary eyes
away,
And hand in hand we wander
Down the old path winding yon-
der
To the orchard where the chil-
dren used to play.

813

MR. FOLEY'S CHRISTMAS

There's nothing sweet in the city
But the patient lives of the poor.
—JOHN BOYLE O'REILLY

I

SINCE pick av them I'm sore de-
nied
'Twixt play or work, I say,
Though it be Christmas, I decide
I'll work whilst others play:
I'll whistle, too, wid Christmas pride
To airn me extry pay.—
It's like the job's more glorified
That's done a-holiday!

Dan, dip a coal in dad's pipe-bowl;
Kate, pass me dinner-can:
Och! Mary woman, save yer sowl,
Ye've kissed a workin'-man—

Ye have, this Christmas mornin',
Ye've kissed a workin'-man!

II

Whisht, Kate an' Dan!—ten thousan'
    grates
There's yon where ne'er a charm
Av childer-faces sanctuates
    The city-homes from harm:
It's cold out there the weather waits
    An' bitter whirls the storm,
But, faith! these arms av little Kate's
    'Ll kape her fayther warm!

Ay, Danny, tight me belt a mite,—
    Kate, aisy wid the can!—
Sure, I'd be comin' home to-night
    A hungry workin'-man—
D'ye moind, this Christmas avenin'—
    A howlin'-hungry man!

III

It's sorry for the boss I be,
    Wid new conthracts to sign
An' hire a sub to oversee
    Whilst he lave off an' dine:
It's sorry for the Company
    That owns the Aarie Line—
What vasht raasponshibility
    They have, compared wid mine!

There, Katy! git me t'other mitt,
    An' fetch me yon from Dan—
(Wid aich one's "Christmas" hid in
    it!)
Lave go me dinner-can!—
Ye'll have me docked this mornin'—
This blessed Christmas mornin',—
    A dishgraced workin'-man!

TO SANTA CLAUS

MOST tangible of all the gods that
    be,
O Santa Claus—our own since In-
    fancy!—
As first we scampered to thee—now,
    as then,
Take us as children to thy heart again.

Be wholly good to us, just as of old;
As a pleased father, let thine arms in-
    fold
Us, homed within the haven of thy
    love,
And all the cheer and wholesomeness
    thereof.

Thou lone reality, when O so long
Life's unrealities have wrought us
    wrong:
Ambition hath allured us,—fame like-
    wise,
And all that promised honor in men's
    eyes.

Throughout the world's evasions, wiles,
    and shifts,
Thou only bidest stable as thy gifts:—
A grateful king re-ruleth from thy lap,
Crowned with a little tinseled soldier-
    cap:

A mighty general—a nation's pride—
Thou givest again a rocking-horse to
    ride,
And wildly glad he groweth as the
    grim
Old jurist with the drum thou givest
    him:

The sculptor's chisel, at thy mirth's
    command,
Is as a whistle in his boyish hand;
The painter's model fadeth utterly,
And there thou standest,—and he
    painteth thee:—

Most like a winter pippin, sound and
    fine
And tingling-red that ripe old face of
    thine,
Set in thy frosty beard of cheek and
    chin
As midst the snows the thaws of spring
    set in.

Ho! Santa Claus—our own since In-
    fancy—
Most tangible of all the gods that be!—
As first we scampered to thee—now, as
    then,
Take us as children to thy heart again.

815

CHRISTMAS ALONG THE WIRES

Scene—Hoosier railway station, Wash-
out Glen

Night—Interior of Telegraph Office—
Single operator's table in some dis-
order—lunch-basket, litter of books
and sheet-music—a flute and a guitar
—Rather good-looking young man,
evidently in charge, talking to com-
mercial traveler.

J UNCTION-Station—Pilot Knob—
    Say "the operator there
Is a *girl*—with auburn hair
And blue eyes, and purty, too,

As they make 'em!"—That'll do!—
They *all* know her 'long the Line—
Railroad men, from President
Of the road to section-hand!—
And she knows *us*—the whole mob
Of us *lightnin'-slingers*—Shoo!—
Brownie's got us all down fine!
Though she's *business,* understand,
Brownie she just beats the band!
Brownie she's held up that job
Five or six years anyhow—
Since her *father's* death, when all
The whole road decided now
Was no time for nothin' small,—
It was *Brownie's* job! Since ten
Years of age she'd been with *him*
In the office. Now, I guess,
She was sixteen, more or less—
Just a girl, but strong and trim,
And as independent, too,
And *reliable* clean through
As the old man when he died
Two mile' up the track beside
His red-light, one icy night
When the line broke down—and yet
He got there in time, you bet,
To shut off a wreck all right!
Yes, *some* life here, and romance—
Pilot Knob, though, and Roachdale,
And this little eight-by-ten
Dinky town of Washout Glen
Have to pool inhabitants
Even for enough young men
To fill out a country dance,—
All chip in on some joint-date,
And whack up and pony down
And *combine* and celebrate,—
Say, on Decoration Day—
Fourth o' July—Easter, or
Circus-Day, or *Christmas,* say—
All *three* towns, and right-o'-way
Fer two extrys,—one from here—
One down from the Knob. Well, then

Roachdale is herself again!
Like *last* Christmas, when all three
Towns collogued, and far and near
Billed things for a Christmas-Tree
At old Roachdale. Now mark here:—
I had leave, last Holidays,
And was goin' home, you see,
Two weeks—and the Company
Sent a man to fill my place—
An old *chum* of mine, in fact,
I'd been coaxin' to arrange
Just to have his dressin'-case
And his latest music packed
And come on here for a change.
He'd been here to visit me
Once before—in *summer then*,—
Come to stay "just two or three
Days," he said—and he stayed *ten*.
When he left here *then*—Well, he
Was clean gone on Brownie—wild
And plum silly as a child!
Name—MacClintock. Most young men
Stood 'way back when Mac was round.
Fact is, he was *fine,* you know—
Silver-tenor voice that went
Up among the stars, and sent
The girls back to higher-tone'
Dreams than they had ever known!
A good-looker—stylish—slim—
And wore clothes that no man
    downed—
Yes, and smoked a good cigar
And smelt right; and used to blow
A smooth flute—And a *guitar*
No man heard till he heard *him!*—
Say, some midnight serenade—
Oomh! how drippin'-sweet he played!
Boys, though, wasn't stuck on Mac
So blame' much,—especially
Roachdale operator.—He
Kind o' had the inside-track
On *all* of us, as to who
Got most talk from Brownie, when

She had nothin' else to do
But to buzz us now and then
Up and down the wires, you know;
And we'd jolly back again
'Bout some dance—and "Would she
    go
With *us* or her *Roachdale* beau?"
(Boys all called him "Roachy"—
    see?)—
Wire her, "Was she 'Happy now'?"
And "How's 'Roachy,' anyhow?"
Or, "Say, Brownie, who's the jay
You was stringin' yesterday?"
And I've sat here when this key
Shot me like a battery,
Just 'cause Brownie wired to say
That "That box o' fruit, or flowers,
That 'I'd' sent her came O. K.,—
To beguile the weary hours
Till we met again!"—Then break
Short off—for the Roachdale cuss
Callin' her, and on to us.
'Course *he'd* sent 'em—no mistake!
Lord, she kept that man awake!
Yet he kept *her* fooled: His cheek
And pure goody-goody gall
Hid from *her*—if not from all—
A quite vivid "*yellow streak.*"—
Awful' jealous, don't you see?—
Felt he had a *right* to be,
Maybe, bein' *engaged.*—And they
Were engaged — that's straight. —
    "G A!" *—
Well: MacClintock when *he* come
Down from York to take this job,
And stopped off at Pilot Knob
For "instructions," there was some
Indications of unrest
At *Roachdale* right from the start,—
"Roachy" wasn't *awful'* smart,
Maybe, but he done his best—

_____
* Telegraphers' abbreviation for "Go ahead."

With such brains as he possessed.—
Anyway he made *one* play
That was brilliant—of its kind—
And *maintained* it.—From the day
That MacClintock took my key
And I left on Number Three,
"Roachy" opened up on Mac
And just *loved* him!—purred and
    whined
'Cross the wires how tickled he
Was to hear that *Mac* was back,
And how glad the *girls* would be
And the young-folks everywhere,
As he'd reason to believe,—
And how, even *then,* they were
"Shapin' things at old Roachdale
For a blow-out, Christmas-eve,
That would turn all others pale!—
First a *Christmas-Tree,* at old
Armory Hall, and then the floor
Cleared, and—"
        "Come in out the cold!"
Breaks MacClintock — "Don't I
    know?—
Dancin', say, from ten till four—
Maybe *daylight* 'fore we go!—
With Ben Custer's Band to pour
Music out in swirlin' rills
And back-tides o' waltz-quadrilles
Level with the window-sills!—
Roachy, you're a *bird!*—But, say,—
How am I to get away
From the office here?"
            Well, then
"Roachy" wires him back again:—
"That's O. K.,—I call a *man*
Up from *Dunkirk;* got it all
Fixed.—So Christmas-eve, you can
Collar the seven-thirty train
For Roachdale—the same that *he*
Comes on.—Leave your office-key
In the door: he'll do the rest."
Then "old Roachy" rattled through

A long list of who'd be there,—
Boys and girls that Mac knew best—
One name, though, that had no bare
Little mention anywhere!
Then he shut off, as he said,
For his supper. . . . About ten
Minutes *Mac* was *called again*—
With a click that flushed him red
As the signal-flag—and then
Came like music in the air—
"Yes, and *Brownie* will be there!"

————

Folks tell *me,* that Christmas-Tree,
Dance and whole blame' jamboree,
Looked like it was goin' to be
A blood-curdlin' tragedy.
People 'long the *roads,* you know—
Well, they've had experience
With all sorts of *accidents,*
And they've learnt *some* things,—and
    so
When an accident or wreck
Happens, they know *some man's*
    "break"
Is responsible, and hence—
Well—they want to *break* his *neck!*
So it happened, Christmas-eve,
At *Roachdale,*—MacClintock there
Cocked back in the barber-chair
At eight-forty, and no train
Down yet from the Knob, and it
Due at eight-ten sharp. The strain
Was a-showin' quite a bit
On the general crowd; and when
Purty soon the rumor spread—
Wreck had probably occurred—
Some one said somebody said
That he'd heard somebody say,
"Operator" at the *Glen*
Was to blame for the delay—
Fact is, he had run away

From his office—Even then
Was in *Roachdale*—there to be
Present at the Christmas-Tree
And the 'shindig' afterward,
Wreck or *no* wreck!" . . . *Mac* sat up,
Whiter than the shavin'-cup. . . .
Back of *his* face in the glass
He staréd into he could see
A big crowd there—and, alas!
Not in all that threatening throng
One friend's face of sympathy—
One friend knowin' right from wrong!
He got on his feet—erect—
Nervy;—faced the crowd, and then
Said: "*I* am MacClintock from
The Glen-office, and I've come
To your Christmas festival
By request of one that all
Of you honor, gentlemen,—
Your most trusted citizen—
Your own operator here
At the station-office—where
He'll acquit *me* of neglect,
And will make it plain and clear
Who the sub. is he sent there
To my office at the Glen—
Or, if *not* one there,—who then
Is indeed the criminal? . . .
I am going now to call
On him.—Join me, gentlemen—
I insist you come with me."
Well, a sense of some respect
Caught 'em,—and they followed, all,
Silently, though sullenly.

Fortunately, half a square
Brought 'em to the station and
The crowd there that packed the small
Waiting-room on every hand,
With a kind o' general stand
Round the half-door window through
Which "old Roachy," in full view,

Sat there, smilin' in a sick
Sort o' way, yet gloryin', too,
In the work he had to do.
Mac worked closer, breathin' quick
At the muttered talk of some
Of the toughest of the crowd;
Till, above the growl and hum
Of the ominous voices, he
Heard the click of "Roachy's" key,—
And his heart beat 'most out 'loud
As he heard him wirin':—"Yes,
Trouble down at *Glen,* I guess.
Glen's fool-operator *here*—
What's-his-name? — MacClintock. —
  Fear
Mob will hang him.—Mob knows he
Left his office.—And no doubt
Wreck there on account of it.
People worked-up here—and shout
Now and then to 'Take him out!'—
'Hang him!'—and so forth." . . . Mac
  lit
Through the half-door window at
"Roachy's" table like a cat:—
He was *white,* but *"Roachy's"* face
Made a brunette out o' *his!* . . .
Mac had pinned him in his chair
Helpless—and a message there
Clickin' back from Pilot Knob.—
"Tell these people, word-for-word,"
Mac says, "what this message is!—
"Tell 'em.—Hear me?" "Roachy"
  heard
And obeyed:—" 'We sized your job
On MacClintock.—*Knob* here sent
A sub. there.—And all O. K.
At Glen-office.—Tie-up *here*—
One hour's wait—all fault of *mine.*
"Hang MacClintock," did you say?
"Hang MacClintock?"—Certainly,—
Hang him on the Christmas-Tree,
With a label on for *me,*—
I'll be there on Number Nine.'"

816

TO THE BOY WITH A COUNTRY

DAN WALLINGFORD

DAN WALLINGFORD, my jo
Dan!—
Though but a child in years,
Your patriot spirit thrills the land
And wakens it to cheers,—
You lift the flag—you roll the drums—
We hear the bugle blow,—
Till all our hearts are one with
yours,
Dan Wallingford, my jo!

817

AT CROWN HILL

LEAVE him here in the fresh green-
ing grasses and trees
And the symbols of love, and the
solace of these—
The saintly white lilies and blossoms
he keeps
In endless caress as he breathlessly
sleeps.
The tears of our eyes wrong the scene
of his rest,
For the sky's at its clearest—the sun's
at its best—
The earth at its greenest—its wild bud-
and-bloom
At its sweetest—and sweetest its
honey'd perfume.
Home! home!—Leave him here in
his lordly estate,
And with never a tear as we turn
from the gate!

Turn back to the home that will know
him no more,—
The vines at the window—the sun
through the door.—
Nor sound of his voice, nor the light
of his face! . . .
But the birds will sing on, and the
rose, in his place,
Will tenderly smile till we daringly
feign
He is home with us still, though the
tremulous rain
Of our tears reappear, and again all is
bloom,
And all prayerless we sob in the long-
darkened room.
Heaven portions it thus—the old
mystery dim,—
It is midnight to us—it is morning
to him.

818

SNOW IN THE AIR

SNOW is in the air—
Chill in blood and vein,—
Winter everywhere
Save in heart and brain!
Ho! the happy year will be
Mimic as we've found it,—
Head of it—and you, and me—
With the holly round it!

Frost and sleet, alack!—
Wind as bleak as wrath
Whips our faces back
As we foot the path;—
But the year—from there to here—
Copy as we've found it,—
Heart up—like the head, my dear,
With the holly round it!

819

THE NAME OF OLD GLORY

1898

I

OLD Glory! say, who,
　By the ships and the crew,
And the long, blended ranks of the
　gray and the blue,—
Who gave you, Old Glory, the name
　that you bear
With such pride everywhere
As you cast yourself free to the rap-
　turous air
And leap out full-length, as we're
　wanting you to?—
Who gave you that name, with the
　ring of the same,
And the honor and fame so becoming
　to you?—
Your stripes stroked in ripples of white
　and of red,
With your stars at their glittering best
　overhead—
By day or by night
Their delightfulest light
Laughing down from their little
　square heaven of blue!—
Who gave you the name of Old Glory?
　—say, who—
　　Who gave you the name of Old
　　Glory?

The old banner lifted, and faltering then
In vague lisps and whispers fell silent
　again.

II

Old Glory,—speak out!—we are ask-
　ing about
How you happened to "favor" a name,
　so to say,

That sounds so familiar and careless
　and gay
As we cheer it and shout in our wild
　breezy way—
We—the *crowd,* every man of us, call-
　ing you that—
We—Tom, Dick, and Harry—each
　swinging his hat
And hurrahing "Old Glory!" like you
　were our kin,
When—*Lord!*—we all know we're as
　common as sin!
And yet it just seems like you *humor*
　us all
And waft us your thanks, as we hail
　you and fall
Into line, with you over us, waving
　us on
Where our glorified, sanctified betters
　have gone.—
And this is the reason we're wanting
　to know—
(And we're wanting it *so!*—
Where our own fathers went we are
　willing to go.)—
Who gave you the name of Old Glory
　—Oho!—
　　Who gave you the name of Old
　　Glory?

The old flag unfurled with a billowy
　thrill
For an instant, then wistfully sighed
　and was still.

III

Old Glory: the story we're wanting to
　hear
Is what the plain facts of your chris-
　tening were,—
For your name—just to hear it,

Repeat it, and cheer it, 's a tang to
    the spirit
As salt as a tear;—
And seeing you fly, and the boys
    marching by,
There's a shout in the throat and a
    blur in the eye
And an aching to live for you always
    —or die,
If, dying, we still keep you waving
    on high.
And so, by our love
For you, floating above,
And the scars of all wars and the sor-
    rows thereof,
Who gave you the name of Old Glory,
    and why
    Are we thrilled at the name of
      Old Glory?

Then the old banner leaped, like a
    sail in the blast,
And fluttered an audible answer at
    last.—

IV

And it spake, with a shake of the
    voice, and it said:—
By the driven snow-white and the liv-
    ing blood-red
Of my bars, and their heaven of stars
    overhead—
By the symbol conjoined of them all,
    skyward cast,
As I float from the steeple, or flap at
    the mast,
Or droop o'er the sod where the long
    grasses nod,—
My name is as old as the glory of God.
    . . . So I came by the name of
      Old Glory.

820

ONE WITH A SONG

FRANK L. STANTON

HE sings: and his song is heard,
    Pure as a joyous prayer,
Because he sings of the simple things—
    The fields, and the open air,
The orchard-bough, and the mock-
    ing-bird,
    And the blossoms everywhere.

He sings of a wealth we hold
    In common ownership—
The wildwood nook, and the laugh of
    the brook,
And the dewdrop's drip and drip,
The love of the lily's heart of gold,
    And the kiss of the rose's lip.

The universal heart
    Leans listening to his lay
That glints and gleams with the glim-
    mering dreams
    Of children at their play—
A lay as rich with unconscious art
    As the first song-bird's of May.

Ours every rapturous tone
    Of every song of glee,
Because his voice makes native choice
    Of Nature's harmony—
So that his singing seems our own,
    And ours his ecstasy.

Steadfastly, bravely glad
    Above all earthly stress,
He lifts his line to heights divine,
    And, singing, ever says,—

This is a better world than bad—
God's love is limitless.

He sings: and his song is heard,
  Pure as a joyous prayer,
Because he sings of the simple things—
  The fields, and the open air,
The orchard-bough, and the mock-
      ing-bird,
  And the blossoms everywhere.

821

INDIANA

OUR Land—our Home!—the com-
    mon home indeed
  Of soil-born children and adopted
      ones—
  The stately daughters and the stal-
      wart sons
Of Industry:—All greeting and god-
    speed!
O home to proudly live for, and, if
    need
  Be, proudly die for, with the roar
      of guns
  Blent with our latest prayer.—So
      died men once. . . .
Lo, Peace! . . . As we look on the
    land THEY freed—
Its harvest all in ocean-overflow
  Poured round autumnal coasts in
      billowy gold—
  Its corn and wine and balmèd
      fruits and flow'rs,—
We know the exaltation that they
    know
  Who now, steadfast inheritors, be-
      hold
    The Land Elysian, marveling
    "This is ours!"

822

CHRISTMAS AFTERTHOUGHT

AFTER a thoughtful, almost pain-
    ful pause,
Bub sighed, "I'm sorry fer old *Santy
    Claus:*—
They *wuz* no Santy Claus, ner *couldn't*
    be,
When *he* wuz ist a little boy like me!"

823

THE CHRISTMAS LONG AGO

COME, sing a hale Heigh-ho
  For the Christmas long ago!—
When the old log-cabin homed us
    From the night of blinding snow,
  Where the rarest joy held reign,
  And the chimney roared amain,
With the firelight like a beacon
    Through the frosty window-pane.

Ah! the revel and the din
From without and from within,
The blend of distant sleigh-bells
  With the plinking violin;
  The muffled shrieks and cries—
  Then the glowing cheeks and eyes—
The driving storm of greetings,
  Gusts of kisses and surprise.

824

EXCEEDING ALL

LONG life's a lovely thing to know,
  With lovely health and wealth,
      forsooth,
And lovely name and fame—But O
    The loveliness of Youth!

825

CLAUDE MATTHEWS

STEADFASTLY from his child-
hood's earliest hour—
From simplest country life to state and
power—
His worth has known advancement,
each new height
A newer glory in his fellow's sight.

So yet his happy fate—though mute
the breath
Of thronging multitudes and thun-
drous cheers,—
Faith sees him raised still higher,
through our tears,
By this divine promotion of his death.

826

THE SERMON OF THE ROSE

WILFUL we are, in our infirmity
Of childish questioning and
discontent.
Whate'er befalls us is divinely
meant—
Thou Truth the clearer for thy mys-
tery!
Make us to meet what is or is to be
With fervid welcome, knowing it is
sent
To serve us in some way full ex-
cellent,
Though we discern it all belatedly.
The rose buds, and the rose blooms,
and the rose
Bows in the dews, and in its fulness,
lo,
Is in the lover's hand,—then on
the breast

Of her he loves,—and there dies.—
And who knows
What fate of all a rose may under-
go
Is fairest, dearest, sweetest, love-
liest?

Nay, we are children: we will not
mature.
A blessed gift must seem a theft;
and tears
Must storm our eyes when but a joy
appears
In drear disguise of sorrow; and how
poor
We seem when we are richest,—most
secure
Against all poverty the lifelong years
We yet must waste in childish
doubts and fears
That, in despite of reason, still endure!
Alas! the sermon of the rose we will
Not wisely ponder; nor the sobs of
grief
Lulled into sighs of rapture, nor
the cry
Of fierce defiance that again is still,
Be patient—patient with our frail
belief,
And stay it yet a little ere we die.

O opulent life of ours, though dis-
possessed
Of treasure after treasure! Youth
most fair
Went first, but left its priceless coil
of hair—
Moaned over, sleepless nights, kissed
and caressed
Through drip and blur of tears the
tenderest.
And next went Love—the ripe rose
glowing there,

Her very sister! . . . *It* is here, but
     where
Is *she,* of all the world the first and
     best?
And yet how sweet the sweet earth
     after rain—
  How sweet the sunlight on the gar-
     den-wall
    Across the roses—and how sweetly
     flows
The limpid yodel of the brook again!
  And yet—and yet how sweeter, after
     all,
    The smoldering sweetness of a
     dead red rose!

827

THE ONWARD TRAIL

MYRON W. REED, DENVER, JANUARY
30, 1899

JUST as of old,—with fearless foot
  And placid face and resolute,
He takes the faint, mysterious trail
That leads beyond our earthly hail.

We would cry, as in last farewell,
But that his hand waves, and a spell
Is laid upon our tongues: and thus
He takes unworded leave of us.

And it is fitting:—As he fared
Here with us, so is he prepared
For any fortuning the night
May hold for him beyond our sight.

The moon and stars they still attend
His wandering footsteps to the end,—
He did not question, nor will we,
Their guidance and security.

So, never parting word nor cry:—
We feel, with him, that by and by
Our onward trails will meet and then
Merge and be ever one again.

828

TO LESLEY

BURNS sang of bonny Lesley
  As she gaed o'er the border,—
Gaed like vain Alexander,
To spread her conquests farther.

I sing another Lesley,
Wee girlie, more alluring,
Who stays at home, the wise one,
Her conquests there securing.

A queen, too, is my Lesley,
And gracious, though blood-royal,
My heart her throne, her kingdom,
And I a subject loyal.

Long shall you reign, my Lesley,
My pet, my darling dearie,
For love, oh, little sweetheart,
Grows never old or weary.

829

THE NATURALIST

OLIVER DAVIE

IN gentlest worship has he bowed
  To Nature. Rescued from the
     crowd
And din of town and thoroughfare,
He turns him from all worldly care
Unto the sacred fastness of

The forests, and the peace and love
That breathes there prayer-like in the
  breeze
And coo of doves in dreamful trees—
Their tops in laps of sunshine laid,
Their lower boughs all slaked with
  shade.

With head uncovered has he stood,
Hearing the Spirit of the Wood—
Hearing aright the Master speak
In trill of bird, and warbling creek;
In lisp of reeds, or rainy sigh
Of grasses as the loon darts by—
Hearing aright the storm and lull,
And all earth's voices wonderful,—
Even this hail an unknown friend
Lifts will he hear and comprehend.

830

HER WAITING FACE

IN some strange place
  Of long-lost lands he finds her
    waiting face—
Comes marveling upon it, unaware,
Set moonwise in the midnight of her
  hair.

831

A SONG OF THE ROAD

O I will walk with you, my lad,
    whichever way you fare,
You'll have me, too, the side o' you,
  with heart as light as air;
No care for where the road you take's
  a-leadin'—anywhere,—

It can but be a joyful ja'nt the whilst
  you journey there.
The road you take's the path o' love,
  an' that's the bridth o' two—
And I will walk with you, my lad—O
  I will walk with you.

    Ho! I will walk with you, my
      lad,
      Be weather black or blue
    Or roadsides frost or dew, my
      lad—
      O I will walk with you.

Ay, glad, my lad, I'll walk with you,
  whatever winds may blow,
Or summer blossoms stay our steps,
  or blinding drifts of snow;
The way that you set face and foot's
  the way that I will go,
And brave I'll be, abreast o' you, the
  Saints and Angels know!
With loyal hand in loyal hand, and
  one heart made o' two,
Through summer's gold, or winter's
  cold, it's I will walk with you.

    Sure, I will walk with you, my
      lad,
      As love ordains me to,—
    To Heaven's door, and through,
      my lad,
      O I will walk with you.

832

THE ENDURING

A MISTY memory—faint, far away
  And vague and dim as child-
    hood's long lost day—
Forever haunts and holds me with a
  spell

Of awe and wonder indefinable:—
A grimy old engraving tacked upon
A shoe-shop wall.—An ancient temple,
    drawn
Of crumbling granite, sagging portico,
And gray, forbidding gateway, grim
    as woe;
And o'er the portal, cut in antique
    line,
The words—cut likewise in this brain
    of mine—
    "Wouldst have a friend?—Wouldst
        know what friend is best?
    Have GOD thy friend: He passeth
        all the rest."

Again the old shoemaker pounds and
    pounds
Resentfully, as the loud laugh resounds
And the coarse jest is bandied round
    the throng
That smokes about the smoldering
    stove; and long,
Tempestuous disputes arise, and then—
Even as all like discords—die again;
The while a barefoot boy more gravely
    heeds
The quaint old picture, and tiptoeing
    reads
There in the rainy gloom the legend
    o'er
The lowering portal of the old church
    door—
    "Wouldst have a friend?—Wouldst
        know what friend is best?
    Have GOD thy friend: He passeth
        all the rest."

So older—older—older, year by year,
The boy has grown, that now, an old
    man here,
He seems a part of Allegory, where
He stands before Life as the old print
    ·   there—

Still awed, and marveling what light
    must be
Hid by the door that bars Futurity:—
Though, ever clearer than with eyes
    of youth,
He reads with his *old* eyes—and tears
    forsooth—
    "Wouldst have a friend?—Wouldst
        know what friend is best?
    Have GOD thy friend: He passeth
        all the rest."

833

A HUMBLE SINGER

A MODEST singer, with meek soul
    and heart,
Sat, yearning that his art
Might but inspire and suffer him to
    sing
Even the simplest thing.

And as he sang thus humbly, came a
    Voice:—
"All mankind shall rejoice,
Hearing thy pure and simple melody
Sing on immortally."

834

THE NOBLEST SERVICE

DR. WYCKLIFFE SMITH, LATE SURGEON
161ST REGIMENT INDIANA VOLUN-
TEERS, DELPHI, DECEMBER 29,
1899

I F all his mourning friends unsel-
    fishly
Might speak, high over grief, in one
    accord,

What voice of joy were lifted to the
Lord
For having lent our need such min-
istry
As this man's life has ever proved to
be!
Yea, even through battle-crash of
gun and sword
His steadfast step still found the
pathway toward
The noblest service paid Humanity
O ye to whose rich firesides he has
brought
A richer light! O watcher at the
door
Of the lone cabin! O kindred!
Comrades!—all!
Since universal good he dreamed and
wrought,
Be brave, to pleasure him, as, on
before,
He leads us, answering Glory's
highest call.

835

OLD MAN WHISKERY-WHEE-
KUM-WHEEZE

OLD Man Whiskery-Whee-Kum-
Wheeze
Lives 'way up in the leaves o' trees.
An' wunst I slipped up-stairs to play
In Aunty's room, while she 'uz away;
An' I clumbed up in her cushion-
chair
An' ist peeked out o' the winder
there;
An' there I saw—wite out in the
trees—
Old Man Whiskery - Whee - Kum -
Wheeze!

An' Old Man Whiskery-Whee-Kum-
Wheeze
Would bow an' bow, with the leaves
in the breeze,
An' waggle his whiskers an' raggledy
hair,
An' bow to me in the winder there!
An' I'd peek out, an' he'd peek in
An' waggle his whiskers an' bow ag'in,
Ist like the leaves 'u'd wave in the
breeze—
Old Man Whiskery - Whee - Kum -
Wheeze!

An' Old Man Whiskery-Whee-Kum-
Wheeze,
Seem-like, says to me: "See my bees
A-bringin' my dinner? An' see my
cup
O' locus'-blossoms they've plum filled
up?"
An' "Um-yum, honey!" wuz last he
said,
An' waggled his whiskers an' bowed
his head;
An' I yells, "Gimme some, won't you,
please,
Old Man Whiskery - Whee - Kum -
Wheeze?"

836

LITTLE-GIRL-TWO-LITTLE-
GIRLS

I'M twins, I guess, 'cause my Ma say
I'm two little girls. An' one o' me
Is *Good* little girl; an' th' other 'n'
she
Is *Bad little girl as she can be!*
An' Ma say so, 'most ever' day.

An' she's the *funniest* Ma! 'Cause
      when
   My Doll won't mind, and I ist
      cry,
   W'y, nen my Ma she sob an' sigh,
   An' say, "Dear *Good* little girl,
      good-by!—
Bad little girl's comed here again!"

Last time 'at Ma act' thataway,
   I cried all to myse'f a while
Out on the steps, an' nen I smile,
An' git my Doll all fix' in style,
An' go in where Ma's at, an' say:
   Morning to you, Mommy dear!
   Where's that Bad little girl wuz
      here?
   Bad little girl's goned clean away,
   An' Good little girl's comed back
      to stay."

837

THE PENALTY OF GENIUS

WHEN little 'Pollus Morton he's
      A-go' to speak a piece, w'y,
         nen
The Teacher smiles an' says 'at she's
   Most proud, of all her little men
An' women in her school—'cause 'Poll
He allus speaks the best of all.

An' nen she'll pat him on the cheek,
   An' hold her finger up at you
Before he speak'; an' *when* he speak'
   It's ist some piece *she* learn' him to!
'Cause he's her favor-ite. . . . An' she
Ain't pop'lar as she *ust* to be.

When 'Pollus Morton speaks, w'y, nen
   Ist all the other childern knows
They're smart as him an' smart-
      again!—
   Ef they *can't* speak an' got fine
      clo'es,
   Their Parunts loves 'em more'n 'Poll-
Us Morton, Teacher, speech, an' all!

838

A PARENT REPRIMANDED

SOMETIMES I think 'at Parunts
      does
Things ist about as bad as *us*—
   Wite 'fore our vurry eyes, at that!
Fer one time Pa he scold' my Ma
   'Cause he can't find his hat;
An' she ist *cried*, she did! An' I
Says, "Ef you scold my Ma
Ever again an' make her cry,
   W'y, you shan't *be* my Pa!"
An' nen he laugh' an' find his hat
Ist wite where Ma she said it's at!

839

IN FERVENT PRAISE OF
PICNICS

PICNICS is fun 'at's purty hard to
      beat.
I purt' nigh ruther go to them than
      eat.—
I purt' nigh ruther go to them than
      go
With our Char*lot*ty to the Trick-Dog
      Show!

840

THE HOME-VOYAGE

GENERAL HENRY W. LAWTON—FELL AT
SAN MATEO, DECEMBER 19, 1899.
IN STATE, INDIANAPOLIS, FEB-
RUARY 6, 1900

BEAR with us, O Great Captain, if
    our pride
Show equal measure with our grief's
    excess
In greeting you in this your help-
    lessness
To countermand our vanity or hide
Your stern displeasure that we thus
    had tried
To praise you, knowing praise was
    your distress:
But this home-coming swells our
    hearts no less—
Because for love of home you proudly
    died.
Lo! then, the cable, fathoms 'neath the
    keel
That shapes your course, is eloquent
    of you;
The old flag, too, at half-mast
    overhead—
We doubt not that its gale-kissed rip-
    ples feel
A prouder sense of red and white
    and blue,—
The stars—Ah, God, were *they*
    interpreted!

In strange lands were your latest hon-
    ors won—
In strange wilds, with strange dan-
    gers all beset;
With rain, like tears, the face of day
    was wet,

As rang the ambushed foeman's fate-
    ful gun:
And as you felt your final duty done,
    We feel *that* glory thrills your spirit
    yet,—
When at the front, in swiftest death,
    you met
The patriot's doom and best reward
    in one.
And so the tumult of that island war,
    At last, for you, is stilled forever-
    more—
    Its scenes of blood blend white as
        ocean foam
On your rapt vision as you sight afar
    The sails of peace, and from that
        alien shore
    The proud ship bears you on your
        voyage home.

Or rough or smooth the wave, or
    lowering day
    Or starlit sky—you hold, by native
        right,
    Your high tranquillity—the silent
        might
Of the true hero—so you led the
    way
To victory through stormiest battle-
    fray,
    Because your followers, high above
        the fight,
    Heard your soul's lightest whisper
        bid them smite
For God and man and space to kneel
    and pray.
And thus you cross the seas unto your
    own
    Beloved land, convoyed with honors
        meet,
    Saluted as your home's first heri-
        tage—

Nor salutation from your State alone,
But *all* the States, gathered in
    mighty fleet,
Dip colors as you move to anchor-
    age.

841

TO THE QUIET OBSERVER

ERASMUS WILSON, AFTER HIS LONG
                SILENCE

DEAR old friend of us all in need
    Who know the worth of a friend
        indeed,
How rejoiced are we all to learn
    Of your glad return.

We who have missed your voice so
        long—
Even as March might miss the song
    Of the sugar-bird in the maples
        when
            They're tapped again.

Even as the memory of these
Blended sweets,—the sap of the trees
    And the song of the birds, and the
        old camp too,
            We think of you.

Hail to you, then, with welcomes deep
As grateful hearts may laugh or
        weep!—
    You give us not only the bird that
        sings,
            But all good things.

842

PROEM TO "HOME-FOLKS"

YOU Home-Folks: — Aid your
    grateful guest—
Bear with his pondering, wandering
        ways:
When idlest he is busiest,
    Being a dreamer of the days.

Humor his silent, absent moods—
    His restless quests along the shores
Of the old creek, wound through the
        woods,
    The haws, papaws, and sycamores:

The side-path home—the back-way
        past
    The old pump and the dipper there;
The afternoon of dreamy June—
    The old porch, and the rocking-
        chair.

Yea, bear with him a little space—
    His heart must smolder on a while
Ere yet it flames out in his face
    A wholly tearless smile.

843

OUR BOYHOOD HAUNTS

HO! I'm going back where
    We were youngsters.—Meet me
        there,
Dear old barefoot chum, and we
Will be as we used to be,—
Lawless rangers up and down
The old creek beyond the town—
Little sunburnt gods at play,
Just as in that far-away:—

Water nymphs, all unafraid,
Shall smile at us from the brink
Of the old mill-race and wade
Tow'rd us as we kneeling drink
At the spring our boyhood knew,
Pure and clear as morning-dew:
And, as we are rising there,
Doubly dow'r'd to hear and see,
We shall thus be made aware
Of an eery piping, heard
High above the happy bird
In the hazel: And then we,
Just across the creek, shall see
(Hah! the goaty rascal!) Pan
Hoof it o'er the sloping green,
Mad with his own melody,
Ay, and (bless the beasty man!)
Stamping from the grassy soil
Bruisèd scents of fleur-de-lis,
Boneset, mint, and pennyroyal.

844

UNCLE SIDNEY'S LOGIC

PA wunst he scold' an' says to me,—
"Don't *play* so much, but try
To *study* more, and nen you'll be
A great man, by an' by."
Nen Uncle Sidney says, "You let
Him *be* a boy an' play.—
The greatest man on earth, I bet,
'Ud trade with him to-day!"

845

HIS LOVE OF HOME

"AS love of native land," the old
man said,
"Er stars and stripes a-wavin' over-
head,

Er nearest kith-and-kin, er daily bread,
A Hoosier's love is fer the old home-
stead."

846

TO "UNCLE REMUS"

WE love your dear old face and
voice—
We're *all* Miss Sally's Little Boys,
Climbin' your knee,
In ecstasy,
Rejoicin' in your Creeturs' joys
And trickery.

The Lord who made the day and
night,
He made the Black man and the
White;
So, in like view,
We hold it true
That He hain't got no favor*ite*—
Onless it's you.

847

THE BALLADE OF THE
COMING RAIN

WHEN the morning swoons in its
highest heat,
And the sunshine dims, and no dark
shade
Streaks the dust of the dazzling street,
And the long straw splits in the
lemonade;
When the circus lags in a sad parade,
And the drum throbs dull as a pulse
of pain,
And the breezeless flags hang limp
and frayed—
O then is the time to look for rain.

When the man on the watering-cart
    bumps by,
Trilling the air of an old fife-tune,
With a dull, soiled smile, and one shut
    eye,
    Lost in a dream of the afternoon;
    When the awning sags like a lank
      balloon,
And a thick sweat stands on the win-
    dow-pane,
    And a five-cent fan is a priceless
      boon—
O then is the time to look for rain.

When the goldfish tank is a grimy
    gray,
    And the dummy stands at the cloth-
      ing-store
With a cap pulled on in a rakish way,
    And a rubber-coat with the 'hind
      before;
    When the man in the barber chair
      flops o'er
And the chin he wags has a telltale
    stain,
    And the bootblack lurks at the open
      door—
O then is the time to look for rain.

848

TO THE JUDGE

A VOICE FROM THE INTERIOR OF OLD
HOOP-POLE TOWNSHIP

FRIEND of my earliest youth,
    Can't you arrange to come down
And visit a fellow out here in the
    woods—
    Out of the dust of the town?
Can't you forget you're a Judge
    And put by your dolorous frown

And tan your wan face in the smile
    of a friend—
    Can't you arrange to come down?

Can't you forget for a while
    The arguments prosy and drear,—
To lean at full-length in indefinite rest
    In the lap of the greenery here?
Can't you kick over "the Bench,"
    And "husk" yourself out of your
      gown
To dangle your legs where the fishing
    is good—
    Can't you arrange to come down?

Bah! for your office of State!
    And bah! for its technical lore!
What does our President, high in his
    chair,
    But wish himself low as before!
Pick between peasant and king,—
    Poke your bald head through a
      crown
Or shadow it here with the laurels of
    Spring!—
    Can't you arrange to come down?

"Judge it" out *here*, if you will,—
    The birds are in session by dawn;
You can draw, not *complaints*, but a
    sketch of the hill
    And a breath that your betters have
      drawn;
You can open your heart, like a case,
    To a jury of kine, white and brown,
And their verdict of "Moo" will just
    satisfy you!—
    Can't you arrange to come down?

Can't you arrange it, old Pard?—
    Pigeonhole Blackstone and Kent!—
Here we have "Breitmann," and
    Ward,
    Twain, Burdette, Nye, and content!

Can't you forget you're a Judge
And put by your dolorous frown
And tan your wan face in the smile
    of a friend—
Can't you arrange to come down?

849

A WHOLLY UNSCHOLASTIC OPINION

PLAIN hoss-sense in poetry-writin'
    Would jes' knock sentiment
    a-kitin'!
Mostly poets is all star-gazin'
And moanin' and groanin' and para-
    phrasin'!

850

A SHORT'NIN' BREAD SONG —PIECED OUT

BEHINE de hen-house, on my
    `knees,
Thought I hearn a chickin sneeze—
Sneezed so hard wi' de whoopin'-
    cough
I thought he'd sneeze his blame' head
    off.

Chorus

*Fotch dat dough fum the kitchin-
    shed—
Rake dem coals out hot an' red—
Putt on de oven an' putt on de led,—
Mammy's gwineter cook some short'-
    nin' bread.*

O I' got a house in Baltimo'—
Street-kyars run right by my do'—
Street-kyars run right by my gate,
Hit's git up soon an' set up late.

(Chorus)

De raincrow hide in some ole tree
An' holler out, all hoarse, at me—
Sayes, "When I sing, de rain hit po'
So's you ain't 'bleedged to plow no
    mo'!"

(Chorus)

Ole man Toad, on High-low Hill,
He steal my dram an' drink his fill,—
Heels in the path, an' toes in the
    grass—
Hit ain't de fus' time an' shain't be
    de las'!

(Chorus)

When corn-plantin' done come roun',
Blackbird own de whole plowed-
    groun',—
Corn in de grain, as I've hearn said,
Dat's de blackbird's short'nin' bread.

(Chorus)

De sweetes' chune what evah I heard
Is de sairanade o' de mockin'-bird;
Whilse de mou'nfullest an' de least I
    love
Is de Sund'y-song o' de ole woods-dove.

(Chorus)

I nevah ain't know, outside o' school,
A smartah mare dan my ole mule,—
I holler "Wo," an' she go "gee,"
Des lak, de good Lord chast'nin' me.

(Chorus)

Hit's no houn'-pup I taken to raise
Hain't nevah jes'ly airn' my praise:
De mo' cawn-pone I feed dat pup,
De mo' he des won't fattnin up.

(Chorus)

I hangs a hoss-shoe ovah my head,
An' I keeps a' ole sieve under de bed,
So, quinchiquently, I sleep soun',
Wid no ole witches pester'n' roun'.

(Chorus)

I jine de chu'ch las' Chuesday night,
But when Sis' Jane ain't treat me right
I 'low her chu'ch ain' none o' mine,
So I 'nounce to all I done on-jine.

(Chorus)

851

THE UNHEARD

I

ONE in the musical throng
   Stood forth with his violin;
And warm was his welcome, and long
   The later applause and the din.—
He had uttered, with masterful skill,
   A melody hailed of men;
And his own blood leapt a-thrill,
   As they thundered again.

II

Another stood forth.—And a rose
   Bloomed in her hair—likewise
One at her tremulous throat—
   And a *rapture* bloomed in her eyes.

Tempests of cheers upon cheers,
   Praises to last a life long;
Roses in showers of tears—
   All for her song.

III

One sat apart and alone,
   Her lips clasped close and straight,
Uttering never a tone
   That the World might hear, elate—
Uttering never a low
   Murmurous verse nor a part
Of the veriest song—But O
   The song in her heart!

852

EQUITY—?

THE meanest man I ever saw
   Allus kep' inside o' the law;
And ten-times better fellers I've
      knowed
The blame' gran'-jury's sent over the
      road.

853

MOONSHINER'S SERENADE

THE night's blind-black, an' I 'low
   the stars's
All skeered at that-air dog's bow-
      wows!
I sensed the woods-road, clumb the
      bars,
An' arrove here, tromplin' over cows.
The mist hangs thick enough to cut,
   But there's her light a-glimmerin'
      through
The mornin'-glories, twisted shut—
   An' shorely there's her shadder too!

Ho! hit's good night,
My Beauty-Bright!
The moon cain't match your
can'le-light—
Your can'le-light with you cain't
shine,
Lau-ree! Lady-love! tiptoe-fine!

Oomh! how them roses soaks the
air!—
Thess drenched with mist an'
renched with dew!
They's a smell o' plums, too, 'round
somewhere—
An' I kin smell ripe apples, too.
Mix all them sweet things into one,—
Yer roses, fruit, an' flower an' vine,
Yit I'll say, "No, I don't choose none,
Ef I kin git that gal of mine!"

Ho! hit's good night,
My Beauty-Bright!
Primp a while, an' blow out the
light—
Putt me in your prayers, an' then
I'll be twic't as good-again!

854

IN A BOX

I SAW them last night in a box at
the play—
Old age and young youth side by
side.—
You might know by the glasses that
pointed that way
That they were—a groom and a
bride;
And you might have known, too, by
the face of the groom,
And the tilt of his head, and the
grim

Little smile of his lip, he was proud
to presume
That we men were all envying him.

Well, she was superb—an Elaine in
the face—
A Godiva in figure and mien,
With the arm and the wrist of a Parian
"Grace,"
And the high-lifted brow of a queen;
But I thought, in the splendor of
wealth and of pride,
And her beauty's ostensible prize,
I should hardly be glad if she sat by
my side
With that far-away look in her eyes.

855

THE EDGE OF THE WIND

YE stars in ye skies seem twinkling
In icicles of light,
And ye edge of ye wind cuts keener
Than ever ye sword-edge might;
Ye footsteps crunch in ye courtway,
And ye trough and ye cask go
"ping!"—
Ye china cracks in ye pantry,
And ye crickets cease to sing.

856

THE HIRED MAN'S FAITH IN
CHILDREN

I BELIEVE *all* childern's good,
Ef they're only *understood,—*
Even *bad* ones, 'pears to me,
'S jes' as good as they kin be!

857

THE LOVELY HUSBAND

Oh a love-ly hus-band he was known, He loved his wife and her a-lone; She reaped the harvest he had sown; She ate the meat; he picked the bone. With mixed admirers ev-'ry size, She smiled on each with

out disguise; This love-ly hus-band closed his eyes Lest he might take her

CHORUS.

by sur-prise. Trot! Run! Was-n't he a han-dy hub-by?

What Fun She could plot and plan! Not One

Oth-er such a dan-dy hub-by As this love-ly man!

II

He answered at her least command:
He fanned her, if she would be
  fanned;
He vanished when she willed it.—
  And
He always coughed behind his hand.
She held him in such high esteem
She let him dope her face with
  "Cream,"—
He'd chink the wrinkles seam-by-
  seam,
And call her "lovely as a dream!"

CHORUS

Hot
Bun!
  Wasn't he a lovey-dovey?
What
Fun
  She could plot and plan!
Not
One
  Other such a dovey-lovey
  As this love-ly man!

III

Her lightest wishes he foreknew
And fell up-stairs to cater to:
He never failed to back from view,
Nor mispronounced *Don't* (   ) *you*
  "Doan chu."
He only sought to fill such space
As her friends left;—he knew his
  place:—
He praised the form she could not
  lace.—
He praised her face before her
  face!

CHORUS

Shot
Gun!
  Wasn't he a lovely fellow?
What
Fun
  She could plot and plan!
Not
One
  Lonesome little streak of yellow
  In this love-ly man!

858

THREE SEVERAL BIRDS

The Romancer, the Poet, and the
Bookman

I

THE ROMANCER

THE Romancer's a nightingale,—
    The moon wanes dewy-dim
And all the stars grow faint and pale
  In listening to him.—
To him the plot least plausible
  Is of the most avail,—
He simply masters it because
  He takes it by the tale.

  O he's a nightingale,—
    His theme will never fail—
  It gains applause of all—because
    He takes it by the tale!

The Romancer's a nightingale:—
  His is the sweetest note—
The sweetest, woe-begonest wail
  Poured out of mortal throat:

So, glad or sad, he ever draws
Our best godspeed and hail;
He highest lifts his theme—because
He takes it by the tale.

O he's a nightingale,—
His theme will never fail—
It gains applause of all—because
He takes it by the tale!

II

THE POET

The bobolink he sings a single song,
Right along,—
And the robin sings another, all his
own—
One alone;
And the whippoorwill, and bluebird,
And the cockadoodle-doo-bird;—
But the mocking-bird he sings in every
tone
Ever known,
Or chirrup-note of merriment or moan.

So the Poet he's the mocking-bird of
men,—
He steals his songs and sings them
o'er again;
And yet beyond believing
They're the sweeter for his thiev-
ing.—
So we'll howl for Mister Mocking-
bird
And have him out again!

It's mighty fond we are of bobolinks,
And chewinks;
And we dote on dinky robins, quite a
few—
Yes, we do;
And we love the dove, and bluebird,
And the cockadoodle-doo-bird,—

But the mocking-bird's the bird for me
and you,
Through and through,
Since he sings as everybody wants him
to.

Ho! the Poet he's the mocking-bird
of men,—
He steals his songs and sings them
o'er again;
And yet beyond believing
They're the sweeter for his thiev-
ing.—
So we'll howl for Mister Mocking-
bird
And have him out again!

III

BOOKMAN'S CATCH

The Bookman he's a humming-bird—
His feasts are honey-fine,—
(With hi! hilloo!
And clover-dew
And roses lush and rare!)
His roses are the phrase and word
Of olden tomes divine;
(With hi! and ho!
And pinks ablow
And posies everywhere!)
The Bookman he's a humming-bird,—
He steals from song to song—
He scents the ripest-blooming rhyme,
And takes his heart along
And sacks all sweets of bursting
verse
And ballads, throng on throng.
(With ho! and hey!
And brook and brae,
And brinks of shade and shine!)

A humming-bird the Bookman is—
Though cumbrous, gray and grim,—
    (With hi! hilloo!
    And honey-dew
    And odors musty-rare!)
He bends him o'er that page of his
As o'er the rose's rim
    (With hi! and ho!
    And pinks aglow
    And roses everywhere!)
Ay, he's the featest humming-bird,—
    On airiest of wings
He poises pendent o'er the poem
    That blossoms as it sings—
God friend him as he dips his beak
    In such delicious things!
    (With ho! and hey!
    And world away
    And only dreams for him!)

859

THE BED

I

"THOU, of all God's gifts the best
    Blessed Bed!" I muse, and rest
Thinking how it havened me
In my dazed Infancy—
Ere mine eyes could bear the kind
Daylight through the window-blind,
Or my lips, in yearning quest,
Groping found the mother-breast,
Or mine utterance but owned
Minor sounds that sobbed and moaned.

II

Gracious Bed that nestled me
Even ere the mother's knee,—
Lulling me to slumber ere

Conscious of my treasure there—
Save the tiny palms that kept
Fondling, even as I slept,
That rare dual-wealth of mine,—
Softest pillow—sweetest wine!—
Gentlest cheer for mortal guest,
And of Love's fare lordliest.

III

By thy grace, O Bed, the first
Blooms of Boyhood-memories burst:—
Dreams of riches, swift withdrawn
As I, wakening, find the dawn
With its glad Spring-face once more
Glimmering on me as of yore:
Then the bluebird's limpid cry
Lulls me like a lullaby,
Till falls every failing sense
Back to sleep's sheer impotence.

IV

Or, a truant, home again,—
With the moonlight through the pane,
And the kiss that ends the prayer—
Then the footsteps down the stair;
And the close hush; and far click
Of the old clock; and the thick
Sweetness of the locust-bloom
Drugging all the enchanted room
Into darkness fathoms deep
As mine own pure childish sleep.

V

Gift and spell, O Bed, retell
Every lovely miracle—
Up from childhood's simplest dream
Unto manhood's pride supreme!—
Sacredness no words express,—
Lo, the young wife's fond caress
Of her first-born, while beside
Bends the husband, tearful-eyed,

Marveling of kiss and prayer
Which of these is holier there.

VI

Trace the vigils through the long,
Long nights, when the cricket's song
Stunned the sick man's fevered brain,
As he tossed and moaned in pain
Piteous—till thou, O Bed,
Smoothed the pillows for his head,
And thy soothest solace laid
Round him, and his fever weighed
Into slumber deep and cool,
And divinely merciful.

VII

Thus, O Bed, all gratefully
I would ever sing of thee—
Till the final sleep shall fall
O'er me, and the crickets call
In the grasses where at last
I am indolently cast
Like a play-worn boy at will.—
'Tis a Bed befriends me still—
Yea, and Bed, belike, the best,
Softest, safest, blessèdest.

860

HOME-FOLKS

HOME-FOLKS! — Well, that-air
name, to me,
Sounds jis the same as *poetry*—
That is, ef poetry is jis
As sweet as I've hearn tell it is!

Home-Folks—they're jis the same as
kin—
All brung up, same as *we* have bin,

Without no over powerin' sense
Of their oncommon consequence!

They've bin to school, but not to git
The habit fastened on 'em yit
So as to ever interfere
With *other* work 'at's waitin' here:

Home-Folks has crops to plant and
plow,
Er lives in town and keeps a cow;
But whether country-jakes er town-,
They know when eggs is up er down!

La! can't you *spot* 'em—when you meet
'Em *anywheres*—in field er street?
And can't you see their faces, bright
As circus-day, heave into sight?

And can't you hear their "Howdy!"
clear
As a brook's chuckle to the ear,
And allus find their laughin' eyes
As fresh and clear as morning skies?

And can't you—when they've gone
away—
Jis feel 'em shakin' hands, all day?
And feel, too, you've bin higher raised
By sich a meetin'?—God be praised!

Oh, Home-Folks! you're the best of all
'At ranges this terreschul ball,—
But, north er south, er east er west,
It's home where you're at your best.—

It's home—it's home your faces shine,
In-nunder your own fig and vine—

Your fambly and your neighbers 'bout
Ye, and the latch-string hangin' out.

    .   .   .   .

Home-Folks—*at home,*—I know o' one
Old feller now 'at hain't got none.—
Invite him—he may hold back some—
But *you* invite him, and he'll come.

861

AMERICA'S THANKSGIVING

1900

FATHER all bountiful, in mercy
    bear
With this our universal voice of
    prayer—
        The voice that needs must be
        Upraised in thanks to Thee,
O Father, from Thy children every-
    where.

A multitudinous voice, wherein we
    fain
Wouldst have Thee hear no lightest
    sob of pain—
        No murmur of distress,
        Nor moan of loneliness,
Nor drip of tears, though soft as sum-
    mer rain.

And, Father, give us first to compre-
    hend,
No ill can come from Thee; lean Thou
    and lend
        Us clearer sight to see
        Our boundless debt to Thee,
Since all thy deeds are blessings, in the
    end.

And let us feel and know that, being
    Thine,
We are inheritors of hearts divine,
        And hands endowed with
            skill,
        And strength to work Thy
            will,
And fashion to fulfilment Thy design.

So, let us thank Thee, with all self
    aside,
Nor any lingering taint of mortal
    pride;
        As here to Thee we dare
        Uplift our faltering prayer,
Lend it some fervor of the glorified.

We thank Thee that our land is loved
    of Thee
The blessèd home of thrift and indus-
    try,
        With ever-open door
        Of welcome to the poor—
Thy shielding hand o'er all abidingly.

Even thus we thank Thee for the
    wrong that grew
Into a right that heroes battled to,
        With brothers long estranged,
        Once more as brothers ranged
Beneath the red and white and starry
    blue.

Ay, thanks—though tremulous the
    thanks expressed—
Thanks for the battle at its worst, and
    best—
        For all the clanging fray
        Whose discord dies away
Into a pastoral song of peace and rest.

862

TO EDMUND CLARENCE STEDMAN

THE AUTHORS' CLUB RECEPTION, NEW
YORK, DECEMBER 6, 1900

IT is a various tribute you command,
     O Poet-seer and World-sage in
     one!—
The scholar greets you; and the stu-
     dent; and
The stoic—and his visionary son:
The painter, harvesting with quiet eye
     Your features; and the sculptor,
     dreaming, too,
A classic marble figure, lifted high
     Where Fame's immortal ones are
     waiting you.

The man of letters, with his wistful
     face;
     The grizzled scientist; the young
     A. B.;
The true historian, of force and grace;
     The orator, of pure simplicity;
The journalist—the editor, likewise;
     The young war-correspondent; and
     the old
War-seasoned general, with sagging
     eyes,
     And nerve and hand of steel, and
     heart of gold.

The serious humorist; the blithe di-
     vine;
     The lawyer, with that twinkling look
     he wears;
The bleak-faced man in the dramatic
     line;
     The social lion—and the bulls and
     bears;

These—these, and more, O favored
     guest of all,
Have known your benefactions, and
     are led
To pay their worldly homage, and to
     call
Down Heaven's blessings on your
     honored head.

Ideal, to the utmost plea of art—
     As real, to labor's most exacting
     need—
Your dual services of soul and heart
     Enrich the world alike in dream and
     deed:
For you have brought to us, from out
     the mine
     Delved but by genius in scholastic
     soil,
The blended treasures of a wealth di-
     vine,—
     Your peerless gift of song—your life
     of toil.

863

WHEN WE FIRST PLAYED "SHOW"

WASN'T it a good time,
     Long Time Ago—
When we all were little tads
     And first played "Show"—
When every newer day
     Wore as bright a glow
As the ones we laughed away—
     Long Time Ago!

Calf was in the back-lot;
     Clover in the red;
Bluebird in the pear tree;
     Pigeons on the shed;

Tom a-chargin' twenty pins
    At the barn; and Dan
Spraddled out just like "The
    'Injarubber'-Man!"

Me and Bub and Rusty,
    Eck and Dunk, and Sid,
'Tumblin' on the sawdust
    Like the A-rabs did;
Jamesy on the slack-rope
    In a wild retreat,
Grappling back, to start again—
    When he chalked his feet!

Wasn't Eck a wonder,
    In his stocking-tights?
Wasn't Dunk—his leaping lion—
    Chief of all delights?
Yes, and wasn't "Little Mack"
    Boss of all the Show,—
Both Old Clown and Candy-Butcher—
    Long Time Ago!

Sid the Bareback-Rider;
    And—oh-me-oh-*my!*—
Bub, the spruce Ring-Master,
    Stepping round so spry!—
In his little waist-and-trousers
    All made in one,
Was there a prouder youngster
    Under the sun!

And NOW—who will tell me,—
    Where are they all?
Dunk's a sanatorium doctor,
    Up at Waterfall;
Sid's a city street-contractor;
    Tom has fifty clerks;
And Jamesy he's the "Iron Magnate"
    Of "The Hecla Works."

And Bub's old and bald now,
    Yet still he hangs on,—

Dan and Eck and "Little Mack,"
    Long, long gone!
But wasn't it a good time,
    Long Time Ago!
When we all were little tads
    And first played "Show!"

864

WILLIAM PINKNEY FISHBACK

SAY first he loved the dear home-
    hearts, and then
He loved his honest fellow citizen—
He loved and honored him, in any post
Of duty where he served mankind the
    most.

All that he asked of him in humblest
    need
Was but to find him striving to suc-
    ceed;
All that he asked of him in highest
    place
Was justice to the lowliest of his race.

When he found these conditions,
    proved and tried,
He owned he marveled, but was satis-
    fied—
Relaxed in vigilance enough to smile
And, with his own wit, flay himself a
    while.

Often he liked real anger—as, per-
    chance,
The summer skies like storm-clouds
    and the glance
Of lightning—for the clearer, purer
    blue
Of heaven, and the greener old earth,
    too.

All easy things to do he did with care,
Knowing the very common danger
there;
In noblest conquest of supreme debate
The facts are simple as the victory
great.

That which had been a task to hardiest
minds
To him was as a pleasure, such as finds
The captive-truant, doomed to read
throughout
The one lone book he really cares
about.

Study revived him: Howsoever dim
And deep the problem, 'twas a joy to
him
To solve it wholly; and he seemed as
one
Refreshed and rested as the work was
done.

And he had gathered, from all wealth
of lore
That time has written, such a treasure-
store,
His mind held opulence—his speech
the rare
Fair grace of sharing all his riches
there—

Sharing with all, but with the greatest
zest
Sharing with those who seemed the
neediest;
The young he ever favored; and
through these
Shall he live longest in men's memo-
ries.

865

A GOOD MAN

I

A GOOD man never dies—
In worthy deed and prayer
And helpful hands, and honest eyes,
If smiles or tears be there:
Who lives for you and me—
Lives for the world he tries
To help—he lives eternally.
A good man never dies.

II

Who lives to bravely take
His share of toil and stress,
And, for his weaker fellows' sake,
Makes every burden less,—
He may, at last, seem worn—
Lie fallen—hands and eyes
Folded—yet, though we mourn and
mourn,
A good man never dies.

866

JOHN CLARK RIDPATH

TO the lorn ones who loved him
first and best,
And knew his dear love at its tender-
est,
We seem akin—we simplest friends
who knew
His fellowship, of heart and spirit too:

We who have known the happy sum-
mertide
Of his ingenuous nature, glorified

With the inspiring smile that ever lit
The earnest face and kindly strength
    of it:

His presence, all-commanding, as his
    thought
Into unconscious eloquence was
    wrought
Until the utterance became a spell
That awed us as a spoken miracle.

Learning, to him was native—was, in
    truth,
The earliest playmate of his lisping
    youth,
Likewise throughout a life of toil and
    stress,
It was as laughter, health and happi-
    ness:

And so he played with it—joyed at its
    call—
Ran rioting with it, forgetting all
Delights of childhood, and of age and
    fame,—
A devotee of learning, still the same!

In fancy, even now we catch the glance
Of the rapt eye and radiant counte-
    nance,
As when his discourse, like a wood-
    land's stream,
Flowed musically on from theme to
    theme:

The skies, the stars, the mountains and
    the sea,
He worshipped as their high divinity—
Nor did his reverent spirit find one
    thing
On earth too lowly for his worship-
    ping.

The weed, the rose, the wildwood or
    the plain,
The teeming harvest, or the blighted
    grain,—
All—all were fashioned beautiful and
    good,
As the soul saw and senses understood.

Thus broadly based, his spacious faith
    and love
Enfolded all below as all above—
Nay, ev'n if overmuch he loved man-
    kind,
He gave his love's vast largess as de-
    signed.

Therefore, in fondest, faithful service,
    he
Wrought ever bravely for humanity—
Stood, first of heroes for the Right al-
    lied—
Foes, even, grieving, when (for them)
    he died.

This was the man we loved—are lov-
    ing yet,
And still shall love while longing eyes
    are wet
With selfish tears that well were
    brushed away,
Remembering his smile of yesterday.—

For, even as we knew him, smiling
    still,
Somewhere beyond all earthly ache or
    ill,
He waits with the old welcome—just
    as when
We met him smiling, we shall meet
    again.

867

HIS HEART OF CONSTANT YOUTH

*And I never hear the drums beat
that I do not think of him.*
—Major Charles L. Holstein

TURN through his life, each word
and deed
Now sacred as it is—
How helped and soothed we are to
read
A history like his!

To turn the years, in far review,
And find him—as To-day—
In orchard-lands of bloom and dew
Again a boy at play:

The jeweled grass—the sumptuous
trees
And flower and fragrance there,
With song of birds and drone of bees
And Spring-time everywhere:

Turn any chapter that we will,
Read any page, in sooth,
We find his glad heart owning still
The freshness of his youth.

With such a heart of tender care
He loved his own, and thus
His home was, to the loved ones there,
A temple glorious.

And, ever youthful, still his love
Enshrined, all manifold,
The people—all the poor thereof,
The helpless and the old.

And little children—Ah! to them
His love was as the sun
Wrought in a magic diadem
That crowned them, every one.

And ever young his reverence for
The laws: like morning-dew
He shone as counsel, orator,
And clear logician, too.

And, as a boy, his gallant soul
Made answer to the trill
Of battle-trumpet and the roll
Of drums that echo still:

His comrades—as his country, dear—
They knew, and ever knew
That buoyant, boyish love, sincere
As truth itself is true:

He marched with them, in tireless
tramp—
Laughed, cheered and lifted up
The battle-chorus, and in camp
Shared blanket, pipe and cup.

His comrades! . . . When you meet
again,
In anguish though you bow,
Remember how he loved you then,
And how he loves you *now*.

868

THE PATHS OF PEACE

MAURICE THOMPSON—FEBRUARY 15,
1901

HE would have holiday—outworn,
in sooth,
Would turn again to seek the old
release,—

The open fields—the loved haunts of
    his youth—
The woods, the waters, and the
    paths of peace.

The rest—the recreation he would
    choose
Be his abidingly! Long has he
    served
And greatly—ay, and greatly let us use
Our grief, and yield him nobly as
    deserved.

Perchance—with subtler senses than
    our own
And love exceeding ours—he listens
    thus
To ever nearer, clearer pipings blown
From out the lost lands of Theoc-
    ritus.

Or haply, he is beckoned from us here,
By night or yeoman of the bosky
    wood,
Or, chained in roses, haled a prisoner
Before the blithe Immortal, Robin
    Hood.

Or, mayhap, Chaucer signals, and with
    him
And his rare fellows he goes pil-
    griming;
Or Walton signs him, o'er the morn-
    ing brim
Of misty waters midst the dales of
    Spring.

Ho! wheresoe'er he goes, or whosoe'er
He fares with, he has bravely earned
    the boon.
Be his the open, and the glory there
Of April-buds, May-blooms and
    flowers of June!

Be his the glittering dawn, the twin-
    kling dew,
The breathless pool or gush of
    laughing streams—
Be his the triumph of the coming true
Of all his loveliest dreams!

869

THE TRIBUTE OF HIS HOME

BENJAMIN HARRISON—INDIANAPOLIS,
MARCH 14, 1901

BOWED, midst a universal grief
    that makes
Columbia's self a stricken mourner,
    cast
In tears beneath the old Flag at half-
    mast,
A sense of glory rouses us and breaks
Like song upon our sorrowing and
    shakes
The dew from our drenched eyes,
    that smile at last
In childish pride—as though the
    great man passed
To his most high reward for our poor
    sakes.
Loved of all men—we muse,—yet ours
    he was—
Choice of the Nation's mighty broth-
    erhood—
Her soldier, statesman, ruler.—
    Ay, but then,
We knew him—long before the world's
    applause
And after—as a neighbor, kind and
    good,
Our common friend and fellow
    citizen.

870

AMERICA

BUFFALO, NEW YORK, SEPTEMBER 14, 1901

*O Thou, America—Messiah of
Nations!*

I

IN the need that bows us thus,
 America!
Shape a mighty song for us—
 America!
Song to whelm a hundred years'
Roar of wars and rain of tears
'Neath a world's triumphant cheers:
 America! America!

II

Lift the trumpet to thy mouth,
 America!
East and West and North and South—
 America!
Call us round the dazzling shrine
Of the starry old ensign—
New baptized in blood of thine,
 America! America!

III

Dying eyes through pitying mists,
 America!
See the Assassin's shackled wrists,
 America!
Patient eyes that turn their sight
From all blackening crime and blight
Still toward Heaven's holy light—
 America! America!

IV

High o'erlooking sea and land,
 America!
Trustfully with outheld hand,
 America!
Thou dost welcome all in quest
Of thy freedom, peace and rest—
Every exile is thy guest,
 America! America!

V

Thine a universal love,
 America!
Thine the cross and crown thereof,
 America!
Aid us, then, to sing thy worth:
God hath builded, from thy birth,
The first nation of the earth—
 America! America!

871

EVEN AS A CHILD

CANTON, SEPTEMBER 19, 1901

EVEN as a child to whom sad
 neighbors speak
 In symbol, saying that his father
 "sleeps"—
Who feels their meaning, even as his
 cheek
 Feels the first tear-drop as it stings
 and leaps—
Who keenly knows his loss, and yet
 denies
 Its awful import—grieves unrecon-
 ciled,
Moans, drowses—rouses, with new-
 drowning eyes—
 Even as a child.

Even as a child; with empty, aimless
    hand
Clasped sudden to the heart all hope
    deserts—
With tears that blur all lights on sea
    or land—
The lip that quivers and the throat
    that hurts:
Even so, the Nation that has known
    his love
Is orphaned now; and, whelmed in
    anguish wild
Knows but its sorrow and the ache
    thereof,
        Even as a child.

872

THE HOOSIER IN EXILE

THE Hoosier in Exile—a toast
    That by its very sound
Moves us, at first, to tears almost,
And sympathy profound;
But musing for a little space,
    We lift the glass and smile,
And poise it with a royal grace—
    The Hoosier in Exile!

The Hoosier in Exile, forsooth!
    For though his steps may roam
The earth's remotest bounds, in truth
    His heart is ever home!
O loyal still to every tie
    Of native fields and streams,
His boyhood friends, and paths
    whereby
He finds them in his dreams!

Though he may fare the thronging
    maze
    Of alien city streets,

His thoughts are set in grassy ways
    And woodlands' cool retreats:
Forever, clear and sweet above
    The traffic's roar and din,
In breezy groves he hears the dove,
    And is at peace within.

When newer friends and generous
    hands
    Advance him, he returns
Due gratefulness, yet, pausing, stands
    As one who strangely yearns
To pay still further thanks, but sighs
    To think he knows not where,
Till—like as life—with misty eyes
    He sees his mother there.

The Hoosier in Exile? Ah, well,
    Accept the phrase, but know
The Hoosier heart must ever dwell
    Where orchard blossoms grow
The whitest, apples reddest, and,
    In cornlands, mile on mile,
The old homesteads forever stand—
    "The Hoosier in Exile!"

873

THE QUEST OF THE FATHERS

WHAT were our Forefathers try-
    ing to find
    When they weighed anchor, that
        desperate hour
They turned from home, and the
    warning wind
    Sighed in the sails of the old May-
        flower?
What sought they that could compen-
    sate
    Their hearts for the loved ones left
        behind—

The household group at the glowing
 grate?—
What were our Forefathers trying
 to find?

What were they trying to find more
 dear
Than their native land and its an-
 nals old,—
Its throne—its church—and its worldly
 cheer—
Its princely state, and its hoarded
 gold?
What more dear than the mounds of
 green
There o'er the brave sires, slumber-
 ing long?
What more fair than the rural scene—
What more sweet than the throstle's
 song?

Faces pallid, but sternly set,
 Lips locked close, as in voiceless
 prayer,
And eyes with never a tear-drop wet—
 Even the tenderest woman's there!
But O the light from the soul within,
 As each spake each with a flashing
 mind—
As the lightning speaks to its kith and
 kin!
 What were our Forefathers trying
 to find?

Argonauts of a godless day—
 Seers of visions, and dreamers vain!
Their ship's foot set in a pathless
 way,—
 The fogs, the mists, and the blind-
 ing rain!—
When the gleam of sun, and moon
 and star
 Seemed lost so long they were half
 forgot—

When the fixed eyes found nor near
 nor far,
And the night whelmed all, and the
 world was not.

And yet, befriended in some strange
 wise,
 They groped their way in the storm
 and stress
Through which—though their look
 found not the skies—
 The Lord's look found *them* ne'er-
 theless—
Found them, yea, in their piteous lot,
 As they in their faith from the first
 divined—
Found them, and favored them—too.
 But what—
 What were our Forefathers trying
 to find?

Numb and agasp, with the frost for
 breath,
 They came on a frozen shore, at
 last,
As bleak and drear as the coasts of
 death,—
 And yet their psalm o'er the wintry
 blast
Rang glad as though 'twere the chim-
 ing mirth
Of jubilant children landing there—
Until o'er all of the icy earth
 The snows seemed warm, as they
 knelt in prayer.

For, lo! they were close on the trail
 they sought:—
 In the sacred soil of the rights of
 men
They marked where the Master-hand
 had wrought;
 And there they garnered and sowed
 again.—

Their land—then *ours,* as to-day it is,
  With its flag of heaven's own light
    designed,
And God's vast love o'er all. . . . . And
    this
Is what our Forefathers were trying
    to find.

874

TO THE MOTHER

THE mother-hands no further toil
    may know;
The mother-eyes smile not on you
    and me;
The mother-heart is stilled, alas!—
    But O
The mother-love abides eternally.

875

NEW YEAR'S NURSERY JINGLE

OF all the rhymes of all the climes
    Of where and when and how,
We best and most can boast and boast
    The Golden Age of NOW!

876

FOOL-YOUNGENS

ME an' Bert an' Minnie-Belle
    Knows a joke, an' we won't tell!
No, we don't—'cause we don't know
Why we got to laughin' so;
But we got to laughin' so,
    We ist kep' a-laughin'.

Wind uz blowin' in the tree—
An' wuz only ist us three
Playin' there; an' ever' one

Ketched each other, like we done,
Squintin' up there at the sun
    Like we wuz a-laughin'.

Nothin' funny anyway;
But I laughed, an' so did they—
An' we all three laughed, an' nen
Squint' our eyes an' laugh' again:
Ner we didn't ist *p'ten'*—
    We wuz *shore-'nough* laughin'.

We ist laugh' an' laugh', tel Bert
Say he *can't* quit an' it hurt.
Nen I *howl,* an' Minnie-Belle
She tear up the grass a spell
An' ist stop her yeers an' *yell*
    Like she'd *die* a-laughin'.

Never sich fool-youngens yit!
Nothin' funny,—not a bit!—
But we laugh' so, tel we whoop'
Purt' nigh like we have the croup—
All so hoarse we'd wheeze an' whoop
    An' ist *choke* a-laughin'.

877

A GUSTATORY ACHIEVEMENT

LAST Thanksgivin'-dinner we
    Et at Granny's house, an' she
Had—ist like she alluz does—
Most an' best pies ever wuz.

Canned *black*burry-pie an' *goose-*
Burry, squshin'-full o' juice;
An' *roz*burry—yes, an' plum—
Yes, an' *churry*-pie—*um-yum!*

Peach an' punkin, too, you bet.
Lawzy! I kin taste 'em yet!
Yes, an' *custard*-pie, an' *mince!*
    . . . .
An'—I—*ain't*—et—no—pie—since!

878

BILLY AND HIS DRUM

HO! it's come, kids, come!
With a bim! bam! bum!
Here's little Billy bangin' on his
big bass drum!
He's a-marchin' round the room,
With his feather-duster plume
A-noddin' an' a-bobbin' with his
big! bom! boom!

Looky, little Jane an' Jim!
Will you only look at him,
A-humpin' an' a-thumpin' with his
bam! bom! bim!
Has the Day o' Judgment come
Er the New Mi-len-nee-um?
Er is it only Billy with his
bim! bam! bum!

I'm a-comin'; yes, I am—
Jim an' Sis, an' Jane an' Sam!
We'll all march off with Billy an' his
bom! bim! bam!
Come hur*raw*in' as you come,
Er they'll think you're deef-an'-dumb
Ef you don't hear little Billy an' his
big bass drum!

879

A DIVERTED TRAGEDY

GRACIE wuz allus a *careless* tot;
But Gracie dearly loved her
doll,
An' played wiv it on the winder-
sill

'Way up-stairs, when she ought to *not,*
An' her muvver *telled* her so an' all;
But she won't *mind* what *she* say
—till,
First thing she know, her dolly fall
Clean spang out o' the winder, plumb
Into the street! An' here Grace come
Down-stairs, two at a time, ist wild
An' a-screamin', "Oh, my child! my
child!"

Jule wuz a-bringin' their basket o'
clo'es
Ist then into their hall down there,—
An' she ist stop' when Gracie
bawl,
An' Jule she say "She ist declare
She's ist in time!" An' what you
s'pose?
She sets her basket down in the
hall,
An' wite on top o' the snowy clo'es
Wuz Gracie's dolly a-layin' there
An' ist ain't bu'st ner hurt a-tall!
Nen Gracie smiled—ist *sobbed* an'
smiled—
An' cried, "My child! my precious
child!"

880

THOMAS THE PRETENDER

TOMMY'S alluz playin' jokes,
An' actin' up, an' foolin' folks;
An' wunst one time he creep
In Pa's big chair, he did, one night,
An' squint an' shut his eyes bofe
tight,
An' say, "Now I'm asleep."
An' nen we knowed, an' Ma know'
too,
He *ain't* asleep no more'n you!

An' wunst he clumbed on our back-
    fence
An' flop his arms an' nen commence
    To crow, like he's a hen;
But when he falled off, like he done,
He didn't fool us children none,
    Ner didn't *crow* again.
An' our Hired Man, as he come by,
Says, "Tom can't *crow,* but he kin
    cry."

An' one time wunst Tom 'tend'-like
    he's
His Pa an' goin' to rob the bees;
    An', first he know—oh, dear!
They ist come swarmin' out o' there
An' sting him, an' stick in his hair—
    An' one got in his yeer!—
An' Uncle sigh an' say to Ma,
An' grease the welts, "Pore Pa! pore
    Pa!"

881

TO MY SISTER

A BELATED OFFERING FOR HER BIRTHDAY

THESE books you find three weeks
    behind
    Your honored anniversary
Make me, I fear, to here appear
    Mayhap a trifle cursory.—
Yet while the Muse must thus refuse
    The chords that fall caressfully,
She seems to stir the publisher
    And dealer quite successfully.

As to our *birthdays*—let 'em run
    Until they whir and whiz!
Read Robert Louis Stevenson,
    And hum these lines of his:—

"The eternal dawn, beyond a doubt,
    Shall break on hill and plain
And put all stars and candles out
    Ere we be young again."

882

THE SOLDIER

THE DEDICATION OF THE SOLDIERS' AND
SAILORS' MONUMENT, INDIANAPOLIS,
MAY 15, 1902

THE Soldier!—meek the title, yet
    divine:
Therefore, with reverence, as with
    wild acclaim,
We fain would honor in exalted line
    The glorious lineage of the glorious
    name:
The Soldier.—Lo, he ever was and is,
    Our Country's high custodian, by
    right
Of patriot blood that brims that heart
    of his
    With fiercest love, yet honor infinite.

The Soldier—within whose inviolate
    care
    The Nation takes repose,—her in-
    most fane
Of Freedom ever has its guardian
    there,
    As have her forts and fleets on land
    and main:
The Heavenward Banner, as its ripples
    stream
    In happy winds, or float in languid
    flow,
Through silken meshes ever sifts the
    gleam
    Of sunshine on its Sentinel below.

The Soldier!—Why, the very utter-
ance
Is music—as of rallying bugles,
blent
With blur of drums and cymbals and
the chants
Of battle-hymns that shake the con-
tinent!—
The thunder-chorus of a world is
stirred
To awful, universal jubilee,—
Yet ever through it, pure and sweet,
are heard
The prayers of Womanhood, and In-
fancy.

Even as a fateful tempest sudden
loosed
Upon our senses, so our thoughts are
blown
Back where The Soldier battled, nor
refused
A grave all nameless in a clime un-
known.—
The Soldier—though, perchance, worn,
old and gray;
The Soldier—though, perchance, the
merest lad,—
The Soldier—though he gave his life
away,
Hearing the shout of "Victory," was
glad;

Ay, glad and grateful, that in such a
cause
His veins were drained at Freedom's
holy shrine—
Rechristening the land—as first it
was,—
His blood poured thus in sacramen-
tal sign
Of new baptism of the hallowed name
"My Country"—now on every lip
once more

And blest of God with still enduring
fame.—
This thought even then The Soldier
gloried o'er.

The dying eyes upraised in rapture
there,—
As, haply, he remembered how a
breeze
Once swept his boyish brow and tossed
his hair,
Under the fresh bloom of the or-
chard-trees—
When his heart hurried, in some wist-
ful haste
Of ecstasy, and his quick breath was
wild
And balmy-sharp and chilly-sweet to
taste,—
And he towered godlike, though a
trembling child!

Again, through luminous mists, he saw
the skies'
Far fields white-tented; and in gray
and blue
And dazzling gold, he saw vast armies
rise
And fuse in fire—from which, in
swiftest view,
The Old Flag soared, and friend and
foe as one
Blent in an instant's vivid mirage.
. . . Then
The eyes closed smiling on the smiling
sun
That changed the seer to a child
again.—

And, even so, The Soldier slept.—Our
own!—
The Soldier of our plaudits, flowers
and tears,—

O this memorial of bronze and stone—
His love shall outlast *this* a thousand
    years!
Yet, as the towering symbol bids us
    do,—
With soul saluting, as salutes the
    hand,
We answer as The Soldier answered to
The Captain's high command.

883

A CHRISTMAS GLEE

FEIGNED AS FROM ELIZABETHAN COMEDY

I

WITH a hey! and a hi! and a hey-
    ho glee!
O a Christmas glass for a sweet-
    lipped lass
To kiss and pass, in her coquetry—
        So rare!
And the lads all flush save the right
    one there—
        So rare—so rare!
With a hey! and a hi! and a ho—oh!
The Christmas holly and the mistle-
    toe!

II

With a hey! and a hi! and a hey-ho
    wile!
    As he lifts the cup and his wan face
        up,
Her eyes touch his with a tender
    smile—
        So rare!
Then his hands grasp out—and her
    own are there—
        So rare—so rare!

With a hey! and a hi! and a ho—
    oh!
The Christmas holly and the mistletoe!

CHORUS

With a hey! and a hi! and a hey-ho-ho!
The wind, the winter and the drifting
    snow!
With a hey! and a hi! and a ho—oh!
The Christmas holly and the mistletoe!

884

NO BOY KNOWS

THERE are many things that boys
    may know—
Why this and that are thus and so,—
Who made the world in the dark and
    lit
The great sun up to lighten it:
Boys know new things every day—
When they study, or when they play,—
When they idle, or sow and reap—
But no boy knows when he goes to
    sleep.

Boys who listen—or should, at least,—
May know that the round old earth
    rolls East;—
And know that the ice and the snow
    and the rain—
Ever repeating their parts again—
Are all just water the sunbeams first
Sip from the earth in their endless
    thirst,
And pour again till the low streams
    leap.—
But no boy knows when he goes to
    sleep.

A boy may know what a long, glad
    while
It has been to him since the dawn's
    first smile,
When forth he fared in the realm
    divine
Of brook-laced woodland and spun-
    sunshine;—
He may know each call of his truant
    mates,
And the paths they went,—and the
    pasture-gates
Of the 'cross-lots home through the
    dusk so deep.—
But no boy knows when he goes to
    sleep.

O I have followed me, o'er and o'er,
From the flagrant drowse on the par-
    lor-floor,
To the pleading voice of the mother
    when
I even doubted I heard it then—
To the sense of a kiss, and a moonlit
    room,
And dewy odors of locust-bloom—
A sweet white cot—and a cricket's
    cheep.—
But no boy knows when he goes to
    sleep.

885

HIS PA'S ROMANCE

ALL 'at I ever want to be
    Is ist to be a man like Pa
When he wuz young an' married Ma!
Uncle he telled us then—'cause they,
My Pa an' Ma, wuz bofe away
To 'tend P'tracted Meetin', where

My Pa an' Ma is allus there
When all the big "Revivals" is,
An' "Love-Feasts," too, an' "Class," an'
    "Prayer,"
An' when's "Comoonian Servicis."
An', yes, an' Uncle said to not
To never tell *them* ner let on
Like we knowed now ist how they
    got
First married. So—while they wuz
    gone—
Uncle he telled us ever'thing—
'Bout how my Pa wuz ist a pore
Farm-boy.—He says, I tell you *what,*
Your Pa *wuz* pore! But neighbors
    they
All liked him—all but one old man
An' his old wife that folks all say
Nobody liked, ner never can!
Yes, sir! an' Uncle purt' nigh swore
About the mean old man an' way
He treat' my Pa!—'cause he's a pore
Farm-hand—but prouder 'an a king—
An' ist work' on, he did, an' wore
His old patched clo'es, ist anyway,
So he saved up his wages—then
He ist worked on an' saved some more,
An' ist worked on, ist night an' day—
Till, sir, he save' up nine er ten
Er hunnerd dollars! But he keep
All still about it, Uncle say—
But he ist thinks—an' thinks a heap!
Though what he wuz a-thinkin', Pa
He never tell' a soul but Ma—
(Then, course, you know, he wuzn't
    Pa,
An', course, you know, she wuzn't
    Ma—
They wuz ist sweethearts, course you
    know);
'Cause Ma wuz ist a girl, about
Sixteen; an' when my Pa he go
A-courtin' her, her Pa an' Ma—

The very first they find it out—
Wuz maddest folks you ever saw!
'Cause it wuz her old Ma an' Pa
'At hate' my Pa, an' toss their head,
An' ist raise Ned!   An' her Pa said
He'd ruther see his daughter dead!
An' said she's ist a child!—an' so
Wuz Pa!—An' ef he wuz man-grown
An' only man on earth below,
His daughter shouldn't marry him
Ef he's a king an' on his throne!
Pa's chances then looked mighty slim
Fer certain, Uncle said.   But he—
He never told a soul but her
What he wuz keepin' quiet fer.
Her folks ist lived a mile from where
He lived at—an' they drove past there
To git to town.   An' ever' one
An' all the neighbers they liked her
An' showed it!   But her folks—no,
        sir!—
Nobody liked her parunts none!
An' so when they shet down, you
        know,
On Pa—an' old man tell' him so—
Pa ist went back to work, an' she
Ist waited.   An', sir! purty soon
Her folks they thought he's turned his
        eye
Some other way—'cause by-an'-by
They heard he'd *rented* the old place
He worked on.   An' one afternoon
A neighber, that had bust' a trace,
He tell' the old man they wuz signs
Around the old place that the young
Man wuz a-fixin' up the old
Log cabin some, an' he had brung
New furnichur from town; an' told
How th' old house 'uz whitewashed
        clean
An' sweet wiv morning-glory vines
An' hollyhawks all 'round the door
An' winders—an' a bran'-new floor

In th' old porch—an' wite-new green-
An'-red pump in the old sweep-well!

An', Uncle said, when he hear tell
O' all them things, the old man he
Ist grin' an' says, he "reckon' now
Some gal, er widder anyhow,
That silly boy he's coaxed at last
To marry him!" he says, says-ee,
"An' ef he has, 'so mote it be'!"
Then went back to the house to tell
His *wife* the news, as he went past
The smokehouse, an' then went on in
The kitchen, where his daughter she
Wuz washin', to tell *her,* an' grin
An' try to worry her a spell!
The mean old thing!   But Uncle said
She ain't cry much—ist pull her old
Sunbonnet forrerds on her head—
So's old man he can't see her face
At all!   An' when he s'pose he scold
An' jaw enough, he ist clear' out
An' think he's boss of all the place!

Then Uncle say, the first you know
They's go' to be a Circus-show
In town; an' old man think he'll take
His wife an' go.   An' when she say
To take their daughter, too, *she* shake
Her head like she don't *want* to go;
An' when he sees she wants to stay,
The old man takes her, anyway!
An' so she went!   But Uncle he
Said she looked mighty sweet that day,
Though she wuz pale as she could be,
A-speshully a-drivin' by
Wite where her beau lived at, you know;
But out the corner of his eye
The old man watch' her; but she throw
Her pairsol 'round so she can't see
The house at all!   An' then she hear
Her Pa an' Ma a-talkin' low
An' kind o' laughin'-like; but she

Ist set there in the seat behind,
P'tendin' like she didn't mind.
An', Uncle say, when they got past
The young man's place, an' 'pearantly
He wuzn't home, but off an' gone
To town, the old man turned at last
An' talked back to his daughter there,
All pleasant-like, from then clean on
Till they got into town, an' where
The Circus wuz, an' on inside
O' that, an' through the crowd, on to
The very top seat in the tent
Wite next the band—a-bangin' through
A tune 'at bu'st his yeers in two!
An' there the old man scrouged an'
      tried
To make his wife set down, an' she
A-yellin'! But ist what she meant
He couldn't hear, ner couldn't see
Till she turned 'round an' pinted.
      Then
He turned an' looked—an' looked
      again! . . .
He ist saw neighbers ever'where—
But, sir, *his daughter* wuzn't there!
An', Uncle says, he even saw
Her beau, you know, he hated so;
An' he wuz with some other girl.
An' then he heard the Clown "Haw-
      haw!"
An' saw the horses wheel an' whirl
Around the ring, an' heard the zipp
O' the Ringmaster's long slim whip—
But that whole Circus, Uncle said,
Wuz all inside the old man's head!

An' Uncle said, he didn't find
His daughter all that afternoon—
An' her Ma says she'll lose her mind
Ef they don't find her purty soon!
But, though they looked all day, an'
      stayed
There fer the night p'formance—not

No use at all!—they never laid
Their eyes on her. An' then they got
Their team out, an' the old man shook
His fist at all the town, an' then
Shook it up at the moon ag'in,
An' said his time 'ud come, some day!
An' jerked the lines an' driv away.

Uncle, he said, he s'pect, that night,
The old man's madder yet when they
Drive past the young man's place, an'
      hear
A fiddle there, an' see a light
Inside, an' shadders light an' gay
A-dancin' 'crosst the winder-blinds.
An' some young chaps outside yelled,
      "Say!
What 'pears to be the hurry—hey?"
But the old man ist whipped the lines
An' streaked past like a runaway!
An' now you'll be su'prised, I bet!—
I hardly ain't quit laughin' yet
When Uncle say, that jamboree
An' dance an' all—w'y, that's a sign
That any old man ort to see,
As plain as 8 and 1 makes 9,
That they's *a weddin'* wite inside
That very house he's whippin' so
To git apast!—An', sir! the bride
There's his own daughter! Yes, an'
      oh!
She's my Ma now—an' young man she
Got married, he's my Pa! *Whoop-ee!*
But Uncle say to not laugh all
The laughin' yet, but please save some
To kind o' spice up what's to come!

Then Uncle say, about next day
The neighbers they begin to call
An' wish 'em well, an' say how glad
An' proud an' tickled ever' way
Their friends all is—an' how they had
The lovin' prayers of ever' one

That had homes of their own! But
    none
Said nothin' 'bout the home that .she
Had run away from! So she sighed
Sometimes—an' wunst she purt' nigh
    cried.

Well, Uncle say, her old Pa, he
Ist like to died, he wuz so mad!
An' her Ma, too! But by-an'-by
They cool down some.
                An', 'bout a week,
She want to see her Ma so bad,
She think she'll haf to go! An' so
She coax him; an' he kiss her cheek
An' say, Lord bless her, *course* they'll
    go!
An', Uncle say, when they're bofe
    come
A-knockin' there at her old home—
W'y, first he know, the door it flew
Open, all quick, an' she's jerked in,
An', quicker still, the door's banged to
An' locked: an' crosst the winder-sill
The old man pokes a shotgun through
An' says to git! "You stold my child,"
He says: "an', now she's back, w'y,
    you
Clear out, this minute, er I'll kill
You! Yes, an' I 'ull kill her, too,
Ef you don't go!" An' then, all wild,
His young wife begs him please to go!
An' so he turn' an' walk'—all slow
An' pale as death, but awful still
An' ca'm—back to the gate, an' on
Into the road, where he had gone
So many times alone, you know!
An', Uncle say, a whipperwill
Holler so lonesome, as he go
On back to'rds home, he say he 'spec'
He ist 'ud like to wring its neck!
An' I ain't think he's goin' back
All by hisse'f—but Uncle say

That's what he does, an' it's a fac'!
An' 'pears-like he's goin' back to
    stay—
'Cause there he stick', ist thataway,
An' don't go nowheres any more,
Ner don't nobody ever see
Him set his foot outside the door—
Till 'bout five days, a boy loped down
The road, a-comin' past from town,
An' he called to him from the gate,
An' sent the old man word: He's
    thought
Things over now; an', while he hate
To lose his wife, he think she ought
To mind her Pa an' Ma an' do
Whatever *they* advise her to.
An' sends word, too, to come an' git
Her new things an' the furnichur
That he had special' bought fer her—
'Cause, now that they wuz goin' to
    quit,
She's free to ist have all of it;—
So, fer his love fer her, he say
To come an' git it, wite away.
An' *spang!* that very afternoon,
Here come her Ma—ist 'bout as soon
As old man could hitch up an' tell
Her "hurry back!" An' 'bout as quick
As she's drove there to where my Pa—
I mean to where her son-in-law—
Lives at, he meets her at the door
All smilin', though he's awful pale
An' trimbly—like he's ist been sick;
He take her in the house—An', 'fore
She knows it, they's a cellar-door
Shet on her, an' she hears the click
Of a' old rusty padlock! Then,
Uncle, he say, she kind o' stands
An' thinks—an' thinks—an' thinks
    ag'in—
An' mayby thinks of her own child
Locked up—like her! An' Uncle
    smiled,

An' I ist laughed an' clapped my
    hands!
An' there she stayed! An' she can cry
Ist all she want! an' yell an' kick
To ist her heart's content! an' try
To pry out wiv a quiltin'-stick!
But Uncle say he guess at last
She's 'bout give up, an' holler through
The door-crack fer to please to be
So kind an' good as send an' tell
The old man, like she want him to,
To come 'fore night, an' set her free,
Er—they wuz rats down there! An' yell
She did, till, Uncle say, it soured
The morning's milk in the back yard!
But all the answer reached her, where
She's skeered so in the dark down there,
Wuz ist a mutterin' that she heard,—
"*I've sent him word!—I've sent him
    word!*"
An' shore enough, as Uncle say,
He *has* "sent word!"

       Well, it's plum night
An' all the house is shet up tight—
Only one winder 'bout half-way
Raised up, you know; an' ain't no light
Inside the whole house, Uncle say.
Then, first you know, there where the
    team
Stands hitched yet, there the old man
    stands—
A' old tin lantern in his hands
An' monkey-wrench; an' he don't seem
To make things out, a-standin' there.
He comes on to the gate an' feels
An' fumbles fer the latch—then hears
A voice that chills him to the heels—
"You halt! an' stand right where you
    air!"
Then, sir! my—my—his son-in-law,
There at the winder wiv his gun,
He tell the old man what he's done:

"You hold *my* wife a prisoner—
An' *your* wife, drat ye! I've got *her!*
An' now, sir," Uncle say he say,
"You ist turn round an' climb wite in
That wagon, an' drive home ag'in
An' bring my wife back wite away,
An' we'll trade then—an' not before
Will I unlock my cellar-door—
Not fer your wife's sake ner your own,
But *my* wife's sake—an' hers alone!"
An', Uncle say, it don't sound like
It's so, but yet it is!—He say,
From wite then, somepin' seem' to strike
The old man's funny-bone some way;
An', minute more, that team o' his
Went tearin' down the road *k'whiz!*
An' in the same two-forty style
Come whizzin' back! An' oh, that-air
Sweet girl a-cryin' all the while,
Thinkin' about her Ma there, shet
In her own daughter's cellar, where—
Ist week or so *she's* kep' house there—
She hadn't time to clean it yet!
So when her Pa an' her they git
There—an' the young man grab' an' kiss
An' hug her, till she make him quit
An' ask him where her mother is.
An' then he smile' an' try to not;
Then slow-like find th' old padlock key,
An' blow a' oat-hull out of it,
An' then stoop down there where he's
    got
Her Ma locked up so keerfully—
An' where, wite there, he say he
    thought
It *ort* to been *the old man*—though
Uncle, he say, he reckon not—
When out she bounced, all tickled so
To taste fresh air ag'in an' find
Her folks wunst more, an' grab' her
    child
An' cry an' laugh, an' even go
An' hug the old man; an' he wind

Her in his arms, an' laugh, an' pat
Her back, an' say he's riconciled,
In such a happy scene as that,
To swap his daughter for her Ma,
An' have so smart a son-in-law
As *they* had! "Yes, an' he's my Pa!"
I laugh' an' yell', "Hooray-hooraw!"

886

TO JOEL CHANDLER HARRIS

YOU who to the rounded prime
    Of a life of toil and stress,
Still have kept the morning-time
    Of glad youth in heart and spirit,
    So your laugh, as children hear it,
    Seems their own, no less,—
Take this book of childish rhyme—
    The Book of Joyous Children.

Their first happiness on earth
    Here is echoed—their first glee:
Rich, in sooth, the volume's worth—
    Not in classic lore, but rich in
    The child-sagas of the kitchen;—
    Therefore, take from me
To your heart of childish mirth
    The Book of Joyous Children.

887

THE BOOK OF JOYOUS
CHILDREN

BOUND and bordered in leaf-green,
    Edged with trellised buds and
        flowers
And glad Summer-gold, with clean
    White and purple morning-glories
    Such as suit the songs and stories
    Of this book of ours,

Unrevised in text or scene,—
    The Book of Joyous Children.

Wild and breathless in their glee—
    Lawless rangers of all ways
Winding through lush greenery
    Of Elysian vales—the viny,
    Bowery groves of shady, shiny
    Haunts of childish days.
Spread and read again with me
    The Book of Joyous Children.

What a whir of wings, and what
    Sudden drench of dews upon
The young brows, wreathed, all un-
        sought,
    With the apple-blossom garlands
    Of the poets of those far lands
    Whence all dreams are drawn
Set herein and soiling not
    The Book of Joyous Children.

In their blithe companionship
    Taste again, these pages through,
The hot honey on your lip
    Of the sun-smit wild strawberry,
    Or the chill tart of the cherry;
    Kneel, all glowing, to
The cool spring, and with it sip
    The Book of Joyous Children.

As their laughter needs no rule,
    So accept their language, pray.—
Touch it not with any tool:
    Surely we may understand it,—
    As the heart has parsed or scanned
        it
    Is a worthy way,
Though found not in any School
    The Book of Joyous Children.

Be a truant—know no place
    Of prison under heaven's rim!

Front the Father's smiling face—
   Smiling, that *you* smile the
     brighter
For the heavy hearts made lighter,
   Since you smile with Him.
Take—and thank Him for His grace—
   The Book of Joyous Children.

888

ELMER BROWN

AWF'LEST boy in this-here town
   Er anywheres is Elmer Brown!
He'll mock you—yes, an' strangers, too,
An' make a face an' yell at you,—
   "*Here's* the way *you* look!"

Yes, an' wunst in School one day,
An' Teacher's lookin' 'wite that way,
He helt his slate, an' hide his head,
An' maked a face at *her,* an' said,—
   "*Here's* the way *you* look!"

An'-sir! when Rosie Wheeler smile
One morning at him 'crosst the aisle,
He twist his face all up, an' black
His nose wiv ink, an' whisper back,—
   "*Here's* the way *you* look!"

Wunst when his Aunt's all dressed to
    call,
An' kiss him good-by in the hall,
An' latch the gate an' start away,
He holler out to her an' say,—
   "*Here's* the way *you* look!"

An' when his Pa he read out loud
The speech he maked, an' feel so proud
It's in the paper—Elmer's Ma
She ketched him—wite behind his
    Pa,—
   "*Here's* the way *you* look!"

Nen when his Ma she slip an' take
Him in the other room an' shake
Him good! w'y, he don't care—no-
    sir!—
He ist look up an' laugh at her,—
   "*Here's* the way *you* look!"

889

THE RAMBO-TREE

WHEN Autumn shakes the
    rambo-tree—
   It's a long, sweet way across the or-
    chard!—
The bird sings low as the bumblebee—
   It's a long, sweet way across the or-
    chard!—
The poor shote-pig he says, says he:
  "When Autumn shakes the rambo-
    tree
There's enough for you and enough
    for me."—
   It's a long, sweet way across the or-
    chard.

For just two truant lads like we,
When Autumn shakes the rambo-tree
There's enough for you and enough
   for me—
   It's a long, sweet way across the or-
    chard.

When Autumn shakes the rambo-
    tree—
   It's a long, sweet way across the or-
    chard!—
The mole digs out to peep and see—
   It's a long, sweet way across the or-
    chard!—
The dusk sags down, and the moon
    swings free,

There's a far, lorn call, "Pig-*gee!*
     Pig-*gee!"*
And two boys—glad enough for
     three.—
  It's a long, sweet way across the or-
     chard.

For just two truant lads like we,
When Autumn shakes the rambo-tree
There's enough for you and enough
     for me—
  It's a long, sweet way across the or-
     chard.

890

FIND THE FAVORITE

OUR three cats is Maltese cats,
     An' they's two that's white,—
An' bofe of 'em's *deef*—an' that's
'Cause their *eyes* ain't right.—

Uncle say that *Huxley* say
   Eyes of *white* Maltese—
When they don't match thataway—
   They're deef as you please!

Girls, they like our white cats best,
   'Cause they're white as snow,
Yes, an' look the stylishest—
   But they're deef, you know!

They don't know their names, an'
     don't
   Hear us when we call
"Come in, Nick an' Finn!"—they
     won't
   Come fer us at all!

But our *other* cat, he knows
   Mister Nick an' Finn,—

Mowg's *his* name,—an' when *he* goes
   Fer 'em, they come in!

Mowgli's *all* his name—the same
   Me an' Muvver took
Like the Wolf-Child's *other* name,
   In "The Jungul Book."

I bet Mowg's the smartest cat
   In the world!—*He's* not
White, but mousy-plush, with that
   Smoky gloss he's got!

All's got little bells to ring,
   Round their neck; but none
Only Mowg *knows* anything—
   He's the only one!

I ist 'spect sometimes he hate
   White cats' stupid ways:—
He won't hardly 'sociate
   With 'em, lots o' days!

Mowg wants in where *we* air,—well,
   He'll ist take his paw
An' ist ring an' ring his bell
   There till me er Ma

Er *some*body lets him in
   Nen an' shuts the door.—
An', when he wants out ag'in,
   Nen he'll ring some more.

Ort to hear our Katy tell!
   She sleeps 'way up-stairs;
An' last night she hear Mowg's bell
   Ringin' round *some*wheres. . . .

Trees grows by her winder.—So,
   She lean out an' see
Mowg up there, 'way out, you know,
   In the clingstone-tree;—

An'-sir! he ist *hint* an' *ring,*—
Till she ketch an' plat
Them limbs;—nen he crawl an' spring
In where Katy's at!

891

THE BOY PATRIOT

I WANT to be a Soldier!—
        A Soldier!—
            A Soldier!—
I want to be a Soldier, with a saber in
    my hand
Or a little carbine rifle, or a musket on
    my shoulder,
Or just a snare-drum, snarling in the
    middle of the band;
I want to hear, high overhead, The
    Old Flag flap her wings
While all the Army, following, in
    chorus cheers and sings;
        I want to hear the tramp and
            jar
        Of patriots a million,
        As gaily dancing off to war
        As dancing a cotillion.

I want to be a Soldier!—
        A Soldier!—
            A Soldier!—
I want to be a Soldier, with a saber in
    my hand
Or a little carbine rifle, or a musket
    on my shoulder,
Or just a snare-drum, snarling in the
    middle of the band.

I want to see the battle!—
        The battle!—
            The battle!—
I want to see the battle, and be in it to
    the end;—

I want to hear the cannon clear their
    throats and catch the prattle
Of all the pretty compliments the
    enemy can send!—
And then I know my wits will go,—
    and where I *shouldn't* be—
Well, there's the spot, in any fight,
    that you may search for me.
        So, when our foes have had
            their fill,
        Though I'm among the
            dying,
        To see The Old Flag flying
            still,
        I'll laugh to leave her flying!

I want to be a Soldier!—
        A Soldier!—
            A Soldier!—
I want to be a Soldier, with a saber in
    my hand
Or a little carbine rifle, or a musket on
    my shoulder,
Or just a snare-drum, snarling in the
    middle of the band.

892

EXTREMES

I

A LITTLE boy once played so loud
    That the Thunder, up in a
        thunder-cloud,
Said, "Since *I* can't be heard, why, then
I'll never, never thunder again!"

II

And a little girl once kept so still
That she heard a fly on the window-
    sill
Whisper and say to a ladybird,—
"She's the stilliest child I ever heard."

893

INTELLECTUAL LIMITATIONS

PARUNTS knows lots more than us,
But they.don't know *all* things,—
'Cause we ketch 'em, lots o' times,
Even on little small things.

One time Winnie ask' her Ma,
At the winder, sewin',
What's the wind a-doin' when
It's a-not a-*blowin'*?

Yes, an' 'Del', that very day,
When we're nearly froze out,
He ask' Uncle *where* it goes
When the fire goes out?

Nen *I* run to ask my Pa,
That way, somepin' funny;
But I can't say ist but "Say,"
When he turn to me an' say,
"Well, what is it, Honey?"

894

A MASQUE OF THE SEASONS

SCENE.—*A kitchen.—Group of Chil-
dren, popping corn.—The Fairy
Queen of the Seasons discovered in
the smoke of the corn-popper.—
Waving her wand, and, with eery,
sharp, imperious ejaculations, ad-
dressing the bespelled auditors, who
neither see nor hear her nor suspect
her presence.*

QUEEN

SUMMER or Winter or Spring or
Fall,—
Which do you like the best of all?

LITTLE JASPER

When I'm dressed warm as warm can
be,
And with boots, to go
Through the deepest snow,
Winter-time is the time for me!

QUEEN

Summer or Winter or Spring or Fall,—
Which do you like the best of all?

LITTLE MILDRED

I like blossoms, and birds that sing;
The grass and the dew,
And the sunshine, too,—
So, best of all I like the Spring.

QUEEN

Summer or Winter or Spring or Fall,—
Which do you like the best of all?

LITTLE MANDEVILLE

O little friends, I most rejoice
When I hear the drums
As the Circus comes,—
So Summer-time's my special choice.

QUEEN

Summer or Winter or Spring or Fall,—
Which do you like the best of all?

LITTLE EDITH

Apples of ruby, and pears of gold,
And grapes of blue
That the bee stings through.—
Fall—it is all that my heart can hold!

QUEEN

Soh! my lovelings and pretty dears,
You've *each* a favorite, it appears,—
Summer and Winter and Spring and
    Fall.
That's the reason I send them *all!*

895

LITTLE DICK AND THE CLOCK

WHEN Dicky was sick
    In the night, and the clock,
As he listened, said "Tick-
    Atty—tick-atty—tock!"
He said that *it* said,
    Every time it said "Tick,"
It said "Sick," instead,
    And he *heard* it say "Sick!"
And when it said "Tick-
    Atty—tick-atty—tock,"
He said it said "Sick-
    Atty—sick-atty—sock!"
And he tried to *see* then,
    But the light was too dim,
Yet he *heard* it again—
    And 'twas *talking* to him!
And then it said "Sick-
    Atty—sick-atty—sick!
You poor little Dick-
    Atty—Dick-atty—Dick!—
Have you got the hick-
    Atties? Hi! send for Doc
To hurry up quick-
    Atty—quick-atty—quock,
And heat a hot brick-
    Atty—brick-atty—brock,
And rickle-ty wrap it
And clickle-ty clap it
    Against his cold feet-
    Al-ty—weep-aty—eepaty—
There he goes, slapit-
    Ty—slippaty—sleepaty!"

896

THE KATYDIDS

SOMETIMES I keep
    From going to sleep,
To hear the katydids "cheep-cheep!"
And think they say
Their prayers that way;
But *katydids* don't have to *pray!*

I listen when
They cheep again;
And so, I think, they're *singing* then!
But, no; I'm wrong,—
The sound's too long
And all-alike to be a song!

I think, "Well, there!
I do declare,
If it is neither song nor prayer,
It's *talk*—and quite
Too vain and light
For me to listen to all night!"

And so, I smile,
And think,—"Now I'll
Not listen for a little while!"—
Then, sweet and clear,
Next *"cheep"* I hear
'S a *kiss.* . . . Good morning,
    Mommy dear!

897

THE NOBLE OLD ELM

O BIG Old Tree, so tall an' fine,
    Where all us childern swings
        an' plays,
Though neighbors says you're on the
        line
Between Pa's house an' Mr. Gray's,—

Us childern used to almost fuss,
  Old Tree, about you when we'd play.
We'd argy you belonged to *us,*
  An' them Gray-kids the other way!

Till *Elsie,* one time *she* wuz here
  An' playin' wiv us—Don't you mind,
Old Mister Tree?—an' purty near
  She scolded us the hardest kind
Fer quar'llin' 'bout you thataway,
  An' say *she'll* find—ef we'll keep
      still—
Whose tree you air *fer shore,* she say,
  An' settle it *fer good,* she will!

So all keep still: An' nen she gone
  An' pat the Old Tree, an' says she,—
"Whose *air* you, Tree?" an' nen let on
  Like she's a-list'nin' to the Tree,—
An' nen she say, "It's settled,—'cause
  The Old Tree says he's *all* our tree—
His *trunk* belongs to bofe your Pas,
  But *shade* belongs to you an' me."

898

EVENSONG

LAY away the story,—
  Though the theme is sweet,
There's a lack of something yet,
  Leaves it incomplete:—
There's a nameless yearning—
  Strangely undefined—
For a story sweeter still
  Than the written kind.

Therefore read no longer—
  I've no heart to hear
But just something you make up,
  O my mother dear.—

With your arms around me,
  Hold me, folded-eyed,—
Only let your voice go on—
  I'll be satisfied.

899

AN IMPROMPTU FAIRY-TALE

*When I wuz ist a little bit o' weenty-
    teenty kid
I maked up a Fairy-tale, all by myse'f,
    I did:—*

I

WUNST upon a time wunst
  They wuz a Fairy King,
An' ever'thing he have wuz *gold*—
  His clo'es, an' *ever'*thing!
An' all the other Fairies
  In his goldun Palace-hall
Had to hump an' hustle—
  'Cause he was bosst of all!

II

He have a golden trumput,
  An' when he blow' on that,
It's a sign he want' his boots,
  Er his coat er hat:
They's a sign fer ever'thing,—
  An' all the Fairies knowed
Ever' sign, an' come a-hoppin'
  When the King blowed!

III

Wunst he blowed an' telled 'em all:
  "Saddle up yer bees—
Fireflies is gittin' fat
  An' sassy as you please!—

Guess we'll go a-huntin'!"
So they hunt' a little bit,
Till the King blowed "Supper-time,"
Nen they all quit.

IV

Nen they have a Banqut
In the Palace-hall,
An' ist et! an' et! an' et!
Nen they have a *Ball;*
An' when the *Queen* o' Fairyland
Come p'omenadin' through,
The King says an' halts her,—
"Guess I'll marry you!"

900

THE TWINS

"IGO AND AGO"

WE'RE The Twins from Aunt
Marinn's,
Igo and Ago.
When Dad comes, the show begins!—
Iram, coram, dago.

Dad he says he named us two
Igo and Ago
For a poem he always knew,
Iram, coram, dago.

Then he was a braw Scotchman—
Igo and Ago
Now he's Scotch-Amer-i-can.
Iram, coram, dago.

"Hey!" he cries, and pats his knee,
"Igo and Ago,
My twin bairnies, ride wi' me—
Iram, coram, dago!"

"Here," he laughs, "ye've each a leg,
Igo and Ago,
Gleg as Tam O'Shanter's 'Meg'!
Iram, coram, dago!"

Then we mount, with shrieks of
mirth—
Igo and Ago,—
The two gladdest twins on earth!
Iram, coram, dago.

Wade and Silas-Walker cry,—
"Igo and Ago—
Annie's kissin' 'em 'good-by'!"—
Iram, coram, dago.

Aunty waves us fond farewells.—
"Igo and Ago,"
Granny pipes, "tak care yersels!"
Iram, coram, dago.

901

THE LITTLE LADY

O THE Little Lady's dainty
As the picture in a book,
And her hands are creamy-whiter
Than the water-lilies look;
Her laugh's the undrown'd music
Of the maddest meadow-brook.—
Yet all in vain I praise The Little
Lady!

Her eyes are blue and dewy
As the glimmering Summer-dawn,—
Her face is like the eglantine
Before the dew is gone;
And were that honied mouth of hers
A bee's to feast upon,
He'd be a bee bewildered, Little Lady!

Her brow makes light look sallow;
　And the sunshine, I declare,
Is but a yellow jealousy
　Awakened by her hair—
For O the dazzling glint of it
　Nor sight nor soul can bear,—
So Love goes groping for The Little
　Lady.

And yet she's neither Nymph nor Fay,
　Nor yet of Angelkind:—
She's but a racing schoolgirl, with
　Her hair blown out behind
And tremblingly unbraided by
　The fingers of the Wind,
As it wildly swoops upon The Little
　Lady.

902

"COMPANY MANNERS"

WHEN Bess gave her Dollies a
　　tea, said she,—
"It's unpolite, when they's Company,
To say you've drinked *two* cups, you
　see,—
But say you've drinked *a couple* of
　tea."

903

THE GOOD, OLD-FASHIONED PEOPLE

WHEN we hear Uncle Sidney
　　tell
About the long-ago
An' old, old friends he loved so well
When *he* was young—My-oh!—
Us childern all wish *we'd* 'a' bin
A-livin' then with Uncle,—so

We could a-kind o' happened in
　On them old friends *he* used to
　　know!—
　The good, old-fashioned people—
　The hale, hard-working people—
　The kindly country people
　　'At Uncle used to know!

They was God's people, Uncle says,
　An' gloried in His name,
An' worked, without no selfishness,
　An' loved their neighbors same
As they was kin: An' when they biled
　Their tree-molasses, in the Spring,
Er butchered in the Fall, they smiled
　An' sheered with all jist ever'thing!—
　The good, old-fashioned people—
　The hale, hard-working people—
　The kindly country people
　　'At Uncle used to know!

He tells about 'em lots o' times,
　Till we'd all ruther hear
About 'em than the Nurs'ry Rhymes
　Er Fairies—mighty near!—
Only, sometimes, he stops so long
　An' then talks on so low an' slow,
It's purt' nigh sad as any song
　To listen to him talkin' so
　Of the good, old-fashioned people—
　The hale, hard-working people—
　The kindly country people
　　'At Uncle used to know!

904

THE BEST TIMES

WHEN Old Folks they wuz
　　young like us
An' little as you an' me,—
Them wuz the best times ever wuz
Er ever goin' ter be!

905

"HIK-TEE-DIK"

THE WAR-CRY OF BILLY AND BUDDY

WHEN two little boys—renowned
    but for noise—
Hik-tee-dik! Billy and Buddy!—
May hurt a whole school, and the head
    it employs,
Hik-tee-dik! Billy and Buddy!
Such loud and hilarious pupils indeed
Need learning—and yet something
    further they need,
Though fond hearts that love them
    may sorrow and bleed.
Hik-tee-dik! Billy and Buddy!

O the schoolmarm was cool, and in
    nowise a fool;
Hik-tee-dik! Billy and Buddy!
And in ruling her ranks it was *her*
    rule to *rule;*
Hik-tee-dik! Billy and Buddy!
So when these two pupils conspired,
    every day,
Some mad piece of mischief, with
    whoop and hoo-ray,
That hurt yet defied her,—how happy
    were they!—
Hik-tee-dik! Billy and Buddy!

At the ring of the bell they'd rush in
    with a yell—
Hik-tee-dik! Billy and Buddy!
And they'd bang the school-door till
    the plastering fell,
Hik-tee-dik! Billy and Buddy!
They'd clinch as they came, and pre-
    tend not to see

As they knocked her desk over—then,
    My! and *O-me!*
How awfully sorry they'd both seem
    to be!
Hik-tee-dik! Billy and Buddy!

This trick seemed so neat and so safe
    a conceit,—
Hik-tee-dik! Billy and Buddy!—
They played it three times—though the
    third they were beat;
Hik-tee-dik! Billy and Buddy!
For the teacher, she righted her desk
    —raised the lid
And folded and packed away each
    little kid—
Closed the incident so—yes, and locked
    it, she did—
Hik-tee-dik! Billy and Buddy!

906

"OLD BOB WHITE"

OLD Bob White's a funny bird!—
    Funniest you ever heard!—
    Hear him whistle,—"Old—Bob—
    White!"
You can hear him, clean from where
He's 'way 'crosst the wheat-field there,
Whistlin' like he didn't care—
    "Old—Bob—*White!*"

Whistles alluz ist the same—
So's we won't fergit his name!—
    Hear him say it?—"Old—Bob—
    White!"
There! he's whizzed off down the
    lane—
Gone back where his folks is stayin'—
Hear him?—There he goes again,—
    "Old—Bob—*White!*"

907

A SESSION WITH UNCLE SIDNEY

[1869]

I

ONE OF HIS ANIMAL STORIES

NOW, Tudens, you sit on *this* knee
  —and 'scuse
It having no side-saddle on;—and,
  Jeems,
You sit on *this*—and don't you wobble
  so
And chug my old shins with your cop-
  pertoes;—
And, all the rest of you, range round
  someway,—
Ride on the rockers and hang to the
  arms
Of our old-time split-bottom carryall!—
Do anything but *squabble* for a place,
Or push or shove or scrouge, or
  breathe *out loud,*
Or chew wet, or knead taffy in my
  beard!—
Do *any*thing almost—act *any*way,—
Only *keep still,* so I can hear myself
Trying to tell you "just one story
  more!"

One winter afternoon my father, with
A whistle to our dog, a shout to us—
His two boys—six and eight years old
  we were,—
Started off to the woods, a half a mile
From home, where he was chopping
  wood. We raced,
We slipped and slid; reaching, at last,
  the north

Side of Tharp's corn-field.—There we
  struck what seemed
'To be a coon-track—so we all agreed:
And father, who was not a hunter, to
Our glad surprise, proposed we follow
  it.
The snow was quite five inches deep;
  and we,   ·
Keen on the trail, were soon far in
  the woods.
Our old dog, "Ring," ran nosing the
  fresh track
With whimpering delight, far on
  ahead.
After following the trail more than a
  mile
To northward, through the thickest
  winter woods
We boys had ever seen,—all suddenly
He seemed to strike *another* trail; and
  then
Our joyful attention was drawn to
Old "Ring"— leaping to this side, then
  to that,
Of a big, hollow, old oak tree, which
  had
Been blown down by a storm some
  years before.
There—all at once—out leapt a lean
  old fox
From the black hollow of a big bent
  limb,—
Hey! how he scudded!—but with our
  old "Ring"
Sharp after him—and father after
  "Ring"—
We after father, near as we could hold.
And father noticed that the fox kept
  just
About four feet ahead of "Ring"—just
  that—
No farther, and no nearer! Then he
  said:—

"There are young foxes in that tree
   back there,
And the mother-fox is drawing 'Ring'
   and us
Away from their nest there!"
            "Oh, le' 's go back!—
Do le' 's go back!" we little vandals
   cried,—
"Le' 's go back, quick, and find the
   little things—
Please, father!—Yes, and take 'em
   home for pets—
'Cause 'Ring' he'll kill the old fox
   anyway!"

So father turned, at last, and back we
   went.
And then he chopped a hole in the
   old tree
About ten feet along the limb from
   which
The old fox ran: and—Bless their little
   lives!—
There, in the hollow of the old tree-
   trunk—
There, on a bed of warm dry leaves
   and moss—
There, snug as any bug in any rug—
We found—one—two—three—four,
   and, yes-sir, *five*
Wee, weenty-teenty baby-foxes, with
Their eyes just barely opened.—*Cute?*
   —my-oh!—
The cutest—the most cunning little
   things
Two boys ever saw, in all their lives!—
"Raw weather for the little fellows
   now!"
Said father, as though talking to him-
   self,—
"Raw weather, and no home *now!*"—
   And off came

His warm old "waumus"; and in that
   he wrapped
The helpless little fellows then, and
   held
Them soft and warm against him as he
   could,—
And home we happy children followed
   him.—

Old "Ring" did not reach home till
   nearly dusk:
The mother-fox had led him a long
   chase—
"Yes, and a *fool's* chase, too!" he
   seemed to say,
And looked ashamed to hear us *prais-
   ing* him
But, *mother*—well, we *could not*
   understand
Her acting as she did—and we so
   pleased!
I can see yet the look of pained sur-
   prise
And deep compassion of her troubled
   face
When father very gently laid his coat,
With the young foxes in it, on the
   hearth
Beside her, as she brightened up the
   fire.
She urged—for the old fox's sake and
   theirs—
That they be taken back to the old
   tree;
But father—for *our* wistful sakes, no
   doubt—
Said we would keep them, and would
   try our best
To raise them.   And at once he set
   about
Building a snug home for the little
   things

Out of an old big bushel-basket, with
Its fractured handle and its stoven
    ribs:
So, lining and padding this all cozily,
He snuggled in its little tenants, and
Called in John Wesley Thomas, our
    hired man,
And gave him in full charge, with
    much advice
Regarding the just care and sustenance
    of
Young foxes.—"John," he said, "you
    feed 'em *milk*—
Warm milk, John Wesley! Yes, and
    keep 'em by
The stove—and keep your stove *a-roar-
    in'*, too,
Both night and day!—And keep 'em
    covered up—
Not *smothered*, John, but snug and
    comfortable—
And now, John Wesley Thomas, first
    and last,—
You feed 'em *milk*—*fresh* milk—and
    always *warm*—
Say five or six or seven times a day—
Of course we'll grade that by the way
    they *thrive*."
But, for all sanguine hope, and care,
    as well,
The little fellows *did not* thrive at
    all.—
Indeed, with *all* our care and vigilance,
By the third day of their captivity
The last survivor of the fated five
Squeaked, like some battered little
    rubber-toy,
Jist clean wore out.—And that's jist
    what 'e wuz!
And—nights,—the cry of the mother-
    fox for her young
Was heard, with awe, for long weeks
    afterward.

And we boys, every night, would go
    to the door
And, peering out in the darkness, lis-
    tening,
Could hear the poor fox in the black
    bleak woods
Still calling for her little ones in vain.
As, all mutely, we returned to the
    warm fireside,
Mother would say: "How would you
    like for *me*
To be out there, this dark night, in
    the cold woods,
Calling for *my* children?"

II

UNCLE BRIGHTENS UP—

UNCLE he says 'at 'way down in
    the sea
Ever'thing's ist like it *used* to be:—
He says they's mermaids an' mermans,
    too,
An' little merchildern, like me an'
    you—
Little merboys, with tops an' balls,
An' little mergirls, with little merdolls.

III

A PET OF UNCLE SIDNEY'S

UNCLE Sidney's vurry proud
    Of little Leslie-Janey,
'Cause she's so smart an' goes to school
    Clean 'way in Pennsylvany!
She print' an' sent a postul-card
    To Uncle Sidney, telling
How glad he'll be to hear that she
    "Toock the onners in Speling."

IV

IN THE KINDERGARTEN OF NOBLE SONG

UNCLE he learns us to rhyme an'
  write
An' all be poets an' all recite:
His little-est poet's his little-est niece,
An' this is her little-est poetry-piece.

V

SINGS A "WINKY-TOODEN" SONG—

O HERE'S a little rhyme for the
  Spring- or Summer-time—
An' a-ho-winky-tooden-an'-a-ho!—
Just a little bit o' tune you can twitter,
  May or June,
An' a-ho-winky-tooden-an'-a-ho!
It's a song that soars and sings,
As the birds that twang their wings
Or the katydids and things
  Thus and so, don't you know,
  An' a-ho-winky-tooden-an'-a-ho!

It's a song just broken loose, with no
  reason or excuse—
An' a-ho-winky-tooden-an'-a-ho!
You can sing along with it—or it mat-
  ters not a bit—
An' a-ho-winky-tooden-an'-a-ho!

It's a lovely little thing
That 'most any one could sing
With a ringle-dingle-ding,
  Soft and low, don't you know,
  An' a-ho-winky-tooden-an'-a-ho!

VI

AND ANOTHER OF OUR BETSY—

US childern's all so lonesome,
  We hardly want to *play*
Or skip or swing or anything,—
  'Cause Betsy she's away!

She's gone to see her people
  At her old home.—But then—
Oh! every child'll jist be wild
  When she's back here again!

CHORUS

Then it's whoopty-doopty dooden!—
  Whoopty-dooden then!
Oh! it's whoopty-doopty dooden,
  When Betsy's back again!

She's like a mother to us,
  And like a sister, too—
Oh, she's as sweet as things to eat
  When all the dinner's through!
And hey! to hear her laughin'!
  And ho! to hear her sing!—
To have her back is all we lack
  Of havin' *everything!*

CHORUS

Then it's whoopty-doopty dooden!—
  Whoopty-dooden then!
Oh! it's whoopty-doopty dooden,
  When Betsy's back again!

Oh! some may sail the northern lakes,
  And some to foreign lands,
And some may seek old Nameless
  Creek,
  Or India's golden sands;
Or some may go to Kokomo,
  And some to Mackinac,—
But I'll go down to Morgantown
  To fetch our Betsy back.

CHORUS

Then it's whoopty-doopty dooden!—
  Whoopty-dooden then!
Oh! it's whoopty-doopty dooden,
  When Betsy's back again!

VII

AND MAKES NURSERY RHYMES

I

THE DINERS IN THE KITCHEN

OUR dog Fred
Et the bread.

Our dog Dash
Et the hash.

Our dog Pete
Et the meat.

Our dog Davy
Et the gravy.

Our dog Toffy
Et the coffee.

Our dog Jake
Et the cake.

Our dog Trip
Et the dip.

And—the worst,
From the first,—

Our dog *Fi*do
Et the pie-dough.

2

THE IMPERIOUS ANGLER

Miss Medairy Dory-Ann
Cast her line and caught a man,
But when he looked so pleased, alack!
She unhooked and plunked him
    back.—
"I never like to catch what I can,"
Said Miss Medairy Dory-Ann.

3

THE GATHERING OF THE CLANS

[*Voice from behind high board-fence.*]

"WHERE's the crowd that dares to go
Where I dare to lead?—you know!"

"Well, here's *one!*"
Shouts Ezry Dunn.

"Count me *two!*"
Yells Cootsy Drew.

"Here's yer *three!*"
Sings Babe Magee.

"Score me *four!*"
Roars Leech-hole Moore.

"Tally—*five!*"
Howls Jamesy Clive.

"I make *six!*"
Chirps Herbert Dix.

"Punctchul!—*seven!*"
Pipes Runt Replevin.

"Mark me *eight!*"
Grunts Mealbag Nate.

"I'm yet *nine!*"
Growls "Lud'rick" Stein.

"Hi! here's *ten!*"
Whoops Catfish Ben.

"And now we march, in daring line,
For the banks of Brandywine!"

4

"IT"

A WEE little worm in a hickory-nut
Sang, happy as he could be,—
"O I live in the heart of the whole
    round world,
And it all belongs to me!"

5

THE DARING PRINCE

A DARING prince, of the realm Rangg
    Dhune,
Once went up in a big balloon
That caught and stuck on the horns
    of the moon,
And he hung up there till next day
    noon—
When all at once he exclaimed, "Hoot-
    toot!"
And then came down in his parachute.

909

THE JAYBIRD

THE Jaybird he's my favor*ite*
    Of all the birds they is!
I think he's quite a stylish sight
    In that blue suit of his:
An' when he 'lights an' shuts his wings,
    His coat's a "cutaway"—
I guess it's only when he sings
    You'd know he wuz a jay.

I like to watch him when he's lit
    In top of any tree,
'Cause all birds git wite out of it
    When *he* 'lights, an' they see
How proud he act', an' swell an'
        spread
    His chest out more an' more,
An' raise the feathers on his head
    Like it's cut pompadore!

908

A SONG OF SINGING

SING! gangling lad, along the brink
    Of wild brook-ways of shoal and
        deep,
Where killdees dip, and cattle drink,
    And glinting little minnows leap!
Sing! slimpsy lass who trips above
    And sets the foot-log quivering!
Sing! bittern, bumblebee, and dove—
    Sing! Sing! Sing!

Sing as you will, O singers all
    Who sing because you *want* to sing!
Sing! peacock on the orchard wall,
    Or tree-toad by the trickling spring!

Sing! every bird on every bough—
    Sing! every living, loving thing—
Sing any song, and anyhow,
    But Sing! Sing! Sing!

910

A BEAR FAMILY

WUNZT, 'way West in Illinoise,
    Wuz two Bears an' their two
        boys:
An' the two boys' names, you know,
Wuz—like *ours* is,—Jim an' Jo;
An' their *parunts'* names wuz same's

All big grown-up people's names,—
Ist *Miz* Bear, the neighbors call
'Em, an' *Mister* Bear—'at's all.
Yes—an' Miz Bear scold him, too,
Ist like grown folks *shouldn't* do!
Wuz a grea'-big river there,
An', 'crosst that, 's a mountain where
Old Bear said some day he'd go,
Ef she don't quit scoldin' so!
So, one day when he been down
The river, fishin', 'most to town,
An' come back 'thout no fish a-tall,
An' Jim an' Jo they run an' bawl
An' tell their ma their pa hain't fetch'
No fish,—she scold again an' ketch
Her old broom up an' biff him, too.—
An' he ist cry, an' say, "Boo-hoo!
I *told* you what I'd do some day!"
An' he ist turned an' runned away
To where's the grea'-big river there
An' ist *splunged* in an' swum to where
The mountain's at, 'way th' other side,
An' clumbed up there. An' Miz Bear
          cried—
An' little Jo an' little Jim—
Ist like their ma—bofe cried fer him!—
But he clumbed on, *clean out o' sight,*
He wuz so mad!—An' served 'em
          right!
Nen—when the Bear got 'way on top
The mountain, he heerd somepin' flop
Its wings—an' somepin' else he heerd
A-rattlin'-like.—An' he wuz *skeered,*
An' looked 'way up, an'—*Mercy sake!*
It wuz a' Eagul an' a SNAKE!
An'-sir! the Snake, he bite an' kill'
The Eagul, an' they bofe fall till
They strike the ground — *k'spang-
          k'spat!*
Wite where the Bear wuz standin' at!
An' when here come the Snake at *him,*
The Bear he think o' little Jim
An' Jo, he did—an' their ma, too,—

All safe at home; an' he ist flew
Back down the mountain—an' could
          hear
The old Snake rattlin', sharp an'
          clear,
Wite clos't behind!—An' Bear he's
          so
All tired out, by time, you know,
He git down to the river there,
He know' he can't *swim* back to where
His folks is at. But ist wite nen
He see a boat an' six big men
'At's been a-shootin' ducks: An' so
He skeered them out the boat. you
          know,
An' ist jumped in—an' Snake *he* tried
To jump in, too, but falled outside
Where all the water wuz; an' so
The Bear grabs one the things you
          row
The boat wiv an' ist whacks the head
Of the old Snake an' kills him dead!—
An' when he's killed him dead, w'y,
          nen
The old Snake's drownded dead again!
Nen Bear set in the boat an' bowed
His back an' rowed—an' rowed—an'
          rowed—
Till he's safe home—so tired he can't
Do nothin' but lay there an' pant
An' tell his childern, "Bresh my coat!"
An' tell his wife, "Go chain my boat!"
An' they're so glad he's back, they say
"They *knowed* he's comin' thataway
To ist su'prise the dear ones there!"
An' Jim an' Jo they dried his hair
An' pulled the burs out; an' their
          ma
She ist set there an' helt his paw
Till he wuz sound asleep, an' nen
She telled him she won't scold again—
          Never—never—never—
          Ferever an' ferever!

911

SOME SONGS AFTER MASTER-SINGERS

I

SONG

[w. s.]

WITH a hey! and a hi! and a hey-
ho rhyme!
O the shepherd lad
He is ne'er so glad
As when he pipes, in the blossom-time,
So rare!
While Kate picks by, yet looks not
there.
So rare! so rare!
With a hey! and a hi! and a ho!
The grasses curdle where the daisies
blow!

With a hey! and a hi! and a hey-ho
vow!
Then he sips her face
At the sweetest place—
And ho! how white is the hawthorn
now!—
So rare!—
And the daisied world rocks round
them there.
So rare! so rare!
With a hey! and a hi! and a ho!
The grasses curdle where the daisies
blow!

II

TO THE CHILD JULIA

[R. H.]

LITTLE Julia, since that we
May not as our elders be,
Let us blithely fill the days
Of our youth with pleasant plays.

First we'll up at earliest dawn,
While as yet the dew is on
The sooth'd grasses and the pied
Blossomings of morningtide;
Next, with rinsèd cheeks that shine
As the enamel'd eglantine,
We will break our fast on bread
With both cream and honey spread;
Then, with many a challenge-call,
We will romp from house and hall,
Gipsying with the birds and bees
Of the green-tress'd garden trees.
In a bower of leaf and vine
Thou shalt be a lady fine
Held in duress by the great
Giant I shall personate.
Next, when many mimics more
Like to these we have played o'er,
We'll betake us home-along
Hand in hand at evensong.

III

THE DOLLY'S MOTHER

[w. w.]

A LITTLE maid, of summers four—
Did you compute her years,—
And yet how infinitely more
To me her age appears:

I mark the sweet child's serious air,
At her unplayful play,—
The tiny doll she mothers there
And lulls to sleep away,

Grows—'neath the grave similitude—
An infant real, to me,
And *she* a saint of motherhood
In hale maturity.

So, pausing in my lonely round,
And all unseen of her,
I stand uncovered—her profound
And abject worshiper.

IV

WIND OF THE SEA

[A. T.]

WIND of the Sea, come fill my
    sail—
Lend me the breath of a freshening
    gale
And bear my port-worn ship away!
For O the greed of the tedious town—
The shutters up and the shutters down!
Wind of the Sea, sweep over the bay
And bear me away!—away!

Whither you bear me, Wind of the
    Sea,
Matters never the least to me:
  Give me your fogs, with the sails
    adrip,
  Or the weltering path thro' the star-
    less night—
On, somewhere, is a new daylight
And the cheery glint of another ship
  As its colors dip and dip!

  Wind of the Sea, sweep over the bay
  And bear me away!—away!

V

SUBTLETY

[R. B.]

WHILST little Paul, convalescing,
    was staying
Close indoors, and his boisterous class-
    mates paying
  Him visits, with fresh school-notes
    and surprises,—
With nettling pride they sprung the
    word "Athletic,"

With much advice and urgings sym-
    pathetic
Anent "athletic exercises." Wise as
Lad might look, quoth Paul: "I've
    pondered o'er that
'Athletic,' but I mean to take, before
    that,
Downstairic and outdooric exercises."

VI

BORN TO THE PURPLE

[W. M.]

MOST-LIKE it was this kingly lad
    Spake out of the pure joy he had
In his child-heart of the wee maid
Whose eery beauty sudden laid
A spell upon him, and his words
Burst as a song of any bird's:—
A peerless Princess thou shalt be,
Through wit of love's rare sorcery:
To crown the crown of thy gold hair
Thou shalt have rubies, bleeding there
Their crimson splendor midst the
    marred
Pulp of great pearls, and afterward
Leaking in fainter ruddy stains
Adown thy neck-and-armlet-chains
Of turquoise, chrysoprase, and mad
Light-frenzied diamonds, dartling glad
Swift spirts of shine that interfuse
As though with lucent crystal dews
That glance and glitter like split rays
Of sunshine, born of burgeoning Mays
When the first bee tilts down the lip
Of the first blossom, and the drip
Of blended dew and honey heaves
Him blinded midst the underleaves.
For raiment, Fays shall weave for
    thee—
Out of the phosphor of the sea

And the frayed floss of starlight, spun
With counterwarp of the firm sun—
A vesture of such filmy sheen
As, through all ages, never queen
Therewith strove truly to make less
One fair line of her loveliness.
Thus gowned and crowned with gems
and gold,
Thou shalt, through centuries untold,
Rule, ever young and ever fair,
As now thou rulest, smiling there.

912

CLIMATIC SORCERY

WHEN frost's all on our winder,
an' the snow's
All out-o'-doors, our "Old-Kriss"- milk-
man goes
A-drivin' round, ist purt' nigh froze to
death,
With his old white mustache froze full
o' breath.

But when it's summer an' all warm
ag'in,
He comes a-whistlin' an' a-drivin' in
Our alley, 'thout no coat on, ner ain't
cold,
Ner his mustache ain't white, ner he
ain't old.

913

THE TREASURE OF THE WISE
MAN

O THE night was dark and the
night was late,
And the robbers came to rob him;

And they picked the locks of his pal-
ace-gate,
The robbers that came to rob him—
They picked the locks of his palace-
gate,
Seized his jewels and gems of state,
His coffers of gold and his priceless
plate,—
The robbers that came to rob him.

But loud he laughed he in the morn-
ing red!—
For of what had the robbers robbed
him?—
Ho! hidden safe, as he slept in bed,
When the robbers came to rob
him,—
They robbed him not of a golden shred
Of the childish dreams in his wise old
head—
"And they're welcome to all things
else," he said,
When the robbers came to rob him.

914

OLD GRANNY DUSK

OLD Granny Dusk, when the sun
goes down,
Here *she* comes into thish-yer town!
Out o' the wet black woods an' swamps
In she traipses an' trails an' tromps—
With her old sunbonnet all floppy an'
brown,
An' her cluckety shoes, an' her old
black gown,
Here *she* comes into thish-yer town!

Old Granny Dusk, when the bats
begin
To flap around, comes a-trompin' in!

An' the katydids they rasp an' whir,
An' the lightnin'-bugs all blink at *her;*
An' the old Hop-toad turns in his
   thumbs,
An' the bunglin' June-bug booms an'
   bums,
An' the Bullfrog croaks, "O here *she*
   comes!"

Old Granny Dusk, though I'm 'feard
   o' you,
Shore-fer-certain I'm sorry, too:
'Cause you look as lonesome an'
   starved an' sad
As a mother 'at's lost ever' child she
   had.—
Yet never a child in thish-yer town
Clings at yer hand er yer old black
   gown,
Er kisses the face you're a-bendin'
   down.

915

FIRE AT NIGHT

FIRE! Fire! Ring! and ring!
   Hear the old bell bang and ding!
Fire! Fire! 'way at night,—
Can't you hear?—I think you might!—
Can't hear them-air clangin' bells?—
W'y, *I* can't hear nothin' else!
Fire! Ain't you 'wake at last!—
Hear them horses poundin' past—
Hear that ladder-wagon grind
Round the corner!—and, behind,
Hear the hose-cart, turnin' short,
And the horses slip and snort,
As the engines clank-and-jar
Jolts the whole street, near and far.
Fire! Fire! Fire! Fire!
Can't you h'ist that winder higher?
La! they've all got past like "scat!" . . .

Night's as black as my old hat—
And it's rainin', too, at that! . . .
Wonder where their old fire's at!

916

THE YOUNG OLD MAN

VOLUNTARY BY ARTLESS "LITTLE
BROTHER"

MAMMA is a widow: There's only
   us three—
Our pretty Mamma, little sister, and
   me:
And we've come to live in this new
   neighborhood
Where all seems so quiet, old-fashioned
   and good.
   Mamma sits and sews at the win-
      dow, and I—
   I'm out at the gate when an old man
      goes by—
Such a *lovely* old man,—though I
   can't tell you why,
   Unless it's his greeting,—"Good
      morning!
Good morning! good morning!" the
   old man will say,—
   "Fine bracing weather we're having
      to-day!—
         And how's little brother—
         And sister—and mother?—
         So dear to each other!—
         Good morning!"

The old man goes by, in his glossy
   high-hat,
And stripe-trousers creased, and all
   turned-up, at that,
And his glancing nose-glasses—and
   pleasantest eyes,
As he smiles on me, always in newer
   surprise:

And though his mustache is as white
   as the snow,
He wears it waxed out and all
   pointed, you know,
And gloves, and high collar and
   bright, jaunty bow,
.   And stylish umbrella.—"Good
   morning!
Good morning! good morning!" the
   old man will say,—
"Fine falling weather we're prom-
   ised to-day!—
      And how's little brother—
      And sister—and mother?—
      So fond of each other!—
      Good morning!"

.   .   .   .

It's Christmas!—it's Christmas! and oh,
   but we're gay!
The postman's been here, and Ma says,
   "Run and play:—
You must leave your Mamma to her-
   self for a while!"
And so sweet is her voice, and so ten-
   der her smile!—
And she looks *so* pretty and happy
   and—Well!—
She's just too delicious for language
   to tell!—
So Sis hugs her *more*—and *I* answer
   the bell,—
      And there in the doorway—
      "Good morning!—
Good morning! good morning! good
   morning, I say!—
Fine Christmas weather we're hav-
   ing to-day!—
      And how's little brother—
      Dear sister—er, ruther—
      Why, here *is* your *mother* . . .
      Good morning!"

917

SOME CHRISTMAS YOUNGSTERS

I

THE STRENGTH OF THE WEAK

*L*AST Chris'mus, little Benny
   Wuzn't sick so bad,—
Now he's had the worst spell
   Ever yet he had.
Ever' Chris'mus-morning, though,
   He'll p'tend as if
He's asleep—an' first you know
   He's got your "Chris'mus-gif' "!

Pa he's good to *all* of us
   All the time; but when,
Ever' time it's *Chris'mus,*
   He's as good-again!—
'Sides our toys an' candy,
   Ever' Chris'mus he
Gives us all a quarter,
   Certain as can be!

Pa, this morning, tiptoe' in
   To make the fire, you know,
Long 'fore it's daylight,
   An' all's ice an' snow!—
An' Benny holler, *"Chris'mus-gif' !"*
   An' Pa jump an' say,
"You'll only get a *dollar* if
   You skeer me thataway!"

II

THE LITTLE QUESTIONER

*B*ABE she's so always
   Wantin' more to hear
All about Santy Claus,
   An' says: "Mommy dear,

Where's Santy's *home* at
    When he ain't *away?*—
An' is they *Mizzuz* Santy Claus
    An' *little* folks—say?—
Chris'mus, Santy's always *here*—
    Don't *they* want him, too?
When it *ain't* Chris'mus
    What does he do?"

III

PARENTAL CHRISTMAS PRESENTS

PARUNTS don't git toys *an'* things,
    Like you'd think they *ruther.*—
Mighty funny Chris'mus-gif's
    Parunts gives each other!—
Pa give Ma a barrel o' flour,
    An' Ma she give to Pa
The nicest dinin'-table
    She know he ever saw!

918

TWILIGHT STORIES

NEITHER *daylight, starlight,*
    moonlight
But a sad-sweet term of some light
By the saintly name of Twilight.

The Grandma Twilight Stories!—Still,
    A childish listener, I hear
The katydid and whippoorwill,
    In deepening atmosphere
Of velvet dusk, blent with the low
    Soft music of the voice that sings
And tells me tales of long ago
    And old enchanted things. . . .

While far fails the last dim daylight,
And the fireflies in the Twilight
Drift about like flakes of starlight.

919

"GO READ YOUR BOOK!"

HOW many times that grim old
    phrase
Has silenced me, in childish days!—
    And *now*—as then it did—
The phantom admonition, clear
And dominant, rings,—and I hear,
    And do as I am bid.

"Go read your book!" my good old sire
Commanded, in affected ire,
    When I, with querying look
And speech, dared vex his studious
    mind
With idle words of any kind.—
    And so I read my book.

Though seldom, in that *wisest* age,
Did I discern on Wisdom's page
    More than the *task:* That led
At least to *thinking,* and at last
To reading less, and not so fast,
    And longing as I read.

And, lo! in gracious time, I grew
To love a book all through and
    through!—
    With yearning eyes I look
On any volume,—old, maybe,
Or new—'tis meat and drink to me.—
    And so I read my book.

Old dog's-eared Readers, scarred and
    inked
With schoolboy hatred, long extinct;—
    Old Histories that bored
Me worst of all the school;—old, worn
Arithmetics, frayed, ripped, and torn—
    Now Ye are all adored.

And likewise I revere and praise
My sire, as now, with vainest gaze
And hearing, still I look
For the old face so grave yet dear—
Nay, still I *see,* and still I *hear!*
And so I read my book.

Next even to my nearest kin,—
My wife—my children romping in
From school to ride my knee,—
I love a book, and dispossess
My lap of it with loathfulness,
For all their love of me.

For, grave or gay the book, it takes
Me as an equal—calms, or makes
Me, laughing, overlook
My little self—forgetful all
Of being so exceeding small.
And so I read my book.

920

WHEN UNCLE DOC WAS YOUNG

THOUGH Doctor Glen—the best of
men—
Is wrinkled, old, and gray,
He'll always smile and stop a while
Where little children play:
And often then he tells us, when
He was a youngster, too,
He was as glad and bad a lad
As old folks ever knew!

As he walks down, no boy in town
But sees him half a block,
And stops to shout a welcome out
With "Here comes Uncle Doc!"
Then all the rest, they look their best
As he lines up among

Us boys of ten—each thinking then
When Uncle Doc was young.

We *run* to him!—Though grave and
grim,
With voice pitched high and thin,
He still reveals the joy he feels
In all that *he* has been:
With heart too true, and honest, too,
To ever *hide* a truth,
He frankly owns, in laughing tones,
He was "a sorry youth!"—

When he was young, he says, he sung
And howled his level-best;
He says he guyed, and sneaked, and
lied,
And wrecked the robin's nest.—
All this, and worse, will he rehearse,
Then smooth his snowy locks
And look the saint he says 'he
ain't. . . .
Them eyes of Uncle Doc's!

He says, when he—like you and me—
Was just too low and mean
To slap asleep, he used to weep
To find his face was clean:
His hair, he said, was just too red
To tell with mortal tongue—
"The Burning Shame" was his nick-
name
When Uncle Doc was young.

921

THE LISPER

ELSIE MINGUS *lisps,* she does!
She lives wite acrosst from us
In Miz. Ayers'uz house 'at she
Rents part to the Mingusuz.—
Yes, an' Elsie plays wiv me.

Elsie lisps so, she can't say
Her own name, ist *anyway!*—
    She say *"Elthy"*—like they wuz
Feathers on her words, an' they
    Ist stick on her tongue like fuzz.

My! she's *purty,* though!—An' when
She *lisps,* w'y, she's purty *nen!*
    When she telled me, wunst, her doll
Wuz so "thweet," an' I p'ten'
    I lisp too,—she laugh'—'at's all!—

She don't never git mad none—
'Cause she know I'm ist in fun.—
    Elsie she ain't one bit sp'iled.—
Of all childerns—ever' one—
    She's the *ladylikest* child!—

My Ma *say* she is! One time
Elsie start to say the rhyme
    "Thing a thong o' thixpenth"—
        Whee!
I ist *yell!* An' Ma say I'm
    Unpolite as I can be!

Wunst I went wiv Ma to call
On Elsie's Ma, an' eat an' all;
    An' nen Elsie, when we've et,
An' we're playin' in the hall,
    Elsie say: It's etikett

Fer young gentlemens, like me,
Eatin' when they's *company,*
    Not to never ever crowd
Down their food, ner "thip their tea
    Ner thup thoop so awful loud!"

922

A MOTTO

THE *Brightest* Star's the *modestest,*
    And more'n likely writes
His motto like the lightnin'-bug's—
    Accordin' To His Lights.

923

A SIMPLE RECIPE

TO be a wholly worthy man,
    As you, my boy, would like to
        be,—
This is to show you how you can—
    This simple recipe:—

Be honest—both in word and act,
    Be strictly truthful through and
        through:
Fact can not fail.—You stick to fact,
    And fact will stick to you.

Be clean—outside and in, and sweep
    Both hearth and heart and hold them
        bright;
Wear snowy linen—aye, and keep
    Your *conscience* snowy-white. ·

Do right, your utmost—good *must*
        come
    To you who do your level-best—
Your very hopes will help you some,
    And work will do the rest.

924

HER LONESOMENESS

WHEN little Elizabeth whispers
    Her morning-love to me,
Each word of the little lisper's,
    As she clambers on my knee—
Hugs me and whispers, "Mommy,
    Oh, I'm so glad it's day
And the night's all gone away!"
How it does thrill and awe me,—
    "The night's all gone away!"

"Sometimes I wake, all listenin','"
    She sighs, "and all's so still!—

The moon and the stars half-glistenin'
Over the window-sill:—
And I look where the gas's pale light
Is all turned down in the hall—
And you ain't here at all!—
And oh, how I wish it was daylight!
—And you ain't here at all!

"And oh," she goes eerily whining
And laughing, too, as she speaks,
"If only the sun kept shining
For weeks and weeks and
weeks!—
For the world's so dark, without you,
And the moon's turned down so
low—
'Way in the night, you know,—
And I get so lonesome about you!—
'Way in the night, you know!"

925

ALMOST BEYOND ENDURANCE

I AIN'T a-goin' to cry no more, no
more!
I'm got ear-ache, an' Ma can't make
It quit a-tall;
An' Carlo bite my rubber-ball
An' puncture it; an' Sis she take
An' poke' my knife down through the
stable-floor
An' loozed it—blame it all!
But I ain't goin' to cry no more, no
more!

An' Aunt Mame *wrote* she's comin',
an' she *can't*—
Folks is come *there!*—An' I don't
care
She *is* my Aunt!
An' my eyes stings; an' I'm
Ist coughin' all the time,

An' hurts me so; an' where my side's
so sore
Grampa felt where, an' he
Says "Mayby it's *pleurasy!*"
But I ain't goin' to cry no more, no
more!

An' I clumbed up an' nen falled off the
fence,
An' Herbert he ist laugh at me!
An' my fi'-cents
It sticked in my tin bank, an' I ist tore
Purt' nigh my thumbnail off,
a-tryin' to git
It out—nen *smash* it!—An' it's in
there yit!
But I ain't goin' to cry no more, no
more!

Oo! I'm so wickud!—An' my breath's
so *hot*—
Ist like I run an' don't res' none
But ist run on when I ought to not;
Yes, an' my chin
An' lips's all warpy, an' teeth's so
fast,
An' 's a place in my throat I can't
swaller past—
An' they all hurt so!—
An' oh, my-oh!
I'm a-startin' ag'in—
I'm a-*startin'* ag'in, but I *won't,* fer
shore!—
*I ist ain't goin' to cry no more, no
more!*

926

THE TOY-BALLOON

THEY wuz a Big Day wunst in
town,
An' little Jason's Pa

Buyed him a little toy-balloon,
    The first he ever saw.—
An' oh! but Jase wuz *more'n* proud,
    A-holdin' to the string
An' scrougin' through the grea'-big
        crowd,
    To hear the Glee Club sing.

The Glee Club it wuz goin' to sing
    In old Masonic Hall;
An' Speakin', it wuz in there, too,
    An' soldiers, folks an' all:
An' Jason's Pa he git a seat
    An' set down purty soon,
A-holdin' little Jase, an' him
    A-holdin' his balloon.

An' while the Speakin' 's startin' up
    An' ever'body still—
The first you know wuz little Jase
    A-yellin' fit to kill!—
Nen Jason's Pa jump on his seat
    An' grab up in the air,—
But little Jason's toy-balloon
    Wuz clean away from there!

An' Jase he yelled; an' Jase's Pa,
    Still lookin' up, clumb down—
While that-air little toy-balloon
    Went bumpin' roun' an' roun'
Ag'inst the ceilin', 'way up there
    Where ever'body saw,
An' *they* all yelled, an' *Jason* yelled,
    An' little Jason's Pa!

But when his Pa he packed him out
    A-screamin'—nen the crowd
Looked down an' hushed—till they
        looked up
    An' howled ag'in out loud;
An' nen the speaker, mad an' pale,
    Jist turned an' left the stand,
An' all j'ined in the Glee Club—"Hail,
    Columby, Happy Land!"

927

THE OLD DAYS

THE old days—the far days—
    The overdear and fair!—
The old days—the lost days—
    How lovely they were!
The old days of Morning,
    With the dew-drench on the flowers
And apple-buds and blossoms
    Of those old days of ours.

Then was the *real* gold
    Spendthrift Summer flung;
Then was the *real* song
    Bird or Poet sung!
There was never censure then,—
    Only honest praise—
And all things were worthy of it
    In the old days.

There bide the true friends—
    The first and the best;
There clings the green grass
    Close where they rest:
Would they were here? No;—
    Would we were there! . . .
The old days—the lost days—
    How lovely they were!

928

TO A POET ON HIS MARRIAGE

MADISON CAWEIN

EVER and ever, on and on,
    From winter dusk, to April
        dawn,
This old enchanted world we range

From night to light—from change to
change—
Or path of burs or lily-bells,
We walk a world of miracles.

The morning evermore must be
A newer, purer mystery—
The dewy grasses, or the bloom
Of orchards, or the wood's perfume
Of wild sweet-williams, or the wet
Blent scent of· loam and violet.

How wondrous all the ways we fare—
What marvels wait us, unaware! . . .
But yesterday, with eyes ablur
And heart that held no hope of Her,
You paced the lone path, but the true
That led to where she waited you.

929

LOCKERBIE FAIR

O THE Lockerbie Fair!—Have you
heard of its fame
And its fabulous riches, too rare for
a name!—
The gold of the noon of the June-time
refined
To the Orient-Night, till the eyes and
the mind
Are dazed with the sights, in the earth
and the air,
Of the opulent splendors of Lockerbie
Fair.

What more fortunate fate might to
mortal befall,
Midst the midsummer beauty and
bloom of it all,
Than to glit with the moon o'er the
rapturous scene

And twink with the stars as they
laughingly lean
O'er the luminous revel and glamour
and glare
Fused in one dazzling glory at Locker-
bie Fair.

The Night, like a queen in her purple
and lace,
With her diamonded brow, and im-
perious grace,
As she leads her fair votaries, train
upon train,
A-dance thro' the feasts of this mystic
domain
To the mandolin's twang, and the
warble and blare
Of voice, flute and bugle at Lockerbie
Fair.

All strange, ever-changing, enchanted
delights
Found now in this newer Arabian
Nights,—
Where each lovely maid is a Princess,
and each
Lucky swain an Aladdin—all treasures
in reach
Of the *"lamps"* and the *"rings"*—and
with *Genii* to spare,
Simply waiting your orders, at Locker-
bie Fair.

930

THE OLD MAN OF THE SEA

I'M The Old Man of the Sea—I
am!—
And this is my secret pride,
That I have a hundred shapes, all
sham,
And a hundred names beside:

They have named me "Habit," and
   "Way," forsooth
"Capricious," and "Fancy-free";—
But to you, O Youth, I confess the
   truth,—
I'm The Old Man of the Sea.

I'm The Old Man of the Sea, yo-ho!
So lift up a song with me,
As I sit on the throne of your shoul-
   ders, alone,
I'm The Old Man of the Sea.

Crowned with the crown of your
   noblest thought,
I'm The Old Man of the Sea:
I reign, rule, ruin, and palter not
In my pitiless tyranny:
You, my lad, are my gay Sindbad,
Frisking about, with me
High on the perch I have always had—
I'm The Old Man of the Sea.

I'm The Old Man of the Sea, yo-ho!
So lift up a song with me,
As I sit on the throne of your shoul-
   ders, alone,
I'm The Old Man of the Sea.

Tricked in the guise of your best in-
   tent,
I am your failures—all—
I am the victories you invent,
And your high resolves that fall:
I am the vow you are breaking now
As the wassail-bowl swings free
And the red guilt flushes your cheek
   and brow—
I'm The Old Man of the Sea.

I'm The Old Man of the Sea, yo-ho!
So lift up a song with me,
As I sit on the throne of your shoul-
   ders, alone,
I'm The Old Man of the Sea.

I am your false dreams of success
And your mythical future fame—
Your life-long lies, and your soul's dis-
   tress
And your slowly-dying shame:
I'm the chattering half of your latest
   laugh,
And your tongue's last perfidy—
Your doom, your tomb, and your
   epitaph . . .
I'm The Old Man of the Sea.

I'm The Old Man of the Sea, yo-ho!
So lift up a song with me,
As I sit on the throne of your shoul-
   ders, alone,
I'm The Old Man of the Sea.

931

PROSE OR VERSE?

PROSE or Verse—or Verse or Prose?
   Ever thus the query goes,—
Which delight do we prefer—
Which the finer—daintier?

Each incites a zest that grows—
Prose or Verse—or Verse or Prose?—
Each a lotus-eater's spell
Wholly irresistible.

All that wit may fashion, free-
Voiced, or piped in melody,—
Prose or Verse—or Verse or Prose—
Which of these the mastery knows?

'Twere as wise to question, friend—
As of this alluring blend,—
The aroma or the rose?—
Prose or Verse—or Verse or Prose?

932

BILLY MILLER'S CIRCUS-SHOW

AT Billy Miller's Circus-Show—
In their old stable where it's at—
The boys pays twenty pins to go,
An' gits their money's-worth at
    that!—
'Cause Billy he can climb and chalk
His stockin'-feet an' purt' nigh walk
A tight-rope—yes, an' *ef* he fall
He'll ketch, an' "skin a cat"—'at's all!

He ain't afeard to swing and hang
    Ist by his legs!—an' mayby stop
An' yell "Look out!" an' nen—
    k-spang!—
    He'll let loose, upside-down, an'
        drop
Wite on his hands! An' nen he'll do
"Contortion-acts"—ist limber through
As "Injarubber Mens" 'at goes
With shore-fer-certain circus-shows!

At Billy Miller's Circus-Show
    He's got a circus-ring—an' they's
A dressin'-room,—so's he can go
    An' dress an' paint up when he plays
He's somepin' else;—'cause sometimes
    he's
"Ringmaster"—bossin' like he please—
An' sometimes "Ephalunt"—er "Bare-
Back Rider," prancin' out o' there!

An' sometimes—an' the best of all!—
    He's "The Old Clown," an' got on
        clo'es
All stripud,—an' white hat, all tall
    An' peakud—like in shore-'nuff
        shows,—
An' got three-cornered red-marks, too,

On his white cheeks—ist like they
    do!—
An' you'd ist die, the way he sings
An' dances an' says funny things!

933

IT'S *GOT* TO BE

"WHEN it's *got* to be,"—like I
    always say,
    As I notice the years whiz past,
And know each day is a yesterday,
    When we size it up, at last,—
Same as I said when my boyhood went
    And I knowed *we* had to quit,—
"It's *got* to be, and it's *goin'* to be!"—
So I said "Good-by" to *it*.

It's *got* to be, and it's *goin'* to be!
    So at least I always try
To kind o' say in a hearty way,—
    "Well, it's *got* to be. Good-by!"

The time just melts like a late, last
    snow,—
    When it's *got* to be, it melts!
But I aim to keep a cheerful mind,
    Ef I can't keep nothin' else!
I knowed, when I come to twenty-one,
    That I'd soon be twenty-two,—
So I waved one hand at the soft young
    man,
    And I said, "Good-by to *you!*"

It's *got* to be, and it's *goin'* to be!
    So at least I always try
To kind o' say, in a cheerful way,—
    "Well, it's *got* to be.—Good-by!"

They kep' a-goin', the years and years,
    Yet still I smiled and smiled,—

For I'd said "Good-by" to my single
    life,
And now had a wife and child:
Mother and son and the father—one,—
Till, last, on her bed of pain,
She jes' smiled up, like she always
    done,—
And I said "Good-by" again.

It's *got* to be, and it's *goin'* to be!
So at least I always try
To kind o' say, in a humble way,—
"Well, it's *got* to be. Good-by!"

And then my boy—as he growed to be
Almost a man in size,—
Was more than a pride and joy to me,
With his mother's smilin' eyes.—
He gimme the slip, when the War
    broke out,
And followed me. And'I
Never knowed till the first fight's
    end . . .
    I found him, and then, . . . "Good-
    by."

It's *got* to be, and it's *goin'* to be!
So at least I always try
To kind o' say, in a patient way,
"Well, it's *got* to be. Good-by!"

I have said, "Good-by!—Good-by!—
    Good-by!"
With my very best good will,
All through life from the first,—and I
Am a cheerful old man still:
But it's *got* to end, and it's *goin'* to
    end!
And this is the thing I'll do,—
With my last breath I will laugh, O
    Death,
And say "Good-by" to *you!* . . .

It's *got* to be! And again I say,—
When his old scythe circles high,
I'll laugh—of course, in the kindest
    way,—
As I say "Good-by!—Good-by!"

934

CHRISTMAS SEASON

TO A FRIEND VISITING ENGLAND

THIS is a Christmas carol—
    A late one, it is true,—
But (dight in Truth's apparel)
    The best that we can do:—
        The best our Muse belated
        Thus offers, antedated,—
        E'en as the old waits waited
    We, waiting, sing for you.

So, haply, you may listen,
    As 'twere, with Fancy's ear,
And shape such songs of this-un
    As were worth worlds to hear,—
        Such anthemings ecstatic
        As scaled The Mermaid's attic
        In midnight's aromatic
    Of choicest Christmas cheer:

Such songs as Marlowe lifted,
    With throstle-throated Will
And rare Ben, as they shifted
    Their laughing voices till
        The   mirth,   with   music
            blended,
        So oversweet ascended,
        It well were never ended—
    And, hark!—you hear it still! . . .

You hear it; aye, and love it!—
    Beyond all voices dear—

Your master's!—none above it.—
    So harken, and so hear!—
    Your master's English.—
        Surely
No other rests so purely
On Fame, or more securely,—
O English of Shakespeare!

935

ART AND POETRY

TO HOMER C. DAVENPORT

WESS he says, and sort o' grins,
    "Art and Poetry is twins!

"Yit, if I'd my pick, I'd shake
Poetry, and no mistake!

"Pictures, allus 'peared to *me,*
Clean laid over Poetry!

"Let me *draw,* and then, i jings,
I'll not keer a straw who sings.

" 'F I could draw as you have drew,
Like to jes' swap pens with you!

"Picture-drawin' 's my pet vision
Of Life-work in Lands Elysian.

"Pictures is first language we
Find hacked out in History.

"Most delight we ever took
Was in our first Picture-book.

" 'Thout the funny picture-makers,
They'd be lots more undertakers!

"Still, as I say, Rhymes and Art
'Smighty hard to tell apart.

"Songs and pictures go together
Same as birds and summer weather."

So Wess says, and sort o' grins,
"Art and Poetry is twins."

936

THE CHILDREN OF THE CHILDLESS

THE Children of the Childless!—
    Yours—and mine.—
Yea, though we sit here in the pitying
        gaze
Of fathers and mothers whose fond
        fingers twine
Their children's locks of living gold,
        and praise
With warm, caressing palms, the head
        of brown,
Or crown
Of opulent auburn, with its amber
        floss
In all its splendor loosed and jostled
        down
Across
The mother-lap at prayer.—Yea, even
        when
These sweet petitioners are kissed, and
        then
Are kissed and kissed again—
The pursed mouths lifted with the
        worldlier prayer
That bed and oblivion spare
Them yet a little while
Beside their envied elders by the glow
Of the glad firelight; or wrestling, as
        they go,
Some promise for the morrow, to be-
        guile
Their long exile

Within the wild waste lands of dream
    and sleep.
Nay, nay, not even these most stably
    real
Of children are more loved than our
    ideal—
More tangible to the soul's touch and
    sight
Than *these—our* children by Divine
    birthright. . . .
These—these of ours, who soothe us,
    when we weep,
With tenderest ministries,
Or, flashing into smiling ecstasies,
Come dashing through our tears—ay,
    laughing leap
Into our empty arms, in Fate's despite,
And nestle to our hearts. O Heaven's
    delight!—
The children of the childless—even
    these!

937

HOOSIER SPRING-POETRY

WHEN ever'thing's a-goin' like
    she's got-a-goin' now,—
The maple-sap a-drippin', and the buds
    on ever' bough
A-sort o' reachin' up'ards all a-trim-
    blin', ever' one,
Like 'bout a million Brownie-fists
    a-shakin' at the sun!
The childern wants their shoes off
    'fore their breakfast, and the
    Spring
Is here so good-and-plenty that the old
    hen has to sing!—
When things is goin' *thisaway,* w'y,
    that's the sign, you know,
That ever'thing's a-goin' like we like
    to see her go!

Oh, ever'thing's a-goin' like we like to
    see her go!
Old Winter's up and dusted, with his
    dratted frost and snow—
The ice is out the crick ag'in, the freeze
    is out the ground,
And you'll see faces thawin' too ef
    you'll jes' look around!—
The bluebird's landin' home ag'in, and
    glad to git the chance,
'Cause here's where he belongs at,
    that's a settled circumstance!
And him and mister robin now's
    a-chunin' fer the show.
Oh, ever'thing's a-goin' like we like to
    see her go!

The sun ain't jes' p'tendin' *now!—*The
    ba'm is in the breeze—
The trees'll soon be green as grass, and
    grass as green as trees;
The buds is all jes' *eechin',* and the
    dogwood down the run
Is bound to bu'st out laughin' 'fore
    another week is done;
The bees is wakin', gap'y-like, and
    fumblin' fer their buzz,
A-thinkin' ever-wakefuler, of other
    days that wuz,—
When all the land wuz orchard-blooms
    and clover, don't you know. . . .
Oh, ever'thing's a-goin' like we like to
    see her go!

938

THE VOICE OF PEACE

INDEPENDENCE BELL: INDIANAPOLIS,
NOVEMBER 17, 1904

THOUGH now forever still
    Your voice of jubilee—
We hear—we hear, and ever will,
    The Bell of Liberty!

Clear as the voice to them
In that far night agone
Pealed from the heavens o'er Bethle-
hem,
The voice of Peace peals on!

Stir all your memories up,
O Independence Bell,
And pour from your inverted cup
The song we love so well!
As you rang in the dawn
Of Freedom—tolled the knell
Of Tyranny,—ring on—ring on—
O Independence Bell!

Ring numb the wounds of wrong
Unhealed in brain and breast;
With music like a slumber-song
Lull tearful eyes to rest.—
Ring! Independence Bell!
Ring on till worlds to be
Shall listen to the tale you tell
Of Love and Liberty!

939

A DEFECTIVE SANTA CLAUS

Little Boy! Halloo!—halloo!
Can't you hear me calling you?—
Little Boy that used to be,
Come in here and play with me.

ALLUS when our Pa he's away
Nen Uncle Sidney comes to stay
At our house here—so Ma an' me
An' Etty an' Lee-Bob won't be
Afeard ef anything at night
Might happen—like Ma says it might.
(Ef *Trip* wuz *big*, I bet you he
'Uz best watch-dog you ever see!)
An' so last winter—ist before

It's go' be Chris'mus-Day—w'y, shore
Enough, Pa had to haf to go
To 'tend a lawsuit—"An' the snow
Ist right fer Santy Claus!" Pa said,
As he clumb in old Ayersuz sled,
An' said he's sorry *he* can't be
With us that night—" 'Cause," he-
says-ee,
"Old Santy *might* be comin' here—
This very night of all the year
I' got to be away!—so all
You kids must tell him—ef he call—
He's mighty welcome, an' yer Pa
He left his love with you an' Ma
An' Uncle Sid!" An' clucked, an' leant
Back, laughin'—an' away they went!
An' Uncle wave' his hands an' yells
"Yer old horse ort to have on bells!"
But Pa yell back an' laugh an' say
"I 'spect when *Santy* come this way
It's time enough for sleighbells nen!"
An' holler back "Good-by!" again,
An' reach out with the driver's whip
An' cut behind an' drive back Trip.

An' so all day it snowed an' snowed!
An' Lee-Bob he ist watched the road,
In his high-chair; an' Etty she
'Ud play with Uncle Sid an' me—
Like she wuz he'ppin' fetch in wood
An' keepin' old fire goin' good,
Where Ma she wuz a-cookin' there
In kitchen, too, an' ever'where!
An' Uncle say, " 'At's ist the way
Yer Ma's b'en workin', night an' day,
Sence she hain't big as Etty is
Er Lee-Bob in that chair o' his!"
Nen Ma she'd laugh 't what Uncle
said,
An' smack an' smoove his old bald
head
An' say "Clear out the way till I
Can keep that pot from b'ilin' dry!"

Nen Uncle, when she's gone back to
The kitchen, says, "We *ust* to do
Some cookin' in the *ashes.—Say,*
S'posin' we try some, thataway!"
An' nen he send us to tell Ma
Send two big 'taters in he saw
Pa's b'en a-keepin' 'cause they got
The premium at the Fair! An' what
You think?—He rake a grea'-big hole
In the hot ashes, an' he roll
Them old big 'taters in the place
An' rake the coals back—an' his face
Ist swettin' so's he purt' nigh swear
'Cause it's so hot! An' when they're
      there
'Bout time 'at we fergit 'em, he
Ist rake 'em out aga;n—an' *gee!*—
He bu'st 'em with his fist wite on
A' old stove-led, while Etty's gone
To git the salt, an' butter, too—
Ist like he said she haf to do,
No matter what *Ma* say! An' so
He salt an' butter 'em, an' blow
'Em cool enough fer us to eat—
An' *me-o-my!* they're hard to beat!
An' Trip 'ud ist lay there an' pant
Like he'd laugh *out loud,* but he can't.
Nen Uncle fill his pipe—an' we
'Ud he'p him light it—Sis an' me,—
But mostly little Lee-Bob, 'cause
"He's the best *Lighter* ever wuz!"
Like Uncle told him wunst when Lee-
Bob cried an' jerked the light from
      me,
He wuz so mad! So Uncle pat
An' pet him (Lee-Bob's ust to that—
'Cause he's the *little*-est, you know,
An' allus has b'en humored so!)
Nen Uncle gits the flat-arn out,
An', while he's tellin' us all 'bout
Old Chris'mus-times when *he's* a kid,
He ist cracked hickernuts, he did,
Till they's a crockful, mighty nigh!

An' when they're all done by an' by,
He raked the red coals out again
An' telled me, "Fetch that popcorn in,
An' old three-leggud skillut—an'
The *led* an' all now, little man,—
An' yer old Uncle here 'ull show
You how corn's popped, long years
      ago
When me an' Santy Claus wuz boys
On Pap's old place in Illinoise!—
An' your Pa, too, wuz chums, all
      through,
With Santy!—Wisht Pa'd be here,
      too!"
Nen Uncle sigh at Ma, an' she
Pat him again, an' say to me
An' Etty,—"You take warning fair!—
Don't talk too much, like Uncle there,
Ner don't fergit, like *him,* my dears,
That 'little pitchers has big ears!'"
But Uncle say to her, "Clear out!—
Yer brother knows what he's about.—
You git your Chris'mus-cookin' done
Er these pore childern won't have
      none!"
Nen Trip wake' up an' raise', an' nen
Turn roun' an' nen lay down again.
An' one time Uncle Sidney say,—
"When dogs is sleepin' thataway,
Like Trip, an' *whimpers,* it's a sign
He'll ketch *eight* rabbits—mayby
      nine—
Afore his fleas'll wake him—nen
He'll bite hisse'f to sleep again
An' *try* to dream he's go' ketch *ten.*"
An' when Ma's gone again back in
The kitchen, Uncle scratch his chin
An' say, "When Santy Claus an' Pa
An' me wuz little boys—an' Ma,
When she's 'bout big as Etty there;—
W'y,—'When we're *growed*—no mat-
      ter *where,'*
Santy he cross' his heart an' say,—

'I'll come to see you, all, some day
When *you'* got childerns—all but me
An' pore old Sid!' " Nen Uncle he
Ist kind o' shade his eyes an' pour'
'Bout forty-'leven bushels more
O' popcorn out the skillut there
In Ma's new basket on the chair.
An' nen he telled us—an' talk' low,
"So Ma can't hear," he say:—"You
      know
Yer *Pa* know', when he drived away,
To-morry's go' be Chris'mus-*Day;*—
Well, nen *to-night,*" he whisper, "see?—
It's go' be Chris'mus-*Eve,*" says-ee,
"An', like yer Pa hint, when he went,
Old Santy Claus (now hush!) he's sent
Yer Pa a postul-card, an' write
He's shorely go' be here to-night. . . .
That's why yer Pa's so bored to be
Away to-night, when Santy he
Is go' be here, sleighbells an' all,
To make you kids a Chris'mus-call!"
An' we're so glad to know *fer shore*
He's comin', I roll on the floor—
An' here come Trip a-waller'n' roun'
An' purt' nigh knock the clo'eshorse
      down!—
An' Etty grab Lee-Bob an' prance
All roun' the room like it's a dance—
Till Ma she come an' march us nen
To dinner, where we're *still* again,
But *tickled* so we ist can't eat
But pie, an' ist the hot mincemeat
With raisins in.—But *Uncle* et,
An' *Ma.* An' there they set an' set
Till purt' nigh supper-time; nen we
Tell him he's got to fix the Tree
'Fore *Santy* gits here, like he said.
We go nen to the old woodshed—
All bundled up, through the deep
      snow—
"An' snowin' yet, *jee-rooshy-O!*"
Uncle he said, an' he'p us wade

Back where's the Chris'mus-Tree he's
      made
Out of a little jackoak-top
He git down at the sawmill-shop—
An' Trip 'ud run ahead, you know,
An' 'tend-like he 'uz *eatin'* snow—
When we all waddle back with it;
An' Uncle set it up—an' git
It wite in front the fireplace—'cause
He says " 'Tain't *so* 'at Santy Claus
Comes down *all* chimblies,—least, to-
      night
He's comin' in *this* house all right—
By the front-door, as ort to be!—
We'll all be hid where we can *see!*"
Nen he look up, an' he see Ma
An' say, "It's ist too bad their *Pa*
Can't be here, so's to see the fun
The childern *will* have, ever' one!"

Well, *we!*—We hardly couldn't wait
Till it wuz dusk, an' dark an' late
Enough to light the lamp!—An' Lee-
Bob light a candle on the Tree—
"Ist one—'cause I'm 'The Lighter'!"—
      Nen
He clumb on Uncle's knee again
An' hug us *bofe;*—an' Etty git
Her little chist an' set on it
Wite clos't, while Uncle telled some
      more
'Bout Santy Claus, an' clo'es he wore
*"All maked o' furs, an' trimmed as
      white
As cotton is, er snow at night!"*
An' nen, all sudden-like, he say,—
*"Hush! Listen there! Hain't that a
      sleigh
An' sleighbells jinglin'?"* Trip go
      "whooh!"
Like *he* hear bells an' *smell* 'em, too.
Nen we all listen. . . . An'-sir, shore
Enough, we hear bells—more an' more

A-jinglin' clos'ter—clos'ter still
Down the old crook-road roun' the
    hill.
An' Uncle he jumps up, an' all
The chairs he jerks back by the wall
An' th'ows a' overcoat an' pair
O' winder-curtains over there
An' says, *"Hide quick, er you're too
    late!—
Them bells is stoppin' at the gate!—
Git back o' them-'air chairs an' hide,
'Cause I hear Santy's voice outside!"*
An' *Bang! bang! bang!* we heerd the
    door—
Nen it flewed open, an' the floor
Blowed full o' snow—that's *first* we
    saw,
Till little Lee-Bob shriek' at Ma
*"There's Santy Claus!—I know him by
His big white mufftash!"*—an' ist cry
An' laugh an' *squeal* an' dance an'
    yell—
Till, when he quiet down a spell,
Old Santy bow an' th'ow a kiss
To him—an' one to me an' Sis—
An' nen go *clos't* to Ma an' stoop
An' kiss her—An' nen give a whoop
That *fainted* her!—'Cause when he
    bent
An' kiss her, he ist backed an' went
Wite 'g'inst the Chris'mus-Tree ist
    where
The candle's at Lee-Bob lit there!—
An' set his white-fur belt afire—
An' blaze streaked roun' his waist an'
    higher
Wite up his old white beard an'
    th'oat!—
Nen Uncle grabs th' old overcoat
An' flops it over Santy's head,
An' swing the door wide back an'
    said,
"Come out, old man!—an' *quick* about

It!—I've ist *got* to put you out!"
An' out he sprawled him in the snow—
"Now *roll!*" he says—*"Hi-roll-ee-O!"*—
An' Santy, sputter'n' *"Ouch! Gee-
    whiz!"*
Ist roll an' roll fer all they is!
An' Trip he's out there, too,—I know,
'Cause I could hear him yappin' so—
An' I heerd Santy, wunst er twic't,
Say, as he's rollin', *"Drat the fice't!"*
Nen Uncle come back in, an' shake
Ma up, an' say, "Fer mercy-sake!—
He hain't hurt none!" An' nen he
    said,—
"You youngsters h'ist up-stairs to bed!
Here! kiss yer Ma 'Good night,' an'
    me,—
We'll he'p old Santy fix the Tree—
An' all yer whistles, horns an' drums
I'll he'p you toot when morning
    comes!"

.   .   .   .

It's long while 'fore we go to sleep,—
'Cause down-stairs, all-time somepin'
    keep
A-kind o' scufflin' roun' the floors—
An' openin' doors, an' *shettin'* doors—
An' could hear Trip a-whinin', too,
Like he don't know ist *what* to do—
An' tongs a-clankin' down *k'thump!*—
Nen some one squonkin' the old
    pump—
An' *Wooh!* how cold it soun' out
    there!—
I could ist *see* the pump-spout where
It's got ice chin-whiskers all wet
An' drippy—An' I see it yet!
An' nen, seem-like, I hear some mens
A-talkin' out there by the fence,
An' one says, "Oh, 'bout twelve
    o'clock!"

"Nen," 'nother'n' says, "Here's to you,
 Doc!—
God bless us ever' one!" An' nen
I heerd the old pump squonk again.
An' nen I say my prayer all through
Like Uncle Sidney learn' me to,—
"O Father mine, e'en as Thine own,
This child looks up to Thee alone:
Asleep or waking, give him still
His Elder Brother's wish and will."
An' that's the last I know . . . Till
 Ma
She's callin' us—an' so is *Pa,*—
He holler *"Chris'mus-gif'!"* an' say,—
"I'm got back home fer Chris'mus-
 Day!—
An' Uncle Sid's here, too—an' he
Is nibblin' roun' yer Chris'mus-Tree!"
Nen *Uncle* holler, "I suppose
Yer Pa's so proud he's froze his nose
He wants to turn it up at us,
'Cause *Santy* kick' up such a fuss—
Tetchin' hisse'f off same as ef
He wuz his own fireworks hisse'f!"

An' when we're down-stairs,—shore
 enough,
Pa's nose *is* froze, an' salve an' stuff
All on it—an' one hand's froze, too,
An' got a old yarn red-and-blue
Mitt on it—"An' he's froze some
 more
Acrost his chist, an' kind o' sore
All roun' his *dy-*fram," Uncle say.—
"But Pa he'd ort a-seen the way
Santy bear up last night when that-
Air fire break out, an' quicker'n *scat*
He's all a-blazin', an' them-'air
Gun-cotton whiskers that he wear
Ist *flashin'!*—till I burn a hole
In the snow with him, an' he roll
The front-yard dry as Chris-mus jokes

Old parents plays on little folks!
But, long's a smell o' tow er wool,
I kep' him rollin' *beautiful!*—
Til I wuz *shore* I *shorely* see
He's *squenched!* W'y, hadn't b'en fer
 me,
That old man might a-burnt clear
 down
Clean—plum'—level with the groun'!"
Nen Ma say, "There, Sid; that'll do!—
Breakfast is ready—*Chris'mus,* too.—
Your voice 'ud soun' best, sayin'
 Grace—
Say it." An' Uncle bow' his face
An' say so long a *Blessing* nen,
Trip bark' *two* times 'fore it's
 "A-men!"

940

WHAT LITTLE SAUL GOT, CHRISTMAS

US parents mostly thinks our own's
 The smartest childern out!
But Widder Shelton's little Saul
Beats all I know about!
He's weakly-like—in p'int o' health,
 But strong in word and deed
And heart and head, and snap and
 spunk,
 And allus in the lead!

Comes honest by it, fer his Pa—
 Afore he passed away—
He was a leader—(Lord, I'd like
 To hear him preach to-day!)
He led his flock; he led in prayer
 Fer spread o' Peace—and when
Nothin' but War could spread it, he
 Was first to lead us then!

So little Saul has grit to take
  Things jes' as they occur;
And Sister Shelton's proud o' him
  As he is proud o' her!
And when she "got up"—jes' fer him
  And little playmates all—
A Chris'mus-tree—they ever'one
  Was there but little Saul.

Pore little chap was sick in bed
  Next room; and Doc was there,
And said the childern might file past,
  But go right back to where
The *tree* was, in the settin'-room.
  And Saul jes' laid and smiled—
Ner couldn't nod, ner wave his hand,
  It hurt so—Bless the child!

And so they left him there with Doc—
  And warm tear of his Ma's . . .
Then—suddent-like—high over all
  Their laughture and applause—
They heerd: "I don't care what you git
  On yer old Chris'mus-tree,
'Cause I'm got somepin' you all
    hain't—
  I'm got the pleurisy!"

In forum—as in battle-field—
  His voice rang for the truth—the
    right—
Keyed with the shibboleth that pealed
  His Soul forth to the fight:
The inspiration of his pen
  Glowed as a star, and lit anew
The faces and the hearts of men
  Watching, the long night through.

A destiny ordained—divine
  It seemed to hosts of those who saw
His rise since youth and marked the line
  Of his ascent with awe:—
From the now-storied little town
  That gave him birth and worth, be-
    hold,
Unto this day of his renown,
  His sword and word of gold.

Serving the Land he loved so well—
  Hailed midsea or in foreign port,
Or in strange-bannered citadel
  Or Oriental Court,—
He—honored for his Nation's sake,
  And loved and honored for his own—
Hath seen his Flag in glory shake
  Above the Pagan Throne.

941

GENERAL LEW WALLACE

FEBRUARY 15, 1905

NAY, Death, thou mightiest of all
    Dread conquerors—thou dread-
est chief,—
Thy heavy hand can here but fall
  Light as the Autumn leaf:
As vainly, too, its weight is laid
  Upon the warrior's knightly sword;—
Still through the charge and cannonade
  It flashes for the Lord.

942

ON READING DR. HENRY VAN DYKE'S VOLUME OF POEMS— MUSIC

MUSIC!—Yea, and the airs you
    play—
Out of the faintest Far-Away
And the sweetest, too; and the dearest
    Here,
With its quavering voice but its bravest
    cheer—
The prayer that aches to be all ex-
    pressed—

The kiss of love at its tenderest:
Music—music, with glad heart-throbs
Within it; and music with tears and
    sobs
Shaking it, as the startled soul
Is shaken at shriek of the fife and roll
Of the drums;—then as suddenly lulled
    again
With the whisper and lisp of the sum-
    mer rain:
Mist of melodies fragrance-fine—
The bird-song flicked from the eglan-
    tine
With the dews when the springing
    bramble throws
A rarer drench on its ripest rose,
And the wingèd song soars up and
    sinks
To the dove's dim coo by the river-
    brinks
Where the ripple's voice still laughs
    along
Its glittering path of light and song.
Music, O Poet, and all your own
By right of capture and that alone,—
For in it we hear the harmony
Born of the earth and the air and the
    sea,
And over and under it, and all
    through,
We catch the chime of The Anthem,
    too.

943

HER SMILE OF CHEER AND
VOICE OF SONG

ANNA HARRIS RANDALL

SPRING fails, in all its bravery of
    brilliant gold and green,—
The sun, the grass, the leafing tree, and
    all the dazzling scene

Of dewy morning—orchard blooms
And woodland blossoms and per-
    fumes
With bird-songs sown between.

Yea, since *she* smiles not any more, so
    every flowery thing
Fades, and the birds seem brooding o'er
    her silence as they sing—
Her smile of cheer and voice of song
Seemed so divinely to belong
    To ever-joyous Spring!

Nay, still she smiles.—Our eyes are
    blurred and see not through
    our tears:
And still her rapturous voice is heard,
    though not of mortal ears:—
Now ever doth she smile and sing
Where Heaven's unending Clime of
    Spring
Reclaims those gifts of hers.

944

THINKIN' BACK

I'VE be'n thinkin' back, of late,
    S'prisin'!—And I'm here to state
I'm suspicious it's a sign
Of age, maybe, er decline
Of my faculties,—and yit
I'm not feelin' old a bit—
Any more than sixty-four
Ain't no young man any more!

Thinkin' back's a thing 'at grows
On a feller, I suppose—
Older 'at he gits, i jack,
More he keeps a-thinkin' back!
Old as old men git to be,
Er as middle-aged as me,

Folks'll find us, eye and mind
Fixed on what we've left behind—
Rehabilitatin'-like
Them old times we used to hike
Out barefooted fer the crick,
'Long 'bout Aprile first—to pick
Out some "warmest" place to go
In a-swimmin'—*Ooh! my-oh!*
Wonder now we hadn't died!
Grate horseradish on my hide
Jes' *a-thinkin'* how cold then
That-'ere worter must 'a' be'n!

Thinkin' back—W'y, goodness me!
I kin call their names and see
Every little tad I played
With, er fought, er was afraid
Of, and so made *him* the best
Friend I had of all the rest!
Thinkin' back, I even hear
Them a-callin', high and clear,
Up the crick-banks, where they seem
Still hid in there—like a dream—
And me still a-pantin' on
The green pathway they have gone!
Still they hide, by bend er ford—
Still they hide—but, thank the Lord
(Thinkin' back, as I have said),
I hear laughin' on ahead!

945

SIS RAPALYE

WHEN rainy-greener shoots the
  grass
And blooms the cherry tree,
And children laugh by glittering
  brooks,
Wild with the ecstasy

Of bursting Spring, with twittering
  bird
And hum of honey-bee,—
"Sis Rapalye!" my spirit shouts . . .
And she is here with me!

As laugh the children, so her laugh
  Haunts all the atmosphere;—
Her song is in the brook's refrain;
  Her glad eyes, flashing clear,
Are in the morning dews; her speech
  Is melody so dear,
The bluebird trills,—"Sis Rapalye!—
  I hear!—I hear!—I hear!"

Again in races, at "Recess,"
  I see her braided hair
Toss past me as I stay to lift
  Her straw hat, fallen there;
The school-bell sends a vibrant pang
  My heart can hardly bear.—
Yet still she leads—Sis Rapalye—
  And leads me everywhere!

Now I am old.—Yet she remains
  The selfsame child of ten.—
Gay, gallant little girl, to race
  On into Heaven then!
Yet gallant, gay Sis Rapalye—
  In blossom-time, and when
The trees and grasses beckon her—
  Comes back to us again.

And so, however long since youth
  Whose raptures wild and free
An old man's heart may claim no
  more,—
  With more than memory
I share the Spring's own joy that brings
  My boyhood back to me
With laughter, blossoms, singing birds
  And sweet Sis Rapalye.

946

TO BLISS CARMAN

HE is the morning's poet—
 The bard of mount and moor,
The minstrel fine of dewy shine,
 The dawning's troubadour:

The brother of the bluebird,
 'Mid blossoms, throng on throng,
Whose singing calls, o'er orchard walls,
 Seem glitterings of song.

He meets, with brow uncovered,
 The sunrise through the mist,
With raptured eyes that range the
 skies
And seas of amethyst:

The brambled rose clings to him;
 The breezy wood receives
Him as the guest she loves the best
 And laughs through all her leaves:

Pan and his nymphs and dryads
 They hear, in breathless pause,
This earth-born wight lilt his delight,
 And envy him because . . .

He is the morning's poet—
 The bard of mount and moor,
The minstrel fine of dewy shine,
 The dawning's troubadour.

947

A SONG O' CHEER

MY Grampa he's a-allus sayin',
 "Sing a song o' cheer!"—
And wunst I says "What kind *is*
 them?"
He says,—"The kind to *hear*.—

'Cause they're the songs that *Nature*
 sings,
 In ever' bird that twitters!"
"Well, *whipperwills* and *doves*," says I,
 "Hain't over-cheery critters!"
"Then don't you sing like *them*," he
 says—
 "Ner *guinny-hens,* my dear—
Ner *peafowls* nuther (drat the boy!)
 You sing a song o' cheer!"
·I can't sing nothin' anyhow;
 But, comin' home, to'rds night,
I kind o' sort o' kep' a-whistlin'
 "Old—Bob—White!"

948

CHILD'S CHRISTMAS CAROL

CHRIST used to be like you and me,
 When just a lad in Galilee,—
So when we pray, on Christmas Day,
He favors first the prayers we say:
Then waste no tear, but pray with
 cheer,
This gladdest day of all the year:

O Brother mine of birth Divine,
Upon this natal day of Thine
Bear with our stress of happiness
Nor count our reverence the less
Because with glee and jubilee
Our hearts go singing up to Thee.

949

I' GOT TO FACE MOTHER
TO-DAY!

I' GOT to face Mother to-day, fer a
 fact!—
 I' got to face Mother to-day!

And jes' how I'll *dare* to, an' how she
    will act,
  Is more than a mortal can say!
But I' *got* to face her—I' *got* to! And so
Here's a' old father clean at the end of
    his row!

And Pink and Wade's gone to the farm
    fer her now—
  And I'm keepin' house fer 'em
    here—
Their purty, new house—and all paid
    fer!—But how
Am *I* goin' to meet her, and clear
Up *my* actchully he'ppin' 'em both to
    elope?—
('Cause Mother wuz set—and wuz no
    other hope!)

I don' think it's *Wade* she's so biased
    ag'in',
  But his *bizness,*—a railroadin' man
'At runs a switch-engine, day out and
    day in,
  And's got to make hay while he
    can,—
It's a *dangersome* job, I'll admit,—but
    see what
A fine-furnished home 'at he's already
    got!

And *Pink*—W'y, the girl wuz just
    pinin' away,—
  So what could her old father do,
When he found her, hid-like, in a loose
    load of hay,
  But jes' to drive on clean into
The aidge of the city, where—singular
    thing!—
Wade switched us away to the Squire,
    i jing!

Now—a-leavin' me here—they're driv
    off, with a cheer,
  On their weddin'-trip—which is to
    drive
Straight home and tell Mother, and tol
    her back here
  And surrender me, dead er alive!
So I'm waitin' here—not so blame'
    overly gay
As I *wuz,*—'cause I' got to face *Mother*
    to-day!

950

NAME US NO NAMES NO MORE

SING, oh, rarest of roundelays!—
  Sing the hilarity and delight
Of our childhood's gurgling, giggling
    days!
  When our eyes were as twinkling-
    keen and bright
And our laughs as thick as the stars
    at night,
And our breasts volcanoes of pent hoo-
    rays!
  When we grouped together in secret
    mirth
  And sniggered at everything on
    earth—
  But specially when strange visitors
    came
  And we learned, for instance, that
    their name
was Fishback—or Mothershead—or
Philpott — or Dalrymple — or Fullen-
wider—or Applewhite—or Hunnicut—
or Tubbs—or Oldshoe!
  *" 'Oldshoe!' — jeminy-jee!" thinks
    we—*
  *"Hain't that a funny name!—tee-
    hee-hee!"*

Barefoot racers from everywhere,
　We'd pelt in over the back-porch
　　floor
For "the settin'-room," and cluster there
　Like a clot of bees round an apple-
　　core,
And sleeve our noses, and pinafore
Our smearcase-mouths, and slick our
　hair,
　And stare and listen, and try to look
　Like "Agnes" does in the old school-
　　book,—
Till at last we'd catch the visitor's
　name,—
Reddinhouse, Lippscomb, or Burlin-
　game,—
or Winkler—or Smock—or Tutewiler
—or Daubenspeck—or Throckmorton
—or Rubottom—or Bixler—
　"'Bixler!' jeminy-jee!" thinks we—
　"Hain't that a funny name!—tee-
　hee-hee!"

　·　　·　　·　　·　　·　　·　　·

Peace!—Let be!—Fall away!—Fetch
　loose!—
We can't have fun as we had fun
　then!—
Shut up, Memory!—what's the use?—
When the girls and boys of 8 and 10
Are now—well, matronly, or old
　men,
And Time has (so to say) "cooked our
　goose"!
But ah! if we only could have back
The long-lost laughs that we now so
　lack
And so vainly long for,—how—we—
　could
Naturely wake up the neigh-ber-
　hood,

over the still heterogenious names
ever unrolling from the endless
roster of orthographic actualities,
—such names—for further instance
of good faith—simply such names
as Vanderlip—or Funkhouser—or
Smoot—or Galbreath—or Frybar-
ger—or Dinwiddie—or Bouslog—
or Puterbaugh—or Longnecker—
or Hartpence—or Wiggins—or
Pangborn—or Bowersox—
　"Bowersox"! Gee!—But alas! now
　we
Taste salt tears in our "tee-hee-
　hee"!

　　　　　　951

　　　　HENRY IRVING

　　　OCTOBER 13, 1905

'TIS Art reclaims him!   By those
　gifts of hers
With which so nobly she endowed his
　mind,
He brought back Shakespeare, in quick
　grief and glee—
Tasting the world's salt tears and sweet
　applause,—
For, even as through his master's, so
　there ran
Through all his multitudinous charac-
　ters
Kinship and love and honor of man-
　kind.
So all mankind shall grace his mem-
　ory
In musing proudly: Great as his genius
　was,
Great likewise was the man.

952

LINCOLN—THE BOY

O SIMPLE as the rhymes that tell
    The simplest tales of youth,
Or simple as a miracle
    Beside the simplest truth—
So simple seems the view we share
With our Immortals, sheer
From Glory looking down to where
    They were as children here.

Or thus we know, nor doubt it not,
    The boy he must have been
Whose budding heart bloomed with the
        thought
    All men are kith and kin—
With love-light in his eyes and shade
    Of prescient tears:—Because
Only of such a boy were made
    The loving man he was.

953

NICHOLAS OBERTING

*A hero of ancient mold is Nicholas
Oberting, of Hardentown, Indiana,
who, a few days ago, in saving three
boys from being gored to death by his
infuriated bull, performed a feat of
daring comparable only with the val-
orous deeds of Roman gladiators. . . .*
        —INDIANAPOLIS STAR.

SING! O Voice of Valor, sing!—
    Sing of Nicholas Oberting!
Giant of the strength of ten,
Yet the gentlest of all men.

He it was that loved the air,
And the green fields everywhere—
Loved the meadow slopes and rills,

And the cattle on the hills—
Loved all out-o'-doors, and took
Off his hat, with reverent look,
As the balmy winds of Spring
Waved the peach-bough, blossoming
At the orchard edge, where he
Paused to mark the minstrelsy
Of the daring first redbreast,
Whose lilt, at its loveliest,
Was not lovelier to hear
Than the laughter, ringing near,
Of child-voices—Truants,—three
Little stragglers, he could see,
Crossing the near pasture-land
Loiteringly, hand in hand,
Laughing as they came. . . . Until—
Sudden ran a sickening chill
Through the strong man's heart! . . .
        He heard
Scarce his own voice, afterward,
For the maddened, bellowing roar
Of the monster beast that bore
Down upon the lads. . . . Out rang
His quick warning.—Then he sprang
Forth to meet them, crying, "Run!—
*Straight for me!—Come on!—Well
        done!"*—
Praised them—cheered them.—*"Good!
    Hooray!
Now, Red-top, you throw away
That cap! but don't"*—And breathless
        hung
The sentence;—for a root had flung
The youngster—stunned—prone on the
    ground . . .
Then—midst a trampling, thund'rous
    sound,
The bellowing beast, with his big bent
    head,
And great horns, white as his eyes
    were red!—
Charged for the lad, as he helpless
    lay . . .

There was a leap then; and—they say
(For but one boy had swooned away)
There was the *leap* and the *laugh* of *a
Man* . . .
And the bravest war of the world be-
gan:
Pinned by the horns in the Hercules
grip
Of his master—the slavering jaws
adrip,
The foaming, steaming, sweltering,
hot-
Mouthed monster raged and charged
and fought,—
But ever the great strong hands were
set
At their horny leverage, bloody-wet;
And ever steadier pressed the hold,
And ever the wild eyes wilder rolled
As the thick neck turned, and the great
hulk grew
Like an o'er-fed engine, shuddering
through—
Yet the thick neck turned—and turned
—and turned—
Till the raw tongue shot from the
throat and burned
The live air foul; and the beast lurched
dead
Crunchingly.
　　　. . . And the youngster said
That the big man just lay there and
cried—
He was so sorry and satisfied!

954

RABBIT

I S'POSE it takes a feller 'at's be'n
　Raised in a country-town, like me,
To *'preciate* rabbits! . . . Eight er ten

Bellerin' boys and two er three
Yelpin' dawgs all on the trail
O' one little pop-eyed cottontail!

'Bout the first good fall o' snow—
So's you kin track 'em, don't you know,
Where they've run,—and one by one
Hop 'em up and chase 'em down
And prod 'em out of a' old bresh-pile
Er a holler log they're a-hidin' roun',
Er, way en-nunder the ricked cord-
wood
Er crosstie-stack by the railroad track
'Bout a mile
Out o' sight o' the whole ding town! . . .
Well! them's times 'at I call good!

Rabbits!—w'y, as my thoughts goes
back
To them old boyhood days o' mine,
I kin sic him now and see "Old Jack"
A-plowin' snow in a rabbit-track
And a-pitchin' over him, head and
heels,
Like a blame' hat-rack,
As the rabbit turns fer the timber-line
Down the County Ditch through the
old cornfields. . . .

Yes, and I'll say right here to you,
Rabbits that boys has *earnt,* like that—
Skinned and hung fer a night or two
On the old back-porch where the
pump's done froze—
Then fried 'bout right, where your
brekfust's at,
With hot brown gravy and shortenin'
bread,—
Rabbits, like *them*—er I ort to 'a' said,
I s'pose,
Rabbits like *those*
Ain't so p'ticalar pore, I guess,
Fer *eatin'* purposes!

955

A SPRING SONG AND A LATER

SHE sang a song of May for me,
    Wherein once more I heard
The mirth of my glad infancy—
    The orchard's earliest bird—
The joyous breeze among the trees
    New-clad in leaf and bloom,
And there the happy honey-bees
    In dewy gleam and gloom.

So purely, sweetly on the sense
    Of heart and spirit fell
Her song of Spring, its influence—
    Still irresistible,—
Commands me here—with eyes ablur—
    To mate her bright refrain,
Though I but shed a rhyme for her
    As dim as Autumn rain.

956

OURS

LOUISVILLE, KENTUCKY, DECEMBER 8,
1906

READ AT A BANQUET IN HONOR OF
HENRY WATTERSON, UPON HIS
DEPARTURE FOR SPAIN

HERE where of old was heard
    The ringing, singing word
That orator and bard
    Alike set free
To soar, through heights profound,
Our land's remotest bound,
Till all is holy ground
    From sea to sea—

Here still, with voice and pen,
One cheers the hopes of men
And gives us faith again—
    This gifted one
We hold here as the guest
Most honored—loved the best—
Wisest and worthiest—
    Our Watterson.

His spirit is the Seer's—
For, though he sees and hears
Through human doubts and fears,
    His heart is one
With Earth's and the Divine—
With his home-hearts—and mine—
And the child's heart is thine,
    Our Watterson!

Give us to touch and praise
His worth in subtlest ways,
Lest even our fondest gaze
    He fain would shun—
Laugh, though a mist appears—
The glad wine salt with tears—
Laugh, as we drain it—"Here's
    Our Watterson!"

957

OLD INDIANY

INTENDED FOR A DINNER OF THE INDIANA
SOCIETY OF CHICAGO

OLD Indiany, 'course we know
    Is first, and best, and most, also,
Of all the States' whole forty-four:—
She's first in ever'thing, that's shore!—
And best in ever'way as yet
Made known to man; and you kin bet
She's most, because she won't confess
She ever was, or will be, less!
And yet, fer all her proud array

Of sons, how many gits away!—
No doubt about her bein' *great*
But, fellers, she's a leaky State!
And them that boasts the most about
Her, them's the ones that's dribbled
out.
Law! jes' to think of all you boys
'Way over here in Illinoise
A-celebratin', like ye air,
Old Indiany, 'way back there
In the dark ages, so to speak,
A-prayin' for ye once a week
And wonderin' what's a-keepin' you
From comin', like you ort to do.
You're all a-lookin' well, and like
You wasn't "sidin' up the pike,"
As the tramp-shoemaker said
When "he sacked the boss and shed
The blame town, to hunt fer one
Where they didn't work fer fun!"
Lookin' *extry* well, I'd say,
Your old home so fur away.—
Maybe, though, like the old jour.,
Fun hain't all yer workin' fer.
So you've found a job that pays
Better than in them old days
You was on The Weekly Press,
Heppin' run things, more er less;
Er a-learnin' telegraph-
Operatin', with a half-
Notion of the tinner's trade,
Er the dusty man's that laid
Out designs on marble and
Hacked out little lambs by hand,
And chewed finecut as he wrought,
"Shapin' from his bitter thought"
Some squshed mutterings to say,—
"Yes, hard work, and porer pay!"
Er you'd kind o' thought the far-
Gazin' kuss that owned a car
And took pictures in it, had
Jes' the snap you wanted—bad!
And you even wondered why

He kep' foolin' with his sky-
Light the same on shiny days
As when rainin'. ('T leaked always.)
Wondered what strange things was hid
In there when he shet the door
And smelt like a burnt drug store
Next some orchard-trees, i swan!
With whole roasted apples on!
That's why Ade is, here of late,
Buyin' in the dear old state,—
So's to cut it up in plots
Of both town and country lots.

958

LONGFELLOW

1807—FEBRUARY 27—1907

O GENTLEST kinsman of Hu-
manity!
Thy love hath touched all hearts,
even as thy Song
Hath touched all chords of music
that belong
To the quavering heaven-strung harp
of harmony:
Thou hast made man to feel and hear
and see
Divinely;—made the weak to be the
strong;
By thy melodious magic, changed
the wrong
To changeless right—and joyed and
wept as we.
Worlds listen, lulled and solaced at the
spell
That folds and holds us—soul and
body, too,—
As though thy songs, as loving
arms in stress

Of sympathy and trust ineffable,
　Were thrown about us thus by one
　　who knew
　Of common human need of kindli-
　　ness.

959

WITH A CHILD-BOOK

TO MASTER PRESTON FROM HIS LONG
INVISIBLE PLAYMATE

THERE is LORE of more devices,
　And ROMANCE that more entices
Higher minds and higher prices;—
But, for "Giggle-boy" or "Cry-sis"
(With some sniffless interstices)
Here's a little tale suffices—
Sweet as oranges in slices
Slobbed in slues o' cream and ices,
Tanged with tingling, spangling
　　spices.—
Ho! there's *no* tale half so nice as
This Old Tailor and his Mice is!

960

THE DOCTOR

He took the suffering human race,
　He read each wound, each weakness
　　clear;
And struck his finger on the place,
　And said: "Thou ailest here, and
　　here!"
　　　—MATTHEW ARNOLD.

WE may idealize the chief of
　men—
Idealize the humblest citizen,—
Idealize the ruler in his chair—

The poor man, or the poorer million-
　aire;
Idealize the soldier—sailor—or
The simple man of peace—at war with
　war;—
The hero of the sword or fife-and-
　drum. . . .
Why not idealize the Doctor some?

The Doctor is, by principle, we know,
Opposed to sentiment. He veils all
　show
Of feeling, and is proudest when he
　hides
The sympathy which natively abides
Within the stoic precincts of a soul
Which owns strict duty as its first con-
　trol,
And so must guard the ill, lest worse
　may come. . . .
Why not idealize the Doctor some?

He is the master of emotions—he
Is likewise certain of that mastery,—
Or dare he face contagion in its ire,
Or scathing fever in its leaping fire?
He needs must smile upon the ghastly
　face
That yearns up toward him in that
　warded place
Where even the Saint-like Sisters' lips
　grow dumb.
Why not idealize the Doctor some?

He wisely hides his heart from you and
　me—
He hath grown tearless, of necessity,—
He knows the sight is clearer, being
　blind;
He knows the cruel knife is very
　kind;
Ofttimes he must be pitiless, for
　thought

Of the remembered wife or child he
  sought
To save through kindness that was
  overcome.
Why not idealize the Doctor some?

Bear with him, trustful, in his darkest
  doubt
Of how the mystery of death comes
  out;
He knows—he knows,—ay, better yet
  than we,
That out of Time must dawn Eternity;
He knows his own compassion—what
  he would
Give in relief of all ills, if he could.—
We wait alike one Master: He will
  come.
Do we idealize the Doctor some?

961

ABE MARTIN

ABE MARTIN!—dad-burn his old
  picture!
P'tends he's a Brown County fixture—
A kind of a comical mixture
  Of hoss-sense and no sense at all!
His mouth, like his pipe, 's allus goin',
And his thoughts, like his whiskers, is
  flowin',
And what he don't know ain't wuth
  knowin'—
  From Genesis clean to baseball!

The artist, Kin Hubbard, 's so keerless
He draws Abe 'most eyeless and ear-
  less
But he's never yet pictured him cheer-
  less
  Er with fun 'at he tries to con-
    ceal,—

Whuther on to the fence er clean over
A-rootin' up ragweed er clover,
Skeert stiff at some "Rambler" er
  "Rover"
  Er newfangled automo*beel!*

It's a purty steep climate old Brown's
  in;
And the rains there his ducks nearly
  drowns in
The old man hisse'f wades his rounds
  in
  As ca'm and serene, mighty nigh
As the old handsaw-hawg, er the mot-
  tled
Milch cow, er the old rooster wattled
Like the mumps had him 'most so well
  throttled
  That it was a pleasure to die.

But best of 'em all's the fool-breaks 'at
Abe don't see at all, and yit makes 'at
Both me and you lays back and shakes
  at
  His comic, miraculous cracks
Which makes him—clean back of the
  power
Of genius itse'f in its flower—
This Notable Man of the Hour,
  Abe Martin, The Joker on Facts.

962

MORNING

BREATH of Morning—breath of
  May—
With your zest of yesterday
And crisp, balmy freshness, smite
Our old hearts with Youth's delight.

Tilt the cap of Boyhood—yea,
Where no "forelock" waves, to-day,—
Back, in breezy, cool excess,
Stroke it with the old caress.

Let us see as we have seen—
Where all paths are dewy-green,
And all human-kind are kin—
Let us be as we have been!

963

THE LOVELINESS

AH, what a long and loitering way
     And ever-lovely way, in truth,
We travel on from day to day
Out of the realms of youth!

How eagerly we onward press
     The lovely path that lures us still
With ever-changing loveliness
     Of grassy vale and hill:

Of groves of May and morning-lands
     Dew-diamonded and gemmed with
          bloom;
With amber streams and golden sands
     And aisles of gleam and gloom;

Where lovely little Fairy-folk,
     In careless ambush, pipe and call
From tousled ferns 'neath elm and oak
     By shoal and waterfall:

Transparent even as the stream,
     The gnarlèd prison-tree reveals
Its lovely Dryad in a dream
     That scarce itself conceals;

The sudden redbird trips the sight
     And tricks the ear—or doubtless we
With happy palms had clapped the
          Sprite
     In new captivity.

On—on, through all the gathering
          years,
     Still gleams the loveliness, though
          seen
Through dusks of loss and mists of
          tears
     That vainly intervene.

Time stints us not of lovely things—
     Old Age hath still a treasure-store,—
The loveliness of songs and wings
     And voices on before.—

And—loveliness beyond all grace
     Of lovely words to say or sing,—
The loveliness of Hope's fair face
     Forever brightening.

964

A PARTING GUEST

WHAT delightful hosts are they—
     Life and Love!
Lingeringly I turn away,
     This late hour, yet glad enough
They have not withheld from me
     Their high hospitality.
So, with face lit with delight
     And all gratitude, I stay
Yet to press their hands and say,
     "Thanks.—So fine a time! Good
          night."

965

"OUT OF REACH"

YOU think them "out of reach,"
    your dead?
Nay, by my own dead, I deny
Your "out of reach."—Be comforted:
'Tis not so far to die.

O by their dear remembered smiles
    And outheld hands and welcoming
        speech,
They wait for us, thousands of miles
    This side of "out of reach."

966

MY FOE

MY Foe? You name yourself, then,
    —I refuse
A term so dark to designate you by.
To me you are most kind and true;
        and I
Am grateful as the dust is for the dews
That brim the dusk, and falter, drip
        and ooze
From the dear darkness of the sum-
        mer sky.
Vex not yourself for lack of moan
        or cry
Of mine. Not any harm, nor ache nor
        bruise
Could reach my soul through any
        stroke you fain
Might launch upon me,—it were as
        the lance
    Even of the lightning did it leap
        to rend
A ray of sunshine—'twould recoil
        again.

So, blessing you, with pitying counte-
        nance,
I wave a hand to you, my helpless
        friend.

967

SOME IMITATIONS

I

POMONA

(*Madison Cawein*)

OH, the golden afternoon!—
    Like a ripened summer day
That had fallen oversoon
    In the weedy orchard-way—
As an apple, ripe in June.

He had left his fishrod leant
    O'er the footlog by the spring—
Clomb the hill-path's high ascent,
    Whence a voice, down showering,
Lured him, wondering as he went.

Not the voice of bee nor bird,
    Nay, nor voice of man nor child,
Nor the creek's shoal-alto heard
    Blent with warblings sweet and wild
Of the midstream, music-stirred.

'Twas a goddess! As the air
    Swirled to eddying silence, he
Glimpsed about him, half aware
    Of some subtle sorcery
Woven round him everywhere.

Suavest slopes of pleasaunce, sown
    With long lines of fruited trees
Weighed o'er grasses all unmown
    But by scythings of the breeze
In prone swaths that flashed and shone

Like silk locks of Faunus sleeked
This, that way, and contrawise,
Through whose bredes ambrosial
        leaked
Oily amber sheens and dyes,
Starred with petals purple-freaked.

Here the bellflower swayed and swung,
        Greenly belfried high amid
Thick leaves in whose covert sung
Hermit-thrush, or katydid,
Or the glowworm nightly clung.

Here the damson, peach and pear;
        There the plum, in Tyrian tints,
Like great grapes in clusters rare;
        And the metal-heavy quince
Like a plummet dangled there.

All ethereal, yet all
        Most material,—a theme
Of some fabled festival—
        Save the fair face of his dream
Smiling o'er the orchard wall.

II

THE PASSING OF A ZEPHYR

(*Sidney Lanier*)

UP from, and out of, and over the
        opulent woods and the plains,
Lo! I leap nakedly loose, as the nudest
        of gods might choose,
For to dash me away through the
        morning dews
And the rathe Spring rains—
Pat and pet the little green leaves of
        the trees and the grass,
Till they seem to linger and cling, as
        I pass,

And are touched to delicate contempo-
        raneous tears of the rain and the
        dew,
That lure mine eyes to weeping like-
        wise, and to laughter, too:
For I am become as the balmiest,
        stormiest zephyr of Spring,
With manifold beads of the marvelous
        dew and the rain to string
On the bended strands of the blos-
        soms, blown
And tossed and tousled and over-
        thrown,
And shifted and whirled, and lifted un-
        furled
In the victory of the blossoming
Of the flags of the flowery world.
Yea, and behold! and a riotous zephyr,
        at last,
I subside; I abate; I pass by; I am past.
And the small, hoarse bass of the bum-
        blebee
Is my requiem-psalm,
And I fling me down to a listless, loiter-
        ing, long eternity
Of amiable calm.

III

EF UNCLE REMUS PLEASE TER 'SCUSEN ME

(*Joel Chandler Harris*)

DEY wunce wuz er time which I
        • gwineter tell you 'bout it—
An' it's easy ter believe it sho'ly ez it is
        ter doubt it!—
So des you pick yer "ruthers" whilse I
        tell how ole Br'er Rabbit
Wunce know de time when he git de
        fightin' habit.
Co'se he ain't no bragger, des a-rippin'
        an' a-rarin'

An' a-darin' all de beestus an' a-des
a-double-darin'
Sich ez Mr. Jonus Lion, er Sir Mr.
Twister Tagger,
Er Sister Hisstopottomus, er A'nt Fer-
jinny Ja'gger!
Yit, des de same, he layin' low an'
know he got de muscle
What sho' ter s'prise mos' any size
what crowd 'im fer a tussle.—
But speshully he 'spise de *Dawg,* an'
sight er one des make 'im
Fergit hisse'f an' run 'em down an'
grab 'em up an' shake 'em!—
An', mo' 'n dat, ef 'twuzn't fer de
Dawg-law den ag'in it,
He'd des a-kilt off ev'y Dawg dat's
chasin' him dis minute!

IV

A RHYME FOR CHRISTMAS

I F *Browning* only were here,
This yule-ish time o' the year—
This mule-ish time o' the year,
Stubbornly still refusing
To add to the rhymes we've been using
Since the first Christmas-glee
(One might say) chantingly
Rendered by rudest hinds
Of the pelt-clad shepherding kinds
Who didn't know Song from b-
U-double-l's-foot!—pah!—
(Haply the old Egyptian *ptah*—
Though I'd hardly wager a baw-
Bee—or a *bumble,* for that—
And that's flat!) . . .
But the thing that I want to get at
Is a rhyme for *Christmas*—
Nay! nay! nay! nay! not *isthmus*—
The t- and the h-sounds covertly are
Gnawing the nice auricular

Senses until one may hear them gnar—
And the terminal, too, for m*as* is m*us,*
So *that* will not do for us.
Try for it—sigh for it—cry for it—die
for it!
O *but* if Browning were here to apply
for it,
He'd rhyme you *Christmas—*
He'd make a *mist pass*
Over—something o' ruther—
Or find you the rhyme's very brother
In lovers that *kissed fast*
To baffle the moon—as he'd lose the
t-final
In fas-t as it blended with *to* (mark the
spinal
Elision—tip-clipt as exquisitely nicely
And hyper-exactingly sliced to precisely
The extremest technical need): Or he'd
twist glass,
Or he'd have a *kissed lass,*
Or shake 'neath our noses some great
giant *fist-mass—*
No matter! If Robert were here, *he*
could do it,
Though it took us till Christmas next
year to see through it.

V

VAUDEVILLE SKITS

I

SERENADE AT THE CABIN

Oh, my little Sadie Sue, I's a-serenadin'
you—
Fer you's de onliest lady-love o' mine;
De White Folk's dance done over, I has
still a chune er two
Below your winder's mohnin'-glory-
vine.

Your good ole mammy's gyarden is, fer
   shore, a ha'nted place,
Dis midnight whilse I's cropin'
   'mongst de bloom;
Yit de moon dah 'bove de chimbly ain'
   no fairer dan de face
What's hidin' 'hind de curtain o'
   your room.

Chorus

Den wake, my colored blonde with
   eyes o' blue,
An' lips ez red ez roses renshed with
   dew;
   Yo' hair ez fair an' fine
   Ez de skeins o' June sunshine,
My little, light-complected Sadie Sue!

In de "Gran's" old dinin'-hall, playin'
   fer de White Folk's ball,
I watch deir pick o' ladies ez dey
   glide,
An' says I, "My Sadie Sue she 'ud
   shorely best you all
Ef she 'uz here a-waltzin' by my
   side!"
Den I laugh all to myse'f-like, ez I
   swipe de twangin' strings
An' shet my eyes in sweetest dreams
   o' you,—
Fer you're my heart's own music dat
   forever beats an' sings—
My soul's own serenade—my Sadie
   Sue!

Chorus

Den wake, my colored blonde with eyes
   o' blue,
An' lips ez red ez roses renshed with
   dew;
   Yo' hair ez fair an' fine
   Ez de skeins o' June sunshine,
My little, light-complected Sadie Sue!

2

CHUCK'S HOODOOS

Chuck's allus had de Hoodoos bad!—
   Do what he kin to lose 'em,
Dey track dat coon, by sun er moon,
   Des like dey cain't uxcuse 'im!
An' more he gyaurd 'em off, more
   hard
Hit 'pear-like dat they press 'im—
De onliest luck dey 'low ole Chuck
   Is dis enough to 'stress 'im!

He taken care—no matter where
   He's walkin' 'long de street an'
See any ladder leanin' there,
   Er cross-eyed man he's meetin'—
Dat eye o' his ketch wher' dey is,
   An', quick as "scat," Chuck's hittin'
De curb outside, an' watch wile-eyed
   Fust lef'-han' place to spit in!

He' got toenails o' bats; an' snails
   Shet hot in deir shell-houses
Wid sealin'-wax; an' little backs
   O' turkles in his trouse's:
A moleskin-pu's'; an' possum's han'—
   Des ever' charm an' wonder—
An' barber-chair o' shore hosshair—
   An' hoss-shoe hangin' under!

"An' yit," says Chuck, "I got no
   luck:—
De Hoodoos still a-bafflin'
Dis po' ole saint what knows he ain't—
   'Twix' shootin' craps an' rafflin'!
No overcoat—ner underwear,—
   Right on de aidge o' winter
I's up aginst de wust layout
   Dey's ever got me inter!"

968

THE ROSE-LADY

TO THE ROSES

I DREAM that you are kisses Allah
sent
In forms material, that all the earth
May taste of you and guess of
Heaven's worth,
Since it can waste such sweetness with
content,—
Seeing you showered o'er the Battle-
ment—
By Angel-hands plucked ripe from
lips of mirth
And flung in lavish clusters, yet no
dearth
Of rapture for the Anthem! . . . I
have bent
Above you, nestled in some low re-
treat,
Pressing your velvet mouths against the
dust,
And, ever nurturing this old con-
ceit,
Have lifted up your lips in perfect
trust
Against my mouth, nor found them
the less sweet
For having kissed the dust beneath
my feet.

969

A HOOSIER CALENDAR

JANUARY

BLEAK January! Cold as fate,
And ever colder—ever keener—
Our very hair cut while we wait
By winds that clip it ever cleaner:

Cold as a miser's buried gold,
Or nether-deeps of old tradition—
Jeems January! you're a cold
Proposition!

FEBRUARY

You, February,—seem to be
Old January's understudy,
But play the part too vaudeville-y,—
With wind too moist and snow too
muddy—
You overfreeze and overthaw—
Your "Hos'ler Jo"-like recitation
But hints that you're, at best, a raw
Imitation.

MARCH

And, March, you've got no friends to
spare—
Warm friends, I mean—unless coal-
dealers,
Or gas-well owners, pipin' where
The piper's paid—above all spielers;
You are a month, too, of complex
Perversities beyond solution—
A sort o' "loveliest of your sex"
Institution!

APRIL

But, April, when you kind o' come
A-sa'nterin' down along our road-
way,
The bars is down, and we're at home,
And you're as welcome as a show-
day!
First thing we know, the sunshine falls
Spring-like, and drenches all Crea-
tion
With that-'ere ba'm the poets calls
"Inspiration."

MAY

And May!—It's warmin' jest to see
  The crick thawed clear ag'in and
    dancin'—
'Pear-like it's tickled 'most as *me*
  A-prancin' 'crosst it with my pants
    on!
And then to hear the bluebird whet
  His old song up and lance it through
    you,
Clean through the boy's heart beatin'
    yet—
      Hallylooya!

JUNE

June—'Ll, I jest git *doped* on June!—
  The trees and grass all at their green-
    est—
The round earth swung 'twixt sun and
    moon,
  Jest at its—so to say—serenest:—
In country,—stars and whipperwills;
  In town,—all night the boys invadin'
Leadin' citizens' winder-sills,
    Sair-a-nadin'.

JULY

Fish still a-bitin'—*some;* but 'most
  Too hot fer anything but layin'
Jest do-less like, and watchin' clos't
  The treetops and the squirrels play-
    in'—
Their tail-tips switched 'bove knot and
    limb,
  But keepin' most in sequestration—
Leavin' a big part to the im-
    Magination.

AUGUST

Now when it's August—I can tell
  It by a hundred signs and over;—

They is a mixed ripe-apple-smell
  And mashed-down grass and musty
    clover;
Bees is as lazy 'most as me—
  Bee-bird eats 'em—gap's his wings
    out
So lazy 'at I don't think he
    Spits their stings out!

SEPTEMBER

September, you appeal to all,
  Both young and old, lordly and low-
    ly;
You stuff the haymow, trough and
    stall,
  Till horse and cow's as roly-poly
As pigs is, slopped on buttermilk
  And brand, shipstuff and 'tater-peel-
    in's—
And folks, too, feelin' fine as silk
    With all their feelin's!

OCTOBER

If I'd be'n asked for my advice,
  And thought the thing out, ca'm
    and sober—
Sizin' the months all once or twice,—
  I'd la'nch'd the year out with *Octo-
    ber.* . . .
All Nature then jest veiled and dressed
  In weddin' gyarments, ornamented
With ripe-fruit-gems—and kissin' jest
    New-invented!

NOVEMBER

I'm 'feared November's hopes is few
  And far between!—Cold as a Mon-
    day-
Washday, er a lodge-man who
  You' got to pallbear for on Sunday;

Colder and colder every day—
The fixed official time for sighin',—
A sinkin' state you jest can't stay
    In, or *die* in!

DECEMBER

December—why, of course we grin
And bear it—shiverin' every minute,
Yet warm from time the month rolls in
Till it skites out with Christmas in
    it;
And so, for all its coldest truths
And chill, goose-pimpled imperfec-
    tions,
It wads our lank old socks with Youth's
    Recollections.

970

THE LITTLE WOMAN

MY little woman, of you I sing
    With a fervor all divine,—
For I know the clasp of the hands that
    cling
So closely here in mine.

Though the rosy palms I used to press
Are faded and worn with care,
And tremulous is the old caress
That nestles in my hair,—

Your heart to me is a changeless page;
I have read it bit by bit,
From the dawn of love to the dusk of
    age,—
And the tale is Holy Writ.

Fold your eyes,—for the twilight bends
As a mother o'er her child—
Even as when, in the long-lost Then,
    You bent o'er ours and smiled. . . .

(Nay, but I spoke all unaware!
    See! I am kneeling, too,
And with mine, dear, is the rose's
    prayer,
    With a blur of tears and dew.)

But O little woman, I often grieve,
    As I think of the vanished years
And trace the course of the cares that
    leave
    Your features dim with tears:

I often grieve, for the frowns I wore
When the world seemed all untrue,—
When my hard, proud heart was sick
    and sore
    And would not come to you!

I often grieve, as I hold your hand—
    As I hold your hand to-night,—
That it takes so long to understand
    The lesson of love aright!

But sing the song that I taught you
    once,
    Dear little woman, as *then*
Away far back in the golden months:—
    Sing me the song again!

For, as under the stars we loved of
    yore
When the nights of love were long,
Your poor, pale lips grow glad once
    more
    And I kiss them into song:—

My little woman's hands are fair
    As even the moonflowers be
When fairies creep in their depths and
    sleep
    Till the sun leaps out o' the sea.

And O her eyes, they are spheres of
*   light—*
So brighter than stars are they,
The brightest day is the darkest night
When my little woman's away.

For my little woman has ever a tear
And a sigh when I am sad;
And I have a thousand smiles for her
When my little woman is glad.

But my little woman is strong and
*   brave,*
For all of her tears and sighs,
Her stanch little heart knows how to
*   behave*
Whenever the storms arise.

My little woman, of you I sing
With a fervor all divine,—
For I know the clasp of the hands that
    cling
So closely here in mine.

971

WHAT TITLE?

WHAT title best befits the man
    We hold our first American?
Or Statesman; Soldier; Hero; Chief,
Whose Country is his first belief:
Or sanest, safest Leader; or
True Patriot; or Orator,
Heard still at Inspiration's height,
Because he speaks for truth and right;
Or shall his people be content
With Our Republic's President,
Or trust his ringing worth to live
In song as Chief Executive?
Nay—his the simplest name—though
    set
Upon him like a coronet,—

God names our first American
The highest, noblest name—The MAN.

972

YOU MAY NOT REMEMBER

In the deep grave's charmèd chamber,
Lying tranced in breathless slumber,
You may haply not remember.

YOU may not remember whether
    It was Spring or Summer
        weather;
But *I* know—we two together
    At the dim end of the day—
How the fireflies in the twilight
Drifted by like flakes of starlight,
    Till o'er floods of flashing moon-
        light
    They were wave-like swept
        away.

You may not remember any
Word of mine of all the many
Poured out for you there, though
    then a
    Soul inspirèd spake my love;—
But *I* knew—and still review it,
    All my passion, as with awe it
    Welled in speech as from a poet
        Gifted of the gods above.

Sleeping here, this hour I grieve in,
You may not remember even
Any kiss I still believe in,
    Or caress of ecstasy,—
May not even *dream*—O can't you?—
    That I kneel here—weep here—want
        you—
    Feign me in your grave, to haunt
        you,
        Since you come not back to me!

Vain! ah, vain is all my yearning
As the West's last embers burning
Into ashes, slowly turning
    Ever to a denser gray!—
While the fireflies in the twilight
  Drift about like flakes of starlight,
    Till o'er wastes of wannest moon-
        light
    They are wave-like swept away.

973

THE REST

v. k.—NATURALIST

HE rests at last, as on the mother-
    breast
The playworn child at evening lies at
  rest,—
For he, a buoyant child, in veriest
  truth,
Has looked on life with eyes of change-
  less youth:—
Has loved our green old earth here
  from the hour
Of his first memory of bud and
  flower—
Of morning's grassy lawns and dewy
  trees
And orchard-blossoms, singing birds
  and bees:

When all the world about him was a
  land
Elysian, with the mother near at hand:
With steadfast gaze of wonder and de-
  light
He marked the miracles of day and
  night:—
Beheld the kingly sun, in dazzling
  reign

By day; and, with her glittering, glim-
  mering train
Of stars, he saw the queenly moon pos-
  sess
Her throne in midmost midnight's
  mightiness.

All living least of things he ever knew
Of mother Earth's he was a brother to:
The lone rose by the brook—or, under,
  where
The swaying water-lilies anchored there;
His love dipped even to the glossy things
That walked the waters and forgot
  their wings
In sheer insanity of some delight
Known but to that ecstatic parasite.

It was enough, thus childishly to sense
All works—since worthy of Omnipo-
  tence—
As worshipful: Therefor, as any child,
He knelt in tenderness of tears, or
  smiled
His gratefulness, as to a playmate glad
To share His pleasures with a poorer lad.
And so he lived: And so he *died?*—
  Ah, no,
We'll not believe that till he tells us so.

974

WE MUST BELIEVE

Lord, I believe: help Thou mine un-
*   belief.*

I

WE must believe—
    Being from birth endowed
      with love and trust—
Born unto loving;—and how simply
  just

That love—that faith!—even in the
  blossom-face
The babe drops dreamward in its rest-
  ing-place,
Intuitively conscious of the sure
Awakening to rapture ever pure
And sweet and saintly as the mother's
  own
Or the awed father's, as his arms are
  thrown
O'er wife and child, to round about
  them weave
  And wind and bind them as one har-
  vest-sheaf
Of love—to cleave to, and *forever*
  cleave. . . .
       Lord, I believe:
       Help Thou mine unbelief.

            II
We must believe—
Impelled since infancy to seek some
  clear
Fulfilment, still withheld all seekers
  here;—
For never have we seen perfection nor
The glory we are ever seeking for:
But we *have* seen—all mortal souls as
  one—
Have seen its *promise,* in the morning
  sun—
Its blest assurance, in the stars of
  night;—
The ever-dawning of the dark to
  light;—
The tears down-falling from all eyes
  that grieve—
  The eyes uplifting from all deeps of
  grief,
Yearning for what at last we shall re-
  ceive. . . .
       Lord, I believe:
       Help Thou mine unbelief.

            III
We must believe:
For still all unappeased our hunger
  goes,
From life's first waking, to its last re-
  pose:
The briefest life of any babe, or man
Outwearing even the allotted span,
Is each a life unfinished—incomplete:
For these, then, of th' outworn, or un-
  worn feet
Denied one toddling step—O there
  must be
Some fair, green, flowery pathway end-
  lessly
Winding through lands Elysian! Lord,
  receive
  And lead each as Thine Own Child
  —even the Chief
Of us who didst Immortal life
  achieve. . . .
       Lord, I believe:
       Help Thou mine unbelief.

                975

THE HIRED MAN'S DOG-STORY

*Twa dogs that were na thrang at hame
Forgather'd ance upon a time.*
                    —BURNS.

DOGS, I contend, is jes' about
     Nigh human—git 'em studied
     out.
I hold, like us, they've got their own
Reasonin' powers 'at's theirs alone—
Same as their tricks and habits too,
Provin', by lots o' things they do,
That instinct's not the only thing
That dogs is governed by, i jing!—

COMPLETE POETICAL WORKS   743

And I'll say furder, on that line,
And prove it, that they's dogs a-
    plenty
Will show intelligence as fine
As ary ten men out o' twenty!

Jevver investigate the way
Sheep-killin' dogs goes at it—hey?
Well, you dig up the facts and you
Will find, first thing, they's always *two*
Dogs goes together on that spree
O' blood and puore dog-deviltry!
And, then, they always go at night—
Mind ye, it's never in daylight,
When folks is up and wide awake,—
No self-respectin' dogs'll make
Mistakes o' judgment on that score,—
And I've knowed fifty head or more
O' slaughtered sheep found in the lot,
Next morning the old farmer got
His folks up and went out to feed,—
And every livin' soul agreed
That all night long they never heerd
The bark o' dog ner bleat o' skeered
And racin', tromplin' flock o' sheep
A-skallyhootin' roun' the pastur',
To rouse 'em from their peaceful sleep
To that heart-renderin' disaster!

Well, now, they's actchul evidence
In all these facts set forth; and hence
When, by like facts, it has been foun'
That these two dogs—colloguin' roun'
At night as thick as thieves—*by day*
Don't go together anyway,
And, 'pearantly, hain't never met
Each other; and the facts is set
On record furder, that these smart
Old pards in crime lives miles apart—
Which is a trick o' theirs, to throw
Off all suspicion, don't you know!—
One's a *town*-dog—belongin' to
Some good man, maybe—er to you!—

And one's a *country*-dog, er *"jay,"*
As you nickname us thataway.
Well, now!—these is the facts I' got
(And, mind ye, these *is* facts—not
    guesses)
To argy on, concernin' what
    Fine reasonin' powers dogs p'sesses.

My idy is,—the dog lives in
The *town*, we'll say, runs up ag'in
The *country*-dog, some Saturday,
Under a' old farm-wagon, say,
Down at the Court-house hitchin'-
    rack.—
Both lifts the bristles on their back
And show their teeth and growl as
    though
They meant it pleasant-like and low,
In case the fight hangs fire. And they
Both wag then in a friendly way,
The town-dog sayin': —"Seems to me,
Last Dimocratic jubilee,
I seen you here in town somewhere?"
The country-dog says:—"Right you
    air!—
And right here's where you seen me,
    too,
Under this wagon, watchin' *you!"*
"Yes," says the town-dog,—"and I
    thought
We'd *both* bear watchin', like as not."
And as he yawns and looks away,
The country-dog says, "What's your
    lay?"
The town-dog whets his feet a spell
And yawns ag'in, and then says,—
    "Well,
Before I answer that—Ain't you
A Mill Crick dog, a mile er two
From old Chape Clayton's stock-farm
    —say?"
"Who *told* you?" says the jay-dog—
    "hey?"

And looks up, real su'prised. *"I
    guessed,"*
The town-dog says—*"You* tell the
    rest,—
How's old Chape's mutton, anyhow?—
How many of 'em's ready now—
How many of 'em's ripe enough fer
    use,
And how's the hot, red, rosy juice?"
" 'Mm!" says the country-dog, "I think
I sort o' see a little blink
O' what you mean." And then he
    stops
And turns and looks up street and
    lops
His old wet tongue out, and says he,
Lickin' his lips, all slobbery,
"Ad-drat my melts! you're jes' my
    man!—
I'll trust you, 'cause I know I can!"
And then he says, "I'll tell you jes'
How things is, and Chape's careless-
    ness
About his sheep,—fer instance, say,
To-morry Chapes'll all be 'way
To Sund'y-meetin'—and ag'in
At night." "At night? That lets us
    in!—
'Better the day' "—the town-dog says—
" 'Better the deed.' We'll pray; Lord,
    yes!—
May the outpourin' grace be shed
Abroad, and all hearts comforted
Accordin' to their lights!" says he,
"And that, of course, means you and
    me."
And then they both snarled, low and
    quiet—
Swore where they'd meet. And both
    stood by it!
Jes' half-past eight on Sund'y night,
Them two dogs meets,—the *town*-dog,
    light

O' foot, though five mile' he had
    spanned
O' field, beech-wood and bottom-land.
But, as books says,—we draw a veil
Over this chapter of the tale! . . .
Yit when them two infernal, mean,
Low, orn'ry whelps has left the scene
O' carnage—chased and putt to death
The last pore sheep,—they've yit got
    breath
Enough to laugh and joke about
The fun they've had, while they sneak
    out
The woods-way fer the old crick where
They both plunge in and wash their
    hair
And rench their bloody mouths, and
    grin,
As each one skulks off home ag'in—
Jes' innardly too proud and glad
    To keep theirselves from kind o'
        struttin',
Thinkin' about the fun they'd had—
    When their blame wizzens needed
        cuttin'!

Dogs is deliber't.—They can bide
Their time till s'picions all has died.
The country-dog don't 'pear to care
Fer town no more,—he's off some-
    where
When the folks whistles, as they head
The team t'ards town. As I jes' said,—
Dogs is deliber't, don't forgit!
So this-here dog he's got the grit
To jes' deprive hisse'f o' town
For 'bout three weeks. But time rolls
    roun'! . . .
Same as they *first* met:—Saturday—
Same Court-house — hitch-rack — and
    same way
The team wuz hitched—same wagon
    where

The same *jay*-dog growls under there
When same *town*-dog comes loafin' by,
With the most innocentest eye
And giner'l meek and lowly style,
As though he'd never cracked a smile
In all his mortal days!—And both
Them dogs is strangers, you'd take
    oath!—
  Both keeps a-lookin' sharp, to see
If folks is watchin'—jes' the way
They acted that first Saturday
  They talked so confidentchully.
"Well"—says the town-dog, in a low
And careless tone—"Well, whatch you
    know?"
" '*Know?*' " says the country-dog—
    "Lots more
Than some smart people knows—that's
    shore!"
And then, in his dog-language, he
Explains how slick he had to be
When some suspicious folks come roun'
A-tryin' to track and run him down—
  Like *he'd* had anything to do
With killin' over fifty head
O' sheep! "Jes' think!—and *me*"—he
    said,
  "And me as innocent as *you,*
That very hour, five mile' away
In this town like you air to-day!"
"Ah!" says the town-dog, "there's the
    beauty
O' bein' *prepared* for what may be,
And *washin'* when you've done your
    duty!—
  No stain o' blood on you er me
Ner wool in *our* teeth!—*Then,*" says
    he,
"When wicked man has wronged us
    so,
  We ort to learn to be forgivin'—
Half the world, of course, don't know
How the other gits its livin'!"

976

PERVERSITY

YOU have more'n likely noticed,
    When you *didn't* when you
    could,
That jes' the thing you *didn't* do
Was jes' the thing you *should.*

977

HER POET-BROTHER

OH! what ef little childerns all
    Wuz big as parunts is!
Nen I'd join pa's Masonic Hall
An' wear gold things like his!
An' you'd "receive," like ma, an' be
My "hostuss"—An', gee-whizz!
We'd *alluz* have ice-cream, ef we
    Wuz big as parunts is!

Wiv all the money mens is got—
    We'd buy a *Store* wiv that,—
Ist candy, pies an' cakes, an' not
    No *drygoods*—'cept a hat-
An'-plume fer *you*—an' "plug" fer me,
    An' clothes like *ma's* an' *his,*
'At on'y ist fit *us*—ef we
    Wuz big as parunts is!

An'—ef *we* had a little boy
    An' girl like me an' you,—
Our Store'd keep ever' kind o' toy
    They'd ever want us to!—
We'd hire "Old Kriss" to 'tend to be
    The boss of all the biz
An' ist *"charge"* ever'thing—ef we
    Wuz big as parunts is!

978

GRAMPA'S CHOICE

FIRST and best of earthly joys,
   I like little girls and boys:
Which of all do I like best?
Why, the one that's happiest.

979

A LITTLE LAME BOY'S VIEWS

ON 'Scursion-days—an' Shows—an'
   Fairs—
They ain't no bad folks anywheres!—
   On street-cars—same as *you*—
Seems like *some*body allus sees
I'm lame, an' takes me on their knees,
   An' holds my crutches, too—
An' asts me what's my name, an' pays
My fare theirse'f—On all Big Days!

The mob all *scrowdges* you an' makes
Enough o' bluffs, fer goodness-sakes!
   But none of 'em *ain't* mad—
They're only *lettin' on.*—*I* know;—
An' I can tell you *why* it's so:
   They're all of 'em too *glad*—
They're *ever' one*, jes' glad as *me*
To be there, er they *wouldn't* be!

The man that sells the tickets snoops
My "one-er" in, but sort o' stoops
   An' grins out at me—then
Looks mean an' business-like an' sucks
His big mustache at me an' chucks
   Too much change out again.—
He's a *smooth citizen*, an' yit
He don't fool *me* one little bit!

An' then, *inside*—fer all the jam—
Folks, seems-like, all knows who I am,
   An' tips me nods an' winks;
An' even country-folks has made
Me he'p eat pie an' marmalade,
   With bottled milk fer "drinks"!—
Folks *all's* so good to me that I—
Sometimes—I nearly purt' near' *cry.*

An' all the *kids,* high-toned er pore,
Seems better than they wuz before,
   An' wants to kind o' "stand
In" with a feller—see him through
The *free* lay-out an' *sideshows,* too,
   An' do the bloomin' "grand"!
On 'Scursion-days—an' Shows   an'
   Fairs—
They ain't no bad folks anywheres!

980

A VERY TALL BOY

THE ONE LONE LIMERICK OF UNCLE
SIDNEY'S

SOME credulous chroniclers tell us
   Of a very tall youngster named
      Ellis.
   Whose Pa said, "Ma-ri-er,
   If Bubb grows much higher,
He'll have to be trained up a trellis."

981

THE RAGGEDY MAN ON
CHILDREN

CHILDERN—take 'em as they
   run—
You kin *bet* on, ev'ry one!—
Treat 'em right and reco'nize
Human souls is all one size.

Jevver think?—the world's best men
Wears the same souls they had when
They run barefoot—'way back where
All these little children air.

Heerd a boy, not long ago,
Say his parents *sassed* him so,
He'd *correct* 'em, ef he could,—
Then be good ef *they'd* be good.

So he says, "It's the vurry best sign
    in the Worl'
That *Goldie Goodwin* is a good little
    girl,"—
An' says, "First she's *gold*—then she's
    good—an' behold,
Good's 'bout 'leventy-*hunnerd* times
    better than *gold!*"

982

'LIZABUTH-ANN ON BAKIN'-DAY

OUR Hired Girl, when it's bakin'-
    day
She's out o' patience allus,
An' tells us "Hike *outdoors* an' play,
An' when the cookies's done," she'll
    say,
"Land sake! she'll come an' call us!"
An' when the little doughbowl's all
Ist heapin'-full, she'll come an' call—
Nen say, "She ruther take a switchin'
Than have a pack o' pesky childern
Trackin' round the kitchen!"

983

GOLDIE GOODWIN

MY old Uncle Sidney *he* says it's a
    sign
All over the Worl', an' ten times out
    of nine,
He can tell by the *name* of a child ef
    the same
Is a good er bad youngun—ist knows
    by their name!—

984

SYMPTOMS

I'M not a-workin' now!—
    I'm jes' a-layin' round
A-lettin' *other* people plow.—
    I'm cumberin' the ground! . . .
I jes' don't *keer!*—I've done my sheer
    O' sweatin'!—Anyhow,
In this dad-blasted weather here,
    I'm not a-workin' *now!*

The corn and wheat and all
    Is doin' well enough!—
They' got clean on from now tel Fall
    To show what kind o' stuff
'At's in their *own* dad-burn backbone;
    So, while the Scriptur's 'low
Man ort to reap as he have sown—
    I'm not a-workin' now!

The grass en-nunder these-
    Here ellums 'long "Old Blue,"
And shadders o' the sugar-trees,
    Beats farmin' quite a few!
As feller says,—I ruther guess
    I'll make my comp'ny bow
And *snooze* a few hours—more er
    less.—
I'm not a-workin' now!

985

BUB SAYS

THE moon in the sky is a custard-
        pie,
An' the clouds is the cream pour'd
        o'er it,
An' all o' the glittering stars in the sky
Is the powdered sugar for it.

.   .   .   .

Johnts—he's   proudest   boy   in
        town—
'Cause his Mommy she cut down
His Pa's pants fer Johnts—an'
        there
Is 'nuff left fer 'nother pair!

.   .   .   .

One time, when her Ma was gone,
Little Elsie she put on
All her Ma's fine clothes—an'
        black
Grow-grain-silk,   an'   sealskin-
        sack;
Nen while she wuz flouncin' out
In the hall an' round about,
Some one knocked, an' Elsie she
Clean forgot an' run to see
Who's there at the door—an' saw
Mighty quick at wuz her Ma.
But ef she ain't saw at all,
She'd a-knowed her parasol!

.   .   .   .

Gran'pas an' Gran'mas is funniest
        folks!—
Don't be jolly, ner tell no jokes,
Tell o' the weather an' frost an' snow

O' that cold New Year's o' long ago;
An' then they sigh at each other an'
        cough
An' talk about suddently droppin' off.

986

THE POOR STUDENT

WITH song elate we celebrate
        The struggling Student wight,
Who seeketh still to pack his pate
        With treasures erudite;
Who keepeth guard and watch and
        ward
        O'er every hour of day,
Nor less to slight the hours of night,
        He watchful is alway.

Though poor in pence, a wealth of
        sense
        He storeth in excess—
With poverty in opulence,
        His needs wax never less.
His goods are few,—a shelf or two
        Of classics, and a chair—
A banjo—with a bird's-eye view
        Of back-lots everywhere.

In midnight gloom, shut in his room,
        His, vigils he protracts,
E'en to the morning's hectic bloom,
        Accumulating facts:
And yet, despite or wrong or right,
        He nurtureth a ban,—
He hath the stanchless appetite
        Of any hirèd man.

On Jason's fleece and storied Greece
        He feeds his hungry mind;
Then stuffs himself like a valise
        With "eats" of any kind:

With kings he feigns he feasts, and
drains
The wines of ages gone—
Then husks a herring's cold remains
And turns the hydrant on.

In Trojan mail he fronts the gale
Of ancient battle-rout,
When, 'las the hour! his pipe must
fail,
And his last "snipe" smush out—
Nor pauses he, unless it be
To quote some cryptic scroll
And poise a sardine pensively
O'er his immortal soul.

987

UNCLE SIDNEY'S RHYMES

LITTLE Rapacity Greed was a glut-
ton:
He'd eat any meat, from goose-livers
to mutton;
All fowl, flesh, or sausage with all
savors through it—
You never saw sausage stuffed as *he*
could do it!
His nice mamma owned, "O he eats
as none other
Than animal kind"; and his bright
little brother
Sighed, pained to admit a phrase non-
eulogistic,
"Rap eats like a—pardon me—Canni-
balistic."
"He eats—like a *boor*," said his sister
—"a shameless
Plebeian, in sooth, of an ancestry
nameless!"

"He eats," moaned his father, despair-
ingly placid
And hopeless,—"he eats like—he eats
like an acid!"

988

"BLUE-MONDAY" AT THE
SHOE SHOP

IN THE EARLY SEVENTIES

OH, if we had a rich boss
Who liked to have us rest,
With a dime's lift for a benchmate
Financially distressed,—
A boss that's been a "jour." himself
And ain't forgot the pain
Of restin' one day in the week,
Then back to work againe!

Chorus

Ho, it's hard times together,
We've had 'em, you and I,
In all kinds of weather,
Let it be wet or dry;
But I'm bound to earn my livelihood
Or lay me down and die!

Poverty compels me
To face the snow and sleet,—
For pore wife and children
Must have a crust to eat.—
The sad wail of hunger
It would drive me insane,
If it wasn't for Blue-Monday
When I git to work againe!

Chorus

Ho, it's hard times together,
We've had 'em, you and I,

In all kinds of weather,
Let it be wet or dry;
But I'm bound to earn my livelihood
Or lay me down and die!

Then it's stoke up the stove, Boss,
And drive off the damps:
Cut out me tops, Boss,
And lend me your clamps;—
Pass us your tobacky
Till I give me pipe a start. . . .
Lor', Boss! how we love ye
For your warm kynd heart!

Chorus

Ho, it's hard times together,
We've had 'em, you and I,
In all kinds of weather,
Let it be wet or dry;
But I'm bound to earn my livelihood
Or lay me down and die!

989

THE THOUGHTS OF YOUTH

THE BOYS'

THE lisping maid,
  In shine and shade
Half elfin and half human,
  We love as such—
  Yet twice as much
Will she be loved as woman.

THE GIRLS'

  The boy we see,
  Of two or three—
Or even as a baby,
  We love to kiss
  For what he is,
Yet more for what he may be.

990

O. HENRY

WRITTEN IN THE CHARACTER OF SHERRARD PLUMMER

O HENRY, Afrite-chef of all de-
  light!—
Of all delectables conglomerate
That stay the starved brain and
    rejuvenate
The mental man. Th' esthetic appe-
    tite—
So long anhungered that its "in'ards"
  fight
And growl gutwise,—its pangs thou
    dost abate
And all so amiably alleviate,
Joy pats its belly as a hobo might
Who haply hath attained a cherry pie
  With no burnt bottom in it, ner no
    seeds—
  Nothin' but crispest crust, and
    thickness fit,
And squshin'-juicy, and jes' mighty
  nigh
  Too dratted drippin'-sweet fer hu-
    man needs,
  But fer the sosh of milk that goes
    with it.

991

WILLIAM McKINLEY

CANTON, OHIO, SEPTEMBER 30, 1907

HE said: "It is God's way:
  His will, not ours be done."
And o'er our land a shadow lay
That darkened all the sun.

The voice of jubilee
That gladdened all the air,
Fell sudden to a quavering key
Of suppliance and prayer.

He was our chief—our guide—
Sprung of our common Earth,
From youth's long struggle proved
    and tried
To manhood's highest worth:
Through toil, he knew all needs
Of all his toiling kind—
The favored striver who succeeds—
The one who falls behind.

The boy's young faith he still
Retained through years mature—
The faith to labor, hand and will,
Nor doubt the harvest sure—
The harvest of man's love—
A nation's joy that swells
To heights of Song, or deeps whereof
But sacred silence tells.

To him his Country seemed
Even as a Mother, where
He rested — slept; and once he
    dreamed—
As on her bosom there—
And thrilled to hear, within
That dream of her, the call
Of bugles and the clang and din
Of war. . . . And o'er it all

His rapt eyes caught the bright
Old Banner, winging wild
And beck'ning him, as to the fight . . .
When—even as a child—
He wakened—And the dream
Was real! And he leapt
As led the proud Flag through a gleam
Of tears the Mother wept.

His was a tender hand—
Even as a woman's is—
And yet as fixed, in Right's command,
As this bronze hand of his:
This was the Soldier brave—
This was the Victor fair—
This is the Hero Heaven gave
To glory here—and There.

992

"MOTHER"

I'M gittin' old—I know,—
    It seems so long ago—
So long sence John was here!
He went so young!—our Jim
'S as old now 'most as him,—
    Close on to thirty year'!

I know I'm gittin' old—
I know it by the *cold,*
    From time 'at first frost flies.—
Seems like—sence John was here—
Winters is more severe;
    And winter I de-spise!

And yet it seems, some days,
John's here, with his odd ways . . .
    Comes soon-like from the corn-
Field, callin' "Mother" at
Me—like he called me that
    Even 'fore Jim was *born!*

When Jim come—La! how good
Was all the neighborhood!—
    And Doctor!—when I heerd
Him joke John, kind o' low,
And say: Yes, folks could go—
    PA needn't be afeard!

When Jim come,—John says-'e—
A-bendin' over me
    And baby in the bed—
    And jes' us three,—says-'e
"Our little family!"
And that was all he said . . .

And cried jes' like a child!—
Kissed me again, and smiled,—
    'Cause I was cryin' too.
And here I am *again*
A-cryin', same as then—
    Yet happy through and through!

The old home's most in mind
And joys long left behind . . .
    Jim's little h'istin' crawl
Acrost the floor to where
John set a-rockin' there . . .
    (I'm *gittin' old*—That's all!)

I'm gittin' old—no doubt—
(*Healthy* as all git-out!)—
    But, strangest thing I do,—
I cry so *easy* now—
I cry jes' anyhow
    The fool-tears wants me to!

But Jim *he* won't be told
'*At* "Mother" 's gittin' old! . . .
    Hugged me, he did, and smiled
This morning, and bragged *"shore"*
He loved me even more
    Than when he was a child!

That's *his* way; but ef *John*
Was here now, lookin' on,
    He'd shorely know and see:
"But, 'Mother,' " s'pect he'd say,
"S'pose you air gittin' gray,
    You're younger yet than *me!*"

I'm gittin' old,—because
Our young days, like they was,
    Keeps comin' back—so clear,
    'At little Jim, once more,
Comes h'istin' crost the floor
    Fer John's old rockin'-cheer!

    .   .   .   .

O *beautiful!*—to be
A-gittin' old, like me! . . .
    Hey, Jim! Come in now, Jim!
Your supper's ready, dear!
(How more, every year,
    He looks and acts like *him!*)

993

THE BOYS OF THE OLD GLEE CLUB

YOU-FOLKS rickollect, I know—
    'Tain't so *very* long ago—
Th' Old Glee Club—was got up here
'Bout first term Grant tuk the Cheer
Fer President four year—and then
Riz—and tuk the thing again!
Politics was runnin' high,
And the *Soldiers* mighty nigh
Swep' the Country—'bout on par
With their rickord through the War.
Glee Club, mainly, Soldiers, too—
Most the Boys had wore the blue,—
So their singin' had the swing—
Kind o' sort o' Shiloh-ring,
Don't you know, 'at kind o' got
Clean *inside* a man and shot
Telegrams o' joy dee-vine
Up and down his mortal spine!
They was jest *boys* then, all young—
And 'bout lively as they sung!
Now they hain't young any more—

('Less the ones 'at's gone before
'S got their youth back, glad and free
'N' keerless as they used to be!)
Burgess Brown's old friends all 'low
He is 'most as lively now,
And as full o' music, too,
As when Old Glee Club was new!
And *John Blake,* you mind, 'at had
The near-sightedness so bad,
When he sung by note, the rest
Read 'em fer him, er he *guessed*
How they run—and *sung* 'em, too,
Clair and sweet as honey-dew!
Harry Adams's here—and he's
Jollyin' ever' man he sees
'At complains o' gittin' gray
Er a-*agein*' anyway.
Harry he jest *thrives* on fun—
"Troubles?" *he* says,—"Nary one!—
Got gran'-children I can play
And keep young with, night and day!"
Then there's *Ozzy Weaver*—he's
Kickin', lively as you please,—
'N' *Dearie Macy.*—Called 'em then
"The Cherubs." Sung "We are two
Men
O' th' Olden Time." Well! their duets
Was jest sweet as violets!
And *Dan Ransdell*—he's still here—
Not jest in the *town,* but near
Enough, you bet, to allus come
Prompt' on time to vote at home!
Dan he's be'n in Washington
Sence he went with Harrison. . . .
And *John Slauson*—(Boys called John
"Sloppy Weather.")—he went on
Once to Washington; and Dan
Intertained him:—Ever' man,
From the President, to all
Other big-guns Dan could haul
In posish 'ud have to shake
Hands with John fer old times' sake.
And to hear *John,* when he got

Home again, w'y, you'd 'a' caught
His own sperit and dry fun
And mis-*chieve*-y-ousness 'at run
Through his talk of all he see:—
"Ruther pokey there, fer *me,"*
John says,—"though, of course, I met
Mostly jest the *Cabinet*
Members; and the President
He'd drop round: and then we went
Incogg fer a quiet walk—
Er sometimes jest set and talk
'Bout old times back here—and how
All *you*-boys was doin' now,
And Old Glee Club songs; and then
He'd say, 'f he *could,* once again,
Jest hear *us*—'once more,' says he,—
'I'd shed Washington, D. C.,
And jest fall in ranks with you
And march home, a-singin', too!' "
And *Bob Geiger*—Now lives down
At Atlanty,—but this town
'S got Bob's *heart*—a permanent
And time-honored resident.
Then there's *Mahlon Butler*—still
Lookin' like he allus will!
"How you feelin'?" s'I, last time
I see Mahlon: 'N' *he* says, "I'm
'Feelin'?' " says, "so peert and gay
'F I's *hitched up* I'd run away!"
He says, " 'Course I'm *bald* a bit,
But not 'nough to *brag* on it
Like *Dave Wallace* does," he says,
"With his *two* shamefacetedness!"
(Dave jest laughs and lifts his "dice"
At the joke, and blushes—twice.)
And *Ed. Thompson, he's* gone on—
They's a whole quartette, 'at's gone—
Yes, a whole quartette, and *more,*
Has crossed on the Other Shore. . . .
Sabold and *Doc Wood'ard's* gone—
'N' *Ward;* and—last,—*Will Tarking-
ton.*—
Ward 'at made an Irish bull

Actchully jest beautiful!—
"'Big-nose Ben,'" says Ward, "I
    s'pose,
Makes an eyesore of his nose!"
And *Will Tarkington*—Ef *he*
Ever had an *inemy,*
The Good Bein's plans has be'n
Tampered with!—because all men,
Women and childern—ever' one—
Loved to love Will Tarkington!

The last time I heerd 'em *all*
Was at Tomilsonian Hall,
As I ŕickollect—and *know,*—
Must be'n fifteen year' ago!—
Big Mass Meetin'—*thousands* here. . . .
Old Dick Thompson in the Cheer
On the stage—and three er four
Other "Silver-Tongues" er more! . . .
Mind Ben Harrison?—Clean, rich,
Ringin' voice—"'bout concert-pitch,"
Tarkington *he* called it, and
Said its music 'clipsed the band
And Glee Club both rolled in one!—
('Course you all knowed *Harrison!*)
Yes, and Old Flag, streamin' clean
From the high arch 'bove the scene
And each side the Speaker's stand.—
And a *Brass,* and *Sheepskin* Band,
('Twixt the speeches 'at was made)
'At cut loose and banged and played—
S'pose, to have the *noise* all through
So's th' crowd could listen to
Some *real* music!—Then Th' Old Glee
Club marched out to victory!—
And sich singin'!—Boys was jest
At their very level-best! . . .
My! to *hear* 'em!—From old "Red-
White-and-Blue," to "Uncle Ned"!—
From "The Sword of Bunker Hill,"
To "Billy Magee-Magaw"!—And—still
The more they sung, the more, you
    know

The crowd jest *wouldn't* let 'em go!—
Till they reached the final notch
O' glory with old "Larboard Watch"!
Well! *that* song's a song my soul
Jest swings off in, past control!—
Allus did and allus will
Lift me clair of earthly ill
And interrogance and doubt
O' what the good Lord's workin' out
Anyway er *anyhow!* . . .
.Shet my eyes and hear it *now!*—
Till, at night, that ship and sea
And wet waves jest wallers me
Into that same sad yet glad
Certainty *the Sailor* had
When waked to his watch and ward
By th' lone whisper of the Lord—
Heerd high 'bove the hoarsest roar
O' any storm on sea er shore!

Time's be'n clockin' on, you know!
Sabold, who was first to go,
Died back East, in ninety-three,
At his old home, Albany:
Ward was next to leave us—Died
New York. . . . How we've laughed
    and cried
Both together at them two
Friends and comards tried and
    true!—
Ner they wasn't, when they died,
Parted long—'most side-by-side
They went singin', you might say,
Till their voices died away
Kind o' into a duet
O' silence they're rehearsin' yet.

Old Glee Club's be'n meetin' less
And less frequenter, I guess,
Sence so many's had to go—
And the rest all miss 'em so!
Still they's calls they' got to make,

Fer old reputation's sake,
So to speak; but, 'course, they all
Can't jest answer *ever'* call—
'Ceptin' Christmas-times, er when
Charity calls on 'em then;
And—not *chargin'* anything—
W'y, the Boys's jest *got* to sing! . . .
Campaign work, and jubilees
To wake up the primaries;
Loyal Legions—G. A. R.'s—
Big Reunions—Stripes-and-Stars
Fer Schoolhouses ever'where—
And Church-doin's, here and there—
And Me-morial Meetin's, when
Our War-Gov'ner lives again!
Yes, and Decoration Days—
Martial music—prayers and praise
Fer the boys 'at marched away
So's *we'd* have a place to stay! . . .
Little childern, 'mongst the flowers,
Learnin' 'bout this Land of Ours,
And the price these Soldiers paid,
Gethered in their last parade. . . .
O that sweetest, saddest sound!—
"Tenting on the old Campground." . . .
The Old Glee Club—singin' so
Quaverin'-like and soft and low,
Ever' listener in the crowd
Sings in *whispers*—but, *out 'loud,*
Sings as ef he didn't keer—
Not fer *nothin'!* . . . Ketch me here
Whilse I'm honest, and I'll say
God's way is the only way! . . .
So I' allus felt, i jing!
Ever' time the Boys 'ud sing
'Bout "A Thousand Years, my Own
Columbia!"—er "The Joys we've
    Known"—
"Hear dem Bells"—er "Hi-lo, Hail!"—
I have felt God must prevail—
Jest like ever boy 'at's gone
Of 'em all, whilse he was on
Deck here with us, seemed to be

Livin', laughin' proof, to *me,*
Of Eternal Life—no more
Will than *them all,* gone before! . . .
Can't I—many-a-time—jest see
Them *all,* like they *used* to be!—
Tarkington, fer instance, clean
Outside o' the man you *seen,*
Singin'—till not only you
Heerd his voice but *felt* it, too,
In back of the bench you set
In—And 'most can feel it yet!
Yes, and Will's the last o' five
Now that's dead—yet still *alive,*
True as Holy Writ's own word
Has be'n spoke and man has heerd!
Them was left when Will went on
Has met once sence he was gone—
Met jest once—but not to sing
Nor to practise anything.—
Facts is, they jest didn't know
Why they *was* a-meetin' so;—
But *John Brush* he had it done
And invited ever' one
Of 'em he could find, to call
At his office, "Music Hall,"
Four o'clock—one Saturd'y
Afternoon.—And this was three
Er four weeks, mind, sence the day
We had laid poor Will away.
Mahlon Butler he come past
My shop, and I dropped my last
And went with him, wonder'n', too,
What new *joke* Brush had in view;—
But, when all got there, and one-
By-one was give' a seat, and none
O' Brush's *twinkles* seemed in sight,
'N' he looked *biz* all right, all right,—
We saw—when he'd locked the door—
What *some* of us, years before,
Had *seen,* and long sence fergot—
(*Seen* but not *heerd,* like as not.)—
How Brush, once when Admiral
    Brown

'S back here in his old home-town
And flags ever'wheres—and Old
Glee Club tellin' George to "Hold
The Fort!" and "We" would "make
     'em flee
By land and sea," et cetery,—
How Brush had got the Boys to
     sing
A song in that-there very thing
Was on the table there to-day—
Some kind o' 'phone, you know.—But
     say!
When John touched it off, and we
Heerd it singin'—No-sir-ee!—
Not the *machine* a-singin'—No,—
Th' *Old Glee Club* o' long ago! . . .
There was *Sabold's* voice again—
'N' *Ward's;*—and, sweet as summer-
     rain,
With glad boy-laughture's trills and
     runs,
Ed. Thompson's voice and *Tarking-
     ton's!* . . .
And *ah,* to *hear* them, through the
     storm
Of joy that swayed each listener's
     form—
Seeming to call, with hail and cheer,
From Heaven's high seas down to us
     here:—
*"But who can speak the joy he feels
While o'er the foam his vessel reels,
And his tired eyelids slumbering fall,
He rouses at the welcome call
Of 'Larboard Watch, Ahoy!'"*
.   .   .   .   .   . And *O*
To *hear* them—same as long ago—
The listeners whispered, still as death,
With trembling lips and broken breath,
As with one voice—and eyes all
     wet,—
"God!—*God!—Thank God, they're
     singing yet!"*

994

"MONA MACHREE"

*Mona Machree, I'm the wanderin'
     creature now,
          Over the sea;
Slave of no lass; but a lover of Nature
     now,
          Careless and free.*
                    —T. A. DALY.

MONA MACHREE! och, the
          sootherin' flow of it,
     Soft as the sea,
Yet, in under the mild, moves the wild
     undertow of it
          Tuggin' at me,
Until both the head and the heart o'
     me's fightin'
For breath, nigh a death all so grandly
     invitin'
That—barrin' your own livin' yet—
     I'd delight in,
     Drowned in the deeps of this bil-
          lowy song to you
Sung by a lover your beauty has
     banned,
Not alone from your love but his dear
     native land,
Whilst the kiss of his lips, and touch
     of his hand,
     And his song—all belong to you,
          Mona Machree!

995

SONG DISCORDANT

I WANT to say it, and I will:—
     You are as sour as you are sweet,
And sweeter than the daffodil
     That blossoms at your feet.—

You are as plain as you are fair;
And though I hate, I love you still,
And so — *confound* you, darling!
There!—
I want to say it, and I will!

I want to ask it, and I do
Demand of you a perfect trust,—
But love me as I want you to—
You must, you minx!—you must!
You blight and bless me, till I swear
And pray—chaotic even as you.—
I curse—Nay, dear,—I *kiss* you.
There!—
I want to, and I do!

996

LARRY NOOLAN'S NEW YEAR

BE-GORRIE, aI wor sorry
When the Ould Year died:
An' aI says, "aI'll shtart to-morry,
Like aI've always thried—
aI'll give yez all fair warnin'
aI'll be shtartin' in the mornin'
From the wakeness aI was born
in—
When the Ould Year died."

The year forninsht the pasht wan,
When the Ould Year died,
Says aI, "This is the lasht wan
aI'll be filled—wid pride."
So says aI til Miss McCarty
aI wor meetin' at the party,
"Lave us both be drinkin' hearty!"
When the Ould Year died.

So we dined an' wined together,
When the Ould Year died,

An' agreed on health an' weather,
An' the whule wurrld wide,
An' says aI,—"aI'm thinkin' very
Much it's you aI'd like to marry."
"Then," says she, "why don't you,
Larry?"
When the Ould Year died.

997

LISPING IN NUMBERS

WE' got a' Uncle writes poetry-
rhymes
Fer me an' Eddie to *speak,* some-
times,—
'Cause *he's* a *poet*—an' he gits *paid*
Fer poetry-writin',—'cause that's his
trade.
An' Eddie says he's goin' to try
To be a poet, too, by an' by
When he's a man!—an' I 'spect he is,
'Cause on his slate wunst he print' this
An' call it

"THE SQUIRL AND THE FUNY LITEL
GIRL"

"A litel girl
Whose name wuz Perl
Went to the woods to play.
The day wuz brite,
An' her hart wuz lite
As she galy skiped a way.

"A queer litel chatter,
A soft litel patter,
She herd in the top of a tree:
The surprized litel Perl
Saw a qute litel squirl,
As cuning as cuning cud be.

"She twisted her curl,
As she looked at the squirl,
An' playfully told it 'good day!'
She calld it 'Bunny'—
Wuzent that funy?
An' it noded an' bounded a way."

Ma read it, an' says "she's *awful*
    proud,"—
An' Pa says "Splen'id!" an' laugh' out
    loud;
But Uncle says, "You can talk as you
    please,
It's a purty good little poetry-piece!"

998

BENJAMIN HARRISON

ON THE UNVEILING OF HIS MONUMENT
AT INDIANAPOLIS—OCTOBER 27, 1908

AS tangible a form in History
    The Spirit of this man stands
        forth as here
He towers in deathless sculpture,
        high and clear
Against the bright sky of his des-
    tiny.
Sprung of our oldest, noblest ancestry,
    His pride of birth, as lofty as sin-
        cere,
    Held kith and kin, as Country, ever
        dear—
Such was his sacred faith in you and
    me.
Thus, natively, from youth his work
        was one
Unselfish service in behalf of all—
    Home, friends and sharers of his
        toil and stress;

Ay, loving all men and despising none,
    And swift to answer every righteous
        call,
    His life was one long deed of
        worthiness.

The voice of Duty's faintest whisper
        found
    Him as alert as at her battle-cry—
    When awful War's battalions thun-
        dered by,
High o'er the havoc still he heard the
        sound
Of mothers' prayers and pleadings all
        around;
    And ever the despairing sob and sigh
    Of stricken wives and orphan chil-
        dren's cry
Made all our Land thrice consecrated
        ground.
So rang his "Forward!" and so swept
        his sword—
    On!—on!—till from the fire-and-
        cloud once more
    Our proud Flag lifted in the glad
        sunlight
As though the very Ensign of the Lord
    Unfurled in token that the strife
        was o'er,
    And victory—as ever—with the
        right.

999

LEE O. HARRIS

CHRISTMAS DAY—1909

O SAY not he is dead,
    The friend we honored so;
Lift up a grateful voice instead
    And say: He lives, we know—

We know it by the light
Of his enduring love
Of honor, valor, truth and right,
And man, and God above.

Remember how he drew
The child-heart to his own,
And taught the parable anew,
And reaped as he had sown;
Remember with what cheer
He filled the little lives,
And stayed the sob and dried the tear
With mirth that still survives.

All duties to his kind
It was his joy to fill;
With nature gentle and refined,
Yet dauntless soul and will,
He met the trying need
Of every troublous call,
Yet high and clear and glad indeed
He sung above it all.

Ay, listen! Still we hear
The patriot song, the lay
Of love, the woodland note so dear—
These will not die away.
Then say not he is dead,
The friend we honor so,
But lift a grateful voice instead,
And say: He lives, we know.

1000

SOMETHING

SITTING by the glimmer
Of the fire to-night,
Though the glowing embers
Sparkle with delight—
There's a sense of something,
Vaguely understood,

Stealing o'er the spirit
As a shadow would.

Is it that the shutter
Shudders in the wind
As a lance of moonshine
Shivers through the blind?
Or the lamplight dancing
In pretended glee
As the keynote whistles
In a minor key?

Footsteps on the sidewalk,
Crunching through the snow,
Seem to whisper something
Of the long ago—
And the merry greetings
Of the passers-by
Seem like truant echoes
Coming home to die.

I have coaxed my pencil
For a smiling face,
But the sketch is frowning
And devoid of grace;
And the airy waltzes
Of my violin
Die away in dirges
Ere I well begin.

Lay away the story—
Though the theme is sweet—
There's a lack of something
Makes it incomplete;
There's a nameless yearning—
Strangely undefined—
For a something better
Than the common kind.

Something! Oh, that something!
We may never know
Why the soul is haunted
Ever thus and so,

Till the longing spirit
Answers to the call
Of the trumpet sounding
Something after all.

1001

A CHRISTMAS-TIME JINGLE

MY dears, do you know, one short
    Christmas ago,
There were two little children named
Jimpsy and Jo,
Who were stolen away by their Uncle
that day,
Who drove round and carted them off
in a sleigh?

And the two little chaps, rolled in buf-
falo wraps,
With their eyes in the furs and their
hands in their laps,
He whizzed down the street, through
the snow and the sleet
At a gait old Kriss Kringle himself
couldn't beat.

And their Uncle yelled "Ho!" all at
once, and then "Whoa!
Mr. Horses, this store is where we must
go."
And as the sleigh stopped, up the heads
popped,
And out on the sidewalk the old Uncle
hopped.

And he took the boys in, with a wink
and a grin,
And had 'em dressed clean up from
toe-tip to chin,

Then he bundled 'em back in the
sleigh, and currack!
Went the whip; and away they all went
whizzin' back.

And Jimpsy and Jo, when they
marched in, you know,
There at home, with new suits, both
their parents says "Oh,
What dee-lishamous rare little children
you air,—
W'y you' got the best Uncle tha' is
anywhere!"

But their Uncle just pats the boys'
heads and says, "Rats!"
In a whisper to them—"Parents purr
same as cats";
Then he kissed 'em and rose and fished
round in his clothes,
And lit his old pipe with the end of
his nose.

1002

WHEN BABY PLAYED

WHEN Baby played,
    The very household tasks were
        stayed
To listen to her voice:—Secrete,
We heard her lisping, low and sweet,
Among her many dolls and pets;
Or, at her window's mignonettes,
Making some butterfly—arrayed
In tremulous gold—all unafraid—
When Baby played. .

When Baby played
Amidst the reapers,—why, they laid
Their work aside, and with loud glee
Tossed her among them tenderly;
And they did single, from the blur

Of tousled grasses, blooms for her—
To wreathe about her throat and wrist,
While for the service each was kissed,
And on till evensong was made
So happier.—When Baby played.

When Baby played,
The lilies down the everglade
Grew purer—where the waters leapt,
The willows laughed instead of wept;
And the glad winds went merrying
To sway the empty grapevine-swing
She needs must leave, in answer to
Our call from home at fall of dew—
And mimicking the call we made.—
When Baby played,—when Baby
   played.

1003

WHEN BABY SLEPT

WHEN weenty-teenty Baby
   slept,—
With voices stilled we lightly stepped
And knelt beside the rug where she
Had fallen in sleep all wearily;
And when a dimpled hand would stir,
We breathlessly bent over her
And kissed the truant strands that
   swept
The tranc'd lids and the dreams that
   kept—
When Baby blinked her Court and
   slept.

When Baby waived her throne and
   slept,
It seemed the sunshine lightlier crept
Along the carpet and the wall,
Her playhouse, tea-set, pets and all:—
A loud fly hushed its hum and made
The faintest Fairy-serenade,

That lulled all waking things except
The goldfish as he flashed and leapt—
When Baby doffed her crown and
   slept.

When sunset veiled her as she slept,
No other sight might intercept
Our love-looks, meant for her alone
The fairest blossom ever blown
In all God's garden-lands below!
Our Spirits whispered, Even so,
And made high mirth in undertone,
In stress of joy all sudden grown
A laugh of tears:—for thus we wept,
When Baby donned her dreams, and
   slept.

1004

WHEN BABY WOKE

WHEN weenty-teenty Baby woke,
   It seemed all summer blos-
      soms broke
In fragrant laughter—that the birds,
Instead of warbles, sang in words!—
Oh, it did seem to us (who, in
Our rapture, dappled cheek and chin
With our warm kisses) to invoke
Our love to break as morning broke!—
When wondrous Baby woke.

When our enraptured Baby woke,—
As when on violets sink and soak
The dewdrops of some glorious
   dawn,—
So seemed the eyes we gazed upon;
And when they smiled, we, bending
   lower,
Knew never sunlight any more
Would be as bright to us—and thus
Forever must they shine for us!
When Baby dewed her eyes and woke.

When Baby danced her eyes and
woke—
The hearts within us, stroke on stroke,
Went throbbing like the pulse of some
High harmony harp-strings might
thrum
In halls enchanted of the lore
Or Arthur's court in days of yore,—
To us she was "a princess fair"—
An "Elfin Queen"—"A ladye rare"—
And we but simple-minded folk—
When Baby woke,—when Baby woke.

1005

A HOBO VOLUNTARY

OH, the hobo's life is a roving life;
  It robs pretty maids of their
heart's delight—
It causes them to weep and it causes
them to mourn
For the life of a hobo, never to return.

The hobo's heart it is light and free,
Though it's Sweethearts all, farewell to
thee!—
Farewell to thee, for it's far away
The homeless hobo's footsteps stray.

In the morning bright, or the dusk so
dim,
It's any path is the one for him!
He'll take his chances, long or short,
For to meet his fate with a valiant
heart.

Oh, it's beauty mops out the side-
tracked-car,
And it's beauty-beaut' at the pigs-feet
bar;

But when his drinks and his eats is
made
Then the hobo shunts off down the
grade.

He camps near town, on the old crick-
bank,
And he cuts his name on the water-
tank—
He cuts his name and the hobo sign,—
"Bound for the land of corn and wine!"

He's lonesome-like, so he gits run in,
To git the hang o' the world again;
But the laundry circles he moves in
there
Makes him sigh for the country air,—

So it's Good-by gals! and he takes his
chance
And wads hisself through the work-
house-fence:
He sheds the town and the railroad,
too,
And strikes mud roads for a change of
view.

The jay drives by on his way to town,
And looks on the hobo in high scorn,
And so likewise does the farmhands
stare—
But what the haids does the hobo
care!

He hits the pike, in the summer's heat
Or the winter's cold, with its snow and
sleet—
With a boot on one foot, and one
shoe—
Or he goes barefoot, if he chooses to.

But he likes the best when the day is
warm,
With his bum prince-albert on his
arm—

He likes to size up a farmhouse where
They haint no man nor bulldog there.

Oh, he gits his meals wherever he can,
So natchurly he's a handy man—
He's a handy man both day and night,
And he's always blest with an appetite!

(Oh, it's I like friends that he'ps me
  through,
And the friends also that he'ps you,
  too,—
Oh, I like all friends, 'most every kind
But I don't like friends that don't like
  mine.)

There's friends of mine when they gits
  the hunch
Comes a swarmin' in, the blasted
  bunch,—
"Clog-step Jonny" and "Flat-wheel
  Bill"
And "Brockey Ike" from Circleville.

With "Cooney Ward" and "Sikes the
  Kid"
And old "Pop Lawson"—the best we
  had—
The rankest mug and the worst for
  lush
And the dandiest of the whole blame
  push.

Oh, them's the times I remembers best
When I took my chance with all the
  rest,
And hogged fried chicken and roastin'
  ears, too,
And sucked cheroots when the feed
  was through.

Oh, the hobo's way is the railroad line,
And it's little he cares for schedule time;
Whatever town he's a-striken for
Will wait for him till he gits there.

And whatever burg that he lands in
There's beauties there just thick for
  him—
There's beauty at "The Queen's Taste
  Lunchstand," sure,
Or "The Last Chance Boardin' House"
  back door.

A tin o' black coffee, and a rhubarb
  pie—
Be they old and cold as charity—
They're hot-stuff enough for the pore
  hobo,
And it's "Thanks, kind lady, for to
  treat me so!"

Then he fills his pipe with a stub cigar
And swipes a coal from the kitchen-
  fire,
And the hired girl says, in a smilin'
  tone,—
"It's good-by John, if you call that
  goin'!"

Oh, the hobo's life is a roving life,
It robs pretty maids of their heart's
  delight—
It causes them to weep and it causes
  them to mourn
For the life of a hobo, never to return.

1006

TO BENJ. S. PARKER

Y OU sang the song of rare delight
  " 'Tis morning and the days are
    long"—
A morning fresh and fair and bright
  As ever dawned in happy song;
A radiant air, and here and there
  Were singing birds on sprays of
    bloom,

And dewy splendors everywhere,
  And heavenly breaths of rose per-
    fume—
All rapturous things were in the song
" 'Tis morning and the days are long."

O singer of the song divine,
  Though now you turn your face
    away
With never word for me or mine
  Nor smile forever and a day,
We guess your meaning, and rejoice
  In what has come to you—the meed
Beyond the search of mortal voice
  And only in the song indeed—
With you forever, as the song,
" 'Tis morning and the days are long."

1007

MY CONSCIENCE

SOMETIMES my Conscience says,
  say he,
"Don't you know me?"
And I, says I, skeered through and
    through,
"Of course I do.
You air a nice chap ever' way,
I'm here to say!
You make me cry—you make me pray,
And all them good things thataway—
That is, at *night.* Where do you stay
Durin' the day?"

And then my Conscience says, onc't
    more,
"You know me—shore?"
"Oh, yes," says I, a-trimblin' faint,

"You're jes' a saint!
Your ways is all so holy-right,
I love you better ever' night
You come around,—tel' plum daylignt,
When you air out o' sight!"

And then my Conscience sort o' grits
His teeth, and spits
On his two hands and grabs, of course,
Some old remorse,
And beats me with the big butt-end
O' *that* thing—tel my clostest friend
'Ud hardly know me. "Now," says he,
"Be keerful as you'd orto be
And *allus* think o' me!"

1008

BLOOMS OF MAY

BUT yesterday! . . .
    O blooms of May,
And summer roses—where away?
O stars above;
And lips of love,
And all the honeyed sweets thereof!—

O lad and lass,
And orchard pass,
And briered lane, and daisied grass!
O gleam and gloom,
And woodland bloom,
And breezy breaths of all perfume!—

No more for me
Or mine shall be
Thy raptures—save in memory—
No more—no more—
Till through the Door
Of Glory gleam the days of yore.

1009

THE DREAM OF DEATH

FROM "AN ADJUSTABLE LUNATIC"

O GENTLE death, bow down and
sip
The soul that lingers on my lip;
O gentle death, bow down and keep
Eternal vigil o'er my sleep;
For I am weary and would rest
Forever on your loving breast.

1010

FANTASY

FROM "AN ADJUSTABLE LUNATIC"

A FANTASY that came to me
As wild and wantonly designed
As ever any dream might be
Unraveled from a madman's mind,—
A tangle-work of tissue, wrought
By cunning of the spider-brain,
And woven, in an hour of pain,
To trap the giddy flies of thought—.

I STOOD beneath a summer moon
All swollen to uncanny girth,
And hanging, like the sun at noon,
Above the center of the earth;
But with a sad and sallow light,
As it had sickened of the night
And fallen in a pallid swoon.
Around me I could hear the rush
Of sullen winds, and feel the whir
Of unseen wings apast me brush
Like phantoms round a sepulcher;
And, like a carpeting of plush,
A lawn unrolled beneath my feet,
Bespangled o'er with flowers as sweet
To look upon as those that nod
Within the garden-fields of God,

But odorless as those that blow
In ashes in the shades below.

And on my hearing fell a storm
Of gusty music, sadder yet
Than every whimper of regret
That sobbing utterance could form,
And patched with scraps of sound
that seemed
Torn out of tunes that demons
dreamed,
And pitched to such a piercing key,
It stabbed the ear with agony;
And when at last it lulled and died,
I stood aghast and terrified.
I shuddered and I shut my eyes,
And still could see, and feel aware
Some mystic presence waited there;
And staring, with a dazed surprise,
I saw a creature so divine
That never subtle thought of mine
May reproduce to inner sight
So fair a vision of delight.

A syllable of dew that drips
From out a lily's laughing lips
Could not be sweeter than the word
I listened to, yet never heard.—
For, oh, the woman hiding there
Within the shadows of her hair,
Spake to me in an undertone
So delicate, my soul alone
But understood it as a moan
Of some weak melody of wind
A heavenward breeze had left be-
hind.

A tracery of trees, grotesque
Against the sky, behind her seen,
Like shapeless shapes of arabesque
Wrought in an oriental screen;
And tall, austere and statuesque
She loomed before it—e'en as though
The spirit-hand of Angelo

Had chiseled her to life complete,
With chips of moonshine round her
    feet.
And I grew jealous of the dusk,
To see it softly touch her face,
As lover-like, with fond embrace,
It folded round her like a husk:
But when the glitter of her hand,
Like wasted glory, beckoned me,
My eyes grew blurred and dull and
    dim—
My vision failed—I could not
    see—
I could not stir—I could but stand,
Till, quivering in every limb,
I flung me prone, as though to
    swim
The tide of grass whose waves of
    green
Went rolling ocean-wide between
My helpless shipwrecked heart and
    her
Who claimed me for a worshiper.

And writhing thus in my despair,
I heard a weird, unearthly sound,
That seemed to lift me from the
    ground
And hold me floating in the air.
I looked, and lo! I saw her bow

Above a harp within her hands;
A crown of blossoms bound her
    brow,
And on her harp were twisted strands
Of silken starlight, rippling o'er
With music never heard before
By mortal ears; and, at the strain,
I felt my Spirit snap its chain
And break away,—and I could see
It as it turned and fled from me
To greet its mistress, where she smiled
To see the phantom dancing wild
And wizard-like before the spell
Her mystic fingers knew so well.

What is it? Who will rightly guess
If it be aught but nothingness
That dribbles from a wayward pen
To spatter in the eyes of men?
What matter! I will call it mine,
And I will take the changeling home
And bathe its face with morning-shine,
And comb it with a golden comb
Till every tangled tress of rhyme
Will fairer be than summer-time:
And I will nurse it on my knee,
And dandle it beyond the clasp
Of hands that grip and hands that
    grasp,
Through life and all eternity!

THE FLYING ISLANDS OF THE NIGHT

FOR the Song's sake; even so:
  Humor it, and let it go
All untamed and wild of wing—
Leave it ever truanting.

    Be its flight elusive!—Lo,
    For the Song's sake—even so.—
    Yield it but an ear as kind
    As thou perkest to the wind

Who will name us what the seas
Have sung on for centuries?
For the Song's sake! Even so—
Sing, O Seas! and Breezes, blow!

    Sing! or Wave or Wind or Bird—
    Sing! nor ever afterward
    Clear thy meaning to us—No!—
    For the Song's sake. Even so.

DRAMATIS PERSONÆ

KRUNG   King—*of the* Spirks
CRESTILLOMEEM   *The* Queen—*Second Consort to* Krung
SPRAIVOLL   *The* Tune-Fool
AMPHINE   Prince—*Son of* Krung
DWAINIE   *A* Princess—*of the* Wunks
JUCKLET   *A* Dwarf—*of the* Spirks
CREECH *and*
GRITCHFANG   Nightmares

Counselors, Courtiers, Heralds, etc.

THE FLYING ISLANDS OF THE NIGHT

ACT I

PLACE—THE FLYING ISLANDS

SCENE I. Spirkland. *Time, Moondawn. Interior Court of* KRUNG. *A vast, pendant star burns dimly in dome above throne.* CRESTILLOMEEM *discovered languidly reclining at foot of empty throne, an overturned goblet lying near, as though just drained. The* Queen, *in seeming dazed, ecstatic state, raptly gazing upward, listening. Swarming forms and features in air above, seen eerily coming and going, blending and intermingling in domed ceiling-spaces of court. Weird music. Mystic, luminous, beautiful faces detached from swarm, float singly forward,—tremulously, and in succession, poising in mid-air and chanting.*

FIRST FACE

And who hath known her—like as *I*
Have known her?—since the envying sky
Filched from her cheeks its morning hue,
And from her eyes its glory, too,
Of dazzling shine and diamond-dew.

SECOND FACE

I knew her—long and long before
High Æo loosed her palm and thought:
"What awful splendor have I wrought
To dazzle earth and Heaven, too!"

THIRD FACE

I knew her—long ere Night was o'er—
Ere Æo yet conjectured what
To fashion Day of—ay, before
He sprinkled stars across the floor

771

Of dark, and swept that form of mine,
E'en as a fleck of blinded shine,
Back to the black where light was not.

Fourth Face

Ere day was dreamt, I saw her face
Lift from some starry hiding-place
Where our old moon was kneeling while
She lit its features with her smile.

Fifth Face

I knew her while these islands yet
Were nestlings—ere they feathered wing,
Or e'en could gape with them or get
Apoise the laziest-ambling breeze,
Or cheep, chirp out, or anything!
When Time crooned rhymes of nurseries
Above them—nodded, dozed and slept,
And knew it not, till, wakening,
The morning stars agreed to sing
And Heaven's first tender dews were wept.

Sixth Face

I knew her when the jealous hands
Of Angels set her sculptured form
Upon a pedestal of storm
And let her to this land with strands
Of twisted lightnings.

Seventh Face

                    And I heard
Her voice ere she could tone a word
Of any but the Seraph-tongue.—
And O sad-sweeter than all sung-
Or word-said things!—to hear her say,
Between the tears she dashed away:—
"Lo, launched from the offended sight
Of Æo!—anguish infinite
Is ours, O Sisterhood of Sin!

Yet is thy service mine by right,
And, sweet as I may rule it, thus
    Shall Sin's myrrh-savor taste to us—
    Sin's Empress—let my reign begin!"

CHORUS OF SWARMING FACES

We follow thee forever on!
Through darkest night and dimmest dawn;
Through storm and calm—through shower and shine,
Hear thou our voices answering thine:
    We follow—*craving* but to be
    Thy followers.—We follow thee—
    We follow, follow, follow thee!

We follow ever on and on—
O'er hill and hollow, brake and lawn;
Through gruesome vale and dread ravine
Where light of day is never seen.—
    We waver not in loyalty,—
    Unfaltering we follow thee—
    We follow, follow, follow thee!

We follow ever on and on!
The shroud of night around us drawn,
Though wet with mists, is wild-ashine
With stars to light that path of thine;—
    The glowworms, too, befriend us—we
    Shall fail not as we follow thee.
    We follow, follow, follow thee!

We follow ever on and on.—
The notchèd reeds we pipe upon
Are pithed with music, keener blown
And blither where thou leadest lone—
    Glad pangs of its ecstatic glee
    Shall reach thee as we follow thee.
    We follow, follow, follow thee!

We follow ever on and on:
We know the ways thy feet have gone,—
The grass is greener, and the bloom

Of roses richer in perfume—
And the birds of every blooming tree
Sing sweeter as we follow thee.
We follow, follow, follow thee!

We follow ever on and on;
For wheresoever thou hast gone
We hasten joyous, knowing there
Is sweeter sin than otherwhere—
Leave still its latest cup, that we
May drain it as we follow thee.
We follow, follow, follow thee!

[*Throughout final stanzas, faces in foreground and forms in background slowly
vanish, and voices gradually fail to sheer silence.—*Crestillomeem *rises and
wistfully gazes and listens; then, evidently regaining wonted self, looks to
be assured of being wholly alone—then speaks.*]

Crestillomeem

The Throne is throwing wide its gilded arms
To welcome me. The Throne of Krung! Ha! ha!
Leap up, ye lazy echoes, and laugh loud!
For I, Crestillomeem, the Queen—ha! ha!
Do fling my richest mirth into your mouths
That ye may fatten ripe with mockery!
I marvel what the kingdom would become
Were I not here to nurse it like a babe
And dandle it above the reach and clutch
Of intermeddlers in the royal line
And their attendant serfs. *Ho!* Jucklet, ho!
'Tis time my knarled warp of nice anatomy
Were here, to weave us on upon our mesh
Of silken villanies. *Ho!* Jucklet, ho!

[*Lifts secret door in pave and drops a star-bud through opening. Enter* Juck-
let *from below.*]

Jucklet

Spang sprit! my gracious Queen! but thou hast scorched
My left ear to a cinder! and my head
Rings like a ding-dong on the coast of death!

For, patient hate! thy hasty signal burst
Full in my face as hitherward I came!
But though my lug be fried to crisp, and my
Singed wig stinks like a little sun-stewed Wunk,
I stretch my fragrant presence at thy feet
And kiss thy sandal with a blistered lip.

CRESTILLOMEEM

Hold! rare-done fool, lest I may bid the cook
To bake thee brown! How fares the King by this?

JUCKLET

Safe couched midmost his lordly hoard of books,
I left him sleeping like a quinsied babe
Next the guest-chamber of a poor man's house:
But ere I came away, to rest mine ears,
I salved his welded lids, uncorked his nose,
And o'er the odorous blossom of his lips
Re-squeezed the tinctured sponge, and felt his pulse
Come staggering back to regularity.
And four hours hence his Highness will awake
And *Peace* will take a nap!

CRESTILLOMEEM

Ha! What mean you?

JUCKLET [*Ominously*]

I mean that he suspects our knaveries.—
Some covert spy is burrowed in the court—
Nay, and I pray thee startle not *aloud,*
But mute thy very heart in its out-throb,
And let the blanching of thy cheeks but be
A whispering sort of pallor!

CRESTILLOMEEM

A spy?—Here?

JUCKLET

Ay, *here*—and haply even *now*. And one
Whose unseen eye seems ever focused keen
Upon our action, and whose hungering ear
Eats every crumb of counsel that we drop
In these our secret interviews!—For he—
The King—through all his talking-sleep to-day
Hath jabbered of intrigue, conspiracy—
Of treachery and hate in fellowship,
With dire designs upon his royal bulk,
To oust it from the Throne.

CRESTILLOMEEM

He spake my name?

JUCKLET

O Queen, he speaks not ever but thy name
Makes melody of every sentence.—Yea,
He thinks thee even true to him as thou
Art fickle, false and subtle! O how blind
And lame, and deaf and dumb, and worn and weak,
And faint, and sick, and all-commodious
His dear love is! In sooth, O wifely one,
Thy malleable spouse doth mind me of
That pliant hero of the bald old catch
"The Lovely Husband."—Shall I wreak the thing?

[*Sings—with much affected gravity and grimace*]

O a lovely husband he was known,
He loved his wife and her a-lone;
She reaped the harvest he had sown;
She ate the meat; he picked the bone.
    With mixed admirers every size,
    She smiled on each without disguise;
    This lovely husband closed his eyes
    Lest he might take her by surprise.

[*Aside, exclamatory*]

Chorious uproarious!

[*Then pantomime as though pulling at bell-rope—singing in pent, explosive utterance*]

> Trot!
>   Run!
>   Wasn't he a handy hubby?
>
> What
>   Fun
>   She could plot and plan!
>
> Not
>   One
>   Other such a dandy hubby
>   As this lovely man!

CRESTILLOMEEM

Or talk or tune, wilt thou wind up thy tongue
Nor let it tangle in a knot of words!
What said the King?

JUCKLET [*With recovered reverence*]

He said: "Crestillomeem—
O that *she* knew this thick distress of mine!—
Her counsel would *anoint* me and her voice
Would flow in limpid wisdom o'er my woes
And, like a love-balm, lave my secret grief
And lull my sleepless heart!" [*Aside*] And so went on,
Struggling all maudlin in the wrangled web
That well-nigh hath cocooned him!

CRESTILLOMEEM

Did he yield
No hint of this mysterious distress
He needs must hold sequestered from his Queen?
What said he in his talking-sleep by which
Some clue were gained of how and when and whence
His trouble came?

JUCKLET

In one strange phase he spake
As though some sprited lady talked with him.—
Full courteously he said: "In woman's guise
Thou comest, yet I think thou art, in sooth,
But woman in thy form.—Thy words are strange
And leave me mystified. I feel the truth
Of all thou hast declared, and yet so vague
And shadow-like thy meaning is to me,
I know not how to act to ward the blow
Thou sayest is hanging o'er me even now."
And then, with open hands held pleadingly,
He asked, "Who *is* my foe?"—And o'er his face
A sudden pallor flashed, like death itself,
As though, if answer had been given, it
Had fallen like a curse.

CRESTILLOMEEM

I'll stake my soul
Thrice over in the grinning teeth of doom,
'Tis Dwainie of the Wunks who peeks and peers
With those fine eyes of hers in our affairs
And carries Krung, in some disguise, these hints
Of our intent! See thou that silence falls
Forever on her lips, and that the sight
She wastes upon our secret action blurs
With gray and grisly scum that shall for aye
Conceal us from her gaze while she writhes blind
And fangless as the fat worms of the grave!
Here! take this tuft of downy druze, and when
Thou comest on her, fronting full and fair,
Say "*Sherzham!*" thrice, and fluff it in her face.

JUCKLET

Thou knowest scanty magic, O my Queen,
But all thou dost is fairly excellent—
An *this* charm work, thou shalt have fuller faith
Than still I must withhold.

[*Takes charm, with extravagant salutation*]

CRESTILLOMEEM

Thou gibing knave!
Thou thing! Dost dare to name my sorcery
As any trifling gift? Behold what might
Be thine an thy deserving wavered not
In stable and abiding service to
Thy Queen!

[*She presses suddenly her palm upon his eyes, then lifts her softly opening hand
upward, his gaze following, where, slowly shaping in the air above them,
appears semblance—or counterself—of* CRESTILLOMEEM, *clothed in most ra-
diant youth, her maiden-face bent downward to a moonlit sward, where
kneels a lover-knight—flawless in manly symmetry and princely beauty,—
yet none other than the counter-self of* JUCKLET, *eerily and with strange
sweetness singing, to some curiously tinkling instrument, the praises of its
queenly mistress:* JUCKLET *and* CRESTILLOMEEM *transfixed below—tran-
cedly gazing on their mystic selves above.*]

SEMBLANCE OF JUCKLET [*Sings*]

Crestillomeem!
Crestillomeem!
Soul of my slumber!—Dream of my dream!
Moonlight may fall not as goldenly fair
As falls the gold of thine opulent hair—
Nay, nor the starlight as dazzlingly gleam
As gleam thine eyes, 'Meema—Crestillomeem!—
Star of the skies, 'Meema—
Crestillomeem!

SEMBLANCE OF CRESTILLOMEEM [*Sings*]

O Prince divine!
O Prince divine!
Tempt thou me not with that sweet voice of thine!
Though my proud brow bear the blaze of a crown,
Lo, at thy feet must its glory bow down,
That from the dust thou mayest lift me to shine
Heaven'd in thy heart's rapture, O Prince divine!—
Queen of thy love ever,
O Prince divine!

SEMBLANCE OF JUCKLET [*Sings*]

Crestillomeem!
                    Crestillomeem!
Our life shall flow as a musical stream—
Windingly—placidly on it shall wend,
Marged with mazhoora-bloom banks without end—
Word-birds shall call thee and dreamily scream,
"Where dost thou cruise, 'Meema—Crestillomeem?
Whither away, 'Meema?—
                    Crestillomeem!"

DUO

[*Vision and voices gradually failing away*]

Crestillomeem!
                    Crestillomeem!
Soul of my slumber!—Dream of my dream!
Star of Love's light, 'Meema—Crestilomeem!
Crescent of Night, 'Meema!—
                    Crestillomeem!

[*With song, vision likewise fails utterly*]

CRESTILLOMEEM

[*To* JUCKLET, *still trancedly staring upward*]

        How now, thou clabber-brainèd spudge!—
Thou squelk!—thou—

JUCKLET

                    Nay, O Queen! contort me not
To more condensèd littleness than now
My shamèd frame incurreth on itself,
Seeing what might fare with it, didst *thou* will
Kindly to nip it with thy magic *here*
And leave it living in that form i' the air,
Forever pranking o'er the daisied sward
In wake of sandal-prints that dint the dews
As lightly as, in thy late maidenhood,
Thine own must needs have done in flighting from
The dread encroachments of the King.

CRESTILLOMEEM

Nay—peace!

JUCKLET

So be it, O sweet Mystic.—But I crave
One service of thy magic yet.—*Amphine!*—
Breed me some special, damnèd philter for
Amphine—the *fair* Amphine!—to chuck it him,
Some serenade-tide, in a sodden slug
O' pastry, 'twixt the door-crack and a screech
O' rusty hinges.—Hey! Amphine, the *fair!*—
And let me, too, elect his doom, O Queen!—
Listed against thee, he, too, doubtless hath
Been favored with an outline of our scheme.—
And I would kick my soul all over hell
If I might juggle his fine figure up
In such a shape as mine!

CRESTILLOMEEM

Then this:—When thou
Canst come upon him bent above a flower,
Or any blooming thing, and thou, arear,
Shalt reach it first and, thwartwise, touch it fair,
And with thy knuckle flick him on the knee,—
Then—his fine form will shrink and shrivel up
As warty as a toad's—so hideous,
Thine own shall seem a marvel of rare grace!
Though idly speak'st thou of my mystic skill,
'Twas that which won the King for me;—'twas **that**
Bereft him of his daughter ere we had
Been wedded yet a haed:—She strangely went
Astray one moonset from the palace-steps—
She went—nor yet returned.—Was it not strange?—
She would be wedded to an alien prince
The morrow midnight—to a prince whose sire
I once knew, in lost hours of lute and song,
When *he* was but a prince—*I* but a mouth
For him to lift up sippingly and drain
To lees most ultimate of stammering sobs
And maudlin wanderings of blinded breath.

JUCKLET [*Aside*]

Twigg-brebblets! but her Majesty hath speech
That doth bejuice all metaphor to drip
And spray and mist of sweetness!

CRESTILLOMEEM [*Confusedly*]

Where was I?
O, ay!—The princess went—she strangely went!—
E'en as I deemed her lover-princeling would
As strangely go, were she not soon restored.—
As so he did:—That airy penalty
The jocund Fates provide our love-lorn wights
In this glad island: So for thrice three nights
They spun the prince his line and marked him pay
It out (despite all warnings of his doom)
In fast and sleepless search for her—and *then*
They tripped his fumbling feet and he fell—UP!—
Up!—as 'tis writ—sheer past Heaven's flinching walls
And topmost cornices.—Up—up and on!—
And, it is grimly guessed of those who thus
For such a term bemoan an absent love,
And so fall *up*wise, they must needs fall on—
And on and on—and on—and on—and on!
Ha! ha!

JUCKLET

Quahh! but the prince's holden breath
Must ache his throat by this! But, O my Queen,
What of the princess?—and—

CRESTILLOMEEM

The princess?—Ay—
The princess! Ay, she went—she strangely went!
And when the dainty vagrant came not back—
Both sire and son in apprehensive throes
Of royal grief—the very Throne befogged
In sighs and tears!—when all hope waned at last,
And all the spies of Spirkland, in her quest,
Came straggling empty-handed home again,—

Why, then the wise King sleeved his rainy eyes
And sagely thought the pretty princess had
Strayed to the island's edge and tumbled off.
I could have set his mind at ease on that—
I could have told him,—*yea,* she tumbled off—
I tumbled her!—and tumbled her so plump,
She tumbled in an under-island, then
Just slow-unmooring from our own and poised
For unknown voyagings of flight afar
And all remote of latitudes of ours.—
Ay, into that land I tumbled her from which
But one charm known to art can tumble her
Back into this,—and *that* charm (guilt be praised!)
Is lodged not in the wit nor the desire
Of my rare lore.

JUCKLET

Thereinasmuch find joy!
But dost thou know that rumors flutter now
Among thy subjects of thy sorceries?—
The art being *banned,* thou knowest; or, unhoused
Is unleashed pitilessly by the grim,
Facetious body of the dridular
Upon the one who fain had loosed the curse
On others.—An my counsel be worth aught,
Then have a care thy spells do not revert
Upon thyself, nor yet mine own poor hulk
O' fearsomeness!

CRESTILLOMEEM

Ha! ha! No vaguest need
Of apprehension there!—While Krung remains—

[*She abruptly pauses—startled first, then listening curiously and with awed
interest. Voice of exquisite melodiousness and fervor heard singing.*]

VOICE

When kings are kings, and kings are men—
    And the lonesome rain is raining!—
O who shall rule from the red throne then,
And who shall covet the scepter when—
    When the winds are all complaining?

When men are men, and men are kings—
    And the lonesome rain is raining!—
O who shall list as the minstrel sings
Of the crown's fiat, or the signet-ring's,
    When the winds are all complaining?

CRESTILLOMEEM

Whence flows such sweetness, and what voice is that?,

JUCKLET

The voice of Spraivoll, an mine ears be whet
And honéd o' late honeyéd memories
Behaunting the deserted purlieus of
The court.

CRESTILLOMEEM

            And who is Spraivoll, and what song
Is that besung so blinding exquisite
Of cadenced mystery?

JUCKLET

                Spraivoll—O Queen,—
Spraivoll The Tune-Fool is she fitly named
By those who meet her ere the day long wanes
And naught but janiteering sparsely frets
The cushioned silences and stagnant dusts
Indifferently resuscitated by
The drowsy varlets in mock servitude
Of so refurbishing the royal halls:
She cometh, alien, from Wunkland—so
Hath she deposed to divers questioners
Who have been smitten of her voice—as rich
In melody as she is poor in mind.
She hath been roosting, pitied of the hinds
And scullions, round about the palace here
For half a node.

CRESTILLOMEEM

And pray, where is she perched—
This wild-bird woman with her wondrous throat?

JUCKLET

Under some dingy cornice, like enough—
Though *wild-bird* she is not, being plumèd in,
Not feathers, but one fustianed stole—the like
Of which so shameth her fair face one needs
Must swear some lusty oaths, but that they shape
Themselves full gentlewise in mildest prayer:—
Not *wild-bird;*—nay, nor *woman*—though, in truth,
She ith a licensed idiot, and drifts
About, as restless and as useless, too,
As any lazy breeze in summer-time.
I'll call her forth to greet your Majesty.
Ho! Spraivoll! Ho! my twittering birdster, flit
Thou hither.

[*Enter* SPRAIVOLL—*from behind group of statuary—singing.*]

SPRAIVOLL

Ting-aling! Ling-ting! Tingle-tee!
The moon spins round and round for me!
Wind it up with a golden key.
Ting-aling! Ling-ting! Tingle-tee!

CRESTILLOMEEM

Who art thou, and what the strange
Elusive beauty and intent of thy
Sweet song? What singest thou, vague, mystic-bird—
What doth The Tune-Fool sing? Ay, sing me what.

SPRAIVOLL [*Singing*]

What sings the breene on the wertling-vine,
And the tweck on the bamner-stem?
Their song, to me, is the same as mine,
As mine is the same to them—to them—
As mine is the same to them.

In star-starved glooms where the plustre looms
   With its slender boughs above,
Their song sprays down with the fragrant blooms,—
   And the song they sing is love—is love—
   And the song they sing is love.

JUCKLET

Your Majesty may be surprised somewhat,
But Spraivoll can not talk,—her only mode
Of speech is melody; and thou might'st put
The dowered fool a thousand queries, and,
In like return, receive a thousand songs,
All set to differing tunes—as full of naught
As space is full of emptiness.

CRESTILLOMEEM

                              A fool?—
And with a gift so all-divine!—A fool?

JUCKLET

Ay, warranted!—The Flying Islands all
Might flock in mighty counsel—molt, and shake
Their loosened feathers, and sort every tuft,
Nor ever most minutely quarry there
One other Spraivoll, itching with her voice
Such favored spot of cuticle as she
Alone selects here in our blissful realm.

CRESTILLOMEEM

Out, jester, on thy cumbrous wordiness!
Come hither, Tune-Fool, and be not afraid,
For I like fools so well I married one:
And since thou art a *Queen* of fools, and he
A *King,* why, I've a mind to bring ye two
Together in some wise. Canst use thy song
All times in such entrancing spirit one
Who lists must so needs list, e'en though the song
Go on unceasingly indefinite?

SPRAIVOLL [*Singing*]

If one should ask me for a song,
  Then I should answer, and my tongue
Would twitter, trill and troll along
  Until the song were done.

Or should one ask me for my tongue,
  And I should answer with a song,
I'd trill it till the song were sung,
  And troll it all along.

CRESTILLOMEEM

Thou art indeed a fool, and one, I think,
To serve my present purposes. Give ear.—
And Jucklet, thou, go to the King and bide
His waking: then repeat these words:—"*The Queen
Impatiently awaits his Majesty,
And craves his presence in the Tower of Stars,
That she may there express full tenderly
Her great solicitude.*" And *then*, end thus,—
"*So much she bade, and drooped her glowing face
Deep in the showerings of her golden hair,
And with a flashing gesture of her arm
Turned all the moonlight pallid, saying 'Haste!'*"

JUCKLET

And would it not be well to hang a pearl
Or twain upon thy silken lashes?

CRESTILLOMEEM

Go!

JUCKLET [*Exit, singing*]

This lovely husband's loyal breast
Heaved only as she might suggest,—
To every whimsy she expressed
He proudly bowed and acquiesced.
  He plotted with her, blithe and gay—

In no flirtation said her nay,—
He even took her to the play,
Excused himself and came away.

CRESTILLOMEEM [*To Spraivoll*]

Now, Tune-Fool, *junior,* let me theme *thee* for
A song:—An Empress once, with angel in
Her face and devil in her heart, had wish
To breed confusion to her sovereign lord,
And work the downfall of his haughty son—
The issue of a former marriage—who
Bellowsed her hatred to the whitest heat,
For that her own son, by a former lord,
Was born a hideous dwarf, and reared aside
From the sire's knowing or his princely own—
That *none,* in sooth, might ever chance to guess
The hapless mother of the hapless child.
The Fiends that scar her thus, protect her still
With outward beauty of both face and form.—
It so is written, and so must remain
Till magic greater than their own is found
To hurl against her. So is she secure
And proof above all fear. Now, listen well!—
Her present lord is haunted with a dream,
That he is soon to pass, and so prepares
(*All havoc hath been wrangled with the drugs!*)
The Throne for the ascension of the son,
His cursèd heir, who still doth baffle all
Her arts against him, e'en as though he were
Protected by a skill beyond her own.
Soh! she, the Queen, doth rule the King in all
Save this affectionate perversity
Of favor for the son whom he would raise
To his own place.—And but for this the King
Long since had tasted death and kissed his fate
As one might kiss a bride! But so his Queen
Must needs withhold, not deal, the final blow,
She yet doth bind him, spelled, still trusting her;
And, by her craft and wanton flatteries,
Doth sway his love to every purpose but
The one most coveted.—And for this end
She would make use of thee;—and if thou dost

Her will, as her good pleasure shall direct,
Why, thou shalt sing at court, in silken tire,
Thy brow bound with wild diamonds, and thy hair
Sown with such gems as laugh hysteric lights
From glittering quespar, guenk and plennocynth,—
Ay, even panoplied as might the fair
Form of a very princess be, thy voice
Shall woo the echoes of the listening Throne.

SPRAIVOLL [*Crooning abstractedly*]

And O shall one—high brother of the air,
In deeps of space—shall he have dream as fair?—
And shall that dream be this?—In some strange place
Of long-lost lands he finds her waiting face—
Comes marveling upon it, unaware,
Set moonwise in the midnight of her hair,
And is behaunted with old nights of May,
So his glad lips do purl a roundelay
Purloinèd from the echo-triller's beak,
Seen keenly notching at some star's blanch cheek
With its ecstatic twitterings, through dusk
And sheen of dewy boughs of bloom and musk.
For him, Love, light again the eyes of her
That show nor tears nor laughter nor surprise—
For him undim their glamour and the blur
Of dreams drawn from the depths of deepest skies.
He doth not know if any lily blows
As fair of feature, nor of any rose.

CRESTILLOMEEM [*Aside*]

O this weird woman! she doth drug mine ears
With her uncanny sumptuousness of song!
[*To Spraivoll*] Nay, nay! Give o'er thy tuneful maunderings
And mark me further, Tune-Fool—ay, and well:—
At present doth the King lie in a sleep
Drug-wrought and deep as death—the after-phase
Of an unconscious state, in which each act
Of his throughout his waking hours is so
Rehearsed, in manner, motion, deed and word,
Her spies (the Queen's) that watch him, serving there
As guardians o'er his royal slumbers, may

Inform her of her lord's most secret thought.
And lo, her plans have ripened even now
Till, *should he come upon this Throne to-night,*
Where eagerly his counselors will bide
His coming,—she, the Queen, hath reason to
Suspect her long-designèd purposes
May fall in jeopardy;—but if he *fail,*
Through *any* means, to lend his presence there,—
Then, by a wheedled mandate, *is his Queen
Empowered with all Sovereignty to reign
And work the royal purposes instead.*
Therefore, the Queen hath set an interview—
A conference to be holden with the King,
Which is ordained to fall on moon to-night,
Twelve star-twirls ere the nick the Throne convenes.—
And with her thou shalt go, and bide in wait
Until she signal thee to sing; and then
Shalt thou so work upon his mellow mood
With that un-Spirkly magic of thy voice—
So all bedaze his waking thought with dreams,—
The Queen may, all unnoticed, slip away,
And leave thee singing to a throneless King.

SPRAIVOLL [*Singing*]

And who shall sing for the haughty son
    While the good King droops his head?—
And will he dream, when the song is done,
    That a princess fair lies dead?

CRESTILLOMEEM

The haughty son hath found *his* "Song"—*sweet curse!—*
And may she sing his everlasting dirge!
She comes from that near-floating land of thine,
Naming herself a princess of that realm
So strangely peopled we would fain evade
All mergence, and remain as strange to them
As they to us. No less this Dwaïnie hath
Most sinuously writhed and lithed her way
Into court favor here—hath glidden past
The King's encharmèd sight and sleeked herself
Within the very altars of his house—

His line—his blood—his very life:—*AMPHINE!*
Not any Spirkland gentlemaiden might
Aspire so high as *she* hath dared to dare!—
For she, with her fair skin and finer ways,
And beauty second only to the Queen's,
Hath caught the Prince betwixt her mellow palms
And stroked him flutterless. Didst ever thou
In thy land hear of *Dwainie of the Wunks?*

SPRAIVOLL [*Singing*]

Ay, Dwainie!—My Dwainie!
        The lurloo ever sings,
A tremor in his flossy crest
        And in his glossy wings.
And Dwainie!—My Dwainie!
        The winno-welvers call;—
But Dwainie hides in Spirkland
        And answers not at all.

The teeper twitters Dwainie!—
        The tcheucker on his spray
Teeters up and down the wind
        And will not fly away:
And Dwainie!—My Dwainie!
        The drowsy oovers drawl;—
But Dwainie hides in Spirkland
        And answers not at all.

O Dwainie!—My Dwainie!
        The breezes hold their breath—
The stars are pale as blossoms,
        And the night as still as death:
And Dwainie!—My Dwainie!
        The fainting echoes fall;—
But Dwainie in Spirkland
        And answers not at all.

CRESTILLOMEEM

A melody ecstatic! and—thy words,
Although so meaningless, seem something more—
A vague and shadowy something, eerie-like,

That maketh one to shiver over-chilled
With curious, creeping sweetnesses of pain
And catching breaths that flutter tremulous
With sighs that dry the throat out icily.—
But save thy music! Come! that I may make
Thee ready for thy royal auditor.   [*Exeunt*]

END ACT I

ACT II

SCENE I. *A garden of* KRUNG'S *Palace, screened from the moon with netted glenk-vines and blooming zhoomer-boughs, all glimmeringly lighted with star-flakes. An arbor, near which is a table spread with a repast—two seats, drawn either side. A playing fountain, at marge of which* AMPHINE *sits thrumming a trentoraine.*

AMPHINE [*Improvising*]

Ah, help me! but her face and brow
Are lovelier than lilies are
Beneath the light of moon and star
That smile as they are smiling now—
White lilies in a pallid swoon
Of sweetest white beneath the moon—
White lilies in a flood of bright
Pure lucidness of liquid light
Cascading down some plenilune
When all the azure overhead
Blooms like a dazzling daisy-bed.—
So luminous her face and brow,
The luster of their glory, shed
In memory, even, blinds me now.

[*Plaintively addressing instrument*]

O warbling strand of silver, where, O where
Hast thou unraveled that sweet voice of thine
And left its silken murmurs quavering
In limp thrills of delight? O golden wire,
Where hast thou spilled thy precious twinkerings?—
What thirsty ear hath drained thy melody,
And left me but a wild, delirious drop
To tincture all my soul with vain desire?

[Improvising]

Her face—her brow—her hair unfurled!—
And O the oval chin below,
Carved, like a cunning cameo,
With one exquisite dimple, swirled
With swimming shine and shade, and whirled
The daintiest vortex poets know—
The sweetest whirlpool ever twirled
By Cupid's finger-tip,—and so,
The deadliest maelstrom in the world.

[Pauses—Enter unperceived, DWAINIE, *behind, in upper bower]*

AMPHINE *[Again addressing instrument]*

O Trentoraine! how like an emptièd vase
Thou art—whose clustering blooms of song have drooped
And faded, one by one, and fallen away
And left to me but dry and tuneless stems
And crisp and withered tendrils of a voice
Whose thrilling tone, now like a throttled sound,
Lies stifled, faint, and gasping all in vain
For utterance.

[Again improvising]

And O mad wars of blinding blurs
And flashings of lance-blades of light,
Whet glitteringly athwart the sight
That dares confront those eyes of hers!
Let any dewdrop soak the hue
Of any violet through and through,
And then be colorless and dull,
Compared with eyes so beautiful!
I swear ye that her eyes be bright
As noonday, yet as dark as night—
As bright as be the burnished bars
Of rainbows set in sunny skies,
And yet as deep and dark, her eyes,
And lustrous black as blown-out stars.

*[Pauses—*DWAINIE *still unperceived, radiantly smiling and wafting kisses down from trellis-window above]*

AMPHINE [*Again to instrument*]
O empty husk of song!
If deep within my heart the music thou
Hast stored away might find an issuance,
A fount of limpid laughter would leap up
And gurgle from my lips, and all the winds
Would revel with it, riotous with joy;
And Dwainie, in her beauty, would lean o'er
The battlements of night, and, like the moon,
The glory of her face would light the world—
For I would sing of love.

DWAINIE

And she would hear,—
And, reaching overhead among the stars,
Would scatter them like daisies at thy feet.

AMPHINE

O voice, where art thou floating on the air?—
O Seraph-soul, where art thou hovering?

DWAINIE

I hover in the zephyr of thy sighs,
And tremble lest thy love for me shall fail
To buoy me thus forever on the breath
Of such a dream as Heaven envies.

AMPHINE

Ah!

[*Turning, discovers* DWAINIE—*she still feigning invisibility, while he, with lifted
eyes and wistful gaze, preludes with instrument—then sings.*]

Linger, my Dwainie! Dwainie, lily-fair,
Stay yet thy step upon the casement-stair—
Poised be thy slipper-tip as is the tine
Of some still star.—Ah, Dwainie—Dwainie mine,
Yet linger—linger there!

Thy face, O Dwainie, lily-pure and fair,
Gleams i' the dusk, as in thy dusky hair
The moony zhoomer glimmers, or the shine
Of thy swift smile.—Ah, Dwainie—Dwainie mine,
        Yet linger—linger there!

With lifted wrist, whereround the laughing air
Hath blown a mist of lawn and clasped it there,
Waft finger-thipt adieus that spray the wine
Of thy waste kisses toward me, Dwainie mine—
        Yet linger—linger there!

What unloosed splendor is there may compare
With thy hand's unfurled glory, anywhere?
What glint of dazzling dew or jewel fine
May mate thine eyes?—Ah, Dwainie—Dwainie mine!
        Yet linger—linger there!

My soul confronts thee: On thy brow and hair
It lays its tenderness like palms of prayer—
It touches sacredly those lips of thine
And swoons across thy spirit, Dwainie mine,
        The while thou lingerest there.

[*Drops trentoraine, and, with open arms, gazes yearningly on* DWAINIE]

DWAINIE [*Raptly*]

Thy words do wing my being dovewise!

AMPHINE

                                Then,
Thou lovest!—O my homing dove, veer down
And nestle in the warm home of my breast!
So empty are mine arms, so full my heart,
The one must hold thee, or the other burst.

DWAINIE [*Throwing herself in his embrace*]

Æo's own hand methinks hath flung me here:
O hold me that He may not pluck me back!

AMPHINE

So closely will I hold thee that not e'en
The hand of death shall separate us.

DWAINIE

So
May sweet death find us, then, that, woven thus
In the corolla of a ripe caress,
We may drop lightly, like twin plustre-buds,
On Heaven's star-strewn lawn.

AMPHINE

So do I pray.
But tell me, tender heart, an thou dost love,
Where hast thou loitered for so long?—for thou
Didst promise tryst here with me earlier by
Some several layodemes which I have told
Full chafingly against my finger-tips
Till the full complement, save three, are ranged
Thy pitiless accusers, claiming, each,
So many as their joinèd number be
Shalt thou so many times lift up thy lips
For mine's most lingering forgiveness.
So, save thee, O my Sweet! and rest thee, I
Have ordered merl and viands to be brought
For our refreshment here, where, thus alone,
I may sip words with thee as well as wine.
Why hast thou kept me so athirst?—Why, I
Am jealous of the flattered solitudes
In which thou walkest.   [*They sit at table*]

DWAINIE

Nay, I will not tell,
Since, an I yielded, countless questions, like
In idlest worth, would waste our interview
In speculations vain.—Let this suffice:—
I stayed to talk with one whom, long ago,
I met and knew, and grew to love, forsooth,
In dreamy Wunkland.—Talked of mellow nights,

And long, long hours of golden olden times
When girlish happiness locked hands with me
And we went spinning round, with naked feet
In swaths of bruisèd roses ankle-deep;
When laughter rang unsilenced, unrebuked,
And prayers went unremembered, oozing clean
From the drowsed memory, as from the eyes
The pure, sweet mother-face that bent above
Glimmered and wavered, blurred, bent closer still
A timeless instant, like a shadowy flame,
Then flickered tremulously o'er the brow
And went out in a kiss.

AMPHINE [*Kissing her*]

Not like to *this!*
O blessèd lips whose kiss alone may be
Sweeter than their sweet speech! Speak on, and say
Of what else talked thou and thy friend?

DWAINIE

We talked
Of all the past, ah me! and all the friends
That now await my coming. And we talked
Of O so many things—so many things—
That I but blend them all with dreams of when,
With thy warm hand clasped close in this of mine
We cross the floating bridge that soon again
Will span the all-unfathomable gulfs
Of nether air betwixt this isle of strife
And my most glorious realm of changeless peace,
Where summer night reigns ever and the moon
Hangs ever ripe and lush with radiance
Above a land where roses float on wings
And fan their fragrance out so lavishly
That Heaven hath hint of it, and oft therefrom
Sends down to us across the odorous seas
Strange argosies of interchanging bud
And blossom, spice and balm.—Sweet—sweet
Beyond all art and wit of uttering.

AMPHINE

O Empress of my listening Soul, speak on,
And tell me all of that rare land of thine!—
For even though I reigned a peerless king
Within mine own, methinks I could fling down
My scepter, signet, crown and royal might,
And so fare down the thornèd path of life
If at its dwindling end my feet might touch
Upon the shores of such a land as thou
Dost paint for me—*thy* realm! Tell on of it—
And tell me if thy sister-woman there
Is like to thee—Yet nay! for an thou didst,
These eyes would lose all speech of sight
And call not back to thine their utter love.
But tell me of thy brothers.—Are they great,
And can they grapple Æo's arguments
Beyond our skill? or wrest a purpose from
The pink side of the moon at Darsten-tide?
Or cipher out the problem of blind stars,
That ever still do safely grope their way
Among the thronging constellations?

DWAINIE

Ay!
Ay, they have leaped all earthland barriers
In mine own isle of wisdom-working Wunks:—
'Twas Wunkland's son that voyaged round the moon
And moored his bark within the molten bays
Of bubbling silver: And 'twas Wunkland's son
That talked with Mars—unbuckled Saturn's belt
And tightened it in squeezure of such facts
Therefrom as even *he* dare not disclose
In full till all his followers, as himself,
Have grown them wings, and gat them beaks and claws,
With plumage all bescienced to withstand
All tensest flames—glaze-throated, too, and lung'd
To swallow fiercest-spurted jets and cores
Of embered and unquenchable white heat:
'Twas Wunkland's son that alchemized the dews
And bred all colored grasses that he wist—
Divorced the airs and mists and caught the trick

Of azure-tinting earth as well as sky:
'Twas Wunkland's son that bent the rainbow straight
And walked it like a street, and so returned
To tell us it was made of hammered shine,
Inlaid with strips of selvage from the sun
And burnished with the rust of rotten stars:
'Twas Wunkland's son that comprehended first
All grosser things, and took our worlds apart
And oiled their works with theories that clicked
In glib articulation with the pulse
And palpitation 'of the systemed facts.—
And, circling ever round the farthest reach
Of the remotest welkin of all truths,
We stint not our investigations to
Our worlds only, but query still beyond.—
For now our goolores say, below these isles
A million million miles, are *other* worlds—
Not like to ours, but *round,* as bubbles are,
And, like them, ever reeling on through space,
And anchorless through all eternity;—
Not like to ours, for our isles, as they note,
Are living things that fly about at night,
And soar above and cling, throughout the day,
Like bats, beneath the bent sills of the skies:
And I myself have heard, at dawn of moon,
A liquid music filtered through my dreams,
As though 'twere myriads of sweet voices, pent
In some o'erhanging realm, had spilled themselves
In streams of melody that trickled through
The chinks and crannies of a crystal pave,
Until the wasted juice of harmony,
Slow-leaking o'er my senses, laved my soul
In ecstasy divine: And afferhaiks,
Who scour our coasts on missions for the King,
Declare our island's shape is like the zhibb's
When lolling in a trance upon the air
With open wings upslant and motionless.
O such a land it is—so all complete
In all wise inhabitants, and knowledge, lore,
Arts, sciences, perfected government
And kingly wisdom, worth and majesty—
And *Art*—ineffably above all else:—
The art of the *Romancer,*—fabulous

Beyond the miracles of strangest fact;
The art of *Poesy,*—the sanest soul
Is made mad with its uttering; the art
Of *Music,*—words may not e'en whimper what
The jewel-sounds of song yield to the sense;
And, last,—the art of *Knowing what to Know,*
And how to zoon straight toward it like a bee,
Draining or song or poem as it brims
And overruns with raciest spirit-dew.—
And, *after,*—chaos all to sense like thine,
Till there, translated, thou shalt know as I. . . .
So furnished forth in all things lovable
Is my Land-Wondrous—ay, and thine to be,—
O Amphine, love of mine, it lacks but thy
Sweet presence to make it a paradise!

[*Takes up trentoraine*]

And shall I tell thee of the home that waits
For thy glad coming, Amphine?—Listen, then!

CHANT-RECITATIVE

A palace veiled in a glimmering dusk;
    Warm breaths of a tropic air,
Drugged with the odorous marzhoo's musk
    And the sumptuous cyncotwaire—
Where the trembling hands of the lilwing's leaves
    The winds caress and fawn,
While the dreamy starlight idly weaves
    Designs for the damask lawn.

Densed in the depths of a dim eclipse
    Of palms, in a flowery space,
A fountain leaps from the marble lips
    Of a girl, with a golden vase
Held atip on a curving wrist,
    Drinking the drops that glance
Laughingly in the glittering mist
    Of her crystal utterance.

Archways looped o'er blooming walks
    That lead through gleaming halls;

And balconies where the word-bird talks
   To the tittering waterfalls:
And casements, gauzed with the filmy sheen
   Of a lace that sifts the sight
Through a ghost of bloom on the haunted screen
   That drips with the dews of light.

Weird, pale shapes of sculptured stone,—
   With marble nymphs agaze
Ever in fonts of amber, sown
   With seeds of gold and sprays
Of emerald mosses, ever drowned,
   Where glimpses of shell and gem
Peer from the depths, as round and round
   The nautilus nods at them.

Faces blurred in a mazy dance,
   With a music, wild and sweet,
Spinning the threads of the mad romance
   That tangles the waltzers' feet:
Twining arms, and warm, swift thrills
   That pulse to the melody,
Till the soul of the dancer dips and fills
   In the wells of ecstasy.

Eyes that melt in a quivering ore
   Of love, and the molten kiss
Jetted forth of the hearts that pour
   Their blood in the molds of bliss.—
Till, worn to a languor slumber-deep,
   The soul of the dreamer lifts
A silken sail on the gulfs of sleep,
   And into the darkness drifts.

[*The instrument falls from her hand*—AMPHINE, *in stress of passionate delight,
embraces her.*]

AMPHINE

Thou art not all of earth, O angel one!
Nor do I far miswonder me an thou
Hast peered above the very walls of Heaven!
What hast thou seen there?—Didst on Æo bask

Thine eyes and clothe Him with new splendorings?
And strove He to fling back as bright a smile
As thine, the while He beckoned thee within?
And, tell me, didst thou meet an angel there
A-linger at the gates, nor entering
Till I, her brother, joined her?

DWAINIE

                    Why, hast thou
A sister dead?—Truth, I have heard of one
Long lost to thee—not dead?

AMPHINE

                    Of her I speak,—
And dead, although we know not certainly,
We moan us ever it must needs be death
Only could hold her from us such long term
Of changeless yearning for her glad return.
She strayed away from us long, long ago.—
O and our memories!—Her wondering eyes
That seemed as though they ever looked on things
We might not see—as haply so they did,—
For she went from us, all so suddenly—
So strangely vanished, leaving never trace
Of her outgoing, that I ofttimes think
Her rapt eyes fell along some certain path
Of special glory paven for her feet,
And fashioned of Æo's supreme desire
That she might bend her steps therein and so
Reach Him again, unseen of our mere eyes.
My sweet, sweet sister!—lost to brother—sire—
And, to *her* heart, one dearer than all else,—
Her *lover*—lost indeed!

DWAINIE

                    Nay, do not grieve
Thee thus, O loving heart! Thy sister yet
May come to thee in some glad way the Fates
Are fashioning the while thy tear-drops fall!
So calm thee, while I speak of thine own self.—

For I have listened to a whistling bird
That pipes of waiting danger. Didst thou note
No strange behavior of thy sire of late?

AMPHINE

Ay, he is silent, and he walks as one
In some fixed melancholy, or as one
Half waking.—Even his worshiped books seem now
But things on shelves.

DWAINIE

              And doth he counsel not
With thee in any wise pertaining to
His ailings, or of matters looking toward
His future purposes or his intents
Regarding thine own future fortunings
And his desires and interests therein?
What bearing hath he shown of late toward thee
By which thou might'st beframe some estimate
Of his mind's placid flow or turbulent?
And hath he not so spoken thee at times
Thou hast been 'wildered of his words, or grieved
Of his strange manner?

AMPHINE

              Once he stayed me on
The palace-stair and whispered, "Lo, my son,
Thy young reign draweth nigh—prepare!"—So passed
And vanished as a wraith, so wan he was!

DWAINIE

And didst thou ever reason on this thing,
Nor ask thyself what dims thy father's eye
And makes a brooding shadow of his form?

AMPHINE

Why, there's a household rumor that he dreams
Death fareth ever at his side, and soon

Shall signal him away.—But *Jucklet* saith
Crestillomeem hath said *the leeches* say
There is no cause for serious concern;
And thus am I assured 'tis nothing more
Than childish fancy of mine aging sire,—
And so, as now, I laugh, full reverently,
And marvel, as I mark his shuffling gait,
And his bestrangered air and murmurous lips,
As by he glideth to and fro, ha! ha!
Ho! ho!—I laugh me many, many times—
Mind, thou, 'tis *reverently* I laugh—ha! ha!—
And wonder, as he glideth ghostly-wise,
If ever *I* shall waver as I walk,
And stumble o'er my beard, and knit my brows,
And o'er the dull mosaics of the pave
Play chequers with mine eyes! Ha! ha!

DWAINIE [*Aside*]

How dare—
How dare I tell him? Yet I must—I must!

AMPHINE

Why, art *thou,* too, grown childish, that thou canst
Find thee waste pleasure talking to thyself
And staring frowningly with eyes whose smiles
I need so much?

DWAINIE

Nay, rather say, their tears,
Poor thoughtless Prince! [*Aside*] (My magic even now
Forecasts his kingly sire's near happening
Of nameless hurt and ache and awful stress
Of agony supreme, when he shall stare
The stark truth in the face!)

AMPHINE

What meanest thou?

DWAINIE

What mean I but thy welfare? Why, I mean,
One hour agone, the Queen, thy mother—

AMPHINE

                                        Nay,
Say only "Queen"!

DWAINIE

                        —The Queen, one hour agone—
As so I learned from source I need not say—
Sent message craving audience with the King
At noon to-night, within the Tower of Stars.—
Thou knowest, only brief space following
The time of her pent session thereso set
In secret with the King alone, *the Throne*
Is set, too, to convene; and that *the King*
Hath lent his seal unto a mandate that,
Should he withhold his presence there, the Queen
Shall be empowered to preside—to reign—
Solely endowed to work the royal will
In lieu of the good King. Now, therefore, I
Have been advised that she, the Queen, by craft
Connives to hold him absent purposely,
That she may claim the vacancy—for what
Covert design I know not, but I know
It augurs peril to you both, as to
The Throne's own perpetuity. [*Aside*] (Again
My magic gives me vision terrible:—
The Sorceress' legions balk mine own.—The King
Still hers, yet wavering. O save the King
Thou Æo!—Render him to us!)

AMPHINE

                              I feel
Thou speakest truth: and yet how know'st thou this?

DWAINIE

Ask me not that; my lips are welded close.—
And, *more,*—since I have dared to speak, and thou

To listen,—Jucklet is accessory,
And even now is plotting for thy fall.
But, Passion of my Soul! think not of me,—
For nothing but sheer magic may avail
To work me harm;—but look thou to thyself!
For thou art blameless cause of all the hate
That rankleth in the bosom of the Queen.
So have thine eyes unslumbered ever, that
No step may steal behind thee—for in this
Unlooked-of way thine enemy will come:
This much I know, but for what fell intent
Dare not surmise.—*So look thou, night and day,*
That none may skulk upon thee in this wise
Of dastardly attack. [*Aside*] (Ha! Sorceress!
Thou palest, tossing wild and wantonly
The smothering golden tempest of thy hair.—
What! lying eyes! ye dare to utter *tears?*
Help! help! Yield us the King!)

AMPHINE

                    And thou, O sweet!
How art thou guarded and what shield is thine
Of safety?

DWAINIE

                 Fear not thou for me at all.—
Possessed am I of wondrous sorcery—
The gift of Holy Magi at my birth:—
Mine enemy must *front* me in assault
And must with mummery of speech assail,
And I will know him in first utterance—
And so may thus disarm him, though he be
A giant thrice in vasty form and force.
                          [*Singing heard*]
But, list! what wandering minstrel cometh here
In the young night?

VOICE [*In distance—singing*]

The drowsy eyes of the stars grow dim;
The wamboo roosts on the rainbow's rim,
And the moon is a ghost of shine:

The soothing song of the crule is done,
But the song of love is a soother one,
And the song of love is mine.
Then, wake! O wake!
For the sweet song's sake,
Nor let my heart
With the morning break!

AMPHINE

Some serenader! Hist!
What meaneth he so early, and what thus
Within the palace garden-close?   Quick; here!
He neareth! Soh! Let us conceal ourselves
And mark his action, wholly unobserved.

[AMPHINE and DWAINIE *enter bower*]

VOICE [*Drawing nearer*]

The mist of the morning, chill and gray,
Wraps the night in a shroud of spray;
The sun is a crimson blot:
The moon fades fast, and the stars take wing;
The comet's tail is a fleeting thing—
But the tale of love is not.
Then, wake! O wake!
For the sweet song's sake,
Nor let my heart
With the morning break!

[*Enter* JUCKLET]

JUCKLET

Eex! what a sumptuous darkness is the Night—
How rich and deep and suave and velvety
Its lovely blackness to a soul like mine!
Ah, Night! thou densest of all mysteries—
Thou eeriest of unfathomable delights,
Whose soundless sheer inscrutability
Is fascination's own ethereal self,
Unseen, and yet embodied—palpable,—

An essence, yet a form of stableness
That stays me—weighs me, as a giant palm
Were laid on either shoulder.—Peace! I cease
Even to strive to grope one further pace,
But stand uncovered and with lifted face.
O but a glamour of inward light
Hath smitten the eyes of my soul to-night!
Groping here in the garden-land,
I feel my fancy's outheld hand
Touch the rim of a realm that seems
Like an isle of bloom in a sea of dreams:
I stand mazed, dazed and alone—alone!—
My heart beats on in an undertone,
And I lean and listen long, and long,
And I hold my breath as I hear again
The chords of a long-dead trentoraine
And the wraith of an old love-song.
Low to myself am I whispering:—
    Glad am I, and the Night knows why—
    Glad am I that the dream came by
    And found me here as of old when I
    Was a ruler and a king.

DWAINIE [*To Amphine*]

What gentle little monster is this dwarf—
Surely not Jucklet of the court?

AMPHINE [*Ironically*]

                 Ay, ay!
But he'll *ungentle* an thy woman's-heart
Yield him but space. Listen: he mouths again.

JUCKLET

It was an age ago—an age
Turned down in life like a folded page.—
See where the volume falls apart,
And the faded book-mark—'tis my heart,—
Nor mine alone, but another knit
So cunningly in the love of it
That you must look, with a shaking head,

Nor know the quick one from the dead.
Ah! what a broad and sea-like lawn
Is the field of love they bloom upon!—
Waves of its violet-velvet grass
Billowing, with the winds that pass,
And breaking in a snow-white foam
Of lily-crests on the shores of home.
Low to myself am I whispering:—
    Glad am I, and the Night knows why—
    Glad am I that the dream came by
    And found me here as of old when I
      Was a ruler and a king.

[*Abruptly breaking into impassioned vocal burst*]

Song

Fold me away in your arm, O Night—
  Night, my Night, with your rich black hair!—
Tumble it down till my yearning sight
And my unkissed lips are hidden quite
And my heart is havened there,—
    Under that mystical dark despair—
    Under your rich black hair.

Oft have I looked in your eyes, O Night—
  Night, my Night, with your rich black hair!—
Looked in your eyes till my face waned white
And my heart laid hold of a mad delight
  That moaned as I held it there
    Under the deeps of that dark despair—
    Under your rich black hair.

Just for a kiss of your mouth, O Night—
  Night, my Night, with your rich black hair!—
Lo! will I wait as a dead man might
Wait for the Judgment's dawning light,
  With my lips in a frozen prayer—
    Under this lovable dark despair—
    Under your rich black hair.

[*With swift change to mood of utter gaiety*]

Ho! ho! what will my dainty mistress say
When I shall stand knee-deep in the wet grass
Beneath her lattice, and with upturned eyes
And tongue out-lolling like the clapter of
A bell, outpour her *that?* I wonder now
If she will not put up her finger thus,
And say, "Hist! heart of mine! the angels call
To thee!" Ho! ho! Or will her blushing face
Light up her dim boudoir and, from her glass,
Flare back to her a flame upsprouting from
The hot-cored socket of a soul whose light
She thought long since had guttered out?—Ho! ho!
Or, haply, will she chastely bend above—
A Parian phantomette, with head atip
And twinkling fingers dusting down the dews
That glitter on the tarapyzma-vines
That riot round her casement—gathering
Lush blooms to pelt me with while I below
All winkingly await the fragrant shower?
Ho! ho! how jolly is this thing of love!
But how much richer, rarer, jollier
Than all the loves is this rare love of mine!
Why, my sweet Princess doth not even dream
I *am* her lover,—for, to here confess,
I have a way of wooing all mine own,
And waste scant speech in creamy compliment
And courtesies all gaumed with winy words.—
In sooth, I do not woo at all—I *win!*
How is it now the old duet doth glide
Itself full ripplingly adown the grooves
Of its quaint melody?—And whoso, by
The *bye,* or by the *way,* or *for the nonce,*
Or, eke ye, *peradventure,* ever durst
Render a duet singly but myself?

[*Singing—with grotesque mimicry of two voices*]

Jucklet's Ostensible Duet

How is it you woo?—and now answer me true,—
   How is it you woo and you win?
Why, to answer you true,—the first thing that you do
Is to simply, my dearest—begin.

But how can I begin to woo or to win
  When I don't know a Win from a Woo?
Why, cover your chin with your fan or your fin,
  And I'll introduce them to you.

But what if it drew from my parents a view
  With my own in no manner akin?
No matter!—your view shall be first of the two,—
  So I hasten to usher them in.

Nay, stay! Shall I grin at the Woo or the Win?
  And what will he do if I *do?*
Why, the Woo will begin with "How pleasant it's been!"
  And the Win with "Delighted with you!"

Then supposing he grew very dear to my view—
  I'm speaking, you know, of the Win?
Why, then, you should do what he wanted you to,—
  And now is the time to begin.

The time to begin? O then usher him in—
  Let him say what he wants me to do.
He is here.—He's a twin of yourself,—I am "Win,"
  And you are, my darling, my "Woo"!

     [*Capering and courtesying to feigned audience*]

That song I call most sensible nonsense;
And if the fair and peerless Dwainie were
But here, with that sweet voice of hers, to take
The part of "Woo," I'd be the happiest "Win"
On this side of futurity! Ho! ho!

     DWAINIE [*Aside to* AMPHINE]
What means he?

     AMPHINE

           Why, he means that throatless head
Of his needs further chucking down betwixt
His cloven shoulders!

    [*Starting forward—*DWAINIE *detaining him*]

DWAINIE

Nay, thou shalt not stir!
See! now the monster hath discovered our
Repast. Hold! Let us mark him further.

JUCKLET [*Archly eying viands*]

What!
A roasted wheffle and a toc-spiced whum,
Tricked with a larvey and a gherghgling's tail!—
And, sprit me! wine enough to swim them in!
Now I should like to put a question to
The *guests;* but as there *are* none, I direct
Mine interrogatory to the host. [*Bowing to vacancy*]
Am I behind time?—Then I can but trust
My tardy coming may be overlooked
In my most active effort to regain
A gracious tolerance by service now:—
Directing rapt attention to the fact
That I have brought mine appetite along,
I can but feel, ho! ho! that further words
Would be a waste of speech.

[*Sits at table—pours out wine, drinks and eats voraciously*]

—There was a time
When I was rather backward in my ways
In courtly company (as though, forsooth,
I felt not, from my very birth, the swish
Of royal blood along my veins, though bred
Amongst the treacled scullions and the thralls
I shot from, like a cork, in youthful years,
Into court favor by my wit's sheer stress
Of fomentation.—*Pah! the stench o' toil!*)
Ay, somehow, as I think, I've all outgrown
That coarse, nice age, wherein one makes a meal
Of two estardles and a fork of soup.
Hey! sanaloo! Lest my starved stomach stand
Awe-stricken and aghast, with mouth agape
Before the rich profusion of this feast,
I lubricate it with a glass of merl
And coax it on to more familiar terms

Of fellowship with those delectables.

[Pours wine and holds up goblet with mock
courtliness]

Mine host!—Thou of the viewless presence and
Hush-haunted lip:—Thy most imperial,
Ethereal, and immaterial health!
Live till the sun dries up, and comb thy cares
With star-prongs till the comets fizzle out
And fade away and fail and are no more!

[Drains and refills goblet]

And, if thou wilt permit me to observe,—
The gleaming shaft of spirit in this wine
Goes whistling to its mark, and full and fair
Zipps to the target-center of my soul!
Why, now am I the veriest gentleman
That ever buttered woman with a smile,
And let her melt and run and drip and ooze
All over and around a wanton heart!
And if my mistress bent above me now,
In all my hideous deformity,
I think she would look over, as it were,
The hump upon my back, and so forget
The kinks and knuckles of my crooked legs,
In this enchanting smile, she needs must leap,
Love-dazzled, and fall faint and fluttering
Within these yawning, all-devouring arms
Of mine! Ho! ho! And yet Crestillomeem
Would have me blight my dainty Dwainie with
This feather from the Devil's wing!—But I
Am far too full of craft to spoil the eyes
That yet shall pour their love like nectar out
Into mine own,—and I am far too deep
For royal wit to wade my purposes.

DWAINIE [*To* AMPHINE]

What can he mean?

AMPHINE [*Chafing in suppressed frenzy*]

            Ha! to rush forward and
Tear out his tongue and slap it in his face!

DWAINIE [*To* AMPHINE]

Nay, nay! Hist what he saith!

JUCKLET

How big a fool—
How all magnificent an idiot
Would I be to blight *her*—(my peerless one!—
My very soul's soul!) as Crestillomeem
Doth instigate me to, for *her* hate's sake—
And inward *jealousy,* as well, belike!—
Wouldst have my Dwainie blinded to my charms—
For charms, good sooth, were every several flaw
Of my malformèd outer-self, compared
With that his Handsomeness the Prince Amphine
Shalt change to at a breath of my puff'd cheek,
E'en were it weedy-bearded at the time
With such a stubble as a huntsman well
Might lose his spaniel in! Ho! ho! Ho! ho!
I fear me, O my coy Crestillomeem,
Thine ancient coquetry doth challenge still
Thine own vain admiration overmuch!
I to crush *her?*—when thou, as certainly,
Hast armed me to smite down the only bar
That lies betwixt her love and mine? Ho! ho!
Hey! but the revel I shall riot in
Above the beauteous Prince, instantuously
Made all abhorrent as a reptiled bulk!
Ho! ho! my princely wooer of the fair
Rare lady of mine own superior choice!
Pah! but my very 'maginings of him
Refinèd to that shamèd, sickening shape,
Do so beloathe me of him there be qualms
Expostulating in my forum now!
Ho! what unprincifying properties
Of medication hath her Majesty
Put in my tender charge! Ho! ho! Ho! ho!
Ah, Dwainie! sweetest sweet! what shock to thee?—
I wonder when she sees the human toad
Squat at her feet and cock his filmy eyes
Upon her and croak love, if she will not
Call me to tweezer him with two long sticks

And toss him from her path.—O ho! Ho! ho!
Hell bend him o'er some blossom quick, that I
May have one brother in the flesh!

[*Nods drowsily*]

DWAINIE [*To* AMPHINE]

                                        Ha! See!
He groweth drunken.—Soh! Bide yet a spell
And I will vex him with my sorcery:
Then shall we hence,—for lo, the node when all
Our subtlest arts and strategies must needs
Be quickened into acts and swift results.
Now bide thou here, and in mute silence mark
The righteous penalty that hath accrued
Upon that dwarfèd monster.

[*She stands, still in concealment from the dwarf, her tense gaze fixed upon him
as though in mute and painful act of incantation.—*JUCKLET *affected drowsily
—yawns and mumbles incoherently—stretches, and gradually sinks at full
length on the sward.—*DWAINIE *moves forward—*AMPHINE, *following, is
about to set foot contemptuously on sleeper's breast, but is caught and held
away by* DWAINIE, *who imperiously waves him back, and still, is panto-
mime, commanding, bids him turn and hide his face—*AMPHINE *obeying as
though unable to do otherwise. Dwainie then unbinds her hair, and throw-
ing it all forward covering her face and bending till it trails the ground,
she lifts to the knee her dress, and so walks backward in a circle round the
sleeping* JUCKLET, *crooning to herself an incoherent song. Then pausing,
letting fall her gown, and rising to full stature, waves her hands above the
sleeper's face, and runs to* AMPHINE, *who turns about and gazes on her with
new wonderment.*]

DWAINIE [*To* AMPHINE]

                        Now shalt thou
Look on such scaith as thou hath never dreamed.

[*As she speaks, half averting her face as with melancholy apprehension, chorus
of lugubrious voices heard chanting discordantly*]

VOICES

When the fat moon smiles,
  And the comets kiss,
    And the elves of Spirkland flit
The Whanghoo twunkers
  A tune like this,
    And the Nightmares champ the bit.

[*As chorus dies away, a comet, freighted with weird shapes, dips from the night
and trails near* JUCKLET's *sleeping figure, while with attendant goblin-forms,
two* Nightmares, CREECH *and* GRITCHFANG, *alight.—The comet kisses,
switches its tail and disappears, while the two goblins hover buzzingly over*
JUCKLET, *who starts wide-eyed and stares fixedly at them, with horribly con-
torted features.*]

CREECH [*To* GRETCHFANG]
Buzz!
  Buzz!
    Buzz!
      Buzz!
Flutter your wings like your grandmother does!
Tuck in your chin and wheel over and *whir-r-r*
Like a dickerbug fast in the web of the wuhrr!
Reel out your tongue, and untangle your toes
And rattle your claws o'er the bridge of his nose;
Tickle his ears with your feathers and fuzz,
And keep up a hum like your grandmother does!

[JUCKLET *moans and clutches at air convulsively*]

AMPHINE [*Shuddering*]

Most gruesome sight! See how the poor worm writhes!
How must he suffer!

DWAINIE
              Ay, but good is meant—
A far voice sings it so.

GRITCHFANG [*To* CREECH]

Let me dive deep in his nostriline caves
And keep an eye out as to how he behaves!

Fasten him down while I put him to rack—
And don't let him flop from the flat of his back!

[*Shrinks to minute size, while goblin attendants pluck from shrubbery a great lily-shaped flower which they invert funnel-wise, with small end at sleeper's nostrils, hoisting* GRITCHFANG *in at top and jostling shape downward gradually from sight, and—removing flower,—voice of* GRITCHFANG *continued gleefully from within sleeper's head*]

Ho! I have bored through the floor of his brains,
And set them all writhing with torturous pains;
And I shriek out the prayer, as I whistle and whiz,
I may be the nightmare that my grandmother is!

[*Reappears, through reversal of flower method, assuming former shape, crosses to* CREECH, *and, joining, the twain dance on sleeper's stomach in broken time to duo*]

Duo

Whing!
Whang!
So our ancestors sang!
And they guzzled hot blood and blew up with a *bang!*—
But they ever tenaciously clung to the rule
To only blow up in the hull of a fool—
To fizz and explode like a cast-iron toad
In the cavernous depths where his victuals were stowed—
When chances were ripest and thickest and best
To burst every buttonhole out of his vest!

[*They pause, float high above, and fusing together into a great square iron weight drop heavily on chest of sleeper, who moans piteously.*]

AMPHINE [*Hiding his face*]

Ah! take me hence!

[DWAINIE *leads him off, looking backward as she goes and waving her hands imploringly to* CREECH *and* GRITCHFANG, *reassuming former shapes, in ecstasies of insane delight*]

CREECH. [*To* GRITCHFANG]

Zipp!
    Zipp!
       Zipp!
          Zipp!
Sting his tongue raw and unravel his lip!
Grope, on the right, down his windpipe, and squeeze
His liver as dry as a petrified wheeze!

[GRITCHFANG—*as before*—*shrinks and disappears at sleeper's mouth*]

Throttle his heart till he's black in the face,
And bury it down in some desolate place
Where only remorse in pent agony lives
To dread the advice that your grandmother gives!

[*The sleeper struggles contortedly, while voice of* GRITCHFANG *calls from within*]

GRITCHFANG

Ho-ho! I have clambered the rungs of his ribs
And beriddled his lungs into tatters and dribs;
And I turned up the tube of his heart like a hose
And squirt all the blood to the end of his nose!!
I stamp on his stomach and caper and prance,
With my tail tossing round like a boomerang-lance!
And thus may success ever crown my intent
To wander the ways that my grandmother went!

[*Reappears, falls hysterically in* CREECH's *outstretched arms.—Then dance and duo.*]

DUO

Whing!
    Whung!
       So our ancestors sung!
And they snorted and pawed, and they hissed and they stung,—
Taking special terrific delight in their work
On the fools that they found in the lands of the Spirk.—
And each little grain of their powders of pain
They scraped up and pestled again and again—
Mixed in quadruple doses for gluttons and sots,
Till they strangled their dreams with gung-jibbrous knots!

[*The comet again trails past, upon which the* Nightmare *leap and disappear.* JUCKLET *staggers to his feet and glares frenziedly around—then starts for opposite exit of comet—is there suddenly confronted with fiend-faces in the air, bewhiskered with ragged purplish flames that flare audibly and huskily in abrupt alternating chill gasps and hot welterings of wind. He starts back from them, reels and falls prostrate, groveling terrifiedly in the dust, and chattering, with eerie music accompanying his broken utterance.*]

JUCKLET

Æo! Æo! Æo!
Thou dost all things know—
        Waving all claims of mine to *dare* to pray,
Save that I needs *must:*—Lo,
        What *may* I pray for? Yea,
        I have not *any* way,
An *Thou* gainsayest me a tolerance so.—
        I dare not pray
                Forgiveness—too great
                My vast o'ertoppling weight
        Of sinning; nor can I
        Pray my
Poor soul unscourged to go.—
Frame *Thou* my prayer, Æo!

What may I pray for? Dare
I shape a prayer,
        In sooth,
        For any canceled joy
        Of my mad youth,
        Or any bliss my sin's stress did destroy?
What may I pray for—What?—
That the wild clusters of forget-me-not
                And mignonette
                And violet
        Be out of childhood brought,
                And in mine hard heart set
                A-blooming now as then?—
                With all their petals yet
        Bediamonded with dews—
        Their sweet, sweet scent let loose
                Full sumptuously again!

What *may* I pray, Æo!
  For the poor hutchèd cot
  Where death sate squat
Midst my first memories?—Lo!
My mother's face—(they, whispering, told me so)—
  That face!—so pinchedly
  It blanched up, as they lifted me—
    Its frozen eyelids would
    Not part, nor could
  Be ever wetted open with warm tears.
    . . . Who hears
The prayers for all dead-mother-sakes, Æo!

Leastwise *one* mercy:—May
I not have leave to pray
All *self* to pass away—
  Forgetful of all needs mine own—
  Neglectful of all creeds;—alone,
  Stand fronting Thy high throne and say:
    To Thee,
  O Infinite, I pray
    Shield *Thou* mine enemy!

[*Music throughout supplication gradually softens and sweetens into utter gentleness, with scene slow-fading into densest night.*]

END ACT II

ACT III

SCENE I. *Court of* KRUNG—*Royal* Ministers, Counselors, *etc., in session.* CRESTILLOMEEM, *in full blazonry of regal attire, presiding. She signals a* Herald *at her left, who steps forward.—Blare of trumpets, greeted with ominous murmurings within, blent with tumult from without.*

HERALD

Hist, ho! Ay, ay! Ay, ay!—Her Majesty,
The All-Glorious and Ever-Gracious Queen,
Crestillomeem, to her most loyal, leal
And right devoted subjects, greeting sends—
Proclaiming, in the absence of the King,
Her royal presence—

[*Voice of* Herald *fails abruptly—utterly.—A breathless hush falls sudden on the court.—A sense oppressive—ominous—affects the throng. Weird music heard of unseen instruments.*]

HERALD [*Huskily striving to be heard*]

Hist, ho! Ay, ay! Ay, ay!—Her Majesty,
The All-Glorious and Ever-Gracious Queen,
Crestillomeem—

[*The Queen gasps, and clutches at* Herald, *mutely signing him to silence, her staring eyes fixed on a shadowy figure, mistily developing before her into wraith-like form and likeness of The Tune-Fool,* SPRAIVOLL. *The shape— evidently invisible and voiceless to all senses but the* Queen's—*wavers vaporishly to and fro before her, moaning and crooning in infinitely sweet-sad minor cadences a mystic song.*]

WRAITH-SONG OF SPRAIVOLL

*I will not hear the dying word
    Of any friend, nor stroke the wing
Of any little wounded bird.
    . . . Love is the deadest thing!*

822

I wist not if I see the smile
Of prince or wight, in court or lane.—
I only know that afterwhile
He will not smile again.

The summer blossom, at my feet,
Swims backward, drowning in the grass.—
I will not stay to name it sweet—
Sink out! and let me pass!

I have no mind to feel the touch
Of gentle hands on brow and hair.—
The lack of this once pained me much,
And so I have a care.

Dead weeds, and husky-rustling leaves
That beat the dead boughs where ye cling,
And old dead nests beneath the eaves—
Love is the deadest thing!

Ah! once I fared not all alone;
And once—no matter, rain or snow!—
The stars of summer ever shone—
Because I loved him so!

With always tremblings in his hands,
And always blushes unaware,
And always ripples down the strands
Of his long yellow hair.

I needs must weep a little space,
Remembering his laughing eyes
And curving lip, and lifted face
Of rapture and surprise.

O joy is dead in every part,
And life and hope; and so I sing:
In all the graveyard of my heart
Love is the deadest thing!

[*With dying away of song, apparition of* SPRAIVOLL *slowly vanishes.* CRESTIL-
OMEEM *turns dazedly to throng, and with labored effort strives to reassume
imperious mien.—Signs for merl and tremulously drains goblet—sinks back
in throne with feigned complacency, mutely waving* Herald *to proceed.*]

HERALD [*Mechanically*]

Hist, ho! Ay, ay! Ay, ay!—Her Majesty,
The All-Glorious and Ever-Gracious Queen,
Crestillomeem, to her most loyal, leal
And right devoted subjects, greeting sends—
Proclaiming, in the absence of the King,
Her royal presence, as by him empowered
To sit and occupy, maintain and hold,
And therefrom rule the Throne, in sovereign state,
And work the royal will—[*Confusion*] *Hist,* ho! Ay, ay!
Ay, ay!—And be it known, the King, in view
Of his approaching dissolution—

[*Sensation among* Counselors, *etc., within, and wild tumult without and cries
of "Long live the* King!" *and "Treason!" "Intrigue!" "Sorcery!"* CRESTIL-
LOMEEM, *in suppressed ire, waving silence, and* Herald *striving to be heard.*]

HERALD

Hist, ho! Ay, ay! Ay, ay!—The King, in view
Of his approaching dissolution, hath
Decreed this instrument—this royal scroll

[*Unrolling and displaying scroll*]

With royal seal thereunto set by Krung's
Most sacred act and sign—

[*General sensation within, and growing tumult without, with wrangling cries of
"Plot!" "Treason!" "Conspiracy!" and "Down with the* Queen!" *"Down
with the usurper!" "Down with the Sorceress!"*]

CRESTILLOMEEM [*Wildly*]

                                        Who dares to cry
"Conspiracy!" Bring me the traitor-knave!

[*Growing confusion without—sound of rioting.—Voice, "Let me be taken! Let
me be taken!" Enter* Guards, *dragging* JUCKLET *forward, wild-eyed and
hysterical—the* Queen's *gaze fastened on him wonderingly.*]

CRESTILLOMEEM [*To* Guards]

Why bring ye Jucklet hither in this wise?

GUARD

O Queen, 'tis he who cries "Conspiracy!"
And who incites the mob without with cries
Of "Plot!" and "Treason!"

CRESTILLOMEEM [*Starting*]

Ha! Can this be true?
I'll not believe it!—Jucklet is my fool,
But not so vast a fool that he would tempt
His gracious Sovereign's ire. [*To* Guards] Let him be freed!

[*Then to* JUCKLET, *with mock service*]

Stand hither, O my Fool!

JUCKLET [*To* Queen]

What! I, thy fool?
Ho! ho! *Thy* fool?—ho! ho!—Why, *thou* art *mine!*

[*Confusion—cries of "Strike down the traitor!"* JUCKLET *wrenching himself
from grasp of officers*]

Back, all of ye! I have not waded hell
That I should fear your puny enmity!
Here will I give ye proof of all I say!

[*Presses toward throne, wedging his opposers left and right—*CRESTILLOMEEM
*sits as though stricken speechless—pallid, waving him back—*JUCKLET, *fairly
fronting her, with folded arms—then to throng continues.*]

Lo! do I here defy her to lift up
Her voice and say that Jucklet speaks a lie.

[*At sign of* Queen, Officers, *unperceived by* JUCKLET, *close warily behind him.*]

And, further—I pronounce the document
That craven Herald there holds in his hand
A forgery—a trick—and dare the Queen,
Here in my listening presence, to command
Its further utterance!

CRESTILLOMEEM [*Wildly rising*]

Hold, hireling!—Fool!—
The Queen thou dost in thy mad boasts insult
Shall utter first thy doom!

[JUCKLET, *seized from behind by* Guards, *is hurled face upward on the dais at her feet, while a minion, with drawn sword pressed close against his breast, stands over him.*]

—Ere we proceed
With graver matters, let this demon-knave
Be sent back home to hell.

[*With awful stress of ire, form quivering, eyes glittering and features twitched and ashen*]

Give *me* the sword,—
The insult hath been mine—so even shall
The vengeance be!

[*As* CRESTILLOMEEM *seizes sword and bends forward to strike,* JUCKLET, *with superhuman effort, frees his hand, and, with a sudden motion and an incoherent muttering, flings object in his assailant's face,—*CRESTILLOMEEM *staggers backward, dropping sword, and, with arms tossed aloft, shrieks, totters and falls prone upon the pave. In confusion following* JUCKLET *mysteriously vanishes; and as the bewildered* Courtiers *lift the fallen* Queen, *a clear, piercing voice of thrilling sweetness is heard singing.*]

VOICE

The pride of noon must wither soon—
The dusk of death must fall;
Yet out of darkest night the moon
Shall blossom over all!

[*For an instant a dense cloud envelops empty throne—then gradually lifts, discovering therein* KRUNG *seated, in royal panoply and state, with* JUCKLET *in act of presenting scepter to him.—Blare of trumpets, and chorus of* Courtiers, Ministers, Heralds, *etc.*]

CHORUS

All hail!! Long live the King!

KRUNG [*To throng, with grave salutation*]

Through Æo's own great providence, and through
The intervention of an angel whom
I long had deemed forever lost to me,
Once more your favored Sovereign, do I greet
And tender you my blessing, O most good
And faith-abiding subjects of my realm!
In common, too, with your long-suffering King,
Have ye long suffered, blamelessly as he:
Now, therefore, know ye all what, until late,
He knew not of himself, and with him share
The rapturous assurance that is his,—
That, for all time to come, are we restored
To the old glory and most regal pride
And opulence and splendor of our realm.

[*Turning with pained features to the strangly stricken* Queen]

There have been, as ye needs must know, strange spells
And wicked sorceries at work within
The very dais boundaries of the Throne.
Lo! then, behold your harrier and mine,
And with me grieve for the self-ruined Queen
Who grovels at my feet, blind, speechless, and
So stricken with a curse herself designed
Should light upon Hope's fairest minister.

[*Motions attendants, who lead away* CRESTILLOMEEM—*the* King *gazing after her, overmastered with stress of his emotions.—He leans heavily on throne, as though oblivious to all surroundings, and, shaping into speech his varying thought, as in a trance, speaks as though witless of both utterance and auditor.*]

I loved her.—Why? I never knew.—Perhaps
Because her face was fair; perhaps because
Her eyes were blue and wore a weary air;—
Perhaps . . . perhaps because her limpid face
Was eddied with a restless tide, wherein
The dimples found no place to anchor and
Abide: perhaps because her tresses beat
A froth of gold about her throat, and poured
In splendor to the feet that ever seemed
Afloat. Perhaps because of that wild way
Her sudden laughter overleapt propriety;
Or—who will say?—perhaps the way she wept.
Ho! have ye seen the swollen heart of summer
Tempest, o'er the plain, with throbs of thunder
Burst apart and drench the earth with rain? She
Wept like that.—And to recall, with one wild glance
Of memory, our last love-parting—tears
And all. . . . It thrills and maddens me! And yet
My dreams will hold her, flushed from lifted brow
To finger-tips, with passion's ripest kisses
Crushed and mangled on her lips. . . . O woman! while
Your face was fair, and heart was pure, and lips
Were true, and hope as golden as your hair,
I should have strangled you!

[*As* KRUNG, *ceasing to speak, piteously lifts his face,* SPRAIVOLL *all suddenly appears, in space left vacant by the* Queen, *and, kneeling, kisses the* King's *hand.—He bends in tenderness, kissing her brow—then lifts and seats her at his side. Speaks then to throng.*]

                                        Good Subjects—Lords:
Behold in this sweet woman here my child,
Whom, years agone, the cold, despicable
Crestillomeem—by baleful, wicked arts
And gruesome spells and fearsome witcheries—
Did spirit off to some strange otherland,
Where, happily, a Wunkland Princess found
Her, and undid the spell by sorcery
More potent—ay, *Divine,* since it works naught
But *good*—the gift of Æo, to right wrong.
This magic dower the Wunkland Princess hath
Enlisted in our restoration here,
In secret service, till this joyful hour

Of our complete deliverance.   Even thus.—
Lo, let the peerless Princess now appear!

[*He lifts scepter, and a gust of melody, divinely beautiful, sweeps through the
court.—The star above the throne loosens and drops slowly downward,
bursting like a bubble on the scepter-tip, and, issuing therefrom,* AMPHINE
and DWAINIE, *hand in hand, kneel at the feet of* KRUNG, *who bends above
them with his blessing, while* JUCKLET *capers wildly round the group.*]

JUCKLET

Ho! ho! but I could shriek for very joy!
And though my recent rival, fair Amphine,
Doth even now bend o'er a blossom, I,
Besprit me! have no lingering desire
To meddle with it, though with but one eye
I slept the while she backward walked around
Me in the garden.

[AMPHINE *dubiously smiles—*JUCKLET *blinks and leers—and* DWAINIE *bites her
finger.*]

KRUNG

Peace! good Jucklet!   Peace!
For this is not a time for any jest.—
Though the old order of our realm hath been
Restored, and though restored my very life—
Though I have found a daughter,—I have lost
A son—for Dwainie, with her sorcery,
Will, on the morrow, carry him away.
'Tis Æo's largess, as our love is His,
And our abiding trust and gratefulness.

CURTAIN

————◆————

INDEX OF TITLES

INDEX OF TITLES

Indicates that the poem appears in this edition under a different title or that the one specified is the subtitle.

INDEX OF FIRST LINES

INDEX OF FIRST LINES

**First lines thus designated do not start a new poem but are
sections of a larger one.*